LIVING  LITURGY™

LIVING ✠ LITURGY™

Spirituality, Celebration, and Catechesis for Sundays and Solemnities

Year C • 2022

Stephanie DePrez
Verna Holyhead, SGS
Orin E. Johnson
John T. Kyler

with
M. Roger Holland, II
and Ferdinand Okorie, CMF

LITURGICAL PRESS
Collegeville, Minnesota

www.litpress.org

✠ CONTENTS

CONTRIBUTORS

Stephanie DePrez is a Catholic writer and educator. She taught theology at Xavier College Preparatory High School in Palm Desert and Arrupe Jesuit High School in Denver, part of the Cristo-Rey network. While pursuing her master's degree in music at UCLA, Stephanie served as the music director at St. Timothy Parish in West LA from 2015 to 2018. She holds a bachelor of arts in music and film production from the University of Notre Dame and recently completed two years as a United States teaching assistant with Fulbright Austria in Vienna. Stephanie is also an accomplished opera singer and has sung in Los Angeles, New York, and Berlin.

Verna Holyhead, SGS (1933–2011), Australian Sister of the Good Samaritan of the Order of St. Benedict, wrote with an emphasis on biblical scholarship, liturgical insight, and pastoral challenge. She is the author of the three-volume collection *Welcoming the Word in Year A, B, and C*, published by Liturgical Press.

Orin E. Johnson has been director of music ministries at Sts. Joachim and Ann Parish in St. Charles, Missouri, since 2012. There, he directs a children's choir, a contemporary ensemble, a funeral choir, and a team of cantors, and supervises two other choirs and liturgical ministries at a K–8 parochial school. He was also coordinator of music and liturgy at the National Shrine of Our Lady of the Snows in Belleville, Illinois, from 1998 to 2012. He resides in St. Louis, Missouri, with his wife, Erin.

John T. Kyler serves as general editor for the parish market at Liturgical Press in Collegeville, Minnesota. In addition to having experience working in parish faith formation and high school and collegiate campus ministry, John is an active liturgical musician, composer, author, and speaker, focusing on the intersection of liturgy, justice, and healthy vulnerability in pastoral ministry. An instructor in the Emmaus Institute for Ministry Formation, John holds a master of education from the University of Notre Dame and a master of theological studies from Saint John's University.

M. Roger Holland, II, is a teaching assistant professor in music and religion and director of The Spirituals Project at the Lamont School of Music, University of Denver. A graduate of Union Theological Seminary in New York City where he received a master of divinity degree, Roger also served as artist-in-residence and director of the Union Gospel Choir for over thirteen years. Roger serves as liturgical music consultant for the Archdiocese of New York's Office of Black Ministry and music director for their special masses at St. Patrick's Cathedral.

Ferdinand Okorie, CMF, is a Catholic priest with the Claretian Missionaries, an assistant professor of New Testament and early Christianity, and the director of Bible Study and Travel Programs at Catholic Theological Union, Chicago. Also, he is the editor-in-chief at *U.S. Catholic*. He writes pastoral reflections on various New Testament topics, notably on theological and pastoral issues in *U.S. Catholic* and peer-review journals. He is the author of *Favor and Gratitude: Reading Galatians in Its Greco-Roman Context* (Fortress Academic, 2020).

 **PREFACE**

Introduction

As a premier Catholic publisher, Liturgical Press remains committed to offering liturgical, spiritual, and scriptural resources rooted in the Benedictine tradition. While these resources have changed and developed over the years, the commitment to sound theology and best pastoral practice remain hallmarks of our mission and ministry. *Living Liturgy*™ is one of our most loved and widely used incarnations of this commitment.

Living Liturgy™ will always help people prepare for liturgy and live a liturgical spirituality—a way of living that is rooted in liturgy. The paschal mystery is the central focus of liturgy, of the gospels, and of this volume. *Living Liturgy*™ is more than a title. Rather, "living liturgy" is a commitment to a relationship with Jesus Christ, embodied in our everyday actions and interactions.

We hope this edition of *Living Liturgy*™ will continue to facilitate this relationship, making liturgical spirituality a lived reality.

Authors

Sr. Verna Holyhead, SGS, and Orin E. Johnson return as authors for this edition of *Living Liturgy*™. Their understanding of Scripture and liturgy provide rich and provocative fodder for reflection and catechesis.

We are also thrilled to introduce a number of authors who are new to *Living Liturgy*™. Stephanie DePrez, M. Roger Holland, II, John T. Kyler, and Fr. Ferdinand Okorie, CMF, write at the intersection of theology and pastoral reality, bringing their own experiences of "living liturgy" to this work.

We know that you will find these contributions to be prayerful, practical, and relevant to our church and world today.

Artwork

This edition features stunning original artwork from Ruberval Monteiro da Silva, OSB. Fr. Ruberval, a native of Brazil, resides in the Benedictine community of Sant'Anselmo in Rome. His colorful mosaics grace the walls of churches around the world, and we are excited to once again include his work in *Living Liturgy*™.

ACKNOWLEDGMENTS for Gospel Reflections

Adapted "Reflecting on the Gospel" sections

Verna Holyhead, *Welcoming the Word in Year C: With Burning Hearts* (2006)
All days except those listed below

Original "Reflecting on the Gospel" sections

M. Roger Holland, II
The Nativity of the Lord (Christmas), Vigil Mass
The Nativity of the Lord (Christmas), Mass at Dawn
The Nativity of the Lord (Christmas), Mass during the Day
Easter Sunday of the Resurrection
Pentecost Sunday

Ferdinand Okorie, CMF
The Immaculate Conception of the Blessed Virgin Mary
Our Lady of Guadalupe
Saint Joseph, Spouse of the Blessed Virgin Mary
The Annunciation of the Lord
Seventh Sunday of Easter
Nativity of Saint John the Baptist
The Most Sacred Heart of Jesus
Saints Peter and Paul, Apostles
The Assumption of the Blessed Virgin Mary
All Saints
The Commemoration of All the Faithful Departed (All Souls' Day)

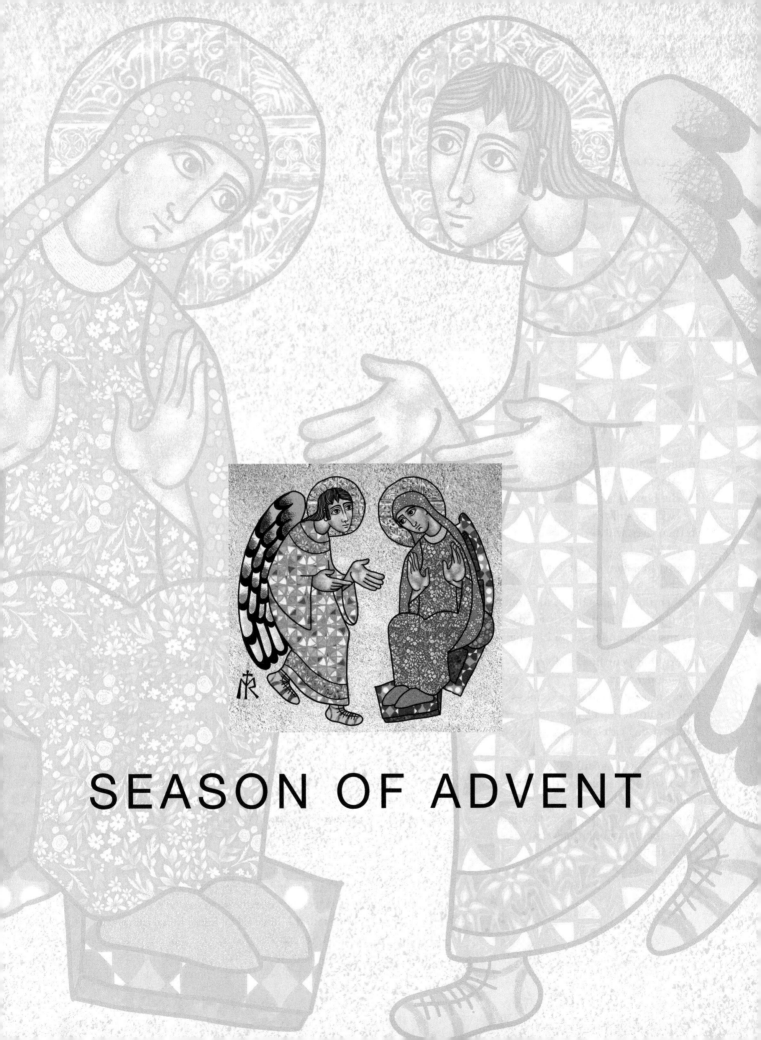

SEASON OF ADVENT

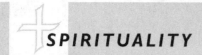

SPIRITUALITY

GOSPEL ACCLAMATION
Ps 85:8

℞. Alleluia, alleluia.
Show us, Lord, your love;
and grant us your salvation.
℞. Alleluia, alleluia.

Gospel

Luke 21:25-28, 34-36; L3C

**Jesus said to his disciples:
"There will be signs in the sun,
    the moon, and the stars,
    and on earth nations will be in
        dismay,
    perplexed by the roaring of
        the sea and the waves.
People will die of fright
    in anticipation of what is com-
        ing upon the world,
    for the powers of the heavens
        will be shaken.
And then they will see the Son
    of Man
    coming in a cloud with power
        and great glory.
But when these signs begin to happen,
    stand erect and raise your heads
    because your redemption is at hand.**

**"Beware that your hearts do not be-
        come drowsy
    from carousing and drunkenness
    and the anxieties of daily life,
    and that day catch you by surprise
        like a trap.
For that day will assault everyone
    who lives on the face of the earth.
Be vigilant at all times
    and pray that you have the strength
    to escape the tribulations that are
        imminent
    and to stand before the Son of Man."**

Reflecting on the Gospel

On this first Sunday of the church year, many of us will gaze on the single flame that is burning on the Advent wreath. It seems so small and insignificant against the background of world events, and even of our own lives. Often, we are so physically and mentally exhausted at the end of the year that we may be skeptical about this tiny, flickering flame and the illumination it can offer us. But as we enter this season, the church encourages us to have hope in the promises of God that can so easily flicker in and out of our consciousness. At first hearing, Luke's gospel may seem to be proclaiming a message of fear and doom; its truth, however, is different. Christ, in his second coming as the glorious Son of Man, will liberate the cosmos and all humanity from fear and menace. Luke uses large, symbolic language for large events. It is the only way to speak of events that have not yet been experienced.

Many people in our world commit themselves to what has not yet happened and to long-range hopes. Medical researchers speak about positive outcomes in decades ahead; ecologists are concerned not just for our planet at this moment, but for its future in the centuries to come; astrophysicists conjecture about developments in terms of millennia. We accept these long-range forecasts and hopes, yet we may feel uncomfortable with, and even dismissive of, the emphasis on the future at the beginning of Advent. We don't mind thinking, with comfortable nostalgia, about the past coming of "baby Jesus"—but that is not where the church wants us to start Advent.

When we take our first plunge into this season, we seem to be caught in a liturgical riptide that drags us away from the comparatively safe and familiar shore of the present into the uncharted end of human history and reflection on the second, and as yet unrealized, coming of Christ.

Advent challenges us to let our hopes reach beyond cozy domesticity to the huge and human hope of a new creation. Just as a woman watches for signs that the birth of her child is imminent, so Jesus urges his disciples to be alert to the birth pangs of the reign of God in all its fullness. In our present time, in the womb of human and cosmic history, God is nurturing and preparing for the birth of the new heaven and new earth. In the midst of any personal suffering, international tension, opportunist politics, or natural disasters that we might experience during these Advent weeks, the word of God urges us to be people of hope. Nor are Christians to be captives of frantic seasonal consumerism. We are called, rather, to be a people awake and alert to the promises of God already revealed, grateful for what has been liberating for us as Jesus's disciples in the year just past, and confident in the gifts of God that are yet to come. Jesus proclaims to us in today's gospel the same good news he spoke to the bent-over woman (cf. Luke 13:10-17). Touched by Jesus, the woman who for eighteen years had only looked at feet and dust was able to "stand up straight" and to see the Sabbath stars shining on his face. Today, we too are urged to lift up our heads and have faith that we will see our redemption drawing near in the Son of Man.

Focusing the Gospel

Key words and phrases: "Beware that your hearts do not become drowsy from carousing and drunkenness and the anxieties of daily life, and that day catch you by surprise like a trap."

To the point: It is interesting that Jesus pairs drunkenness and anxiety in this passage as equal forms of distraction. One uses substance to distance from reality, and the other is a preoccupation with the frustrations of reality. Both are presented as equally harmful, taking our hearts away from focusing on the true reality of the coming of Christ. Drunkenness and anxiety are also both presented as causing us to become "drowsy." Perhaps the vigilance that Jesus speaks of is not a sharp awareness that borders on anxiety or a complacency that removes us from our situation. Perhaps Christian vigilance is more about seeking a balance between noticing the aspects of our life that are not currently life-giving and holding them in a healthy perspective.

Connecting the Gospel

to the first reading: Jeremiah speaks of a nation of Israel that is safe and secure. This is considered "justice." The Lord raises up a leader for Judah and Jerusalem who promotes safety and security.

to experience: In the second reading, Paul equates strength to love, offering love as the key to "strengthen your hearts" in order to please God. Do you view love as a source of strength in your own life?

Connecting the Responsorial Psalm

to the readings: This psalm is brimming with hope and delight. The second reading calls us to justice, and in the psalm, we learn who the just are. They are the humble, who encounter the Lord through kindness and constancy.

to psalmist preparation: When proclaiming these words, you are tying together the gospel and the readings by providing a road map to justice. You are a version of John the Baptist, proclaiming the way to the Lord for your community by sharing the concrete instructions: "All the paths of the LORD are kindness and constancy / toward those who keep his covenant and his decrees. / The friendship of the LORD is with those who fear him, / and his covenant, for their instruction."

PROMPTS FOR FAITH-SHARING

What are a few sources of anxiety in your life? Have you experienced anxiety that causes you to become "drowsy" with distraction?

What are ways in which you seek out "drunkenness"? Do you seek a form of escape that goes beyond self-care?

If we view "justice" as safety and security, how is it present in your own family and wider community? Is your parish a "just" place for parishioners?

How does putting a priority on love contribute to a nation of safety and security?

Model Penitential Act

Presider: In today's gospel Jesus tells us to be mindful about the ways our hearts may grow drowsy. Let us remain awake and aware, asking for God's mercy and forgiveness . . . *[pause]*

> Lord Jesus, you are the Son of God and the Son of Man: Lord, have mercy.
>
> Christ Jesus, you are the Hope for the World: Christ, have mercy.
>
> Lord Jesus, you are our ever-present Redeemer: Lord, have mercy.

Homily Points

• Today we begin a new liturgical year. Marking time through the liturgical year is an important part of our Christian journey, as it allows us to more deeply align our hearts and minds with Christ and enter more fully into the paschal mystery. It is important to remember that the waiting we experience now during this time of preparation for the coming of God is intimately connected to not only Christmas, but also the entirety of Christ's life, death, and resurrection.

• In the second reading, St. Paul prays that God will make God's people "increase and abound in love." While it is easy to speak of this love in a general sense, this is a good time to consider explicit ways in which our community and world need to grow in love for each other and in love for God. This is not a time for shaming or rebuking, but for inviting ways to cultivate the love Paul describes.

• The gospel today reminds us that as Christians, we wait for something more than the celebration of the historical coming of Christ at Christmas. Jesus tells his disciples that a day will come when all must stand before the Son of Man. Like the disciples, we too wait for the coming of Christ at the end of time, a time where sin, fear, and injustice will be no more. This waiting is an important part of the twofold nature of Advent.

Model Universal Prayer (Prayer of the Faithful)

Presider: Jesus tells his disciples not to become drowsy from the anxieties of daily life. Confident in this, we bring our needs before God.

Response: Lord, hear our prayer.

That the church may always radiate the light and hope of Christ . . .

That all leaders of cities and countries may work together for the common good . . .

That all who feel despair may know God's abiding comfort and presence . . .

That all gathered here may begin this season of Advent with renewed hope . . .

Presider: Loving God, hear these prayers we bring before you and grant them according to your will. We ask this through Christ our Lord. **Amen.**

COLLECT

Let us pray.

Pause for silent prayer

Grant your faithful, we pray, almighty God,
the resolve to run forth to meet your Christ
with righteous deeds at his coming,
so that, gathered at his right hand,
they may be worthy to possess the heavenly Kingdom.
Through our Lord Jesus Christ, your Son,
who lives and reigns with you in the unity of the Holy Spirit,
God, for ever and ever. **Amen.**

FIRST READING

Jer 33:14-16

The days are coming, says the LORD,
  when I will fulfill the promise
  I made to the house of Israel and Judah.
In those days, in that time,
  I will raise up for David a just shoot;
  he shall do what is right and just in the land.
In those days Judah shall be safe
  and Jerusalem shall dwell secure;
  this is what they shall call her:
  "The LORD our justice."

RESPONSORIAL PSALM
Ps 25:4-5, 8-9, 10, 14

R̂. (1b) To you, O Lord, I lift my soul.

Your ways, O LORD, make known to me;
  teach me your paths,
guide me in your truth and teach me,
  for you are God my savior,
  and for you I wait all the day.

R̂. To you, O Lord, I lift my soul.

Good and upright is the LORD;
  thus he shows sinners the way.
He guides the humble to justice,
  and teaches the humble his way.

R̂. To you, O Lord, I lift my soul.

All the paths of the LORD are kindness and
    constancy
  toward those who keep his covenant
    and his decrees.
The friendship of the LORD is with those
    who fear him,
  and his covenant, for their instruction.

R̂. To you, O Lord, I lift my soul.

SECOND READING
1 Thess 3:12–4:2

Brothers and sisters:
May the Lord make you increase and
    abound in love
  for one another and for all,
  just as we have for you,
  so as to strengthen your hearts,
  to be blameless in holiness before our
    God and Father
  at the coming of our Lord Jesus with all
    his holy ones. Amen.

Finally, brothers and sisters,
  we earnestly ask and exhort you in the
    Lord Jesus that,
  as you received from us
  how you should conduct yourselves to
    please God
  —and as you are conducting
    yourselves—
  you do so even more.
For you know what instructions we gave
    you through the Lord Jesus.

About Liturgy

Many Modes of Waiting: Somewhere, perhaps in a closet or a basement storeroom, perhaps perched high on a shelf or hidden behind assorted tapestries or various nativity figurines, it is there. Be it wooden or metal, large or small, it remains there for eleven months of the year. Waiting. Waiting to be adorned with greenery, violet and rose candles, perhaps decorative ribbons, and then brought once again into our sacred spaces and into our lives.

Even the Advent wreath spends most of its time waiting.

Yet this wreath's waiting continues even into its time of active purpose. Consider that the wreath's candles are lit for perhaps five or six hours each weekend, and perhaps a couple hours of the days in between. Consider particularly the fourth candle, whose main purpose seems to be standing tall and proclaiming a "not yet" counterbalance to the "soon" of its trio of ever-shorter luminary friends.

Yet, when it is time to be what it was made to be, to do what it is asked to do, this candle easily and capably springs into action—to remind us that our whole lives are a combination of rest, readiness, and activity, all in the name of the Lord. Our whole lives are a combination of "soon" and "not yet" while we wait for that same Lord, already risen in glory, to come again as he promised.

About Liturgical Documents

Revisiting, Reimagining: As a new liturgical year begins, much like when a new calendar year begins, it is a good idea to make some resolutions about our spiritual and liturgical lives. Might I suggest revisiting the myriad documents that inform and guide our public prayer? Some, like *Sacrosanctum Concilium* (SC; the Constitution on the Sacred Liturgy) and Sing to the Lord might initially seem to be known and studied well enough, but revisiting them, especially if it's been some time, might yield some surprising realizations.

Could you say, off the top of your head, what Sing to the Lord, fifteen years old now, says about recorded music? I suspect the nuanced information there would surprise you! And there are many other lesser-known documents, like the various "instructions" following *Sacrosanctum Concilium* over many years—*Varietates Legitimae* and *Liturgiam Authenticam* to name two—along with the occasional *motu proprio* and encyclical to attend to. Which have the full weight of universal liturgical law, and which only provide guidance or suggestions? Which are relevant universally, and which apply only in the United States? Did you know there is a Roman Missal for the Dioceses of Zaire that offers significant adjustments from our ordinary form? What insights might we draw from that rite?

This space will, occasionally during the coming year, delve into these documents, at least briefly, offering some history, context, reminders, new insights, and future possibilities.

About Music

Advent Justice: Advent, scripturally, picks up where the previous cycle finished, painting imagery of end times, often in stark and frightening ways. This cycle adds a layer of justice as well, a justice that, as the weeks progress, transforms into hope—hope for a future of peace only possible through tangible acts of justice.

So, especially this First Sunday of Advent, it's important to use music with texts that pick up on that sense of justice. "This Is Your Justice" by Craig Colson (World Library Publications [WLP]/GIA Publications [GIA]) is one such contemporary offering.

✠ SPIRITUALITY

GOSPEL ACCLAMATION
Luke 3:4, 6

℟. Alleluia, alleluia.
Prepare the way of the Lord, make
   straight his paths:
all flesh shall see the salvation of
   God.
℟. Alleluia, alleluia.

Gospel

Luke 3:1-6; L6C

In the fifteenth year of the
   reign of Tiberius Caesar,
   when Pontius Pilate was
      governor of Judea,
   and Herod was tetrarch of
      Galilee,
   and his brother Philip
      tetrarch of the re-
      gion of Ituraea and
      Trachonitis,
   and Lysanias was tetrarch
      of Abilene,
   during the high priesthood of Annas
      and Caiaphas,
the word of God came to John the
   son of Zechariah in the desert.
John went throughout the whole region
   of the Jordan,
   proclaiming a baptism of repentance
      for the forgiveness of sins,
   as it is written in the book of the
      words of the prophet Isaiah:
   A voice of one crying out in the
      desert:
   "Prepare the way of the Lord,
      make straight his paths.
   Every valley shall be filled
      and every mountain and hill
         shall be made low.
   The winding roads shall be made
      straight,
      and the rough ways made
         smooth,
   and all flesh shall see the salvation
      of God."

Reflecting on the Gospel

Against a backdrop of geography, politics, and history, Luke ushers the adult John the Baptist onto the Jordan stage. Last Sunday's gospel announced the advent or "arrival" of Jesus at the end of human history; today, as watchman and awakener, John announces the advent of salvation and consolation to the people and proclaims that their hope for the dawn of messianic time is near. In searching for ways to communicate John's significance, Luke and the other gospel writers found it most appropriate to use (with minor alterations) the words of Second Isaiah with which that prophet begins his "Book of the Consolation of Israel" (Isa 40-55). John's is the voice that, after four centuries of prophetic silence, heralds the coming of God's salvation not only to Israel, but to all humankind. In an insignificant and troublesome pocket of the Roman Empire, John starts to shout his message throughout the district around the Jordan River.

Son of the priest Zechariah though he may be, John dissociates himself from Jerusalem and the temple and chooses the place where Israel crossed over from its wilderness wandering into the Promised Land. John will call the people to make another crossing: from the exile of unfaithfulness to God into the forgiveness of their sins. He proclaims a baptism of repentance, a conversion of heart (*metanoia*) that looks to future commitment and not merely to regret for the past.

We are used to heavy earth-moving equipment and technology that builds roads to speed travelers on their way—cutting out sharp bends, smoothing treacherous bumps, straightening dangerous curves to give us a clearer and safer view of what is ahead or oncoming. Advent is the season of Christian "road work," with John the Baptist as our overseer. With John's voice, the church asks us both personally and communally to level and straighten out whatever is an obstacle or danger on our journey to God. What are the "potholes" in our discipleship, those sins of omission? From what do we need to be converted if we are to make the way smoother for others who find it difficult to travel to God because of our intolerant or erratic behavior? Do we indulge in outbursts of destructive "road rage" toward our sisters and brothers as we all try to follow the way of the gospel? Have we a kingdom vision that can enable us to see around the twists and turns of personal tragedy or ecclesial failure and to recognize there an advent of Christ—his presence with us in the suffering, dying, and rising from these painful realities?

From the desert of his prison, Paul writes in the second reading to the church at Philippi using words that the liturgy now addresses to us. It is a hopeful letter, full of Paul's confidence in the fidelity of this church to continue in the way of the gospel so that Jesus Christ may bring his work in them to completion by the time he comes again. Out of his tender compassion, Paul prays a threefold prayer: that the Philippians may continue to grow in mutual love; that its members may be discerning of the demands of their Christian life; and that they may be vigilant for Christ's second coming, "filled with the fruit of righteousness that comes through Jesus Christ for the glory and praise of God"

(Phil 1:11). First love, then understanding, then ethics—these are Paul's priorities, for where would the last be without the other two?

Focusing the Gospel

Key words and phrases: "John went throughout the whole region of the Jordan, proclaiming a baptism of repentance for the forgiveness of sins."

To the point: In this gospel, the writer includes a lot of information we might pass over as "fluff" when reading today. The fifteenth year of whom? Tetrarch of what? This setup creates a relevant context for the first few audiences of this gospel. Those in the first century would have known who this Caesar was and where Abeline is. They are road markers, setting the scene for the arrival of Jesus. The writer then immediately references Isaiah, which his first audience would recognize. These pieces of the gospel require us to do more work to encounter the Word as it was intended. How might this be written if it were for today's audience? What historical context would you use to set up the coming of Christ in your hometown this month? What books or lyrics would you use to paint a picture of the Christ that citizens of your country are longing for?

Connecting the Gospel

to the first reading: The first reading reads like a coach's speech to a bedraggled team in the fourth quarter of a losing game. Take off that robe of mourning and misery! Up, Jerusalem! God is leading Israel (you!) into joy!

to experience: This reading is an ancient pump-up speech that, like the first part of the gospel, gives us context. We encounter today's gospel after being reminded here that God is on our side, and we are ultimately going to win. The readings are building the scene for the coming of Christ.

Connecting the Responsorial Psalm

to the readings: This psalm is very blunt. The Lord has done great things for us, and we are filled with joy. Paul uses this certainty in his letter to the Philippians when he tells us, "I am confident of this, / that the one who began a good work in you / will continue to complete it / until the day of Christ Jesus." Paul is speaking of the Holy Spirit, trusting and celebrating that the good things the Spirit has begun will continue to manifest positively.

to psalmist preparation: If you have ever played or coached a sport, or received or given mentorship, this psalm invites you to channel that experience. You are the leader in this moment, giving encouragement to the congregation, reminding them of past victories. "Although they go forth weeping, / carrying the seed to be sown, / they shall come back rejoicing, / carrying their sheaves." You have the opportunity to share God's game plan with your parish, using this beautiful imagery. For you personally, recall a moment when you had to double down on hard work and trust to accomplish a goal. This is the type of moment the psalmist is asking us to remember.

PROMPTS FOR FAITH-SHARING

Have you taken a course or attended a workshop on biblical history? Are there clues in this week's readings that you are able to pick out because of the time you've spent studying the context of the writers? What can you share with your fellow ministers?

_____

_____

_____

_____

Who was a great coach or mentor who helped you develop? What activities or words did this person use to encourage you to grow?

_____

_____

_____

_____

Paul's prayer for us is, "[T]hat your love may increase ever more and more in knowledge and every kind of perception, to discern what is of value, so that you may be pure and blameless for the day of Christ." How does this make you feel? How would you change if you knew this prayer was being said for you constantly?

_____

_____

_____

_____

In light of Paul's words, what is your prayer for your own community?

_____

_____

_____

_____

CELEBRATION

Model Penitential Act

Presider: In today's gospel John cries out, "Prepare the way of the Lord." For the times our lives have not heralded God's coming, we ask for forgiveness and peace . . . *[pause]*

Lord Jesus, you are the Way that beckons us to follow: Lord, have mercy.

Christ Jesus, you speak words of peace when we are afraid: Christ, have mercy.

Lord Jesus, you are light, and in you there is no darkness: Lord, have mercy.

Homily Points

• Both the first reading and the gospel share images of God lowering mountains and exulting valleys. We may have heard these words before without thinking about what they actually mean. Consider putting this into perspective for your community by referencing local natural landmarks that people can visualize and imagine the significance of these works of God.

• The desert imagery in today's gospel may be difficult to imagine during December. Even so, the desert remains an important image in Scripture. Today we hear that John the Baptist leaves his time of prayer and contemplation in the desert to proclaim the words of the prophet Isaiah. Later, Jesus will spend time in the desert praying and preparing for his public ministry. How are we being called to spend time in the desert of prayer and contemplation during this Advent season? How might we carve out some quiet time and stillness in our own lives during these busy weeks leading up toward Christmas? Perhaps part of that time might be spent in contemplating those great works of God that Isaiah and John mention.

• Today's psalm allows for further consideration of the works of God: "The Lord has done great things for us; we are filled with joy." The words of the psalmist speak to our very human emotions: dreaming, laughing, rejoicing, etc. How can we name our response to the works of the Lord in our everyday lives? Meister Eckhart is known for proclaiming, "If the only prayer we ever say is thank you, it would be sufficient." How do today's readings help us cultivate a spirit of gratitude?

Model Universal Prayer (Prayer of the Faithful)

Presider: We offer our prayers in a spirit of gratitude, knowing that God hears us when we call out. With confidence, we bring our prayers to God.

Response: Lord, hear our prayer.

That all members of the church may grow in appreciation and gratitude for the works of God . . .

That lawmakers and politicians may always advocate for peace and justice, even when it is difficult . . .

That all who feel alone or isolated during these days of Advent may find comfort and consolation in family, friends, caregivers, and strangers . . .

That our church community may, like John the Baptist, have the courage to proclaim the works of God . . .

Presider: Loving God, hear and answer these prayers, according to your will, not ours. We ask this through Christ our Lord. **Amen.**

COLLECT

Let us pray.

Pause for silent prayer

Almighty and merciful God,
may no earthly undertaking hinder those
who set out in haste to meet your Son,
but may our learning of heavenly wisdom
gain us admittance to his company.
Who lives and reigns with you in the unity
    of the Holy Spirit,
God, for ever and ever. **Amen.**

FIRST READING

Bar 5:1-9

Jerusalem, take off your robe of mourning
    and misery;
    put on the splendor of glory from God
      forever:
wrapped in the cloak of justice from God,
    bear on your head the mitre
    that displays the glory of the eternal
      name.
For God will show all the earth your
    splendor:
    you will be named by God forever
    the peace of justice, the glory of God's
      worship.

Up, Jerusalem! stand upon the heights;
    look to the east and see your children
gathered from the east and the west
    at the word of the Holy One,
    rejoicing that they are remembered by
      God.
Led away on foot by their enemies they
    left you:
    but God will bring them back to you
    borne aloft in glory as on royal thrones.
For God has commanded
    that every lofty mountain be made low,
and that the age-old depths and gorges
    be filled to level ground,
    that Israel may advance secure in the
      glory of God.
The forests and every fragrant kind of
    tree
    have overshadowed Israel at God's
      command;
for God is leading Israel in joy
    by the light of his glory,
    with his mercy and justice for company.

RESPONSORIAL PSALM

Ps 126:1-2, 2-3, 4-5, 6

℟. (3) The Lord has done great things for us; we are filled with joy.

When the LORD brought back the captives of Zion,
  we were like men dreaming.
Then our mouth was filled with laughter,
  and our tongue with rejoicing.

℟. The Lord has done great things for us; we are filled with joy.

Then they said among the nations,
  "The LORD has done great things for them."
The LORD has done great things for us;
  we are glad indeed.

℟. The Lord has done great things for us; we are filled with joy.

Restore our fortunes, O LORD,
  like the torrents in the southern desert.
Those who sow in tears
  shall reap rejoicing.

℟. The Lord has done great things for us; we are filled with joy.

Although they go forth weeping,
  carrying the seed to be sown,
they shall come back rejoicing,
  carrying their sheaves.

℟. The Lord has done great things for us; we are filled with joy.

SECOND READING

Phil 1:4-6, 8-11

Brothers and sisters:
I pray always with joy in my every prayer
    for all of you,
  because of your partnership for the
      gospel
  from the first day until now.
I am confident of this,
  that the one who began a good work
      in you
  will continue to complete it
  until the day of Christ Jesus.
God is my witness,
  how I long for all of you with the
      affection of Christ Jesus.
And this is my prayer:
  that your love may increase ever more
      and more
  in knowledge and every kind of
      perception,
  to discern what is of value,
  so that you may be pure and blameless
      for the day of Christ,
  filled with the fruit of righteousness
  that comes through Jesus Christ
  for the glory and praise of God.

About Liturgy

Liturgical Justice: As our Scriptures this Advent continue to reveal the coming justice and righteousness of God's son, we are reminded to engage in our ministries, when possible, with the same justice that Jesus lived 2,000 years ago and continues to teach us today.

Justice issues are interwoven into all of these elements. Is a liturgy director using the monetary and human resources of the parish appropriately? Are the materials selected for art and environment environmentally friendly? Are those who are paid for their ministries paid an appropriate amount, and paid promptly upon completing their labors in the vineyard?

Further, directors of music and/or liturgy have responsibilities that demand even more attention to these justice issues. On the personal level, the season can demand so much more time and effort than other times of the year; are you carefully monitoring your workload and your sanity during this time? On the professional and economic level, we should remind ourselves that a parish budget (or a music and liturgy budget within that whole) is a document of priorities more than anything else. Does the music and liturgy budget meet the demands of justice that our faith places upon it? Are you able and willing to be a voice that calls for an appropriate percentage of the parish budget to be put toward creating the fullest and most vibrant celebration of the source and summit of our faith—the liturgy? All the other facets of parish life revolve around this public prayer and within this they find their purpose.

Pursuing justice at our liturgies must go beyond the economic and ecological and into the societal as well. Are all those in your parish community equally represented and heard in the various aspects of the liturgy, as lectors or music ministers? Is the liturgy prepared with inculturation in mind, something much more complicated than ensuring it is multilingual? Are those at the margins more than welcomed—are they seen and heard as an essential part of the Body of Christ?

About Liturgical Documents

Sacrosanctum Concilium's Greatest Hits: The first document to come out of the Second Vatican Council was the Constitution on the Sacred Liturgy. That it was the first indicates the importance of the liturgy in our lives and that those at the council recognized that fact.

Many readers have already heard many times the famous phrases "source" and "summit" (or font and apex) and "full, conscious, and active" participation (SC 10, 14). Some may already be well-versed into how these words have been translated, interpreted, argued over, and hopefully enacted over the last sixty years. Off and on over the next few weeks we'll explore the history of liturgical experimentation preceding the council and some of the other "nooks and crannies" of this foundational document.

About Music

Melodies That Engage: Consider the repetitive *Psallite* refrain "Take Your Place at the Table" (Liturgical Press) or strong and accessible melody of "Prepare Ye the Way of the Lord" by Kenneth Louis (WLP/GIA).

GOSPEL ACCLAMATION
cf. Luke 1:28

R︲. Alleluia, alleluia.
Hail, Mary, full of grace, the Lord is with you;
blessed are you among women.
R︲. Alleluia, alleluia.

Gospel

Luke 1:26-38; L689

The angel Gabriel was sent from God
  to a town of Galilee called Nazareth,
  to a virgin betrothed to a man named
    Joseph,
  of the house of David,
  and the virgin's name was Mary.
And coming to her, he said,
  "Hail, full of grace! The Lord is with
    you."
But she was greatly troubled at what was
    said
  and pondered what sort of greeting
    this might be.
Then the angel said to her,
  "Do not be afraid, Mary,
  for you have found favor with God.
Behold, you will conceive in your womb
    and bear a son,
  and you shall name him Jesus.

Continued in Appendix A, p. 261.

See Appendix A, p. 261, for the other readings.

Reflecting on the Gospel

The Scottish Franciscan Friar John Duns Scotus defends the Catholic faith and promotes and preaches about devotion to the Blessed Virgin Mary, insisting, therefore, on her sinless conception. In addition to the various ways that the Blessed Virgin Mary is honored and venerated in our church, Duns Scotus helps us comprehend her role in God's saving plan for the world to begin from her conception as the daughter of Ann and Joachim. Today, we honor and celebrate the Immaculate Conception of the Blessed Virgin Mary.

The role of the Blessed Virgin Mary in God's saving plan for humanity is supported by the salutation she receives from the angel Gabriel: "'Hail, full of grace! The Lord is with you.' . . . [Y]ou have found favor with God." The Blessed Virgin Mary belongs to a long line of biblical figures who have an experience of divine encounter and communication. Perhaps God's encounter, conversation, and the promise of divine presence to Hagar is known to the Blessed Mother (Gen 16:7-13). But whatever she knows about God's relationship with her ancestors suddenly has become personal. As a maiden, she has become a recipient of divine salutation and it is delivered by an angel of the Lord.

The angel Gabriel delivers the message to the Blessed Mother that she has found favor with God. The Blessed Mother hears in the angelic message the favorable action of God in her life that began at her conception, continues into the present moment, and has become vivid in her self-consciousness. While she ponders in complete wonder and amazement how God's grace has been in her life since childhood, the angel Gabriel reiterates in vivid fashion the divine grace that has been given to the Blessed Mother: "you have found favor with God." As a beneficiary of the gratuitous gift of divine grace, the life of the Blessed Mother has been under the guidance of God. The angel Gabriel confirms that to be the case with an emphatic assurance of God's protection: "The Lord is with you." God's gratuitous gift of divine favor to the Blessed Mother is the moving force in her life to willingly accept to make God's presence reach everyone in the world by becoming the Mother of our Lord. Even though she is unaware of the profundity of God's grace in her life, it has guided and brought her to an expression of total self-professed cooperation with God's saving plan for humanity: "I am the handmaid of the Lord" and let God's will be done in me.

With the Blessed Mother's *fiat*, her role in God's plan for the salvation of the world since the moment of her conception is established. As a maiden, in spite of the difficulties her place in God's saving plan for the world presents to the Blessed Mother, she voices her cooperation, calling herself God's servant. She embraces a universal role that is far beyond her particular interest and ambition as a young woman. Indeed, she gives up everything, takes up her God-given role, and makes her contribution in the divine plan to save the world. On this day that we commemorate her immaculate conception, the Blessed Mother becomes an example for us to discern God's purpose and be disposed to do good deeds toward one another in total collaboration with the divine plan for humanity.

Focusing the Gospel

Key words and phrases: "Hail, full of grace! The Lord is with you."

To the point: With no preparation or expectation, the angel Gabriel bursts into Mary's life and addresses her as "full of grace." This gospel gives us an opportunity to contemplate how we might react in a similar situation. Practicing Catholics have likely been reminded of Mary's *fiat*, her "yes" to the Lord, again and again over the years. This week, take the opportunity to go beyond that obvious question posed in this gospel and focus on the greeting as well. The truth is that we are met with bursts of grace all the time—in our families, daily activities, and community. Do you lean into grace? Accept it? Suspiciously brush it off? How would you react if a friend greeted you, "Hello, full of grace!"? By our Christian baptism, we are indeed full of grace, and the Lord is with us. That is an encouraging thought.

Model Penitential Act

Presider: Today's gospel reminds us of Mary's great trust in God. For the times we have not been who we are called to be, we ask for mercy and forgiveness . . . *[pause]*

Lord Jesus, you are the Son of God and the Son of Man: Lord, have mercy.
Christ Jesus, you are indeed the Son of Justice: Christ, have mercy.
Lord Jesus, you are light and life for a people in darkness: Lord, have mercy.

Model Universal Prayer (Prayer of the Faithful)

Presider: We bring our prayers before our loving God, assured like Mary that nothing is impossible for God.

Response: Lord, hear our prayer.

That the church may continue to listen to and uphold the voices, experience, and expertise of women . . .

That world leaders may work to end violence and oppression and say "yes" to peace and inclusion . . .

That all who are hurting in body, mind, or spirit may know the compassion of God . . .

That all gathered here might commit or recommit themselves to upholding the dignity of life and ending human trafficking . . .

Presider: Loving God, hear these prayers we bring to you today, as well as those intentions we hold in the silence of our hearts. We ask this through Christ our Lord. **Amen.**

About Liturgy

Pray What You Mean: The name of this solemnity is, perhaps understandably, easily misunderstood among the faithful to be about the conception of Jesus instead of the conception of—and indeed a title for—the Blessed Mother. Perhaps a longer or more carefully worded title for the day might have yielded better, clearer results.

When we craft intercessions for Mass, however, we should not be tempted to make them overly long, even in the name of clarity. Rather, we should say only what we need to, and mean to, say. This brevity makes word choice that much more important!

Perhaps you've heard an intercession remembering the young people in the parish preparing for the "special sacraments" of Eucharist or confirmation. Those are indeed special sacraments, but the question that follows is, of course, which sacraments aren't special? Or maybe we pray that church leaders guide us in ways of justice and love—but haven't they been doing that already? Perhaps we should rather pray that they "continue to lead us" in those pursuits.

So, when preparing intercessions, be careful to pray what you mean, so the entire assembly can, together, mean what they pray, and then live it clearly and effectively!

COLLECT

Let us pray.

Pause for silent prayer

O God, who by the Immaculate Conception of
   the Blessed Virgin
prepared a worthy dwelling for your Son,
grant, we pray,
that, as you preserved her from every stain
by virtue of the Death of your Son, which you
   foresaw,
so, through her intercession,
we, too, may be cleansed and admitted to your
   presence.
Through our Lord Jesus Christ, your Son,
who lives and reigns with you in the unity of
   the Holy Spirit,
God, for ever and ever. **Amen.**

FOR REFLECTION

• What are some of the ways you respond to God's call in your own life?

• As difficult as this call of discipleship can be, we rest assured knowing that God chooses us for God's self and that "nothing will be impossible for God." What does it mean for you to be chosen by God?

Homily Points

• Today's celebration, like all Marian celebrations, ultimately helps draw us closer to Jesus. It can be confusing, then, when we hear the term "Immaculate Conception." Today's solemnity honors Mary as one born without sin. It is because of this immaculate conception, however, that she can indeed be the *Theotokos*, or "God-bearer."

• Like Mary, we are called to bear God in the world. What does this look like for us today? Do we, like Mary, bring God's word to fulfillment in our own lives? Mary's "yes," or *fiat*, confirms her willingness to participate in God's plan of salvation. Like Mary, we also say "yes" to participating in the paschal mystery, living Christ's life, death, and resurrection in our own lives. In doing so we remember that the darkness and evil of the world do not have the final word. Life and love always prevail.

GOSPEL ACCLAMATION
cf. Luke 1:28

℟. Alleluia, alleluia.
Blessed are you, holy Virgin Mary, deserving of
all praise;
from you rose the sun of justice, Christ our God.
℟. Alleluia, alleluia.

Gospel   Luke 1:26-38; L690A

The angel Gabriel was sent from God
  to a town of Galilee called Nazareth,
  to a virgin betrothed to a man named
    Joseph,
  of the house of David,
  and the virgin's name was Mary.
And coming to her, he said,
  "Hail, full of grace! The Lord is with
    you."
But she was greatly troubled at what was
  said
  and pondered what sort of greeting
    this might be.
Then the angel said to her,
  "Do not be afraid, Mary,
  for you have found favor with God.
Behold, you will conceive in your womb
  and bear a son,
  and you shall name him Jesus.

Continued in Appendix A, p. 262.

See Appendix A, p. 262, for the other readings.

12

Note from the Liturgical Calendar:
"Sunday, December 12, 2021 is the Third Sunday of Advent, and the Feast of Our Lady of Guadalupe is omitted this year. Our Lady of Guadalupe may be appropriately honored in the Homily, Universal Prayer, and hymns during the Sunday liturgy. If pastoral advantage calls for it (cf. GIRM, no. 376), a Votive Mass of Our Lady of Guadalupe may be celebrated on a weekday before or after December 12, with the proper readings and prayers."

Reflecting on the Gospel
During the cold winter month of December 1531, when daylight was shorter, the air drier, and the environment arid, the community was spending more time indoors around the fireplace. It had been ten years since the Aztecs were colonized by Spanish conquistadors. They were denied the freedom for self-determination, and their way of life was hybridized by a foreign power that established itself on their soil through conquest that took the lives of loved ones, relatives, and friends.

In this environment of resentment and a discomforting presence of an invader arrived another visitor, a celestial visitor to the land and its people. She arrived as one of the locals, and not as a foreigner. After the gospel reading, the Blessed Mother arrives at the home of Elizabeth and Zechariah (Luke 1:40), her first ever known public visit since her encounter with the angel of the Lord, bringing joy to Elizabeth and her unborn child. Onwards, she makes visits and appearances all over the world, arriving to the Americas as Our Lady of Guadalupe. She comes to this community as an evangelizer to proclaim the good news of God's loving presence among God's children, especially the vulnerable and the disenfranchised.

At the home of Elizabeth and Zechariah, Elizabeth hears Mary's greeting and recognizes it, calling the Blessed Virgin Mary "the mother of my Lord" (1:43). Similarly, Juan Diego heard the Blessed Mother speak to him in his native language and she identified herself as his mother in a famous statement linked to the Blessed Mother: "Am I not here, I who am your Mother?" Just as the Blessed Mother fills the home of Elizabeth and Zechariah with joy because she has been endowed with divine favor and God is with her, likewise, during the winter month of torpidity and inertia, she visited a people under the weight of foreign occupation, bringing joy and hope. Appearing to Juan Diego, an indigenous commoner, and speaking to him in his native language of Nahuatl, she brought a renewed sense of dignity and hope to the Aztecs.

When the leaders of our church gathered at the Second Vatican Council, they recognized the Blessed Virgin Mary as a "model in faith and charity" (*Lumen Gentium* 53). Indeed, the Blessed Mother travels in haste to rejoice with the household of Elizabeth and Zechariah, providing whatever help, physical and emotional, that she can to Elizabeth for three months while carrying the pregnancy of her own child. Similarly, her presence to the exploited and marginalized Aztecs restored dignity and self-worth and elevated their imagination beyond their present life experiences in the hands of the Spanish conquistadors. For the Aztecs, the power and the presence of God through the Blessed Mother brought a renewed sense of freedom and commitment to social justice.

Our Lady of Guadalupe is venerated as a symbol of national unity and she is a Mother who unites God's children in the Americas and beyond. The devotion to her identity as Our Lady of Guadalupe indeed is one of unity for all God's children. By her exemplary life of faith in God and charity toward God's children, the Blessed Mother teaches us that our faith in God should match our disposition to charitable deeds toward one another. Our devotion and veneration of her motherhood demands from us a spirituality that honors our common humanity and siblinghood as God's children.

Focusing the Gospel
Key words and phrases: "Do not be afraid, Mary, for you have found favor with God."

To the point: In today's gospel we witness an exchange between an angel of God and Mary, a young girl. Though Gabriel has existed for millennia, when he notices Mary's fear, he tells her, "Do not be afraid, Mary." There is a deep tenderness in this exchange. One of the most powerful beings created by God comes directly to a teenage girl and, as they are speaking, is aware enough of her shock and hesitation to tell her that she's full of grace and favored by God. Mary asks a very direct question about the possibility of bearing a child outside of the act of sex, and Gabriel explains it to her. He treats her as an equal or, perhaps, as the Mother of God, with all of the respect that deserves.

Model Penitential Act
Presider: As we begin today's celebration, let us take a moment to ask for God's pardon and peace . . . *[pause]*

　　Lord Jesus, you are Son of God and son of Mary: Lord, have mercy.
　　Christ Jesus, you rule over the house of Jacob forever: Christ, have mercy.
　　Lord Jesus, your kingdom is eternal and has no end: Lord, have mercy.

Model Universal Prayer (Prayer of the Faithful)
Presider: God's love for God's people is evident in today's celebration. Let us bring our prayers to God, knowing they will be heard by one who loves us.

Response: Lord, hear our prayer.

That the church might always stand with people who are poor and relegated to any of the margins of society . . .

That all civil and world leaders may find inspiration for leadership in Mary's humility . . .

That all who are discriminated against because of their race or nationality may find the authentic acceptance and encounter that comes from God . . .

That all gathered here may commit ourselves to reaching beyond our walls of wood and stone to build relationships with all of God's people . . .

Presider: Loving God, hear the prayers we bring before you this day. Like Mary, we are your servants. Answer these prayers according to your Word. We ask this through Christ our Lord. **Amen.**

About Liturgy
Calendar Quirks: There is such a richness in the typical celebrations of Our Lady of Guadalupe! This year the challenge, indeed the opportunity, is to allow Sunday to be Sunday and also honor our Blessed Mother in ways that harmonize well with the liturgical calendar.

　　See the "About Music" note on December 12 for a brief thought about the canticle (in the place of the responsorial psalm) for this solemnity.

FOR REFLECTION

• What images of Mary do you most resonate with? Why?

• What about the story of Our Lady of Guadalupe speaks to you?

Homily Points
• Today's celebration of the feast of Our Lady of Guadalupe gives us even deeper insight into Mary's maternal nature. In the story of the interaction between Mary and Juan Diego, we hear Mary speak using words like "My child" and "My dearest one."

• Our Lady of Guadalupe took the appearance of an Indigenous woman dressed in traditional Aztec garb. With this, Mary's physical representation was not one of dominance but of familial togetherness, intensified by the fact that she spoke in Juan Diego's own language. Mary always stands on the side of the poor and vulnerable. This is the central theme of Mary's *Magnificat* and the message of the incarnation.

• As we celebrate the patron of the Americas in today's feast, let us take this opportunity to name and remember the poverty, oppression, and injustice that still pervade our country and world. May we find inspiration in the story of Our Lady of Guadalupe to grow in common community.

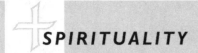

SPIRITUALITY

GOSPEL ACCLAMATION
Isa 61:1 (cited in Luke 4:18)

R̸. Alleluia, alleluia.
The Spirit of the Lord is upon me,
because he has anointed me
to bring glad tidings to the poor.
R̸. Alleluia, alleluia.

Gospel Luke 3:10-18; L9C

The crowds asked John the Baptist,
    "What should we do?"
He said to them in reply,
    "Whoever has two cloaks
    should share with the person who
        has none.
And whoever has food should do
    likewise."
Even tax collectors came to be baptized
    and they said to him,
    "Teacher, what should we do?"
He answered them,
    "Stop collecting more than what is
        prescribed."
Soldiers also asked him,
    "And what is it that we should do?"
He told them,
    "Do not practice extortion,
    do not falsely accuse anyone,
    and be satisfied with your wages."

Now the people were filled with
    expectation,
    and all were asking in their hearts
    whether John might be the Christ.
John answered them all, saying,
    "I am baptizing you with water,
    but one mightier than I is coming.
I am not worthy to loosen the thongs of
    his sandals.
He will baptize you with the Holy Spirit
    and fire.
His winnowing fan is in his hand to
    clear his threshing floor
    and to gather the wheat into his barn,
    but the chaff he will burn with un-
        quenchable fire."
Exhorting them in many other ways,
    he preached good news to the people.

Reflecting on the Gospel

In the gospel a shout is heard: urgent, loud, seeming at first to be discordant with the joy of the other readings. John the Baptist is with us again, a lean and eager man, his life pared down to essentials by his wilderness experience, his tongue sharpened by silence. Listening to his prophetic and passionate words, the crowds wonder if he might be the long-awaited Messiah. They come to

John with their practical questions: "[W]hat is it that we should do?" they ask, and John has practical answers for them. He does not suggest that they dissociate themselves from their everyday lives, but rather that they be converted to just living and sharing in their ordinary relationships. John does not call them into the desert but urges them to be sensitive to the wilderness of poverty around them and among them, responding by cloth-ing the needy with their extra cloak and shar-ing food with the hungry.

There is nothing of elitism in the Baptist's ministry. In the crowds are two of the most despised groups in Palestinian society: tax collectors and soldiers, both of whom worked for the Roman occupying force. The tax collectors are not told to resign, but to stop exploiting the people; the soldiers (probably police who served as security guards for the tax collectors) are not commanded to leave the force, but to avoid violence, intimidation, and grumbling about their pay—they at least get a wage. One way the imperial system of Rome or any global power then or now can be changed is through a change of heart of those within it or concerned about it, or through informed, responsible voting for or against it. This is gospel "people power."

John comes to us this third week of Advent as the awakener of our sense of social justice, the one who points to the clutter of selfish concerns and material-ism that can suffocate our practical love for our brothers and sisters in the stale air of indifference or greed. We are called to be concerned not only with the material clothing of the naked, but also with covering with love the naked vul-nerability of someone in need. Feeding the hungry is not only about the soup kitchen, but also about nourishing one another with our compassionate concern. How can we, individually, or in our families, parishes, or other communities, respond today to John the Baptist? How can we plan ways in which we can give Christmas back to the ones to whom it really belongs: the homeless, the refu-gees, the elderly, the sick, the hopeless young people, those with disabilities, all of whom are so often discarded like our cast-off Christmas wrappings?

It is not easy to hear prophetic voices over the outer noise of the shopping centers or the inner noise of our rehearsals of what still needs to be done by Christmas Eve. Yet these are the days when we are encouraged by Isaiah, whose song is today's responsorial, to take at least some time to be water-drawers as well as shoppers. In a few moments of prayer or sacred reading, we can reach into our inner depths where the well of salvation flows and drink joyfully and confidently from its sustenance. Or we can draw water so that we may quench the thirst of a brother or sister for companionship, for compassion, for something to hope for—and discover that, in our so doing, God renews the springs of his grace within us.

Focusing the Gospel

Key words and phrases: "Whoever has two cloaks should share with the person who has none. And whoever has food should do likewise."

To the point: John the Baptist does not mince words. He gets right to the heart of concrete values, providing a perfect preamble to the Beatitudes. He challenges his community when they request his critique, but instead of feeling insult or trepidation, Luke tells us that, "Now the people were filled with expectation, and all were asking in their hearts whether John might be the Christ." What if, when we encounter an admonition in response to our actions, we react with expectation? What if we are able to view honest critique with curiosity, as opposed to shame and excuses? Parishes are a cornerstone of community. How do you solicit and receive critique from your colleagues?

Connecting the Gospel

to the first and second readings: The gospel, on the surface, seems to be in conflict with the joy and satisfaction expressed in the first and second readings. While John the Baptist is telling his community to go against self-protective habits of the day, the prophet Zephaniah and the apostle Paul tell us to rejoice, feel peace, and exalt the Lord. This is a classic spiritual conundrum, that in humility we will find the most joy and the most peace. "Whoever has two cloaks should share with the person who has none. And whoever has food should do likewise."

to experience: If you gave up half of all you own—your belongings, clothes, phone, books, jewelry, even half of the value of your house, or half of your retirement fund—to your local homeless shelter or women's crisis center, what would it feel like? Does the thought fill you with fear or outrage? Does it feel like it's too big of an ask for Christ to make? Why does it feel this way?

Connecting the Responsorial Psalm

to the readings: The Nativity is at hand, and this week's psalm accompanies the first and second readings in their anticipation of joy and peace.

to psalmist preparation: "God indeed is my savior; / I am confident and unafraid." When you proclaim these words, allow yourself to truly embody that sentiment. When you stand in front of the congregation, feel the weight of your worthiness and allow yourself to fully believe what you sing. Recall moments of consolation and peace in your life, when you have felt confident and unafraid.

PROMPTS FOR FAITH-SHARING

What do you think John the Baptist's answer would be if you asked him, "What should I do?"

_____

_____

_____

_____

_____

_____

When in your life do you feel, as the psalmist says, most "confident and unafraid"?

_____

_____

_____

_____

_____

_____

It's Gaudete Sunday. How are you balancing the material demands of secular consumerism with Paul's call to "Have no anxiety at all"? Are there areas of your day when you can focus on putting "everything, by prayer and petition, with thanksgiving," in a request to God?

_____

_____

_____

_____

_____

_____

Model Penitential Act

Presider: In today's letter from Paul to the Philippians, we hear that the peace of God will guard our hearts and minds in Jesus. With prayer and petition let us acknowledge the times we have sinned . . . *[pause]*

Lord Jesus, you are the one in whom we rejoice: Lord, have mercy.

Christ Jesus, you baptize us with the Holy Spirit: Christ, have mercy.

Lord Jesus, you renew us in your love: Lord, have mercy.

Homily Points

• Our readings today on this Gaudete Sunday are filled with images of rejoicing. The prophet Zephaniah tells us to shout for joy, for the Lord is in our midst. Likewise, St. Paul insists that the Lord is near and exhorts us to rejoice in the Lord. Although it takes a more somber tone, even the gospel reading speaks of rejoicing as John the Baptist warns his followers that there is still time to turn to God before the wheat is gathered and the chaff is burned.

• These Advent readings emphasize an important element of discipleship: The kingdom of God is both "here" and "not yet." God is present in our lives, yet we still look for the time when God's kingdom will come to full fruition. We are never not in the presence of God, yet we know there will be a time when wars and poverty and injustice and division will be no more. We wait in hope but must also commit ourselves to spreading the reign of God.

• Emmanuel, "God with us," is such a powerful reality that is far beyond what we can possibly comprehend. Even so, we can reflect on the idea that God loves us so intimately that God becomes one of us. If we really lived this notion of Emmanuel, would we not treat all people with dignity and respect? Would we not live as stewards of the earth, working to care for our common home? As we continue this season of Advent, how might we be called to more fully live this certainty of Emmanuel, God with us?

Model Universal Prayer (Prayer of the Faithful)

Presider: Paul tells us to practice gratitude and have no anxiety as we make our requests known to God. Trusting that God hears us, we bring our prayers and petitions.

Response: Lord, hear our prayer.

That the church may continue to be a source of joy for all peoples . . .

That local and world leaders may practice gratitude and compassion in their actions and decisions . . .

That all people who find this season particularly joyless may find consolation in Emmanuel, God with us . . .

That all gathered here may discern how to best use their gifts to bring about the kingdom of God . . .

Presider: God who knows us intimately, listen to our prayers. We ask this through Christ our Lord. **Amen.**

COLLECT

Let us pray.

Pause for silent prayer

O God, who see how your people
faithfully await the feast of the Lord's
    Nativity,
enable us, we pray,
to attain the joys of so great a salvation
and to celebrate them always
with solemn worship and glad rejoicing.
Through our Lord Jesus Christ, your Son,
who lives and reigns with you in the unity
    of the Holy Spirit,
God, for ever and ever. **Amen.**

FIRST READING

Zeph 3:14-18a

Shout for joy, O daughter Zion!
    Sing joyfully, O Israel!
Be glad and exult with all your heart,
    O daughter Jerusalem!
The LORD has removed the judgment
    against you,
    he has turned away your enemies;
the King of Israel, the LORD, is in your
    midst,
    you have no further misfortune to fear.
On that day, it shall be said to Jerusalem:
    Fear not, O Zion, be not discouraged!
The LORD, your God, is in your midst,
    a mighty savior;
he will rejoice over you with gladness,
    and renew you in his love,
he will sing joyfully because of you,
    as one sings at festivals.

CATECHESIS

RESPONSORIAL PSALM
Isa 12:2-3, 4, 5-6

R℣. (6) Cry out with joy and gladness: for
among you is the great and Holy One
of Israel.

God indeed is my savior;
   I am confident and unafraid.
My strength and my courage is the LORD,
   and he has been my savior.
With joy you will draw water
   at the fountain of salvation.

R℣. Cry out with joy and gladness: for
among you is the great and Holy One
of Israel.

Give thanks to the LORD, acclaim his name;
   among the nations make known his
   deeds,
   proclaim how exalted is his name.

R℣. Cry out with joy and gladness: for
among you is the great and Holy One
of Israel.

Sing praise to the LORD for his glorious
   achievement;
   let this be known throughout all the
   earth.
Shout with exultation, O city of Zion,
   for great in your midst
   is the Holy One of Israel!

R℣. Cry out with joy and gladness: for
among you is the great and Holy One
of Israel.

SECOND READING
Phil 4:4-7

Brothers and sisters:
Rejoice in the Lord always.
I shall say it again: rejoice!
Your kindness should be known to all.
The Lord is near.
Have no anxiety at all, but in everything,
   by prayer and petition, with
      thanksgiving,
   make your requests known to God.
Then the peace of God that surpasses all
   understanding
   will guard your hearts and minds in
   Christ Jesus.

About Liturgy

Truth with Intensity: We hear more from John the Baptist this weekend, one of the more colorful personae in our Scriptures. We're given some insight into his attire, into his diet even, and perhaps into his whole aesthetic. We can even imagine him sharing his fiery rhetoric—or can we? Luke's gospel—all of the gospels—neglect to tell us how he proclaimed his warnings and prophesies, only that he said them.

I often like to imagine the Old Testament prophets, and specifically John the Baptist, not screaming, eyes set ablaze, but speaking with an intensity that can only be found in the softest voice. Many of us have experienced our parents being angry and yelling at us, but then, when they were *really* angry, their volume would drop way down, and we all knew what that meant too.

I'm reminded of a lesson I learned a while back, most useful typically in a rehearsal or classroom setting, that seems appropriate for anyone who is called to speak truth from any sort of platform. If folks are being too loud or noisy and not listening to you, sometimes speaking softer is the solution. Whisper. Make people have to be quiet to hear you. For a conductor, if your choir or ensemble isn't following your tempo, conduct smaller, down to just your pointer finger keeping time an inch from your chest. Make people watch you; make people pay attention. God wasn't in the storm or the earthquake; God was in the whispering wind. Jesus was at his most strong when silent in front of the Sanhedrin and Pilate.

As we continue pondering divine justice and how our liturgies themselves embody that facet of God, we must hold as true that brash voices are needed sometimes—and that sometimes kinder voices are needed. While we are not in any position to dictate to other people how they speak truth, we can decide for ourselves, in any given context, what manner of speaking the truth might be best received, might best achieve a desired result. Those whose hearts and minds are most in need of change are, from our perspective, often both the folks we think we might need to speak most forcefully to, and those most likely to walk away from pondering the subject matter *because* they feel they are being yelled at. Even when being a voice for the voiceless, you might not want to be as loud as possible. Volume doesn't make a truth any more true.

Similarly, those who might most need to hear bold and sustained voices of justice and equity should not tune out the message because it is bold and sustained. It is important for all of us to hear and truly understand such voices, perhaps only to recognize and affirm the humanity and dignity that has not always (or rarely) been recognized and affirmed; perhaps that's so someday—or sooner—we all together will be part of building a just world, the reign of God.

About Music

The Highest Honor of Our Race: It seems a good moment to talk about the text of the canticle (in the place of the responsorial psalm) for the solemnity of Our Lady of Guadalupe, which is typically, though not this year, on December 12. The refrain from Judith 13 says, "You are the highest honor of our race." You can quickly see where that final word could become problematic. It's worth taking time with any music ministers this weekend to discuss and pray over how the word is being used in this context and to reflect on any issues of racial justice especially that need to be addressed in the current moment.

✠ SPIRITUALITY

GOSPEL ACCLAMATION
Luke 1:38

℟. Alleluia, alleluia.
Behold, I am the handmaid of the Lord.
May it be done to me according to your word.
℟. Alleluia, alleluia.

Gospel

Luke 1:39-45; L12C

Mary set out
  and traveled to the hill
     country in haste
to a town of Judah,
where she entered the
     house of Zechariah
and greeted Elizabeth.
When Elizabeth heard
  Mary's greeting,
the infant leaped in her
    womb,
and Elizabeth, filled with
    the Holy Spirit,
cried out in a loud voice
    and said,
"Blessed are you among
    women,
and blessed is the fruit of your
    womb.
And how does this happen to me,
  that the mother of my Lord should
    come to me?
For at the moment the sound of your
    greeting reached my ears,
  the infant in my womb leaped for joy.
Blessed are you who believed
  that what was spoken to you by the
    Lord
  would be fulfilled."

Reflecting on the Gospel

The large mysteries of the first three weeks of Advent converge this Sunday into the truth that the Christ who will rule the cosmos was once carried in the small world of Mary's womb. John the Baptist, whose strong voice we heard on the Jordan riverbank last week, today has no voice and can only announce the good news of Jesus's equally silent advent by an exultant leap of joy in Elizabeth's womb. There are no crowds pressing forward, asking questions. There are only two pregnant women as the first and most intimate audience for the meeting of the Messiah with his precursor, and the one question Elizabeth asks of Mary is: "How does this happen to me, that the mother of my Lord should come to me?"

As the ark of the covenant was being taken up to Jerusalem, David danced before it in joyful reverence for the sacred artifacts of Israel it contained (2 Sam 6:14-15). John now dances before Mary, the new "ark" of a new covenant, sealed in the flesh and blood of the child she carries in her womb—the most holy possession of Israel. When the six-month-old baby leaps in Elizabeth's womb, she too becomes a prophet. Filled with the Holy Spirit, she reads the signs of the times, the "something more" of an ordinary human event—the stirring of the child in her womb—and proclaims the blessedness that God has bestowed on Mary and the One she carries.

The Advent mystery tells us so clearly that God has a special love for apparently unimportant people and places: for backwater Nazareth and its young woman; for the unnamed village of an old country priest and his aging wife; for the town of Bethlehem-Ephrathah which, by the time of the prophet Micah, whom we heard in the first reading, had been eclipsed by Jerusalem in importance, even though the former was David's birthplace. The word of the Lord that came to Micah in the eighth century BCE announces that a new future awaits this town for, like a woman in labor, its pain (of neglect) will be changed when it brings forth a future king who will fulfill the dreams as yet unrealized by the Davidic lineage. The one to come will be shepherd of his flock, caring for them in the strength of the Lord and bringing peace and security. In such unimportant places and in unexpected ways, the Son of David will be born as this fulfillment of the dreams of his people. In us, too, such dreams will be fulfilled if we offer Jesus hospitality.

Do we recognize the glory of God in unimportant people and places? Or do we drop a veil over the poverty and pain that can exist not only in far-off places, but also nearby, and even in our own hearts? Some people dread the approach of Christmas. The loneliness, for example, of those suffering the pain of broken relationships or distance from loved ones is intensified by viewing the joyful companionship and family gatherings of those around them. In many places, the rates of suicide and domestic violence rise during this "season of goodwill" when not much goodwill is experienced by some people. This is a challenge to our parishes and families, and one that many Christians are meeting with great generosity and hospitality.

God has given us the most wonderful of Christmas gifts: his own Son, wrapped in our human flesh. But the whole Christ, head and members, is not yet fully formed. Until the end of the ages, he continues to wrap himself in the love and fidelity of his disciples.

Focusing the Gospel

Key words and phrases: "Elizabeth, filled with the Holy Spirit, cried out in a loud voice."

To the point: Elizabeth is so overwhelmed with joy when Mary comes to her that her body reacts in two physical ways. First, the child she's carrying moves. If you've carried a child, you can imagine what that big kick may have felt like. Second, she cries out. The gospel writer is very specific with this action: she doesn't simply "greet" or "speak," as we may expect. Instead, she "cried out in a loud voice." There's a lack of inhibition in Elizabeth's joy that is unexpected, if not jarring. She expresses loud joy at not only seeing a member of her family whom she loves, but simultaneously making the connection that her cousin is *carrying her Messiah.* That realization does not elicit demur wonder, but a vocal exclamation. Do you have a family member or friend who expresses joy in a similar way? Do you find this delightful, or does it give you some anxiety when a person greeting you "makes a scene"? Do you think Mary was overwhelmed, or ran right into her arms?

Connecting the Gospel

to the first reading: The first reading paints a picture of the coming of a grand ruler, who will "stand firm" and "shepherd his flock by the strength of the Lord." Words like "majestic" and "greatness" suggest a ruler who is intimidating, and yet the passage ends with the declaration, "[H]e shall be peace." The prophet Micah gives us a classic moment of biblical irony: the leader described with warrior-like words is, in fact, peace on earth.

to experience: This week's readings are a juxtaposition of traditionally feminine and masculine imagery: In the gospel, Elizabeth has an experience directly tied to her pregnancy, and in the first reading, Micah describes a leader who is a "firm" and "majestic" shepherd. However, both passages hinge on an unexpected turn: Elizabeth cries out loudly and says exactly what she's thinking, and Micah's Ruler is the embodiment of peace. By pairing these two passages in this week's liturgy, we are invited to contemplate a Messiah who speaks to the nuanced experience of both women and men.

Connecting the Responsorial Psalm

to the readings: The psalm gives us a command to use in prayer: "[L]et us see your face." This direct ask is helpful, but what might that "face" be? The first reading describes a shepherd who is firm and majestic, and the second reading describes the body of Jesus, consecrated and offered as a "holocaust" for us. The gospel gives us an example of someone's reaction at the anticipation of seeing the actual, physical face of Jesus, the child being carried by Elizabeth, Mary's cousin.

to psalmist preparation: What does "the face" of Jesus look like to you? Is it what was left on Veronica's cloth? Is it a literal rendition of the Shroud of Turin? Or could "seeing" the face of the Lord be noticing his work in your life? Think about moments of peace or triumph, grace or clarity. Let those moments map your own experience of the face of God. When you share these words, invite the congregation to seek the face of the Lord in their own lives. This week's psalm is a petition to the Lord. Enjoy the satisfaction of asking a direct question.

PROMPTS FOR FAITH-SHARING

When was the last time you were so filled with joy and delight that you yelled about it, loudly?

_____

_____

_____

_____

_____

How do you express sudden joy? How do you greet people you haven't seen in a while? What kind of greeting makes you feel most comfortable and loved?

_____

_____

_____

_____

_____

Do you contemplate God in your personal devotion with more feminine or masculine imagery? How does this imagery inform your prayer?

_____

_____

_____

_____

What is the face of God? Do you see the face of God in your own life and work? Who shows the face of God to you?

_____

_____

_____

_____

_____

CELEBRATION

Model Penitential Act

Presider: Today's gospel is about the importance of relationships. For the times we have not lived in right relationship with ourselves, others, and God, we ask for forgiveness . . . *[pause]*

Lord Jesus, you show us how to love each other: Lord, have mercy.

Christ Jesus, you are the peace the world cannot give: Christ, have mercy.

Lord Jesus, you are the Son of God and the son of Mary: Lord, have mercy.

Homily Points

• Relationship is at the core of today's gospel. Mary travels to be with her cousin Elizabeth to accompany her during her pregnancy. When Mary speaks, John leaps in Elizabeth's womb. There is a visceral, tangible reaction when the two women embrace. Part of this encounter highlights the significance of the familial relationship between Mary and Elizabeth, where the two offer support and solidarity. Even more fundamental, however, is Mary's and Elizabeth's relationship with God. Mary agrees to be the Mother of God, and Elizabeth recognizes the presence of God in her midst. Do we recognize God in our relationships with family members, friends, and co-workers? Do we react when we encounter God in our midst?

• It can be very easy for us, as humans, to limit our understanding of God and God's working in our lives. The first reading from the prophet Micah calls Bethlehem-Ephrathah "too small to be among the clans of Judah." Historically, the population of Bethlehem was probably small in number and perhaps easily overlooked in comparison to the larger cities. Even so, it is in Bethlehem that Jesus of Nazareth is born. It is in Bethlehem that the world changes forever when God becomes human. We must be willing to encounter God where God presents God's self, even in the most unlikely of places.

• Throughout Scripture, God continually chooses people who are humble and lowly to raise up and work through. At a time when everyone is preparing for Christmas, humility might be in short supply. How can you live this humility of Mary and Elizabeth and Christ in the coming days?

Model Universal Prayer (Prayer of the Faithful)

Presider: With faith like that of Mary and Elizabeth, let us lift up our prayers to God.

Response: Lord, hear our prayer.

That all members of the church may grow in humility, following the example of Mary . . .

That state, national, and world leaders will work to meet the physical, social, and spiritual needs of the most vulnerable . . .

That all survivors of abuse may know the immense love of God, even when they feel betrayed by people and institutions . . .

That our community, inspired by the interaction of Mary and Elizabeth, may actively build relationships of love and hope . . .

Presider: Loving God, our prayers are no secret to you, yet we raise them to grow in relationship and transparency. Hear these prayers and answer them according to your will. We ask this through Christ our Lord. **Amen.**

COLLECT

Let us pray.

Pause for silent prayer

Pour forth, we beseech you, O Lord,
your grace into our hearts,
that we, to whom the Incarnation of Christ
    your Son
was made known by the message of an
    Angel,
may by his Passion and Cross
be brought to the glory of his
    Resurrection.
Who lives and reigns with you in the unity
    of the Holy Spirit,
God, for ever and ever. **Amen.**

FIRST READING
Mic 5:1-4a

Thus says the LORD:
You, Bethlehem-Ephrathah
    too small to be among the clans of
        Judah,
from you shall come forth for me
    one who is to be ruler in Israel;
whose origin is from of old,
    from ancient times.
Therefore the Lord will give them up, until
    the time
    when she who is to give birth has
        borne,
and the rest of his kindred shall return
    to the children of Israel.
He shall stand firm and shepherd his flock
    by the strength of the LORD,
    in the majestic name of the LORD, his
        God;
and they shall remain, for now his
    greatness
    shall reach to the ends of the earth;
    he shall be peace.

RESPONSORIAL PSALM

Ps 80:2-3, 15-16, 18-19

℟. (4) Lord, make us turn to you; let us see
your face and we shall be saved.

O shepherd of Israel, hearken,
from your throne upon the cherubim,
shine forth.
Rouse your power,
and come to save us.

℟. Lord, make us turn to you; let us see
your face and we shall be saved.

Once again, O LORD of hosts,
look down from heaven, and see;
take care of this vine,
and protect what your right hand has
planted,
the son of man whom you yourself
made strong.

℟. Lord, make us turn to you; let us see
your face and we shall be saved.

May your help be with the man of your
right hand,
with the son of man whom you yourself
made strong.
Then we will no more withdraw from you;
give us new life, and we will call upon
your name.

℟. Lord, make us turn to you; let us see
your face and we shall be saved.

SECOND READING

Heb 10:5-10

Brothers and sisters:
When Christ came into the world, he said:
"Sacrifice and offering you did not
desire,
but a body you prepared for me;
in holocausts and sin offerings you took
no delight.
Then I said, 'As is written of me in the
scroll,
behold, I come to do your will, O God.'"

First he says, "Sacrifices and offerings,
holocausts and sin offerings,
you neither desired nor delighted in."
These are offered according to the law.
Then he says, "Behold, I come to do your
will."
He takes away the first to establish the
second.
By this "will," we have been consecrated
through the offering of the body of
Jesus Christ once for all.

About Liturgy

ERO CRAS: On December 17, the "O" antiphons began appearing at our liturgies at the gospel acclamation, helping us notice and shift into the last few days of Advent preparations for Christmas. They are not antiphons when used in that way at Mass, however; they were first the antiphons to the *Magnificat* at Evening Prayer for each day. Each one offers a specific messianic title for the coming Christ:

> December 17—Sapientia (Wisdom)
> December 18—Adonai (Hebrew rendering of YHWH)
> December 19—Radix Jesse (Flower of Jesse's Stem)
> December 20—Clavis David (Key of David)
> December 21—Oriens (Dawn, literally "The East")
> December 22—Rex Gentium (King of All People)
> December 23—Emmanuel (God with Us)

If one takes the first letter of each Latin title, working in reverse from December 23 to 17, two Latin words emerge: *ERO CRAS*—which means, in English, "Tomorrow, I will be [there]." The familiar hymn "O Come, O Come, Emmanuel" is based on the "O" antiphons. Because their proper appearance in the church's liturgy is so late in the season, many music directors choose not to use this hymn (or others based on the "O" antiphons) until the Third or Fourth Sunday of Advent.

About Liturgical Documents

Sacrosanctum Concilium's *Context:* With only a few words allowed here for what ought to be a multivolume effort, an important piece of context to mention is that Vatican II and especially the Constitution on the Sacred Liturgy and its calls for reform did not emerge out of a vacuum and are not the "rupture" some have described them as. Indeed, for a century there were legitimate liturgical "experiments" happening all around the world, in places like the Benedictine Abbey in Solesmes and at St. John's Abbey (also Benedictine) in Minnesota. Much of the work being done was a recovery of Gregorian chant, research into the patristic era of the church, and an exploration of the liturgical practices of that same time.

Pope Pius X, elected in 1903, issued a *motu proprio* (more on what those are another time!) on sacred music, wishing the laity to participate actively in the liturgy and called for more frequent reception of Holy Communion as well. Efforts between then and the council included recognizing that liturgy is a human action as well as a religious and divine action, recalling the importance of Scripture in our worship, and many liturgical reforms by Pope Pius XII in the 1950s. These included broader permissions to use the vernacular at liturgies in certain situations, allowing the use of vernacular hymns, shortening the eucharistic fast and significant changes to the rites of Holy Week, including moving the Holy Thursday liturgy to the evening, the Good Friday service to the afternoon, and making permanent the evening Easter Vigil liturgy first used experimentally in 1951.

The church indeed had much to talk about—the liturgical items mentioned here and so much more, liturgically and not—when Pope John XXIII convened the council he would not see finish. None of the conversations, decisions, and following implementations pertaining to our liturgy would have happened without the preceding work and ministries that gave and continue to give context to them. We are still hard at work implementing the reforms, liturgical and otherwise, of Vatican II, and will be for many years to come.

SEASON OF
CHRISTMAS

"It comes down to this, down to all this littleness,
to the tiny, fragile flesh of a newborn child in whom God
dares to immerse himself in human history:
fully human and fully divine."

The Vigil Mass

GOSPEL ACCLAMATION

R̸. Alleluia, alleluia.
Tomorrow the wickedness of the
    earth will be destroyed:
the Savior of the world will reign
    over us.
R̸. Alleluia, alleluia.

Gospel

Matt 1:1-25; L13ABC

The book of the genealogy of
    Jesus Christ,
    the son of David, the son
        of Abraham.

Abraham became the father
    of Isaac,
    Isaac the father of Jacob,
    Jacob the father of Judah
        and his brothers.
Judah became the father of
    Perez and Zerah,
    whose mother was Tamar.
Perez became the father of Hezron,
    Hezron the father of Ram,
    Ram the father of Amminadab.
Amminadab became the father of
    Nahshon,
    Nahshon the father of Salmon,
    Salmon the father of Boaz,
    whose mother was Rahab.
Boaz became the father of Obed,
    whose mother was Ruth.
Obed became the father of Jesse,
    Jesse the father of David the king.

David became the father of Solomon,
    whose mother had been the wife of
        Uriah.
Solomon became the father of Rehoboam,
    Rehoboam the father of Abijah,
    Abijah the father of Asaph.

Continued in Appendix A, p. 263, or
Matt 1:18-25 in Appendix A, p. 263.

See Appendix A, p. 264, for the other readings.

Reflecting on the Gospel

In many cultures, family holds a particular place of importance. Knowledge of and reverence for ancestors have significance. Historically, it was not uncommon for Jewish and African peoples to be known not only by their given name but also in relation to their parent(s). Hence, a person was known as the individual and the son/daughter of the person's father and/or mother (e.g., Rachel, the daughter of Laban). Through such nomenclature we are given familial connection and context. By knowing who one's parents are, we get a sense of how someone was raised, with what values, any economic advantages or disadvantages, honor or dishonor associated with the family, and other such information. Individuals were often seen through the lens of their parents, family, and ancestors.

The author of Matthew's gospel begins the accounts by tracing the genealogy of Jesus. It is logical to conclude, therefore, that the author thinks it is important. Many scholars view the presentation of this lineage as a justification for the reader—proof of the eminence from which Jesus is a descendant. Of preeminence among the line of descendants are Abraham and David. Abraham is recognized as the father of the nation and father of the faith, and David as preeminent king, "a man after [God's] own heart" (1 Sam 13:14). Tracing Jesus's lineage back to two such luminaries within Judean history grants Jesus a certain legitimacy, both as King and Messiah. In the Matthean gospel account, the writer reinforces the tie to the Davidic line when an angel of the Lord addresses the human father of Jesus as "Joseph, son of David." The writer of Matthew's gospel uses the reference to Joseph as the "son of David" to further establish the Davidic connection of the family line, as the people of Jesus's time would have understood Joseph to be the biological father.

Of further note in the Matthean genealogy is the patriarchal litany, wherein we have four women highlighted: Tamar, Rahab, Ruth, and the wife of Uriah, Bathsheba. Each of these women, in turn, introduces complicated familial information into the genealogy. Tamar disguises herself as a prostitute and seduces her father-in-law, Judah. Rahab is a Canaanite woman of faith and also a prostitute who hides Israelite spies in her home. Ruth is a Moabite woman of faith who attaches herself to Naomi, a Jew. The wife of Uriah, Bathsheba, has an affair with David, who in turn has Uriah killed in battle in an attempt to hide his sin and indiscretion. These four women of the Hebrew Bible (Old Testament) are joined by a fifth in the New Testament: Mary, the human Mother of God. The Matthean narrative, by including the women, not only highlights and uplifts the role of women in the birth of Jesus but it also conveys the sometimes less than ideal history within families.

The gospel for the Vigil Mass at Christmas serves to convey several things. First, it is made clear that family is important, both for the ancestral roots that ground us and in the way family history serves to contribute to who we are and will become. Second, family can substantiate and legitimize our existence. Third, family history can be complicated and is not always neat and tidy. This, however, does not negate our access to greatness and blessings. Finally, the introduction of non-Jewish blood in the lineage foretells of the accessibility of the Gospel promise of hope and salvation for the Gentiles and all nations, as through baptism we are adopted into the family of God and made coheirs with Jesus, our brother.

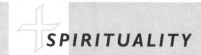

SPIRITUALITY

Mass at Midnight

GOSPEL ACCLAMATION
Luke 2:10-11

℟. Alleluia, alleluia.
I proclaim to you good news of
    great joy:
today a Savior is born for us,
Christ the Lord.
℟. Alleluia, alleluia.

Gospel

Luke 2:1-14; L14ABC

**In those days a decree
    went out from Caesar
    Augustus
that the whole world
    should be enrolled.
This was the first
    enrollment,
when Quirinius was gover-
    nor of Syria.
So all went to be enrolled,
    each to his own town.
And Joseph too went up from Galilee
    from the town of Nazareth
    to Judea, to the city of David that is
    called Bethlehem,
because he was of the house and
    family of David,
    to be enrolled with Mary, his be-
    trothed, who was with child.
While they were there,
    the time came for her to have her
    child,
    and she gave birth to her firstborn
    son.**

Continued in Appendix A, p. 264.

See Appendix A, p. 265, for the other readings.

Reflecting on the Gospel

It comes down to this, down to all this littleness, to the tiny, fragile flesh of a newborn child in whom God dares to immerse himself in human history: fully human and fully divine. Luke's gospel genius brings together heaven and earth, human longing and divine response in a narrative that cuts through often incomprehensible discussions of the divine sonship of Jesus. The story of Christ's birth is told as a nighttime event, and so we celebrate Christmas with candles and lights and under the stars. But none of these eliminate the darkness; they shine within it. So it is with this Child. Here is a mystery of divine concealment and divine revelation, darkness and light.

Jesus was not born in the familiarity of his own home, not surrounded by celebrating family and friends. Mary's birth pangs and Joseph's shared pain come as they are on a journey and among strangers. The traditional interpretation of "no room for them in the inn" has been one of negative refusal to help an obviously pregnant, near-to-full-term woman and her husband, something that would be abhorrent to Middle Eastern hospitality. Could it be that Luke is already emphasizing that it is the poor who are willing to give whatever they have, even if this is only the humble hospitality of a room shared with the animals and a feeding-trough bed for the newborn rather than more conventional guest accommodations? Given that he is writing fifty or so years after the resurrection of Jesus, Luke has surely experienced this, been moved by it, and challenges his more affluent communities with it. How often, to our shame, have the poor witnessed this to us in our own times?

The child is twice described as "wrapped in swaddling clothes," revealed as bound into a real, enfleshed humanity by the birth customs and culture of his particular time and place. As the Book of Wisdom proclaims, these are the same for king or commoner (Wis 7:4-5). Yet what is concealed is sung to the shepherds by the peaceful militia of angels: "Today in the city of David a savior has been born for you who is Christ and Lord." And this is a great joy for all the people. This is the good news that will turn the shepherds from a terrified, ostracized huddle on a Bethlehem hillside into seekers and proclaimers of what they find.

By the proclamation to the shepherds, Luke again chooses to make the poor and marginalized the first people who hear the good news of Christ's birth. For the first time in his gospel, he uses the word "today." When we hear this word as a eucharistic assembly, it becomes a present call to us to respond out of the poverty of our human and holy longings: to go and find the child of peace, to share the joy of our finding, to gaze with the eyes of faith on what the shepherds saw, to glorify and praise God—and go home changed. We find the Child laid "today" not only in the feeding place of the eucharistic table but also in our sisters and brothers, those to whom we also say "Amen" when we receive the body of Christ, and especially those whom Luke's Christmas gospel is all about: the hospitable, the peaceful, the poor and disregarded.

✝ SPIRITUALITY

Mass at Dawn

GOSPEL ACCLAMATION
Luke 2:14

Ry. Alleluia, alleluia.
Glory to God in the highest,
and on earth peace to those
on whom his favor rests.
Ry. Alleluia, alleluia.

Gospel

Luke 2:15-20; L15ABC

When the angels went away
    from them to heaven,
the shepherds said to one
    another,
"Let us go, then, to
    Bethlehem
to see this thing that has
    taken place,
which the Lord has made
    known to us."
So they went in haste and
    found Mary and Joseph,
and the infant lying in the manger.
When they saw this,
    they made known the message
    that had been told them about this
    child.
All who heard it were amazed
    by what had been told them by the
    shepherds.
And Mary kept all these things,
    reflecting on them in her heart.
Then the shepherds returned,
    glorifying and praising God
    for all they had heard and seen,
    just as it had been told to them.

See Appendix A, p. 265, for the other readings.

Reflecting on the Gospel

Good news travels fast! Consider how in our own communities good news is shared as someone purchases a new home, gets a new job with a raise, gets married, or has a baby. Today, the news of such events travels quickly as it is shared via social media. In biblical times, no such technology existed. Word of mouth was the social media of the day.

It is not a stretch to imagine that God wanted news of Jesus's birth, Emmanuel's arrival, to reach the people. Earlier in chapter 2 of Luke's gospel we are told that an angel of the Lord appeared to the shepherds as they worked

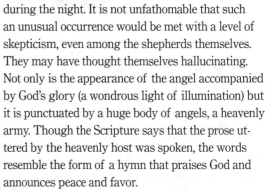

during the night. It is not unfathomable that such an unusual occurrence would be met with a level of skepticism, even among the shepherds themselves. They may have thought themselves hallucinating. Not only is the appearance of the angel accompanied by God's glory (a wondrous light of illumination) but it is punctuated by a huge body of angels, a heavenly army. Though the Scripture says that the prose uttered by the heavenly host was spoken, the words resemble the form of a hymn that praises God and announces peace and favor.

We are told in verses 15 and 16 of Luke's second chapter that the shepherds decided to travel to Bethlehem and see this news that the angel shared firsthand. The result of their journey is fourfold. First, the shepherds are able to witness for themselves this great and wondrous event, the birth of the child who is both Messiah and Lord. Second, their presence allows them to share in the joy of this family, celebrating with Mary and Joseph. Third, their firsthand witness of the child now makes them valuable evangelists who can testify to their community as to what they have seen and not simply what they have heard. Finally, they offer their testimony first to Mary and Joseph, who have each also received a visitation from an angel. In Luke's account only Joseph receives a visit from an angel. In the Matthean account it is Mary who receives the visitation, and in Matthew's gospel the purveyor of the news is identified as the archangel Gabriel, one of the few angels identified by name in the Bible. The shepherds' sharing with Mary and Joseph of their visitation by an angel further confirms what had been previously told to Mary and Joseph in their encounters. One may interpret from Mary's response to the shepherds' news an air of comfort as she seems to be receptive and further considers the implications of her son's miraculous birth.

Like the shepherds in Luke's account of the nativity of the Lord, we are also called to share the Good News with all whom we encounter, making known all we have experienced, heard, and seen along our pilgrim journey. We can share the joy and miracle of Jesus who has come into the world, he who is both Messiah and Lord. We can witness of the saving, transformative power of the Word made flesh who dwells among us. Our witness need not rise to the proportion of a grand hymn as with the heavenly host. All we need to do is make known what has been told to us and what we have experienced for ourselves.

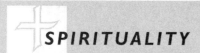

SPIRITUALITY

Mass during the Day

GOSPEL ACCLAMATION

R̷. Alleluia, alleluia.
A holy day has dawned upon us.
Come, you nations, and adore the Lord.
For today a great light has come upon the earth.
R̷. Alleluia, alleluia.

Gospel

John 1:1-18; L16ABC

In the beginning was the Word,
    and the Word was with God,
    and the Word was God.
He was in the beginning with God.
All things came to be through him,
    and without him nothing came to be.
What came to be through him was life,
    and this life was the light of the human
        race;
the light shines in the darkness,
    and the darkness has not overcome it.

A man named John was sent from God.
He came for testimony, to testify to the
        light,
    so that all might believe through him.
He was not the light,
    but came to testify to the light.
The true light, which enlightens everyone,
    was coming into the world.
He was in the world,
    and the world came to be through him,
    but the world did not know him.
He came to what was his own,
    but his own people did not accept him.

But to those who did accept him
    he gave power to become children of
        God,
    to those who believe in his name,
    who were born not by natural
        generation
    nor by human choice nor by a man's
        decision
    but of God.

*Continued in Appendix A, p. 266, or
John 1:1-5, 9-14 in Appendix A, p. 266.*

See Appendix A, p. 266, for the other readings.

Reflecting on the Gospel

Comic book heroes always have an origin story. It allows us, the readers, a glimpse of how the heroes came into being and how they received their powers. We also learn of the circumstances that set them on their path. Of the Synoptic Gospels, only Matthew and Luke give us a nativity with details and circumstances surrounding Jesus's birth. Mark's gospel begins with Jesus's earthly ministry in his adult years. John's gospel is unique among the four gospel books of the New Testament. Rather than a nativity, John's "origin story" goes all the way to the beginning: the beginning of existence. John does not speak of Jesus as a babe or an infant, but rather as Word (*Logos*) and Light (*Phōs*). John's gospel introduces Jesus as the conduit or facilitator through which all things are made possible. Jesus's duality as both God and human is also established.

John's gospel opens with a beginning reminiscent of the first book of the Bible, Genesis, and the creation story. In fact, both books begin with the phrase "In the beginning." Another connection can be found in how light factors prominently in this "beginning." In John's gospel we are told, "In the beginning was the Word, / and the Word was with God, / and the Word was God. / He was in the beginning with God. / All things came to be through him, / and without him nothing came to be." Verses 4-9 go on to identify this Word (*Logos*), also the Light (*Phōs*). In the first chapter of Genesis, God speaks and creates. Through the word of God, light comes into being: "Let there be light" (Gen 1:3). John's opening verses would therefore seem to be in line with the opening verses of Genesis. Essentially, all of creation came into being (is created) in the Genesis account through the spoken word of God. Hence, "All things came to be through him, / and without him nothing came to be."

Jesus as the light is also a focal point of John's gospel. In the opening verses of the gospel John asserts that Jesus is not only the light that "shines in the darkness" but also "[t]he *true* light, which enlightens everyone," and has now come into the world (emphasis added). What is perhaps most important to note is the intimate way in which the *Logos* and *Phōs* has entered the world, for the Word (*Logos*) has become flesh (human). In this very intimate manner, the Word has also become "the light of the human race."

Also unique to John's gospel are the series of self-revelatory statements— the "I am" revelations. Among them is the proclamatory statement found in chapter 8, "I am the light of the world. Whoever follows me will not walk in darkness, but will have the light of life" (8:12). This "light" that followers of Jesus will possess is meant to serve a purpose. It is meant to reflect the source of that light. Jesus describes this light in the fifth chapter of Matthew: "You are the light of the world. A city set on a mountain cannot be hidden. Nor do they light a lamp and then put it under a bushel basket; it is set on a lampstand, where it gives light to all in the house. Just so, your light must shine before others, that they may see your good deeds and glorify your heavenly Father" (5:14-16). As followers of Christ, we must reflect the light of Christ that has come into the world.

Model Penitential Act

Presider: Today we rejoice at the birth of Jesus Christ, our Emmanuel. As we prepare to celebrate the mystery of the incarnation, we ask for pardon and peace for the times we have not lived as God incarnate . . . *[pause]*

Lord Jesus, you are Son of God and son of Mary: Lord, have mercy.

Christ Jesus, you are Emmanuel, God with us: Christ, have mercy.

Lord Jesus, you are the Savior of the world who comes as a baby in the manger: Lord, have mercy.

Model Universal Prayer (Prayer of the Faithful)

Presider: Loving God, you became human in the incarnation and know the needs of your people. Hear us now as we offer our prayers and petitions.

Response: Lord, hear our prayer.

That today's celebration of the incarnation may inspire the church to see God in all people, regardless of nationality, race, religion, sexuality, or sexual orientation . . .

That all local and world leaders may work tirelessly to uphold human dignity in all forms, from conception to natural death . . .

That all who are alone this day may know they are loved, valued, and upheld as the children of a loving God . . .

That all gathered here today may use our gifts for the service of others, following the example Jesus gives us . . .

Presider: Emmanuel, God with us, hear our prayers this day as we stand in gratitude for the gift of the incarnation. May our lives radiate the light and peace of your birth. We ask this through Christ our Lord. **Amen.**

About Liturgy

Seasonal Symbolism: Christmas falls just a few days after the winter solstice, the shortest day—and longest night—of the year. Christmas then, in our experience, takes a lot of symbolism from light entering into the darkness. The Advent wreath leads us to that, and then at Christmas, trees are typically adorned with lights, as are many of the homes in our neighborhoods and businesses too, even if in a more secular way.

We would do well to remember that this is tied to life in the northern hemisphere; in the southern hemisphere, for instance in Australia, Christmas falls near the summer solstice, and the meteorological season brings with it not darkness and chill, but heat, dryness, and the longest days of the year.

Just as much of our Christmas music might not make sense to sing in Sydney at Christmas, might we examine how our music, art and environment, and other traditions may not readily cross cultures in our own local communities and open up more widely those conversations and practices?

COLLECT

(from the Mass during the Day)
Let us pray.

Pause for silent prayer

O God, who wonderfully created the dignity
   of human nature
and still more wonderfully restored it,
grant, we pray,
that we may share in the divinity of Christ,
who humbled himself to share in our
   humanity.
Who lives and reigns with you in the unity of
   the Holy Spirit,
God, for ever and ever. **Amen.**

FOR REFLECTION

• The incarnation is an act of God's self-gift. At a time where we put so much emphasis on the exchange of presents, today's celebration is an invitation to refocus on the gifts of life and love and relationship. How do we share ourselves with others? Do we listen attentively when someone speaks to us, or are we distracted by our laundry list of to-dos? Do we value opportunities for interactions with cashiers at the grocery store, or do we wish they would stop talking and work faster? Some serious self-reflection might reveal that we could more generously share our gift of self.

Homily Points

• The mystery of the incarnation is at the core of our Christian identity. The implications of this are almost unbelievable—namely, that humans now participate in God's divinity. Do we live this reality by treating all people with respect and working to protect human dignity in all forms?

• As we each discern how God calls us to live lives of Christian discipleship, we must also ask ourselves what gifts God has so generously given us and how we might use those gifts to make a difference in the world. While financial gifts are important and necessary, the sharing of one's talents for the good of others is just as, if not more, significant.

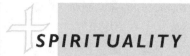

SPIRITUALITY

GOSPEL ACCLAMATION
Col 3:15a, 16a

℟. Alleluia, alleluia.
Let the peace of Christ control your
    hearts;
let the word of Christ dwell in you
    richly.
℟. Alleluia, alleluia.

Gospel

Luke 2:41-52; L17C

Each year Jesus' parents went
    to Jerusalem for the feast
    of Passover,
    and when he was twelve
        years old,
    they went up according to
        festival custom.
After they had completed
    its days, as they were
    returning,
    the boy Jesus remained be-
        hind in Jerusalem,
    but his parents did not know it.
Thinking that he was in the caravan,
    they journeyed for a day
    and looked for him among their rela-
        tives and acquaintances,
    but not finding him,
    they returned to Jerusalem to look
        for him.
After three days they found him in the
    temple,
    sitting in the midst of the teachers,
    listening to them and asking them
        questions,
    and all who heard him were
        astounded
    at his understanding and his
        answers.

Continued in Appendix A, p. 267.

Reflecting on the Gospel

"Family" today has many cultural and moral connotations and challenges for Christians. The "Holy Family of Jesus, Mary, and Joseph" may seem to exist on another planet or, at least, be light-years away from twenty-first-century relevance. Yet the gospel truth that the word of God for this feast affirms is that family life is "a kind of school of deeper humanity" that is penetrated by the spirit of Christ. It is a challenge to live in mutual respect and love: for parents to honor the dignity of their children, and children to respect the dignity of their parents, each one bound to the other in the love that God has lavished upon us, as John writes in today's second reading.

Our understanding of what we usually call "the finding in the temple" has often been sabotaged by artistic depictions of a precocious child Jesus, haloed and white-clad, lecturing (and even berating!) the religious teachers. Yet if we are attentive to the text, Jesus is described as first listening to the temple teachers before asking questions at what was a customary festival and Sabbath question-and-answer session (as opposed to a judicial one). "Searching" and "finding" are important gospel themes in Luke. They reflect the human experience that our questing so often involves questioning in the hope of finding that something more: more love, more wisdom, more truth.

Any parent can appreciate Mary and Joseph's desperate search for and relief at finding Jesus, but there is another search, another finding that is of central importance. It hangs painfully on Jesus's response to his mother's question, "Son, why have you done this to us?" The first words of Jesus in Luke's gospel are his response: "Why were you looking for me? Did you not know that I must be in my Father's house?"—the affairs that will take Jesus through a life of obedience, through another Passover of pain, another three-day loss in the tomb and into his new and risen life. The most significant developmental task of adolescence is the search for and gradual finding of one's identity, and as R. Alan Culpepper comments in the introduction to *The New Interpreter's Bible*: "What defines one's identity—family ties, religious experience, a sense of vocation, a personal creed, or one's dreams and ideals? Jesus found his identity by affirming his relationship with God."

For Mary and Joseph, as for all parents, there is the pain of allowing this child his independence, his identity, loving him, not possessing him or punishing him, but not fully understanding him. Surely a sword passes also through Joseph's heart as, in response to Mary's words about "your father and I," and as if gently contradicting her, Jesus refers to "my Father." For us, as for Joseph, commitment to gospel priorities will always cause some pain. Parents know this in a special and poignant way. For now, this "passover" of the adolescent Jesus is a theological sign of what is to come.

After this, Jesus returns to Nazareth with Mary and Joseph and is obedient to them. In the verse preceding this gospel (Luke 2:40), Luke had written of Jesus's growth in human and divine wisdom after his presentation in the temple. The last verse of this temple incident with which Luke ends his narrative of Jesus's childhood is again a comment that it was in this human family that such growth continued. An aspect of doing his Father's will was his openness to being graced by the precious relationships of his family at Nazareth. Children and parents in every age and culture are meant to be grace for one another.

Focusing the Gospel

Key words and phrases: "Your father and I have been looking for you with great anxiety."

To the point: This is one of the most relatable passages in all of the gospels. It doesn't take a lot of historical context to understand the fear and dread Mary and Joseph must have felt when they realized their precious baby boy was gone.

This gospel signifies the movement of Jesus from being Mary's miracle baby to a self-reflective adult. The entirety of his childhood, adolescence, and young adulthood is covered in a few short sentences. What we know of Jesus's upbringing is contained in the words that he "was obedient to [his parents]" and "advanced in wisdom and age and favor before God and man." Like last week, this is an opportunity to reflect on what the gospel writer must have heard about Jesus's life. Since the gospel contains accounts and parables of remarkable things, often turning the mundane remarkable, we are invited to wonder at the notion that Jesus's upbringing was probably fairly normal for a boy of his place and time. Whatever personal relationship Jesus may have developed with his Father in heaven, while here on earth, he was raised by a young mother and a father who likely built furniture for a living. He grew up a religious minority in an occupied territory. The lack of information given to us by the gospels is, in fact, information. Jesus was a child, then a teenager, then a twentysomething, and when he began his public ministry, he still lived with his mom.

Connecting the Gospel

to the second reading: John tells us in the second reading that we are the children of God, called to love one another as Jesus commanded us. Paired with this gospel, we are invited to consider that the call to "be like children" is not outside the scope of normal human experience. We've all been children. Perhaps we, like Jesus before his ministry, are also waiting with the knowledge that we belong to God, but "what we shall be has not yet been revealed."

to experience: If you knew you were destined to inherit everything your heart desires, how would you act in everyday life? If you knew that, ultimately, you will be taken care of, how would that knowledge alter your daily disposition? This is what John tells us. "Beloved, if our hearts do not condemn us, we have confidence in God and receive from him whatever we ask, because we keep his commandments and do what pleases him." If we truly believe this, daily anxieties can be put in a healthy perspective.

Connecting the Responsorial Psalm

to the readings: This week's readings are all about children in the house of the Lord. Mary and Joseph find Jesus in the temple, Hannah presents her son Samuel in the temple, and John tells us that we are God's children.

to psalmist preparation: You are telling the congregation that the blessed are in the house of the Lord while they are actually sitting in the house of the Lord. When you exclaim, "How lovely is your dwelling place, O LORD of hosts!" you can look around at real space. This is not purely metaphorical. Allow yourself to be drawn into the wonder of your church's particular art and architecture.

PROMPTS FOR FAITH-SHARING

Imagine Jesus as a peer in your elementary school or high school. How do you think he would have been received? Would you have been friends?

Have you ever had a conflict with a parent or authority figure because of misunderstood communication? How does it feel to know Jesus had the same interaction with his parents?

What do you consider the "house of the Lord," and how do you choose to "dwell" there in everyday life? Is it the physical church? A moment of prayer and meditation? A garden or walk?

31

Model Penitential Act

Presider: Today we celebrate the Holy Family, the relationship between Jesus, Mary, and Joseph. For the times we have failed to live in communion with others as one human family, we ask for pardon and peace . . . *[pause]*

> Lord Jesus, with Mary and Joseph you are a member of the Holy Family: Lord, have mercy.
>
> Christ Jesus, you call us to share the love of your Holy Family: Christ, have mercy.
>
> Lord Jesus, you invite us to grow in holiness: Lord, have mercy.

Homily Points

• Family relationships are not always easy, and even the Holy Family encountered the challenges of family life. Mary and Joseph must have been so worried when they could not find Jesus. It is not unreasonable to believe they experienced other emotions as well, perhaps some of the same feelings we have in our families today. There must have been frustration, concern, self-doubt, and maybe even some anger. We can find comfort knowing that the Holy Family was in fact a family, a human family.

• Today's gospel also shows the importance of communication within the family, as there must have been some sort of miscommunication between Mary, Joseph, and Jesus. Mary asks, "[W]hy have you done this to us?" and Jesus simply responds, "Why were you looking for me?" Luke even tells us that Jesus's parents did not understand what Jesus said to them. Misunderstandings are unavoidable in any relationship. We must be mindful, however, how we respond to these misunderstandings. Do we become angry or frustrated? Or do we respond with patience and compassion? Sometimes family life is a combination of both!

• As we celebrate and seek to emulate the Holy Family, we must also be aware that not all familial relationships are positive. Some family relationships are filled with mistrust, abuse, or any other number of negative feelings or experiences. Additionally, we must recognize that families take different forms and are not necessarily homogeneous. With this, the language we use in talking about family relationships must be inclusive and loving. We can take comfort knowing that the Holy Family demonstrates these realities.

Model Universal Prayer (Prayer of the Faithful)

Presider: Loving God, as we celebrate the Holy Family we bring our prayers to you without reservation or hesitation, for we know that you hear the prayers of your family.

Response: Lord, hear our prayer.

That the church may continue to grow in its understanding of the needs and realities of families today . . .

That local and national leaders may enact legislation that supports families and provides livable wages and healthy working conditions . . .

That all who feel separated or isolated from their families may find love and support, knowing they are never alone . . .

That all victims of domestic abuse may find support, healing, and justice . . .

Presider: Loving God, hear the prayers we bring before you today through the intercession of the Holy Family. May we find comfort in the support of Jesus, Mary, and Joseph as we strive to live lives of holiness in our own families. We ask this through Christ our Lord. **Amen.**

COLLECT

Let us pray.

Pause for silent prayer

O God, who were pleased to give us
the shining example of the Holy Family,
graciously grant that we may imitate them
in practicing the virtues of family life and
    in the bonds of charity,
and so, in the joy of your house,
delight one day in eternal rewards.
Through our Lord Jesus Christ, your Son,
who lives and reigns with you in the unity
    of the Holy Spirit,
God, for ever and ever. **Amen.**

FIRST READING

1 Sam 1:20-22, 24-28

In those days Hannah conceived, and at
    the end of her term bore a son
    whom she called Samuel, since she had
    asked the LORD for him.
The next time her husband Elkanah was
    going up
with the rest of his household
to offer the customary sacrifice to the
    LORD and to fulfill his vows,
Hannah did not go, explaining to her
    husband,
    "Once the child is weaned,
I will take him to appear before the LORD
and to remain there forever;
I will offer him as a perpetual nazirite."

Once Samuel was weaned, Hannah
    brought him up with her,
along with a three-year-old bull,
an ephah of flour, and a skin of wine,
and presented him at the temple of the
    LORD in Shiloh.
After the boy's father had sacrificed the
    young bull,
Hannah, his mother, approached Eli and
    said:
    "Pardon, my lord!
As you live, my lord,
I am the woman who stood near you
    here, praying to the LORD.
I prayed for this child, and the LORD
    granted my request.
Now I, in turn, give him to the LORD;
    as long as he lives, he shall be dedicated
    to the LORD."
Hannah left Samuel there.

RESPONSORIAL PSALM

Ps 84:2-3, 5-6, 9-10

℟. (cf. 5a) Blessed are they who dwell in
    your house, O Lord.

How lovely is your dwelling place, O LORD
     of hosts!
  My soul yearns and pines for the courts
     of the LORD.
My heart and my flesh cry out for the
     living God.

R℣. Blessed are they who dwell in your
     house, O Lord.

Happy they who dwell in your house!
  Continually they praise you.
Happy the men whose strength you are!
  Their hearts are set upon the
     pilgrimage.

R℣. Blessed are they who dwell in your
     house, O Lord.

O LORD of hosts, hear our prayer;
  hearken, O God of Jacob!
O God, behold our shield,
  and look upon the face of your
     anointed.

R℣. Blessed are they who dwell in your
     house, O Lord.

SECOND READING
1 John 3:1-2, 21-24

Beloved:
See what love the Father has bestowed
     on us
  that we may be called the children of
     God.
And so we are.
The reason the world does not know us
  is that it did not know him.
Beloved, we are God's children now;
  what we shall be has not yet been
     revealed.
We do know that when it is revealed we
     shall be like him,
  for we shall see him as he is.

Beloved, if our hearts do not condemn us,
  we have confidence in God and receive
     from him whatever we ask,
  because we keep his commandments
     and do what pleases him.
And his commandment is this:
  we should believe in the name of his
     Son, Jesus Christ,
  and love one another just as he
     commanded us.
Those who keep his commandments
  remain in him, and he in them,
  and the way we know that he remains
     in us
  is from the Spirit he gave us.

*See Appendix A, p. 267, for optional
readings.*

CATECHESIS

About Liturgy

Receiving Gifts: Many of us likely exchanged gifts the last day or two and may continue to do so over the next several days as Christmas celebrations continue. For those of us who lead a team of liturgical volunteers, be they musicians, lectors, servers, or any other grouping, it's prudent to occasionally reflect on the gift that they are to the worshiping community.

Of course, on the surface level that seems obvious: we are accustomed to speaking of gifts of time and talent to the parish, and it is so. Without those in our families of faith ministering to one another, the liturgy would be much less vibrant, and perhaps more than hollow—not even possible!

Yet I know at times in my roles as director of music ministries and as a church choir director, I sometimes forget that what volunteer music ministers offer must be seen as a gift. We can rightly become frustrated when rehearsal attendance begins to falter, for instance, and begin pondering if attendance policies might be needed. Such approaches might be valid, but only if first the offering that choir members show by choosing to join a music ministry is seen as a gift. Gifts can really only be graciously accepted, and particularly in these instances seen as a love offering. Love can never be forced or expected; it can at most be invited. It can certainly be received amiably and returned or offered first in kindness.

May we choose to see the volunteer liturgical ministers and their activities as gift: to us, to the community, and to God.

About Liturgical Documents

Sacrosanctum Concilium's *Emergence and Key Facets:* This first document to come from Vatican II (December 3, 1963) was approved by a nearly unanimous vote of the council (2,147 to 4). The Constitution on the Sacred Liturgy put into writing the principles emerging from the previous work of liturgical experimentations and adaptions, and set forth a road map, broadly, for implementation.

As I have already mentioned, the concepts of "source" and "summit" and "full, conscious, and active" participation found within are lynchpins of modern expressions of worship. The document also brought forth concepts that, some sixty years later, may seem like second nature to us: the paschal mystery (Christ's death, resurrection, and second coming, in a nutshell) (see SC 47 and 61) and inculturation far beyond mere use of the vernacular (SC 37–40).

Constitution on the Sacred Liturgy 37 is particularly worth revisiting frequently: "Even in the liturgy the church does not wish to impose a rigid uniformity in matters which do not affect the faith or the well-being of the entire community. Rather does it cultivate and foster the qualities and talents of the various races and nations. Anything in people's way of life which is not indissolubly bound up with superstition and error the church studies with sympathy, and, if possible, preserves intact. It sometimes even admits such things into the liturgy itself, provided they harmonize with its true and authentic spirit." We will return to this paragraph—and these critical concepts—in this space soon!

About Music

Hidden Gems on Families: The wide diversity of Scripture available today make it difficult to briefly suggest hymnody based on the readings. Some non-Christmas selections that might not be immediately obvious include "Center of My Joy" (found in GIA's *Lead Me Guide Me* hymnal) and "The Hands That First Held Mary's Child" (found in WLP's *One in Faith* hymnal), a rare text focusing on St. Joseph to the tune RESIGNATION.

DECEMBER 26, 2021
THE HOLY FAMILY OF JESUS, MARY, AND JOSEPH

GOSPEL ACCLAMATION

Heb 1:1-2

R⁊. Alleluia, alleluia.
In the past God spoke to our ancestors through
    the prophets;
in these last days, he has spoken to us through
    the Son.
R⁊. Alleluia, alleluia.

Gospel

Luke 2:16-21; L18ABC

The shepherds went in haste to Bethle-
    hem and found Mary and Joseph,
  and the infant lying in the manger.
When they saw this,
  they made known the message
    that had been told them about this
      child.
All who heard it were amazed
  by what had been told them by the
    shepherds.
And Mary kept all these things,
  reflecting on them in her heart.
Then the shepherds returned,
  glorifying and praising God
  for all they had heard and seen,
  just as it had been told to them.

When eight days were completed for
    his circumcision,
  he was named Jesus, the name given
      him by the angel
  before he was conceived in the
      womb.

See Appendix A, p. 268, for the other readings.

Reflecting on the Gospel

The mention of the circumcision and naming of Jesus in today's gospel is the first emphasis in Luke on the Jewishness of Jesus, and on Mary's and Joseph's obedience to the Mosaic Law. The first obedience Luke describes, however, is that of the shepherds. For the sake of their flocks, they were familiar with reading the skies and stars and listening to the singing of the winds; then one night they hear and see hosts of angels leading them over to Bethlehem.

Marginalized by the self-righteous who considered them irreligious because of their handling of their animals, and especially because their work did not permit them to leave their flocks unsupervised in order to participate in regular worship, these are the first people who are called to a new "worship," to a new "leaving all" of their flocks in order to go to the Christ Child. They risk a hasty journey down from the hills to the town. Perhaps it is the unexpectedness of the choice of themselves, poor and marginalized, as hearers of the angel's proclamation that urges them and opens them to faith in what they see there: a man and woman with a newborn child, "a savior . . . who is Messiah and Lord" (Luke 2:11). And when they return to their flocks, to their ordinary life, they return as people of praise, giving glory on their small piece of earth to what the angels had glorified in the vast heavens above them.

Mary hears what the shepherds repeat to her and, in contrast to their rush and excitement, around her there is silence. For a second time, she is "reflecting on" what she has heard. The Greek word that Luke uses is from *symballo*, "throwing together." Mary tries to "throw things together": her own human experience, the divine power she knows is working in her, the vulnerable child of her womb, and what the shepherds have told her. Before her there lies a lifetime of such pondering. She is surely the model for our pondering of the Word, for the times of reflective silence that we all need, for the challenge that disciples of Jesus accept: to constantly try to treasure the good news about Jesus, even in spite of the often contradictory voices we hear.

Mary had already been greeted by the angel of the annunciation as "favored one," and by Elizabeth as "blessed" (Luke 1:28, 42). The first reading chosen for today is the most solemn blessing of the First Testament, a Jewish blessing that, by its transplantation into the liturgy of this feast, serves to bless Mary as the one upon whom God's face has shone in a unique way; the woman whom God has favored with the joy and pain of the motherhood of Christ and the members of his body; the woman to whom God gives not just the peace of Christmas, but also that of the resurrection morning.

For those of us who view today not only as the octave of Christmas but also as the civil New Year's Day, this is a day of partying and pleasure, of seeing out the old and seeing in the new. What this newness also means for Christians is reflected in Luke's portrait both of the active, excited shepherds, obedient to the word of God, and of Mary, in his cameo, still and silent with the Word made flesh. We need both activity and excitement, stillness and silence in our lives if we are to recognize the Christ and tell this good news to others throughout this year.

Focusing the Gospel

Key words and phrases: "All who heard it were amazed by what had been told them by the shepherds."

To the point: This must have been an exciting scene, with shepherds shocked to find a family staying in a barn, and Mary and Joseph shocked that they had been found! The conversation that took place probably included many explanations, and a lot of, "Well, that's what the angels told us to do." Imagine the delight of everyone to realize that these strange happenings were not isolated. It was probably very comforting to Mary and Joseph to receive outside confirmation that their miracle child was indeed blessed.

Model Penitential Act

Presider: As we begin this new calendar year and celebrate this great solemnity of Mary, the Holy Mother of God, we pause and pray, mindful of our own sinfulness and need for God's mercy . . . *[pause]*

    Lord Jesus, you are Son of God and son of Mary: Lord, have mercy.
    Christ Jesus, your name was given by the angel: Christ, have mercy.
    Lord Jesus, you intercede for us at the right hand of the Father: Lord, have mercy.

Model Universal Prayer (Prayer of the Faithful)

Presider: Just as the shepherds went in haste to Bethlehem to find Jesus, let us also make haste in bringing our prayers to the God who intimately knows us and generously hears us.

Response: Lord, hear our prayer.

That the church may imitate Mary's contemplation through authentic discernment about important issues . . .

That all peoples and powers will know peace in this new year . . .

That all who are incarcerated may find support as they work toward rehabilitation and re-entrance into society . . .

That all gathered here may find time for quiet prayer in this new year . . .

Presider: Loving God, hear our prayers as we begin this new year and consecrate it to you, trusting that you know all our hopes, dreams, anxieties, and fears. We ask this through Christ our Lord. **Amen.**

About Liturgy

Liturgical Moderation: The title "Mary, Mother of God" was only arrived at after a few centuries of debate on the theological essence of Christ: fully God and fully human. The path to this doctrine was not always easy and was troubled with sometimes harsh arguments and public declarations of several heresies, Arianism perhaps chief among them.

Today, a growing inability, or perhaps a lack of desire, to engage in nuanced discussions and make critical distinctions can be placed alongside an inability (or again, an unwillingness) to listen or read carefully for content—instead focusing only on figuring out how to respond, retort, and argue back. Frequently, we need more nuance, more distinction, more listening. We, most often, need more "both/and" and less "either/or."

That said, of course there are some very binary moments in life, some moments of either right or wrong, either this or that. Additionally, the maxim "everything in moderation, including moderation" rings true. The art of it all is sorting out when to be nuanced and when not to be, when to be "both/and" and when to be "either/or," and when to be moderate and when to not be, even in our discussions over and executions of liturgical ideals and practices.

COLLECT
Let us pray.

Pause for silent prayer

O God, who through the fruitful virginity of
    Blessed Mary
bestowed on the human race
the grace of eternal salvation,
grant, we pray,
that we may experience the intercession of her,
through whom we were found worthy
to receive the author of life,
our Lord Jesus Christ, your Son.
Who lives and reigns with you in the unity of
    the Holy Spirit,
God, for ever and ever. **Amen.**

FOR REFLECTION

• Do we, like Mary, leave room in our hearts to contemplate God and God's incredible works?

• What are your prayers for this new calendar year?

Homily Points

• Some people are surprised by the number of Marian celebrations that occur during the seasons of Advent and Christmas. If we think about it, however, we realize that Mary's response to God is what facilitated the incarnation. We cannot celebrate Jesus's birth without also acknowledging and uplifting the one who bore him. This does not diminish our honor and reverence for Christ. Instead it offers us another lens through which we can understand Jesus. Mary is present at Jesus's birth, throughout his childhood and ministry, and even at the foot of the cross. Just as we can learn more about someone by knowing their family members, the same is true for Jesus.

• After her encounter with the shepherds in Bethlehem, the evangelist Luke tells us, "Mary kept all these things, / reflecting on them in her heart." As Mary continued to discern and understand the reality of the incarnation, she took time to quiet herself, reflect, and pray. May we also be willing to take time in reflection and prayer when we encounter something new or challenging.

✝ SPIRITUALITY

GOSPEL ACCLAMATION
Matt 2:2

℞. Alleluia, alleluia.
We saw his star at its rising
and have come to do him homage.
℞. Alleluia, alleluia.

Gospel

Matt 2:1-12; L20ABC

When Jesus was born in
    Bethlehem of Judea,
  in the days of King Herod,
  behold, magi from the
      east arrived in Jeru-
      salem, saying,
  "Where is the newborn king
      of the Jews?
  We saw his star at its rising
    and have come to do him
      homage."
When King Herod heard
    this,
  he was greatly troubled,
  and all Jerusalem with
      him.
Assembling all the chief priests and
    the scribes of the people,
  he inquired of them where the Christ
      was to be born.
They said to him, "In Bethlehem of
    Judea,
  for thus it has been written through
      the prophet:
  *And you, Bethlehem, land of
      Judah,*
    *are by no means least among
        the rulers of Judah;*
    since from you shall come a ruler,
      *who is to shepherd my people
          Israel."*

Continued in Appendix A, p. 268.

Reflecting on the Gospel

The magi may be historically controversial, but there is no doubt about the way in which they thrill our imagination and make us wonder about their visit to the child. Wonder and excitement about journeying to Jesus are important for every Christian, king or commoner. It is not from the Bible but from a legend recorded by the eighth-century saint and first English historian Bede the Venerable that we have numbered and named the magi Melchior, Caspar, and Balthasar. Artists, especially after the discovery of the New World, have often made the magi a multiracial trio, with black, red, and yellow faces, and the presumption of a one-to-one correspondence with their three gifts. The scholars may rightly debate historical issues; as listeners to the biblical word proclaimed in the assembly, and prayed in our sacred reading, we simply accept the narrative of the feast as story, but as story laden with symbols and rich in theological associations. And a story is often the surest, straightest line to the truth.

Guided by their natural and scientific wisdom, equipped with wealth and readiness to take risks, the magi—learned ones, possibly Persian astronomers—discover that following a star and searching for the truth can lead one into a political minefield. (Some things never change!) It was a widespread belief that heavenly portents marked the birth of great leaders, and so they come to Jerusalem to look for a baby whom they describe as the "newborn king of the Jews."

Panicking at the suggestion of any threat to his power, Herod gathers around him his "yes" men, those whom Matthew names as the same opponents of Jesus in the passion narrative (Matt 26:57), and inquires of them where the Messiah was to be born. For his own theological purposes, Matthew modifies the prophet Micah's text with the Davidic text from 2 Samuel 5:2 to add a royal note to the search for the newborn king. The wisdom of the word of God in the Hebrew Scriptures is thus offered and accepted by the magi. They have the humility to know that they are not self-sufficient, that they need help on their search; and they have the discernment that sees through Herod's hypocritical and vicious suggestion that, when the magi have found the child, they return to tell Herod the whereabouts of the child so that he, too, can go and pay him homage.

In the Gentile magi, the divisions of culture, religion, and nation are reconciled because, as we respond with the antiphon to Psalm 72, "Lord, every nation on earth will adore you." If we believe that every nation, every religion has some gift to offer God, can we dare refuse to accept the gifts that strangers bring us? A multicultural society and church are witnesses to the inclusiveness that Christ asks of us.

The most important gift we can offer Christ—the gift that is richer than any gold, frankincense, or myrrh—is, of course, the wealth of our love and the fragrant readiness of suffering that this will inevitably entail. In the gifts that the wise ones offer to the Christ Child, there is again the hint of the paschal mystery: the myrrh of embalming, the frankincense that fragranced the temple sacrifices and burned before the holy of holies, the gold of precious value. The magi go home by another route when they realize that they are being manipulated by hypocrisy and jealous power-seeking. It is, Matthew suggests, often the strangers and outsiders—and today read the asylum seekers or the unpretentious poor or those who work for justice—who reveal to us, as individuals and as nations, how and what we should be seeking and how to come home to this truth.

Focusing the Gospel

Key words and phrases: "When Jesus was born in Bethlehem of Judea, in the days of King Herod, behold, magi from the east arrived in Jerusalem."

To the point: This is the first instance of God expanding the Abrahamic covenant beyond the Israelites. For nearly two thousand years, the Hebrews have been God's chosen people. Now, with the arrival of Jesus, the promise of God's kingdom expands to include all of humanity. This is modeled to us when the emissaries from a completely different country arrive to honor him and claim Jesus as their Lord too.

Connecting the Gospel

to the first and second readings: This week's readings are all about people from different cultures and tribes coming together to celebrate the Lord. In the first reading, Isaiah describes a caravan of nations gathering in the light of the Lord. In the second reading, Paul makes the case for salvation outside of the Jewish faith when he tells the Ephesians that "Gentiles are coheirs, members of the same body, and copartners in the promise in Christ Jesus through the gospel."

This is a relatively pedestrian concept for modern Catholics, but for Christians in the years after Christ's resurrection, this notion is radical. The special covenant between God and Abraham now extends to all nations, including those outside of the Hebrew faith. This isn't something Paul proposes for the first time in his letter to the Ephesians. It begins the week Jesus is born, when the leaders of nations with no ethnic relation to Israel come and pay a tiny Hebrew boy homage.

to experience: We are often caught up in how our faith affects (and is affected by) the culture and politics of the country where we live. This week's readings give us an opportunity to reflect on the international aspect of salvation. Catholics have a tendency to "get into the weeds" when it comes to living the gospel. This week, we have an opportunity to take in a much wider view of our church and celebrate the universality of Christ's message.

Connecting the Responsorial Psalm

to the readings: The psalm contains imagery to address nationality and geography. The line "May he rule from sea to sea, / and from the River to the ends of the earth" is followed by "The kings of Tarshish and the Isles shall offer gifts; / the kings of Arabia and Seba shall bring tribute." When you proclaim that every nation on earth shall adore the Lord, you are painting a vivid picture of what this means, with multiple aspects.

to psalmist preparation: As you approach this week's psalm, think about the "nations" in your own life. Are there differing political tribes within your family? Do you live in a community that seeks to separate itself from others through location or economics? As you declare these words, make it a prayer for unity within your own life, drawing together the many nations you navigate as a person of faith.

PROMPTS FOR FAITH-SHARING

Which "nations" do you consider yourself a part of? Which "nations" are distant to you?

_____

_____

_____

_____

Imagine someone opposite from you in every way: geographically, financially, culturally. How does knowing that person is a coheir of heaven, along with you, make you feel?

_____

_____

_____

_____

If Christ's second coming happened this week, on your church's block, which international emissary would you find the most shocking? What if representatives from China, India, and Ethiopia showed up on your doorstep, offering gifts?

_____

_____

_____

_____

If the church is truly universal, what implications does that have for how your parish and neighborhood live out their Catholic faith?

_____

_____

_____

_____

_____

Model Penitential Act

Presider: Today's feast of the Epiphany celebrates the arrival and homage of the magi. We, too, give Jesus homage by our lives. For the times we have not lived according to our call, we ask God for forgiveness and peace . . . *[pause]*

Lord Jesus, the magi from the east traveled to Jerusalem to pay homage to you: Lord, have mercy.

Christ Jesus, you are priest, prophet, and king: Christ, have mercy.

Lord Jesus, you are the star that leads us to light and life: Lord, have mercy.

Homily Points

• Today's readings are excellent reminders that we encounter God in a variety of people, places, circumstances, and situations. In the letter to the Ephesians, Paul explicitly states that both Jews and Gentiles are welcome in God's kingdom: "[T]he Gentiles are coheirs, members of the same body, / and copartners in the promise in Christ Jesus through the gospel." This statement of welcome and inclusivity reminds us that all people bear God's image. Do we treat others with the God-given dignity they deserve?

• Likewise, the magi travel from their home country to the home of Jesus where they meet Jesus Christ, the Savior and Lord. They were outsiders in Judea, with different beliefs, customs, and culture. Even so, God transcends these differences and the magi warmly interact with Mary, Joseph, and Jesus. Rather than fearing people who were different, Mary and Joseph welcomed these magi into their home and showed them hospitality, remaining open to a sharing of words and gifts.

• Just as God is encountered through people, the feast of Epiphany is a prime celebration of God present and active in nature. The magi notice God's presence in the beauty and wonder of a star in the night sky. God speaks to these travelers from the east via creation. How do we encounter God in creation? Do we take the time to not only acknowledge God's creative works but to also dedicate ourselves to stewardship of these gifts? Care for our common home is an important element of Catholic social teaching, for we respect and honor God's presence in the created world. If they were not deeply attuned to this reality, the magi would not have found the Christ Child they were seeking. May we, like the magi, be willing to see God's presence in all people, places, and things.

Model Universal Prayer (Prayer of the Faithful)

Presider: Just as the magi from the east brought gifts of gold, frankincense, and myrrh to Jesus, we bring our prayers and petitions to the same God who hears and answers when we call out.

Response: Lord, hear our prayer.

That the church may always radiate the light of Christ . . .

That all countries and peoples may practice hospitality, welcoming people who are strangers, immigrants, and refugees . . .

That all who are excluded or marginalized because of who they are may know God's self-gift and presence in their lives . . .

That our community may be a living sign of hope to all and actively seek ways to illumine the darkness of anger, fear, and hatred . . .

Presider: Loving God, you communicate yourself to us in a myriad of ways. Hear these prayers we bring before you and help us to remain open to your work and presence in our lives. We ask this through Christ our Lord. **Amen.**

COLLECT
Let us pray.

Pause for silent prayer

O God, who on this day
revealed your Only Begotten Son to the
nations
by the guidance of a star,
grant in your mercy
that we, who know you already by faith,
may be brought to behold the beauty of
your sublime glory.
Through our Lord Jesus Christ, your Son,
who lives and reigns with you in the unity
of the Holy Spirit,
God, for ever and ever. Amen.

FIRST READING
Isa 60:1-6

Rise up in splendor, Jerusalem! Your light
has come,
the glory of the Lord shines upon you.
See, darkness covers the earth,
and thick clouds cover the peoples;
but upon you the LORD shines,
and over you appears his glory.
Nations shall walk by your light,
and kings by your shining radiance.
Raise your eyes and look about;
they all gather and come to you:
your sons come from afar,
and your daughters in the arms of their
nurses.

Then you shall be radiant at what you see,
your heart shall throb and overflow,
for the riches of the sea shall be emptied
out before you,
the wealth of nations shall be brought
to you.
Caravans of camels shall fill you,
dromedaries from Midian and Ephah;
all from Sheba shall come
bearing gold and frankincense,
and proclaiming the praises of the LORD.

RESPONSORIAL PSALM
Ps 72:1-2, 7-8, 10-11, 12-13

R̸. (cf. 11) Lord, every nation on earth will adore you.

O God, with your judgment endow the king,
  and with your justice, the king's son;
he shall govern your people with justice
  and your afflicted ones with judgment.

R̸. Lord, every nation on earth will adore you.

Justice shall flower in his days,
  and profound peace, till the moon be no more.
May he rule from sea to sea,
  and from the River to the ends of the earth.

R̸. Lord, every nation on earth will adore you.

The kings of Tarshish and the Isles shall offer gifts;
  the kings of Arabia and Seba shall bring tribute.
All kings shall pay him homage,
  all nations shall serve him.

R̸. Lord, every nation on earth will adore you.

For he shall rescue the poor when he cries out,
  and the afflicted when he has no one to help him.
He shall have pity for the lowly and the poor;
  the lives of the poor he shall save.

R̸. Lord, every nation on earth will adore you.

SECOND READING
Eph 3:2-3a, 5-6

Brothers and sisters:
You have heard of the stewardship of God's grace
  that was given to me for your benefit,
  namely, that the mystery was made known to me by revelation.
It was not made known to people in other generations
  as it has now been revealed
  to his holy apostles and prophets by the Spirit:
  that the Gentiles are coheirs, members of the same body,
  and copartners in the promise in Christ Jesus through the gospel.

About Liturgy

Holding Precious Things: Scripture doesn't offer much descriptive information about the magi, like how many of them there were or exactly where they were from. What we do hear is that the gifts they offer were precious and symbolic: gold, which recognized Christ's kingship; frankincense, which recognized his divinity; myrrh, which recognized his coming sacrificial death and burial.

During our eucharistic liturgies, many objects are necessarily handled and perhaps moved from one location to another: a processional cross, candles, the Roman Missal, Lectionary, and book of the gospels, bread and wine (become Body and Blood) and the vessels they are held in, and more. Some of these items are precious because of their materials and earthly value: a gold paten or chalice, for instance; and many of us know how surprisingly expensive some of the necessary liturgical books can be! All of the items that are held or carried during liturgy are precious in a theological and symbolic way: a processional cross is a sign of our faith in the paschal mystery; a book of the gospels is our written account of the things Jesus said to us and did for us.

All of our sacred ministers, during whatever training they receive, should be taught to handle and carry these liturgical objects with the utmost reverence and awareness of their precious nature, rather than using a utilitarian approach that might lend itself to irreverence and, further, that may extend outside of the liturgy itself. We've all seen (or perhaps even been guilty of ourselves) the tucking of the Missal under an arm so that something else might be picked up too, or perhaps we've seen the sacred vessels, post-Communion, stacked up precariously so one server can remove them from the altar in one trip. There's no rush, especially within Mass, when we enter into *kairos*, God's time. Reverence easily supersedes convenience.

Think of the precious objects in your life, in your homes, held and carried with the greatest sense of their worth to you, with just a bit of fear that you don't want to be the one to drop the item, or worse, break it. So, too, let the items that help us express our faith and worship together be treated with similar dignity and reverence.

About Liturgical Documents

Sacrosanctum Concilium—*Source and Summit:* That the liturgy of the church (not just the Eucharist, but all our liturgies) be seen as source and summit rests in the vision of the Constitution on the Sacred Liturgy as to what liturgy should be and do. It is—always—about Jesus's act of redemption and our living it out through worship and daily life. Any other activities of the church point to and draw strength from liturgy. Christ's presence at liturgy affirm this: his presence especially in the consecrated eucharistic species, but also in priest, Word, and the gathered assembly (SC 7).

There is, too, a renewed emphasis on discipleship and evangelization; that is, liturgy as testimony, repeated weekly and daily to both create church and form faith. It is meant to be a present reality and anamnesis (SC 5), and not ever private but belonging to the whole church (SC 26). All devotions, which are by nature not liturgical and private, should direct the faithful back to the liturgy of the church and begin from that same point (SC 13). Succinctly, the liturgy embodies all these things, so it can be an act that achieves the glorification of God and the sanctification of the people (see SC 61). Therefore, people should fully and actively participate in and understand the liturgy!

JANUARY 2, 2022
THE EPIPHANY OF THE LORD

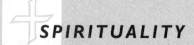

SPIRITUALITY

GOSPEL ACCLAMATION
cf. Luke 3:16

R⁊. Alleluia, alleluia.
John said: One mightier than I is
    coming;
he will baptize you with the Holy Spirit
    and with fire.
R⁊. Alleluia, alleluia.

Gospel

Luke 3:15-16, 21-22; L21C

The people were filled with
    expectation,
  and all were asking in their
      hearts
    whether John might be the
        Christ.
John answered them all,
    saying,
  "I am baptizing you with
      water,
  but one mightier than I is
      coming.
I am not worthy to loosen the
    thongs of his sandals.
He will baptize you with the Holy Spirit
    and fire."

After all the people had been baptized
  and Jesus also had been baptized and
      was praying,
    heaven was opened and the Holy
        Spirit descended upon him
  in bodily form like a dove.
And a voice came from heaven,
    "You are my beloved Son;
    with you I am well pleased."

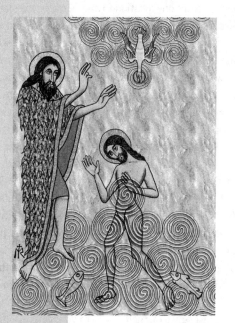

Reflecting on the Gospel

Hopefully, we have often witnessed it: the priest rolling up his sleeves in readiness for the ministry of the waters, the invitation of the children in the assembly to gather around the font, the reverent taking of the naked, tiny, and vulnerable scrap of humanity, and the holding up of him or her to the people into whose faith this child will be baptized. Then there is the triple immersion: in the name of the Father, the Son, and the Holy Spirit—sometimes with slightly outraged protest, more often with the quietness of pleasant familiarity with the waters of the womb. Then another elevation, and this child of God is shown with a new christened identity to the assembly. There is always applause, always a smile on even the most bored faces, and a moment in which human and holy solidarity is felt, not only by the proud parents but also by the gathered local church. It is a moment that is truly "sacramental," a sign of some greater and hidden mystery of God's extraordinary love; and it is a humbling realization. The child has done nothing to deserve this, except for the wonderful obedience of being born. One can almost hear the biblical question echoing down the centuries, with all its hopes and fears: "What, then, will this child be?" (Luke 1:66). In Luke's gospel, that question had been asked about John the Baptist at his circumcision. It is the adult John whom we meet again in today's gospel, and it is in the context of water and baptism.

The solidarity of a parish baptism, the communal event that it is, reflects Luke's narrative. Jesus is surrounded by people who had been baptized by John. John the Baptist is humble and strong, for when the people express a wondering expectancy that he might be the promised Messiah, John resists the temptation to self-aggrandizement and is quick to dispel any illusions about his status. He is only a servant, he says, who is not even worthy to perform the menial task of doing up the sandal straps of the coming One. He points out to the crowd the differences between himself and the One who is to come: his is a baptism of water and repentance; the Messiah's will be a baptism of transformation through fire and the Holy Spirit. John the Baptist is probably referring to the end time, but Luke announces this with the insight of a post-Pentecost evangelist and the experience of the transformation of that fire and wind-struck day (Acts 2:1-4).

To the good news of solidarity and humility, Luke adds the significance of prayer. Several times in his gospel, Luke sets important events in Jesus's life and mission in the context of prayer (e.g., Luke 6:12-13; 9:28; 22:42-46). Jesus dies with the words of Psalm 31:5 on his lips. The baptism of the Lord could be called a prayer event, for Luke does not describe the moment of baptism but rather its aftermath. It is Jesus's prayer that tears open the heavens for the descent of the Holy Spirit and the revelation of his true identity by the Father's voice that acclaims him as the beloved Son on whom God's favor rests.

It is the same for us. Prayer is a necessary part of our identity as baptized sons and daughters of God. It opens heaven to us and reveals who we are—for, in a very real sense, we are who we pray. At prayer, we struggle to hear what God is calling us to be, to know who we are in our deepest truth, at the still point where the Spirit has descended into our depths and anointed us for mission.

Focusing the Gospel

Key words and phrases: "After all the people had been baptized and Jesus also had been baptized and was praying, heaven was opened and the Holy Spirit descended upon him in bodily form like a dove."

To the point: Jesus joins us to him in baptism. The Trinity is on full display here, as Jesus, beginning his public ministry, is baptized *by the Holy Spirit*. Jesus receives his baptism through John, who, it is worth noting, is not God. Not only do we witness Jesus participating in an act that will become the cornerstone of the Christian faith, but we see it facilitated by a human whose divinity is as precarious as our own.

It is through Jesus's humanity that we are saved. He is both fully human and fully divine, and in this scene, his humanity is on display for us. He receives the sacrament of baptism, and thus participates in the act that our own lives require to gain entry to heaven. He's God. Why should Jesus bother getting baptized, if he is one with the Holy Spirit already? Because the very act of God entering into humanity is to participate in it fully, unto death, and thus dignify human life and make it worthy of heaven.

Connecting the Gospel

to the first reading: The first reading from Isaiah is full of contradicting imagery. Comfort for the people is followed by the scene of mountains falling down and valleys being raised—not necessarily a comforting natural event. Zion goes to the top of a mountain to cry out, loudly, and yet the Lord being heralded is a shepherd, gathering his flock into his arms. This imagery creates a dichotomy of physical stress (mountains falling, crying out) with comfort and safety (being brought into a hug). This reading accompanies the baptism of Jesus, which is also an ironic event.

to experience: Why does God need to be baptized by God? Because it is within this seeming contradiction that our own salvation lies. Because God is fully human and fully divine, it is through this act of living as one of us, alongside other humans, that our own lives are sanctified. Paul tells us in the second reading, "he saved us through the bath of rebirth and renewal by the Holy Spirit, whom he richly poured out on us through Jesus Christ our savior, so that we might be justified by his grace and become heirs in hope of eternal life."

Connecting the Responsorial Psalm

to the readings: This week's psalm is full of magnificent imagery: God robed in light, heaven spread like a tent, God traveling on clouds and opening his hands and spilling food onto all of the earth. It is a love poem, an ode to our Creator. This imagery gives God human traits like being clothed, having a palace, traveling, and opening a hand. This poetic personification of God comes to fruition in the person of Jesus, long after the psalmist proclaimed his glory using the imagery of humanity.

to psalmist preparation: Psalms that contain poetic imagery can often feel too esoteric to be easily accessible. Take time this week to really focus on what these images mean and how describing God with human traits is a way of bringing our Creator closer to us.

PROMPTS FOR FAITH-SHARING

Why do you think Jesus was baptized, if he is God?

What is your favorite image of God in this week's readings? What about that image brings you comfort?

What is your relationship with the Holy Spirit like? Do you ever pray to the Holy Spirit? Why or why not?

How do you prepare the way of the Lord in your family, neighborhood, career, and community?

Model Rite for the Blessing and Sprinkling of Water

Presider: In baptism you claim us for yourself. As we are sprinkled with these waters, let us prepare ourselves to enter this celebration . . . *[pause]*

   [*continue with* The Roman Missal, *Appendix II*]

Homily Points

• In the sacrament of baptism, God claims us for God's self. In today's gospel when Jesus was baptized, a voice from heaven said: "You are my beloved Son; with you I am well pleased." God says the same thing to us at our baptism: "You are my beloved sons and daughters; with you I am well pleased."

• When we realize we are chosen by God, we come to see that we are a special people. From the moment we recognize this we are charged with the responsibility to become who we are meant to be. It is one thing to simply say, "I am beloved," but it is an entirely different reality to embody those words and truly make them our own. Belovedness is not about superiority or acclaim. Rather, it is a humble acknowledgment that God lives and moves in each of us.

• In the reading from the Acts of the Apostles, Peter tells the community that Jesus "went about doing good and healing all those oppressed." We share the same call by virtue of our common baptism. This universal call to holiness, grounded in God's love for us, is the duty of each and every Christian. We pray that we can tear down any forms of division among us, for as Peter says, "God shows no partiality." This is true even within the church. While our lives may take different directions and forms, all of us share a common call.

Model Universal Prayer (Prayer of the Faithful)

Presider: Knowing that God claims us for God's self, we are unafraid to bring our prayers and petitions to the one who intimately knows and loves us.

Response: Lord, hear our prayer.

That the church may uphold our common baptismal vocation and recognize the importance and gifts of the laity . . .

That national and world leaders may defend the dignity of all persons, especially people who are relegated to the margins of our society . . .

That all who suffer from depression and other forms of mental illness may be reminded of their self-worth and importance in our community . . .

That all of us gathered here may commit ourselves to the conservation of God's gift of water and work to ensure all people have access to the food and drink they need . . .

Presider: Loving God, hear and answer these prayers according to your will. Bless us with peace and a renewed commitment to living our baptismal call. We ask this through Christ our Lord. **Amen.**

COLLECT

Let us pray

Pause for silent prayer

Almighty ever-living God,
who, when Christ had been baptized in the
   River Jordan
and as the Holy Spirit descended upon
   him,
solemnly declared him your beloved Son,
grant that your children by adoption,
reborn of water and the Holy Spirit,
may always be well pleasing to you.
Through our Lord Jesus Christ, your Son,
who lives and reigns with you in the unity
   of the Holy Spirit,
God, for ever and ever. **Amen.**

FIRST READING
Isa 40:1-5, 9-11

Comfort, give comfort to my people,
   says your God.
Speak tenderly to Jerusalem, and proclaim
      to her
   that her service is at an end,
   her guilt is expiated;
indeed, she has received from the hand of
      the LORD
   double for all her sins.

   A voice cries out:
In the desert prepare the way of the LORD!
   Make straight in the wasteland a
      highway for our God!
Every valley shall be filled in,
   every mountain and hill shall be made
      low;
the rugged land shall be made a plain,
   the rough country, a broad valley.
Then the glory of the LORD shall be
      revealed,
   and all people shall see it together;
   for the mouth of the LORD has spoken.

Go up onto a high mountain,
   Zion, herald of glad tidings;
cry out at the top of your voice,
   Jerusalem, herald of good news!
Fear not to cry out
   and say to the cities of Judah:
   Here is your God!
Here comes with power
   the Lord GOD,
   who rules by a strong arm;
here is his reward with him,
   his recompense before him.
Like a shepherd he feeds his flock;
   in his arms he gathers the lambs,
carrying them in his bosom,
   and leading the ewes with care.

RESPONSORIAL PSALM
Ps 104:1b-2, 3-4, 24-25, 27-28, 29-30

℞. (1) O bless the Lord, my soul.

O Lord, my God, you are great indeed!
    You are clothed with majesty and glory,
robed in light as with a cloak.
    You have spread out the heavens like a
        tent-cloth.

℞. O bless the Lord, my soul.

You have constructed your palace upon
        the waters.
    You make the clouds your chariot;
you travel on the wings of the wind.
    You make the winds your messengers,
and flaming fire your ministers.

℞. O bless the Lord, my soul.

How manifold are your works, O Lord!
    In wisdom you have wrought them all—
    the earth is full of your creatures;
the sea also, great and wide,
    in which are schools without number
    of living things both small and great.

℞. O bless the Lord, my soul.

They look to you to give them food in due
        time.
When you give it to them, they gather it;
    when you open your hand, they are
        filled with good things.

℞. O bless the Lord, my soul.

If you take away their breath, they perish
        and return to the dust.
When you send forth your spirit, they are
        created,
    and you renew the face of the earth.

℞. O bless the Lord, my soul.

SECOND READING
Titus 2:11-14; 3:4-7

See Appendix A, p. 269.

See Appendix A, p. 269, for additional readings.

About Liturgy
The More Things Stay the Same, the More They Change: The rite of baptism (outside Mass), as revised at Vatican II, is a fine window into how the liturgies of the church both stayed the same and were dramatically reenvisioned, resymbolized, and have a significantly different understanding of the people of God.

Yes, the form (trinitarian) and matter (water) remained the same. But even quick glimpses into the structure and content of the rite as a whole illustrate the above concepts.

Before Vatican II, there was only one rite of baptism for any age and context; now there are many varying rites that take into account various ages and other contexts. Vestments of the presider changed: in the former rite, the priest would begin the sacrament vested in purple, indicative of the sacrament's forgiveness of original sin, only later changing to white vestments; today the presider wears white the whole time (see Order of Baptism of Children 74), recognizing resurrection in Christ and the fullness of the paschal mystery.

The former rite said nothing of any rite of gathering and did not even include Scripture; the present rites do both (see 75–83). The blessing of water formerly was a prayer that was rather exorcistic, essentially without epiclesis, and, consistently with other facets of the rite, focused on forgiveness of sins. Our current water blessing (see 91) is one of the fullest examples of anamnesis that readily invokes the Spirit and has pronounced imagery of both cleansing and new life.

Many in practice today use immersion in the water as a fuller sign of death in Christ and rising with him to new life, where in the former rite a simpler pouring of water (still valid today) was typical. The use of chrism today has a fuller symbolism of being formed into Christ as priest, prophet, and king (see 98). The light of the candle given the baptized once represented sinlessness; now a fuller symbolism of life in faith is described (see 100). Finally, today, there is a blessing where there had been none (see 105), which reminds the people of the many and varied themes of the rite.

We see, then, that baptism, at Vatican II, was reoriented to call the faithful to their rights and obligations as members of Christian community. From baptism the whole life of the faithful proceeds, sustained by the Eucharist and the other sacraments. It's not only about washing away the stain of original sin, but so much more.

Today's celebration should remind us of all of this, perhaps especially for those who do not remember their baptism as infants. Substitute in a sprinkling rite in place of the penitential rite, make sure the preaching says as much about the assembly as it does about Christ, and in picking hymnody, seek out texts that balance the historical event with its implications for who it is we are today, the baptized faithful and adopted children of God!

About Music
Singing of Initiation: Music with texts that speak well to this richer, fuller understanding of baptism and initiation include "Covenant Hymn" (GIA), a lengthy and beautiful poem by Rory Cooney of lifelong belonging with stirring melody by Gary Daigle, and a much shorter text and tune, "Take, O Take Me As I Am" by John Bell of the Iona Community (GIA). Both lean on Scripture and allow the singer to pray a hymn of Christian community and of joyful hope for the future, in very different ways.

ORDINARY TIME I

✝ SPIRITUALITY

GOSPEL ACCLAMATION
See 2 Thess 2:14

℟. Alleluia, alleluia.
God has called us through the Gospel
to possess the glory of our Lord Jesus Christ.
℟. Alleluia, alleluia.

Gospel   John 2:1-11; L66C

There was a wedding at Cana in Galilee,
and the mother of Jesus was there.
Jesus and his disciples were also invited
to the wedding.
When the wine ran short,
the mother of Jesus said to him,
"They have no wine."
And Jesus said to her,
"Woman, how does your concern affect
me?
My hour has not yet come."
His mother said to the servers,
"Do whatever he tells you."
Now there were six stone water jars there
for Jewish ceremonial washings,
each holding twenty to thirty gallons.
Jesus told them,
"Fill the jars with water."
So they filled them to the brim.
Then he told them,
"Draw some out now and take it to the
headwaiter."
So they took it.
And when the headwaiter tasted the
water that had become wine,
without knowing where it came from
—although the servers who had drawn
the water knew—,
the headwaiter called the bridegroom
and said to him,
"Everyone serves good wine first,
and then when people have drunk
freely, an inferior one;
but you have kept the good wine until
now."
Jesus did this as the beginning of his
signs at Cana in Galilee
and so revealed his glory,
and his disciples began to believe in him.

Reflecting on the Gospel

At Cana we meet Mary for the first time in John's gospel, and we hear the first and last words that she speaks in this gospel. Already there is a sense of separateness between the mother and the son. They are at the same wedding, but come independently, Jesus being described as also invited with his disciples. John never refers to Jesus's mother by her personal name, nor does he do this when speaking of "the beloved disciple." Both the ideal woman disciple and the ideal man are described only by their relationship to Jesus. The mother of

the Lord is the discerning one who notices that the wine has run out. She stands before Jesus in the privileged role of mother and presents him with the problem. Jesus's reply to her words have a note of rebuke as he calls her "Woman," not the expected response to one's own mother.

The mother is loved, but she is also an outsider—outside of Jesus's free, unique relationship to God, his Father (John 7:4; 8:19; 12:27). This pain will thrust through her most deeply when she is again named as "woman" on Golgotha and is the beloved and last gift from whom Jesus dispossesses himself before he hands over his breath to his Father. Then will be the "hour" that Jesus tells his mother has not yet come at Cana.

His mother is persevering, even in the pain of Jesus's response that amounts to telling her to keep out of it! How readily do we persevere in our discipleship when faced with what seems to be a rebuke to our faith? The mother's faith in the words of the Word goes beyond understanding. Not understanding, not hoping, but believing—because "hope that sees for itself is not hope" (Rom 8:24)—the mother speaks to the stewards, "Do whatever he tells you." We never hear her speak again in John's gospel. Even on Golgotha, there is nothing more to be spoken out of her motherhood and discipleship. These words are enough for her, enough for John's community—and enough for us. In obedience to Jesus's words, the servants fill to the brim the six water jars used for the Jewish purificatory rites; then they draw and take the water-become-wine to the steward. The steward, who has not heard the words of Jesus or his mother, implies that it is the bridegroom who is responsible for this best wine. The Cana bridegroom is a shadowy, silent, and inactive presence, a foil for the next time a bridegroom is mentioned in John 3:29, when John the Baptist acclaims Jesus to be the Bridegroom of his people, and himself as the best man who, according to cultural practice, presents the Bridegroom to the bride Israel and then withdraws.

The purificatory jars at Cana numbered six, a symbolic number of incompleteness. At Jesus's "hour," there will be a seventh jar, when from the clay of his passion-fired humanity there will flow the wine of his blood, not only for purification but for exultant transformation.

The wine-become-blood redeems and purifies his bride, the church, sanctifying and deifying her. It allows her to participate in the Lord's own death and transformation, and nourishes her with the life of the resurrection. Accordingly, the wine of "the wedding of the Lamb" is the mystical image for the entire paschal feast of the Lord, the feast of the new and eternal covenant-making in the loving blood of the Lamb. It is this mystery of word and wine, this paschal celebration, which we celebrate at every Sunday Eucharist. We are now the wedding guests waiting to be filled with the sacramental wine.

Focusing the Gospel

Key words and phrases: "Jesus and his disciples were also invited to the wedding. When the wine ran short, the mother of Jesus said to him, 'They have no wine.'"

To the point: Let all the mamas rejoice! This week we see that even Jesus fulfills the fourth commandment to honor his mother. One of the many questions we can ask this week is, why would Mary make such a big deal about wine? In order to understand this, we have to look at the context. Mary and Jesus are at a wedding, which is a celebration for the entire community. Mary notices they have run out of wine. Could the bride and groom not afford more? Did they make a miscalculation when purchasing? Whatever the situation, Mary anticipates their embarrassment, realizes this community celebration will be impacted, and makes a very big ask of her son.

Connecting the Gospel

to the first reading: In the first reading, Isaiah sings a litany of praise to the nation of Israel, foretelling its future glory, fulfilled in the person of Jesus. God makes Israel's land "his spouse," signifying a relationship come to fruition. The church ultimately becomes Christ's bride, an image that describes the depth and dependence of our relationship to Jesus Christ. It is fitting, then, to pair this vivid imagery with Jesus's first miracle, his public debut, which took place at a wedding.

to experience: A marriage is one of the strongest bonds humans have. We are born to parents and have no choice in siblings, but a marriage is a choice, one that is made between two separate hearts, to join together before the Lord and create a domestic church. If you are married, imagine reading the first reading to your spouse as a love poem. In Paul's letter to the Corinthians, he speaks of the many gifts given by the Spirit. How do your gifts, and the gifts of your spouse, balance each other?

Connecting the Responsorial Psalm

to the readings: This week's psalm doesn't speak to marriage directly, but the joy with which the psalmist praises the Lord can easily be applied to a spouse. The church is the bride of Christ, and we are called to participate in that relationship.

to psalmist preparation: Are you a fan of a certain team? Do you know someone who is a radical supporter of a professional or collegiate sports team? That's the kind of fervor the psalmist is sharing with us this week. This is a rallying cry, a litany of support for our Lord.

PROMPTS FOR FAITH-SHARING

What do you think your gifts of the Holy Spirit are?

Within your parish planning committee, what gifts of the Holy Spirit do you see colleagues bringing?

Think of your favorite team sport and how you support your team. What would it feel like to apply the same "fan" activities you do in sports to your faith? Do you wear team colors? Do you make space in your week to watch games with other fans?

If you were at the wedding at Cana, how do you think you'd respond if you watched the interaction between Mary and her son?

Model Penitential Act

Presider: In today's gospel we hear the story of the wedding at Cana in Galilee where Jesus's disciples first began to know him. For the times we have failed to prioritize our relationship with you, we ask for forgiveness and healing . . . *[pause]*

    Lord Jesus, you are the Son of God and the son of Mary: Lord, have mercy.

    Christ Jesus, you share signs of yourself that reveal the kingdom of God: Christ, have mercy.

    Lord Jesus, you meet the needs of your people: Lord, have mercy.

Homily Points

• We can probably recite elements of today's gospel from memory. For example, we know that Jesus turned water into wine at the request of his mother. While these details are not insignificant, it is important to look beyond these elements. What does this wedding celebration reveal about Jesus?

• The wedding at Cana in Galilee is often referred to as the start of Jesus's public ministry. John writes, "Jesus did this as the beginning of his signs at Cana in Galilee and so revealed his glory, and his disciples began to believe in him." Essentially, Jesus reveals two essential elements of his nature. First, we see that Jesus is fully human, as he attended the wedding party with his mother, just like many of us have. Second, Jesus reveals that he is the Son of God, performing signs that disclose his divine nature and the nature of the kingdom of God.

• In the kingdom of God there will be no more thirsting. In fact, we will come to see throughout John's gospel that there will also be no hunger or sickness or death. The second reading from Paul to the Corinthians begins, "There are different kinds of spiritual gifts but the same Spirit; there are different forms of service but the same Lord; there are different workings but the same God who produces all of them in everyone." As Jesus does in today's gospel, we must all use the unique gifts God has given to us so that we might build up the kingdom of God. Just like the accounts of today's gospel, the kingdom of God is both "here" and "not yet."

Model Universal Prayer (Prayer of the Faithful)

Presider: Just as Mary put her trust in her son, telling the servers to do whatever Jesus says, we also bring our needs to the God who hears and answers our prayers.

Response: Lord, hear our prayer.

That the church may continue to listen to and uphold the voices of women, just as Jesus does . . .

That countries can work together to bring peace and healing to the parts of the world most in need . . .

That all who suffer from any form of mental, physical, or spiritual illness may know the healing compassion of Christ . . .

That our local community may serve others with attitudes of abundance rather than scarcity . . .

Presider: Loving God, hear the prayers we bring before you today. Just as you reveal the kingdom of God through your signs, may we also reveal the kingdom through our works of service for others. We ask this through Christ our Lord. **Amen.**

COLLECT

Let us pray.

Pause for silent prayer

Almighty ever-living God,
who govern all things,
both in heaven and on earth,
mercifully hear the pleading of your
    people
and bestow your peace on our times.
Through our Lord Jesus Christ, your Son,
who lives and reigns with you in the unity
    of the Holy Spirit,
God, for ever and ever. **Amen.**

FIRST READING
Isa 62:1-5

For Zion's sake I will not be silent,
    for Jerusalem's sake I will not be quiet,
until her vindication shines forth like the
    dawn
    and her victory like a burning torch.

Nations shall behold your vindication,
    and all the kings your glory;
you shall be called by a new name
    pronounced by the mouth of the LORD.
You shall be a glorious crown in the hand
    of the LORD,
    a royal diadem held by your God.
No more shall people call you "Forsaken,"
    or your land "Desolate,"
but you shall be called "My Delight,"
    and your land "Espoused."
For the LORD delights in you
    and makes your land his spouse.
As a young man marries a virgin,
    your Builder shall marry you;
and as a bridegroom rejoices in his bride
    so shall your God rejoice in you.

RESPONSORIAL PSALM
Ps 96:1-2, 2-3, 7-8, 9-10

R℣. (3) Proclaim his marvelous deeds to all the nations.

Sing to the LORD a new song;
  sing to the LORD, all you lands.
Sing to the LORD; bless his name.

R℣. Proclaim his marvelous deeds to all the nations.

Announce his salvation, day after day.
Tell his glory among the nations;
  among all peoples, his wondrous deeds.

R℣. Proclaim his marvelous deeds to all the nations.

Give to the LORD, you families of nations,
  give to the LORD glory and praise;
  give to the LORD the glory due his name!

R℣. Proclaim his marvelous deeds to all the nations.

Worship the LORD in holy attire.
  Tremble before him, all the earth;
say among the nations: The LORD is king.
  He governs the peoples with equity.

R℣. Proclaim his marvelous deeds to all the nations.

SECOND READING
1 Cor 12:4-11

Brothers and sisters:
There are different kinds of spiritual gifts
    but the same Spirit;
  there are different forms of service but
    the same Lord;
  there are different workings but the
    same God
  who produces all of them in everyone.
To each individual the manifestation of
    the Spirit
  is given for some benefit.
To one is given through the Spirit the
    expression of wisdom;
  to another, the expression of knowledge
    according to the same Spirit;
  to another, faith by the same Spirit;
  to another, gifts of healing by the one
    Spirit;
  to another, mighty deeds;
  to another, prophecy;
  to another, discernment of spirits;
  to another, varieties of tongues;
  to another, interpretation of tongues.
But one and the same Spirit produces all
    of these,
  distributing them individually to each
    person as he wishes.

About Liturgy

Christmastime or Wintertime: I have written before about the value in helping our assemblies develop a "liturgical spirituality" by, among other ways, helping them notice the changing seasons of our liturgical year in as many ways as possible: changing the art and environment, and changing the music (for instance, the musical setting of the ordinary of the Mass), along with the prescribed changes like vestment colors. Doing this work in a timely and complete way helps all to notice the cyclical progression of the year and could even help frame your congregation's reception of Scripture and communal prayer, if only in subconscious ways.

Yes, the church itself can be a little fuzzy about some of the time-keeping involved. Last Sunday, the Baptism of the Lord, typically known liturgically as the end of Christmastide, is mentioned in the Universal Norms on the Liturgical Year and the Calendar this way: "Christmas Time runs from First Vespers (Evening Prayer I) of the Nativity of the Lord up to and including the Sunday after Epiphany or after January 6" (33) and "The Sunday falling after January 6 is the Feast of the Baptism of the Lord" (38). There are occasions where the celebration is transferred to Monday, but that is not the norm.

Yet, alongside this directive, the Lectionary includes this tidbit on the First Sunday in Ordinary Time: "The First Sunday in Ordinary Time is the Feast of the Baptism of the Lord." And if one thinks perhaps there would be clarity in the introduction to the Lectionary, that isn't the case either: "The Sunday on which the Feast of the Baptism of the Lord falls replaces the first Sunday in Ordinary Time" (104). Suffice it to say, lest this be more confusing and less helpful—that's not why you're reading this, after all—is that, liturgically speaking, in the current calendar, Christmastide ended last Sunday.

Returning to the present moment, and the focus on helping our assemblies navigate the changing seasons by adjusting what they perceive with their senses as much as we can, is there any difference between an art and environment that is specifically "Christmas" and one that is "winter" in character? For instance, poinsettias. Are they Christmas flowers, or winter flowers? Many parishes allow the red and white flowers, if they are in healthy condition, to remain in place, perhaps even up until Ash Wednesday. Perhaps there is value in showing that there is some connection from season to season, scripturally, prayerfully. Perhaps the distinction between Christmas and winter is a bit of a false dichotomy, as our liturgical seasons have reason to follow the meteorological seasons—at least in the Northern Hemisphere, as mentioned before.

If the matter of "shall we leave the poinsettias out, they seem in good shape" has not been examined for a while, perhaps it's worth considering with your liturgical leaders and team this time around.

About Music

Love and Unity: As we hear of Jesus's first miracle at the wedding at Cana this weekend, some music typical for assembly singing at weddings might make a rare Sunday appearance, particularly music with texts of unity, considering the epistle. Consider "How Beautiful" by Twila Paris (in several hymnals) or various settings of "Ubi Caritas" / "Where Charity and Love Prevail," which also vary from resource to resource.

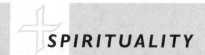

✠ SPIRITUALITY

GOSPEL ACCLAMATION
See Luke 4:18

℟. Alleluia, alleluia.
The Lord sent me to bring glad tidings to the poor,
and to proclaim liberty to captives.
℟. Alleluia, alleluia.

Gospel   Luke 1:1-4; 4:14-21; L69C

Since many have undertaken to com-
    pile a narrative of the events
    that have been fulfilled among us,
    just as those who were eyewitnesses
        from the beginning
    and ministers of the word have
        handed them down to us,
    I too have decided,
    after investigating everything accu-
        rately anew,
    to write it down in an orderly se-
        quence for you,
    most excellent Theophilus,
    so that you may realize the certainty
        of the teachings
    you have received.

Jesus returned to Galilee in the power
    of the Spirit,
    and news of him spread throughout
        the whole region.
He taught in their synagogues and was
    praised by all.

He came to Nazareth, where he had
    grown up,
    and went according to his custom
    into the synagogue on the sabbath day.
He stood up to read and was handed a
    scroll of the prophet Isaiah.
He unrolled the scroll and found the
    passage where it was written:
The Spirit of the Lord is upon me,
    because he has anointed me
    to bring glad tidings to the poor.

Continued in Appendix A, p. 270.

Reflecting on the Gospel

As we begin to journey with Luke through the semi-continuous gospel readings of Year C, it is appropriate that the first four verses are read to remind us
of Luke's purpose in writing his two-part good news, the gospel and Acts of
the Apostles. In the latter, the church is committed to doing in the power of the
Spirit of Jesus what he himself did in the days of his flesh. Theophilus ("God-
lover"), who is addressed in verse 3, was probably a significant Christian and
a patron of Luke. God-lover though he
may be, there is always more truth to
be discovered, a greater commitment
to be made, a new excitement about the
tradition that has been handed down by
those who were both eyewitnesses and
servants of the word. Luke is not one
of these, but he is respectful of what he
has received from them. Using his own
human gifts and guided by the Holy
Spirit, he is eager to record, order, and interpret the Jesus tradition for the sake of
his patron and the wider community of
believers. "Today" we are among those
believers, gathered into the Liturgy of
the Word, into the presence of Christ.

In the reading, Jesus is called up to
the reading desk in the Nazareth synagogue. The people are expectant: here
is the hometown boy made good, with a
teaching reputation already established
throughout Galilee. They think they
know him, but Jesus is the Messiah, the
anointed One, with the fullness of the Spirit upon him. Born, baptized, proved
the faithful Israelite par excellence in the wilderness, Jesus speaks forth as the
prophet the words of Isaiah as a summary of his mission that he is about to
begin. The prophet, he proclaims, is called to announce good news to the poor—
their liberty, healing, freedom from all oppression—as in the Jubilee year of
release described in Leviticus 25 and Deuteronomy 15. Whether such a year was
ever actually celebrated in Israel is uncertain, but it persisted as a symbol of the
possibilities found in a new era of empowerment for the disadvantaged.

Then comes the climax, the moment of interpretation of the word of God:
"Today this scripture passage is fulfilled in your hearing," says Jesus (Luke
4:21). That Jesus is the Word in our human flesh is what we have so recently
celebrated in our Christmas festivities. In the weeks of Ordinary Time, what
will the "Amen, amen!" in the first reading mean for us in our lives? Will the
tears and joy of Ezra's and Nehemiah's community, the amazement of the Nazareth synagogue in response to the word of God, be reflected in our responses
to what we hear proclaimed in the Liturgy of the Word? (Next Sunday we will
hear how fickle and fleeting the response to Jesus can be.)

Around the time of the Jubilee year 2000, there were some great initiatives
related to remitting debts of the poorest nations and adopting compassionate
policies toward those detained as asylum seekers. More than two decades later,
have we, as people baptized into prophecy, retained the urgency in advocating
that our politicians continue this work? What local church initiatives for justice

and peace will keep Jubilee dreams alive through the decades of the third millennium? And what do we as individuals do in order to be "good news" to the poor?

Focusing the Gospel

Key words and phrases: "I too have decided, after investigating everything accurately anew, to write it down in an orderly sequence for you."

To the point: This opening passage from the Gospel of Luke centers us in the context of this story. Luke informs us that these are stories that go back to the eyewitnesses of Christ. This framing at the beginning of his gospel helps us understand how to approach the "reality" of the life of Christ. Luke tells us this isn't a magnificent fairy tale, but tells us, "I too have decided, after investigating everything accurately anew, to write it down in an orderly sequence for you."

This week's gospel also gives us a daring scene that could fit in any modern-day film. Jesus goes to his hometown synagogue, where we can assume everyone knows him, walks up to read, is handed the scroll with the exact prophecy of his coming, and then he reads it out loud, to his friends and neighbors. "Rolling up the scroll, he handed it back to the attendant and sat down, and the eyes of all in the synagogue looked intently at him. He said to them, 'Today this Scripture passage is fulfilled in your hearing.'" Imagine the wonder that everyone seated must have felt. It reads like a movie script.

Connecting the Gospel

to the first reading: In the first reading Ezra leads what seems like a normal liturgy. He stands at a podium and reads from the Torah. However, the Israelites in this story have just returned from the Babylonian exile to find Jerusalem destroyed. This isn't a normal Sabbath for them; this is a moment to take a deep breath after realizing the destruction that has happened in their homeland. Giving this moment even more weight is the fact that the audience is specifically mentioned, twice: men, women, and children old enough to understand. There's a universal aspect to this narrative, because the writer of this passage went out of the way to describe ages and genders in a scene in which Ezra's shell-shocked community comes together to pray.

to experience: Both the first reading and the gospel are moments when a community, gathered in prayer together, receives an unexpected message. In the gospel, Jesus outs himself as the Messiah. In the first reading, Ezra looks at his community of fellow refugees, who've finally returned home, and tells them to stop weeping and start celebrating.

Both of these cinematic scenes take place during a religious service. The primacy of delivery is given to this community event, a gathering of faithful. This is where key information is shared.

Connecting the Responsorial Psalm

to the readings: This week's psalm is very self-aware. You are telling the congregation that the words they are hearing are spirit, life, true, favorable, and refreshing. This is an invitation to help them really "hear with new ears."

to psalmist preparation: The words of the fourth stanza are very tender: "Let the words of my mouth and the thought of my heart / find favor before you, / O LORD, my rock and my redeemer." When you proclaim this, it's a personal prayer, but you are doing it on behalf of your parish. Hold them with you in that moment.

PROMPTS FOR FAITH-SHARING

If someone were writing the story of your life, what sources would you want them to look at? Journals? Interviews with family members? Social media? Why or why not?

_____

_____

_____

_____

If you were sitting in the synagogue when your neighbor Jesus stood up and read this passage from Isaiah, how do you think you would react?

_____

_____

_____

_____

If you had to name the "part of the body" that you are in your parish, what would it be?

_____

_____

_____

_____

Ezra's words tell us, "Today is holy to the LORD your God. Do not be sad, and do not weep." Is there a situation in your life that can be reframed by this command?

_____

_____

_____

_____

Model Penitential Act

Presider: In today's letter from Paul to the Corinthians we hear that we are all part of Christ's body. For the times we have not fully lived this calling, we ask our loving God for pardon and peace . . . *[pause]*

Lord Jesus, you returned to Galilee in the power of the Spirit: Lord, have mercy.

Christ Jesus, your words are spirit and life: Christ, have mercy.

Lord Jesus, you are the fulfillment of the prophets: Lord, have mercy.

Homily Points

• "If one part suffers, all the parts suffer with it; / if one part is honored, all the parts share its joy." These words from our second reading remind us of our intricate and intimate interconnectedness with others and all of God's creation. There is power and strength in community. If we are willing to accept help from others during our difficult times, we must also stand ready to assist others when they experience challenges and hardship. We cannot opt in to community when it is convenient. Rather, part of living and working in communion with others is recognizing that we all succeed together or fail together.

• Part of the communal reality is recognizing and naming our own gifts. When we can name our strengths without self-absorption or false humility, we are able to better recognize how we can use these gifts for the service of others. Paul writes, "God placed the parts, each one of them, in the body as he intended." When each person uses their individual gifts for the common good, the community grows and flourishes. The same is true for the workings of our human body.

• Today's gospel offers an example of this, as we hear the very beginning of Luke's writings. Luke tells us that he, like others before him, has compiled a narrative of the life of Jesus. Luke relies on the witness of others in the construction of this story; he himself was not an eyewitness. Rather, Luke uses the gifts God has given him to listen to the stories of those who walked and talked and ate with Jesus so that he may compile them for Theophilus and other future generations. How do we use our own gifts and talents to share the life of Jesus with others?

Model Universal Prayer (Prayer of the Faithful)

Presider: Trusting that the Scriptures are fulfilled in Jesus Christ, we are confident as we raise our prayers and petitions to the God of life and love.

Response: Lord, hear our prayer.

That the church may strive to uplift the voices of all people, especially people who might be otherwise ignored or overlooked . . .

That national and world leaders may work together to develop and uphold just immigration policies that serve the needs of the people . . .

That all who experience homelessness or live without a home may find places of shelter, safety, and rest . . .

That all gathered here might work together to bring about the kingdom of God and build up the Body of Christ . . .

Presider: Loving God, we are members of one body, and when one of us suffers, all of us suffer. Hear these prayers we bring before you so that we might all grow in fellowship and community, rejoicing in our common mission. We ask this through Christ our Lord. **Amen.**

COLLECT

Let us pray.

Pause for silent prayer

Almighty ever-living God,
direct our actions according to your good
        pleasure,
that in the name of your beloved Son
we may abound in good works.
Through our Lord Jesus Christ, your Son,
who lives and reigns with you in the unity
        of the Holy Spirit,
God, for ever and ever. **Amen.**

FIRST READING

Neh 8:2-4a, 5-6, 8-10

Ezra the priest brought the law before the
        assembly,
    which consisted of men, women,
    and those children old enough to
        understand.
Standing at one end of the open place that
        was before the Water Gate,
    he read out of the book from daybreak
        till midday,
    in the presence of the men, the women,
    and those children old enough to
        understand;
    and all the people listened attentively to
        the book of the law.
Ezra the scribe stood on a wooden
        platform
    that had been made for the occasion.
He opened the scroll
    so that all the people might see it
    —for he was standing higher up than
        any of the people—;
    and, as he opened it, all the people rose.
Ezra blessed the LORD, the great God,
    and all the people, their hands raised
        high, answered,
    "Amen, amen!"
Then they bowed down and prostrated
        themselves before the LORD,
    their faces to the ground.
Ezra read plainly from the book of the law
        of God,
    interpreting it so that all could
        understand what was read.
Then Nehemiah, that is, His Excellency,
        and Ezra the priest-scribe
    and the Levites who were instructing
        the people
    said to all the people:
    "Today is holy to the LORD your God.
Do not be sad, and do not weep"—
    for all the people were weeping as they
        heard the words of the law.

He said further: "Go, eat rich foods and
    drink sweet drinks,
    and allot portions to those who had
        nothing prepared;
    for today is holy to our LORD.
Do not be saddened this day,
    for rejoicing in the LORD must be your
        strength!"

RESPONSORIAL PSALM

Ps 19:8, 9, 10, 15

R̄. (cf. John 6:63c) Your words, Lord, are
    Spirit and life.

The law of the LORD is perfect,
    refreshing the soul;
the decree of the LORD is trustworthy,
    giving wisdom to the simple.

R̄. Your words, Lord, are Spirit and life.

The precepts of the LORD are right,
    rejoicing the heart;
the command of the LORD is clear,
    enlightening the eye.

R̄. Your words, Lord, are Spirit and life.

The fear of the LORD is pure,
    enduring forever;
the ordinances of the LORD are true,
    all of them just.

R̄. Your words, Lord, are Spirit and life.

Let the words of my mouth and the
        thought of my heart
    find favor before you,
O LORD, my rock and my redeemer.

R̄. Your words, Lord, are Spirit and life.

SECOND READING

1 Cor 12:12-14, 27

Brothers and sisters:
As a body is one though it has many parts,
    and all the parts of the body, though
        many, are one body,
    so also Christ.
For in one Spirit we were all baptized into
        one body,
    whether Jews or Greeks, slaves or free
        persons,
    and we were all given to drink of one
        Spirit.
Now the body is not a single part, but
        many.
You are Christ's body, and individually
        parts of it.

or 1 Cor 12:12-30

See Appendix A, p. 270.

About Liturgy

When in Rome: Today's gospel describes how Jesus "came to Nazareth, where he had grown up, and went according to his custom into the synagogue on the sabbath day" (Luke 4:16). Many of us might not be aware, even though there are many universal and national documents that prescribe how liturgy is to be carried out, just how much the lived implementation of liturgies varies from church to church. At one time or another, most of us have attended liturgy far from home and noticed several differences between our familiar home and wherever we've found ourselves that particular Sunday.

You know the expression "When in Rome, do as the Romans do"? It's a maxim with origins in a very different period of church life, attributed to St. Ambrose. St. Augustine and his mother, St. Monica, were visiting Rome and discovered that Saturday was observed as a day of fasting there. This was not the practice in Milan, where they lived. Seeking wisdom on the matter, they asked St. Ambrose, who purportedly replied "When I am here (in Milan) I do not fast on Saturday, when in Rome I do fast on Saturday."

There was a vast period of church life, centuries ago, when many rites were part of the Roman Catholic Church—the Ambrosian Rite, the Dominican Rite, and dozens more. It would take more space than available here to delve into that history, but one of the reforms of the Council of Trent was, in effect, to disallow most other rites of Eucharist outside the Roman Rite. (It's more complex than that, of course.)

Following the Second Vatican Council and its desire "for legitimate variations and adaptations to different groups, regions and peoples, especially in mission countries . . . provided that the substantial unity of the Roman rite is preserved" (SC 38), the Zaire Rite (or Zaire Use) came to be, incorporating various changes, some reflective of elements of the local culture: alterations to the calendar, standing instead of kneeling, a relocation of the penitential act to following the homily or the creed, liturgical dance, and additional assembly responses.

About Liturgical Documents

Sacrosanctum Concilium—*Further Instructions:* Several instructional documents have been a part of our unpacking and implementing the liturgical directives of the Constitution on the Sacred Liturgy. In 1967, *Musicam Sacram* was issued, striving to clarify norms and values in modern sacred music. One of its key lines is this: "It is desirable that the assembly of the faithful should participate in the songs of the Proper as much as possible, especially through simple responses and other suitable settings" (33).

In 1994, *Varietates Legitimae*: Inculturation and the Roman Liturgy was given, which further refined the principles of inculturation mentioned earlier, the particular areas of liturgy that could be adapted, and the procedures and structures that can appropriately do so.

Liturgiam Authenticam arrived in 2001, speaking to efforts to continue revising translations of the Roman Missal: "the original text, insofar as possible, must be translated integrally and in the most exact manner, without omissions or additions in terms of their content, and without paraphrases or glosses" (20).

About Music

Reflecting the Gospel: "You Have Anointed Me" by Darryl Ducote, Mike Balhoff, and Gary Daigle (Oregon Catholic Press [OCP]) should be considered this weekend, with lyrics straight from the gospel. Also look at the *Psallite* refrain "You Are God's Temple" (Liturgical Press), which reminds us the church is more than brick and mortar—it, too, is built of living stones.

SPIRITUALITY

GOSPEL ACCLAMATION
Matt 4:18

R̸. Alleluia, alleluia.
The Lord sent me to bring glad tidings to the
poor,
to proclaim liberty to captives.
R̸. Alleluia, alleluia.

Gospel

Luke 4:21-30; L72C

Jesus began speaking in the synagogue, saying:
"Today this Scripture passage is
fulfilled in your hearing."
And all spoke highly of him
and were amazed at the gracious
words that came from his
mouth.
They also asked, "Isn't this the
son of Joseph?"
He said to them, "Surely you will
quote me this proverb,
'Physician, cure yourself,' and
say,
'Do here in your native place
the things that we heard were
done in Capernaum.'"
And he said, "Amen, I say to you,
no prophet is accepted in his
own native place.
Indeed, I tell you,
there were many widows in Israel in the
days of Elijah
when the sky was closed for three and a
half years
and a severe famine spread over the entire land.
It was to none of these that Elijah was sent,
but only to a widow in Zarephath in the
land of Sidon.
Again, there were many lepers in Israel
during the time of Elisha the prophet;
yet not one of them was cleansed, but
only Naaman the Syrian."
When the people in the synagogue heard this,
they were all filled with fury.
They rose up, drove him out of the town,
and led him to the brow of the hill
on which their town had been built,
to hurl him down headlong.
But Jesus passed through the midst of them
and went away.

Reflecting on the Gospel

On January 27, 1980, only two months before he was murdered, Archbishop Oscar Romero referred to the gospel we hear today: "In the most sublime homily ever given, Christ closes the book and says, 'These things have been fulfilled today.'" That is what a homily is: saying that God's word is not a reading about times past, but a living and spiritual word that is being fulfilled here today. Hence our effort to apply God's eternal message to people's concrete circumstances.

Romero did this and died for it because he was doing what Jesus was doing in his hometown synagogue at Nazareth: helping the people to understand the "today" implications of the biblical word. Last Sunday, the gospel proclaimed how Jesus as the prophet, the forth-teller, was approved by the people—but not for long! This week we hear how the implications of what he said begins to dawn on them and how their provincialism begins to assert itself. Here is someone they have known (or think they have known) from childhood, the boy who has Joseph for his father. Luke's communities, however, have heard the proclamation of Jesus's beloved sonship of the Father at his baptism (Luke 3:22) and his genealogy that ends with the proclamation "son of God" (Luke 3:38). The Nazareth assembly would like to own Jesus, make him conform to their expectations, perhaps do good for their businesses by enticing the crowds to Nazareth for some of the miracle-working he has done in Capernaum. But he is the free prophet, bound by nothing but the compassion for the poor that he has announced. Accepted or not in his own country, it must be enough that he has spoken out.

The animosity that Jesus will encounter throughout his life, the opposition that will lead him to that terrible mission of martyrdom, seems to be concentrated into this event as the Lukan sign of what is to come. Jesus dares to confront the synagogue assembly with the memory of God's grace shown to those beyond the community of Israel by referring to two other prophets: Elijah and Elisha. For the poor widow of Zarephath, a Gentile, Elijah miraculously replenished her meager store of oil and grain during a famine (1 Kgs 17:8-16); when commanded by Elisha to wash in the waters of the Jordan, the Syrian leper Naaman was healed (2 Kgs 5:9-14). None of us likes to lose an argument by having our own traditions used against us, especially those traditions we have strenuously defended. When Jesus tries to make the people face the truth and consequences of their own Scriptures—and his ministry—this unwelcome reproach to their consciences enrages them. They choose, as religious communities may so often do, to have a selective memory about their tradition. On this occasion, the crowd drives Jesus beyond the city walls to a hill from which they can either throw him down or stone him. But Jesus passes through their midst and "went away." Where he is walking is to another hill, another angry crowd, to be thrown down onto a cross and lifted high. If today's Christian communities are closed or divided, Jesus will pass again through their midst and walk away.

Focusing the Gospel

Key words and phrases: "When the people in the synagogue heard this, they were all filled with fury. . . . But Jesus passed through the midst of them and went away."

To the point: For Jesus's neighbors and colleagues in his hometown, a routine visit to the synagogue has turned into a shocking reveal. Jesus has stood up and read the prophecy from Isaiah about himself. He then looks up and tells those gathered that the prophecy is fulfilled. He's telling his neighbors that he is, in fact, the Messiah. You can imagine how this may have come across as humorous, and then perhaps a little awkward for those listening. They knew Jesus. They've known him his whole life. They knew him so well that someone even whispered, "Isn't this Joseph's kid?"

Anticipating their rejection, he references the history of Elijah and Elisha, who were also rejected from their hometowns. But this is too much for the men of the town in the synagogue. "They rose up, drove him out of the town, and led him to the brow of the hill on which their town had been built, to hurl him down headlong." They've got Jesus backed up to a cliff, with the intention of throwing him over. That's how immediate and all-consuming the threat of something radically new is to these townspeople. Jesus, the Messiah?

Connecting the Gospel

to the first and second readings: The first reading is one of the most tender and personal moments in all of Scripture: "Before I formed you in the womb I knew you, before you were born I dedicated you, a prophet to the nations I appointed you." Our Lord is deeply personal, and this tender attention moves directly into the second reading.

The section of Paul's first letter to the Corinthians sums up most of our faith. It does so in a poetic way, and it's no surprise that this reading is often chosen by couples for a wedding liturgy. Paul states over and over, in a myriad of beautiful images, that you can be the most successful person alive, but it means nothing if it isn't done with love.

to experience: We get a nice list today of the things that love is not. "It is not jealous, it is not pompous, it is not inflated, it is not rude, it does not seek its own interests, it is not quick-tempered, it does not brood over injury, it does not rejoice over wrongdoing but rejoices with the truth." Sit with this list awhile and think over your day.

Connecting the Responsorial Psalm

to the readings: The psalm's stanzas move through three stages: in the first, the psalmist is saved by the Lord. In the second, refuge is found within the Lord's fortress. In the final stanza, there is hope. This hope is borne of trust, and the psalmist tells us, "On you I depend from birth; / from my mother's womb you are my strength." This ties into Jeremiah's words, "Before I formed you in the womb I knew you."

to psalmist preparation: Think of the intimacy between a mother and the child in her womb. You have probably witnessed this relationship, whether through giving birth, accompanying your spouse, or being near nieces, nephews, and godchildren. That is the intimacy with which God accompanies us.

PROMPTS FOR FAITH-SHARING

What are areas where you have failed to "be" love? Where do you tend to succeed?

If someone from your parish stood up this weekend, walked to the ambo, read this gospel, and told you they were the second coming of Christ, what would you do? Is there any situation in which you would believe your neighbor if they imitated Jesus in this week's gospel?

God knew you the moment of your conception. How does this intimacy inform your reverence for the vulnerable within your society?

What does it mean that love never fails? People die, war continues, greed perseveres, and yet this isn't a failure of love. Is it love's absence? Do we simply reject love?

Model Penitential Act

Presider: In today's gospel, Jesus is rejected for being prophetic. For the times we have ignored or shunned prophetic voices we encounter, we ask for God's pardon and peace . . . *[pause]*

Lord Jesus, your words are spirit and life: Lord, have mercy.

Christ Jesus, you are the fulfillment of the prophets: Christ, have mercy.

Lord Jesus, you are all we hope and long for: Lord, have mercy.

Homily Points

• God delights us with surprises. In today's gospel, after Jesus speaks in the synagogue, all were amazed and asked, "Isn't this the son of Joseph?" It was difficult for those gathered to see Jesus as anything beyond what they already knew about him and his family. They became even more enraged when Jesus proclaimed that prophets are not accepted in their native place. Filled with fury, outrage, and at least some bewilderment, the crowd attempted to kill Jesus because he did not meet their expectations. They did not allow God to surprise them. Do we allow ourselves to be surprised by God?

• Undaunted by the crowds, however, Jesus does not shirk from his message. Rather, he remains confident and committed to his words and does not fight back when the people rebuke him and try to throw him over a cliff. This is similar to the Christian message proclaimed by Paul in the letter to the Corinthians. Paul writes, "At present we see indistinctly, as in a mirror, but then face to face. At present I know partially; then I shall know fully, as I am fully known." As humans we do not know everything. When the kingdom of God is fulfilled, however, we will know and see as God does.

• While this reading from Paul is often associated with weddings, it is important to remember that the faith, hope, and love that are described are essential elements for all aspects of Christian life. We must embody faith, hope, and love in our everyday actions and interactions, so much so that what we do and say is incomplete if we do not cling to these gifts that remain. When we do this we live the prophetic lives to which we are called.

Model Universal Prayer (Prayer of the Faithful)

Presider: Confident that our God loves us and lavishly gifts and blesses us, we raise our prayers and petitions.

Response: Lord, hear our prayer.

That the church may always be a prophetic witness in the world, giving voice to the voiceless and power to the powerless . . .

That all local, national, and world leaders will work to protect the dignity and rights of their people . . .

That all people who are unemployed or underemployed may find dignified and justly compensated work . . .

That our local community may work to embody God's gifts of faith, hope, and love through how we live with each other . . .

Presider: Loving God, hear these prayers we bring before you today. Just as you did in the synagogue, speak to us today and open our ears to hear your voice in our midst. We ask this through Christ our Lord. **Amen.**

COLLECT

Let us pray.

Pause for silent prayer

Grant us, Lord our God,
that we may honor you with all our mind,
and love everyone in truth of heart.
Through our Lord Jesus Christ, your Son,
who lives and reigns with you in the unity
    of the Holy Spirit,
God, for ever and ever. **Amen.**

FIRST READING
Jer 1:4-5, 17-19

The word of the LORD came to me, saying:
    Before I formed you in the womb I knew
        you,
        before you were born I dedicated you,
        a prophet to the nations I appointed
            you.

But do you gird your loins;
    stand up and tell them
    all that I command you.
Be not crushed on their account,
    as though I would leave you crushed
        before them;
for it is I this day
    who have made you a fortified city,
a pillar of iron, a wall of brass,
    against the whole land:
against Judah's kings and princes,
    against its priests and people.
They will fight against you but not
        prevail over you,
    for I am with you to deliver you, says
        the LORD.

RESPONSORIAL PSALM
Ps 71:1-2, 3-4, 5-6, 15, 17

℟. (cf. 15ab) I will sing of your salvation.

In you, O LORD, I take refuge;
    let me never be put to shame.
In your justice rescue me, and deliver me;
    incline your ear to me, and save me.

℟. I will sing of your salvation.

Be my rock of refuge,
    a stronghold to give me safety,
    for you are my rock and my fortress.
O my God, rescue me from the hand of the
        wicked.

℟. I will sing of your salvation.

For you are my hope, O Lord;
    my trust, O God, from my youth.
On you I depend from birth;
    from my mother's womb you are my
        strength.

℟. I will sing of your salvation.

My mouth shall declare your justice,
    day by day your salvation.
O God, you have taught me from my
    youth,
    and till the present I proclaim your
    wondrous deeds.

R̸. I will sing of your salvation.

SECOND READING

1 Cor 13:4-13

Brothers and sisters:
Love is patient, love is kind.
It is not jealous, it is not pompous,
    it is not inflated, it is not rude,
    it does not seek its own interests,
    it is not quick-tempered, it does not
        brood over injury,
    it does not rejoice over wrongdoing but
        rejoices with the truth.
It bears all things, believes all things,
    hopes all things, endures all things.

Love never fails.
If there are prophecies, they will be
    brought to nothing;
    if tongues, they will cease;
    if knowledge, it will be brought to
        nothing.
For we know partially and we prophesy
    partially,
    but when the perfect comes, the partial
        will pass away.
When I was a child, I used to talk as a
    child,
    think as a child, reason as a child;
    when I became a man, I put aside
        childish things.
At present we see indistinctly, as in a
    mirror,
    but then face to face.
At present I know partially;
    then I shall know fully, as I am fully
        known.
So faith, hope, love remain, these three;
    but the greatest of these is love.

or 1 Cor 12:31–13:13

See Appendix A, p. 270.

About Liturgy

I Am Patient, I Am Kind: Last week's epistle ("As a body is one though it has many parts, and all the parts of the body, though many, are one body, so also Christ.") immediately precedes this week's passage—a passage that is likely familiar to us mainly from the sacrament of matrimony. I can say I was one of those who lamented its overuse at weddings, once upon a time. But no more. Here's why.

A while back, I learned from my one of my best friends (who I think had learned this from someone else) that a good spiritual exercise is to insert one's own name (or "I") in the second paragraph of this passage wherever you see the word "love" (or "it"). Those few sentences, prayed that way, make for a nice examination of conscience. "I am patient, I am kind," and so on. This practice makes you think about how you lived your faith that day, week, or month.

God is love and can only be so because God is also relationship—three persons, in love, loving. And we are created in that image too. We are meant to be in relationship, in love, loving.

These words can be so helpful to us, whatever our role in crafting and executing the liturgy. It might help as we sort out how to converse with a zealous pastor with whom we might not agree, or with a volunteer minister who "doesn't play in the sandbox well" with his or her peers. Thinking back to last week's epistle paired with this one, this approach might also be a powerful and faith-filled way to address any jealousy and envy that might arise between various people in your charge.

Perhaps, too, we know ourselves, at least on occasion, to be the one others might call "difficult"—this is one way to self-examine and perhaps take such criticism and make it positive and helpful, even if it wasn't initially offered that way.

A different friend related to me the story of how her family fought for this passage to be included at an elderly relative's funeral Mass, even though it is not one of the prescribed choices in the Lectionary. The pastor, who had initially pushed back, used exactly this approach to the passage in the homily, remembering the life of love that was truly lived by that departed soul. May we strive to live so that one day these words be true for us all!

Many times in recent years I have noticed that this passage, once overlooked and perhaps even ignored due to its ubiquity, appears in my life at just the right moment, and I have found this particular way to pray it most helpful. Perhaps you might as well.

About Music

Intimacy and Relationship: The Old Testament passage today reminds us that God has always known us, before we were even being formed in our mother's womb. This imagery is also found in countless settings of Psalm 139: Bernadette Farrell's "O God You Search Me" (OCP) and Eugene Englert's "Secrets of My Heart" (WLP/GIA) are but two of many.

The gospel, on the other hand, has Jesus not recognized by those who ought to know him best, those from his own "native place." A piece that might speak to those feelings of misunderstandings and even isolation is "Restless" by Audrey Assad and Matt Maher, echoing the familiar St. Augustine prayer, found in several contemporary resources.

✝ SPIRITUALITY

GOSPEL ACCLAMATION
Matt 4:19

℟. Alleluia, alleluia.
Come after me
and I will make you fishers of men.
℟. Alleluia, alleluia.

Gospel   Luke 5:1-11; L75C

While the crowd was
    pressing in on Jesus
    and listening to the
    word of God,
he was standing by the
    Lake of Gennesaret.
He saw two boats there
    alongside the lake;
the fishermen had
    disembarked and
    were washing their
    nets.
Getting into one of the
    boats, the one be-
    longing to Simon,
he asked him to put out
    a short distance
    from the shore.
Then he sat down and
    taught the crowds from the boat.
After he had finished speaking, he said
    to Simon,
    "Put out into deep water and lower
        your nets for a catch."
Simon said in reply,
    "Master, we have worked hard all
        night and have caught nothing,
    but at your command I will lower the
        nets."
When they had done this, they caught a
    great number of fish
    and their nets were tearing.
They signaled to their partners in the
    other boat
    to come to help them.
They came and filled both boats
    so that the boats were in danger of
        sinking.

Continued in Appendix A, p. 271.

Reflecting on the Gospel

As we started to journey through Ordinary Time, we met Jesus beginning his public ministry. Today, we hear his call to his first disciples to follow him and companion him in this ministry. All three of the readings for this Sunday contain a story of a call: different people, in different circumstances, with different social and religious status, yet all are touched by the divine initiative. Isaiah, perhaps daydreaming, was in the Jerusalem temple; Paul, certainly persecuting, was on the road to Damascus; the fishermen, at the lake of Gennesaret (the Sea of Galilee), were washing their nets.

In the gospel, Jesus is standing on the lakeside with a crowd pressing around him to hear the word of God. Significantly, Peter and his companions are not part of this crowd. They are tending to their nets after an unprofitable night's fishing. Then Jesus himself becomes a "fisherman" for, as Proverbs 20:5 says, "The intention of the human heart is deep water, / but the intelligent draw it forth." He gets into Simon's boat, hauls this probably nonplussed man in with him, and puts out a short way from the shore to continue teaching the crowd. After that, Jesus addresses his words to Simon only, telling him to launch out into the deep and put down his nets for a catch. Something that Simon Peter had heard as he sat with Jesus must have made an impression, for he responds to Jesus as "Master," and although he cannot resist reminding Jesus that their nets were empty the night before, in obedience to Jesus's words he casts them into the water.

Then a great reversal happens, as it does so often in the gospels and as it will for all those who are obedient to Jesus. Empty nets become full to the breaking point, and Peter's personal encounter with Jesus leads to the call of James and John to help with the catch; emptiness becomes fullness in not only one boat but two. Peter is as overwhelmed as the boats. He falls down at Jesus's feet, now calling him "Lord," the post-resurrection title that Luke throws back into this early episode so that those who hear this narrative will recognize the presence of the risen One throughout the whole of his gospel. Peter begs Jesus to leave him because he is a sinner. We may admire this as Peter's humble profession of his unworthiness to associate with Jesus. But if we read our own experiences, could there not also be a fear of the deep waters that Peter might be letting himself into, waters that would be less troubled if Jesus just went away and left the fishermen to their nets, empty or full? Are there times when we have said to God, "Why me?" when being asked to cope with this commitment, this vocation, this suffering? One day a young woman whose daughter had just given birth to a child with Down syndrome, said in tears to her mother, "Why me?" Her mother replied, "Why? Because of all my children, you are the one whom I would choose—and God has chosen—to be the mother of this child who needs so much love."

At the dawn of the third millennium, John Paul II reminded the church of this section of Luke's gospel: *Duc in altum!* Put out into the deep! These words ring out for us today, and they invite us to remember the past with gratitude, to live the present with enthusiasm, and to look forward to the future with confidence: "Jesus Christ is the same yesterday, today, and forever" (Heb 13:8). Now after more than two decades into the third millennium, how are we measuring up to this challenge?

Focusing the Gospel

Key words and phrases: "They signaled to their partners in the other boat to come to help them."

To the point: This is a story of unexpected gifts, of the irony of following the Lord, and perhaps less discussed, a story of involving community in success.

We've all heard the gospel of Jesus telling Simon to "[p]ut out into deep water," even though Simon is certain, based on his experience, that there's nothing to catch. However, he gives it a try. This deference to Jesus is exemplary of our faith, but this week, maybe focus on the final event of this story: once Simon's boat begins to fill, he calls his colleagues to help him.

Simon could have kept this to himself. He had a big take. He'd likely be the only person with fish to sell the next day. Instead, his reaction is to tell his colleagues about the opportunity he's found. They set out into the water, and both boats are filled so heavy with fish that they can barely keep them afloat.

How often do we get "bogged down" in our professional lives? Whether it is a job or a volunteer position, once we have routine obligations, we quickly form a habit of expectation. What Jesus does is crush Simon's expectations. Simon, like any fisherman, has learned how to read the signs of the sea and knows what works and what doesn't. But Jesus encourages him to try one more time. The result is abundance.

Connecting the Gospel

to the second reading: In the gospel, Jesus reaches out to a fisherman. His choice of a common profession that's not particularly glamorous exemplifies Jesus's commitment to everyone, not just kings and priests. It draws us closer to him. In the second reading, Paul drops another line that brings us close to the real person of Jesus: "After that, he appeared to more than five hundred brothers at once, most of whom are still living." Paul was a contemporary of Jesus. He knows people who knew Jesus during Jesus's ministry.

to experience: We are not speaking of prophecies and prayers. We are speaking about an actual human who walked around the Middle East, had friends, and was executed by his community for speaking out. Paul knows people who were there and gave him firsthand accounts of not only being with Jesus during his ministry, but *being with the risen Lord.* Paul references these encounters as evidence as if to say, *You don't think Jesus rose from the dead? I've got five hundred accounts of people who saw him.* And then the kicker: Paul himself saw the risen Christ. What did he do with an experience like that? He wrote about it like he was running out of time.

Connecting the Responsorial Psalm

to the readings: In the first reading, Isaiah has a very intense vision in which an angel burns his lips with an ember from holy fire to purify them. This visceral experience is physical and shocking. Can you imagine how overwhelming it would be not only to see a vision of God in heaven with the angels, but to have one of them burn your lips with fire? This certainly gives new meaning to the phrase "word on fire."

to psalmist preparation: In this week's psalm, you are describing to the congregation what this may have felt like for Isaiah. Imagine the angels. Imagine "the Lord seated on a high and lofty throne, / with the train of his garment filling the temple." This is the image you are describing through the words of praise. Can you muster up the kind of courage Isaiah had when he declared, "Here I am . . . send me!"?

PROMPTS FOR FAITH-SHARING

What are the "deep waters" of your career that you've grown to expect? Do you leave space for the Lord to surprise you?

What would you do if you had a dream or waking vision similar to the one Isaiah describes?

If Paul walked into the room right now, what would you ask him about the risen Christ?

If an angel handed you an ember and told you to purge one sinful tendency from your life, what would you choose?

Model Penitential Act

Presider: In today's gospel Peter exclaims, "Depart from me, Lord, for I am a sinful man." Like Peter, we at times recognize our own sinfulness and dependence on God's love, pardon, and peace . . . *[pause]*

> Lord Jesus, you filled the nets to bursting: Lord, have mercy.
>
> Christ Jesus, you remind us not to be afraid: Christ, have mercy.
>
> Lord Jesus, you make us fishers of people: Lord, have mercy.

Homily Points

• If we are honest with ourselves, we often tend to operate out of one of two mindsets, where the daily decisions we make are influenced by either what we have or what we do not have. Simply put, do we act with a mindset of scarcity or a mindset of abundance? While we may rightly fluctuate between the two, our gospel today reminds us that Jesus provides us more than enough, more than we can possibly ever imagine. We have the opportunity each day to choose to see what God has given us, rather than lamenting what we do not have.

• How do we respond to God's generosity? In both the first reading and the gospel, Isaiah and Peter respond in fear and trepidation when they see God's marvelous works. Isaiah shouts, "Woe is me, I am doomed!" and Peter exclaims, "Depart from me, Lord, for I am a sinful man." After some time, however, their attitudes shift. Isaiah and Peter change from a hesitancy to doing the work of God because of their own shortcomings to acknowledging the power of God and their willingness to participate in it. Isaiah says, "Here I am, send me." And Luke writes that Peter "left everything and followed him."

• Jesus tells Peter and each of us, "Do not be afraid." While fear is a natural and necessary part of life, with prayer and the support of our community, we can become who we are called to be: people of awe, people of gratitude, people of abundance.

Model Universal Prayer (Prayer of the Faithful)

Presider: Jesus heard and answered the prayers of Peter and his partners, blessing them abundantly beyond their belief. We, too, bring our prayers and petitions to God, knowing that they will be heard.

Response: Lord, hear our prayer.

That the church, following the example of Peter, will be fishers of all people . . .

That civil servants work to ensure a sharing of goods with those who are in need . . .

That all who experience self-doubt may know they are beloved by God . . .

That our local community may stand in awe and gratitude of the works of God . . .

Presider: Loving God, hear these prayers we bring before you today. We trust that in your great kindness and generosity you will hear and answer them according to your will. We ask this through Christ our Lord. **Amen.**

COLLECT

Let us pray.

Pause for silent prayer

Keep your family safe, O Lord, with
  unfailing care,
that, relying solely on the hope of
  heavenly grace,
they may be defended always by your
  protection.
Through our Lord Jesus Christ, your Son,
who lives and reigns with you in the unity
  of the Holy Spirit,
God, for ever and ever. **Amen.**

FIRST READING
Isa 6:1-2a, 3-8

In the year King Uzziah died,
  I saw the Lord seated on a high and
    lofty throne,
  with the train of his garment filling the
    temple.
Seraphim were stationed above.

They cried one to the other,
  "Holy, holy, holy is the LORD of hosts!
All the earth is filled with his glory!"
At the sound of that cry, the frame of the
  door shook
  and the house was filled with smoke.

Then I said, "Woe is me, I am doomed!
For I am a man of unclean lips,
  living among a people of unclean lips;
  yet my eyes have seen the King, the
    LORD of hosts!"
Then one of the seraphim flew to me,
  holding an ember that he had taken
    with tongs from the altar.

He touched my mouth with it, and said,
  "See, now that this has touched your
    lips,
  your wickedness is removed, your sin
    purged."

Then I heard the voice of the Lord saying,
  "Whom shall I send? Who will go for
    us?"
"Here I am," I said; "send me!"

RESPONSORIAL PSALM
Ps 138:1-2, 2-3, 4-5, 7-8

℟. (1c) In the sight of the angels I will
  sing your praises, Lord.

I will give thanks to you, O LORD, with all
  my heart,
  for you have heard the words of my
    mouth;
  in the presence of the angels I will sing
    your praise;

I will worship at your holy temple
and give thanks to your name.

R℣. In the sight of the angels I will sing
your praises, Lord.

Because of your kindness and your truth;
for you have made great above all things
your name and your promise.
When I called, you answered me;
you built up strength within me.

R℣. In the sight of the angels I will sing
your praises, Lord.

All the kings of the earth shall give
thanks to you, O LORD,
when they hear the words of your mouth;
and they shall sing of the ways of the LORD:
"Great is the glory of the LORD."

R℣. In the sight of the angels I will sing
your praises, Lord.

Your right hand saves me.
The LORD will complete what he has
done for me;
your kindness, O LORD, endures forever;
forsake not the work of your hands.

R℣. In the sight of the angels I will sing
your praises, Lord.

SECOND READING

1 Cor 15:3-8, 11

Brothers and sisters,
I handed on to you as of first
importance what I also received:
that Christ died for our sins
in accordance with the Scriptures;
that he was buried;
that he was raised on the third day
in accordance with the Scriptures;
that he appeared to Cephas, then to the
Twelve.
After that, he appeared to more
than five hundred brothers at once,
most of whom are still living,
though some have fallen asleep.
After that he appeared to James,
then to all the apostles.
Last of all, as to one born abnormally,
he appeared to me.
Therefore, whether it be I or they,
so we preach and so you believed.

or 1 Cor 15:1-11

See Appendix A, p. 271.

About Liturgy

Expansive Language: "Jesus said to Simon, 'Do not be afraid; from now on you will be catching men'" (Luke 5:10b). I don't expect that any of us, today, believe what Jesus meant here is to describe a future where the apostles, led by Simon Peter, would be catching only men and not women. "Masculine pronouns have always been used in a collective manner to refer to both men and women," some argue. This of course is not always true and the language has not always been consistent or helpful. Instances have arisen where the masculine language, initially meant to be inclusive, was later reframed to try to exclude. That the language is unclear, requiring speaker and receiver to have a joint understanding of context, implications, and inferences, is easily solved with clearer language. Inclusive language isn't always sufficient, for both language and acts of inclusion almost always also create exclusions, even unintentionally.

A contemporary (yet timeless) paradox also relevant here is the "gendering" of God. Surely we comprehend that God has no gender, even while also understanding that the Word Incarnate was male and used a masculine title, "Abba," for God the Father. Often, in fact, when people talk about, or pray to God, they really mean God the Father without realizing it. Yet we struggle here, because the names for God should depend on who God (or each of the persons of the Trinity) is, not what God does. All three persons of the Trinity, for instance, were vital to creation and redemption.

No image of God that humans create will ever be complete; every analogy we create will be more unlike God than it is like God. There is, though, perhaps no other way for our human senses and logic to grow in understanding of the divine and for our hearts to grow into relationship with God.

Jesus never invoked his masculinity as necessary for his mission. Gender issues did arise, but Jesus always landed on the side of empowering and elevating women and all those on the fringes of society. Let us consider being more conscious, more careful with our language, our images, and our understandings in our faith expressions.

About Liturgical Documents

Authors, Authority, Recipients, Weight: When considering the many documents that shape our liturgical practices, it is important, even foundational, to keep in mind the context of the document to inform the reader about how to receive it and "use" it. Where did it come from: the Vatican, the United States Conference of Catholic Bishops (USCCB), your local ordinary? Who is it addressed to: priests, or all the faithful? Is it universal law, or instruction, or suggestion? Is it operating on a practical level or more on a theological one, or both? If one document comes out later in time than another, does the more recent document automatically displace the earlier one?

Among the more typical documents in our liturgical universe are constitutions (like the one we've been glancing at so far), instructions (also briefly mentioned), introductions, decrees, apostolic letters, and occasionally other texts like messages, directories, guidelines, circular letters . . .

Over the coming weeks, this space will delve into these questions to help inform our reception and understanding of the many writings that seek to form our divine worship.

About Music

Responding to Christ's Call: We probably all have favorites when it comes to music to pair with Jesus calling and gathering his apostles. Some perhaps lesser-known pieces to consider include "To Follow You" by Chris de Silva (GIA) and "We Will Go, Lord" by Shannon Cerneka and Orin Johnson (GIA).

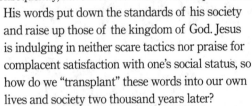

SPIRITUALITY

GOSPEL ACCLAMATION
Luke 6:23ab

℟. Alleluia, alleluia.
Rejoice and be glad,
your reward will be great in heaven.
℟. Alleluia, alleluia.

Gospel

Luke 6:17, 20-26; L78C

Jesus came down with the Twelve
and stood on a stretch of level
ground
with a great crowd of his
disciples
and a large number of the
people
from all Judea and Jerusalem
and the coastal region of Tyre
and Sidon.
And raising his eyes toward his
disciples he said:
"Blessed are you who are poor,
for the kingdom of God is
yours.
Blessed are you who are now
hungry,
for you will be satisfied.
Blessed are you who are now weeping,
for you will laugh.
Blessed are you when people hate you,
and when they exclude and insult you,
and denounce your name as evil
on account of the Son of Man.
Rejoice and leap for joy on that day!
Behold, your reward will be great in heaven.
For their ancestors treated the prophets in
the same way.
But woe to you who are rich,
for you have received your consolation.
Woe to you who are filled now,
for you will be hungry.
Woe to you who laugh now,
for you will grieve and weep.
Woe to you when all speak well of you,
for their ancestors treated the false
prophets in this way."

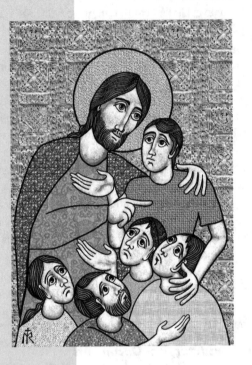

Reflecting on the Gospel

Luke's Beatitudes are part of a sermon on the plain, not on a mountain as was Matthew's chosen setting. It is not geography that governs each evangelist's choice, but rather theology and the particular challenge each emphasizes for different communities. Luke's setting reflects Jesus's very down-to-earth ground rules for inclusion in the kingdom of God. The Lukan Beatitudes are less spiritualized than Matthew's and, consequently, have more concrete social implications.

His words put down the standards of his society and raise up those of the kingdom of God. Jesus is indulging in neither scare tactics nor praise for complacent satisfaction with one's social status, so how do we "transplant" these words into our own lives and society two thousand years later?

For Luke, the poor were not just the poor in spirit (as in Matt 5:3); they were the economically impoverished, the people on the margins, pushed there by a society that did not take seriously the covenant responsibility to which Moses and the prophets had called them. The poor are specially loved by God, not so much because of what they are, but because of what God is—the compassionate defender of the weak and powerless (Deut 10:18; Amos 2:6-7). As the liberation theologian Gustavo Gutiérrez wrote in his 1991 essay in *Voices from the Margin*: "God has a preferential love for the poor not because they are necessarily better than others, morally or religiously, but simply because they are living in an inhuman situation that is contrary to God's will. The ultimate basis for the privileged position of the poor is not in the poor themselves but in God, in the graciousness and universality of God's agapeic love."

As individuals, church, governments, our justice re-presents God's justice to the world. The poor, hungry, weeping, and persecuted people are those for whom the church calls us to make a special option, one that will have both personal and political consequences. In their pastoral letter Economic Justice for All, the US bishops offer a finely balanced statement about the economy: "Decisions must be judged in the light of what they do for the poor, what they do to the poor, and what they enable the poor to do for themselves" (24). Our option for the poor is to be preferential not exclusive, respectful not denigrating, enabling not patronizing.

Since the poor do not need to be told that they are poor, it seems that Luke has very much in mind the audience of affluent, comfortable, and self-satisfied Christians in his communities. To make sure that poverty is not romanticized, Jesus speaks the next two beatitudes to the hungry and weeping. Jesus and the early church, in his Spirit, will provide for the hungry (Luke 9:17; 16:21; Acts 6:1-4), and tears are more precious in God's sight than derisive laughter (Luke 7:32, 38). Discipleship is not to be domesticated; it may demand the high price of hatred, exclusion, scorn, and eviction from the places of the privileged. It is the struggle for justice when, for example, low-income housing estates are gentrified or when those who fear a drop in their land value protest about group homes for people with disabilities being built in their "neighborhood" (the term that, ironically, is often used). When governments ignore the potential impact of climate change on the small land holdings of subsistence farmers, when their social welfare budget is insignificant when compared to the money spent on war, and when we—as citizens not only of our own nations but also of the kingdom of God—do nothing to advocate justice, then our ears need to be dug out by the "woes" of Jesus.

Focusing the Gospel

Key words and phrases: "Blessed are you who are poor, for the kingdom of God is yours."

To the point: This is one of those times in the gospel when Jesus doesn't mince words, but gets right to the point. The kingdom of God belongs to the poor. The hungry will be satisfied. Those who are weeping will laugh. On the flip side, the rich have nothing left to receive, the full will be hungry, and those who are laughing will weep. This makes no sense in a world built around consuming for convenience, media impact, purchasing power, and the accumulation of wealth. What are we supposed to do with these words?

This week's gospel invites us to focus on the end game. Our purpose in this earthly life is to get to heaven, and bring as many people with us as possible. Do not let the physical and material goals of your career and family distract you from that ultimate goal. You are trying to love others, especially your family, in such a way that you condition your soul and theirs for heaven. That's what we're doing on Sunday. That's what you're invited to do in your vocation. That's the reason we seek good, rich, healthy relationships with friends, family, and colleagues. When we live with our eyes on heaven, this life becomes far more vibrant and satisfying. Shift your focus from earthy achievements to those of a love much greater.

Connecting the Gospel

to the first reading: Jeremiah is equally fervent about directing one's attention away from "his strength in flesh" and instead toward the Lord. The first reading is two contrasting metaphors: one of a bush in the desert that cannot change with the seasons, and one of a tree with growing roots that are watered by the Lord.

to experience: Do you ever feel like you're standing in a parched desert, unable to let the seasons change you? This is a common experience that we're bound to have multiple times in our lives. Allow yourself, this week, to pinpoint areas where you need to water your roots.

Connecting the Responsorial Psalm

to the readings: The psalmist provides imagery to complement Jeremiah. "He is like a tree / planted near running water, / that yields its fruit in due season, / and whose leaves never fade." It's winter in the northern hemisphere. How are you experiencing this season? Do you feel like you're in a spiritual hibernation, or are you blooming?

to psalmist preparation: Take some time this week to imagine moments in your own spiritual life when you have experienced each of the four seasons. When was winter, a dark time when you perhaps lost someone or experienced a trial? Can you recall a spring, when your faith began to open more and bloom? Have you lived through a summer in your faith, when prayer was easy and you felt God "in sync" with your life? What was autumn like, watching the leaves turn glorious colors as your faith matured?

PROMPTS FOR FAITH-SHARING

Have you ever been spiritually hungry? Have you ever been physically hungry?

What season of faith are you currently in?

When was the last time your faith felt like a barren bush in the desert? Or a tree being fed by the waters of the Lord?

What are specific actions you can take to align yourself more fully with Jesus's call in the gospel?

Model Penitential Act

Presider: Today we hear the prophet Jeremiah proclaim, "Blessed is the one who trusts in the LORD, whose hope is in the LORD." For the times we have not trusted in God and instead placed our hope in things not of God, we ask for forgiveness and healing . . . *[pause]*

Lord Jesus, you satisfy the hungry: Lord, have mercy.

Christ Jesus, you bring hope to those who grieve and weep: Christ, have mercy.

Lord Jesus, you share an abundance of good things with the poor: Lord, have mercy.

Homily Points

• Today's gospel tells us that Jesus means business. His words are not mere lip service or some sort of easy consolation for those who are hurting. In Luke's version of the Beatitudes, Jesus shares four statements of blessedness, not unlike Matthew's account. What follows, however, is different. Not only does Jesus say, "Blessed are you who are poor, for the kingdom of God is yours," but he continues, "[W]oe to you who are rich, for you have received your consolation."

• Scripture scholars often refer to this passage, among others in the gospel of Luke, as indicating a sort of "great reversal." Luke consistently situates the narrative of Jesus within the framework of the real world. This temporal element of Luke's writing is not insignificant, especially as today's gospel points to a great reversal where those who have will be humbled and those who have nothing will be exalted. Expected and "normal" social structures are challenged in favor of a new way of life in Christ.

• We see this notion in other places throughout Luke's gospel. Consider Mary's great *Magnificat* we heard during Advent. In that first chapter of Luke, Mary foreshadows the reality of the kingdom of God where the voiceless are given positions of power, the poor live in abundance, and those who weep and mourn will laugh and rejoice. What does this mean for us today? As we hear Jesus's words today, perhaps we can all take some time to think about how we might lower our own voices so the voices of others may be heard. Maybe we can name our own positions of privilege and help lift up others. If we follow today's command, we will indeed "[r]ejoice and leap for joy on that day!"

Model Universal Prayer (Prayer of the Faithful)

Presider: Today's psalm reminds us, "Blessed are they who hope in the Lord." Trusting in the God of all goodness, we raise our prayers and petitions.

Response: Lord, hear our prayer.

That the church may always stand on the side of people who are hurting and oppressed . . .

That public authorities may always build up citizens by working for the common good . . .

That all who have experienced loss may know the comfort of Jesus through loved ones . . .

That our community may work tirelessly for inclusivity in all forms . . .

Presider: Loving God, we rejoice for in you we come to know all that is good. Hear the prayers we make today and answer them according to your will so we may be a people who are poor, hungry, sad, and excluded in order to better know you and build your kingdom. We ask this through Christ our Lord. **Amen.**

COLLECT

Let us pray.

Pause for silent prayer

O God, who teach us that you abide
in hearts that are just and true,
grant that we may be so fashioned by
    your grace
as to become a dwelling pleasing to you.
Through our Lord Jesus Christ, your Son,
who lives and reigns with you in the unity
    of the Holy Spirit,
God, for ever and ever. **Amen.**

FIRST READING

Jer 17:5-8

Thus says the LORD:
    Cursed is the one who trusts in human
        beings,
        who seeks his strength in flesh,
        whose heart turns away from the
            LORD.
    He is like a barren bush in the desert
        that enjoys no change of season,
    but stands in a lava waste,
        a salt and empty earth.
    Blessed is the one who trusts in the
        LORD,
        whose hope is the LORD.
    He is like a tree planted beside the
        waters
        that stretches out its roots to the
            stream:
    it fears not the heat when it comes;
        its leaves stay green;
    in the year of drought it shows no
        distress,
        but still bears fruit.

RESPONSORIAL PSALM
Ps 1:1-2, 3, 4 and 6

R̸. (40:5a) Blessed are they who hope in
the Lord.

Blessed the man who follows not
the counsel of the wicked,
nor walks in the way of sinners,
nor sits in the company of the insolent,
but delights in the law of the Lᴏʀᴅ
and meditates on his law day and night.

R̸. Blessed are they who hope in the Lord.

He is like a tree
planted near running water,
that yields its fruit in due season,
and whose leaves never fade.
Whatever he does, prospers.

R̸. Blessed are they who hope in the Lord.

Not so the wicked, not so;
they are like chaff which the wind
drives away.
For the Lᴏʀᴅ watches over the way of the
just,
but the way of the wicked vanishes.

R̸. Blessed are they who hope in the Lord.

SECOND READING
1 Cor 15:12, 16-20

Brothers and sisters:
If Christ is preached as raised from the
dead,
how can some among you say there is no
resurrection of the dead?
If the dead are not raised, neither has
Christ been raised,
and if Christ has not been raised, your
faith is vain;
you are still in your sins.
Then those who have fallen asleep in
Christ have perished.
If for this life only we have hoped in
Christ,
we are the most pitiable people of all.

But now Christ has been raised from the
dead,
the firstfruits of those who have fallen
asleep.

About Liturgy

Black and Red: Jesus's insistence today that one's yes means yes and no means no might bring to mind a maxim popular in some liturgical circles: "Say the black, do the red." This refers to the Roman Missal itself, which has words meant to be said printed in black ink, and actions to be done printed in red. The broader principle is that one should not adapt or change the universal liturgy, ever. There is no reason, ever, to make changes in the Missal, nor is there ever a need to interpret anything in the Missal. It's all there—just say it and do it. Done.

In practice (and dare I say reality), it just isn't quite that simple. The Missal frequently uses phrases like "these or similar words," "according to circumstances and local conditions," or "where a pastoral reason suggests" along with other conditional words like "may" or "should." Further, there are places where the Missal doesn't tell us to do anything at all. You know the threefold sign of the cross the faithful do before the gospel proclamation? That wasn't included in the Missal until the 2012 edition, at least not for the faithful to do. And, in our current Missal, the relevant instruction reads, "At the ambo, the Priest opens the book and, with hands joined, says, *The Lord be with you,* to which the people reply, *And with your spirit.* Then he says, *A reading from the holy Gospel,* making the Sign of the Cross with his thumb on the book and on his forehead, mouth, and breast, which everyone else does as well" (GIRM 134). A strict reading here, for those who profess "Say the black, do the red" as their liturgical guide, would indicate that the faithful should each take a turn signing the Lectionary or book of the gospels before signing themselves! Or, to be even a bit silly about it, that everyone would make the threefold sign of the cross on the priest instead of themselves.

The Missal is indeed much more complex than "say the black, do the red." While we should be careful to not adjust the universal liturgy, especially the immutable portions of it, for personal reasons or "on a whim," the liturgy does have substantial room for local pastoral adaptations and implementations.

About Liturgical Documents

Liturgical Documents from the Vatican: In addition to the Constitution on the Sacred Liturgy, other documents that have the full weight of universal church law include the General Instruction of the Roman Missal, decrees (for instance, In Time of Covid-19 was issued in 2020 to guide Holy Week ritual adjustments around the world), and, to some extent, clarifying instructions put forth from the Holy See, like the two already mentioned.

Apostolic letters also have full weight, if a document says it does. Sometimes these documents are merely instructional, or bestowing an honor. Circular letters are outside the usual structure of the church, legislatively speaking, but are still common and often are used to explain norms and sometimes add context to the document's intent and purpose.

We should note, too, that many legislative documents, from the Vatican and elsewhere, often have an introductory *praetonda,* which is more theological and contextual, before the actual legislative (practical) portion of the writings.

While other various documents on liturgy can come from the Vatican from time to time, these are the most frequent and impactful on our worship.

About Music

Foundational Love: "How Firm a Foundation" (FOUNDATION) is in several hymnals, as is "Love Divine, All Loves Excelling" (various tunes); either may be a good fit in your circumstance this weekend.

SPIRITUALITY

GOSPEL ACCLAMATION
John 13:34

R⁊. Alleluia, alleluia.
I gave you a new commandment, says the Lord:
love one another as I have loved you.
R⁊. Alleluia, alleluia.

Gospel Luke 6:27-38; L81C

Jesus said to his disciples:
"To you who hear I say,
  love your enemies, do
    good to those who
      hate you,
  bless those who curse
    you, pray for those
    who mistreat you.
To the person who strikes
    you on one cheek,
  offer the other one as
    well,
  and from the person who
    takes your cloak,
  do not withhold even
    your tunic.
Give to everyone who asks
    of you,
  and from the one who
    takes what is yours
    do not demand it
      back.
Do to others as you would have them do
    to you.
For if you love those who love you,
  what credit is that to you?
Even sinners love those who love them.
And if you do good to those who do
    good to you,
  what credit is that to you?
Even sinners do the same.
If you lend money to those from whom
    you expect repayment,
  what credit is that to you?
Even sinners lend to sinners,
  and get back the same amount.

Continued in Appendix A, p. 271.

Reflecting on the Gospel

Shortly after the 1989 murder in San Salvador of six Jesuits and their house-keeper and her daughter, the theologian Jon Sobrino, SJ, spoke in London about the tragedy. As a member of the same community, he would also have been killed except for the fact that he was lecturing elsewhere on that tragic day. During his talk, he described his experience at a celebration of All Saints' Day in a Salvadoran refuge. Around the altar were cards with the names of deceased family members and friends of those in the refuge. Since they were not allowed to go to the cemetery to put flowers on the graves, they had painted flowers around the names. One card with no flowers read: "Our dead enemies." At the conclusion of the Eucharist, an old man explained to Jon: "As we are Christians, you know, we believe that our enemies should be on the altar, too. They are our brothers, in spite of the fact that they kill and murder us."

To love our enemies is surely hard, unreasonable, yet it is also the most radical obedience that Jesus asks of his disciples as he continues his Sermon on the Plain. To love our enemies who victimize us makes us no longer victims; we become free people whose behavior is determined by no one else—except the Christ of whom we are disciples.

In *Man's Search for Meaning,* Viktor Frankl, the Austrian Jewish psychiatrist imprisoned in the Nazi death camps, wrote about "the last of human freedoms," the ability "to choose one's attitude to a given set of circumstances." It was this ultimate freedom that had helped him and others to survive even the most inhuman of situations. To love and not hate, to bless and not curse, to be generous and not demanding, to be compassionate and not self-centered—the choice is always there. For Christians, the strength to make such a choice depends on neither psychiatric theory nor theology (although both can support it); it is as simple and demanding as the words of the old Salvadoran refugee: "As we are Christians . . ."

This is the good news that, paradoxically, seems such "bad news." "Bad" because it goes against our spontaneous inclination to give as good as we get from those who are our enemies, and we all have them! It is good news "to you who hear," because it is the word of Jesus. It is not hypothetical morality, but realistic Christian challenge to people who know what it is like to be slapped down, psychologically if not physically, whose generosity can be abused, and who find it difficult to extend love beyond friends, admirers, or benefactors.

The only motivation for this love is our kinship with God as daughters and sons, kinship with a God who is compassionate. *Mercy* is a most privileged gospel word. In Jesus's mother tongue it derives from the word for "womb." It is like the womb-love that a mother has for her child, fiercely protective and lavishly loving. That Jesus chooses in today's gospel to describe his Father's love as this mother-love—"Be merciful, just as your Father is merciful"—is not only a startling reinterpretation of what the "Fatherhood" of God means, but also a challenge to what it means to be a daughter or son of such a Father. The responsorial Psalm 103 calls us to remember the mercy and love of God who forgives and removes our sins. Our gratitude to God for this should urge us to try to be worthy sons and daughters of God, likewise compassionate and forgiving of others.

Focusing the Gospel

Key words and phrases: "Stop judging and you will not be judged. Stop condemning and you will not be condemned. Forgive and you will be forgiven."

To the point: This week's gospel is a part of the centerpiece of Jesus's ministry. For the entire history of the Hebrew people, there has been an understanding of retribution. If someone fails the community, he or she is punished. The laws laid out in Leviticus govern everyday life, because these laws have kept the people of Israel intact, despite all odds. Here, Jesus presents a new law that is in radical opposition to what the Hebrew people expect from the Lord who chose them. In Matthew's gospel, Jesus tells his disciples that he has "come not to abolish but to fulfill" the law (5:17). Here, in Luke's gospel, is where that happens.

It's not only radical for Jesus's time. This week it is worth the time to read the gospel a few times over, maybe even out loud. This is God's word. This is what Jesus is telling you to do. There's no asterisk or extra context. This is it. Love your enemies. Pray for those who mistreat you. Lend expecting nothing back. Stop judging. Stop condemning. Forgive. That's it. That's the point. That's how we get to heaven.

Connecting the Gospel

to the second reading: It is fitting that in this week with the gospel calling us to radical, unending love there is also a letter from Paul reminding the Corinthians of the divinity of Jesus as the New Adam, the one who restores us to our pre-Fall state. If the gospel is meant to make us uncomfortable and challenge our inherently sinful nature, the second reading reminds us that it is because of Adam that we have this nature, and a tendency to hate our enemies. We need Jesus not only because his words are our spiritual nourishment, but because through his death he undoes original sin and gives us the opportunity to be participants in the kingdom of heaven.

to experience: Paul tells us, "Just as we have borne the image of the earthly one, we shall also bear the image of the heavenly one." We are called to "bear the image" of Christ in our words and deeds. This is intimidating, but it isn't impossible, or else we wouldn't be asked to do it. Go back to the gospel and find the line that bothers you the most. Maybe it's something you're not great at doing every day, like being good to the people who aren't kind to you. Maybe you have a tendency to judge those you interact with a lot. Pick the line that speaks to you, in your current situation, and sit with it for a while.

Connecting the Responsorial Psalm

to the readings: This week's psalm centers us back in the love and acceptance of the Lord. If the gospel is our marching orders, full of (really hard) tasks, the psalm is our comfort, reminding us that "[m]erciful and gracious is the Lord, / slow to anger and abounding in kindness." This is the kind of person the gospel is calling us to be: kind and merciful.

to psalmist preparation: This psalm contains one of the thesis statements of all of salvation history, and you have the privilege of sharing it with your congregation. "The Lord is kind and merciful." How free would we feel if we were able to accept this, to truly believe it? How much easier would it be to love our enemies if we ourselves knew we are loved, no matter what?

PROMPTS FOR FAITH-SHARING

Who are your enemies? How do you love them?

Have you had a friend or family member skip out on repaying you for something? Did you forgive that person? Do you hold a grudge?

In what area of life do you find it the hardest not to judge people? Religious? Political? Academic?

Jesus is the New Adam, and through our baptism, we are wiped clean of original sin. Does this feel intimidating or empowering?

Model Penitential Act

Presider: In today's gospel, Jesus gives us an overview of the Christian moral life. For the times we have done wrong and for the times we have failed to do good, we ask for God's pardon, healing, and peace . . . *[pause]*

    Lord Jesus, you open the doors of new life: Lord, have mercy.

    Christ Jesus, you are the hope for which we long: Christ, have mercy.

    Lord Jesus, you call us to be merciful, just as the Father is merciful: Lord, have mercy.

Homily Points

• Most people don't like being told what to do, especially when that means being told not to do a certain something. Fortunately for us the Christian way of life is not about what we cannot do, as Jesus makes abundantly clear in today's reading. Jesus does not say, "Don't take revenge on those who hurt you," but instead says, "[L]ove your enemies, do good to those who hate you." Jesus does not say, "Do not hold back in what you give." Rather, Jesus says, "Give to everyone who asks of you, and from the one who takes what is yours do not demand it back."

• Moral theologians speak of two types of happiness: morality of happiness and morality of obligation. As Christians, we act because we find true happiness in living as God calls us to live. We find joy in following Jesus's command to love our enemies and do good to those who hate us because we know that is how we grow in relationship with God and others. The Christian life is not about following a strict set of rules because we have to. The Christian life is about making choices because they bring us joy and ultimate fulfillment.

• Fortunately for us, we have a model for this way of living. Jesus simply says, "Be merciful, just as your Father is merciful." We learn how to live and love by following the example of the God who loves us beyond our wildest imagination. We find support and hope in the example of Jesus who literally embodied the words he preached, so much so that he was killed. Christian love is *agapic*, a love that is self-giving and "others-centered." The way of God is giving ourselves for others. May we have the courage to live this reality.

Model Universal Prayer (Prayer of the Faithful)

Presider: Trusting in the incredible mercy of a God who loves us, we raise our prayers and petitions to the one who hears our every need.

Response: Lord, hear our prayer.

That the church may always embody the mercy of God . . .

That local and world leaders may make decisions based on the good of others rather than self-interest . . . .

That all who are hurting in body, mind, or spirit may know the compassion of God . . .

That those gathered here may challenge the systems of injustice that pervade our communities and world . . .

Presider: Loving God, you are the example of perfect love and mercy. As we work to become more like you, may we live and act in your image so that we can continue to make your kingdom present in the world. We ask this through Christ our Lord. **Amen.**

COLLECT

Let us pray.

Pause for silent prayer

Grant, we pray, almighty God,
that, always pondering spiritual things,
we may carry out in both word and deed
that which is pleasing to you.
Through our Lord Jesus Christ, your Son,
who lives and reigns with you in the unity
    of the Holy Spirit,
God, for ever and ever. **Amen.**

FIRST READING

1 Sam 26:2, 7-9, 12-13, 22-23

In those days, Saul went down to the
    desert of Ziph
    with three thousand picked men of Israel,
    to search for David in the desert of Ziph.
So David and Abishai went among Saul's
    soldiers by night
    and found Saul lying asleep within the
    barricade,
    with his spear thrust into the ground at
    his head
    and Abner and his men sleeping around
    him.

Abishai whispered to David:
    "God has delivered your enemy into
    your grasp this day.
Let me nail him to the ground with one
    thrust of the spear;
    I will not need a second thrust!"
But David said to Abishai, "Do not harm
    him,
    for who can lay hands on the LORD's
    anointed and remain unpunished?"
So David took the spear and the water jug
    from their place at Saul's head,
    and they got away without anyone's
    seeing or knowing or awakening.
All remained asleep,
    because the LORD had put them into a
    deep slumber.

Going across to an opposite slope,
    David stood on a remote hilltop
    at a great distance from Abner, son of
    Ner, and the troops.
He said: "Here is the king's spear.
Let an attendant come over to get it.
The LORD will reward each man for his
    justice and faithfulness.
Today, though the LORD delivered you into
    my grasp,
    I would not harm the LORD's anointed."

RESPONSORIAL PSALM

Ps 103:1-2, 3-4, 8, 10, 12-13

R̸. (8a) The Lord is kind and merciful.

Bless the LORD, O my soul;
  and all my being, bless his holy name.
Bless the LORD, O my soul,
  and forget not all his benefits.

R̸. The Lord is kind and merciful.

He pardons all your iniquities,
  heals all your ills.
He redeems your life from destruction,
  crowns you with kindness and
    compassion.

R̸. The Lord is kind and merciful.

Merciful and gracious is the LORD,
  slow to anger and abounding in
    kindness.
Not according to our sins does he deal
  with us,
  nor does he requite us according to our
    crimes.

R̸. The Lord is kind and merciful.

As far as the east is from the west,
  so far has he put our transgressions
    from us.
As a father has compassion on his
  children,
  so the LORD has compassion on those
    who fear him.

R̸. The Lord is kind and merciful.

SECOND READING

1 Cor 15:45-49

Brothers and sisters:
It is written, *The first man, Adam, became
  a living being,*
  the last Adam a life-giving spirit.
But the spiritual was not first;
  rather the natural and then the spiritual.
The first man was from the earth, earthly;
  the second man, from heaven.
As was the earthly one, so also are the
  earthly,
  and as is the heavenly one, so also are
    the heavenly.
Just as we have borne the image of the
  earthly one,
  we shall also bear the image of the
    heavenly one.

About Liturgy

Both Justice and Mercy: The Scripture today dwells quite heavily on mercy, which in this instance might be described as the act of being generous with someone beyond what they might have merited. The gospel presents example after example of how the Lord is merciful with each of us, and calls us to love in the same way.

Yet we know our God is one of justice as well. Where justice exists without mercy, a legalistic culture can emerge; where mercy exists without justice, we chance losing pursuit of equity and fairness. Said another way, by St. Thomas Aquinas, "Mercy without justice is the mother of dissolution; justice without mercy is cruelty."

In some ways, we who pursue liturgical ministries can get lost in a sea of rubrics and laws that can turn our liturgies, if we are not careful and aware, into cold, legalistic performances that lack the warmth and radiance of God's merciful love, shared with us and which we are called to share with each other, both inside the church and outside. Perhaps this is one reason Divine Mercy Sunday was added to the church calendar in recent times, to remind us of this.

Further, Pope Francis, quoting Aquinas, has recently reminded us that mercy is not something altogether different from justice, but rather is the fullness of justice, united in God's sacrificial love which we, too, are daily called to imitate.

There are circumstances where some have strayed perhaps too far from the liturgical rubrics, perhaps in the name of merciful love, and may need to remind themselves that even in liturgy justice and mercy must coexist; they temper one another and reveal a fuller sign of holiness and indeed a fuller sign of our God. What are the liturgical practices where you are that may be in need of a second look this weekend?

About Liturgical Documents

Liturgical Documents from the USCCB and Dioceses: The bishop is the chief liturgist in his diocese and can, within the context of universal law, make liturgical decisions for the whole of that territory. Sometimes bishops work in concert, such that a whole state or region shares similar practices—we saw that frequently during the liturgical adjustments made during the COVID-19 crisis. Similarly, priests have the same function in terms of liturgical decisions in their parishes.

The USCCB occasionally provides liturgical guidance, frequently without the weight of liturgical law but drawing on such sources, to offer what might be called "best practices" or at least suggestions on how to implement a vision of worship across the entire country. These are often not written by the bishops themselves, but by wise and experienced experts in the field, after which the bishops discuss, amend, and ultimately approve the guidance for dissemination.

One such significant document is celebrating its fifteenth anniversary this year, *Sing to the Lord*, which put forth the USCCB's vision for music at worship. Over the coming weeks, we will remind ourselves here what it called for, evaluate the reception of it, and examine where more work needs to be done.

About Music

Singing of God's Mercy: "There's a Wideness in God's Mercy" is found in several hymnals; Ed Bolduc has a recent contemporary arrangement (WLP/GIA) with some bright energy and an added refrain. "Amazing Grace" is another well-known option; it, too, has been rearranged and given a refrain; in this case Chris Tomlin added words that are relevant today: "And like a flood, his mercy reigns." This arrangement can be found in Worship Now (WN) and other contemporary resources.

FEBRUARY 20, 2022

SEVENTH SUNDAY IN ORDINARY TIME

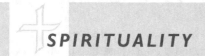

SPIRITUALITY

GOSPEL ACCLAMATION
Phil 2:15d, 16a

R⍀. Alleluia, alleluia.
Shine like lights in the world
as you hold on to the word of life.
R⍀. Alleluia, alleluia.

Gospel

Luke 6:39-45; L84C

Jesus told his disciples a parable,
  "Can a blind person guide a blind
    person?
Will not both fall into a pit?
No disciple is superior to the teacher;
  but when fully trained,
    every disciple will be like his teacher.
Why do you notice the splinter in your
    brother's eye,
  but do not perceive the wooden beam
    in your own?
How can you say to your brother,
  'Brother, let me remove that splinter
    in your eye,'
  when you do not even notice the
    wooden beam in your own eye?
You hypocrite! Remove the wooden
    beam from your eye first;
  then you will see clearly
    to remove the splinter in your broth-
      er's eye.

"A good tree does not bear rotten fruit,
  nor does a rotten tree bear good
    fruit.
For every tree is known by its own
    fruit.
For people do not pick figs from
    thornbushes,
  nor do they gather grapes from
    brambles.
A good person out of the store of good-
    ness in his heart produces good,
  but an evil person out of a store of
    evil produces evil;
  for from the fullness of the heart the
    mouth speaks."

Reflecting on the Gospel

"Look, I just want to say this for your own good. . . ." Do these or similar words press the "BEWARE" button for us? The answer probably depends on those speaking and the tone in which they speak. If we recognize the speakers as people of good heart and great integrity, we will be willing to listen to constructive criticism; if we sense destructive superiority and self-righteousness in their words, we do not want them as our teachers. What Jesus teaches, he

lives, and in today's continuation of the Sermon on the Plain he is the wisdom teacher who voices his expectation of this same integrity in his disciples. If we are blind to our own shortcomings, yet judgmental about those of our sisters and brothers, we have no right to guide them with our advice; we will only succeed in dragging them down into the metaphorical "ditch" rather than helping them out of their difficulties. The church, the community of disciples, can contain such blind guides and ditches, as both Luke and we ourselves know.

The good teacher, the wise parent, often makes a point by exaggeration, as does Jesus in some of his parables, including the mini-parables in this reading. To have a wooden beam in our own eye does not make us a very efficient splinter-remover for someone else's eye. Smug superiority distorts our vision of ourselves and our neighbor. Some of us would have no trouble winning a black belt for innuendo and faint praise, so quick are we on the offensive against others, and even faster on the defensive about ourselves.

Using the familiar biblical image of a tree whose quality is judged by the good or bad fruit it produces, Jesus teaches his listeners that the quality of people is judged by their actions. There is more involved here than "spiritual eye surgery" to get rid of the judgmental log that blinds us. It is a matter of the biblical heart, that deepest personal reality, the storehouse of our dreams and desires. Good will be drawn from the good-hearted person, evil from the heart that is morally diseased. One of the surest indicators of good or bad people is their words: words that are honest and match their deeds, as did Jesus's words, or words that are a sadly hypocritical script for playacting.

The mass media and politicians are a source of many words in contemporary society. The "doublespeak" we get so much of is dishonest and dangerous. We need the wisdom and discernment of which Jesus speaks. Recent history offers many examples of "doublespeak" that may be so familiar to our ears that our hearts no longer have a Christian reaction. "The final solution" meant the genocide of six million Jews; "collateral damage" in war means the killing of innocent civilians; a prison's "management unit" is a solitary confinement block. We need to take the pulse of our newspapers, TV, and governments to make a Christian diagnosis of such language and its reporters.

We can use our words to praise and give thanks to God for his love as we do in the responsorial Psalm 92. Worshipping in the house of the Lord and planted in God's fidelity, the faithful are like a fertile palm, or as enduring in their love of God as a great Lebanon cedar. Designated as a "Sabbath song," this psalm is an appropriate response for us as we gather as a Sunday community of faith and worship in God's house and as a temple of living stones.

Focusing the Gospel

Key words and phrases: "A good person out of the store of goodness in his heart produces good, but an evil person out of a store of evil produces evil; for from the fullness of the heart the mouth speaks."

To the point: The only thing you have to give is what you already have. This week's gospel has a lot of great one-liners, but if we take each on its own terms, there's a larger picture here that shows us we can't focus on others before we focus on bringing the best out of ourselves. You can't guide a blind person until you, yourself, can see. You can't point out someone else's faults until you have identified your own shortcomings. And you can't give people the good fruit of your own labor if you haven't made any good fruit. Last week's gospel was about how we treat others, and this week is about how we treat ourselves. In these words, Jesus is inviting us to be honest and assess ourselves with a critical eye.

Connecting the Gospel

to the first reading: The first reading from Sirach, a Wisdom book, emphasizes this gospel message of self-awareness. "So too does one's speech disclose the bent of one's mind." When we are tested, the decisions we make are a reflection of what's going on in our hearts and minds.

to experience: It's easy to become overwhelmed by the poetic presentation used in much of Scripture. We're reading words that have been handed down over centuries and translated into English from Hebrew and Greek. When you read the sentence "As the test of what the potter molds is in the furnace, so in tribulation is the test of the just," it looks overwhelming. This isn't usual word order for English. Instead of rushing through it, take it a phrase at a time. The tribulation of good people is like a potter putting a clay mold into a furnace. Will it stay together, or will it crack under the pressure? Reading Scripture is not easy, and the Old Testament is frequently intimidating. This text has already gone through one translation before coming to you. You are always invited to move words around in your personal prayer, relishing what moves your heart.

Connecting the Responsorial Psalm

to the readings: We all want to bear good fruit! After reflecting on this week's readings, which are focused on our own actions, this psalm is time for us to reflect on the goodness of the Lord. We are reminded why we're trying so hard to bear good fruit in our own lives.

to psalmist preparation: This week's readings are centered by the psalm. The words you proclaim are the basis for the self-reflection that the gospel invites us to take on. Why are we working so hard to take the wooden beam out of our own eyes? Because it is good to give thanks to the Lord, our rock, in whom there is no wrong.

PROMPTS FOR FAITH-SHARING

What do you think is your biggest spiritual shortcoming? What is an area where you feel you succeed?

If your words produced fruit as you spoke, what kind of fruit do you think would tumble out? Would the fruit be ripe? Would it be satisfying, or shriveled?

How does it make you feel to know that death is swallowed up in victory? How do you view the loss of loved ones, and your own mortality, in light of this?

Are you preoccupied with the "splinter" in someone's eye these days? How can you turn that focus on yourself, someone you can actually change?

71

Model Penitential Act

Presider: In today's gospel Jesus reminds us that every tree is known by its own fruit. For the times we have not borne fruit, or borne fruit that is rotten, we ask God for pardon and peace . . . *[pause]*

Lord Jesus, you cultivate life and love: Lord, have mercy.
Christ Jesus, you show us by example how to grow in relationship: Christ, have mercy.
Lord Jesus, you destroy sin and death: Lord, have mercy.

Homily Points

• In *The Horse and His Boy* from the Chronicles of Narnia series, C. S. Lewis writes, "If you do one good deed your reward usually is to be set to do another and harder and better one." As Christians, we live lives rooted in more than words. Christ shows us by example that discipleship is a way of life that involves not only thinking and speaking but also acting.

• The first reading from the book of Sirach tells us that a person is known by their words and actions: "The fruit of a tree shows the care it has had; so too does one's speech disclose the bent of one's mind." Likewise, Jesus proclaims in the gospel: "[E]very tree is known by its own fruit." The agrarian metaphors here help us understand exactly what Jesus says, so that there might be little confusion. The ways we grow, what nurtures and nourishes us, directly affect how we live. Our words and actions reveal what is on our hearts, for "[a] good person out of the store of goodness in his heart produces good, but an evil person out of a store of evil produces evil." If our hearts are not in relationship with Christ, it will be revealed through our actions.

• With Ash Wednesday only a few days away, how will you make time to prioritize your relationship with Christ? Jesus's words today offer one possibility: "Remove the wooden beam from your eye first; then you will see clearly to remove the splinter in your brother's eye." In what ways do we need to grow in our relationship with God and others so that we may remove the beams from our eyes? While we are certainly a relational community and we care for each other, we must first recognize our own shortcomings before being critical of others.

Model Universal Prayer (Prayer of the Faithful)

Presider: Knowing our call to bear fruit both as individuals and as a community, we bring our prayers and petitions to the one who loves us.

Response: Lord, hear our prayer.

That the church may always bear fruit that benefits others, rather than the fruit of selfish interests . . .

That community and world leaders might prioritize care for our common home . . .

That all who are questioning their faith may find comfort throughout the process . . .

That the actions of our community may always reflect our belief in the risen Christ . . .

Presider: Loving God, everything you give us is a gift. Help us to not only recognize these gifts but to cultivate them through lives of service for others. We ask this through Christ our Lord. **Amen.**

COLLECT

Let us pray.

Pause for silent prayer

Grant us, O Lord, we pray,
that the course of our world
may be directed by your peaceful rule
and that your Church may rejoice,
untroubled in her devotion.
Through our Lord Jesus Christ, your Son,
who lives and reigns with you in the unity
of the Holy Spirit,
God, for ever and ever. **Amen.**

FIRST READING
Sir 27:4-7

When a sieve is shaken, the husks appear;
so do one's faults when one speaks.
As the test of what the potter molds is in
the furnace,
so in tribulation is the test of the just.
The fruit of a tree shows the care it has
had;
so too does one's speech disclose the
bent of one's mind.
Praise no one before he speaks,
for it is then that people are tested.

RESPONSORIAL PSALM
Ps 92:2-3, 13-14, 15-16

℟. (cf. 2a) Lord, it is good to give thanks
    to you.

It is good to give thanks to the LORD,
    to sing praise to your name, Most High,
to proclaim your kindness at dawn
    and your faithfulness throughout the
      night.

℟. Lord, it is good to give thanks to you.

The just one shall flourish like the palm
    tree,
    like a cedar of Lebanon shall he grow.
They that are planted in the house of the
    LORD
    shall flourish in the courts of our God.

℟. Lord, it is good to give thanks to you.

They shall bear fruit even in old age;
    vigorous and sturdy shall they be,
declaring how just is the LORD,
    my rock, in whom there is no wrong.

℟. Lord, it is good to give thanks to you.

SECOND READING
1 Cor 15:54-58

Brothers and sisters:
When this which is corruptible clothes
    itself with incorruptibility
    and this which is mortal clothes itself
      with immortality,
    then the word that is written shall come
      about:
Death is swallowed up in victory.
    Where, O death, is your victory?
    Where, O death, is your sting?
The sting of death is sin,
    and the power of sin is the law.
But thanks be to God who gives us the
    victory
    through our Lord Jesus Christ.

Therefore, my beloved brothers and
    sisters,
    be firm, steadfast, always fully devoted
      to the work of the Lord,
    knowing that in the Lord your labor is
      not in vain.

CATECHESIS

About Liturgy

Asking the Right Questions: A wise person once told me, "If you ask the wrong question, you get the wrong answer." Here's an example: Suppose you walk down to the river one day, only to see a baby floating down the stream in a basket. You can just barely reach out to snag the basket and save the child, when you see another basket heading your way from upstream. You quickly find a place to set the first baby down safely and race back to save the next—and when you do, you see another. Followed by another. And another. You look around for help, but you find yourself all alone.

As you frantically work to save all the children in the river, you think to yourself, "Surely there's got to be someone around to help me! There must be a better way to save all these babies!" These aren't bad questions, but the pressing nature of the situation prevents you from asking an even more important question: "How are all these babies ending up in the river in the first place?"

This brief fable usually points to the difference between acts of mercy and acts of justice: acts of mercy put bandages on wounds; acts of justice strive to prevent wounds in the first place. Jesus frequently gives, through parables, some instructions on living a Christian life, as in this weekend's gospel. His teachings are prompted by questions he asks of his disciples, rhetorically: "Can a blind person guide a blind person? Will not both fall into a pit?" (Luke 6:39).

We should take care that those we ask to direct or lead liturgies, or even some smaller component of them, have proper training and experience to accomplish these tasks. Several ministerial organizations, like the National Association of Pastoral Musicians (NPM) and the National Federation on Catholic Youth Ministry (NFCYM), offer occasional workshops, seminars, or online learning opportunities. Your local diocesan office of worship may also offer opportunities or be able to point you in the right direction as well. Without formation we are asking those who help shape our worship to do so while "blind" so to speak, which can lead to poor results, even when such a leader has good instincts.

We should be reminded, by Jesus's queries, to consider how we evaluate liturgies and our liturgical practices, by ensuring we ask the right questions, in very specific and critical and helpful ways. Often, questions like "What did everyone think of Christmas this year?" will only lead to generic and uncritical responses: "It was fine," and the like. Instead, questions might be constructed to elicit both some thought and longer, more concrete answers: "Did our music this year reflect well the changing demographics of the parish?" or "Did our hospitality ministry serve in such a way that an infrequent visitor might wish to return to us someday soon?" In turn, digging into such questions and their answers can yield quite actionable statements that can bring our liturgical ministries to new and impactful heights.

About Music

"Burying the Alleluia": Some parishes have a practice, this last Sunday before Lent begins, of including many "Alleluias" during the music at liturgy, as it will be several weeks before that acclamation of praise will be sung again. Consider the *Psallite* refrain "Let all the Earth Sing Out Your Praises" (Liturgical Press) for a jaunty and syncopated tune of joy and jubilation.

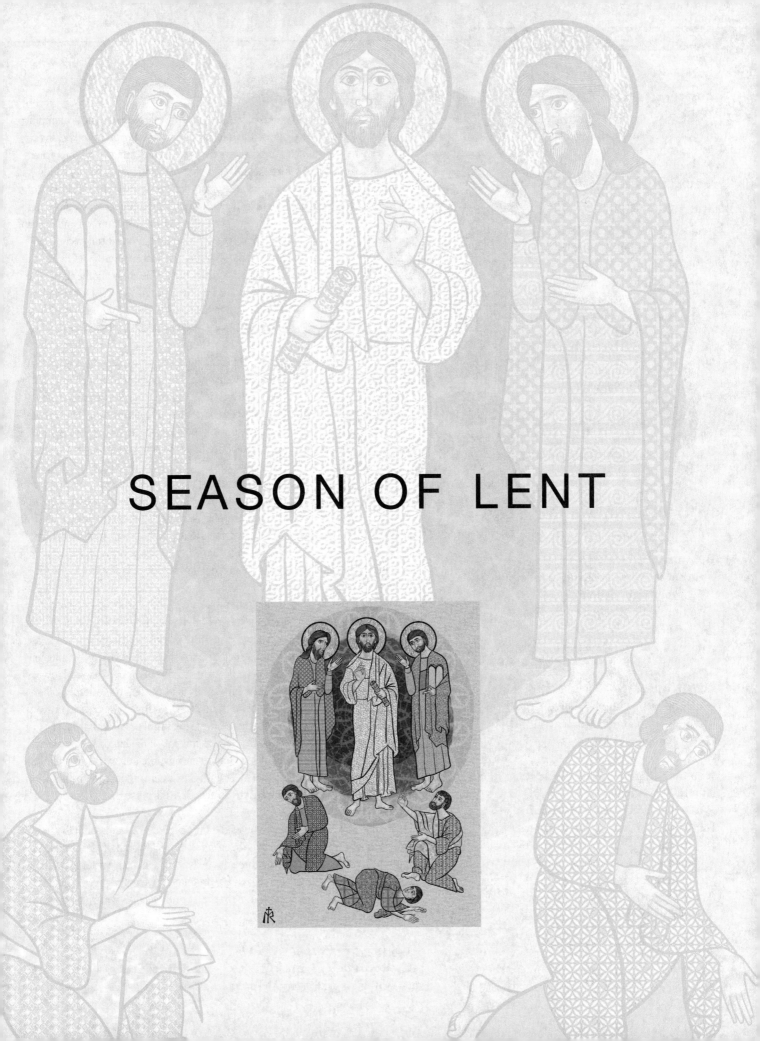

SEASON OF LENT

GOSPEL ACCLAMATION
See Ps 95:8

If today you hear his voice,
harden not your hearts.

Gospel

Matt 6:1-6, 16-18; L219

Jesus said to his disciples:
   **"Take care not to perform
      righteous deeds
   in order that people may
      see them;
   otherwise, you will have
      no recompense from
      your heavenly Father.**
**When you give alms,
   do not blow a trumpet be-
      fore you,
   as the hypocrites do in the
      synagogues and in the
      streets
   to win the praise of
      others.
Amen, I say to you,
   they have received their
      reward.
But when you give alms,
   do not let your left hand know what
      your right is doing,
   so that your almsgiving may be
      secret.
And your Father who sees in secret
   will repay you.**

**"When you pray,
   do not be like the hypocrites,
   who love to stand and pray in the
      synagogues and on street
      corners
   so that others may see them.
Amen, I say to you,
   they have received their reward.
But when you pray, go to your inner
      room,
   close the door, and pray to your
      Father in secret.
And your Father who sees in secret
   will repay you.**

Continued in Appendix A, p. 272.

See Appendix A, p. 272, for the other readings.

Reflecting on the Gospel

We are fond of logos. Schools, businesses, sporting clubs and teams, community groups, travel agencies—all use them to say, often superficially: "You belong to us, and we belong to each other." As we prepare to enter into the season of Lent, the church presents us with a "logo." Not a very elegantly designed logo, this cruciform smudge of ash on our foreheads, but then neither was the crucifixion of Jesus elegant. Nor is the cross of ash gentle and fragrant like the first cross that was traced on us with the oils of catechumens and chrism at baptism. Our first liturgical fingerprinting recorded our identity as "Christian," as one committed to living and dying and rising with Christ. The cross another brother or sister fingers on us today is rougher, grittier, dirtier than the cross of baptismal oils—because that it how our lives have become. As we receive the ashes, the words of both options are stark and urgent: "Repent, and believe in the Gospel" or "Remember that you are dust, and to dust you shall return." Remember what Lent is all about.

The ritual of Ash Wednesday speaks of realities that our glossy personal and social masks usually try to hide, and perhaps so many people come to receive the ashes because it is a relief to admit in ritual what we find so difficult to put into words—that there are the "tears of things" within and around us: the grief and tragedy, the despair and deaths that are part of the dust and ashes of human life. In many parishes, today's ashes are made of the burnt palms from last year. Here are the palms that we held in our hands a year ago when, on Palm Sunday, we sang our "Hosannas." And yet we know that so often we have been unfaithful to the king we hailed. Many times our commitment to Christ has become as insubstantial as ash. But as those who live in bushfire-prone areas know, ash is also the regenerating remnant of what was once alive and can again bring forth prolific new life.

Many things that were once alive in us have probably died and turned to ash: loved ones have died, illness has struck, friendships have been broken, illusions about ourselves or others have been destroyed. It is out of such ashes that we hope Christ will raise us up to new life with him at Easter. In the season of Lent, therefore, the church calls us to traditional Christian practices: to prayer, fasting, and almsgiving. The Japanese have a beautiful proverb that says: "Something of the fragrance of the flowers lingers on the hands of the giver." Whatever we do in Lent should seep unobtrusively into our world and relationships, and yet it will also transform us with the lingering "odor of the knowledge of him" (2 Cor 2:14) and our attempts to live his mystery more deeply during this season.

Just as every human birth involves the breaking of the waters and the flowing of blood, so it is when we have been carried in the womb of the church through the days of Lent to the three-day feast of the Easter Triduum. In those days, for which all the Lenten days are a pregnancy, we will again participate in the mystery of our passage through the water and blood as we are reborn in the spirit of the risen Christ.

Focusing the Gospel

Key words and phrases: "[D]o not be like the hypocrites, who love to stand and pray in the synagogues and on street corners so that others may see them."

To the point: Our world is filled with spiritual "posturing." Even in the midst of the pursuit of heaven, humans tend to judge one another and create an arbitrary hierarchy of spiritual "success." That may be an interesting game, but it has nothing to do with our salvation and may even jeopardize it. Our relationship with God and the Eucharist is one of the most tender and personal we can have. As with a romantic relationship, showing it off to others for their affirmation of its existence isn't how it is nurtured. We can't expect a relationship to grow if we're measuring its validity by how it is viewed by others.

Model Penitential Act

Presider: As we begin this holy season of Lent, a time of prayer, fasting, and almsgiving, we take a moment to recall our sins and ask for God's forgiveness . . . *[pause]*

Lord Jesus, you have the words of spirit and life: Lord, have mercy.
Christ Jesus, you call sinners back to you: Christ, have mercy.
Lord Jesus, you intercede for us at the right hand of the Father:
    Lord, have mercy.

Model Universal Prayer (Prayer of the Faithful)

Presider: As we begin the season of Lent, we raise our prayers and petitions to the God who loves us and invites us into relationship.

Response: Lord, hear our prayer.

That the church may recommit itself to upholding the baptismal vocation of every person . . .

That all leaders may govern with humility and kindness . . .

That all who go without food, water, clothing, and shelter may find refuge in communities that support the vulnerable and protect life . . .

That our local community may enter this season of Lent with an openness to God's call in our lives . . .

Presider: Loving God, you yourself are mercy and compassion. Hear these prayers we bring before you, as well as the ones we hold in the silence of our hearts, so that our prayer, fasting, and abstinence may be pleasing to you. We ask this through Christ our Lord. **Amen.**

About Liturgy

Lent Can Be Habit-Forming: Ash Wednesday is one of those days that brings large numbers of people to church, including many who don't go to church very regularly. Care should be taken to prepare a schedule of Masses (and other services that include imposition of ashes) to allow as many people as possible to gather together on this annual journey of repentance and conversion.

Further, attention should be given in a more focused way to ministries of hospitality, preaching, ritual, and music. The first step in forming habits—for instance, regular worship attendance—is creating a worship experience that people will want to return to. Lent is a perfect time to help those potential habits flourish, as people often commit to a more conscious and active faith life during these weeks. We would do well to support those goals and to welcome all into our spiritual homes with warmth and sincerity.

COLLECT
Let us pray.

Pause for silent prayer

Grant, O Lord, that we may begin with holy fasting
this campaign of Christian service,
so that, as we take up battle against spiritual evils,
we may be armed with weapons of self-restraint.
Through our Lord Jesus Christ, your Son,
who lives and reigns with you in the unity of the Holy Spirit,
God, for ever and ever. **Amen.**

FOR REFLECTION

• How do you hope to grow in your relationship with God and others throughout this season of Lent?

• What self-constructed ideologies or practices seem to separate you from God's infinite love, mercy, and forgiveness?

Homily Points

• There is a difference between secrecy and humility. Secrecy within the church has destroyed the lives of innocent people and protected unjust aggressors. There are certainly times where we must speak up and raise our voices. This is not what Jesus is talking about in today's gospel. Rather, when Jesus says, "[C]lose the door, and pray to your Father in secret," and "[D]o not let your left hand know what your right is doing, so that your almsgiving may be secret," he is telling his disciples to remember why they are doing what they are doing.

• When we pray, fast, and give alms, we do so because we are called to perform these acts to grow in relationship with God and others. It is not about accolade or self-promotion. Last Sunday's gospel about the splinter in the eye transitions perfectly to today's. This Lenten season is a great opportunity to live humbly and examine the motives behind our actions, especially our actions of piety.

✚ SPIRITUALITY

One does not live on bread alone,
but on every word that comes forth from the
   mouth of God.

Gospel   Luke 4:1-13; L24C

**Filled with the Holy Spirit, Jesus returned
      from the Jordan
   and was led by the Spirit into the desert
      for forty days,
   to be tempted by the devil.
He ate nothing during those days,
   and when they were over he was hungry.
The devil said to him,
   "If you are the Son of God,
   command this stone to become bread."
Jesus answered him,
   "It is written, *One does not live on bread
      alone."*
Then he took him up and showed him
   all the kingdoms of the world in a single
      instant.
The devil said to him,
   "I shall give to you all this power and glory;
   for it has been handed over to me,
   and I may give it to whomever I wish.
All this will be yours, if you worship me."
Jesus said to him in reply,
   "It is written:
   *You shall worship the Lord, your God,
      and him alone shall you serve."*
Then he led him to Jerusalem,
   made him stand on the parapet of the
      temple, and said to him,
   "If you are the Son of God,
   throw yourself down from here, for it is
      written:
   *He will command his angels concern-
      ing you, to guard you,*
   and:
   *With their hands they will support you,
      lest you dash your foot against a stone."*
Jesus said to him in reply,
   "It also says,
   *You shall not put the Lord, your God, to
      the test."*
When the devil had finished every
      temptation,
   he departed from him for a time.**

Reflecting on the Gospel

Jesus is alone, hungry, poised at the edge of decision making before his Father and his own truth. With perfect timing, the tempter arrives with three attractive propositions.

If Jesus would turn stones into bread, it would bring great personal and social advantages: neither he nor the poor of the land need be hungry anymore, the tempter implies. But Jesus answers that it is not bread alone, but the word of God that is life-giving food. People of every generation must transplant the wilderness tempta- tions into their own life and times, and the first contemporary temptation is to neglect the word of God and allow ourselves to be seduced by so many other words: texts, emails, mass media, the flood of digital in- formation, our often mindless and heartless inner and outer conversations. The word of God feeds our deepest hungers. Our obedi- ence to this Word is expressed in our atten- tive listening to its proclamation, especially in the Sunday liturgy, in our prayerful read- ing of Holy Scripture (*lectio divina*), and our efforts to make this Word "living and effec- tive" (Heb 4:12) from day to day.

The people of first-century Palestine who were living under the oppression of the Roman Empire were hoping for political redemption. If Jesus seizes power and glory, suggests the devil in his second temptation, what he could do for them! But Jesus knows what this would mean: power and authority handed to him by the tempter would also bring op- pression and violence (Luke 4:1-14). Jesus will go the longer, less immediate, and more sacrificial way of service to others rather than domination over them. He will wait to receive the kingdom from the hand of his Father rather than from the devil, the ruler of a "counter-kingdom." Jesus will establish a healing reign over sick bodies, tormented psyches, and a troubled cosmos. We are only too familiar with scenarios of unjust wars and political compromise that accompany the lust for power. We certainly need to take a stand against these, but perhaps we are less conscious of the compromises we make ourselves: that bargaining for a little more status and authority at the expense of others and the effect that this has on world history—whose time we share. We can often be tempted to serve personal success rather than fidelity to God, our own reputation rather than the needs of our brothers and sisters, political expediency rather than justice. *"God . . . alone shall you serve"* will involve Christians in the self-sacrificing obedience of Jesus.

The third temptation is for Jesus to launch his messianic career with a spec- tacular stunt—throwing himself from the high point of the Jerusalem temple. The tempter assures Jesus that, since he is a privileged Son, God will certainly deliver him from any human and airborne limitations by sending angels to catch him and carry him to safety. And what religious authority his survival would give him! But Jesus will be true to his sonship not by flamboyant acts but by suffering an impoverished death on a cross, a commonplace punishment for criminals. Only then will come Jesus's leap of faith, not from the temple pinnacle, but from the raised cross on Calvary; not into angels' hands but into the hands of his Father (Luke 23:46), who will lift him up in the resurrection. Often we would like God to treat us as "different," "special" people who deserve miraculous intervention and deliverance from the limitations of our humanity. This will be offered to us, but only in the same way it was offered to Jesus: through suffering, dying, and rising with him.

Focusing the Gospel

Key words and phrases: "When the devil had finished every temptation, he departed from him for a time."

To the point: In this gospel Jesus grapples with the most basic state of humanity: temptation. Jesus, being fully human, experiences temptation just like the rest of us. This scene is grand in scope, but it gets at the heart of Jesus's story. Do you want food? Do you want power? Do you want safety? Jesus is fasting, so he's already hungry. He's the single most powerful human to ever walk the earth, and yet his life is that of an ethnic minority in an occupied region. Even though Jesus is God, he's still bound by the political and social systems of his own time, even as he's working to upend them. So to be met with these temptations of physical satisfaction and immediate power isn't something we should dismiss lightly. Does Jesus send the devil away? Of course. But does the devil get the chance to make his case? Yes. It should hearten us to know that Jesus, like all of us, went through the whole experience of temptation.

Connecting the Gospel

to the second reading: Paul's letter to the Romans centers around words, mouths, and calling out. Paul tells us that if the Word is in our mouth, we should confess with our mouth, and if we call upon the Lord, we are saved. These aren't just actions of the mind and heart, but words said out loud to align oneself with the Lord. And it's not just for the Jews! Paul designates this recipe for holiness to everyone, because Christ makes "no distinction between Jew and Greek." This is an issue that causes the early church much frustration. For a people conditioned to understand their centrality in salvation history, the notion that Jesus has saved everyone, and not just the Hebrew people, is hard to accept.

to experience: In this week's gospel, Jesus directly interfaces with evil, experiences temptation, and responds to it. He is not "above" it. In the second reading, Paul invites all people to engage in their own salvation by using words and speaking aloud, as Jesus spoke aloud to dismiss the devil.

Connecting the Responsorial Psalm

to the readings: You will likely recognize the lyrics to Michael Joncas's "On Eagle's Wings" this week. Chances are your congregation will too. Whether or not you use that hymn in your own parish, it's comforting to recognize lines from Scripture in their original context.

This week's readings are all about temptation and actively choosing the Lord. The psalm gives us relevant, urgent words that can be used in many situations throughout our day that involve temptation. In the midst of the beautiful poetry of being saved and protected by God, we get the refrain, "Be with me, Lord, when I am in trouble."

to psalmist preparation: Can you think of a situation in your life when you were in trouble? Whether it was big, small, tragic, or inconsequential, how did you involve God in it? Did you pray, did you ask others to pray, or did you muscle through it and hope God was involved anyway? Draw upon your own experience using the words of this psalm today.

PROMPTS FOR FAITH-SHARING

What is your biggest everyday temptation? Why do you think this happens? How do you usually deal with it?

Imagine Jesus dealing with your most habitual temptation. How would he respond? How does imagining this make you feel? Is it intimidating or empowering?

Do you ever reject temptation verbally? For example, if you want chocolate, do you ever say, "No, I'm not going to eat that chocolate." Do you think verbalizing your rejection of temptation, as Paul calls us to do in cases big and small, may help?

Model Penitential Act

Presider: Today's gospel reminds us of the importance of prioritizing God in our lives, even over comfort and riches. For the times we have not made God a priority, we ask for forgiveness . . . *[pause]*

   Confiteor: I confess . . .

Homily Points

• Jesus's temptations in the gospel are quite extraordinary, which is exactly the point. Not many of us would necessarily be tempted by the ability to turn stones to bread or jump from high precipices. Sure, they might be fun tricks but those are not the types of temptation we encounter every day. They are not basic human temptations. Instead, these temptations were specific for the Son of God.

• Throughout Luke's gospel, the demons know who Jesus is and are quick to call him the Son of God. These temptations in the desert are especially significant because the devil knows and proclaims Jesus as the Son of God. At the beginning of his public ministry, Jesus makes it abundantly clear that he will not take the easy way out. Rather than succumbing to the temptations of comfort, convenience, and power, Jesus is already showing us that the path to life is through the cross. It is not an easy journey and there will be ample difficulties. Even so, Jesus chooses the way of suffering and ultimate death.

• Today's gospel ends on an interesting note. Luke writes, "When the devil had finished every temptation, he departed from him for a time." There will be more struggles and obstacles that Jesus must overcome on the way to resurrected glory. Like Jesus, we will encounter challenges. However, Jesus shows by example how to overcome them: staying close to the word of God. He quotes Scripture throughout today's gospel and throughout the rest of his life and ministry. May we follow Jesus's example and Paul's profession in today's letter to the Romans: "The word is near you, in your mouth and in your heart."

Model Universal Prayer (Prayer of the Faithful)

Presider: Just as Jesus entered the desert to fast and pray, on this first Sunday of Lent we bring our prayers to our loving God.

Response: Lord, hear our prayer.

That the church may be a beacon of hope as we begin this season of Lent . . .

That all local and national leaders resist the temptations of comfort, wealth, and power . . .

That all who struggle and live with addiction may know the presence of God and support of others . . .

That we might recommit ourselves to our baptismal call this Lenten season . . .

Presider: Loving God, you are true power and true glory. We bring our prayers to you today at the beginning of Lent. Walk with us during these forty days so that we may rejoice with you in the resurrection on Easter. We ask this through Christ our Lord. **Amen.**

Let us pray.

Pause for silent prayer

Grant, almighty God,
through the yearly observances of holy Lent,
that we may grow in understanding
of the riches hidden in Christ
and by worthy conduct pursue their effects.
Through our Lord Jesus Christ, your Son,
who lives and reigns with you in the unity of the Holy Spirit,
God, for ever and ever. **Amen.**

FIRST READING
Deut 26:4-10

Moses spoke to the people, saying:
   "The priest shall receive the basket from you
   and shall set it in front of the altar of the LORD, your God.
Then you shall declare before the LORD, your God,
   'My father was a wandering Aramean
   who went down to Egypt with a small household
   and lived there as an alien.
But there he became a nation
   great, strong, and numerous.
When the Egyptians maltreated and oppressed us,
   imposing hard labor upon us,
   we cried to the LORD, the God of our fathers,
   and he heard our cry
   and saw our affliction, our toil, and our oppression.
He brought us out of Egypt
   with his strong hand and outstretched arm,
   with terrifying power, with signs and wonders;
   and bringing us into this country,
   he gave us this land flowing with milk and honey.
Therefore, I have now brought you the firstfruits
   of the products of the soil
   which you, O LORD, have given me.'
And having set them before the LORD, your God,
   you shall bow down in his presence."

RESPONSORIAL PSALM
Ps 91:1-2, 10-11, 12-13, 14-15

R⁊. (cf. 15b) Be with me, Lord, when I am
    in trouble.

You who dwell in the shelter of the Most
    High,
    who abide in the shadow of the
        Almighty,
say to the LORD, "My refuge and fortress,
    my God in whom I trust."

R⁊. Be with me, Lord, when I am in trouble.

No evil shall befall you,
    nor shall affliction come near your tent,
for to his angels he has given command
        about you,
    that they guard you in all your ways.

R⁊. Be with me, Lord, when I am in trouble.

Upon their hands they shall bear you up,
    lest you dash your foot against a stone.
You shall tread upon the asp and the
        viper;
    you shall trample down the lion and the
        dragon.

R⁊. Be with me, Lord, when I am in trouble.

Because he clings to me, I will deliver him;
    I will set him on high because he
        acknowledges my name.
He shall call upon me, and I will answer
        him;
    I will be with him in distress;
I will deliver him and glorify him.

R⁊. Be with me, Lord, when I am in trouble.

SECOND READING
Rom 10:8-13

Brothers and sisters:
What does Scripture say?
    The word is near you,
        in your mouth and in your heart
    —that is, the word of faith that we
        preach—,
    for, if you confess with your mouth that
        Jesus is Lord
and believe in your heart that God
        raised him from the dead,
    you will be saved.
For one believes with the heart and so is
        justified,
    and one confesses with the mouth and
        so is saved.

Continued in Appendix A, p. 273.

About Liturgy

Liturgical Cognitive Dissonance: With apologies to Bob Hurd, a few years ago, I wrote these parody lyrics to his popular Lenten hymn text "Led by the Spirit," which in the original speaks of Jesus's forty days in the desert and temptation there. These parody lyrics . . . do not.

> Led by the Spirit of our God, / We go this day of days
> Down to the cafeteria / For long johns, maybe glazed,
> Or cake or fritters, sprinkles too—Have yours most any way!
> Rejoice my friends, as Lent begins: It is Donut Sunday!

Many parishes, like the one I serve at, have a regular "Donut Sunday" or some other form of fellowship and socializing following Sunday Masses. Ours is once a month, and I was struck by some cognitive dissonance a few years ago when Donut Sunday aligned with the First Sunday of Lent, at which we sang Bob Hurd's hymn at the end of Mass.

The gospel this first Sunday of Lent, in every cycle, relates Jesus's self-exile following his baptism, during which he fasts, prays, is tempted by Satan, rebukes him, and is ministered to by angels. This time in the desert, we all know, is one of the patterns of our approach to Lent each year, walking in spiritual solidarity with those preparing for the sacraments of initiation in a few weeks' time at the Easter Vigil.

Lent need not be a morose and depressed season; indeed, our liturgical prayers call it a joyful season. Yet there is at least potential for disconnect between our liturgical spirituality and singing, in Bob Hurd's words, "Led by the Spirit of our God / we go to fast and pray," if our first stop when the hymn concludes is Donut Sunday. Similarly, many parishes have fish fries or similar dinners during Lent, with copious amounts of seafood, pasta, and other savory non-meat dishes available for the whole family—but sometimes that feast is available on Good Friday too, which again points to a disconnect that does not help the faithful live what they pray or pray what they live.

To be clear, I'm not suggesting that parishes forsake fellowship, hospitality, or fundraising! I am suggesting a couple things: (1) that parishes take these activities on intentionally and with an awareness of the changing contexts in the liturgical year, and (2) perhaps those responsible for picking music for liturgy take note (as we did not, a few years ago) of the amusing dissonance that might arise should Donut Sunday align with the First Sunday of Lent!

About Music

Entering the Journey: In addition to "Led by the Spirit" (OCP) mentioned above, other pieces that can help frame the day and the Lenten journey include Alan Hommerding's well-crafted "From Ashes to the Living Font" (WLP/GIA), which helps keep before the assembly, and on their lips, the bookends of the season and the journey. For something more contemporary, "Desert Song" by Brooke Ligertwood (Hillsong United, found in WN) offers a more personal and intimate text of prayer and Lenten praise. *Psallite*'s "Lord, Cleanse My Heart" (Liturgical Press) is another appropriate choice.

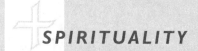

SPIRITUALITY

GOSPEL ACCLAMATION

cf. Matt 17:5

From the shining cloud the Father's voice is
  heard:
This is my beloved Son, hear him.

Gospel   Luke 9:28b-36; L27C

**Jesus took Peter, John, and James
  and went up the mountain to pray.
While he was praying his face changed
    in appearance
  and his clothing became dazzling
      white.
And behold, two men were conversing
    with him, Moses and Elijah,
  who appeared in glory and spoke of
      his exodus
  that he was going to accomplish in
      Jerusalem.
Peter and his companions had been
    overcome by sleep,
  but becoming fully awake,
  they saw his glory and the two men
    standing with him.
As they were about to part from him,
    Peter said to Jesus,
  "Master, it is good that we are here;
  let us make three tents,
  one for you, one for Moses, and one
    for Elijah."
But he did not know what he was
    saying.
While he was still speaking,
  a cloud came and cast a shadow over
    them,
  and they became frightened when
    they entered the cloud.
Then from the cloud came a voice that
    said,
  "This is my chosen Son; listen to
    him."
After the voice had spoken, Jesus was
    found alone.
They fell silent and did not at that time
  tell anyone what they had seen.**

Reflecting on the Gospel

Luke describes Jesus's transfiguration as happening "while he was praying," emphasizing the power of prayer to mediate the presence of God and the consequent transformation of the one who prays. Jesus is joined by two of his ancestors, Moses and Elijah. The first of these, Moses, had to cope with his people who frequently grumbled about their exodus out of Egyptian slavery and into freedom. After spending forty days on Mount Sinai where God had called him to receive the divine teaching, Moses was transformed by his encounter and his face had become so radiant that when he came down from the mountain to his people, he needed to veil himself lest his brightness blind them (Exod 34:29-35). Elijah had encountered God in the silence outside the cave on Mount Horeb/Sinai after his forty-day flight from Jezebel, his too vicious slaughter of the false prophets she favored, and his arrogant ignoring of the other hundred true and hidden prophets of God (1 Kgs 18–19).

The glory of the transfiguration eventually penetrates the fog of sleep that resulted from the disciples' mountain climb. As it will be in Gethsemane, such sleep is the faithless opposite of watching and praying—a reality with which we may be all too familiar. As Moses and Elijah leave, Peter has what he considers his own moment of dazzling brilliance. He does not want to take any holy risks. A safer, more familiar solution, he suggests, would be to "house" the glory of Jesus, Moses, and Elijah in three tents (or "tabernacles") set up on this mountain. As observant Jews, Jesus and the disciples had all celebrated the feast of Tabernacles/Booths from their childhood. That feast commemorates not only the wilderness wandering of Israel when the people lived in fragile, portable tents, but also the later dwelling of the cloud of God's glory, the Shekinah, in the Jerusalem temple. We have often been very pious about Peter's words, "Master, it is good that we are here," but inattentive to Luke's following comment that Peter did not know what he was saying. Jesus's disciples are never to be frozen in the familiar. For Peter, James, and John, there is another mountain to be climbed, another transfiguration in blood and pain to be experienced before the glory of the resurrection is revealed.

Then God, not Peter, takes the initiative—tenting over Jesus and the disciples with divine glory, overshadowing them with a cloud, and calling them into its mystery. Over Moses on Mount Sinai, over Daniel's Son of Man, over Mary of Nazareth, the cloud was witness to and symbol of God's transfiguring presence. Now it embraces the tabernacle of Jesus's body and those who are his companions. Terrified, they enter and hear the Father's assurance, given only to Jesus at his baptism but now announced to disciples of all times: "This is my chosen Son; listen to him." Then there is silence, and Jesus alone is with them. They will go down from the mountain, onto the plain; and the struggle to understand Jesus goes on. On the plains of our everyday life, we struggle to respond to the Father's command: to listen to the Son, to become children of the light in his light, brothers and sisters who are ready to risk the unfamiliar and new because we are enveloped in the security of God's presence and promise. After the mountain of Jesus's transfiguration comes the hill of his crucifixion. Our pilgrim legs have to be strong for both climbs, and though we may not always recognize it, the "mountaintop" experiences are often occasions where God allows us to catch our breath for the next and harder ascents.

Focusing the Gospel

Key words and phrases: "Peter and his companions had been overcome by sleep, but becoming fully awake, they saw his glory and the two men standing with him."

To the point: This was probably an awesome and terrifying scene for Peter, John, and James. They wake up and their friend Jesus is talking with long-dead heroes, in a cloud of glory. It's almost as if they stumbled into a private meeting of the divine. Peter's reaction is rash but not illogical; he suggests building tents (what we would call altars) to honor the three superheroes standing in front of him. What else could he do? We get another encounter with Peter's humanity when Luke tells us, "But he did not know what he was saying."

Have you ever been this excited? We call life-changing experiences "mountaintop" experiences because of this gospel passage. Whether it's a retreat or a vacation, it's the mountaintop experiences that give us the inspiration and courage to carry on with regular life.

Connecting the Gospel

to the first reading: The first reading is another "mountaintop" moment, in which God makes a covenant with Abram. Abram's scene includes shocking theatrics, like Peter's. Abram sets up his sacrifice of animals, and then the sun sets. "When the sun had set and it was dark, there appeared a smoking fire pot and a flaming torch, which passed between those pieces." In the midst of this otherworldly experience, God makes a promise to Abram and sets in motion a relationship with Abram's family that will come to fruition in the person of Jesus, 1,800 years later.

to experience: Have you ever had a "mountaintop" experience? Maybe it was a retreat when you were young, or your wedding day, or a time in your life when you were so removed from the mundanity of everyday life that you felt you were touching the divine. You are connected to both Abram and Peter in this. Having a mountaintop experience is part of being a Christian and living through the ebb and flow of intellectual and emotional connection to faith. Sometimes we're on fire. Sometimes we can't be bothered to do more than go through the motions. But it is in this movement that we condition ourselves for heaven by choosing God, and choosing love, no matter where we feel we are.

Connecting the Responsorial Psalm

to the readings: It's Lent, a time of reflection and abstinence. So where can we turn to be satisfied, regardless of the season? We are reminded in the psalm that, no matter what, the Lord is our light and our salvation.

to psalmist preparation: The first verse is self-reflection, the second and third are petitions, and the final verse is a call outward for others to also wait for the Lord with courage. This four-stanza prayer has a thorough process through which you guide the congregation.

Model Penitential Act

Presider: In today's gospel we encounter the transfiguration of Jesus. Knowing our own need for transformation, we ask for God's healing and forgiveness for the times we have sinned . . . *[pause]*

    Confiteor: I confess . . .

Homily Points

• Sylvia Dunstan, an incredibly gifted hymn text author, writes, "Transform us as you, transfigured." These words are our prayer today. In the gospel, Jesus reveals to the disciples that he is the Son of God. The revelation is extraordinary, but this event is not one of passivity. We, too, are invited into a life of transformation as we strive to become the people we are called to be.

• Part of our own transformation, just like that of the disciples, is our awareness and alertness of the presence of God. Luke writes, "Peter and his companions had been overcome by sleep, but becoming fully awake, they saw his glory and the two men standing with him." What keeps our own minds from being fully awake? Do our own experiences and prejudices and biases keep us from fully encountering God? Do we have difficulty recognizing the belovedness of others? Are we simply going through the motions of prayer because we are exhausted? This Second Sunday of Lent is a great opportunity to reflect on our own self-awareness.

• Today we pray that we may embody the words of Paul in the letter to the Philippians: "He will change our lowly body to conform with his glorified body by the power that enables him also to bring all things into subjection to himself." May we allow God to transform us in God's image so that our light may shine in radiant glory.

Model Universal Prayer (Prayer of the Faithful)

Presider: Paul urges us today to stand firm in the Lord. We do so by bringing God our prayers and petitions.

Response: Lord, hear our prayer.

That the church may facilitate and sustain interreligious and ecumenical dialogue to promote the greater glory of God . . .

That all who are in positions of social power may use their privilege to lift up people who are hurting and excluded . . .

That all who live in fear of persecution may find comfort and relief in the presence of others . . .

That our local community may listen to the voice of God and always treat others as God's beloved . . .

Presider: Loving God, we are your people who long to see your face. Help us continue to grow in relationship with you and others through our words and actions, knowing that you alone are our light and life. We ask this through Christ our Lord. **Amen.**

COLLECT

Let us pray.

Pause for silent prayer

O God, who have commanded us
to listen to your beloved Son,
be pleased, we pray,
to nourish us inwardly by your word,
that, with spiritual sight made pure,
we may rejoice to behold your glory.
Through our Lord Jesus Christ, your Son,
who lives and reigns with you in the unity
    of the Holy Spirit,
God, for ever and ever. **Amen.**

FIRST READING
Gen 15:5-12, 17-18

The Lord God took Abram outside and
    said,
    "Look up at the sky and count the stars,
        if you can.
Just so," he added, "shall your descendants
        be."
Abram put his faith in the LORD,
    who credited it to him as an act of
        righteousness.

He then said to him,
    "I am the LORD who brought you from
        Ur of the Chaldeans
    to give you this land as a possession."
"O Lord GOD," he asked,
    "how am I to know that I shall possess
        it?"
He answered him,
    "Bring me a three-year-old heifer, a
        three-year-old she-goat,
    a three-year-old ram, a turtledove, and a
        young pigeon."
Abram brought him all these, split them
    in two,
    and placed each half opposite the other;
    but the birds he did not cut up.
Birds of prey swooped down on the
    carcasses,
    but Abram stayed with them.
As the sun was about to set, a trance fell
    upon Abram,
    and a deep, terrifying darkness
        enveloped him.

When the sun had set and it was dark,
    there appeared a smoking fire pot and a
        flaming torch,
    which passed between those pieces.
It was on that occasion that the LORD made
    a covenant with Abram,
    saying: "To your descendants I give this
        land,
    from the Wadi of Egypt to the Great
        River, the Euphrates."

RESPONSORIAL PSALM

Ps 27:1, 7-8, 8-9, 13-14

℟. (1a) The Lord is my light and my
   salvation.

The LORD is my light and my salvation;
   whom should I fear?
The LORD is my life's refuge;
   of whom should I be afraid?

℟. The Lord is my light and my salvation.

Hear, O LORD, the sound of my call;
   have pity on me, and answer me.
Of you my heart speaks; you my glance
   seeks.

℟. The Lord is my light and my salvation.

Your presence, O LORD, I seek.
   Hide not your face from me;
do not in anger repel your servant.
   You are my helper: cast me not off.

℟. The Lord is my light and my salvation.

I believe that I shall see the bounty of the
   LORD
   in the land of the living.
Wait for the LORD with courage;
   be stouthearted, and wait for the LORD.

℟. The Lord is my light and my salvation.

SECOND READING

Phil 3:17—4:1

Join with others in being imitators of me,
   brothers and sisters,
   and observe those who thus conduct
      themselves
   according to the model you have in us.
For many, as I have often told you
   and now tell you even in tears,
   conduct themselves as enemies of the
      cross of Christ.
Their end is destruction.
Their God is their stomach;
   their glory is in their "shame."
Their minds are occupied with earthly
   things.
But our citizenship is in heaven,
   and from it we also await a savior, the
      Lord Jesus Christ.
He will change our lowly body
   to conform with his glorified body
   by the power that enables him also
   to bring all things into subjection to
      himself.

Therefore, my brothers and sisters,
   whom I love and long for, my joy and
      crown,
   in this way stand firm in the Lord.

or Phil 3:20—4:1, see Appendix A, p. 273.

About Liturgy

God's Light: There is a fable told about a king who needed to choose which of his three sons would be the next ruler of the land. His older two sons had roles in the government as minister of war and minister of finance; the youngest son eschewed that life and instead lived a life of solitude and prayer, as a hermit, far from home.

The king could not decide among the three, so he devised a test: they each in turn would have from sundown to sunrise to fill a dungeon room in the castle completely, from floor to ceiling, with whatever and however they chose.

The eldest son, the minister of war, began by ordering the many military troops of the land to bring every rock and boulder they could find to the castle. By morning, the room appeared to be completely full; the king, though, noted he could place his fingers, and sometimes his whole hand, in various crevices and gaps between the stones. This son would not be the next king.

The next son, the minister of finance, knew the country had grown prosperous under his father's rule, so he had those under his command gather all of the paper money, the coins, the jewels and precious metals of the land to bring to the dungeon. But, by sunrise, even all of the affluence of the land only filled the room halfway. He, too, would not be the next king.

The last son, when it came his turn, did not know how to proceed. He didn't have authority to command thousands of troops, nor did he possess any amount of money or riches of his own. So, at sundown, as the door shut behind him, leaving him in complete darkness, he did what he knew: he pulled a candle from his knapsack, and a prayer book, and began to pray. He prayed with such fervor that before he knew it, it was sunrise, and his father was opening the door.

"Father, I'm sorry," the son said. "My son, whatever for?" the father replied. "Your two brothers tried to fill this room with power, with wealth—and they failed. You, however, succeeded—by filling this room with light."

The transfiguration we celebrate today, and each Second Sunday of Lent, is sometimes viewed as a revelation, where Jesus shares more of who he was (and is) with trusted friends. It's also sometimes seen as a glimpse of glory that might help steel these three chosen apostles against witnessing the passion and death that was to come.

Liturgically, we may be tempted to make our liturgies better through use of authority and power, be that from whatever position we hold at the parish or by appealing to the liturgical documents and the weight they have. Sometimes we might try to buy our way to better liturgies, be that through hiring professional musicians or by being especially lavish with spending toward art and environment. May I suggest today we ponder this fable, and today's gospel, and reimagine how our liturgies, in our various contexts, might be improved by instead bringing God's light to the study, preparation, and execution of divine worship?

About Music

Miraculous Mysteries: We can probably name from the top of our heads several hymns that focus on "light" imagery, likely appropriate for the weekend. Brian Wren has a beautiful transfiguration text, given an appealing melody in one case by Ricky Manalo (OCP), which, by methodical phrasing and judicious interludes, gives each singer time to contemplate the mysteries embedded in this miraculous revelation.

MARCH 13, 2022
SECOND SUNDAY OF LENT

ST. JOSEPH, SPOUSE OF THE BLESSED VIRGIN MARY

GOSPEL ACCLAMATION
Ps 84:5

Blessed are those who dwell in your house,
O Lord;
they never cease to praise you.

Gospel Matt 1:16, 18-21, 24a; L543

Jacob was the father
of Joseph, the
husband of Mary.
Of her was born
Jesus who is
called the Christ.

Now this is how the
birth of Jesus
Christ came
about.
When his mother
Mary was
betrothed to
Joseph,
but before they
lived together,
she was found with
child through
the Holy Spirit.
Joseph her husband,
since he was a
righteous man,
yet unwilling to expose her to shame,
decided to divorce her quietly.
Such was his intention when, behold,
the angel of the Lord appeared to him
in a dream and said,
"Joseph, son of David,
do not be afraid to take Mary your wife
into your home.
For it is through the Holy Spirit
that this child has been conceived in
her.
She will bear a son and you are to name
him Jesus,
because he will save his people from
their sins."
When Joseph awoke,
he did as the angel of the Lord had
commanded him
and took his wife into his home.

or Luke 2:41-51a in Appendix A, p. 274.

See Appendix A., p. 274, for the other readings.

Reflecting on the Gospel

St. Joseph is one of several biblical figures who collaborated with God in the divine plan to ensure God's continuous presence in the world. The angelic messages he received through dreams urged obedience from him on the events enfolding in his life that have been divinely assigned to him. St. Joseph did not disappoint—he acquiesced to the angelic instructions. For this reason, we celebrate him as a man of humility and docility who displays an unalloyed disposition and openness to God's presence in his life.

Within a short period of time, St. Joseph's engagement to the Blessed Mother turns into a discreet plan to call off the engagement because the Blessed Mother is pregnant with Jesus by the power of the Holy Spirit. But a visit from the angel Gabriel reverses St. Joseph's plan and he becomes a faithful spouse to the Blessed Mother (Matt 1:24). At the birth of Jesus Christ, St. Joseph readies the manger in which baby Jesus comfortably rests. At the visit of the magi, he stands next to the Blessed Mother and the baby Jesus playing his God-given role, as numerous iconic images of the magi's visitation in our tradition portray.

When the life of baby Jesus rests on the hands of St. Joseph, he follows the instruction of the angel of the Lord, making the difficult journey to Egypt to save Jesus (Matt 2:13-15). This event is enriched with extrabiblical messages in Christian icons and paintings of St. Joseph on foot, leading the donkey carrying the new mother and her baby. These images of the Holy Family leaving the Judean region without being spotted by Herod and his armies should reveal to us the considerable level of Joseph's commitment to the responsibility God has given him. Indeed, with no relative at the city gate to welcome the Holy Family, except the Jewish community to seek out for support, St. Joseph has to provide comfort for his family in a foreign land and keep them safe in case information has spread far and wide of Herod's murderous search for the newborn king of the Jews.

Back home in Nazareth, St. Joseph remains a steadfast companion to Mary and a role model to Jesus by his exemplary life of righteousness and humility. Listening to Simeon's words to Mary, St. Joseph offers her reassurance and support (Luke 2:33-35), and he leads in the effort to find Jesus after his disappearance in Jerusalem. St. Joseph is an exemplary husband and father who is present to his family, overseeing the challenges that come into his life with poise. His humble demeanor rubs off on the Blessed Mother and Jesus, as they draw strength and encouragement from this righteous man who is a husband and a father.

St. Joseph teaches us that a husband and a father ought to have a steady and discerning relationship with God, which builds him up into an exemplary man for his household. He teaches every household the value of active listening skills that deepen our love for one another. He listens to the messages of the angel; he listens to the magi rave about Jesus; he listens to what Simeon says about Mary and Jesus; and he listens to the conversation between Mary and Jesus at the temple in Jerusalem after three days of searching for him. Therefore, St. Joseph teaches us the value in active listening and acting in good faith for the people we love.

Focusing the Gospel

Key words and phrases: "Joseph her husband, since he was a righteous man, yet unwilling to expose her to shame, decided to divorce her quietly."

To the point: The focus on today's gospel tends to be on the angel appearing to Joseph in a dream; however, this line from Matthew is equally notable. When Joseph finds out his fiancée is pregnant without his involvement, he doesn't react in anger, or publicly shame her, or do any of the things we would expect from a man in this situation. Instead of wielding his anger against his "unfaithful" fiancée, he decides to end things privately and avoid ruining her future. We get a glimpse of Joseph's holiness in this scene. Even though society would find it perfectly within his rights to call her out, he anticipates the social shame she's bound to endure as a single pregnant woman and chooses to avoid adding to it.

Model Penitential Act

Presider: Today as we honor St. Joseph, we remember that he lived as a dedicated and loving family member. For the times we have not lived and loved in this same way, we bring our prayers to the God who hears us . . . *[pause]*

Lord Jesus, you are Son of God and son of Mary: Lord, have mercy.

Christ Jesus, you knew the demands of family life: Christ, have mercy.

Lord Jesus, you intercede for us at the right hand of the Father:
Lord, have mercy.

Model Universal Prayer (Prayer of the Faithful)

Presider: Following the example of Jesus who taught us to call on God our Father, we bring our prayers and petitions to the one who knows us and loves us well.

Response: Lord, hear our prayer.

That the church may follow the example of St. Joseph's faith and be an ever-living witness to God working in our lives . . .

That leaders of cities and countries may work to protect the most vulnerable, especially women and children . . .

That all survivors of physical or sexual abuse may find the healing for which they long . . .

That all gathered here may welcome Christ in their lives, whether at home, at school, or in the workplace . . .

Presider: Loving God, hear the prayers that we bring to you today. May we follow St. Joseph's example of humility and dedication to Christ, always striving to live our lives with a similar generosity of Spirit. We ask this through Christ our Lord. **Amen.**

About Liturgy

Silent Leadership: Around this date each year, memes appear on social media pointing out that St. Joseph, in our Scriptures, never is quoted. While he certainly embodies a person with great influence in the nativity narratives, and surely did speak from time to time, none of his words are recorded for us. We are left to observe how Joseph leads by example instead of by words.

Those of us who hold leadership roles in liturgy would do well to learn such a lesson—that leadership by example, rather than by decree or "orders," is a very powerful and Christian model of leadership, especially when coupled with acts of humble service. Too often, in our church, people offer only one mode of leadership, sometimes seemingly blind to its ill effects.

Leadership by example, by service: perhaps a lesson Jesus learned from his earthly father, and one for us today as well.

COLLECT

Let us pray.

Pause for silent prayer

Grant, we pray, almighty God,
that by Saint Joseph's intercession
your Church may constantly watch over
the unfolding of the mysteries of human
    salvation,
whose beginnings you entrusted to his
    faithful care.
Through our Lord Jesus Christ, your Son,
who lives and reigns with you in the unity
    of the Holy Spirit,
God, for ever and ever. **Amen.**

FOR REFLECTION

• So often when we consider the Holy Family, St. Joseph is easily overlooked. Even so, his participation in God's plan was paramount. How might you better emulate St. Joseph's humility, virtue, and trust in God?

• Luke tells us that Joseph "was a righteous man." What does righteousness look like in your life today?

Homily Points

• Internationally acclaimed Scripture scholar Raymond Brown challenges us to encounter today's gospel with fresh ears and eyes. So often we think about Joseph's intention to divorce Mary as a form of self-preservation. But what if Joseph's fears stem from feelings of inadequacy? There are many times we feel underqualified or even downright unqualified to do the will of God; these are natural human reactions. May we, like Joseph, be willing to listen to the word of God and respond with confidence.

• This was just the beginning of St. Joseph's foray into the challenging realities of family life with Mary and Jesus. If we are honest with ourselves, family can be exhausting, even frustrating. When we are tired from caring for children, or parents, or spouses or siblings, may we remember today's gospel and echo St. Joseph's "yes."

SPIRITUALITY

GOSPEL ACCLAMATION
Matt 4:17

Repent, says the Lord;
the kingdom of heaven is at hand.

Gospel   Luke 13:1-9; L30C

**Some people told Jesus about the
   Galileans
   whose blood Pilate had mingled with
      the blood of their sacrifices.
Jesus said to them in reply,
   "Do you think that because these
      Galileans suffered in this way
   they were greater sinners than all
      other Galileans?
By no means!
But I tell you, if you do not repent,
   you will all perish as they did!
Or those eighteen people who were
   killed
   when the tower at Siloam fell on
      them—
   do you think they were more guilty
   than everyone else who lived in
      Jerusalem?
By no means!
But I tell you, if you do not repent,
   you will all perish as they did!"**

**And he told them this parable:
   "There once was a person who had a fig
      tree planted in his orchard,
   and when he came in search of fruit on
      it but found none,
   he said to the gardener,
   'For three years now I have come in
      search of fruit on this fig tree
   but have found none.
So cut it down.
Why should it exhaust the soil?'
He said to him in reply,
   'Sir, leave it for this year also,
   and I shall cultivate the ground around
      it and fertilize it;
   it may bear fruit in the future.
If not you can cut it down.'"**

*Year A readings may be used, see Appendix A,
pp. 276–277.*

Reflecting on the Gospel

In today's gospel, the crowd reminds Jesus about the tragedy of what happened to a group of Galileans who had been standing at the altar worshiping God when they themselves became sacrificial offerings at the hands of Pilate's henchman. Although not historically recorded outside the gospel, this incident

would have been as politically explosive as those tragedies that are still too familiar in volatile and unreconciled parts of our world and in acts of indiscriminate terrorism. Jesus recognizes the unspoken but implied question: *Big sinners, big suffering?* and answers with an explicit *No.* He himself raises the issue of eighteen people who were killed when the tower of Siloam accidentally collapsed on them. Neither of these incidents, says Jesus, is about God's punishment of the victims' sinfulness, although human nature is sometimes and mistakenly quick to make such a judgment. They show, rather, the fragility of our lives and the suddenness with which death can overwhelm us. We can be tempted to query, privately or publicly, the truth of our response to Psalm 103, "The Lord is kind and merciful," but the laws of nature are not to be equated with the laws of morality.

Jesus uses these events to make one point: what happened was sudden, with no time to avoid the catastrophes. But there is a much greater catastrophe on which the people need to focus: their unpreparedness for the merciful yet just judgment of God. So Jesus tells a parable about an unproductive fruit tree. A healthy fruit tree is interdependent, not self-sufficient; it takes nourishment from the soil in which it is planted and is further nourished by the work of the gardener who fertilizes it. In turn, the tree gives back fruit.

In the judgment of the orchard owner, time has run out for the tree that had not borne fruit for three years, and it deserves to be cut down. It is all "take" from the soil that must also nourish the other trees, and no "give." But the gardener begs his master to be patient and allow him another year of extra effort, of digging around and fertilizing the tree to see if it will bear some fruit. If it still does not, then it can be cut down. By choosing this reading for Lent, the church suggests that the loving patience of our God is giving us another chance to do some seasonal gardening on ourselves: to loosen the soil around our personal and communal earthbound roots with the tools of prayer, fasting, and almsgiving; to fertilize our lives with the rich Lenten liturgy of word and sacrament; and to strengthen, not weaken, one another by mutual care and kindness.

The tree is a fig, a sturdy tree. Unlike some of our indoor plants, fig trees do not droop and die overnight. It takes a long drought, continuous and insidious gnawing at the roots, or protracted neglect to make a fig tree barren. And what about us? What has gradually dried up and withered our Christian lives? Are there small infidelities gnawing away at the roots of our baptismal commitment? Are we failing to cultivate or prune our discipleship so that the sap of the Christ-life may continue to rise within us? Like the Galileans and the victims of the Siloam collapse, we can never be sure how many "next years" lie ahead of us. "Today," this Lent, is the important time of conversion.

Focusing the Gospel

Key words and phrases: "[D]o you think they were more guilty than everyone else who lived in Jerusalem? By no means!"

To the point: Jesus references a local accident that resulted in the death of eighteen people. It was probably a big news story, and as in any community, the Jewish people probably discussed at great length how and why it happened. At the time of Jesus's arrival in salvation history, there is still a strong notion that good things happen to good people, and bad things happen to bad people. Jesus challenges this way of thinking throughout his ministry, but here he specifically calls out this false theology. He explicitly states that those who died in an accident were no more guilty than everyone else who lives in Jerusalem. Bad things happen to good people, and vice versa. Jesus is well aware of this.

Then he tells us about a fig tree that will bear no fruit. The owner's reaction is to cut it down, but the gardener cautions him not to, because even though the fig tree isn't bearing fruit, it is contributing to the soil and retains the possibility of producing fruit in the future. How many times do we write someone off as a sinner or bad influence? Though sometimes this creates healthy distance for our own growth, we must remember everyone who is alive retains the possibility of bearing good fruit. No one's path to sainthood is the same.

Connecting the Gospel

to the first and second readings: In the second reading, Paul references the story of Moses and the Israelites in the first reading directly and reminds his audience that "[t]hese things happened as examples for us, so that we might not desire evil things, as they did."

to experience: When we read the Old Testament, we are reading the same literature that the Jews read in Jesus's time and that the first Christians read after Jesus's resurrection. There is a direct through line in our experience of salvation history, because every community's chapter is aware of the chapter before. When Paul is telling the Corinthians about Moses and the Israelites, he says, "These things happened to them as an example, and they have been written down as a warning to us, upon whom the end of the ages has come. Therefore, whoever thinks he is standing secure should take care not to fall." Paul may as well be speaking to twenty-first-century Christians. In fact, he is.

Connecting the Responsorial Psalm

to the readings: Today's readings have a lot of warnings and call us to recontextualize our own actions in light of the fact that bad things happen to good people, and we've got a firm narrative of how those good people should act, regardless. Conversely, the psalm deals with God's actions toward us and reminds us that, regardless of the mess we make, he is kind and merciful. "The LORD secures justice / and the rights of all the oppressed. / He has made known his ways to Moses, / and his deeds to the children of Israel." Regardless of how much fruit our tree is bearing, "Merciful and gracious is the LORD, / slow to anger and abounding in kindness."

to psalmist preparation: Think of a situation in your life when you or someone you love went through a hard time that appeared to be very unfair—sickness, job loss, financial constraint. Were you able to feel God's mercy and kindness? Why or why not?

PROMPTS FOR FAITH-SHARING

Do you get frustrated when you do all you can to live a holy life, and bad things still happen? Has there been a particularly frustrating situation recently? How do you deal with earthly suffering?

Do you have any experience watching a fruitless fig tree finally begin to bloom? Did you give up on it, or fight to keep it planted?

Has God ever broken into your life in a radical scene, like Moses encountering the burning bush?

Is there anyone in your life who lives as an example to you of how to grow in holiness? How did you encounter this person's story? How does looking at the story of someone else's faith influence your own growth?

Model Penitential Act

Presider: In today's reading from Exodus, Moses responds to God's call on the mountain in the burning bush. For the times we have remained indifferent to God's call in our own lives, we ask God for peace and healing . . . *[pause]*

Confiteor: I confess . . .

Homily Points

• There is nothing quite like an unambiguous warning, especially when it forces a reality check. This is exactly what happens in Paul's letter to the Corinthians. Paul writes: "[W]hoever thinks he is standing secure should take care not to fall." Confidence is important. Overconfidence is vicious. As we celebrate this Third Sunday of Lent, in what ways have we become complacent in confidence?

• Likewise, in today's parable we see that complacency is unacceptable. Jesus gives us two choices: grow or die. While this may sound overly dramatic, we encounter this very choice every single day. After the years without bearing fruit, it makes sense that the owner of the garden would want to stop wasting resources on something that was not producing. The gardener's words are just as foreboding as Paul's: "[L]eave it for this year also, and I shall cultivate the ground around it and fertilize it; it may bear fruit in the future. If not you can cut it down." Our God is a God of second chances. We see that often throughout Jesus's ministry. There will come a time, however, when we will have to answer before God. Did we use the resources God has given us to bear fruit in the world?

• Today's gospel is a good checkpoint of sorts as we enter this third week of our Lenten journey. Have we been using the time we have to cultivate our relationship with God and others? Have we generously and selflessly shared our gifts and resources with others? Are we making the most of each day? Jesus tells us we have another chance to step it up. Repentance and God's life-giving forgiveness are possible. Let us not squander that opportunity.

Model Universal Prayer (Prayer of the Faithful)

Presider: Just as the gardener petitions the garden owner to give the fig tree another chance, we come to our loving God, unafraid to bring our own petitions.

Response: Lord, hear our prayer.

That the church, like Moses, might respond to God's call with the words, "Here I am." . . .

That leaders of communities, cities, and nations may work to end the modern-day slavery occurring in our midst, especially mindful of victims of human trafficking . . .

That all farmers experience good weather this season so to bear a bountiful harvest . . .

That we might respond to Jesus's invitation to repentance this Lenten season, confident in God's love for us . . .

Presider: Loving God, you spoke to Moses in the burning bush. Speak to us today and answer the prayers we bring to you. We trust that you will answer these needs according to your will. We ask this through Christ our Lord. **Amen.**

COLLECT

Let us pray.

Pause for silent prayer

O God, author of every mercy and of all
    goodness,
who in fasting, prayer and almsgiving
have shown us a remedy for sin,
look graciously on this confession of our
    lowliness,
that we, who are bowed down by our
    conscience,
may always be lifted up by your mercy.
Through our Lord Jesus Christ, your Son,
who lives and reigns with you in the unity
    of the Holy Spirit,
God, for ever and ever. **Amen.**

FIRST READING

Exod 3:1-8a, 13-15

Moses was tending the flock of his father-
    in-law Jethro,
    the priest of Midian.
Leading the flock across the desert, he
    came to Horeb,
    the mountain of God.
There an angel of the LORD appeared to
    Moses in fire
    flaming out of a bush.
As he looked on, he was surprised to see
    that the bush,
    though on fire, was not consumed.
So Moses decided,
    "I must go over to look at this
        remarkable sight,
    and see why the bush is not burned."

When the LORD saw him coming over to
    look at it more closely,
    God called out to him from the bush,
        "Moses! Moses!"
He answered, "Here I am."
God said, "Come no nearer!
Remove the sandals from your feet,
    for the place where you stand is holy
        ground.
I am the God of your fathers," he
    continued,
    "the God of Abraham, the God of Isaac,
        the God of Jacob."
Moses hid his face, for he was afraid to
    look at God.
But the LORD said,
    "I have witnessed the affliction of my
        people in Egypt
    and have heard their cry of complaint
        against their slave drivers,
    so I know well what they are suffering.
Therefore I have come down to rescue
    them
    from the hands of the Egyptians

and lead them out of that land into a
    good and spacious land,
    a land flowing with milk and honey."

Moses said to God, "But when I go to the
    Israelites
and say to them, 'The God of your
    fathers has sent me to you,'
if they ask me, 'What is his name?'
    what am I to tell them?"
God replied, "I am who am."
Then he added, "This is what you shall tell
    the Israelites:
    I AM sent me to you."

God spoke further to Moses, "Thus shall
    you say to the Israelites:
The Lord, the God of your fathers,
    the God of Abraham, the God of Isaac,
    the God of Jacob,
has sent me to you.

"This is my name forever;
    thus am I to be remembered through all
    generations."

RESPONSORIAL PSALM
Ps 103:1-2, 3-4, 6-7, 8, 11

R̸. (8a) The Lord is kind and merciful.

Bless the Lord, O my soul;
    and all my being, bless his holy name.
Bless the Lord, O my soul,
    and forget not all his benefits.

R̸. The Lord is kind and merciful.

He pardons all your iniquities,
    heals all your ills.
He redeems your life from destruction,
    crowns you with kindness and
    compassion.

R̸. The Lord is kind and merciful.

The Lord secures justice
    and the rights of all the oppressed.
He has made known his ways to Moses,
    and his deeds to the children of Israel.

R̸. The Lord is kind and merciful.

Merciful and gracious is the Lord,
    slow to anger and abounding in
    kindness.
For as the heavens are high above the
    earth,
    so surpassing is his kindness toward
    those who fear him.

R̸. The Lord is kind and merciful.

SECOND READING
1 Cor 10:1-6, 10-12

See Appendix A, p. 275.

About Liturgy

From Station to Station: A brief word here about a common Lenten devotional practice, the Stations of the Cross. While not strictly a liturgy, this prayer can indeed be public and has some sort of broad "ritual" attached to its celebration. What I wish to call attention to here is that this prayer is, by its name and form, stational: that is, it requires the person praying to move from place to place. This form of prayer has roots in liturgical practices in Jerusalem centuries ago, where liturgies would trace historical moments in the Christian story by physically gathering at the places those events were believed (or known) to have happened. For instance, Holy Thursday would be celebrated one place, Good Friday another, and Easter yet another, corresponding to the historical locations of those particular moments of Christ's life and ministry.

It may be common practice in your circumstance that the Stations of the Cross be led with everyone stationary in the pews, with leader(s) stationary at the ambo or some other prominent location. This practice, though, removes the processional and stational nature of this devotion, moving through both time and space. Perhaps consider whether a more mobile Stations of the Cross, if not already your practice, might be possible in your circumstance. Even so, the unique pastoral situation within your community may prevent this.

About Liturgical Documents

Sing to the Lord: As previously mentioned, Sing to the Lord, the document from the USCCB on liturgical music in the United States, turns fifteen years old this year. Without bearing the weight of liturgical law, this document puts forth a robust and comprehensive vision for music ministry, from theological underpinnings to personnel, structures, practicalities, and more.

It draws frequently on other church liturgical documents and in particular its ancestor from the USCCB, Music in Catholic Worship (1972), seeing itself as a revision of that foundational document.

Sing to the Lord early on shares a number of reasons why the updated guidelines, and indeed any guidance on sacred music, are so important:

> God has bestowed upon his people the gift of song. God dwells within each human person, in the place where music takes its source. Indeed, God, the giver of song, is present whenever his people sing his praises. (STL 1)

> This common, sung expression of faith within liturgical celebrations strengthens our faith when it grows weak and draws us into the divinely inspired voice of the Church at prayer. Faith grows when it is well expressed in celebration. Good celebrations can foster and nourish faith. Poor celebrations may weaken it. Good music "make[s] the liturgical prayers of the Christian community more alive and fervent so that everyone can praise and beseech the Triune God more powerfully, more intently and more effectively." (STL 5)

That God is present in the singing assembly is an important, sometimes overlooked sub-point of the divine presences enumerated in the Constitution on the Sacred Liturgy (SC 7). The weight that STL puts on the quality of liturgical celebrations is a lens through which the rest of the document can be read and interpreted: the well-done ministry of music is indeed always one of the factors directly related to whether a liturgy might be called "poor" or "good," and a broad range of factors impact that quality. We will break open some of these factors, as discussed in STL, over the coming weeks.

MARCH 20, 2022
THIRD SUNDAY OF LENT

GOSPEL ACCLAMATION
John 1:14ab

The Word of God became flesh and made his
dwelling among us;
and we saw his glory.

Gospel   Luke 1:26-38; L545

The angel Gabriel was sent from God
  to a town of Galilee called Nazareth,
  to a virgin betrothed to a man named
      Joseph,
  of the house of David,
  and the virgin's name was Mary.
And coming to her, he said,
  "Hail, full of grace! The Lord is with you."
But she was greatly troubled at what was said
  and pondered what sort of greeting this
      might be.
Then the angel said to her,
  "Do not be afraid, Mary,
  for you have found favor with God.
Behold, you will conceive in your womb and
      bear a son,
  and you shall name him Jesus.
He will be great and will be called Son of
      the Most High,
  and the Lord God will give him the throne
      of David his father,
  and he will rule over the house of Jacob
      forever,
  and of his Kingdom there will be no end."

Continued in Appendix A, p. 278.

See Appendix A, p. 278, for the other readings.

Reflecting on the Gospel

The solemnity of the Annunciation of our Lord reveals in a profound way God's desire for relationship with humankind, so that being among us and through sharing in human experience, God elevates us into the state we share. Both the plan and the annunciation are from God, who sent his angel at the appointed time to disclose to the Blessed Virgin Mary the incarnation of God as "Emmanuel, God is among us" (Matt 1:23). The message of the angel of the Lord to the Blessed Virgin Mary reveals the vulnerability and compassion of God toward humankind as God takes on human nature in order to redeem humanity. The annunciation of our Lord, therefore, is the beginning of the divine plan to bring to fulfillment God's desire to enter into relationship with humanity for the benefit of the human family.

The angel Gabriel announces that our Lord Jesus Christ will sit on the throne of his father David. Just as David exercised his leadership as God's Son, likewise Jesus Christ will rule the world forever in his capacity as the Son of the Most High God for the benefit of humankind. As one after God's heart, David was humble and he united the tribes of Israel throughout his leadership. Israel and its surrounding neighbors witnessed a long period of peace, harmony, and diplomacy of shared respect and mutuality because David used his military success to end acrimony among Israel and its neighbors. Similarly, the angel Gabriel's revelation that Jesus Christ will sit on the throne of David means that the leadership of the Son of God will usher in peace and harmony in the world. Jesus's leadership on the throne of David will establish a time of universal mutuality on the basis of our common humanity, fellowship, and equality. The angel Gabriel discourses that his reign of peace, joy, and harmony will last forever. Just as David led God's people, Jesus Christ will lead the world through his presence among us, for God has taken on human flesh (John 1:14).

The presence of the Son of God among us is sure proof that God is determined to reenter into human affairs and reunite humanity with God through participating and sharing in our experiences. We know this to be the case because St. Paul tells us that, though Jesus Christ is divine, sharing in God's nature, he chooses also to be part of the human family by taking on human nature (Phil 2:6-7). Becoming human and dwelling in our midst, he chooses humility and service (Phil 2:8) as his model of leadership on the throne of David. In Jesus's life of leadership through service, he teaches us the extraordinary meaning of our relationship with God and the virtues that build and sustain every relationship—namely, humility and service. Indeed, Jesus Christ lives among us as the One who serves (Luke 22:27).

As we commemorate the Annunciation of our Lord, let us celebrate with an outstretched and opened arm ready to welcome our Lord Jesus Christ into our lives at his birth. Our Savior is coming into our lives as the leader who will prepare and lead us to God. In the same way, let us take every opportunity that has been given to us to lead others through service and Christian charity to experience God's presence in their lives and to be renewed by the encounter.

Focusing the Gospel

Key words and phrases: "Do not be afraid, Mary, for you have found favor with God."

To the point: In the midst of the most jarring and overwhelming moment of Mary's life thus far, it is interesting that instead of a shocked reaction to the angel who has burst into her bedroom, she questions the logic of Gabriel's proposal. "How can this be, since I have no relations with a man?"

Mary demonstrates an openness to wonder and the impossible. Even when she's face-to-face with an angel of God, Mary is able to hold a conversation, to follow the instructions, and to give a response. We are quite lucky that in one of humanity's pinnacle moments, our advocate kept her head.

Model Penitential Act

Presider: On today's feast of the Annunciation, we celebrate Mary's "yes" to God. For the times we have not been open to God's work in our lives, we ask for grace, pardon, and peace . . . *[pause]*

Lord Jesus, you are the Son of God and the son of Mary: Lord, have mercy.

Christ Jesus, in your incarnation you took on human form: Christ, have mercy.

Lord Jesus, you call us to live our vocation of discipleship: Lord, have mercy.

Model Universal Prayer (Prayer of the Faithful)

Presider: Just as the angel tells Mary, "Do not be afraid . . . for you have found favor with God," we confidently bring our needs to the God of life and love.

Response: Lord, hear our prayer.

That the church may echo Mary's fiat by upholding the voices of women . . .

That local and world leaders may practice true humility and genuine openness to others . . .

That all who experience infertility, miscarriage, or stillbirth may find comfort in their communities of faith and find hope in the Christian family . . .

That our local community may work to meet the needs of the most vulnerable in our midst, especially women and children . . .

Presider: Loving God, like Mary we are your servants who work to do your will. Hear our prayers and answer them in ways that bear fruit for a barren world. We ask this through Christ our Lord. **Amen.**

About Liturgy

Praying Vocationally: We are perhaps accustomed to the organization of the Lectionary where, on Sundays, the first reading (from the Old Testament or Acts, typically) bears some connection to the gospel reading, sometimes illuminated by the responsorial psalm, while the second reading is drawn from the epistles and continues more or less chronologically, independent of the other readings.

So it's worth noting on today's solemnity that the readings, set up in form like a Sunday, all work so well in concert with one another. Further, the responsorial psalm and the epistle are the pair that are most interwoven, with the Letter to the Hebrews directly quoting Psalm 40.

Aligning our will to the divine will is the ultimate and everyday goal of discipleship. While not listed as an option for the responsorial psalm, this is a psalm I sometimes suggest for other places within the wedding liturgy, indicative of the vocation the couple is preparing to embody by their vows and their lives together. Liturgically, crafting the liturgy around that aspect of Mary's fiat could help all discern their Christian vocation in whatever form they are being called to.

FOR REFLECTION

• Mary's response to God is both an act of faith and a statement of consent. How might Mary's example help us to better listen to the voices of women who have been hurt or abused by people and powers?

• The angel proclaims, "Hail, full of grace! The Lord is with you." How do we experience God's presence in our lives today? How might we make ourselves more ready and willing to listen to God's voice?

Homily Points

• More than any other evangelist, Luke upholds the presence and importance of women in the story of Jesus. Mary is a profound example, as her "yes" allows for Emmanuel, "God with us." But Luke's inclusion of women does not end with Mary. It continues with Elizabeth, Anna in the temple, and a number of disciples who are healed by Jesus. The faithful women were even the first to bear witness to the resurrection! Their presence is not coincidental or insignificant.

• Each of the women in Luke's gospel teach us about growing in relationship with God. Here, when Mary asks the angel, "How can this be?" she offers a model of faith. As Christians, we are called to grapple with our faith rather than blindly accept what we have been taught. It is through questions and conversations that our seeds of faith find fertile ground to grow and flourish.

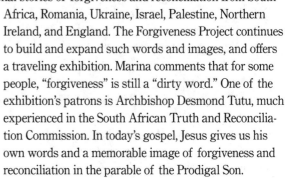

✝ SPIRITUALITY

GOSPEL ACCLAMATION
Luke 15:18

I will get up and go to my Father and shall say to him:
Father, I have sinned against heaven and against you.

Gospel   Luke 15:1-3, 11-32; L33C

Tax collectors and sinners were all
    drawing near to listen to Jesus,
but the Pharisees and scribes
    began to complain, saying,
"This man welcomes sinners and
    eats with them."
So to them Jesus addressed this
    parable:
"A man had two sons, and the
    younger son said to his father,
    'Father give me the share of your
    estate that should come to me.'
So the father divided the property be-
    tween them.
After a few days, the younger son col-
    lected all his belongings
    and set off to a distant country
    where he squandered his inheri-
    tance on a life of dissipation.
When he had freely spent everything,
    a severe famine struck that
        country,
    and he found himself in dire need.
So he hired himself out to one of the
    local citizens
    who sent him to his farm to tend
    the swine.
And he longed to eat his fill of the pods on
    which the swine fed,
    but nobody gave him any.
Coming to his senses he thought,
    'How many of my father's hired workers
    have more than enough food to eat,
    but here am I, dying from hunger.
I shall get up and go to my father and I shall
    say to him,
    "Father, I have sinned against heaven and
    against you.

Continued in Appendix A, p. 279.

Year A readings may be used, see Appendix A, pp. 280–281.

Reflecting on the Gospel

The journalist Marina Cantacuzino founded in England the Forgiveness Project, a group that works with grassroots organizations for reconciliation, conflict resolution, and restorative justice through victim support. In 2004, they held what they called "The F Word" exhibition in the Oxo Gallery of London's South Bank. It was neither pornographic nor a study of popular slang usage. The "f" stood for "forgiveness" and consisted of a collection of photographs matched with twenty-six personal stories of forgiveness and reconciliation from South Africa, Romania, Ukraine, Israel, Palestine, Northern Ireland, and England. The Forgiveness Project continues to build and expand such words and images, and offers a traveling exhibition. Marina comments that for some people, "forgiveness" is still a "dirty word." One of the exhibition's patrons is Archbishop Desmond Tutu, much experienced in the South African Truth and Reconciliation Commission. In today's gospel, Jesus gives us his own words and a memorable image of forgiveness and reconciliation in the parable of the Prodigal Son.

The compassionate love of God in Christ is always ready to forgive sinners and welcome them home. This is the challenging truth that Jesus proclaims—to the consolation of the tax collectors and sinners, and the dismay of the Pharisees and scribes who were his audience. Today we are Jesus's Lenten audience. We are called to listen to the story of two brothers, neither of whom really knows what it means to be the son of a father who is prodigal in his love.

The parable begins with the "want" of the younger son, a demand to have his share of his inheritance. In Middle Eastern context, this amounted to wishing that his father was dead, since that was the rightful time for inheritance. As a foolish lover, the father gives not only the younger son what he demands, but "divided his property between them"—that is, he included the older brother. In fact, the latter, as the elder, would receive double the share (Deut 21:17-21). This son, therefore, skulks selfishly, hypocritically in the background until the end of the parable when he is revealed for what he really is. Even though he remains physically at home, he is also in the "far country" of misunderstanding and intolerance of either his father or his brother. And contrary to social expectations of an elder brother in his culture, he does nothing to promote understanding or reconciliation between them.

The father is only concerned with being a loving father, and so he allows his younger son the freedom to reject his love. The wants of this boy lead him where he certainly did not intend to go when he left home: to enslavement to a Gentile boss in a Gentile pigsty, to starvation, and to physical and spiritual impoverishment. By looking after pigs, he makes himself ritually unclean, so squandering a second inheritance: his Jewish faith. At this crisis point, the boy sits down, "[c]oming to his senses"—working it all out in the first person: *I* will do this and that; *I* will go home and do the work of a hired hand so that *I* can pay back my debts; *I* will explain everything to my father and express my regret at what *I* have done. But coming to his senses doesn't reconcile the son; coming to his father will.

During Lent, the church calls us to remember the gifts of God that we have squandered and that have led us into the small or greater mess of our spiritual "pigsty." With great wisdom, the church also knows that we need this time of heightened awareness of our compassionate Father who embraces us in the outstretched arms of the Crucified.

Focusing the Gospel
Key words and phrases: "This man welcomes sinners and eats with them."

To the point: Today's gospel is well known for the value it places on welcoming those who have turned away. However, it is worth looking at where Jesus stands when he shares this parable: in the midst of tax collectors and sinners. Jesus isn't preaching to faithful Jews; he's preaching to a group of people whom the faithful Jews want nothing to do with. By physically aligning himself with sinners, Jesus delivers his message in a way that the Pharisees find threatening. They are used to avoiding sinners and keeping themselves "clean" by staying away from those who threaten their holiness. Jesus does not espouse this mindset. He goes into a crowd of sinners and shares a story of a sinner being accepted.

How do you think the father in this parable felt during the time that his son was away? Do you think the father turned all of his attention to the second, faithful son? Do you think the father thought and prayed about his far-off son? "While he was still a long way off, his father caught sight of him, and was filled with compassion." His father saw him coming before he had arrived. Perhaps the father was even waiting. Perhaps he had been waiting a long time. Jesus does not stand in a crowd of faithful to welcome home sinners. He goes to the sinners, seeing them even though they are a long way off.

Connecting the Gospel
to the second reading: Paul tells us, "Whoever is in Christ is a new creation: the old things have passed away; behold, new things have come." When a sinner comes to Christ, that sinner is made new. "And all this is from God, who has reconciled us to himself through Christ and given us the ministry of reconciliation." We hear much about the sacrament of reconciliation, but do you participate in the ministry of reconciliation? Do you wait for sinners to return to Christ? Do you go out and accompany those who do not feel invited into God's message? Do you sit beside those who cling to the "old things" because they fear encountering the new?

to experience: The readings today give us the opportunity to place ourselves in the midst of the sinner. It is one thing to welcome a sinner back into the fold, but an entirely different experience to go out into the world—our neighborhoods, schools, communities—and share space with sinners. This is the ministry of reconciliation, so that we, like the father in today's gospel, can see someone coming from a long way off.

Connecting the Responsorial Psalm
to the readings: "Look to him that you may be radiant with joy, / and your faces may not blush with shame." When the son returns to his father, he is filled with shame, but the father lifts him from it. The psalm reminds us of this salvific love, which is so full of goodness that it welcomes us without shame.

to psalmist preparation: How would you pray if you knew you did not need to have shame? How would you speak to the Lord if you truly believed that everything you shared, God considered sacred? Bring this openness and confidence to your congregation today. Truly see the goodness of the Lord.

PROMPTS FOR FAITH-SHARING

Who do you consider to be a "sinner"? Do you avoid people like this? Why or why not?

What do you think is the benefit of placing yourself beside sinners?

When was a time you were the Prodigal Son? Or the father? Or the other brother?

How do you participate in the ministry of reconciliation?

CELEBRATION

Model Penitential Act

Presider: In today's gospel, Jesus shares a parable to illustrate the immense love God has for us. For the times we have rejected that love, we ask God for forgiveness and mercy . . . *[pause]*

Confiteor: I confess . . .

Homily Points

• How often have we heard this parable and tried to place ourselves in the position of one of the two brothers? So often we can be quick to recognize our own sinfulness and shortcomings and take the position of the younger brother. Likewise, there are probably times when we have acted more like the older brother, quick to condemn someone and point out that person's flaws and shortcomings. Like all of Jesus's parables, however, the story is not about us.

• Instead, this story reveals something spectacular about the nature of God. The father in today's story would be well within his authority to ignore the return of his younger son. Why shouldn't he? The son asked for his share of inheritance, basically telling his father, "I wish you were dead." It would be perfectly understandable for the father to resist the son's vain and self-concerned apology. Even so, the father patiently kept watch for the return of his son, ready to welcome him back. Luke writes, "While he was still a long way off, his father caught sight of him, and was filled with compassion." In sharing this parable, Jesus tells us about the incredible nature of the God who loves us beyond any of our faults and shortcomings. Even when we are a long way off from who we are called to be, God waits for us to return.

• In the second reading, Paul implores his followers to be reconciled to God. We are called to return to God, recognizing that we are sinful and will fail again. We fall short no matter how hard we try. We can rest, however, knowing that God waits for us to return, ready to greet us from a long way off and hold us in love and esteem. As Pope Francis says in *Evangelii Gaudium,* "God never tires of forgiving us; we are the ones who tire of seeking [God's] mercy." We pray that we may have the strength and courage to always accept God's loving embrace.

Model Universal Prayer (Prayer of the Faithful)

Presider: Knowing that our God hears us and wraps us in mercy, we confidently share our needs and petitions:

Response: Lord, hear our prayer.

That the church may witness the mercy of God, always sharing love and forgiveness with people who might be often excluded or marginalized in our society . . .

That local and world leaders might lead efforts toward reconciliation between peoples, families, communities, and nations . . .

That all who believe that they are undeserving of God's love may know their own beloved-ness in God's eyes . . .

That all gathered here might open their hearts and minds to God's love and mercy, and stand ready and willing to share this love and mercy with all peoples . . .

Presider: Loving God, our needs are no surprise to you. In your love and mercy, hear these prayers and answer them according to your will, that we might always grow in relationship with you. We ask this through Christ our Lord. **Amen.**

COLLECT
Let us pray.

Pause for silent prayer

O God, who through your Word
reconcile the human race to yourself in a
 wonderful way,
grant, we pray,
that with prompt devotion and eager faith
the Christian people may hasten
toward the solemn celebrations to come.
Through our Lord Jesus Christ, your Son,
who lives and reigns with you in the unity
 of the Holy Spirit,
God, for ever and ever. **Amen.**

FIRST READING
Josh 5:9a, 10-12

The LORD said to Joshua,
 "Today I have removed the reproach of
 Egypt from you."

While the Israelites were encamped at
 Gilgal on the plains of Jericho,
 they celebrated the Passover
 on the evening of the fourteenth of the
 month.
On the day after the Passover,
 they ate of the produce of the land
 in the form of unleavened cakes and
 parched grain.
On that same day after the Passover,
 on which they ate of the produce of the
 land, the manna ceased.
No longer was there manna for the
 Israelites,
 who that year ate of the yield of the
 land of Canaan.

RESPONSORIAL PSALM

Ps 34:2-3, 4-5, 6-7

R). (9a) Taste and see the goodness of the Lord.

I will bless the LORD at all times;
  his praise shall be ever in my mouth.
Let my soul glory in the LORD;
  the lowly will hear me and be glad.

R). Taste and see the goodness of the Lord.

Glorify the LORD with me,
  let us together extol his name.
I sought the LORD, and he answered me
  and delivered me from all my fears.

R). Taste and see the goodness of the Lord.

Look to him that you may be radiant with joy,
  and your faces may not blush with shame.
When the poor one called out, the LORD heard,
  and from all his distress he saved him.

R). Taste and see the goodness of the Lord.

SECOND READING

2 Cor 5:17-21

Brothers and sisters:
Whoever is in Christ is a new creation:
  the old things have passed away;
  behold, new things have come.
And all this is from God,
  who has reconciled us to himself
    through Christ
  and given us the ministry of
    reconciliation,
  namely, God was reconciling the world
    to himself in Christ,
  not counting their trespasses against
    them
  and entrusting to us the message of
    reconciliation.
So we are ambassadors for Christ,
  as if God were appealing through us.
We implore you on behalf of Christ,
  be reconciled to God.
For our sake he made him to be sin who
    did not know sin,
  so that we might become the
    righteousness of God in him.

About Liturgy

Eyelash to Eyelash: In last year's edition of *Living Liturgy*, I noted that the Latin roots of the word "reconciliation" are, syllable by syllable, "re," which means again; "con," which means with; and "cilia," which is the Latin word for eyelash. So then "re-con-cilia-tion" means "to again be eyelash to eyelash with [someone]."

Ask yourself, on a weekend when the readings so strongly point us toward that kind of true reconciliation, can you imagine being so intimately close to the person with whom you most strongly disagree? If you're like me, that's a hard image to conjure. Yet it is that kind of intimacy and union which we're all called to, with those we simply can't stand, and even with those we have not met yet.

In the liturgical realm, we might have disagreements with many people, particularly concerning styles of ritual practice and music and musical forms suitable for worship. The disagreements in themselves are not bad, and can even be healthy—if we are willing to, by love, be eyelash to eyelash with those same individuals. When it comes to linguistic or cultural experiences in liturgy, one of the typical questions is whether to include a particular language in our liturgies *because* those who speak the language are already in the pews, or whether to adapt that practice as a way to be more welcoming to those who are so often kept on the margins? The church is universal after all, in every time and place.

About Liturgical Documents

Sing to the Lord—Diversity and Inclusion: We can see, with so many references to music and singing in our sacred Scriptures, that music is an integral part of not only our human experience, but our faith experience as well. It encompasses all human emotions; it encompasses all human prayer to the divine including prayers of praise, thanksgiving, petition, and lament—all is made even more communicative and indeed more holy through our voices raised in song. You may have heard a quote attributed to St. Augustine: "Who sings well prays twice."

Sing to the Lord, which we began looking at last week, offers a few practical and tangible ideas and guidelines for the fullness of what a music ministry can and should be—for as successful as any ministry already is, there are always ways to be a more expansive and complete ministry. Much of what STL offers is likely already common practice where you are. Some details, though, may be surprising, or at least not well represented in many parishes. For instance, STL offers these instructions:

> Liturgical music today must reflect the multicultural diversity and intercultural relationships of the members of the gathered liturgical assembly. The varied use of musical forms . . . can assist in weaving the diverse languages and ethnicities of the liturgical assembly into a tapestry of sung praise. (60)

> The use of the vernacular is the norm in most liturgical celebrations in the dioceses of the United States "for the sake of a better comprehension of the mystery being celebrated." However, care should be taken to foster the role of Latin in the Liturgy, particularly in liturgical song. (61)

STL suggests that parishes—ones with a multicultural congregation already or indeed ones not (yet) as diverse—ought to consider praying and singing in languages, occasionally, beyond English, including Latin and other languages represented in the church universal.

About Music

Music for Reconciliation and Feasting: Hymns that speaks well to the gospel passage include "I Come with Joy," text by Brian Wren, and "As We Gather at Your Table" by Carl Daw (both from Hope Publishing), found in several hymnals.

MARCH 27, 2022
FOURTH SUNDAY OF LENT

✝ SPIRITUALITY

GOSPEL ACCLAMATION
Joel 2:12-13

Even now, says the Lord,
return to me with your whole heart;
for I am gracious and merciful.

Gospel   John 8:1-11; L36C

Jesus went to the Mount of Olives.
But early in the morning he arrived again
    in the temple area,
    and all the people started coming to him,
    and he sat down and taught them.
Then the scribes and the Pharisees
    brought a woman
who had been caught in adultery
and made her stand in the middle.
They said to him,
    "Teacher, this woman was caught
    in the very act of committing adultery.
Now in the law, Moses commanded us to
    stone such women.
So what do you say?"
They said this to test him,
    so that they could have some charge to
        bring against him.
Jesus bent down and began to write on
    the ground with his finger.
But when they continued asking him,
    he straightened up and said to them,
    "Let the one among you who is without
        sin
    be the first to throw a stone at her."
Again he bent down and wrote on the
    ground.
And in response, they went away one by
    one,
    beginning with the elders.
So he was left alone with the woman be-
    fore him.
Then Jesus straightened up and said to her,
    "Woman, where are they?
Has no one condemned you?"
She replied, "No one, sir."
Then Jesus said, "Neither do I condemn
    you.
Go, and from now on do not sin any more."

*Year A readings may be used, see Appendix A,
pp. 282–283.*

Reflecting on the Gospel

A woman has been dragged from the act of intercourse with a man not her husband and now cowers in the temple court before her accusers, the scribes and Pharisees. They approach Jesus with the dilemma they have carefully orchestrated. Jesus is actually the first one they want to put on trial.

With mock reverence for the "Teacher," they put the case to Jesus. If Jesus argues that the woman should not be stoned, he violates the Mosaic teaching and the community tradition. If he says she should be stoned, he will violate his own compassionate teaching and be regarded by many as a charlatan who preaches one thing and does another. "So what do you say?" they ask Jesus. The stones that the Mosaic teaching dictated should be hurled at both the woman and her male sexual partner (Lev 20:10; Deut 22:22) are already heaped up in the hearts of her accusers.

Bent over, silent, eyes fixed on the ground, Jesus assumes the same stance as the woman. But then he straightens up and tosses at the accusers of both of them his conclusion: "Let the one among you who is without sin be the first to throw a stone at her" (John 8:7). The scribes and Pharisees realize suddenly that they themselves are now on trial. One by one they drift away. Is their exit according to seniority, a last clutch at remnants of their respectability? Or is it that the older they are, the more they may have to read in their hearts about a wife, a daughter, a granddaughter, an unknown woman in a brothel?

Now, for the first time, the woman is addressed as a human being. Jesus speaks to her as more than just a heap of evil that has been dumped in the temple and must be cleaned out as soon as possible. There is only one stone thrown in this incident: the stone of mercy which Jesus casts at the devastated and violated woman as he assures her that no one has condemned her, especially not himself. His concern is more for the woman's future than for her past: "Go, and from now on do not sin any more." This is no moralizing lecture, simply the powerful command of love lived for her at a moment of great risk for both of them.

Sometimes, especially as we read and pray the Scriptures reflectively, we can allow our imagination to lead us deeper into the heart of Jesus, into his human memory and experience. Reflecting on this gospel, might we wonder if, on that temple morning, he remembered his own mother: the fear—holy yet human—she must have experienced, the gossip she probably endured about her pregnancy. And did Jesus also remember the gentle and just man named Joseph, who would not cast a stone?

Far away from the temple, in our own experience, are we tempted to use the sins of others to mask our own self-righteousness, our personal failures and limitations? What attitude do we show to those who believe they have the right to arbitrarily dispense death by war, capital punishment, euthanasia, abortion, or subtle defamation? Are we brave enough to oppose their ethic, in personal encounter or by the ballot box? Do we pray that they will read their own hearts and change them? And are some of us still most condemnatory about those who sin against the two commandments that seem to be written larger than the other eight in our Christian psyches because they are concerned with things sexual? What we need to heap up in our own hearts and in our church is compassion that heals, not stones that hurt.

Focusing the Gospel

Key words and phrases: "So he was left alone with the woman before him. Then Jesus straightened up and said to her, 'Woman, where are they? Has no one condemned you?' She replied, 'No one, sir.'"

To the point: In today's gospel, we hear that Jesus went off to pray alone, then returned and was swarmed by those who wanted to hear him speak. In the midst of this bout of celebrity, the Pharisees, already uncomfortable with what Jesus is doing in the Jewish community, try to use theatrical punishment to turn the mood. They're trying to catch him in a lie and make him resort to violence. He does neither of these things. Instead, he ignores them, and when pestered, he flips their judgment back on them. It's not only an extremely deft moment of rhetoric, but a way to completely diffuse the tension. And what's the result? A sinner repents. The woman who committed adultery and was being manipulated by social shame in order to make a point, who could have been violently harmed, walks away a better person.

Connecting the Gospel

to the second reading: Paul also gives us an unexpected reaction, when he states, "For his sake I have accepted the loss of all things and I consider them so much rubbish, that I may gain Christ and be found in him." Accepting the loss of all things, and calling them trash, is a bold statement to make. More and more, our world hinges on the transient currency of material and capital, instead of the necessary realities of truth and justice. Paul reminds us that detachment is not the goal in itself, but only a step along the way to maturity. "It is not that I have already taken hold of it or have already attained perfect maturity, but I continue my pursuit in hope that I may possess it, since I have indeed been taken possession of by Christ Jesus."

to experience: "For his sake I have accepted the loss of all things." Is there something that you have recently lost? Perhaps you've lost a family member or friend to illness, or a job or opportunity. Perhaps you've had an argument with someone close to you. Think about the things you have "lost" recently and put them in the context of Paul's words. Lost things are not truly lost if our pursuit is heaven.

Connecting the Responsorial Psalm

to the readings: In this week's gospel, the Lord "does great things" for a sinner, even saving her from physical violence. "Although they go forth weeping, / carrying the seed to be sown, / they shall come back rejoicing, / carrying their sheaves."

to psalmist preparation: Call to mind recent events or relationships that have brought you consolation. Spend some time going over these great things, and let the joy of them resonate in you.

PROMPTS FOR FAITH-SHARING

When have you been the adulterous woman? When have you been the Pharisee?

Have you ever been in the middle of a heated situation and then diffused the anger? How did you accomplish this? What does it take to encourage indignant people to calm down?

What is one way that you can detach yourself from material things this week?

What is one "great thing" the Lord has done for you recently? Why did it bring you consolation?

Model Penitential Act

Presider: In today's gospel an angry crowd stands ready to condemn and punish the woman caught in adultery. For the times we have condemned others and sought punishment instead of reconciliation, we ask for God's pardon and peace . . . *[pause]*

    Confiteor: I confess . . .

Homily Points

• Today's gospel challenges us on a number of levels, as it always seems easier to point out someone else's sins rather than recognizing our own need for conversion. What is it about human nature that makes this so? In describing the differences and growing tensions between people, John Steinbeck writes in *The Grapes of Wrath*, "They reassured themselves that they were good and the intruders bad, as a man must do before he fights." It is so easy to create "the other," the outsider. *She is not like us. She is other. They believe something different than we do. They are other.*

• So many of the difficult situations we encounter stem from creating a sense of otherness. We do this in the workplace, in schools, and even in church. But Isaiah speaks to the promise that Jesus brings to fulfillment: "Remember not the events of the past, the things of long ago consider not; see, I am doing something new!" Rather than focusing on what separates us from others or increasing the chasm of difference, Jesus offers another way. Jesus points to forgiveness and reconciliation.

• Today's gospel foreshadows what we will experience next week in Holy Week. Just as Jesus transforms the situation with the woman from violence to forgiveness, he himself will show the life that springs from death. Jesus did not condemn but forgives, loves, and welcomes. He tells the woman and each of us, "Go, and from now on do not sin any more." As we come to the end of this Lenten season, are we willing to extend the forgiveness Jesus offers to others? Perhaps more importantly, are we willing to accept Jesus's forgiveness ourselves?

Model Universal Prayer (Prayer of the Faithful)

Presider: Knowing that God is full of mercy and kindness, we bring our prayers and petitions to the God of love.

Response: Lord, hear our prayer.

That clergy and church leaders live as authentic messengers of mercy . . .

That world leaders and nations may seek peaceful resolutions and end the use of nuclear weapons and weapons of mass destruction . . .

That all who feel guilt or shame may know their self-worth and the gifts they share . . .

That all gathered here might witness to the mercy of Christ in these final days of Lent . . .

Presider: Hear our prayers, O God, and in your great mercy answer them according to your will. We ask this through Christ our Lord. **Amen.**

COLLECT

Let us pray.

Pause for silent prayer

By your help, we beseech you, Lord our
    God,
may we walk eagerly in that same charity
with which, out of love for the world,
your Son handed himself over to death.
Through our Lord Jesus Christ, your Son,
who lives and reigns with you in the unity
    of the Holy Spirit,
God, for ever and ever. **Amen.**

FIRST READING
Isa 43:16-21

Thus says the LORD,
    who opens a way in the sea
    and a path in the mighty waters,
who leads out chariots and horsemen,
    a powerful army,
till they lie prostrate together, never to rise,
    snuffed out and quenched like a wick.
Remember not the events of the past,
    the things of long ago consider not;
see, I am doing something new!
    Now it springs forth, do you not
        perceive it?
In the desert I make a way,
    in the wasteland, rivers.
Wild beasts honor me,
    jackals and ostriches,
for I put water in the desert
    and rivers in the wasteland
    for my chosen people to drink,
the people whom I formed for myself,
    that they might announce my praise.

RESPONSORIAL PSALM
Ps 126:1-2, 2-3, 4-5, 6

℟. (3) The Lord has done great things for
    us; we are filled with joy.

When the LORD brought back the captives
    of Zion,
    we were like men dreaming.
Then our mouth was filled with laughter,
    and our tongue with rejoicing.

℟. The Lord has done great things for us;
    we are filled with joy.

Then they said among the nations,
    "The LORD has done great things for
        them."
The LORD has done great things for us;
    we are glad indeed.

℟. The Lord has done great things for us;
    we are filled with joy.

Restore our fortunes, O Lord,
    like the torrents in the southern desert.
Those that sow in tears
    shall reap rejoicing.

℟. The Lord has done great things for us;
    we are filled with joy.

Although they go forth weeping,
    carrying the seed to be sown,
they shall come back rejoicing,
    carrying their sheaves.

℟. The Lord has done great things for us;
    we are filled with joy.

SECOND READING
Phil 3:8-14

Brothers and sisters:
I consider everything as a loss
    because of the supreme good of
        knowing Christ Jesus my Lord.
For his sake I have accepted the loss of all
        things
    and I consider them so much rubbish,
    that I may gain Christ and be found in
        him,
    not having any righteousness of my
        own based on the law
    but that which comes through faith in
        Christ,
    the righteousness from God,
    depending on faith to know him and the
        power of his resurrection
    and the sharing of his sufferings by being
        conformed to his death,
    if somehow I may attain the
        resurrection from the dead.

It is not that I have already taken hold of it
    or have already attained perfect maturity,
    but I continue my pursuit in hope that I
        may possess it,
    since I have indeed been taken
        possession of by Christ Jesus.
Brothers and sisters, I for my part
    do not consider myself to have taken
        possession.
Just one thing: forgetting what lies behind
    but straining forward to what lies
        ahead,
    I continue my pursuit toward the goal,
    the prize of God's upward calling, in
        Christ Jesus.

About Liturgical Documents

Sing to the Lord—Style Wars: "'The Church recognizes Gregorian chant as being specially suited to the Roman Liturgy. Therefore, other things being equal, it should be given pride of place in liturgical services.' . . . The 'pride of place' given to Gregorian chant by the Second Vatican Council is modified by the important phrase 'other things being equal.' . . . In considering the use of the treasures of chant, pastors and liturgical musicians should take care that the congregation is able to participate in the Liturgy with song. They should be sensitive to the cultural and spiritual milieu of their communities, in order to build up the Church in unity and peace" (STL 72–73).

Many parishes occasionally sing some Gregorian chant: an *Agnus Dei* during Lent perhaps, or an *Ave Maria* at funerals. It is likely an error to do too much chant, especially if that's not a parish's present practice; nor though do we want to abandon completely the church's musical tradition and history. Similarly, with regard to instrumentation:

> Among all other instruments which are suitable for divine worship, the organ is "accorded pride of place" because of its capacity to sustain the singing of a large gathered assembly, due to both its size and its ability to give "resonance to the fullness of human sentiments, from joy to sadness, from praise to lamentation." Likewise, "the manifold possibilities of the organ in some way remind us of the immensity and the magnificence of God." (STL 87)

> However, from the days when the Ark of the Covenant was accompanied in procession by cymbals, harps, lyres, and trumpets, God's people have, in various periods, used a variety of musical instruments to sing his praise. Each of these instruments, born of the culture and the traditions of a particular people, has given voice to a wide variety of forms and styles through which Christ's faithful continue to join their voices to his perfect song of praise upon the Cross. Many other instruments also enrich the celebration of the Liturgy, such as wind, stringed, or percussion instruments "according to longstanding local usage, provided they are truly apt for sacred use or can be rendered apt." (STL 89–90)

Again, these words from Sing to the Lord are guidelines, not laws, but they hopefully give any parish some room to consider questions like these: Is our parish music ministry successful in every way it can be? Which aspects of our music ministries do we do well? Which aspects need improvement, or are not represented at all? How can I be a part of creating a growing and expansive music ministry—one that draws from all times, geographies, languages, and cultures, and one that is relevant, welcoming, and prayerful for all God's people?

About Music

Forgiveness: There are any number of songs that speak to the nature of forgiveness and life in Christ. Consider "Take from My Heart" or "The Path of Mercy" by John T. Kyler and Karen Schneider Kirner (WLP/GIA).

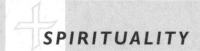

SPIRITUALITY

GOSPEL ACCLAMATION
Phil 2:8-9

Christ became obedient to the point of death,
even death on a cross.
Because of this, God greatly exalted him
and bestowed on him the name which is above
    every name.

Gospel at the Procession with Palms
Luke 19:28-40; L37C

Jesus proceeded on his journey up to
    Jerusalem.
As he drew near to Bethphage and
    Bethany
  at the place called the Mount of Olives,
  he sent two of his disciples.
He said, "Go into the village opposite you,
  and as you enter it you will find a colt
    tethered
  on which no one has ever sat.
Untie it and bring it here.
And if anyone should ask you,
  'Why are you untying it?'
  you will answer,
  'The Master has need of it.'"
So those who had been sent went off
  and found everything just as he had
    told them.
And as they were untying the colt, its
    owners said to them,
  "Why are you untying this colt?"
They answered,
  "The Master has need of it."
So they brought it to Jesus,
  threw their cloaks over the colt,
  and helped Jesus to mount.
As he rode along,
  the people were spreading their cloaks
    on the road;
  and now as he was approaching the
    slope of the Mount of Olives,
  the whole multitude of his disciples
  began to praise God aloud with joy
  for all the mighty deeds they had seen.

Continued in Appendix A, p. 284.

Gospel at Mass   Luke 22:14–23:56; L38ABC
or Luke 23:1-49 *in Appendix A, pp. 284–287.*

Reflecting on the Gospel

Just before the Last Supper, "Satan entered into Judas, the one surnamed Iscariot" (Luke 22:3), and we recognize that the sword of Simeon's prophecy hangs over those whom we meet in the Last Supper narrative. Even with Jesus's chosen disciples, some will fall, some will rise, some will both fall and rise. We can identify with all of them in large or small ways. Jesus sits at table and announces at the beginning of the meal that this is to be his last. Bread and cup become an event of Body and Blood, of the whole person and presence of Jesus, which establishes a new relationship of participating in and sharing his life. Tonight the disciples recline around the table with him; tomorrow they will decline to be guests at the board of the cross.

And then it is off to the Mount of Olives: to agony among the generations of olive trees where Jesus lies among them like a protruding root, struggling in prayer to surrender to his Father's will. For the three apostles with him, it is escapism into sleep. Then comes the pain of betrayal by a friend, the sword-slashing panic by the awakened apostles, and the command of nonviolence from Jesus. Arrested and parceled up in false accusations, Jesus is sent from one judgment seat to another: from Pilate to Herod, from Herod back to Pilate, wrapped in insult.

All Jesus's friends are scattered; even Peter follows only "at a distance." He, too, is put on trial by a servant girl outside Pilate's courtroom, and a cock's crow brings in the verdict of shameful guilt. But when Jesus is brought out, he passes by Peter, turns and looks at him . . . and Peter is saved. He realizes that his master will never turn away from him. Then he remembers his master's words and weeps bitterly at their truth and his untruthfulness. The same realization, the same remembering, the same tears will save every disciple.

Scourged and mocked, Jesus is led out to his death—the innocent, nonviolent victim of the sin of the world. A man from the country, Simon of Cyrene, is made to help him carry his cross, but Jesus is the Servant who will still reach out to others. When some of the women of Jerusalem follow him like a mourning chorus, Jesus ministers to their grief but begs them to make it a larger lamentation for all those who are unfaithful to their God. On Golgotha, Jesus ministers also to the poor criminal who recognizes him as a just one. Lover of sinners to the end, Jesus allows this thief to "steal" Paradise from him. Then Luke puts on Jesus's lips the words of Psalm 31: "Into your hands I commend my spirit," a gentler dying prayer than Mark's or Matthew's cry of "My God, my God, why have you abandoned me?" (Ps 22:2). Quietly, Jesus escapes, like a bird freed from a trap, into his Father's hands.

For a moment, then, we go down silently on our knees, rising up to hear the faith of a non-Gentile proclaim before the human wreck of a dead man: "This man was innocent beyond doubt." This is the faith that will take us through Holy Week and through the killing fields in our own world. Hopefully, too, we will minister like Joseph of Arimathea: taking the wounded body of Christ, our suffering sisters and brothers, off their crosses, wrapping them in our compassion, and advocating for them before the powerful with gentle but brave persistence.

Focusing the Gospel

Key words and phrases: "Just as he was saying this, the cock crowed, and the Lord turned and looked at Peter; and Peter remembered the word of the Lord."

To the point: Jesus is about to die, and he knows it, but the thing he is most concerned with is keeping his friends safe. He knows they will desert him when he needs them most. Jesus knows Peter isn't up to the task of vouching for him. But Jesus still tells them what's going to happen, because they are his friends, and he loves them.

This gospel is an opportunity for us to sympathize with Jesus. If your best friends stopped talking to you in the middle of a time you were going through a personal tragedy, would you still reach out to them? Would you forgive them? Or would you blame them for not having the strength to accompany you through your loss? Jesus is about to go through great physical and mental peril, and his primary concern is preparing his friends to help him, even though he knows they probably won't step up and follow through. There is a deep tenderness in these friendships— filial, platonic, and masculine—that exemplify the depth of Jesus's fraternal love for his friends. Jesus knows that Judas is going to hurt him, but Jesus doesn't call him out or shame him. Jesus lets Judas exercise free will, because Jesus loves every single one of those men praying with him, and he wants them to try.

Connecting the Gospel

to the first and second readings: Isaiah exemplifies the commitment that Jesus is hoping to receive from his friends. Even though Judas makes a terrible decision and Peter goes aloof, Jesus still calls them to the type of resolve Isaiah describes, because Jesus knows that it is possible, even if it won't happen. The standard doesn't change.

to experience: Jesus never once in his ministry waters down his message to make it more attainable. He elevates the standards of his friends over and over, and when they fail, he still loves them. Peter, a grand failure by all accounts, becomes the first pope. Because Peter keeps coming back. It would be wonderful to have the resolve of Isaiah, who has "a well-trained tongue, that [he] might know how to speak to the weary a word that will rouse them." But even when we fail, as Peter failed, and we let our friends down, "The Lord God is [our] help, therefore [we are] not disgraced."

Connecting the Responsorial Psalm

to the readings: Today's psalm is a glimpse into the mind of Jesus headed to Calvary. In between a declaration of abandonment is the narrative of someone who continues to rely on the Lord. The refrain is one of anguish, but the verses are steadfast in trust.

to psalmist preparation: It's likely that, since parishioners sing the refrain, they will focus on the imagery of being abandoned. It's your job to lean into the verses and really stress the trust the psalmist has. "But you, O LORD, be not far from me; / O my help, hasten to aid me."

Model Penitential Act

Presider: As we celebrate Palm Sunday, our proclamations of joy and acclamation quickly turn to shouts of condemnation and death. For the times when our words and actions have been inconsistent with who we are called to be, we ask for God's mercy and forgiveness . . . *[pause]*

   Confiteor: I confess . . .

Homily Points

• Blessed Basil Moreau, the founder of the Congregation of Holy Cross, wrote: "Human life is like a great way of the cross. We do not have to go to the chapel or church to go through the different stations. This Way of the Cross is everywhere, and we travel it every day, even in spite of ourselves and without being aware of it." Today we hear the Way of the Cross, the journey of Jesus's suffering and death. But as Moreau notes, the Way of the Cross is also something that we deeply embody in our everyday actions and interactions.

• When we think of the crosses we encounter today, it is easy to name events of death and destruction where people die of disease and famine and lack of resources. We see the greed and hate present in the ways people talk to and treat each other, especially people with different ideologies and beliefs. We see systemic racism and xenophobia that is so commonplace in our lives that we might even be unaware of it. But the cross is more than death and destruction. The cross is life. We see examples of this life when people practice humility and kindness in solidarity with each other. We encounter this life in self-gift, like Jesus who gave of himself for others. This *agapic* love is an essential and unavoidable part of the cross.

• Do we recognize this self-gift in our midst? Are we willing to see examples of this self-giving love in those we encounter? In teachers, in doctors, in first responders? In the self-giving love of parents caring for their children and children caring for their parents? In those who listen and hear us when we need to talk? Do we practice this self-gift we see in Jesus's suffering, death, and resurrection? When we do, we realize that suffering and death never win. Life and love always prevail.

Model Universal Prayer (Prayer of the Faithful)

Presider: The God who took on human form intimately knows our needs. With trust in this loving humility, we raise our prayers and petitions:

Response: Lord, hear our prayer.

That church leaders may dedicate themselves to the service of others and persevere through pain and difficulties to share Christ with the world . . .

That national and world leaders put an end to executions and the use of the death penalty as a means of punishment . . .

That all who suffer at the hands of government and civil leaders may find strength and resolve in Jesus Christ . . .

That our local community may recommit to recognizing the life and light that spring from death . . .

Presider: Loving God, you always hear our prayers. Journey with us this week as we commemorate the events of your life, death, and resurrection so that we might more fully enter into your paschal mystery. We ask this through Christ our Lord. **Amen.**

COLLECT
Let us pray.

Pause for silent prayer

Almighty ever-living God,
who as an example of humility for the
   human race to follow
caused our Savior to take flesh and submit
   to the Cross,
graciously grant that we may heed his
   lesson of patient suffering
and so merit a share in his Resurrection.
Who lives and reigns with you in the unity
   of the Holy Spirit,
God, for ever and ever. **Amen.**

FIRST READING
Isa 50:4-7

The Lord God has given me
   a well-trained tongue,
that I might know how to speak to the
   weary
   a word that will rouse them.
Morning after morning
   he opens my ear that I may hear;
and I have not rebelled,
   have not turned back.
I gave my back to those who beat me,
   my cheeks to those who plucked my
     beard;
my face I did not shield
   from buffets and spitting.

The Lord God is my help,
   therefore I am not disgraced;
I have set my face like flint,
   knowing that I shall not be put to
     shame.

RESPONSORIAL PSALM
Ps 22:8-9, 17-18, 19-20, 23-24

℟. (2a) My God, my God, why have you
   abandoned me?

All who see me scoff at me;
   they mock me with parted lips, they
     wag their heads:
"He relied on the Lord; let him deliver him,
   let him rescue him, if he loves him."

℟. My God, my God, why have you
   abandoned me?

Indeed, many dogs surround me,
   a pack of evildoers closes in upon me;
they have pierced my hands and my feet;
   I can count all my bones.

R℣. My God, my God, why have you
   abandoned me?

They divide my garments among them,
   and for my vesture they cast lots.
But you, O LORD, be not far from me;
   O my help, hasten to aid me.

R℣. My God, my God, why have you
   abandoned me?

I will proclaim your name to my brethren;
   in the midst of the assembly I will
      praise you:
"You who fear the LORD, praise him;
   all you descendants of Jacob, give glory
      to him;
   revere him, all you descendants of
      Israel!"

R℣. My God, my God, why have you
   abandoned me?

SECOND READING
Phil 2:6-11

Christ Jesus, though he was in the form
      of God,
   did not regard equality with God
   something to be grasped.
Rather, he emptied himself,
   taking the form of a slave,
   coming in human likeness;
   and found human in appearance,
   he humbled himself,
   becoming obedient to the point of
      death,
   even death on a cross.
Because of this, God greatly exalted him
   and bestowed on him the name
   which is above every name,
   that at the name of Jesus
   every knee should bend,
   of those in heaven and on earth and
      under the earth,
   and every tongue confess that
   Jesus Christ is Lord,
   to the glory of God the Father.

About Liturgy

Regarding Evaluating Liturgy: With Holy Week upon us, we will want to be attuned to the upcoming celebrations and gauge their execution, effectiveness, and many other details. We should always strive to ensure our liturgies are the best they can possibly be. Effective evaluation of liturgy, broadly, includes three steps.

First, in advance, we should set goals and principles that can be either qualitatively or quantitatively measured; second, we must pledge not to evaluate the liturgy *while it is happening*; third, we ought to engage in critical discussions soon after the liturgies, specifically about the particular goals and principles set ahead of time.

Setting goals about what will be evaluated helps to focus later discussion and can help create actionable results from that discussion, especially if the evaluation includes the "right" people and occurs soon after the liturgies so the memories are still fresh in everyone's minds.

It's tempting to, at least personally, evaluate the liturgies while they are occurring, but our first focus must be the prayer of these moments or our leadership of them. A helpful practice here is keeping one worship aid (or perhaps a small notebook or a smartphone note) separate, on which, after liturgy, you can jot down some notes to help your evaluation process later.

About Liturgical Documents

Sing to the Lord—Recorded Music: Regarding the complications that necessarily arise when considering an outdoor procession (for instance, on Palm Sunday), we should always remember that the church wishes for authenticity in all things: liturgical objects, postures, gestures, furnishings, etc. Yet a couple paragraphs in Sing to the Lord, while noting this ideal, might surprise you with their approach to prerecorded music:

> Recorded music lacks the authenticity provided by a living liturgical assembly gathered for the Sacred Liturgy. While recorded music might be used advantageously outside the Liturgy as an aid in the teaching of new music, it should not, as a general norm, be used within the Liturgy.

> Some exceptions to this principle should be noted. Recorded music may be used to accompany the community's song during a procession outside and, when used carefully, in Masses with children. Occasionally, it might be used as an aid to prayer, for example, during long periods of silence in a communal celebration of reconciliation. However, recorded music should never become a substitute for the community's singing. (STL 93–94)

About Music

Jesus Christ Is Lord: One of the trickiest scriptural texts to set to music is the Philippians canticle, which is today's epistle reading. It is tricky for at least a couple reasons. First, the tone of the music can take various "feels" and one of those, say "jubilantly victorious," may be appropriate in one liturgical context but not another. Second, the subtleties of the text do not lend themselves well to poetic adaptation, or at least risk losing particular meaning or worse— drifting into vaguely heretical places!

A couple settings of this text that might serve congregations well today include, in a contemporary style, "Jesus, Only Jesus" (Redman, Tomlin, et al., WN) and "At the Name of Jesus" by James E. Clemens, set as a memorable canon, perhaps also useful as processional music.

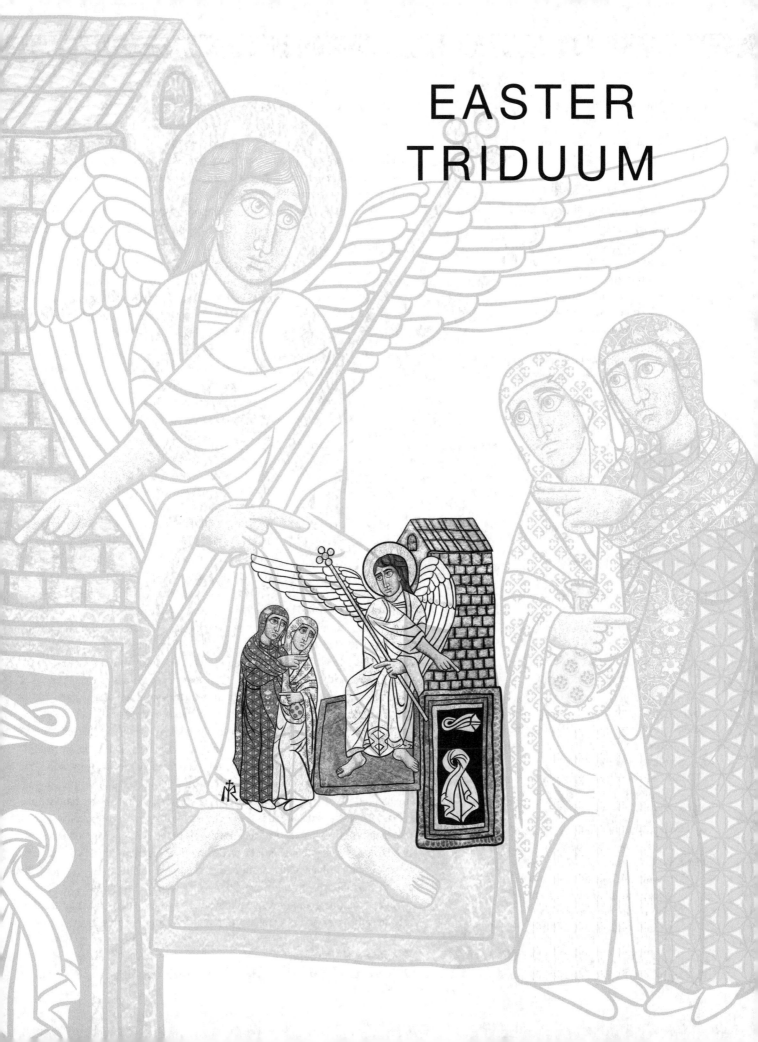

EASTER
TRIDUUM

GOSPEL ACCLAMATION
John 13:34

I give you a new commandment, says the Lord:
love one another as I have loved you.

Gospel   John 13:1-15; L39ABC

Before the feast of Passover, Jesus knew
      that his hour had come
   to pass from this world to the Father.
He loved his own in the world and
      he loved them to the end.
The devil had already induced
      Judas, son of Simon the Is-
      cariot, to hand him over.
So, during supper,
   fully aware that the Father had
      put everything into his
      power
   and that he had come from God
      and was returning to God,
   he rose from supper and took
      off his outer garments.
He took a towel and tied it around
      his waist.
Then he poured water into a basin
   and began to wash the disciples'
      feet
   and dry them with the towel
      around his waist.
He came to Simon Peter, who said
      to him,
   "Master, are you going to wash my
      feet?"
Jesus answered and said to him,
   "What I am doing, you do not
      understand now,
   but you will understand later."
Peter said to him, "You will never wash
      my feet."
Jesus answered him,
   "Unless I wash you, you will have no
      inheritance with me."
Simon Peter said to him,
   "Master, then not only my feet, but my
      hands and head as well."
Jesus said to him,
   "Whoever has bathed has no need
      except to have his feet washed,
   for he is clean all over;
   so you are clean, but not all."

Continued in Appendix A, p. 288.
See Appendix A, p. 288, for the other readings.

Reflecting on the Gospel

Tonight we do not hear a Synoptic Gospel with a narrative of the institution of the Eucharist. The institution tradition is left to Paul to proclaim in the second reading. The gospel is John's description of the last meal that Jesus shares with his friends, his washing of their feet, and his command that his disciples, like him, be loving servants of one another.

The backdrop to this night is the description of the Jewish Passover and the memory of this feast of freedom for God's people. The ritual is outlined in detail in the first reading: the date of its celebration as a spring moon feast; the selection, slaughter, and eating of the unblemished lamb or kid; the marking of the Hebrew houses with its blood so that God would pass over them and not destroy them.

The Passover was to become the defining experience for Judaism. It testified to the truth that human beings are meant to be free and that God is concerned when they are not. But it also meant that God required an active response from the oppressed people: not passive acceptance of the status quo, but a willingness to set out on a dangerous way, trusting in God's protection. The fact that the people called Israel had once been strangers and slaves in Egypt, who were liberated by their God, was to have historical, religious, and ethical reverberations for the Jewish people down through the generations. They were to remember liturgically this Jewish Passover in every generation, a remembrance that pulls past, present, and future into a personal and communal "we" and a glorious but demanding "today."

Every Eucharist is a celebration of the Passover of the Lord, accomplished definitively in the blood of Christ, the Lamb of God, which marks us for salvation. As a nighttime community, we come together on this Holy Thursday to share the meal of salvation and commit ourselves once again to the journey into which Christ calls us: into freedom and away from the slavery of sin (Gal 5:1, 13). With the words of Psalm 116 on our lips, we toast the goodness of God, no longer as the psalmist does from a cup of sacrificial libation at the temple, but from the blessing cup of the sacramental blood of the risen Christ. We pledge ourselves publicly in the liturgical assembly to keep our promises to God.

It is Paul in his First Letter to the Corinthians who proclaims the words of institution of the Eucharist. With the Jewish remembrance of the Passover, the story becomes the storyteller's story; so the memorial of the broken bread and the poured cup becomes the Corinthians' own story, their own covenant with Christ. Christ says the bread is his body "that is for you," a communion with all the members of his body. And as Paul writes to the Romans, "If God is for us, who can be against us?" (8:31). From this moment, through Christ's death and resurrection until his return at the end of the ages, God in Christ is *for us*. When we, the members of his body live the mystery we celebrate, and if, like Christ, we are bread broken and consumed for others and wine poured out for the thirst of the world, we witness to the world the holy mystery of this night.

Focusing the Gospel

Key words and phrases: "He loved his own in the world and he loved them to the end."

To the point: As in last week's gospel from Luke, John tells the story of the Last Supper. In this version, Jesus washes the feet of his disciples. The same care and tenderness we encountered in Luke is on full display here, as Jesus physically humbles himself in front of his best friends. The scene is delicate in the gospel and was probably even more delicate in person. Jesus—best friend, charismatic speaker, and reliable travel partner—is getting down on his knees and picking up the feet of his friends to wash them. Can you imagine one of your friends doing this?

Model Penitential Act

Presider: As we begin this Sacred Triduum and commemorate your acts of humility and service, we call to mind the times we have not lived and loved in your example . . . *[pause]*

Lord Jesus, you are the Paschal Lamb: Lord, have mercy.

Christ Jesus, you feed us with your Body and Blood: Christ, have mercy.

Lord Jesus, you show us how to love: Lord, have mercy.

Model Universal Prayer (Prayer of the Faithful)

Presider: Paul reminds us when we eat the bread and drink the cup, we proclaim the death and resurrection of Jesus. With this, we humbly bring our prayers to God as we participate in this act of thanksgiving.

Response: Lord, hear our prayer.

That the pope, bishops, and all disciples of Christ may serve with a spirit of service and humility . . .

That leaders of peoples will make decisions out of selflessness and gratitude to best protect the people they serve . . .

That all who go without adequate food, shelter, or other resources may find support in the generosity of others and reform of the broken systems that perpetuate deprivation and disparity . . .

That our local community might grow in our understanding of Christ in the Eucharist through our shared liturgical prayer . . .

Presider: Loving God, you give us an example to follow. Hear the prayers we bring today as we strive to imitate the humility and self-gift of the paschal victory of Jesus. We ask this through Christ our Lord. **Amen.**

About Liturgy

Mantras and Litanies: Entering into the Triduum, we might use any number of mantras (e.g., music in Taizé style) or litanies (e.g., the Litany of the Saints) at our liturgies of the next several days to embody our prayer. Music in this style is perhaps uniquely able to communicate in at least two if not three directions simultaneously: we talk with God, God talks with us, and the Christian community talks with one another.

The form of prayer isn't by definition communicative in that way, however. Taizé music must, for instance, be given several repetitions to create that space and must be given swells and releases, even to the point of humming or stopping singing altogether, for the various directions of prayerful communication to occur.

Similarly with litanies, care should be taken to ensure nothing in the presentation of them "takes one out of the moment"—too many voices of leadership or sudden entrances of various accompanying instruments can be jarring and take one away from the environment where sincere and powerful prayer is occurring.

COLLECT

Let us pray.

Pause for silent prayer

O God, who have called us to participate
in this most sacred Supper,
in which your Only Begotten Son,
when about to hand himself over to death,
entrusted to the Church a sacrifice new for all
    eternity,
the banquet of his love,
grant, we pray,
that we may draw from so great a mystery,
the fullness of charity and of life.
Through our Lord Jesus Christ, your Son,
who lives and reigns with you in the unity of
    the Holy Spirit,
God, for ever and ever. **Amen.**

FOR REFLECTION

• Today's liturgy often begins with a procession of the holy oils that were recently consecrated at the diocesan chrism Mass. What do the oil of the sick, the oil of the catechumens, and the chrism mean for your life and for you as a follower of Christ?

• How do you think ritual anointings in our community connect to the command Jesus issues today?

Homily Points

• It might seem strange that as we celebrate Christ's institution of the Eucharist, we do not explicitly hear about it in today's gospel. Jesus's action and command, "I have given you a model to follow, so that as I have done for you, you should also do," is essentially Jesus saying, "Do this in memory of me." Humility, service, and self-gift is so intimately connected to Jesus's mission, ministry, and identity that this is one of his final commands.

• Any disconnect between Eucharist and the service of others is impossible. Today, Jesus shows us that the Eucharist is not only about a personal relationship with God. Rather, Eucharist is the communal act of living for others, following the example of Christ.

GOSPEL ACCLAMATION
Phil 2:8-9

Christ became obedient to the point of death,
even death on a cross.
Because of this, God greatly exalted him
and bestowed on him the name which is above
    every other name.

Gospel   John 18:1–19:42; L40ABC

Jesus went out with his disciples across
    the Kidron valley
  to where there was a garden,
  into which he and his disciples entered.
Judas his betrayer also knew the place,
  because Jesus had often met there with
    his disciples.
So Judas got a band of soldiers and guards
  from the chief priests and the
    Pharisees
  and went there with lanterns, torches,
    and weapons.
Jesus, knowing everything that was going
    to happen to him,
  went out and said to them, "Whom are
    you looking for?"
They answered him, "Jesus the Nazorean."
He said to them, "I AM."
Judas his betrayer was also with them.
When he said to them, "I AM,"
  they turned away and fell to the ground.
So he again asked them,
  "Whom are you looking for?"
They said, "Jesus the Nazorean."
Jesus answered,
  "I told you that I AM.
So if you are looking for me, let these
    men go."
This was to fulfill what he had said,
  "I have not lost any of those you gave me."
Then Simon Peter, who had a sword,
    drew it,
  struck the high priest's slave, and cut
    off his right ear.
The slave's name was Malchus.
Jesus said to Peter,
  "Put your sword into its scabbard.
Shall I not drink the cup that the Father
    gave me?"

Continued in Appendix A, pp. 289–290.
See Appendix A, p. 291, for the other readings.

Reflecting on the Gospel

Self-possessed and undefeated, the Son of God strides toward the accomplishment of his Passover. John has no Simon of Cyrene; Jesus carries his own cross, the cross that belongs to him and that, for that very reason, will be raised up as

a sign of victory. On the cross is the description of Jesus's "crime": "Jesus the Nazarene, the King of the Jews." Writing in Greek (the language of trade and commerce), in Latin (the language of Roman government), and in Hebrew (the language of Jesus's own Jewish people), John turns what Pilate wrote to salve his conscience into a proclamation of Christ's universal kingship. Beside Jesus hang "two others," not named as criminals nor insurgents as in the other gospels, but merely two attendant shadows who fade into anonymity in Jesus's royal presence.

The crucified is dispossessed of everything: first of his clothing, then of his mother and the beloved disciple, the woman and man who are his two ideal disciples. But this hour of patient pain and separation will become the hour of new communion as these two are given into each other's care by the dying Jesus. Here is the model for the Johannine church and every Christian community: women and men as equal disciples, welcoming each other and caring for each other in Jesus's name and as his gifts, and all this under the shadow of the cross, the glory tree. Then Jesus was "aware that everything was now finished." Thirsting to the end, he is offered sour wine on a sprig of hyssop. Here John deliberately evokes the "Lamb of God" memory, for it was with the fernlike hyssop that Exodus describes the sprinkling of the doorposts on the night of the Hebrews' Passover (12:22).

In this gospel, there is no dying cry, only the silent triumph of one who has accomplished that for which he came into the world. Jesus hands over his breath to his Father, the breath that will animate the new creation. No bones of this Paschal Lamb are broken; no cosmic darkness falls over the earth. From Christ's pierced side flow blood and water, John's signs of the Eucharist and baptism through which all peoples and nations will enter into the new temple of the body of the crucified and risen One.

With deliberate irony, John proclaims that it is with the dead body of Jesus in their arms that hesitant Israel first finds life and faith. Joseph of Arimathea and Nicodemus bind Jesus in the swaddling bands of death, surround him with the amount of costly spices and oils that would be considered a fitting extravagance for a king's burial, and, in a solemn cortege, place Jesus in a garden and a new tomb. Hidden in the heart of the earth, the grain of Christ's body awaits the fruiting of Easter morning.

Then we go up to venerate the cross: young people glad to be doing something; adults walking independently, children carried on their parents' shoulders; the frail, aged, and disabled heading with determination for what they are so familiar with. Together we become the people who pass by, looking and remembering that there is no sorrow like this sorrow. We kiss or touch or reverence the cross and hope that its sap will drip salvation on us. This is Easter Triduum; this is our paschal faith. Today the church is even dispossessed of the eucharistic action, offering us the hosts that were consecrated at last evening's Mass. And so we leave the church to wait for the night of nights. . . .

Focusing the Gospel

Key words and phrases: "[T]hey took Jesus, and, carrying the cross himself, he went out to what is called the Place of the Skull, in Hebrew, Golgotha."

To the point: Jesus is a charismatic speaker and an openhearted healer. Somehow, his work is seen as a threat to certain people in his community. Their suspicion turns to fear, and they execute the one person they have spent centuries waiting for. The irony and tragedy of Jesus's crucifixion and death have been with us for two millennia. Hope is coming upon us quickly, but today we dwell on the loss of this beautiful human. Jesus was a good man, son, and friend. We often see the big-picture tragedy of the crucifixion and salvation, but it's also fruitful to remember Jesus the man. God loves us so much, he died for us. Do not let today's gospel be familiar. Let it shock you. It's awful, and let it be awful.

About Liturgy

Lamenting, Hoping: Every liturgy we celebrate is in the context of the fullness of the paschal mystery—that is, we know the end of the story, or at least as much that has happened by this point, even on Good Friday.

Still, one of the modes of prayer most lacking in our church experience, and therefore one of the modes we do most poorly, is lament. It's just not "fun" or "exciting," so to speak, to pray together in times of lament. It is, though, perhaps the most necessary time.

We must not, though, pray in times of lament as if we are without hope. The psalms show us this in their structure. Psalm 31 today shows us the progression, the pivot, from despair to hope. Let us approach the "changeable" portions of this liturgy (music, preaching, etc.) in just that way: fully entering into lament at the death of the Messiah, yet with hope in his promises soon to be fulfilled.

Let us pray.

Remember your mercies, O Lord,
and with your eternal protection sanctify your
    servants,
for whom Christ your Son,
by the shedding of his Blood,
established the Paschal Mystery.
Who lives and reigns for ever and ever.
Amen.

or:

O God, who by the Passion of Christ your
    Son, our Lord,
abolished the death inherited from ancient sin
by every succeeding generation,
grant that just as, being conformed to him,
we have borne by the law of nature
the image of the man of earth,
so by the sanctification of grace
we may bear the image of the Man of heaven.
Through Christ our Lord.
Amen.

FOR REFLECTION
• Mary and the beloved disciple stay with Jesus throughout his crucifixion and death. Who constantly stays by your side and supports you in your life?

• In the accounts of his passion and death, Jesus's dignity is beyond violated. Where do you encounter such violations of human dignity in the world today?

Homily Points

• Jesus is in complete control of the events of today's gospel. John omits the part of the passion where Jesus prays that this suffering might pass. Similarly, when his accusers arrive in the garden, Jesus speaks first and greets them. Later, immediately before he dies, Jesus proclaims, "It is finished."

• Why would a God of love, force God's own son to die? Theologian Elizabeth Johnson argues that Jesus died because he proclaimed the kingdom of God, a challenging concept many were unwilling to accept. It was because of this commitment to solidarity with the poor and making peace with enemies and inclusion of sinners that Jesus was killed. Where are we in our own commitment to continuing the mission and ministry of Jesus?

Gospel   Luke 24:1-12; L41ABC

At daybreak on the first day of the week
    the women who had come from Gali-
        lee with Jesus
    took the spices they had prepared
    and went to the tomb.
They found the stone rolled away
        from the tomb;
    but when they entered,
    they did not find the body of
        the Lord Jesus.
While they were puzzling over
        this, behold,
    two men in dazzling garments
        appeared to them.
They were terrified and bowed
        their faces to the ground.
They said to them,
    "Why do you seek the living
        one among the dead?
He is not here, but he has been
        raised.
Remember what he said to you
        while he was still in Galilee,
    that the Son of Man must be
        handed over to sinners
    and be crucified, and rise on
        the third day."
And they remembered his words.
Then they returned from the tomb
    and announced all these things to the
        eleven
    and to all the others.
The women were Mary Magdalene,
    Joanna, and Mary the mother of
        James;
    the others who accompanied them
        also told this to the apostles,
    but their story seemed like nonsense
    and they did not believe them.
But Peter got up and ran to the tomb,
    bent down, and saw the burial cloths
        alone;
    then he went home amazed at what
        had happened.

See Appendix A, pp. 292–297, for the other
readings.

Reflecting on the Gospel

It is dawn, and the first cosmic light is breaking. Silently, attentively, but disregarded, the women who had faithfully followed Jesus from Galilee have noted
the place of burial so they can return after the Sabbath and complete the burial
rites. Soon the inner landscape of the memory and faith of these women will also

be enlightened. They are doing what
they should do according to the Jewish
funeral ritual, but they are about to
enter into the new and most profound
ritual that is at the service of the new
temple of Jesus's risen body. At first
there is just empty space, an empty
tomb, and the women are disoriented
and don't know what to do. Then two
dazzling messengers of God proclaim
to them the Easter message that will
echo down the ages, to be heard with
all its consequences by every Christian community that also enters into
the mystery of the resurrection: "Why
do you seek the living one among the
dead? / He is not here, but he has been
raised. Remember . . ."

The church gathers us so that we,
too, will remember—after the fire
and song and joy of this Easter are
over. When sorrow has intruded into
our joy; when we have laid the body of a loved one in the grave; when the loss
of friendship or health seems to cut us off from any good future or past happiness—then we need to remember Jesus's Galilee predictions of his passion, his
words about the new life that would rise from pain and death, and the Easter
gospel where prediction becomes proclamation.

Remember Galilee, say the messengers, and the people to whom Jesus gave new
healed bodies, new peace of mind, new hope. These graveside women are Galilee
women, and they do remember. It is this remembrance that returns them eagerly
back "to the / eleven / and to all the others" with the good news of the resurrection.
Poignantly, Luke reminds us that his dearest followers are no longer the Twelve
but eleven. With them, however, is a larger, more inclusive group that has been
gathered into their company. On the execution place of the skull, Luke had not
named any of the women who "stood at a distance" (23:49). Now, no longer distant
from but in the midst of the mystery of the crucified and risen Jesus, three of these
women are named as Mary Magdalene, Joanna, and Mary the mother of James.

Then, as so often today, the women's witness on their return is regarded as
"nonsense," not worthy of serious consideration. Yet they have personally experienced the reality of resurrection, not by seeing the risen body of Jesus but
through faith in the words of God's messengers and the memory of the Galilee
experiences. Peter runs to the tomb and sees the linen burial cloths, but his response is described as amazement, not faith. Not until Luke 24:34 is the Lord's appearance to Peter announced, and with this personal experience, no doubt is left.

The gospels do not ground our faith in empty tombs or discarded burial
cloths. Gospel faith in the resurrection is built on the presence and witness of

the risen Lord in human experience, in women and men who have received God's gift of faith and have had it nourished in the community of believers. This is the truth to which, as church, we will loudly and constantly sing "Alleluia" for the next fifty days.

Focusing the Gospel
Key words and phrases: "[T]heir story seemed like nonsense and they did not believe them."

To the point: Jesus's friends gave up. They watched Jesus die in a grotesque, public way. They buried him. They were in the first wave of grief, the shock of loss. Jesus's female friends go to the tomb to care for his body and are very confused. Two angels tell them that their friend is no longer among the dead. What on earth could that mean? If you've experienced the loss of someone close, the idea that an angel tells you it's all a mistake and your loved one is alive is the most vibrant fantasy you can have. It's just too good to be true. But here we find the women sitting in an empty tomb hearing this impossible news.

Model Universal Prayer (Prayer of the Faithful)
Presider: As we celebrate Christ's victory over sin and death, we confidently bring our needs to the God of life and love.

That the church might be willing to boldly proclaim the resurrection of Christ and the light that springs from darkness . . .

That local, national, and world leaders might seek opportunities to protect the life and dignity of all people, from conception until natural death . . .

That all those who grieve and mourn during this season of resurrection may find comfort in the embrace of Christ who conquers death . . .

That all members of our community who will be fully welcomed into the church today, (especially Name[s]) may find support from each of us as they continue their journey of faith in Jesus the Christ . . .

Presider: God of life and of the living, hear these prayers we bring to you. Knowing that your love is stronger than sin and death, we are unafraid to make these petitions known. Hear and answer them according to your will. We ask this through Christ our Lord. **Amen.**

About Liturgy
The Exodus Canticle: The only required Old Testament reading for the Easter Vigil Liturgy of the Word is the third reading, the telling of the crossing of the Red Sea in Exodus. It's prescribed because it prefigures so powerfully our salvation by Christ's death as well as our being claimed by that same Christ in baptism. We pass, through water, from death to life and are set free from the bondage of sin.

Have you noticed that the end of this reading brings us immediately to the same canticle sung in response? While it is not described so in our liturgical documents, many parishes have taken the creative liberty to begin singing the canticle where it would otherwise have been read. Other parishes begin an extended introduction to the canticle at that point of the reading, to help underscore (literally) the connection.

FOR REFLECTION

• The men in dazzling garments ask, "Why do you seek the living one among the dead?" How is God calling you to leave behind the tombs of death in your own life?

• Just as we often make resolutions of prayer, fasting, and abstinence during Lent, we might also make resolutions for this season of Easter. How might you intentionally practice this Easter joy in the coming weeks?

Homily Points
• In today's gospel we hear that the women were the first people to hear and proclaim that Jesus had risen from the dead. This is consistent with Luke's entire narrative, as it holds women in a place of primacy. It was the women who stayed with Jesus throughout his passion, and it was the women who were first to know of the resurrection. When they tried to share this with the others, however, their story was deemed as "nonsense."

• Perhaps this is difficult for us to grasp, as we know how the story ends. We know that Jesus rises three days after his death. But those first disciples did not know this. With that, the voices of proclamation were essentially ignored. The gospel today invites us to consider which voices we ignore in our church and lives today. Do we listen to the experiences of women, of people of color, of immigrants and refugees, of the LGBTQ community? Or do we condemn their experiences as nonsense? Let us proclaim the resurrection by listening to the voices and experiences of all we encounter.

GOSPEL ACCLAMATION
cf. 1 Cor 5:7b-8a

℟. Alleluia, alleluia.
Christ, our paschal lamb, has been sacrificed;
let us then feast with joy in the Lord.
℟. Alleluia, alleluia.

Gospel   John 20:1-9; L42ABC

On the first day of the week,
 Mary of Magdala came
  to the tomb early in
  the morning,
 while it was still dark,
 and saw the stone re-
  moved from the
  tomb.

So she ran and went to
 Simon Peter
 and to the other disciple
  whom Jesus loved,
  and told them,
 "They have taken the
  Lord from the tomb,
 and we don't know
  where they put
  him."
So Peter and the other
 disciple went out and
 came to the tomb.
They both ran, but the
 other disciple ran
 faster than Peter
 and arrived at the tomb first;
 he bent down and saw the burial cloths
  there, but did not go in.
When Simon Peter arrived after him,
 he went into the tomb and saw the burial
  cloths there,
 and the cloth that had covered his head,
 not with the burial cloths but rolled up in
  a separate place.
Then the other disciple also went in,
 the one who had arrived at the tomb first,
 and he saw and believed.
For they did not yet understand the
 Scripture
 that he had to rise from the dead.

or

Luke 24:1-12; L41C *in Appendix A, p. 298,*

or, at an afternoon or evening Mass
Luke 24:13-35; L46 *in Appendix A, p. 298.*

See Appendix A, p. 299, for the other readings.

Reflecting on the Gospel

How does one extract hope from tragedy? How is one able to move on from trauma and find the strength and courage to keep living? In John's account of the discovery of the empty tomb on what we have come to know as Easter morning, Mary Magdalene (Mary of Magdala), planning to prepare the body of Jesus for burial, discovers an empty tomb. Beyond simply shock and surprise, this experience was trauma on top of trauma.

James Cone in his book *The Cross and the Lynching Tree* equates crucifixion with the lynching of Black bodies, most prolific post-slavery and through the Jim Crow era. Much like the crucifixion of Jesus, the lynching of Black men and women were public spectacles, a traumatic event for members of the Black community, especially for members of the victim's family. Lynchings in the United States, like crucifixions by the Roman Empire, were intended as a deterrent, a public warning and display of oppressive, institutional power.

In May 2020, the country witnessed what was essentially a public lynching when George Floyd was murdered by a police officer who placed his knee on Floyd's neck for 9 minutes and 29 seconds. The incident was recorded by a young girl of seventeen years for the world to see. This incident occurred during a global pandemic that put a spotlight on various failings in American society and highlighted what many called the pandemic within the pandemic: racism. The murder (or public lynching) of George Floyd occurred not long after other incidents of the murder of Black bodies. In early May 2020, the country became aware of the vigilante death of Ahmaud Arbery, followed by an announcement of the police killing of Breonna Taylor a few weeks later, followed by the weaponizing of the police in New York City's Central Park as a white woman threatened an innocent Black man, and then finally, on the same day, the death of George Floyd. Especially for the Black community, this was trauma after trauma. One hadn't fully processed one murder before another had taken place. For Mary, who was present when Jesus was crucified (John 19:25), to arrive at the tomb two days later and find the body of Jesus missing must have been more than surprise or shock. It was traumatic: trauma added to trauma. Verse 11 of chapter 20 tells us that Mary stood outside the tomb weeping. To witness the public execution of your Lord and Savior, then days later go for closure through the ritual tending to the body only to find the body missing, is nothing short of traumatic.

Yet, it is in the midst of great tragedy that God's power is revealed. It is through God's grace that we are able to experience hope in the midst of tragedy and trauma. From the public lynching of George Floyd we saw people across racial lines come together in protest. In fact, Floyd's murder sparked a worldwide movement for justice and a recognition that Black people are disproportionately affected by police brutality. The resurrection of Jesus not only represents hope in the midst of tragedy but also the transformation of physical and spiritual death to life. It is the special gift of God to do a good work in the midst of the valley. It is the promise of God to "comfort all who mourn," to offer "a diadem instead of ashes" ("beauty for ashes" in some translations), "oil of gladness instead of mourning," and "a glorious mantle instead of a faint spirit" (Isa 61:2-3).

Focusing the Gospel
Key words and phrases: "They have taken the Lord from the tomb, and we don't know where they put him."

To the point: Mary Magdalene is not running back to her friends and telling them Jesus has risen from the dead. Instead, she's mortified that someone has stolen his body from his grave. The apostles are in devastating grief when they encounter the reality of Jesus's resurrection. They watched someone they love dearly die violently. Not only are they experiencing the trauma of losing Jesus but there's also the fear that they will be next. To be presented with the reality that Jesus actually rose from the dead, and is really the Messiah, requires emotional whiplash. Peter and John are putting the pieces together slowly. As you encounter the celebration of Easter this year, allow yourself to sympathize with the apostles' human journey throughout the Triduum.

Model Penitential Act
Presider: This is resurrection day! Alleluia! Knowing that we do not always walk in the light of the resurrection, we ask for God's healing presence in our lives . . . *[pause]*

Lord Jesus, you rose from the dead: Lord, have mercy.
Christ Jesus, you destroy sin and death: Christ, have mercy.
Lord Jesus, your love gives us life: Lord, have mercy.

Model Universal Prayer (Prayer of the Faithful)
Presider: Through his death and resurrection, Jesus brings us life. With this gift of life, we bring our prayers and petitions to the God who loves us.

That the church may boldly proclaim the joy of the resurrection . . .

That people in power resolve misunderstandings with compassion and peace . . .

That all who were baptized at the Easter Vigil continue to grow in their relationship with Christ . . .

That all gathered here may renew our baptismal promises with courage and conviction . . .

Presider: Loving God, on this day of resurrection we rejoice in your triumph over sin and death. Hear the prayers we bring before you, through the risen Christ our Lord. **Amen.**

About Liturgy
Pulling Out All the Stops: We are likely familiar with the expression "pull out all the stops." It implies that we should do everything possible, to make an experience or pursuit of a particular goal as full and complete as possible. And, if there's ever a time to liturgically pull out all the stops, it's Easter!

Did you know the phrase has origins in sacred music? An organ has several ranks of pipes, typically, each of which makes a different sort of sound: flutes, reeds, strings, etc. And, at the organ console, the organist decides on a registration for each piece—that is, which combinations of ranks are used to create the desired sound. So, an organist who pulls out all the stops is literally making the organ play as forcefully and as fully as possible. May our celebrations of resurrection and new life be strong and full as well!

COLLECT
Let us pray.

Pause for silent prayer

O God, who on this day,
through your Only Begotten Son,
have conquered death
and unlocked for us the path to eternity,
grant, we pray, that we who keep
the solemnity of the Lord's Resurrection
may, through the renewal brought by your Spirit,
rise up in the light of life.
Through our Lord Jesus Christ, your Son,
who lives and reigns with you in the unity of
the Holy Spirit,
God, for ever and ever. **Amen.**

FOR REFLECTION
• The Beloved Disciple "saw and believed" without yet understanding. When have you believed something without understanding the fullness of the reality?

• Mary ran to Peter and the Beloved Disciple to tell them that the tomb was empty. In your own life, who are the people you turn to when you are experiencing difficult times or new challenges?

Homily Points
• There are details in today's gospel that may seem a bit strange. The passage begins, "On the first day of the week, Mary of Magdala came to the tomb early in the morning, while it was still dark." Likewise, the account of the disciples racing to the tomb also has very specific elements: "They both ran, but the other disciple ran faster than Peter and arrived at the tomb first." The detail John provides in his resurrection account gives credibility and grounding to the story, as they were specific details observed by those first witnesses.

• The first reading from the Acts of the Apostles also emphasizes this notion of witness. Peter proclaims, "We are witnesses of all that he did." The word "witness" comes from the Latin *testimonium*, or one who testifies. While we may not be called to spread the gospel across the country or world, we still must testify to the death and resurrection of Jesus by our daily actions.

SEASON
OF EASTER

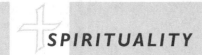

SPIRITUALITY

GOSPEL ACCLAMATION
John 20:29

Ry. Alleluia, alleluia.
You believe in me, Thomas, because you have
    seen me, says the Lord;
blessed are those who have not seen me, but still
    believe!
Ry. Alleluia, alleluia.

Gospel   John 20:19-31; L45C

On the evening of that first day of the
    week,
    when the doors were locked, where the
        disciples were,
    for fear of the Jews,
    Jesus came and stood in their midst
    and said to them, "Peace be with you."
When he had said this, he showed them
    his hands and his side.
The disciples rejoiced when they saw the
    Lord.
Jesus said to them again, "Peace be with
    you.
As the Father has sent me, so I send
    you."
And when he had said this, he breathed
    on them and said to them,
    "Receive the Holy Spirit.
Whose sins you forgive are forgiven them,
    and whose sins you retain are retained."

Thomas, called Didymus, one of the
    Twelve,
    was not with them when Jesus came.
So the other disciples said to him, "We
    have seen the Lord."
But he said to them,
    "Unless I see the mark of the nails in
        his hands
    and put my finger into the nailmarks
    and put my hand into his side, I will
        not believe."

Now a week later his disciples were again
    inside
    and Thomas was with them.
Jesus came, although the doors were locked,
    and stood in their midst and said,
        "Peace be with you."

Continued in Appendix A, p. 299.

Reflecting on the Gospel

A dispirited, frightened group of disciples huddles together behind closed doors on the evening of Easter day. They have realized, only too painfully, that by deserting Jesus in the hour of his passion and death they have also betrayed themselves. They are wounded people who may believe that Jesus has risen from the dead, but what that means, and what it means *for them,* given their unfaithfulness, leaves them in panicking ignorance. Then the Tomb Breaker himself, with his wounded, living body, is among them, breaking not only into their closed room but also into their despair.

The first gift of his resurrection that Jesus offers them is peace. Jesus breathes on them, and the word that John uses here for "breathe" is used nowhere else in the New Testament. It has all the nuances of the spirit/breath/wind of Genesis, which brooded over the primeval chaos to bring forth new life (Gen 1:2). In Genesis, too, the Creator God breathes into the nostrils of human dust, and this dust becomes a living person (2:7). When Jesus breathes over the disciples, their humanity is raised from the dust of disappointment and fear. This Easter day is the first day of the new creation (or the "eighth day" in the Genesis timeline).

On the following "eighth day," there is also a new beginning for Thomas, who was absent the week before. Nowhere in the gospels is Thomas ever described as "doubting." He has been outspoken, generous, ready to face death with his master (John 11:16). At the Last Supper, he is honest enough to say aloud what the other disciples were most likely thinking: that none of them *is* sure where Jesus is heading. But like his companions who did not accept the testimony of Mary Magdalene about Jesus's resurrection, Thomas also wants a personal experience. His post-resurrection challenge is: "Do not be unbelieving, but believe." In both his disbelief and his faith, Thomas represents us, the future generations who are called to blessedness because we believe without having seen Jesus in the flesh.

Jesus invites Thomas to touch the wounds in his risen body, for in this opened body is the way, the truth, and the life that Thomas was seeking (John 14:5-7). As Jesus and his disciple stand before each other in the midst of the community, it is Thomas's faith, not his hands, that digs deeply into the mystery of his risen Lord, and he cries out the most profound and personal proclamation of gospel faith: "My Lord and my God!" In return, Jesus speaks the greatest of all beatitudes that will resound beyond that Jerusalem room, into our assembly today, and to the end of the ages: "Blessed are those who have not seen and have believed."

A visitor to the Vietnam Veterans Memorial in Washington, DC, described watching a man stand before the wall into which are carved more than 58,000 names of Americans who sacrificed their lives or are missing in action because of that tragic war. The man moved slowly along the wall, stopping now and then to run his fingers over some of the names. Tears streamed down his face as he touched one he recognized. The wall is a place of gathered memories. The name that Thomas gave to Jesus is carved into our hearts at our baptism. We often need to rub the fingers of our Christian memory over it, recognizing with gratitude the peacemaking sacrifice of Jesus that is our salvation. We also need to recognize that Christ still shows himself to us in the wounds of the suffering members of his body: ourselves, and our sisters and brothers, known and unknown.

Focusing the Gospel

Key words and phrases: "Now Jesus did many other signs in the presence of his disciples that are not written in this book."

To the point: We are given two dramatic scenes in this week's gospel. Jesus's friends are terrified and afraid of the religious authorities looking for them, perhaps to try them as they tried Jesus. While they are hiding, Jesus comes and stands in their midst. He doesn't knock, he doesn't stand at the front of the room, but instead he comes of his own accord and stands in their midst, as an equal. There's no big announcement or exclamation. Instead, Jesus tells them, "Peace be with you."

Jesus's disciples are exhausted. They've watched the brutal execution of one of their own, found his body stolen, and are now in hiding. They were likely at the peak of despair. The first thing Jesus offers them is peace. He doesn't enter and immediately give an explanation, or an escape plan. He gives them peace. Perhaps, when our own anxiety is high and we do not understand a situation, instead of constantly seeking a solution, we can, as Jesus offers, focus our energy on finding peace in the midst of the turmoil.

Connecting the Gospel

to the first reading: Today's first reading is from Acts, the sequel to Luke's gospel. It answers many of the questions posed by the gospel—mainly, what did the disciples do after Jesus came back? First, they gather all together at Solomon's home. Then they begin performing signs and wonders. The Holy Spirit, given to them in John's gospel this week, works through them. They gain a bit of celebrity. "None of the others dared to join them, but the people esteemed them." People in their community hear of their words and works, and come to see what all the fuss is about. "Yet more than ever, believers in the Lord, great numbers of men and women, were added to them."

to experience: If you lived in Jerusalem in the first century and heard of these wonderful things, would you believe they were of the Lord? Would you ignore them as impossible, convinced that the Lord will only operate the way you've been taught? Take time this week to think about how you would react to a miracle on earth. Do you leave space for God to surprise you?

Connecting the Responsorial Psalm

to the readings: In today's gospel we witness Jesus passing on the Lord's love everlasting in the person of the Holy Spirit. When we sing the words "Give thanks to the Lord for he is good, / his love is everlasting," it is not a poetic metaphor, but instead very literal and very real. God's love for us existed before we existed, and it will remain forever.

to psalmist preparation: There are two options for refrain this week and throughout the season, and one of them is simply the word Alleluia. It's interesting to think about how the word "Alleluia" is another way of saying, "Give thanks to the Lord for he is good, / his love is everlasting." That's what we mean when we say Alleluia: we are grateful, we are joyful, we are loved.

PROMPTS FOR FAITH-SHARING

When you are feeling anxious, do you focus on solving the problem leading to your anxiety, or do you focus on finding peace in the situation? How might finding peace before all else benefit you?

Have you ever experienced a miracle or something miraculous in your life?

What is a "rejected cornerstone" in your life—something you dismissed early on but later came to realize was essential?

The apostles in today's reading gather in "Solomon's portico." Is there a home or meeting space where you usually gather with your community? What is the benefit of having a gathering place to be and pray?

CELEBRATION

Model Rite for the Blessing and Sprinkling of Water

Presider: In today's gospel Jesus shares the gift of peace with his disciples. May this water remind us of God's healing presence in our lives . . . *[pause]*

    [continue with The Roman Missal, *Appendix II]*

Homily Points

• We know from the creation narratives in Genesis that God breathed life into God's people. Likewise, Jesus breathes on his disciples when he greets them in the locked room. Life comes from God, and as we see throughout this passage, there are several instances where Jesus is named and claimed as God.

• Today's gospel passage is generally considered the conclusion of the Gospel of John. While an epilogue follows, scholars believe it was added to the original text. The verses we hear today punctuate the narrative, as the evangelist specifically states the purpose of his work: "Now Jesus did many other signs in the presence of his disciples that are not written in this book. But these are written that you may come to believe that Jesus is the Christ, the Son of God, and that through this belief you may have life in his name." John makes it abundantly clear that life in Christ is what the gospel is all about.

• From the very beginning of John's gospel, we know that Jesus is the Son of God, the Word that was from the beginning. Today's gospel puts that theological reality in a lived context. In his profession of faith, Thomas makes a clear and concise christological statement, based not on theological discourses but on relationship and belief: "My Lord and my God!" What an incredibly powerful "end" to the story.

Model Universal Prayer (Prayer of the Faithful)

Presider: As we profess Jesus Christ as the Son of God, we confidently raise up our prayers:

Response: Lord, hear our prayer.

That the church may work to uphold the dignity of all people, especially people who are relegated to the margins of our society . . .

That local and world leaders may work for lasting peace grounded in humility and justice . . .

That all who struggle with their belief in God may know that they are never alone . . .

That all gathered here may renounce the stereotypes that surround our brothers and sisters who are immigrants and refugees . . .

Presider: Loving God, you heard the prayers of your disciples and you hear us today. Listen to the prayers we offer to you and answer them according to your will. We ask this through Christ our Lord. **Amen.**

COLLECT

Let us pray.

Pause for silent prayer

God of everlasting mercy,
who in the very recurrence of the paschal
    feast
kindle the faith of the people you have
    made your own,
increase, we pray, the grace you have
    bestowed,
that all may grasp and rightly understand
in what font they have been washed,
by whose Spirit they have been reborn,
by whose Blood they have been redeemed.
Through our Lord Jesus Christ, your Son,
who lives and reigns with you in the unity
    of the Holy Spirit,
God, for ever and ever. **Amen.**

FIRST READING
Acts 5:12-16

Many signs and wonders were done
    among the people
    at the hands of the apostles.
They were all together in Solomon's portico.
None of the others dared to join them, but
    the people esteemed them.
Yet more than ever, believers in the Lord,
    great numbers of men and women,
        were added to them.
Thus they even carried the sick out into
    the streets
    and laid them on cots and mats
    so that when Peter came by,
    at least his shadow might fall on one or
        another of them.
A large number of people from the towns
    in the vicinity of Jerusalem also
        gathered,
    bringing the sick and those disturbed
        by unclean spirits,
    and they were all cured.

RESPONSORIAL PSALM
Ps 118:2-4, 13-15, 22-24

℞. (1) Give thanks to the Lord for he is
    good, his love is everlasting.
    or:
℞. Alleluia.

Let the house of Israel say,
    "His mercy endures forever."
Let the house of Aaron say,
    "His mercy endures forever."
Let those who fear the Lord say,
    "His mercy endures forever."

℞. Give thanks to the Lord for he is good,
    his love is everlasting.
    or:
℞. Alleluia.

I was hard pressed and was falling,
  but the LORD helped me.
My strength and my courage is the LORD,
  and he has been my savior.
The joyful shout of victory
  in the tents of the just.

℞. Give thanks to the Lord for he is good,
  his love is everlasting.
  or:
℞. Alleluia.

The stone which the builders rejected
  has become the cornerstone.
By the LORD has this been done;
  it is wonderful in our eyes.
This is the day the LORD has made;
  let us be glad and rejoice in it.

℞. Give thanks to the Lord for he is good,
  his love is everlasting.
  or:
℞. Alleluia.

SECOND READING
Rev 1:9-11a, 12-13, 17-19

I, John, your brother, who share with you
  the distress, the kingdom, and the
    endurance we have in Jesus,
  found myself on the island called
    Patmos
  because I proclaimed God's word and
    gave testimony to Jesus.
I was caught up in spirit on the Lord's day
  and heard behind me a voice as loud as
    a trumpet, which said,
  "Write on a scroll what you see."
Then I turned to see whose voice it was
    that spoke to me,
  and when I turned, I saw seven gold
    lampstands
  and in the midst of the lampstands one
    like a son of man,
  wearing an ankle-length robe, with a
    gold sash around his chest.

When I caught sight of him, I fell down at
    his feet as though dead.
He touched me with his right hand and
    said, "Do not be afraid.
I am the first and the last, the one who
    lives.
Once I was dead, but now I am alive
    forever and ever.
I hold the keys to death and the
    netherworld.
Write down, therefore, what you have
    seen,
  and what is happening, and what will
    happen afterwards."

About Liturgy

My Lord and My God: Thomas's prayer today in the gospel, "My Lord and My God!" (John 20:28), is also a popular devotional prayer at the elevation of the sacred species during the eucharistic prayer. It mimics the "doubting" apostle's recognition of the Lord truly present in his midst.

It's worth considering that while gathered at the altar, we are anamnetically at the Last Supper and the crucifixion as well as at a foretaste of the eternal heavenly banquet. At the fraction rite, when the Body of Christ is broken to be shared with the many for the forgiveness of sins, we sing, "Lamb of God, you take away the sins of the world, / have mercy on us. / . . . grant us peace."

Hopefully, we can't help but notice these liturgical connections, if done with intent and with the conscious participation of the faithful. We see that signs of the real presence abound in our liturgies, if we pause to recognize them. This sort of liturgical spirituality is so much more approachable and beneficial than a classroom philosophical discussion on transubstantiation.

Let the liturgy serve its catechetical role, that what we pray reinforces what we believe, and what we believe is found in our corporate prayer!

About Liturgical Documents

Sing to the Lord—Progressive Solemnity: One thought regarding liturgical celebrations that Sing to the Lord puts before the church again is the concept of progressive solemnity, which is found in several previous liturgical documents. The notion extends beyond the music of the liturgy to elements like vestments, candles, and which of the various and rich options in liturgies are utilized, based on the hierarchy of memorials, feasts, solemnities, etc. Sing to the Lord is quick to add that "solemnity should never be allowed to devolve to an empty display of ceremony, however" (113).

Musically, one concept of musical progressive solemnity seems to have not gotten much traction in the United States—the ranking of various parts of Mass to be sung. In order, these parts are: a) Dialogues and Acclamations, b) Antiphons and Psalms, c) Refrains and Repeated Responses, and d) Hymns (STL 115). That is, when doing only a minimal amount of singing at a liturgy (say, a weekday of Ordinary Time), start with singing dialogues and acclamations. Then, as the solemnity of any celebration increases (along with an ability to provide music ministry), add items from category B, then C, and finally D. These categories, notably, are different from what is listed in *Musicam Sacram* (28–32), which was also not widely accepted. The usual experience before STL (in 2007) and since is nearly the opposite of these suggestions. This is not to say one manner of music ministry is better than the other; rather, it is just to note that on this occasion the reception of this part of this particular liturgical document was cool at best, or practically nonexistent.

About Music

More Mercy: Earlier this year a couple songs of mercy were mentioned for an appropriate Sunday. Other pieces to consider today include "Your Grace Is Enough" by Matt Maher (in several contemporary resources) and "As We Forgive" by James Marchionda (WLP/GIA), which is also a fine musical reflection on the Lord's Prayer.

APRIL 24, 2022
SECOND SUNDAY OF EASTER
(or of DIVINE MERCY)

✦ SPIRITUALITY

GOSPEL ACCLAMATION

℞. Alleluia, alleluia.
Christ is risen, creator of all;
he has shown pity on all people.
℞. Alleluia, alleluia.

Gospel   John 21:1-19; L48C

At that time, Jesus revealed himself
    again to his disciples at the Sea of
    Tiberias.
He revealed himself in this way.
Together were Simon Peter, Thomas
    called Didymus,
    Nathanael from Cana in Galilee,
    Zebedee's sons, and two others of his
    disciples.
Simon Peter said to them, "I am going
    fishing."
They said to him, "We also will come
    with you."
So they went out and got into the boat,
    but that night they caught nothing.
When it was already dawn, Jesus was
    standing on the shore;
    but the disciples did not realize that it
    was Jesus.
Jesus said to them, "Children, have you
    caught anything to eat?"
They answered him, "No."
So he said to them, "Cast the net over the
    right side of the boat
    and you will find something."
So they cast it, and were not able to pull
    it in
    because of the number of fish.
So the disciple whom Jesus loved said to
    Peter, "It is the Lord."
When Simon Peter heard that it was the
    Lord,
    he tucked in his garment, for he was
    lightly clad,
    and jumped into the sea.
The other disciples came in the boat,
    for they were not far from shore, only
    about a hundred yards,
    dragging the net with the fish.

Continued in Appendix A, p. 300,

or John 21:1-14, p. 300.

Reflecting on the Gospel

Most commentators consider John 20:31 to be the end of the gospel as that evangelist wrote it; the Good News we hear today is a part of the epilogue to John's gospel, certainly inspired as all Scripture is, but probably a "mosaic" created from various pieces of ecclesial tradition by a close disciple of John. It gives the early Christian communities a picture of some important aspects

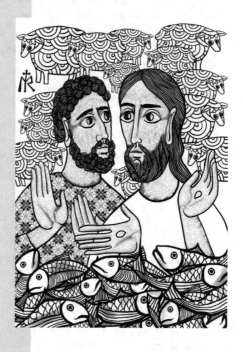

of life for *all* disciples after the "hour" of Jesus's death and resurrection: the primacy and mission of Peter, the place of the Beloved Disciple, the responsibility of all believers to be fishers of people.

Peter, the leader, has gone back to the everyday, the familiar way of being a fisherman, taking with him six other disciples. There is Thomas, who hovered between disbelief and belief until his experience with his wounded and risen Lord; Nathanael, the true Israelite without guile who had to decide whether anything good had really come out of Nazareth; James and John, who had their own problems with status seeking; and two unnamed disciples, one of whom is later revealed as the Beloved Disciple. Into the shoes of the seventh unnamed disciple we may step, while still at times recognizing that we also walk in the footsteps of the others. These seven, the number of fullness, symbolize more than just a part of the apostolic group; they represent the whole community of believers down through the centuries who will encounter the risen Lord, be called by him to let down their nets into the sea of humanity, eat with him, profess their love for him, and follow him in many different ways.

The gospel begins as a night scene of failure, with no fish caught. Then the sun rises, and the disciples are hailed from the shore by someone who calls them "[c]hildren." They are the "children" of John 13:33 who are loved but still have much to learn. The stranger tells them to let down their nets, and emptiness is filled with a great catch. Then with the sun rising and the dawn of faith breaking, the disciple whom Jesus loves, who rested his head on the heart of Jesus, who stood his ground at the cross and holds the preeminent place of intimate contemplation giving him the keen eyes of faith, sees and proclaims with deference to Peter: "It is the Lord." It is Peter, the model for pastoral leadership, but leadership that is also dependent on contemplative insight, who plunges into the water. Always eager and impetuous, he makes his way to Jesus. Again we are reminded that the way to the risen Lord is through the waters, through the baptism into which we are plunged.

When they come to the shore, the disciples are invited to breakfast at a charcoal fire on which bread and fish are cooking. As with an earlier feeding, the disciples, too, are to be involved in the preparation of this meal (John 6:5-13). Jesus tells them to bring some of the fish they have just caught, and it is Peter, in his leadership role, who hauls the net, heavy with fish, from the water's edge. The word used for "drag" is the same word that John used to describe how the

Father will "draw" people to Jesus (6:44) and how Jesus himself will "draw" others to himself when he is exalted on the cross (12:32). Such a "drawing" or "gathering" is the pastoral effort Peter is to make as leader of the church.

Focusing the Gospel

Key words and phrases: "When Simon Peter heard that it was the Lord, he tucked in his garment, for he was lightly clad, and jumped into the sea."

To the point: When Peter recognizes Jesus, he is so filled with excitement that he jumps off the side of the boat and swims to Jesus, his dear friend. He's overseeing a net full of fish, but instead of checking in with his colleagues, he dives into the sea to get to his friend as fast as possible. There is an unfettered humanity about Peter and in Peter's desire to be close to the Lord in whatever way he can. It is this pure, almost childish, desire for the goodness of Jesus that becomes the face of the church on earth. Jesus even calls those in the boat "Children," naming and valuing their childlike reaction to him.

Connecting the Gospel

to the first reading: Despite their original efforts to hide, the apostles are noticed by the Sanhedrin and brought before them, much like Jesus was before being condemned to death. The high priest asks them, "We gave you strict orders, did we not, to stop teaching in that name?" Here we see Peter claim his full authority as our first pope, and instead of hiding or denying, he responds, "We must obey God rather than men." He even goes so far as to be critical of them: "The God of our ancestors raised Jesus, though you had him killed by hanging him on a tree." Who is this Peter, so firm in his words and so unafraid to speak them?

to experience: Through the readings last week and this week, we are able to watch Peter's transformation from a timid and impulsive "sidekick" into the leader Jesus always knew he would be. Peter has fumbled his way through the gospel since we met him, and Jesus never, ever stopped drawing him close. Even after denying Jesus at the crucial moment, and then hiding in a house after Jesus died, Peter finally finds the guts to stand up, in front of the highest authorities in his community, and call them out.

Connecting the Responsorial Psalm

to the readings: The psalm tells us, "For his anger lasts but a moment; / a lifetime, his good will." The Lord's anger is brief but his love is constant. We can see this exemplified in how Jesus treats Peter, when Peter blurts out that Jesus is the Messiah, denies Jesus is his friend, and then hides after Jesus is killed. At each of these moments, the human reaction is to be angry with Peter, or at least disappointed. Instead, Jesus's compassion is constant.

to psalmist preparation: "You changed my mourning into dancing." This is one of the most vivid and beloved images we receive from the psalms. What does this experience look like to you? Have you ever found moments of "dancing" in the midst of great grief?

PROMPTS FOR FAITH-SHARING

Is there someone in your life worth jumping out of a boat to hug? How does it feel to know that Jesus would do this for you?

Have you ever felt you failed at something so badly, you couldn't possibly try it again? Viewing Peter's transformation through this framework of overcoming what appears to be total failure, can you imagine a situation in which you might revisit your "failed" work?

What is one example of when the Lord was your helper (as opposed to the other way around)?

Have you ever had your grief turned into dancing? What was the "dancing"?

CELEBRATION

Model Rite for the Blessing and Sprinkling of Water

Presider: In today's gospel Jesus calls his disciples "Children" and cares for them with tender love. May this water remind us of our special relationship with God . . . *[pause]*
   [continue with The Roman Missal, *Appendix II]*

Homily Points

• Composer Rory Cooney writes, "If you love me, feed my lambs. Be my heart, my voice, my hands." These lines seem to summarize the entirety of today's gospel passage, for they reiterate the concrete realities of loving Jesus. We do not love Jesus in isolation from the rest of the world or as a practice of individualism. Rather, our love for Jesus must compel us to be the heart, voice, and hands of Christ for others.

• Like he does so often throughout the gospels, Jesus shows by example how we are to treat others. Notice first his warm words to the disciples, "Children, have you caught anything to eat?" Of course, Jesus knows the answer to that question, but by asking it Jesus continues to show the love and concern for others that is so fundamental to his mission. Later, when he invites the disciples to breakfast, Jesus again recognizes their fundamental human needs and satiates their hunger. This is the moment when the disciples recognize Jesus. They realized it was the Lord by the way he loved and cared for others. As we seek to imitate Christ, we have this same responsibility.

• Even so, this life of discipleship is not always easy. The reading from the Acts of the Apostles illustrates the very real difficulties the early disciples faced. When the apostles were brought before the court officials, the Sanhedrin ordered that they stop speaking in the name of Jesus. Rather than renouncing Jesus, the disciples "left the presence of the Sanhedrin, rejoicing that they had been found worthy to suffer dishonor for the sake of the name." All of our actions have consequences. Are we prepared for the consequences of following Christ, serving as the heart, voice, and hands of the Shepherd?

Model Universal Prayer (Prayer of the Faithful)

Presider: We know that, just as Jesus provides for the needs of his disciples, Jesus will also provide for us. With confidence we raise our prayers to our God of life and love.

Response: Lord, hear our prayer.

That all shepherds within the church may take Jesus's command to heart and feed the flock with patient understanding and love . . .

That local, national, and world leaders may work for an equitable distribution of resources so to end hunger and poverty . . .

That all may form their conscience and participate in the political process to ensure a society that protects life in all stages . . .

That our local community may continue to support our sisters and brothers who were initiated at the Easter Vigil . . .

Presider: Loving God, our needs are no surprise, yet we raise them as we strive to grow in relationship with you. Hear these prayers we offer today and answer them according to your will. We ask this through Christ, the risen Lord. **Amen.**

COLLECT

Let us pray.

Pause for silent prayer

May your people exult for ever, O God,
in renewed youthfulness of spirit,
so that, rejoicing now in the restored glory
      of our adoption,
we may look forward in confident hope
to the rejoicing of the day of resurrection.
Through our Lord Jesus Christ, your Son,
who lives and reigns with you in the unity
      of the Holy Spirit,
God, for ever and ever. **Amen.**

FIRST READING

Acts 5:27-32, 40b-41

When the captain and the court officers had
      brought the apostles in
   and made them stand before the
      Sanhedrin,
   the high priest questioned them,
   "We gave you strict orders, did we not,
   to stop teaching in that name?
Yet you have filled Jerusalem with your
      teaching
   and want to bring this man's blood
      upon us."
But Peter and the apostles said in reply,
   "We must obey God rather than men.
The God of our ancestors raised Jesus,
   though you had him killed by hanging
      him on a tree.
God exalted him at his right hand as
      leader and savior
   to grant Israel repentance and
      forgiveness of sins.
We are witnesses of these things,
   as is the Holy Spirit whom God has given
      to those who obey him."

The Sanhedrin ordered the apostles
   to stop speaking in the name of Jesus,
      and dismissed them.
So they left the presence of the Sanhedrin,
   rejoicing that they had been found
      worthy
   to suffer dishonor for the sake of the
      name.

RESPONSORIAL PSALM

Ps 30:2, 4, 5-6, 11-12, 13

R̝. (2a) I will praise you, Lord, for you
      have rescued me.
   or
R̝. Alleluia.

I will extol you, O LORD, for you drew me
      clear
   and did not let my enemies rejoice over
      me.

124

O LORD, you brought me up from the
     netherworld;
   you preserved me from among those
     going down into the pit.

R⁄. I will praise you, Lord, for you have
     rescued me.
   or
R⁄. Alleluia.

Sing praise to the LORD, you his faithful
     ones,
   and give thanks to his holy name.
For his anger lasts but a moment;
   a lifetime, his good will.
At nightfall, weeping enters in,
   but with the dawn, rejoicing.

R⁄. I will praise you, Lord, for you have
     rescued me.
   or
R⁄. Alleluia.

Hear, O LORD, and have pity on me;
   O LORD, be my helper.
You changed my mourning into dancing;
   O LORD, my God, forever will I give you
     thanks.

R⁄. I will praise you, Lord, for you have
     rescued me.
   or
R⁄. Alleluia.

SECOND READING
Rev 5:11-14

I, John, looked and heard the voices of
     many angels
   who surrounded the throne
   and the living creatures and the elders.
They were countless in number, and they
     cried out in a loud voice:
      "Worthy is the Lamb that was
        slain
        to receive power and riches,
           wisdom and strength,
        honor and glory and blessing."
Then I heard every creature in heaven and
     on earth
   and under the earth and in the sea,
   everything in the universe, cry out:
      "To the one who sits on the throne
        and to the Lamb
        be blessing and honor, glory and
           might,
        forever and ever."
The four living creatures answered,
     "Amen,"
   and the elders fell down and worshiped.

CATECHESIS

About Liturgy

Avoiding Overworking and Burnout, Part I: Previously on these pages I have written about the extravagance and fullness of liturgies we all strive for and the need to "pull out all the stops" on Easter. All of this is true: our liturgy demands the fullness of signs and symbols, and is worthy of every effort to make the public prayer of the church lavishly cared for, prepared, and executed.

All of that said, anyone in a leadership role for any portion of an institution's liturgy—or all of the liturgy—must be cautious to avoid overworking oneself or burning out in that role. Further, those who labor in the vineyard under those in liturgical leadership should be on the lookout for leaders who exhibit signs of burnout: stress that leads to being tired, anxious, angry, or perhaps even confused or withdrawn.

There are two techniques I'd like to share today to help anyone avoid fatigue and burnout. These took many years for me to learn; I am still working to master both of them. They often do not come naturally to people in positions of authority, nor to perfectionists, which I'm afraid describe many of us who work in liturgy.

The first technique is delegation. The art of leaving to another person the responsibilities that you oversee is more complicated than it might first appear. You must find someone responsible and adequately trained and/or experienced with a role, or be willing to mentor or send someone to various workshops as needed. For tasks such as "scheduling lectors," that might not be so challenging. For other responsibilities like "training lectors," that might be more difficult. You must also be willing to hand over near-complete authority, lest the person be in the difficult spot of having responsibilities without power. You must be willing to let that person sometimes make mistakes or decide something differently than you would, often a "right" decision, just not the one you would make. (You must also be willing, of course, to correct "wrong" decisions that are truly wrong.) These last elements of delegation are the toughest to internalize.

A further benefit of delegation is that it can help create a broad sense of "ownership" in a parish's corporate worship. "Liturgy" is, after all, the "work of the people" and should be achieved by making it truly so. Sharing such responsibility can also help ensure that the liturgical practices faithfully reflect the local community, including the details and vision that those in the community find important and meaningful—again, quite possibly "right" even if not the choices we individually might make.

The second technique will be addressed in next Sunday's writing, the Pareto Principle: in short, not letting the perfect become the enemy of the good.

About Music

Rising for Mission: Today's Scripture should instill in our congregations a strong sense of mission and evangelization. To help the music reinforce that call during the continuing celebrations of resurrection, consider "Arise, O Church, Arise" (WLP/GIA) with text by Paul Nienaber, SJ, and a lively tune by John Angotti. From the *Lead Me, Guide Me* hymnal (GIA), "I'm Available to You" by Carlis Moody Jr. is a strong personal affirmation of willingness to serve and speak God's truth.

SPIRITUALITY

GOSPEL ACCLAMATION
John 10:14

℟. Alleluia, alleluia.
I am the good shepherd, says the Lord;
I know my sheep, and mine know me.
℟. Alleluia, alleluia.

Gospel

John 10:27-30; L51C

Jesus said:
"My sheep hear my voice;
  I know them, and they follow me.
I give them eternal life, and they shall
    never perish.
No one can take them out of my hand.
My Father, who has given them to me,
    is greater than all,
  and no one can take them out of the
      Father's hand.
The Father and I are one."

Reflecting on the Gospel

In the western Indian state of Gujarat, many of the shepherds gather their various flocks together at night in one place. This enables the shepherds to share the night watches and more easily protect the sheep. At daybreak, each shepherd calls his sheep to take them to water and then move on. The call of each shepherd is different, and as the sheep hear it, they disentangle themselves from the large flock and follow their own shepherd. This may not sound very surprising until we discover that as many as 5,000 sheep can be gathered in the one nighttime flock. Each shepherd is so familiar with his own sheep, and they with him, that when the sheep answer his voice, the shepherd recognizes the weak as needing extra care and notices and looks for the strays.

In today's gospel, John describes Jesus as the Shepherd who gathers us into the flock of his community, aware of our weaknesses and strengths and our tendency to wander away from him yet calling us by name and to life. We can say nothing more moving about human beings than that they call each other to life. It is the beautiful reality behind the fidelity of husband and wife or the steadfastness of friends; it is what helps relationships to endure through good times and bad. Yet all this is a faint echo of the creating word that God has whispered over the dust of each human person, a word that in its intimacy is unutterable by anyone except our Creator and the Son who was sent to make it flesh among us. In the Easter garden, the risen Jesus speaks the one most personal word to Mary Magdalene—her name, "Mary!" And she turns to him from whom she will never turn away, responding to the voice of the Shepherd with his name: "'Rabbouni,' which means Teacher" (20:16).

In today's gospel, Jesus is speaking in the portico of Solomon's temple during the winter feast of the Dedication (Hanukkah), a winter festival that commemorates God's deliverance of Israel from the Syrian tyrant, Antiochus Epiphanes, through the resistance of the Maccabees. After its profanation, the temple was purified and rededicated in 164 BCE, and so this feast was one that remembered and renewed hope for deliverance from Israel's enemies. Jesus is not the powerful political leader that many were waiting for when Israel was again under occupation, a messiah who would save them from civil and religious tyranny. Jesus offers the people a different security: the safety of eternal life if they commit their lives into his hands and obey his voice. Jesus can do this because the Father has given him the flock for its safekeeping and shepherding. The Easter Triduum tells us how costly Jesus's care of his flock will be, but the body of the Shepherd that is ravaged in death is also raised in glory to know and name his sheep and call them into a share of that glory. With the responsorial Psalm 100 we profess our faith in this and recognize ourselves as belonging to God as his flock. That God's steadfast love for us endures forever is most clearly revealed in the Christ who is both compassionate Shepherd and obedient Lamb.

The voice of the Shepherd is heard now in that of his disciples.

Focusing the Gospel

Key words and phrases: "My sheep hear my voice; I know them, and they follow me."

To the point: This gospel appears short, yet it contains the doctrine of salvation, as well as the Trinity. It is through Jesus that we receive eternal life. Jesus receives us through the Father, and yet he and the Father are one. Recall that two weeks ago, Jesus sent the apostles the Holy Spirit. John, who writes this gospel, is giving us the through line of experiences that are summed up and codified in the doctrine of the Trinity.

Jesus is the Good Shepherd, who draws us with his voice, which is quite literal. Jesus was a human being who walked around this earth and used a physical voice to share stories, heal members of his community, and laugh with friends. This literal accounting continues when Jesus tells us, "I give them eternal life, and they shall never perish." This isn't a metaphor, either. We believe that we can share in eternal life with the Lord, in the communion of saints, and that in the kingdom of heaven we won't perish.

Connecting the Gospel

to the first reading: This week's passage from Acts continues the story of Peter boldly proclaiming the works of Jesus. They've gained a lot of followers who weren't born Jewish. These are the Gentiles. In order to follow Peter, they've converted to Judaism. Later it will be decided that one doesn't need to convert to Judaism to be a Christian, but keep in mind that this was probably a few months to years after the death of Jesus, and Christianity is in its infancy.

This, understandably, bothers those born Jewish. Not only is this religious minority accustomed to being left alone, this influx of Jewish converts is following the suspicious upstarts who had followed Jesus.

to experience: Paul and Barnabas are challenging the existing way of doing things and blatantly rebuking the religious standards of the day. They see that there are certain members of their community who are not interested in the message of Jesus, because they fear it threatens their precariously balanced freedom under Roman rule. The freedom through Jesus being offered to them doesn't make sense. They're comfortable, and any threat to their comfort is suspect. Do you ever refuse a call to Christian charity because it upsets your comfort? If you put being a disciple above being comfortable, how would your life have to change?

Connecting the Responsorial Psalm

to the readings: In the gospel this week, Jesus says, "My sheep hear my voice; I know them, and they follow me. . . . No one can take them out of my hand." This is another instance of the Trinity. The psalm speaks of the Lord as the shepherd, and here, Jesus is explaining that he is the shepherd. They are one and the same.

to psalmist preparation: "Know that the Lᴏʀᴅ is God; / he made us, his we are; / his people, the flock he tends." Internet culture has recently taken the term "sheep" as derogatory, one who follows blindly. However, in this psalm we are reminded that a sheep is one who is tended lovingly by a shepherd. We desire to be sheep, and claim our place in Christ's flock.

PROMPTS FOR FAITH-SHARING

Have you ever been invited to participate in an activity, party, or group that makes you uncomfortable because it requires you to challenge yourself? Why did you hold reservations? Did you eventually join?

_____

_____

_____

Recall a time you turned down an opportunity to be charitable in word or deed because it would have upset your routine. (We have all done this.) Looking back on it, would you do things differently? Why or why not?

_____

_____

_____

_____

Who is your shepherd? Is it material success? Professional gain? Social acclaim? How can you reorient your tendencies to follow Christ?

_____

_____

_____

_____

If you were a first-century Jew, how do you think you would have reacted to Peter in the square in the first reading? Would you have listened with curiosity, suspicion, or interest?

_____

_____

_____

_____

Model Rite for the Blessing and Sprinkling of Water

Presider: In today's gospel we encounter Christ, the Good Shepherd. May this water remind us whose we are . . . *[pause]*

   [continue with The Roman Missal, *Appendix II]*

Homily Points

• In *Waiting for God,* Simone Weil writes that love is a direction. This image is interesting, as instead of insisting that love is manifest in the same static, unchanging actions, it suggests that love looks different in different times and different circumstances. The way we are called to love when we are children looks different from the way we are called to love as we grow in age and faith. The way a single father loves his children might look different than the love a woman has for her elderly mother. And that is OK! The particulars of love can change from situation to situation, but the source and direction of authentic love is always God.

• We discern the direction of love throughout our lives. In today's gospel Jesus proclaims, "My sheep hear my voice; I know them, and they follow me." Notice that Jesus does not say, "My sheep do what I tell them. They have an obligation to me." As we continue to discern God's call in our lives, we listen not for specific instructions for every possible scenario we encounter. Instead, we listen to the voice of Jesus by following his command: Do this to remember me. We can love because we have known love.

• This is the intimacy that is often associated with the image of the Good Shepherd. When Pope Francis said that shepherds must smell like the sheep, he reminds us of the intimate relationship between the two. This is our model *par excellence.* In order to love and serve others we must be close to them, keenly aware of their unique and individual needs, hopes, fears, and dreams. These are not the same for each person. The Good Shepherd shows us how love is a direction.

Model Universal Prayer (Prayer of the Faithful)

Presider: With confidence that the Shepherd hears us, we confidently raise our prayers and petitions.

Response: Lord, hear our prayer.

That the church may listen to the voice of the Shepherd, guided by his example of tenderness and love . . .

That civic leaders may create legislation that protects the most vulnerable . . .

That all who feel abandoned by God or the church may know that they always have a home in the arms of the Shepherd . . .

That our local community may follow the example of shepherds and coexist peacefully with the natural world that surrounds us . . .

Presider: Loving God, hear the prayers we bring to you this day. We know your voice and strive to be attentive to it, living lives in intimate union with you. We ask this through Christ our Lord. **Amen.**

COLLECT

Let us pray.

Pause for silent prayer

Almighty ever-living God,
lead us to a share in the joys of heaven,
so that the humble flock may reach
where the brave Shepherd has gone before.
Who lives and reigns with you in the unity
   of the Holy Spirit,
God, for ever and ever. **Amen.**

FIRST READING
Acts 13:14, 43-52

Paul and Barnabas continued on from
   Perga
   and reached Antioch in Pisidia.
On the sabbath they entered the
   synagogue and took their seats.
Many Jews and worshipers who were
   converts to Judaism
   followed Paul and Barnabas, who spoke
     to them
   and urged them to remain faithful to the
     grace of God.

On the following sabbath almost the whole
   city gathered
   to hear the word of the Lord.
When the Jews saw the crowds, they were
   filled with jealousy
   and with violent abuse contradicted
     what Paul said.
Both Paul and Barnabas spoke out boldly
   and said,
   "It was necessary that the word of God
     be spoken to you first,
   but since you reject it
   and condemn yourselves as unworthy
     of eternal life,
   we now turn to the Gentiles.
For so the Lord has commanded us,
   I have made you a light to the Gentiles,
   that you may be an instrument of
     salvation
   to the ends of the earth."

The Gentiles were delighted when they
   heard this
   and glorified the word of the Lord.
All who were destined for eternal life came
   to believe,
   and the word of the Lord continued to
     spread
   through the whole region.
The Jews, however, incited the women of
   prominence who were worshipers
   and the leading men of the city,
   stirred up a persecution against Paul
     and Barnabas,
   and expelled them from their territory.

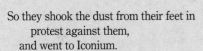

So they shook the dust from their feet in
   protest against them,
   and went to Iconium.
The disciples were filled with joy and the
   Holy Spirit.

RESPONSORIAL PSALM
Ps 100:1-2, 3, 5

℟. (3c) We are his people, the sheep of his
   flock.
   or
℟. Alleluia.

Sing joyfully to the LORD, all you lands;
   serve the LORD with gladness;
   come before him with joyful song.

℟. We are his people, the sheep of his
   flock.
   or
℟. Alleluia.

Know that the LORD is God;
   he made us, his we are;
   his people, the flock he tends.

℟. We are his people, the sheep of his
   flock.
   or
℟. Alleluia.

The LORD is good:
   his kindness endures forever,
   and his faithfulness, to all generations.

℟. We are his people, the sheep of his
   flock.
   or
℟. Alleluia.

SECOND READING
Rev 7:9, 14b-17

See Appendix A, p. 300.

About Liturgy

Avoiding Overworking and Burnout, Part II: Continuing from the writings of last week, the second technique I'll mention here is the Pareto Principle. Usually used to talk about cause and effect, the application to liturgy is the same. The idea is, roughly, that 80 percent of an effect comes from 20 percent of the causes, and vice versa. For example, it might take you twenty minutes to make a worship aid for a liturgy that is 80 percent complete—all but the fine-tuning and proofing, for instance—but it will then take you another eighty minutes to finish those details. Especially for those of us who strive for perfection in even the smallest tasks, "powering through" that last 20 percent of a job that asks for 80 percent of our labor can be exhausting!

Here's the secret: not all our day-to-day responsibilities in liturgical ministries have to be done to a full 100 percent. It's often worthwhile to do a cost-benefit analysis, especially this time of year with First Communions, confirmations, weddings, graduations: it can get overwhelming. For instance, perhaps confirmation would be absolutely perfect if you, as music director, swapped in that one new hymn you just discovered for the preparation of the gifts. But that requires time to order the piece, update the worship aid, rehearse the choir . . . And the piece you did last year? It could stand one more year of use probably; it's largely a different congregation than last year who won't even know what they're missing.

Note carefully I'm not saying it's fine to do all your liturgical tasks at only 80 percent—not at all! That will only lead to poor and unfulfilling liturgies, and, if you are in a professional role, likely job loss. Recalling and using the Pareto Principle is necessarily contextual, not an everyday endeavor. We should still note, moment to moment, if we have reached a point in our labors of diminishing returns, where inefficiency begins to rule the day. Similarly, as Shakespeare noted, we might find ourselves in a situation where "Striving to better, oft we mar what's well." More colloquially, if it ain't broke, we might not want to be fixing it, lest our efforts for perfection accidentally create something not as good as what we already had.

Let us often strive for perfection, and simultaneously not let perfection be the enemy of the good.

About Music

Good Shepherd Sunday: We have once again reached Good Shepherd Sunday, as this Fourth Sunday of Easter is nicknamed. Your first instinct may be to search your parish's repertoire for various settings of Psalm 23, and of course there will be many settings of this beloved text to pick from. The psalm in this particular cycle is Psalm 100, and there are many fine paraphrases and settings of this appropriate psalm too.

You can keep the Easter spirit alive by singing settings of Psalm 118 as well, perhaps at the communion procession. Settings by Trevor Thompson (OCP) and Marty Haugen (GIA) are popular, but explore lesser known settings by Shannon Cerneka (GIA) or Timothy R. Smith (OCP). Lastly, consider the *Psallite* refrain "You Are the Shepherd" (Liturgical Press).

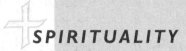

SPIRITUALITY

GOSPEL ACCLAMATION
John 13:34

℟. Alleluia, alleluia.
I give you a new commandment, says the Lord:
love one another as I have loved you.
℟. Alleluia, alleluia.

Gospel

John 13:31-33a, 34-35; L54C

When Judas had left them, Jesus said,
  "Now is the Son of Man glorified,
      and God is glorified in him.
If God is glorified in him,
  God will also glorify him in himself,
  and God will glorify him at once.
My children, I will be with you only a
      little while longer.
I give you a new commandment: love
      one another.
As I have loved you, so you also should
      love one another.
This is how all will know that you are
      my disciples,
  if you have love for one another."

Reflecting on the Gospel

The shadow of Judas falls over the first verse of today's gospel. The words about glory and love are spoken only after this chosen disciple has gone out into the night that is already within him. Jesus speaks gently to his own, to "[m]y children." In the five verses of this gospel, two words are constantly repeated: "glory" and "love." Judas walks away from both. In the prologue to his gospel, John proclaims that the glory of God was revealed in the descent of the Word into our humanity, "glory as of the Father's only Son, / full of grace and truth" (John 1:14). Now as Jesus comes to his "hour," the love that will be his ultimate self-sacrifice becomes also his hour of glory, a new prologue to his ascent to the Father in the glory of the resurrection. This is the life and love and glory that Jesus will share with his disciples.

This is the "hour" and this is the "today" in which past, present, and future flow together and are redefined as the reality in which all disciples, both at and beyond this gospel table, are to live Jesus's love command. This commandment is "new," not because the Old Testament was lacking in love but because, first, it is a commandment given with the authority of Jesus himself who loved his own to the end (John 13:1). Second, it is "new" because it is about the love that is to be practiced in the new Christian communities of Jesus's disciples. This does not mean these communities will be elitist or exclusive, but is a recognition of the truth that Christian life and mission depend mainly on the witness of those who love one another as Jesus has loved, with the radical love that takes him to death and resurrection.

The loss of faith that so often results from the lack or distortion of this love is tragically evident in the past and present history of the church. Sexual, physical, or psychological abuse by those called Christian—and especially those in whom great trust has been placed—denominational division and bickering, human rights ignored or violated: all these are failure in obedience to Jesus's command to love one another as he has loved us.

One of the significant New Testament words for resurrection is *anastasis*, "standing up." Jesus stood up for the insignificant, dispossessed, and disadvantaged people; he stood up against the lack of love in powerful people and places, both civil and religious, and he died because this is the way he lived. This is why God "stood up" for Jesus by raising him from the dead to the glory of his resurrection. In our parish communities, we may have wonderful liturgies and eager ministers, but if there is also jealousy, possessiveness, status seeking, and more judgment passed than love given by both laity and clergy, if there are subtle policies of exclusion rather than inclusion, shadows fall over us. We become death-dealing individuals rather than life-giving communities.

Focusing the Gospel

Key words and phrases: "This is how all will know that you are my disciples, if you have love for one another."

To the point: This is it: the finale, the final word, the last message that Jesus leaves with us before ascending into heaven. It's simple and straightforward. There isn't a lot of room to wonder what he's talking about. Love one another. That's it. That's the endgame. Our job is to love one another. How? "As I have loved you."

Throughout the gospel, Jesus has modeled this love for us. He could have ended everything by reminding us that we are loved, and always will be. Instead of choosing words to soothe, Jesus gives us a new commandment. In Jesus's last moments with his best friends, he essentially tells them, "Go and do for others what I did for you."

Connecting the Gospel

to the first reading: Catholics often ignore this gap of time between the resurrection and the Nicene Creed. In the three hundred years in between Jesus walking around on earth and the codified national acceptance of Christianity by Constantine, it grew throughout the Middle East, Africa, and southern Europe by word of mouth. Paul and Barnabas go into cities telling people about Jesus, their dear personal friend. Paul and Barnabas pick a few leaders from the community and perform the first ordinations when they, "with prayer and fasting, commended them to the Lord."

to experience: When we walk into a church to attend Mass, we are participating in a work that has been going on for more than 2,000 years. While this is impressive, we need to leave space to marvel at how small it began. The church was not handed to us fully formed. Paul and Barnabas, guided by the Holy Spirit, are seeing it through its infancy.

Connecting the Responsorial Psalm

to the readings: "Let all your works give you thanks, O LORD, / and let your faithful ones bless you." One of the main ways we "give thanks" to the Lord is doing exactly what Jesus tells us to do in the gospel: love one another. We don't need to do grand works of sacrifice or ministry; we need to love one another as Jesus has loved us.

to psalmist preparation: Jesus performed miracles and great acts of healing, but he also shared meals with his friends, listened to his mom, and made space for the members of society everyone else wanted to ignore. These are ways to participate in the "discourse of the glory of your kingdom." How do you, in your ministry, show your fellow Catholics love? In what ways does your call to share the psalm embody Christ's love?

PROMPTS FOR FAITH-SHARING

How did Jesus love his disciples?

Do you feel that you love others as Jesus loves you? Why or why not?

What is one concrete example of Jesus's love for you in your life?

If you were in Antioch in the first century, how do you think you would have reacted to Paul and Barnabas?

Model Rite for the Blessing and Sprinkling of Water

Presider: In today's gospel Jesus calls us to love others as he has loved us. May this water remind us of our call to live in God's love . . . *[pause]*

    [continue with The Roman Missal, *Appendix II]*

Homily Points

• The Johannine narrative is much more than a simple historical account of the life of Jesus of Nazareth. Rather, John uses a number of literary forms to help his readers understand the reality of life in Christ. Specifically, John's gospel boasts a high Christology where it is abundantly clear that Jesus is indeed the Son of God. One of the primary examples of this occurs in today's reading where Jesus gives a new commandment to his disciples. Prior to Jesus, it was only YHWH who issued commandments. In giving this new command, it is clear that Jesus is God.

• The command itself, like many of Jesus's teachings, is easier said than done. In saying: "As I have loved you, so you also should love one another," Jesus calls us to love as God loves. This is not a love that is individualistic, nor is it grounded in fanfare and exultation. Instead, this love is profoundly communal and rooted in the humility and vulnerability of self-gift.

• Christ's own example of self-gift shows us how to share this love with others. We love as God loves when we lower our voices to listen to people whose voices might be typically ignored or forgotten. We love as God loves when we recognize our own limitations and need for a community of people to support us. We love as God loves when we share our gifts with others, unafraid of the consequences. Are you happy with how you have loved today?

Model Universal Prayer (Prayer of the Faithful)

Presider: As we pray to more fully embody the love that Jesus shares, we raise our prayers for our community and world.

Response: Lord, hear our prayer.

That all who call themselves Christian may practice and share the love of Christ . . .

That all people in positions of power follow Jesus's example of humility and self-gift . . .

That all who are suffering the pain of loss may find comfort and care in the hearts and hands of others . . .

That all gathered here may be a living witness to the God of love through the way we treat each other . . .

Presider: Loving God, you are the source of all love. May we relish the example you give us and find the strength to practice the faith in you that we profess. We ask this through Christ our Lord. **Amen.**

COLLECT

Let us pray.

Pause for silent prayer

Almighty ever-living God,
constantly accomplish the Paschal
    Mystery within us,
that those you were pleased to make new
    in Holy Baptism
may, under your protective care, bear
    much fruit
and come to the joys of life eternal.
Through our Lord Jesus Christ, your Son,
who lives and reigns with you in the unity
    of the Holy Spirit,
God, for ever and ever. **Amen.**

FIRST READING

Acts 14:21-27

After Paul and Barnabas had proclaimed
    the good news to that city
    and made a considerable number of
      disciples,
    they returned to Lystra and to Iconium
      and to Antioch.
They strengthened the spirits of the
    disciples
    and exhorted them to persevere in the
      faith, saying,
    "It is necessary for us to undergo many
      hardships
    to enter the kingdom of God."
They appointed elders for them in each
    church and,
    with prayer and fasting, commended
      them to the Lord
    in whom they had put their faith.
Then they traveled through Pisidia and
    reached Pamphylia.
After proclaiming the word at Perga they
    went down to Attalia.
From there they sailed to Antioch,
    where they had been commended to the
      grace of God
    for the work they had now
      accomplished.
And when they arrived, they called the
    church together
    and reported what God had done with
      them
    and how he had opened the door of
      faith to the Gentiles.

RESPONSORIAL PSALM

Ps 145:8-9, 10-11, 12-13

℟. (cf. 1) I will praise your name for ever,
    my king and my God.
    or
℟. Alleluia.

The Lord is gracious and merciful,
 slow to anger and of great kindness.
The Lord is good to all
 and compassionate toward all his
  works.

R⫽. I will praise your name for ever, my
  king and my God.
 or
R⫽. Alleluia.

Let all your works give you thanks,
 O Lord,
 and let your faithful ones bless you.
Let them discourse of the glory of your
  kingdom
 and speak of your might.

R⫽. I will praise your name for ever, my
  king and my God.
 or
R⫽. Alleluia.

Let them make known your might to the
  children of Adam,
 and the glorious splendor of your
  kingdom.
Your kingdom is a kingdom for all ages,
 and your dominion endures through all
  generations.

R⫽. I will praise your name for ever, my
  king and my God.
 or
R⫽. Alleluia.

SECOND READING
Rev 21:1-5a

Then I, John, saw a new heaven and a new
  earth.
The former heaven and the former earth
  had passed away,
 and the sea was no more.
I also saw the holy city, a new Jerusalem,
  coming down out of heaven from God,
  prepared as a bride adorned for her
  husband.
I heard a loud voice from the throne
  saying,
 "Behold, God's dwelling is with the
  human race.
He will dwell with them and they will be
  his people
 and God himself will always be with
  them as their God.
He will wipe every tear from their eyes,
 and there shall be no more death or
  mourning, wailing or pain,
 for the old order has passed away."

The One who sat on the throne said,
 "Behold, I make all things new."

About Liturgy

Love One Another: "This is how all will know that you are my disciples, / if you have love for one another" (John 13:35). This passage, which ends today's gospel, must stand as a reminder to each of us: in all things we do—not some of the things, not most of the things—in all things we do, there must be humble and sacrificial love. Even in lament or righteous anger, there must be love. If that love is absent, we are not living and proclaiming Christ. An end, no matter how noble or fruitful, cannot justify a loveless means. The elevation of even the most marginalized and cast aside cannot be accomplished by lowering the worth of any other individual or group of people. May this wisdom, this spirituality fill all we do as we lead the church universal in communal prayer!

About Liturgical Documents

Sing to the Lord—Three Judgments, One Evaluation: One last bit of writing on Sing to the Lord for now, that of evaluating the music chosen for liturgy. Music in Catholic Worship introduced the three judgments when picking music for liturgy: the liturgical, the pastoral, and the musical. Sing to the Lord takes effort to further these judgments by reminding us, "All three judgments must be considered together, and no individual judgment can be applied in isolation from the other two" (126). We cannot pick a piece of music for a liturgical moment unless it can satisfy all three facets of this single assessment.

The liturgical judgment is described in terms of structure and text in Sing to the Lord; a facet of the textual judgment not explicitly mentioned is assessing whether the text of a piece meets the liturgical moment. For instance, the "entrance chant," as the Missal calls it, is meant to "open the celebration, foster the unity of those who have been gathered, introduce their thoughts to the mystery of the liturgical time or festivity, and accompany the procession of the Priest and ministers" (GIRM 47). We need to ensure, by text and tune, all these conditions are met.

The pastoral judgment necessitates some knowledge of who will be gathered in prayer (STL 130). Aspects like sanctification, formation, and culture are noted, as is the need to determine whether the music truly bears the weight of the faith the text it sets. "The pastoral question, finally, is always the same: Will this composition draw this particular people closer to the mystery of Christ, which is at the heart of this liturgical celebration?" (STL 133).

The musical judgment is the most subjective of the lot, by its nature, so it's best to let the words of Sing to the Lord speak on their own:

> This judgment requires musical competence. Only artistically sound music will be effective and endure over time. To admit to the Liturgy the cheap, the trite, or the musical cliché often found in secular popular songs is to cheapen the Liturgy, to expose it to ridicule, and to invite failure.
>
> Sufficiency of artistic expression, however, is not the same as musical style, for "the Church has not adopted any particular style of art as her own. She has admitted styles from every period, in keeping with the natural characteristics and conditions of peoples and the needs of the various rites." Thus, in recent times, the Church has consistently recognized and freely welcomed the use of various styles of music as an aid to liturgical worship. (135–36)

Selecting music for liturgy requires quite a lot more than determining the "theme" of the readings and locating community favorites to match. Reminded of the three judgments in one evaluation, let us pursue our sung prayer with additional vigor and intentionality!

✝ SPIRITUALITY

GOSPEL ACCLAMATION
John 14:23

℟. Alleluia, alleluia.
Whoever loves me will keep my word,
    says the Lord,
and my Father will love him and we will
    come to him.
℟. Alleluia, alleluia.

Gospel   John 14:23-29; L57C

Jesus said to his disciples:
   "Whoever loves me will keep
      my word,
   and my Father will love him,
   and we will come to him and
      make our dwelling with
      him.
Whoever does not love me does
   not keep my words;
   yet the word you hear is not
      mine
   but that of the Father who sent
      me.

"I have told you this while I am
   with you.
The Advocate, the Holy Spirit,
   whom the Father will send in my
      name,
   will teach you everything
   and remind you of all that I told you.
Peace I leave with you; my peace I give
   to you.
Not as the world gives do I give it to
   you.
Do not let your hearts be troubled or
   afraid.
You heard me tell you,
   'I am going away and I will come
      back to you.'
If you loved me,
   you would rejoice that I am going to
      the Father;
   for the Father is greater than I.
And now I have told you this before it
   happens,
   so that when it happens you may
      believe."

Reflecting on the Gospel

In today's gospel Jesus continues to speak reassuring words about love. He knows the unspoken questions in the hearts of his disciples—not only those around the Last Supper table, but all those of future generations. How will we be able to do what we heard Jesus tell us last Sunday: love one another as he has loved us? "Whoever loves me will keep my word," says Jesus, and this word is

what he has received from the Father who sent him. Obedience and love are bound together, not by any external law, but by the love that Jesus lived and now speaks to our hearts from the depths of his heart. He is in our hearts, to be loved freely, without compulsion. Jesus is present and loved when his disciples remember his words and release them from the past by allowing them to make a claim on their present and their future.

Nostalgia for what life was like when Jesus was present in first-century Palestine imprisons us in the past. The new way of remembering him will be powerful, real, and yet invisible, as present as the life-giving air we breathe. Jesus names this *Parakletos*, the Paraclete, the Holy Spirit. The word *parakletos* has been variously and richly translated as "encourager," "advocate," "counselor." The Holy Spirit is all of these for Jesus's disciples, individually, and corporately as church. The Spirit is both conservative and creative, the memory and future of the church, enabling us to reach back to the memory of what Jesus said and did and bring this to that life, which is constantly renewed with new understanding and experience of his mystery.

On this night of gifts, Jesus next offers his disciples the gift of peace. As with the new love commandment, this peace is also new; it is not sentimental, complacent, secure, or conflict-free because it is, Jesus says, "my peace"—a peace that comforts the afflicted and afflicts the comfortable. It is a gift given not in the context of cozy table talk, but on the cold eve of his death, when one friend has already become an enemy and left the companionship of the table, and Jesus is saying his last goodbyes to those who, with one exception, will fail to stand by him during his passion and death. He assures them that they should not be afraid but find new courage in his peace. This peace is *shalom*, the right relationship that flows from our loving union with God through Jesus and the Holy Spirit. The Holy Spirit makes connections, establishes unlikely partnerships, and breaks down barriers between people—if we are open and welcoming to the Spirit's advocacy for this in us.

Jesus's life has been all about the God who sent him, not about himself, and in this sense he can say, "[T]he Father is greater than I." Jesus is leaving his disciples because of his obedient love of the Father that will take him through death into the glory of the resurrection that the Father will bestow upon him. Jesus and his Father will share this glory and love with his disciples through the Holy Spirit. These Last Supper words, therefore, are not about absence but about presence: the abiding presence of the Father and the Son with the community of disciples in the power of the Spirit, until the end of time. If the disciples' love is generous, not possessive, they will rejoice in the departure of

Jesus for this is the accomplishment of his life's work. Tonight they only hear Jesus's words; when the risen Jesus again offers his peace and his Spirit-Breath moves over the chaos of their disillusionment and fears, they will understand (John 20:19-23).

Focusing the Gospel

Key words and phrases: "Peace I leave with you; my peace I give to you."

To the point: After explaining the arrival of the Holy Spirit, Jesus declares that he is giving us peace. Have you ever considered that peace, true peace, may be the primary work of the Holy Spirit? When we are at peace in our relationships, in our communities, and in our world, we are making present the kingdom of heaven on earth. We achieve that peace with the aid and guidance of the Holy Spirit, the presence of God on earth. Jesus tells us that even without immediate peace in all areas of our lives, we can still let go of our anxiety. The Holy Spirit brings peace, and the Holy Spirit is with us.

Connecting the Gospel

to the first reading: We continue to see the early church forming in Acts. The issue of whether Gentiles need to first become Jews to follow Christ is slowly being decided based on very young tradition and the needs of the moment. We believe these things to be guided by the Holy Spirit, working through the early church in the decisions of Paul, Barnabas, and the elders. They're making the best decisions they can at any given moment, in the hopes that they can keep their burgeoning flock together and live as Jesus instructed. What they end up doing is creating foundational tradition that is written down by Luke, included in the canon of the New Testament, and that establishes church teaching.

to experience: Have you ever had an experience that you didn't pay attention to but that ended up being very impactful? Paul and Barnabas probably weren't making every decision with the weight of two thousand years on their shoulders. They thought Jesus was going to return any minute, and so they had better keep his followers in line and supported. The modern church is built upon very human decisions (guided by the Holy Spirit) that were made by the early church concerned with what was in front of them, not how it would impact people two millennia later. If we approached our anxieties with this sentiment, taking each need on its own terms without being constantly distracted by repercussions, would that perhaps afford us all a little more peace?

Connecting the Responsorial Psalm

to the readings: This week's psalm speaks about nations. We can view the gospel as Jesus's call for our personal peace, but the psalm draws that desire for peace into the national sphere. "[Y]ou rule the peoples in equity." Every nation is different, but the Lord loves every nation, even nations which enact laws that harm human rights and promote economies that are unjust. Likewise, when we are unjust in our own lives, God is waiting to grant us peace.

to psalmist preparation: Think of a prayer that your own nation needs to hear and hold it in your heart as you proclaim these words. Allow yourself to be specific with your intentions, so that when you are proclaiming, "So may your way be known upon earth; among all nations, your salvation," you know exactly what you are asking for.

Model Rite for the Blessing and Sprinkling of Water

Presider: Today Jesus tells us, "Peace I leave with you; my peace I give to you." May these waters remind us of the peace for which we live and long . . . *[pause]*

  [continue with The Roman Missal, *Appendix II]*

Homily Points

• One does not need to look far to find division in our world. It sometimes even seems that our current obsession with social media contributes to this sense of division, as it is certainly easy to create "the other." *She believes something different than me. She is other. He looks different than I do. He is other.* As it is true for us today, division and disagreement were not uncommon in the early church. Today's reading from Acts places us in the middle of a heated conversation about what it takes to be a Christian.

• In what ways do we see these separations in our own church? When do we make it difficult for someone to fully participate in our parish and liturgical life? How do we exclude people with different ideologies? The divisions Paul and Barnabas experienced in antiquity remain, though they may look a bit different. These divisions might look like systemic injustice, systems of racism, xenophobia, and sexism that have become so commonplace in our community that we are not even aware of them.

• Jesus's words in the gospel are what will move us forward: "Peace I leave with you; my peace I give to you." It is impossible to grow past division and distinction without embracing this peace. This peace of Christ begins in our own hearts before it is shared with others and comes only from a relationship with the God of love. Although Jesus tells his disciples that he must go away, we rest in the warm embrace of the Advocate, our Spirit and guide. Come, Holy Spirit. Breathe in us a new resolve.

Model Universal Prayer (Prayer of the Faithful)

Presider: Jesus tells us not to let our hearts be troubled. With confidence, we bring our cares and concerns to the God who loves us and listens to our prayer.

Response: Lord, hear our prayer.

That the church may seek to unify the divisions that exist within our own ecclesial communities . . .

That world leaders may address divisions with a sense of openness and humility . . .

That all who live in constant anxiety and fear may find calm in the presence of God and the people of God . . .

That all Christian churches may work toward peace and unity in Christ Jesus, the Lord . . .

Presider: Loving God, you are the peace that surpasses all division and destruction. May we grow in our relationship with you so to imitate the peace you freely give. We ask this through Christ our Lord. **Amen.**

COLLECT

Let us pray.

Pause for silent prayer

Grant, almighty God,
that we may celebrate with heartfelt
    devotion these days of joy,
which we keep in honor of the risen Lord,
and that what we relive in remembrance
we may always hold to in what we do.
Through our Lord Jesus Christ, your Son,
who lives and reigns with you in the unity
    of the Holy Spirit,
God, for ever and ever. **Amen.**

FIRST READING
Acts 15:1-2, 22-29

Some who had come down from Judea were
    instructing the brothers,
  "Unless you are circumcised according
      to the Mosaic practice,
  you cannot be saved."
Because there arose no little dissension
    and debate
  by Paul and Barnabas with them,
  it was decided that Paul, Barnabas, and
      some of the others
  should go up to Jerusalem to the
      apostles and elders
  about this question.

The apostles and elders, in agreement
    with the whole church,
  decided to choose representatives
  and to send them to Antioch with Paul
      and Barnabas.
The ones chosen were Judas, who was
    called Barsabbas,
  and Silas, leaders among the brothers.
This is the letter delivered by them:

"The apostles and the elders, your brothers,
  to the brothers in Antioch, Syria, and
      Cilicia
  of Gentile origin: greetings.
Since we have heard that some of our
    number
  who went out without any mandate
      from us
  have upset you with their teachings
  and disturbed your peace of mind,
  we have with one accord decided to
      choose representatives
  and to send them to you along with our
      beloved Barnabas and Paul,
  who have dedicated their lives to the
      name of our Lord Jesus Christ.
So we are sending Judas and Silas
  who will also convey this same message
      by word of mouth:
  'It is the decision of the Holy Spirit and
      of us

not to place on you any burden beyond
   these necessities,
namely, to abstain from meat sacrificed
   to idols,
from blood, from meats of strangled
   animals,
and from unlawful marriage.
If you keep free of these,
   you will be doing what is right. Farewell.'"

RESPONSORIAL PSALM
Ps 67:2-3, 5, 6, 8

R̸. (4) O God, let all the nations praise you!
   or
R̸. Alleluia.

May God have pity on us and bless us;
   may he let his face shine upon us.
So may your way be known upon earth;
   among all nations, your salvation.

R̸. O God, let all the nations praise you!
   or
R̸. Alleluia.

May the nations be glad and exult
   because you rule the peoples in equity;
   the nations on the earth you guide.

R̸. O God, let all the nations praise you!
   or
R̸. Alleluia.

May the peoples praise you, O God;
   may all the peoples praise you!
May God bless us,
   and may all the ends of the earth fear
      him!

R̸. O God, let all the nations praise you!
   or
R̸. Alleluia.

SECOND READING
Rev 21:10-14, 22-23

See Appendix A, p. 301.

About Liturgy

All Are Welcome: Today's reading from the Acts of the Apostles briefly relates the church's discussions, in its earliest days, on whether converts to Christianity need to follow the complete Mosaic Law in order to follow Christ. The determination was that if Gentiles ascribed to a certain few commands, they would be "doing what is right" (Acts 15:29); the focus, then, of the rest of Acts, and to a large extent Paul's mission of evangelization, became the Gentiles opening the church doors much wider and revealing the fullness of Christ's salvation.

Pope Francis said in his apostolic exhortation *Evangelii Gaudium* (The Joy of the Gospel), "The Eucharist, although it is the fullness of sacramental life, is not a prize for the perfect but a powerful medicine and nourishment for the weak" (47). This echoes St. Ambrose, who wrote, "If, whenever Christ's blood is shed, it is shed for the forgiveness of sins, I who sin often, should receive it often: I need a frequent remedy." More explicitly at the end of that same paragraph, Pope Francis concludes, "[T]he Church is not a tollhouse; it is the house of the Father, where there is a place for everyone, with all their problems."

Paul wrote, describing what was passed onto him regarding the Eucharist, "Therefore whoever eats the bread or drinks the cup of the Lord unworthily will have to answer for the body and blood of the Lord. A person should examine himself, and so eat the bread and drink the cup. For anyone who eats and drinks without discerning the body, eats and drinks judgment on himself" (1 Cor 11:27-29). The judgment on who receives worthily, in Paul's regard, is left to that person alone and his or her relationship with God, it seems.

Too often we place artificial limits on who is welcome in our houses of worship. Too often we pass frail and human judgment on others' worthiness when it isn't our place to do so. The church (and the capital-C Church) always welcomes sinners, the lost, the cast aside, the ones who do not or cannot recognize their own worth because this was integral to Christ's ministry as well.

Sometimes we can sadly apply such litmus tests to those who want to share ministry with us, and sometimes the harshest human judgments are erroneously passed from one person to another not when positions or beliefs are far apart, but when agreement on some matter is almost-but-not-quite the same. Sometimes these verdicts are reached not because of what someone believes, but because of how that person speaks or acts (or chooses not to) on those beliefs. These sorts of sad divisions must be healed, or not created in the first place. In the words of "Ubi Caritas," "Lest we be divided in mind, let us beware. / Let cease malicious quarrels, let strife give way. / And in the midst of us be Christ our God."

It is easy to forget, in church, in ministry, that we are all on the same team! Christ himself taught that "whoever is not against us is for us" (Mark 9:40). Let us not place any artificial restrictions on who can pray, minister, teach, heal, sing, or love in Christ's name, especially at liturgy.

About Music

Music of Welcome: Consider two different "All Are Welcome" pieces this weekend: one by Marty Haugen (GIA), the other by Jesse and Jennah Manibusan (OCP). Several various settings of "Ubi Caritas" would also be appropriate, and would be a nice reminder of Holy Thursday a few weeks ago.

✝ SPIRITUALITY

GOSPEL ACCLAMATION
Matt 28:19a, 20b

℟. Alleluia, alleluia.
Go and teach all nations, says the Lord;
I am with you always, until the end of the world.
℟. Alleluia, alleluia.

Gospel

Luke 24:46-53; L58C

Jesus said to his disciples:
  "Thus it is written that
      the Christ would
      suffer
  and rise from the dead on
      the third day
  and that repentance, for
      the forgiveness of
      sins,
  would be preached in his
      name
  to all the nations, begin-
      ning from Jerusalem.
You are witnesses of these
      things.
And behold I am sending the promise
      of my Father upon you;
  but stay in the city
  until you are clothed with power
      from on high."

Then he led them out as far as
      Bethany,
  raised his hands, and blessed them.
As he blessed them he parted from
      them
  and was taken up to heaven.
They did him homage
  and then returned to Jerusalem with
      great joy,
  and they were continually in the
      temple praising God.

Reflecting on the Gospel

We all have experienced having to say goodbye and return home without some-one we love: a sick parent, a son or daughter beginning college, a soldier depart-ing for active service, the airport farewell to a dear friend. We have to leave each other, but it's hard to go. The aspect of the Easter mystery of the ascension is about not only Jesus's departure and homecoming, but also ours.

In the readings for this feast we have two accounts of the ascension: one at the end of Luke's gospel, closing the period of his earthly ministry; the other at the beginning of the Acts of the Apostles ("part two" of Luke's gospel) and the beginning of the church's mission. Through these two accounts, Luke em-phasizes the historical continuity of the mystery of the risen Christ. Jesus's departure is a continuing challenge to the disciples of the "in-between-time" of the church. In the gospel, the ascension takes place on Easter day; in Acts, it is forty days later. Again, there is symbolism in this number. Forty days recalls the experience of the two prophet ances-tors who had spoken with Jesus on the mount of transfiguration. For forty days God instructed Moses in the law on Mount Sinai; for forty days Elijah journeyed to Sinai/Horeb before encountering God in the "light" silence outside the cave. "Forty" is also a biblical number of transition to a new stage of salvation history: from desert wanderings to the land of Canaan; from Jesus's wilderness experience to his public ministry; from the earthly pres-ence of Jesus to his presence in the Spirit in the community of believers.

For forty days the apostles are to be in the company of the risen Jesus, eat with him, and wait for the Holy Spirit, the promise of the Father, who will be given to them. They are to do this in Jerusalem, the city of prophets and the end point of Jesus's earthly journey in Luke's gospel. The earthly ministry of Jesus having been completed, in these "forty days" Jesus instructs his apostles about the beginning and continuing mission of the church. It is to be in the power of the Holy Spirit, its members believing in his risen presence, eating at table, wit-nessing beyond Jerusalem to the ends of the earth, and gathering and waiting together in joyful expectation.

As children (and perhaps still as adults, if we take the time), we may have often been fascinated to watch the clouds and see how quickly they formed new shapes, new "pictures," especially on windy days. Above us there seemed to be a "becoming world" of surprises, where nothing was fixed or static. The cloud that is described as enveloping Jesus at his ascension wraps him in the glory of God and reveals, even as it hides, another aspect of the Beloved Son: that there is no place for his disciples to just look "intently at the sky" (as the first reading puts it). The words of the two messengers who spoke to the apostles after Jesus ascended, men whose dress and words remind us of the two angels at the resur-rection tomb, suggest that this is the wrong kind of waiting, a dawdling that will never harvest the fruits of Jesus's resurrection. The time for eye-witnessing is past; now is the time for proclamation. The ascension points to the need for

Pentecost and the driving, Spirit-filled passion that will make the disciples the witnesses of Jesus throughout the world until he comes again.

Focusing the Gospel

Key words and phrases: "They did him homage and then returned to Jerusalem with great joy, and they were continually in the temple praising God."

To the point: Jesus begins with a quick recap of salvation history: "Thus it is written that the Christ would suffer and rise from the dead on the third day and that repentance, for the forgiveness of sins, would be preached in his name to all the nations, beginning from Jerusalem." He places his apostles firmly within this story and charges them to begin from their position as Jews and go forth to preach his name to all nations.

Once Jesus departs, they return home and are "continually in the temple praising God." How can they preach to all nations if they are inside a building? Because the temple they are in is Christ, whom they bring wherever they go.

Connecting the Gospel

to the first reading: Luke, who wrote Acts as well as the gospel in his name, provides more detail about the scene that took place at the ascension, and it is from his words that we have the image of Jesus being lifted up on a cloud and the apostles standing and staring at the sky. Along with the grace of the Holy Spirit, we also receive one of the hardest truths of our faith: "It is not for you to know the times or seasons that the Father has established by his own authority." Two thousand years later, we still don't know.

to experience: "He presented himself alive to them by many proofs after he had suffered, appearing to them during forty days and speaking about the kingdom of God." Luke spends a great deal of time on Jesus's words about the kingdom of God. The kingdom of God is what Christians are charged to make manifest in the world, right now. It is when we are following Jesus's words and living with the guidance of the Holy Spirit that we are bringing about Christ's kingdom.

Connecting the Responsorial Psalm

to the readings: The image of God mounting his throne to shouts of joy is the culminating scene of generations of anticipation. As Jesus ascends into heaven, his disciples, charged with bringing his message to all nations, witness the final act of this part of the story. It is God mounting his throne.

to psalmist preparation: The act of watching Jesus leave likely left his apostles a bit forlorn. Two men from heaven tell them to stop staring at the sky, because Jesus will one day return. The psalm today gives us an opportunity to rejoice and be grateful, and not focus on the very human emotion of loss. You have the opportunity to invite the congregation into the celebration of Jesus's ascension, which is a celebration we continue to have, two thousand years later.

PROMPTS FOR FAITH-SHARING

Are you continually in the temple, praising God? What would this look like in your life?

What does the kingdom of God look like to you? How do you bring it about in your own life?

If you were one of the apostles who watched Jesus ascend into heaven, how do you think you would react? Would you feel a loss? Would it be excitement? Would you be thrilled with the call of spreading his word to all nations?

Have you ever felt "clothed with power from on high"? If you imagine this "power" as the presence of the Holy Spirit, what do you think it would feel like to have it physically wrap around you, like clothing?

Model Rite for the Blessing and Sprinkling of Water

Presider: As we celebrate the ascension, Jesus tells his disciples in today's gospel that they are called to give witness by their lives. May these waters strengthen our witness in Christ . . . *[pause]*

    [continue with The Roman Missal, *Appendix II]*

Homily Points

• Endings are never easy. Think about some of the times in your own life when you experienced something good coming to an end. Perhaps you were nearing the end of a wonderful family vacation. Maybe you were ending a job or possibly retiring after a long career. You might even remember the moments when you were saying goodbye to a loved one who was dying. While there is certainly sadness and perhaps some fear and anxiety, those endings also signal the start of something new. Although the disciples were parting with Jesus, the new stage of their relationship with Christ was just beginning.

• Being a witness of Christ certainly means emulating what we have seen Jesus do in the gospels. It involves standing with people who are marginalized or ignored by society. It means forgiving people who have hurt us. It includes giving of ourselves for the good of others. But today's celebration of the ascension reveals another important aspect of giving witness to Christ. The ascension celebrates not so much Jesus leaving earth as it does the depth of his relationship with the Father. Jesus, fully God and fully human, enters the glory of heaven.

• The last line of today's gospel highlights our call as disciples of Christ. Luke writes, "They did him homage and then returned to Jerusalem with great joy." After their encounter with Christ, the disciples returned home to the places where they lived and worked and recreated full of the joy of Christ. Are we filled with this same joy in our own lives? Does our relationship with God the Father and Christ the Son translate to joyful witness? If not, perhaps we need to ask God for the grace to grow in relationship with God so that we might better know the joy God promises.

Model Universal Prayer (Prayer of the Faithful)

Presider: In today's reading from Acts the disciples were "looking at the sky," not understanding where Jesus was going. Knowing that our relationship with Christ transcends time and space, we are able to lift our prayers today, confident that they will be heard.

Response: Lord, hear our prayer.

That our church may grow in intimacy with God through witnessing Jesus's life and sharing the joy of relationship . . .

That all who work for peace may find support and nourishment for their work, sustained always by the Holy Spirit . . .

That all who are at places of transition in their lives may look forward with courage to the future, relying on the strength of their relationship with others in Christ . . .

That all who feel abandoned, especially children who are orphans or separated from their families, may know the warmth of love in relationship and community . . .

Presider: Loving God, our prayers are no secret to you. We raise them today to grow in intimacy with you, trusting that you are always with us, no matter the circumstances. We ask this through Christ our Lord. **Amen.**

COLLECT
Let us pray.

Pause for silent prayer

Gladden us with holy joys, almighty God,
and make us rejoice with devout
    thanksgiving,
for the Ascension of Christ your Son
is our exaltation,
and, where the Head has gone before in
    glory,
the Body is called to follow in hope.
Through our Lord Jesus Christ, your Son,
who lives and reigns with you in the unity
    of the Holy Spirit,
God, for ever and ever. **Amen.**

or

Grant, we pray, almighty God,
that we, who believe that your Only
    Begotten Son, our Redeemer,
ascended this day to the heavens,
may in spirit dwell already in heavenly
    realms.
Who lives and reigns with you in the unity
    of the Holy Spirit,
God, for ever and ever. **Amen.**

FIRST READING
Acts 1:1-11

In the first book, Theophilus,
    I dealt with all that Jesus did and taught
    until the day he was taken up,
    after giving instructions through the
        Holy Spirit
    to the apostles whom he had chosen.
He presented himself alive to them
    by many proofs after he had suffered,
    appearing to them during forty days
    and speaking about the kingdom of God.
While meeting with them,
    he enjoined them not to depart from
        Jerusalem,
    but to wait for "the promise of the
        Father
    about which you have heard me speak;
    for John baptized with water,
    but in a few days you will be baptized
        with the Holy Spirit."

When they had gathered together they
    asked him,
    "Lord, are you at this time going to
        restore the kingdom to Israel?"
He answered them, "It is not for you to
    know the times or seasons
    that the Father has established by his
        own authority.
But you will receive power when the Holy
    Spirit comes upon you,
    and you will be my witnesses in
        Jerusalem,

throughout Judea and Samaria,
 and to the ends of the earth."
When he had said this, as they were
 looking on,
 he was lifted up, and a cloud took him
 from their sight.
While they were looking intently at the
 sky as he was going,
 suddenly two men dressed in white
 garments stood beside them.
They said, "Men of Galilee,
 why are you standing there looking at
 the sky?
This Jesus who has been taken up from
 you into heaven
 will return in the same way as you have
 seen him going into heaven."

RESPONSORIAL PSALM

Ps 47:2-3, 6-7, 8-9

R̊. (6) God mounts his throne to shouts of
 joy: a blare of trumpets for the Lord.
 or:
R̊. Alleluia.

All you peoples, clap your hands,
 shout to God with cries of gladness,
for the LORD, the Most High, the awesome,
 is the great king over all the earth.

R̊. God mounts his throne to shouts of joy:
 a blare of trumpets for the Lord.
 or:
R̊. Alleluia.

God mounts his throne amid shouts of joy;
 the LORD, amid trumpet blasts.
Sing praise to God, sing praise;
 sing praise to our king, sing praise.

R̊. God mounts his throne to shouts of joy:
 a blare of trumpets for the Lord.
 or:
R̊. Alleluia.

For king of all the earth is God;
 sing hymns of praise.
God reigns over the nations,
 God sits upon his holy throne.

R̊. God mounts his throne to shouts of joy:
 a blare of trumpets for the Lord.
 or:
R̊. Alleluia.

SECOND READING

Eph 1:17-23

or Heb 9:24-28; 10:19-23

See Appendix A, p. 301.

CATECHESIS

About Liturgy

Peaceful Tension: The celebration of the Ascension is perhaps the most obvious liturgical example of Christian paradox. Our salvation and eternal life with and in God is achieved, and is also incomplete and not fully accomplished until the Second Coming.

Paradox is necessarily uncomfortable; it demands holding two seemingly opposi-tional concepts together in a peaceful tension. Many people avoid conflict at nearly any cost. Many have a worldview that could be called excessively "black and white" with very little patience for any gray. Yet our faith is not only full of paradox, it depends on them!

Our messiah was not one of political might but rather a suffering servant who washed feet and preached that the last would be first. Paul wrote that, for some, Christ's glory through suffering and death would be a stumbling block and be seen as foolishness, yet God's foolishness is stronger than anything humanity can offer.

That Mary is known as *Theotokos,* the God-bearer, is paradox: how can a woman give birth to God? As much a claim about Christ and his being both human and of the same substance of God the Father, it is argued to be necessary for our salvation that the hypostatic union—the two natures residing in one human person—be accurate and true.

How can God, that which the whole world cannot contain, come to dwell within con-secrated bread and wine and so come to dwell within us, to feed and sustain us?

As we prepare and pray liturgies today we, too, are mindful that the liturgy is itself divine and a work of humanity. It's comforting to remember that there is no greater evidence of liturgy being the work of the people as when something goes "wrong"—or at least not as planned. Moments like these can be frustrating or worse sometimes, but viewed through the proper lens, they are also moments of grace and holiness.

Further, we must examine the components and ministers of our liturgies, and assess if there are opportunities to express more of the "peaceful tension" that paradox is. Some lament that, in the last sixty or so years, our faith has lost a bit of the "mystery" it once had, particular via the Tridentine expression of the Eucharist. That "mystery" isn't always aligned with Christian paradox, but often it is, and it is likely more benefi-cial than not to help our assemblies know and live within that peaceful tension.

About Music

Risen in Glory: Christian Cosas recently penned a powerful litany expressing the prayer of the church dealing with tough issues of abuse, denials, and other struggles. "Rise Again" (WLP/GIA) was also named the 2019 Song of the Year by Association of Catholic Publishers and is well worth your consideration.

"Revelation Song" by Jennie Lee Riddle (WN) is a contemporary expression of Christ's ascended glory, adapting familiar words from the book of Revelation. The same text is used as the foundation of the *Psallite* refrain "Worthy Is the Lamb Who Was Slain" (Liturgical Press), with a typically easy-to-learn and repetitive (in a good way!) melody.

Lastly, consider today Melvin L. Farrell's hymn text "Let the Earth Rejoice and Sing" (WLP/GIA), paired with the festive LLANFAIR tune so prevalent on ascension day, due to its connection to the more familiar words "Hail the day that sees him rise," found in many hymnals.

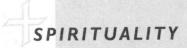

SPIRITUALITY

GOSPEL ACCLAMATION
cf. John 14:18

R℣. Alleluia, alleluia.
I will not leave you orphans, says the Lord.
I will come back to you, and your hearts will
 rejoice.
R℣. Alleluia, alleluia.

Gospel   John 17:20-26; L61C

Lifting up his eyes to heaven, Jesus
  prayed, saying:
  "Holy Father, I pray not only for them,
  but also for those who will believe in
    me through their word,
  so that they may all be one,
  as you, Father, are in me and I in you,
  that they also may be in us,
  that the world may believe that you
    sent me.
And I have given them the glory you gave
    me,
  so that they may be one, as we are one,
  I in them and you in me,
  that they may be brought to perfection
    as one,
  that the world may know that you sent
    me,
  and that you loved them even as you
    loved me.
Father, they are your gift to me.
I wish that where I am they also may be
    with me,
  that they may see my glory that you
    gave me,
  because you loved me before the foun-
    dation of the world.
Righteous Father, the world also does not
    know you,
  but I know you, and they know that you
    sent me.
I made known to them your name and I
    will make it known,
  that the love with which you loved me
  may be in them and I in them."

Reflecting on the Gospel

Ultimately, our baptism makes us members of the community of God's children
in fellowship with one another because of the conviction that the unity of the
Trinity is the foundation upon which our Christian unity is established, which
makes us appreciate our own union as God's children. Through ritual celebration and storytelling, Eastertide offers us an opportunity to reflect deeply on
our union with the Trinity. This celebration fills and prepares us in hope of an
eternal glory in God's presence.

In the gospel reading, Jesus's
prayer for unity between God and
humankind reveals the main features
of the story of our salvation—
namely, God becoming human so
that God will renew humanity from
within, from participation in human
life in order to elevate humanity to
the status that we share with God at
the time of creation because we bear
God's image. Our union with God
is certainly not far removed from
our relationship with one another.
For this reason, Jesus recognizes
the importance of our union with
one another and prays that it will
be the same as the union he shares
with God. Our fellowship with one
another testifies to our siblinghood
as God's children. It shows that we
belong to God and Jesus Christ, and that we are disposed to reflect in our lives
the same elements of unity that bind God and Jesus Christ together. Just as God
and Jesus Christ are working together for the benefit of humankind, likewise we
must approach our fellowship with one another with a spirit of benevolence and
goodwill, which is the intention of Jesus's prayer to God on our behalf.

Another important intention in Jesus's prayer for us is that the love of God,
which Jesus Christ experienced in his life and death on the cross, may also be
experienced by believers. Jesus is among us as God made flesh manifesting the
love of God in his ministry of calling our attention to the presence of God in
the world. Christian love originates in God loving us first, and God's love for
us is manifested in the self-giving of Jesus Christ on the cross. The love of God
toward Jesus Christ is displayed in Christ's love for us by accepting to die on the
cross (Gal 2:20). It is in this context that Jesus's prayer to love one another as I
have loved you (John 13:34) finds its invitation to replicate in believers' relationships with one another the love with which we have been divinely loved by God
through Christ, and to make whatever sacrifices are necessary to respect and
honor the dignity of each other.

Jesus expresses his greatest desire for humanity, for whose sake he took
human nature and for the fulfillment of the saving plan of God in us, when
he says, "I wish that where I am they also may be with me." The unity of the
Trinity with believers comes to fulfillment at the heavenly habitation. The ministry of Jesus Christ for our sake carries within it the invitation to live on earth
with the same mind that is in Jesus Christ (Phil 2:5) in order for believers to

prepare for life in the heavenly kingdom. The ultimate end of our earthly life is to be with God and share eternity with Jesus Christ. Easter season invites us to prepare for this life through acts of love, humility, and compassion toward one another, which are the virtues of our Christian life and holiness.

Focusing the Gospel
Key words and phrases: "Father, they are your gift to me."

To the point: John gives us Jesus's final prayer and, in doing so, gives us a glimpse into the loving heart of this fully human, fully divine Lord. As with much of John's gospel, Jesus is speaking not only with a command but with deep, tender love. Jesus is from the Lord, and prays that we know it, but he also reflects on the gift he has received in us. We are God's gift to Jesus. What do you think of that? We spend so much time and energy on the knowledge that Jesus is a gift, and that our lives are a gift, and that God showers us with gifts, but how often do we reflect on the notion that we, ourselves, are a gift to God? Do you ever wonder about how the way we choose to live our lives, and be in relationship with God and one another, is our gift to God? Jesus offers this tender, precious reflection on the value we hold simply by being ourselves. We are a gift to Jesus. You, without any qualifying act, are a gift to the Lord. And you are valued as such.

Connecting the Gospel
to the first reading: Stephen sees the reality of Jesus with God in heaven, and speaks of it to his community. They block out this information (they "covered their ears") and reject both Stephen's words and Stephen himself. The implications of Stephen's message are so inflammatory that they kill him.

to experience: Jesus says in the gospel, "I wish that where I am they also may be with me, that they may see my glory that you gave me." Stephen does indeed see this glory. The first reading tells us, "Stephen, filled with the Holy Spirit, looked up intently to heaven and saw the glory of God and Jesus standing at the right hand of God." Have you ever had an experience of truly witnessing the glory of God? Was it shocking? Were you filled with awe or peace? Were you able to notice in that moment that you were filled with the Holy Spirit?

Connecting the Responsorial Psalm
to the readings: The psalm this week has a narrative structure that gives us an opportunity to reflect on Jesus's return to the Father. The first verse tells us that the Lord is king and his kingdom is built on justice. The second verse tells us how everyone responds: the heavens and all peoples proclaim justice and see his glory. The final verse can be read as the prayer spoken back to God, in acknowledgment of this.

to psalmist preparation: This week the psalm provides the congregation an opportunity to celebrate and revel in Jesus's return to the Father. It is a reminder to us that regardless of our earthly constraints, the Lord remains king above all. It is a declaration of hope.

PROMPTS FOR FAITH-SHARING

When in your life do you feel that you are a gift to others? What are some moments or tasks you remember in which you were being a gift to those around you?

Have you ever had a moment in which you were certain you were "filled with the Holy Spirit"? Perhaps the birth of a child, or a delicate exchange with a friend?

When you think of Jesus sitting on a throne of justice, does it fill you with hope, or does it make you nervous? Why do you think you feel this way?

If Jesus came back to earth tomorrow, how confident would you feel in the way you've lived your life and the decisions you've made?

CELEBRATION

Model Rite for the Blessing and Sprinkling of Water

Presider: Today Jesus prays that all may know the love of the Father. May this water remind us of God's immense love for us.

[continue with The Roman Missal, *Appendix II*]

Homily Points

• In today's gospel Jesus prays that all his followers may be one, just as Jesus and the Father are one. It seems that two thousand years later this prayer is just as urgent in our lives today, for it is not difficult to see the division that permeates even our own church. Rather than working for unity, many Catholics are quick to point out the flaws in someone else's theology or even in their relationship with Christ. Social media continues to divide people of faith, hastily creating labels and exacerbating differences.

• We must remember, however, that Jesus calls us to unity, not uniformity. Oneness in Christ does not mean that everyone's relationship with Christ will look the same. Oneness in Christ also does not necessitate everyone living out their vocation in the exact same way. The Spirit blesses all of us with manifold gifts. Sometimes we ignore these different gifts and perspectives, prioritizing some standardization of what it means to be Christian. Jesus does not call us to be the same. Rather, Jesus prays that we may be one. It is important that we work to highlight what we have in common rather than what divides us.

• Jesus's prayer in today's gospel is not only for the first disciples who heard him speak those words. Instead, Jesus prays for all who will believe in him; he prays for all of us. The renowned Irish novelist James Joyce wrote that Catholic means "Here comes everybody." May we work to grow in communion with each other through Christ, so that we might better recognize God's presence in everyone.

Model Universal Prayer (Prayer of the Faithful)

Presider: Just as Jesus prays to the Father in today's gospel, we lift our prayers to the God of life and love.

Response: Lord, hear our prayer.

That the church might grow in unity by listening to all voices, especially the voices of people who are excluded or marginalized . . .

That local and world leaders may set aside their political differences so to work for the common good of all people . . .

That we might continue to uphold the prophetic voices in our midst, allowing all people to speak truth to power even when it might be uncomfortable or unwelcome . . .

That all who are wounded, suffering, or scared may find the courage to be themselves and always find a place of welcome in our local community . . .

Presider: Loving God, hear the prayers we bring before you today. We trust that you will hear us, just as you hear the voices of all who call out to you. Give us the courage to work for unity, following the example you set before us. We ask this through Christ our Lord. **Amen.**

COLLECT

Let us pray.

Pause for silent prayer

Graciously hear our supplications, O Lord,
so that we, who believe that the Savior of
    the human race
is with you in your glory,
may experience, as he promised,
until the end of the world,
his abiding presence among us.
Who lives and reigns with you in the unity
    of the Holy Spirit,
God, for ever and ever. **Amen.**

FIRST READING

Acts 7:55-60

Stephen, filled with the Holy Spirit,
    looked up intently to heaven and saw
        the glory of God
    and Jesus standing at the right hand of
        God,
    and Stephen said, "Behold, I see the
        heavens opened
    and the Son of Man standing at the
        right hand of God."
But they cried out in a loud voice,
    covered their ears, and rushed upon him
        together.
They threw him out of the city, and began
    to stone him.
The witnesses laid down their cloaks
    at the feet of a young man named Saul.
As they were stoning Stephen, he called
        out,
    "Lord Jesus, receive my spirit."
Then he fell to his knees and cried out in a
        loud voice,
    "Lord, do not hold this sin against
        them";
    and when he said this, he fell asleep.

RESPONSORIAL PSALM

Ps 97:1-2, 6-7, 9

R̸. (1a and 9a) The Lord is king, the most
        high over all the earth.
    or
R̸. Alleluia.

The Lᴏʀᴅ is king; let the earth rejoice;
    let the many islands be glad.
Justice and judgment are the foundation
        of his throne.

R̸. The Lord is king, the most high over all
        the earth.
    or
R̸. Alleluia.

144

The heavens proclaim his justice,
    and all peoples see his glory.
All gods are prostrate before him.

℟. The Lord is king, the most high over all
    the earth.
    or
℟. Alleluia.

You, O LORD, are the Most High over all
    the earth,
    exalted far above all gods.

℟. The Lord is king, the most high over all
    the earth.
    or
℟. Alleluia.

SECOND READING
Rev 22:12-14, 16-17, 20

I, John, heard a voice saying to me:
    "Behold, I am coming soon.
I bring with me the recompense I will give
    to each
    according to his deeds.
I am the Alpha and the Omega, the first
    and the last,
    the beginning and the end."

Blessed are they who wash their robes
    so as to have the right to the tree of life
    and enter the city through its gates.

"I, Jesus, sent my angel to give you this
    testimony for the churches.
I am the root and offspring of David,
    the bright morning star."

The Spirit and the bride say, "Come."
Let the hearer say, "Come."
Let the one who thirsts come forward,
    and the one who wants it receive the gift
        of life-giving water.

The one who gives this testimony says,
    "Yes, I am coming soon."
Amen! Come, Lord Jesus!

About Liturgy

Completeness, Wholeness, and Unity: The texts for today's Scriptures speak, in different ways, of completeness, of wholeness, and of unity. Though from their different vantage points, in one manner of pondering, these three themes are all one in the same. Completeness, wholeness, and unity are who God is and who the Christian community is, then, called to be. When someone or many someones are left out or allowed to fall behind or be forgotten, there can be no completeness, no wholeness, no unity.

It is a broadly known concept that liturgical music serves the liturgy, a liturgy intended to be sung and sung more fully (Sing to the Lord showed us in its discussion of progressive solemnity), in more of our experiences most of the time. One way in which music serves the liturgy is in the accompaniment of liturgical actions. The entrance chant accompanies a procession; a hymn or antiphon accompanies a sprinkling rite; the gospel acclamation accompanies the procession to the ambo; another hymn (or instrumental music) accompanies the presentation of the gifts and the preparation of both them and the altar; another hymn or antiphon accompanies the duration of the communion procession . . .

It is usually best if the music at these moments is roughly similar in length to the time it takes to accomplish the particular ritual action. A piece of music that is either too short or too long for a ritual moment is quickly noticed to be out of place. (It's worth noting that at the Easter Vigil liturgy the church prescribes a much longer gospel acclamation, with three verses from Psalm 118, than at any other liturgy—an opportunity for a much longer procession to the ambo, perhaps taking the book of the gospels through each aisle of church, bringing the Word close to God's people!)

With many hymns, violence is done to them if they are presented in an incomplete way, by either ending them early or by skipping verses. Obvious examples include singing hymns with the Beatitudes as their text: it only makes sense to sing all the verses. Similarly, if the hymn chosen has a trinitarian text with one verse dedicated to each person of the trinity, leaving a verse out leaves an assembly to sing an incomplete vision of the triune God.

Subtler examples include pieces that tell the story of the paschal mystery, where ending early might neglect the resurrection or ascension. If a text writer or the composer working with a text has decided to sing verse 1 again as a final verse, there is likely a very good reason for that choice, and we should respect it and probably even spend some time in prayer and reflection on that choice, either on our own or on rehearsal night with our choirs and ensembles.

The prayers we sing at liturgy deserve their own completeness, wholeness, and unity. It is there that holiness abides; it is there where we can truly lift our voices in the fullest expressions of our faith and honor those who help us do so.

About Music

Hymns of Unity: Hymns that speak of this wholeness and unity include, as recently mentioned, "Ubi Caritas" in any of a variety of incarnations. Consider, too, "Many and Great" by Ricky Manalo (OCP) or Somos el Cuerpo de Cristo by Jaime Cortez (OCP).

SPIRITUALITY

GOSPEL ACCLAMATION

℟. Alleluia, alleluia.
Come, Holy Spirit, fill the hearts of your faithful
and kindle in them the fire of your love.
℟. Alleluia, alleluia.

Gospel John 14:15-16, 23b-26; L63C

Jesus said to his disciples:
"If you love me, you will keep my
commandments.
And I will ask the Father,
and he will give you another Advocate to
be with you always.

"Whoever loves me will keep my word,
and my Father will love him,
and we will come to him and make our
dwelling with him.
Those who do not love me do not keep my
words;
yet the word you hear is not mine
but that of the Father who sent me.

"I have told you this while I am with you.
The Advocate, the Holy Spirit whom the
Father will send in my name,
will teach you everything
and remind you of all that I told you."

or John 20:19-23

On the evening of that first day of the
week,
when the doors were locked, where the
disciples were,
for fear of the Jews,
Jesus came and stood in their midst
and said to them, "Peace be with you."
When he had said this, he showed them his
hands and his side.
The disciples rejoiced when they saw the
Lord.
Jesus said to them again, "Peace be with
you.
As the Father has sent me, so I send you."
And when he had said this, he breathed on
them and said to them,
"Receive the Holy Spirit.
Whose sins you forgive are forgiven them,
and whose sins you retain are retained."

Reflecting on the Gospel

The Holy Spirit is described as the Comforter or Paraclete, which translates from the Greek as Helper or Advocate. Earlier in John's gospel, Jesus tells the disciples that he will leave them, but that the Father will send them another Advocate, one that will teach them everything and remind them of all they

have been taught (John 14:26). This Advocate that will come to them is "the Spirit of truth" who will be with them always (John 14:16-17). As the third person of the Holy Trinity, one way the Holy Spirit may be understood is as the active presence of God that enacts the will of God. In Genesis as the world was formed, we are told that a mighty wind swept over the waters before God spoke light into existence. With the Word, creation came into being, and God's Spirit caused it to be so.

It could be argued that the presence or the anointing of the Holy Spirit is an essential ingredient at the beginning of ministry and for its success. In John's gospel, before Jesus begins his public ministry, John the Baptist testifies, "I saw the Spirit come down like a dove from the sky and remain upon him" (John 1:32). This confirmed for John that the one he just baptized was indeed the prophesized Son of God, the one whom John heralded. Luke's gospel gives the account of Jesus announcing to those gathered in the synagogue the words of the prophet Isaiah, "The Spirit of the Lord is upon me, / because he has anointed me . . ." (Luke 4:18). This, after he was tempted in the desert by the devil. Luke informs us that not only was Jesus filled with the Spirit (through baptism) but he was also in the *power* of the Spirit: filled with the indwelling power of the Spirit and anointed. To anoint is to confer a special and specific designation, one that denotes separation and is intended for use that is holy. While one is typically anointed with oil, to be anointed with the Spirit is particular, indeed, and implies a designation and capacity that comes from God.

Just as Jesus began his public ministry after being imbued (filled) with the power of the Spirit, the disciples, newly reconstituted as twelve, were told to journey to Jerusalem where they would receive "power" when the Holy Spirit came upon them. Now that Jesus had physically departed, it was important that the disciples receive the power of the Holy Spirit as they began public ministry in Jesus's stead. Of course, as conveyed in the first reading, the Spirit of God was poured out on all who were present on the day of Pentecost, for in Scripture we see the physical manifestation of the Spirit as wind or breath, fire, and a dove.

We, too, are "sealed" with the Spirit through the sacrament of confirmation, which prepares and strengthens us for ministry, our service to the Body of Christ. Pentecost is often viewed as the birth of the church. Jesus empowered the disciples to continue his work when he breathed on them and empowered them. Our bodies are even temples of the Holy Spirit, according to St. Paul. Pentecost Sunday serves as a reminder of the gift of God's Spirit, bestowed so that we may have power for service and guidance from the Advocate who will remind us of all truth and be with us always.

Focusing the Gospel
Key words and phrases: "Jesus said to them again, 'Peace be with you.'"

To the point: This week's gospel reminds us of the gift we received in a special way at confirmation that we continue to receive anytime we pray, "Come, Holy Spirit." The presence of God on earth exists in a concrete and specific way in the person of the Holy Spirit. The Holy Spirit comes upon the apostles right after Jesus says, "Peace be with you." It is through the Holy Spirit that we do find peace.

Connecting the Gospel
to the first reading: The first reading this week is a manifestation of Christ's salvation intended for all nations. When the apostles receive the Holy Spirit, the first result of this new grace is their ability to speak with people from all over the world. The initial grace experienced by receiving the Holy Spirit is communication. It isn't power; it isn't humility; it's an opportunity to engage with people from every culture and ethnic background. This is the beginning of the universal church.

to experience: What does it mean that the first act of the Holy Spirit after being made manifest to the apostles is the gift of tongues? This should inform our call to personal ministry. No matter what our gifts are, whether they be words, presence, or deeds, we should always remember that the primary work of the Holy Spirit at Pentecost is to get Christ's message out to everyone.

Connecting the Responsorial Psalm
to the readings: What does the Holy Spirit do? Renew the face of the earth. Think about this word: "renew," or to make new again. Jesus died, and has been made new through the resurrection. The coming of the Holy Spirit is the earth's opportunity to be made new, through the work of those guided by the Holy Spirit. "When you send forth your spirit, they are created, / and you renew the face of the earth."

to psalmist preparation: What in your own life needs to be made new again? Is there a relationship or area of discipleship where you can bring this sentiment of renewal forward? How can you spend time this week allowing for renewal of your own faith? Bring all of this with you when you proclaim these words.

PROMPTS FOR FAITH-SHARING

What is one area of your life that can benefit from intentional renewal?

How do you work to bring Christ's message to those who "speak a different language" than you, perhaps in politics or career? How do you engage those who are different from you?

Knowing that the first act of the Holy Spirit when sent to the apostles is the work of communication, how can you renew the way you speak with family, friends, and colleagues?

Have you ever gone to Mass in another country and heard the words you know so well spoken in a different language? What was this experience like?

Model Rite for the Blessing and Sprinkling of Water

Presider: On this Pentecost Sunday we celebrate the coming of the Holy Spirit and Jesus entrusting his mission to his apostles then and to us today. May this water remind us of our call and mission.

[*continue with* The Roman Missal, *Appendix II*]

Homily Points

• Today's readings are filled with images we have seen before in Scripture. One of the most prominent is the tongues of fire that descend upon the apostles. We have seen fire as a presence of the divine when Moses encounters God in the burning bush. Likewise, the tongues of fire today also represent the divine, descending upon the apostles and charging them with a mission to proclaim God's saving work.

• Another image from Hebrew Scripture that we encounter today is that of breath. Jesus breathes on the disciples as they are gathered, saying, "Peace be with you." Jesus breathes life into the disciples, allowing them to overcome their fears. Likewise, in the second creation story in Genesis, God breathes life into the nostrils of the living being God creates. God's creative breath continues from the time of creation to Jesus and extends to our lives as well.

• This notion of creation is significant. So often we think of creation as being completed when God rests on the seventh day, but we need to remember that God's creation is still unfolding and will continue to unfold until the end of time. When Jesus breathes on the apostles, he renews and charges them to continue the work of creation by building up the kingdom of God. Likewise, the same Spirit moves in us today and allows us to participate in the creative work of the triune God. What power and responsibility! We pray that we may be open to the Spirit's work in our lives and thus remain attentive to God's voice.

Model Universal Prayer (Prayer of the Faithful)

Presider: Confident that we are filled with the Spirit, we are unafraid to call upon God as we strive to grow in relationship with God.

Response: Lord, hear our prayer.

That church leaders may remain open to God working in the world, especially the renewal and restoration that comes from the Spirit . . .

That all may grow as stewards of the earth and prioritize care for God's creation and our common home . . .

That we may work to welcome all people in our church and in our world, especially those who speak different languages or hold different cultural beliefs and values . . .

That all gathered here might continue to invoke the Spirit as they participate in the continual unfolding of God's creation . . .

Presider: Loving God, you breathe on us today just as you breathed in that first breath of creation and on the apostles that day of Pentecost. Give us the strength to respond to your call, knowing that you are with us in all we do and encounter. We ask this through Christ our Lord. **Amen.**

COLLECT

Let us pray.

Pause for silent prayer

O God, who by the mystery of today's
     great feast
sanctify your whole Church in every
     people and nation,
pour out, we pray, the gifts of the Holy Spirit
across the face of the earth
and, with the divine grace that was at work
when the Gospel was first proclaimed,
fill now once more the hearts of believers.
Through our Lord Jesus Christ, your Son,
who lives and reigns with you in the unity
     of the Holy Spirit,
God, for ever and ever. **Amen.**

FIRST READING

Acts 2:1-11

When the time for Pentecost was fulfilled,
     they were all in one place together.
And suddenly there came from the sky
     a noise like a strong driving wind,
     and it filled the entire house in which
          they were.
Then there appeared to them tongues as
     of fire,
     which parted and came to rest on each
          one of them.
And they were all filled with the Holy Spirit
     and began to speak in different tongues,
     as the Spirit enabled them to proclaim.

Now there were devout Jews from every
     nation under heaven staying in
     Jerusalem.
At this sound, they gathered in a large
     crowd,
     but they were confused
     because each one heard them speaking
          in his own language.
They were astounded, and in amazement
     they asked,
     "Are not all these people who are
          speaking Galileans?
Then how does each of us hear them in
     his native language?
We are Parthians, Medes, and Elamites,
     inhabitants of Mesopotamia, Judea and
          Cappadocia,
     Pontus and Asia, Phrygia and
          Pamphylia,
     Egypt and the districts of Libya near
          Cyrene,
     as well as travelers from Rome,
     both Jews and converts to Judaism,
          Cretans and Arabs,
     yet we hear them speaking in our own
          tongues
     of the mighty acts of God."

RESPONSORIAL PSALM

Ps 104:1, 24, 29-30, 31, 34

R̸. (cf. 30) Lord, send out your Spirit, and
    renew the face of the earth.
    or:
R̸. Alleluia.

Bless the Lᴏʀᴅ, O my soul!
    O Lᴏʀᴅ, my God, you are great indeed!
How manifold are your works, O Lᴏʀᴅ!
    The earth is full of your creatures.

R̸. Lord, send out your Spirit, and renew
    the face of the earth.
    or:
R̸. Alleluia.

If you take away their breath, they perish
    and return to their dust.
When you send forth your spirit, they are
    created,
    and you renew the face of the earth.

R̸. Lord, send out your Spirit, and renew
    the face of the earth.
    or:
R̸. Alleluia.

May the glory of the Lᴏʀᴅ endure forever;
    may the Lᴏʀᴅ be glad in his works!
Pleasing to him be my theme;
    I will be glad in the Lᴏʀᴅ.

R̸. Lord, send out your Spirit, and renew
    the face of the earth.
    or:
R̸. Alleluia.

SECOND READING

Rom 8:8-17

or

1 Cor 12:3b-7, 12-13

SEQUENCE

See Appendix A, p. 302.

About Liturgy

The Gift of Reverence: Several times a year, I lead confirmation retreats with a close friend of mine. We believe strongly in interactive components to these days, to allow the young people an opportunity to approach the faith more than just intellectually but with their hearts and souls, and their whole selves.

One of the activities we often do on these retreats is to divide the participants into seven smaller groups and assign each group one gift of the Holy Spirit. We then ask each group to come up with a business that offers a product or a service somehow connected to or a part of the gift they were assigned. Once they have come up with that idea, we invite them to create a logo or an ad for that business on poster board—something that would convey just what that particular gift of the Spirit is and how in practical ways it can help people in their day-to-day life.

I mention all this because one of the gifts of the Spirit is reverence, something we liturgists could probably always spend more time considering. Reverence is not something exclusive to church buildings and liturgy, though that is perhaps where it is practiced the most, and in the most public way. Often the businesses our retreat participants create that embody the gift of reverence include makers of incense or kneelers, both objects used liturgically to show reverence, deep respect, in the divine presence.

There are, of course, other ways to show reverence, and many of them vary from culture to culture, or from religion to religion. Christians stand, typically, when the gospel is proclaimed as a sign of reverence focused more tightly on the respect for and acknowledged importance of Christ's words and deeds. Our Jewish siblings sit when the Torah is read, however—not out of a lack of reverence, but as a posture more conducive to listening and study.

Within our own assemblies, we might in one church find the pews filled with people a few minutes before Mass begins but completely silent, but then travel to the next church over and find their gathering much more conversational and informal. While it might be tempting to call the second instance "irreverent," we might also consider whether one could be observing the Body of Christ by recognizing that in one another and by communication entering into true communion and true community. One version isn't necessarily right and the other wrong—it depends, ultimately, on the vision of and realization of reverence for each particular parish.

You can also examine the other gifts of the Spirit, liturgically, in similar fashion: how are wisdom, courage, or right judgment embodied in your congregations and your communal prayer? How might these gifts be embodied differently, more fully, by the expressions of liturgy and music?

About Music

Singing the Sequence: This solemnity is one of two (the other being Easter Day) that require the sequence between the second reading and the gospel acclamation. Singing it is almost always preferable. Ricky Manalo's "By the Waking of Our Hearts" (OCP) is a gentle and easily learned pentatonic melody, with verses that could be sung by the assembly or by a solo voice, with all joining on the refrain.

ORDINARY
TIME II

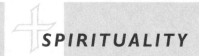

SPIRITUALITY

GOSPEL ACCLAMATION
Cf. Rev 1:8

℟. Alleluia, alleluia.
Glory to the Father, the Son, and the Holy Spirit;
to God who is, who was, and who is to come.
℟. Alleluia, alleluia.

Gospel

John 16:12-15; L166C

**Jesus said to his disciples:
"I have much more to tell you, but
 you cannot bear it now.
But when he comes, the Spirit
 of truth,
 he will guide you to all truth.
He will not speak on his own,
 but he will speak what he hears,
 and will declare to you the things
 that are coming.
He will glorify me,
 because he will take from what is
 mine and declare it to you.
Everything that the Father has is mine;
 for this reason I told you that he will
 take from what is mine
 and declare it to you."**

Reflecting on the Gospel

We mark our foreheads with the sign of the cross and name the Three Persons so often, but does anything of their mystery plow its significance into our hearts? At the beginning of our Christian lives, at baptism, we are named for them; at the beginning and end of each Eucharist we sign ourselves with their memory; when our bodies are signed in death, we hope they claim us; when we bless our children, we remember the creativity the Trinity shares with us. All these moments of naming the Trinity are occasions of life and love. When we are blessed "in the name of," we are incorporated into the personal history of the one named. The sign of the cross and the invocation of the Trinity, a prayer of gesture and words that we learned in childhood, are a simple yet profound statement that we belong to Father, Son, and Holy Spirit and are called to live in communion with them.

In the short reading from John's gospel, part of the Last Supper discourse, Jesus speaks about the Spirit, the great encourager, who will enable future communities of believers to have access to him and his Father after he is no longer with them in the flesh. For the Spirit there are no limitations of one place, one moment in history, one gathering of disciples. The Spirit gives the church a future and a hope. When Christian communities encounter new ecclesial, social, and global challenges, the Spirit enables past, present, and future to converge. The past and privileged words of Jesus will be remembered, but the Spirit will pluck the strings of memory so that a new melody is played, a new meaning will sound in the present context, and this song at the heart of the church will accompany disciples into the future.

The Spirit guides the teaching, interpretation, and witness of the church throughout the ages. It also places a great responsibility on those whose ministry is to spark a creative conversation between believers and the words of Jesus, especially those who, week after week, break open the Scriptures in the homily. Likewise, each member of the assembly has a responsibility to enter into that conversation with openness to the Spirit.

Theology has developed a word to describe the dynamic relationship between the Persons of the Trinity and the community of believers—*perichoresis*, or "dance." In this metaphorical language, the Trinity is a partnership of encircling and embracing, a graceful movement of loving attentiveness into which we are invited as partners who must, in our turn, draw others into the dance by our loving outreach to them. With the imagery of the dance we cannot think of God as solitary.

Theology, preaching, metaphor may all help toward gaining some understanding of who and what we celebrate on this feast, but perhaps it is again the poet who has the insight to realize that it is only in the communion of death—when we are drawn into the community of those whom the poet George Herbert calls the "unnumbered Three"—that we will truly see and understand because it is only then, in death, that the dust we are will be transformed. No longer will it blow into our eyes to blind us, but it will become a seeing dust that sparkles with a revelation of the mystery of the Three in our mutually unveiled presence.

Focusing the Gospel

Key words and phrases: "He will not speak on his own, but he will speak what he hears, and will declare to you the things that are coming."

To the point: The Holy Spirit interacts with us in a different way than Jesus interacts with us. Jesus lived a full life as a human and is present to us fully in the Eucharist. The Holy Spirit "will take from what is mine [Jesus's] and declare it to you." We are all loved by God and invited to live a life worthy of heaven. What the Holy Spirit does is bring out those parts of us that are oriented toward God, and shower us with grace. The Holy Spirit brings out the intrinsic possibility for salvation that we all have, as heirs of the resurrection of Christ. As an active person of the triune God, the Holy Spirit weaves through our hearts and thoughts, drawing us toward actions that follow Jesus's message and spread love and goodness. This isn't a metaphor; it's an action, performed by a person. The Holy Spirit is a person with agency, who is available for us to call upon at every moment, as one of the three persons of God.

Connecting the Gospel

to the first reading: This reading from Proverbs can be read as a monologue from the Holy Spirit. Within the construct of temporality and linear history, the notion of one God in three persons is very confusing and has proven to be one of the most frustrating aspects of our faith throughout Christian history. This passage offers those of us confined to linear time a poetic understanding of the Holy Spirit at the creation of the world. "The LORD possessed me, the beginning of his ways, / the forerunner of his prodigies of long ago; / from of old I was poured forth, / at the first, before the earth."

to experience: What is your understanding of the Holy Spirit? Most of us learn about the Holy Spirit with the imagery of a dove as children, and later as the agent of grace during sacraments. Because of the lack of a physical image, it's harder to explain the Holy Spirit in satisfying terms when explaining the Trinity. We know that the Holy Spirit is a person sent to us by God, after the ministry and resurrection of Jesus. We know the Holy Spirit continues to facilitate the active work of our Lord on earth today. We know the Holy Spirit is with us always, and can be called upon at any time. But in many ways, the esoteric understanding of this person of God isn't satisfactory, especially for Catholics who find the source and summit of faith in the physical presence of Christ in the Eucharist.

This week, we have the opportunity to read about the Holy Spirit as wisdom, in the first reading. Read these words as if they are the biography of the Holy Spirit, who has always existed as a person of the Trinity, with God, "beside him as his craftsman, / and I was his delight day by day, / playing before him all the while, / playing on the surface of his earth; / and I found delight in the human race."

Connecting the Responsorial Psalm

to the readings: Today's psalm, like the first reading, offers a poetic view of the work of the Holy Spirit. "When I behold your heavens, the work of your fingers, / the moon and the stars which you set in place." The Holy Spirit was present at the creation of the world and joined in the work of God's fingers.

to psalmist preparation: This week you share a series of scenes from the heavens to the beasts of the earth. Take time this week to reflect on the beauty and specificity of the psalmist. Your job is to share some of the most beautiful poetry ever written by human beings with your congregation. It's a privilege to share these words. Embrace that task and allow yourself to feel empowered by beauty.

PROMPTS FOR FAITH-SHARING

What images do you use for the Holy Spirit in prayer? What prayers have you found most helpful?

What is the context you usually find when you pray, "Come, Holy Spirit"? Do you reserve these words for collective prayer, or do you ever pray, "Veni, sancte spiritus" on your own?

How has the Holy Spirit been active in your life? Where have you seen the concrete impact of the work of this person of the Trinity?

If you think of the Holy Spirit as the active "agent" of God in the world today, how does that change your approach to the Trinity? How does knowing that God is constant and working, not only in the Eucharist but in all parts of life, impact your faith?

Model Penitential Act

Presider: As we celebrate the Most Holy Trinity, we delve deeper into the relationship between the Father, Son, and Holy Spirit. We, too, are called to participate in this relationship. For the times we have failed to live as we are called, we ask the triune God for pardon and peace . . . *[pause]*

Lord Jesus, you are the Son of the Father: Lord, have mercy.

Christ Jesus, you are our unending light and life: Christ, have mercy.

Lord Jesus, you are both fully God and fully human: Lord, have mercy.

Homily Points

• When we think about the word "mystery," we often associate it with a problem to be solved. It might even conjure up images of Sherlock Holmes or Scooby Doo or Angela Lansbury. But mystery in the theological sense is different from our typical understanding of the word. Rather than something to be solved, Christian mystery is something that is infinitely knowable. Instead of having a single, finite answer, such as Colonel Mustard in the kitchen with the candlestick, Christian mystery is mysterious in the sense that no matter how much we learn about something, there is still much more for us to know.

• As we celebrate the Most Holy Trinity today, we celebrate a God who always reveals more of God's self to us. No matter how much time we spend in prayer or studying theological texts, it is impossible for us to fully encapsulate our description or understanding of God. Fortunately, today's gospel gives us some helpful insight: "Everything that the Father has is mine; for this reason I told you that [the Spirit of Truth] will take from what is mine and declare it to you." Relationship, namely the relationship between the Father, Son, and Holy Spirit, is the foundation of the Trinity.

• God is relational by God's very nature, and the triune God also invites us into this relationship. As we are created in the image and likeness of God, we take part in this relationship of love that is constantly poured and shared between members. We hear this in today's second reading: "[T]he love of God has been poured out into our hearts through the Holy Spirit that has been given to us." When we respond to this love and share this love, we actively participate in the mystery of the Trinity.

Model Universal Prayer (Prayer of the Faithful)

Presider: Invited into relationship with the triune God, we freely share our prayers with the one who loves us.

Response: Lord, hear our prayer.

That the relational love of the Trinity might inspire church leaders to teach and preach with kindness and mercy . . .

That all local, national, and world leaders may work for the common good of all people by upholding laws based in justice and human relationship . . .

That all who are sick and all who care for them may experience the compassion of others in simple acts of love and connection . . .

That all people who are exploited, especially sex workers and victims of human trafficking, may know their God-given dignity and find safety, comfort, and peace . . .

Presider: Loving God, you call us into relationship with you. Created in your image, we know the love that flows between Father, Son, and Spirit. Help us embody this love in our own lives and know the joy of life in you. We ask this through Christ our Lord. **Amen.**

COLLECT

Let us pray.

Pause for silent prayer

God our Father, who by sending into the
world
the Word of truth and the Spirit of
sanctification
made known to the human race your
wondrous mystery,
grant us, we pray, that in professing the
true faith,
we may acknowledge the Trinity of
eternal glory
and adore your Unity, powerful in majesty.
Through our Lord Jesus Christ, your Son,
who lives and reigns with you in the unity
of the Holy Spirit,
God, for ever and ever. **Amen.**

FIRST READING
Prov 8:22-31

Thus says the wisdom of God:
"The LORD possessed me, the beginning of
his ways,
the forerunner of his prodigies of long
ago;
from of old I was poured forth,
at the first, before the earth.
When there were no depths I was brought
forth,
when there were no fountains or springs
of water;
before the mountains were settled into
place,
before the hills, I was brought forth;
while as yet the earth and fields were not
made,
nor the first clods of the world.

"When the Lord established the heavens
I was there,
when he marked out the vault over the
face of the deep;
when he made firm the skies above,
when he fixed fast the foundations of
the earth;
when he set for the sea its limit,
so that the waters should not transgress
his command;
then was I beside him as his craftsman,
and I was his delight day by day,
playing before him all the while,
playing on the surface of his earth;
and I found delight in the human race."

RESPONSORIAL PSALM

Ps 8:4-5, 6-7, 8-9

R̷. (2a) O Lord, our God, how wonderful
your name in all the earth!

When I behold your heavens, the work of
your fingers,
the moon and the stars which you set in
place—
what is man that you should be mindful
of him,
or the son of man that you should care
for him?

R̷. O Lord, our God, how wonderful your
name in all the earth!

You have made him little less than the
angels,
and crowned him with glory and honor.
You have given him rule over the works of
your hands,
putting all things under his feet.

R̷. O Lord, our God, how wonderful your
name in all the earth!

All sheep and oxen,
yes, and the beasts of the field,
the birds of the air, the fishes of the sea,
and whatever swims the paths of the
seas.

R̷. O Lord, our God, how wonderful your
name in all the earth!

SECOND READING

Rom 5:1-5

Brothers and sisters:
Therefore, since we have been justified by
faith,
we have peace with God through our
Lord Jesus Christ,
through whom we have gained access
by faith
to this grace in which we stand,
and we boast in hope of the glory of God.
Not only that, but we even boast of our
afflictions,
knowing that affliction produces
endurance,
and endurance, proven character,
and proven character, hope,
and hope does not disappoint,
because the love of God has been
poured out into our hearts
through the Holy Spirit that has been
given to us.

About Liturgy

The Relationship between Music and Preaching, Part I: Having recently here embarked on a brief journey through Sing to the Lord and other considerations on hymn texts and the foundational importance of fully active and conscious participation in the liturgy, I'd like to spend the next few weeks pondering the relationship between liturgical music and preaching. These thoughts were initially formed a few years ago at the request of Dr. Rhodora Beaton, who was at the time the professor of Liturgical and Sacramental Theology at Aquinas Institute of Theology in St. Louis, Missouri. It was presented to and discussed with her students in both her Theology of Worship class and the DMin in Preaching cohort.

The first question, of course, is why bother exploring this relationship at all? Isn't there already preaching at Eucharist, at least, if not other liturgies? Certainly, there is, but the power music has to impart a message and allow it to remain in someone's heart and soul cannot be denied, and sung music is often a more successful agent in that regard than preaching alone.

The relationship music shares with preaching is, first of all, scriptural. Paul wrote, "Let the word of Christ dwell in you richly, as in all wisdom you teach and admonish one another, singing psalms, hymns, and spiritual songs with gratitude in your hearts to God" (Col 3:16). Further, we already saw earlier in these pages the maxim attributed to St. Augustine, "Who sings well prays twice." But what does that mean? Music amplifies the text it carries, both sonically (acoustically, that is) and in meaning and profundity. When the melody, harmony, and style of a piece of music perfectly matches the text it bears, the communicative value of both the music and text is multiplied several times over.

We remind ourselves, too, what the Constitution on the Sacred Liturgy imparted regarding the "active participation" of assemblies: "To promote active participation, the people should be encouraged to take part by means of acclamations, responses, psalmody, antiphons, and songs, as well as by actions, gestures, and bodily attitudes. And at the proper times all should observe a reverent silence" (SC 30). This means the music sung, especially "songs," is putting a form of preaching directly on congregants' lips and into their eyes, engaging at least three senses, counting hearing. It is natural, then, that the structures and rhythms of the whole of liturgy should be resonant with the music that permeates the celebration.

If the prescribed liturgical preaching is musical in structure, borrowing structural forms and techniques, it may become more memorable. Yet, who leaves the church building humming a few bars from the preaching? That seems unlikely. Alternatively, a test: who can, from memory, recite a few lines of Psalm 91? Your first answer is likely, "Not many." But we can all sing it, if we call to mind any memorable line from Michael Joncas's "On Eagle's Wings."

In future weeks, continuing this exploration, we'll examine the types of liturgical music mentioned above in the Constitution on the Sacred Liturgy, what it tells us of preaching, and then delve into the relationship of music and preaching and the importance of such an endeavor.

About Music

Fullness of Praise: Recall from writings a few pages ago: take care not to damage the integrity of any Trinitarian hymn texts today by omitting any of their verses.

One lesser known piece to consider today is Robert E. Kreutz's "Hymn to the Trinity" (WLP/GIA), a simple, sweet melody of praise.

JUNE 12, 2022
THE MOST HOLY TRINITY

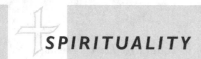

SPIRITUALITY

GOSPEL ACCLAMATION
John 6:51

℟. Alleluia, alleluia.
I am the living bread that came down from heaven,
says the Lord; / whoever eats this bread will live
forever.
℟. Alleluia, alleluia.

Gospel

Luke 9:11b-17; L169C

**Jesus spoke to the crowds about the
kingdom of God,
and he healed those who needed to
be cured.
As the day was drawing to a close,
the Twelve approached him and said,
"Dismiss the crowd
so that they can go to the surrounding villages and farms
and find lodging and provisions;
for we are in a deserted place here."
He said to them, "Give them some food
yourselves."
They replied, "Five loaves and two fish
are all we have,
unless we ourselves go and buy food
for all these people."
Now the men there numbered about
five thousand.
Then he said to his disciples,
"Have them sit down in groups of
about fifty."
They did so and made them all sit down.
Then taking the five loaves and the two
fish,
and looking up to heaven,
he said the blessing over them, broke
them,
and gave them to the disciples to set
before the crowd.
They all ate and were satisfied.
And when the leftover fragments were
picked up,
they filled twelve wicker baskets.**

Reflecting on the Gospel

What we celebrate today is God's hospitality in the gift of Jesus, shared with the world in his personal fullness, in his "body and blood." Luke's account of the feeding of the five thousand is situated in the part of his gospel that focuses on mission (9:1-50), and it can be seen as symbolic of the outreach of the church. There is no special invitation to this Bethsaida meal, no house or dining hall in which to eat. Even though Jesus had planned a kind of ministry "debriefing" session with his apostles, everyone who had found out where they were and followed them is welcomed at Bethsaida, and Jesus teaches and heals them until late in the day. The Twelve tell Jesus to send the crowd away to find shelter and food, neither of which is available in the lonely place, but Jesus responds with the challenge: "Give them some food yourselves." Having just completed their first missionary field work of preaching, healing, and exorcising, the apostles are now called to partnership with Jesus in another apostolic mission: feeding the hungry crowds.

Jesus's command that the Twelve seat the crowd in a hundred groups of fifty each is an image of the local churches gathered as the church universal. Just as Jesus has taught the crowd throughout the day, so he will now teach his disciples something more about the kingdom in action when he takes, blesses, breaks, and places the five loaves and two fishes into the hands of the disciples to give to the crowd.

Luke obviously wants his community, and all hearers of the gospel, to connect this meal with the feeding traditions of his ancestors: the miraculous manna in the wilderness (Exod 16:15) and the story of Elisha who fed a smaller crowd with loaves of bread, some of which were left over (2 Kgs 4:42-44). Into this past, the present of the Gospel Bethsaida and all our eucharistic "Bethsaidas" are gathered.

When the fragments of the meal are collected, they fill twelve baskets. Such is the superabundant hospitality of God in Christ, that there will always be more than enough to feed the future church of the Twelve when it gathers for its "Bethsaida" meal. But one thing is needed: hands to give the food to the people. The church, guided by the Spirit (about whom we have heard so much on the last two Sundays), needs a creative conversation with the words of Jesus at Bethsaida about the present shortage of ordained ministers to feed the hungry people of God and the right of the people to the have access to the Eucharist.

There are other "Bethsaida" questions this gospel prompts us to raise: how are we to celebrate Eucharist in a world wounded by so much injustice? Before Jesus fed the people, he taught and healed and exorcised. What are the paralyzing hungers of people who are physically starving, spiritually deprived, or psychologically damaged that we need to feed? What are the "demons" that need to be exorcised from ourselves and our communities so our celebration of the Eucharist is not hypocritical?

Focusing the Gospel

Key words and phrases: "Then taking the five loaves and the two fish, and looking up to heaven, he said the blessing over them, broke them, and gave them to the disciples to set before the crowd."

To the point: Entire books have been written on this passage. It is one of the most moving stories of the Christian imagination. There is something deeply comforting about a God who provides, and who does so in a surprising way using mundane materials. Jesus doesn't conjure up a feast, nor does he tell the apostles what will happen. His directions amount to, "Keep doing what you're doing, and it will be okay." Also, Jesus doesn't tell them that God will provide; he tells them, "Give them some food yourselves." Jesus wants the apostles to do what they can with what they have to feed the community, and to trust that God will take care of the rest.

Connecting the Gospel

to the first and second readings: The first and second readings this week are both scenes of bread being blessed and broken. It is one of the great aspects of our faith that the central symbol of community is sharing a meal, and a meal as simple and universal as bread. From Genesis to St. Paul, blessing bread and sharing it is an act that unites us.

to experience: The central gift of our Catholic faith is the Eucharist, the "thanksgiving" we share when we invite Christ's real presence into our bodies. This physical reality is also the aspect of Catholicism that separates us from most other Christian denominations. And yet, today's readings show us just how seamless the elevation of this act is, from the establishment of God's relationship with Abraham to the first Christian communities.

Connecting the Responsorial Psalm

to the readings: Who is the priest in this psalm? Is it Jesus? Is it those in the line of apostolic succession? Or could it be all of us, who are called to be priests, prophets, and kings in our own ways to our communities? Though only certain members of our community are called to the sacrament of holy orders, we can all participate in the "common priesthood" of service to lead by Christian example.

to psalmist preparation: Reflect on ways that being the psalmist is a participation in the call to common priesthood. You stand before your congregation and invite them to reflect on Scripture, while joining their voices together. This is one of the most precious and powerful acts we have in the liturgy.

PROMPTS FOR FAITH-SHARING

How do you break bread with others? Do you plan meals with your family? Take a break together with your team at work? Get a drink with a recreational sports team?

What do you find significant about Jesus's choice to use bread in the Eucharist? Why do you think Jesus is called the Bread of Life?

How do you live aspects of the vocation to be a priest within your community, among others who share the same call?

Model Penitential Act

Presider: Nourished by God in Word and sacrament, we take a moment to recall the times we have failed to follow Christ's example in our lives, asking for peace and healing . . . *[pause]*

Lord Jesus, you are the Bread of Life: Lord, have mercy.

Christ Jesus, you feed us with yourself: Christ, have mercy.

Lord Jesus, the food you give never leaves us wanting: Lord, have mercy.

Homily Points

• As with the Trinity, our understanding of Eucharist is fundamentally grounded in relationship. At the Last Supper, Jesus gathered with his friends and gave an example of how to continue to grow in relationship with God and each other. His words are both a statement of truth and a call to action: "This is my body. . . . [This is] my blood. . . . Do this in remembrance of me."

• As Christians, our remembering is not a passive event where we simply recall what has happened in the past. Rather, our remembering is active. Our remembering is *anamnetic*. When we follow Jesus's command to break the bread and share the cup, we not only remember the historical Jesus of the past, but with these words and actions we also celebrate Jesus's presence with us today as he continues to nourish and sustain us. We remember the past, celebrate in the present, and look forward to the future where the reign of God will be fulfilled.

• We see this vividly in today's gospel. When the disciples state that they only have five loaves and two fish to feed the gathered crowds, they do not realize that the Bread of Life is in their midst. As Jesus prays, breaks, and shares today, he foreshadows his future death and resurrection. Likewise, Jesus makes it abundantly clear that his disciples must follow this example in their own lives. When Jesus says, "Give them some food yourselves," he shows that they must take an active role in bringing about the kingdom of God. The paschal mystery is deeply communal. So is the Eucharist. To limit our understanding of Eucharist to an individual or private relationship with Jesus is insufficient.

Model Universal Prayer (Prayer of the Faithful)

Presider: You give of yourself to us, sustaining us and giving us life in you. Confident in this, we raise our prayers to you, knowing you will hear and answer them.

Response: Lord, hear our prayer.

That all members of the church might better recognize and embrace the communal element of Christ's sharing of himself in the Eucharist . . .

That leaders of cities and nations may work to ensure all people have access to healthy food and clean water . . .

That all who are hungry may find the resources they need to grow and flourish as dignified people of God . . .

That we might work to reduce waste and our overconsumption of food and resources to ensure that all people might eat, drink, and flourish as dignified individuals . . .

Presider: Loving God, you feed us with yourself. Strengthen us to do your will in our lives and hear the prayers we bring to you this day. We ask this through Christ our Lord. **Amen.**

COLLECT

Let us pray.

Pause for silent prayer

O God, who in this wonderful Sacrament have left us a memorial of your Passion, grant us, we pray, so to revere the sacred mysteries of your Body and Blood that we may always experience in ourselves the fruits of your redemption. Who live and reign with God the Father in the unity of the Holy Spirit, God, for ever and ever. **Amen.**

FIRST READING

Gen 14:18-20

In those days, Melchizedek, king of Salem, brought out bread and wine, and being a priest of God Most High, he blessed Abram with these words: "Blessed be Abram by God Most High, the creator of heaven and earth; and blessed be God Most High, who delivered your foes into your hand." Then Abram gave him a tenth of everything.

RESPONSORIAL PSALM

Ps 110:1, 2, 3, 4

R̸. (4b) You are a priest forever, in the line of Melchizedek.

The Lᴏʀᴅ said to my Lord: "Sit at my right hand
   till I make your enemies your footstool."

R̸. You are a priest forever, in the line of Melchizedek.

The scepter of your power the Lᴏʀᴅ will stretch forth from Zion:
   "Rule in the midst of your enemies."

R̸. You are a priest forever, in the line of Melchizedek.

"Yours is princely power in the day of your birth, in holy splendor;
   before the daystar, like the dew, I have begotten you."

R̸. You are a priest forever, in the line of Melchizedek.

The Lᴏʀᴅ has sworn, and he will not repent:
   "You are a priest forever, according to the order of Melchizedek."

R̸. You are a priest forever, in the line of Melchizedek.

SECOND READING

1 Cor 11:23-26

Brothers and sisters:
I received from the Lord what I also handed on to you,
   that the Lord Jesus, on the night he was handed over,
   took bread, and, after he had given thanks,
   broke it and said, "This is my body that is for you.
Do this in remembrance of me."
In the same way also the cup, after supper, saying,
   "This cup is the new covenant in my blood.
Do this, as often as you drink it, in remembrance of me."
For as often as you eat this bread and drink the cup,
   you proclaim the death of the Lord until he comes.

OPTIONAL SEQUENCE

See Appendix A, p. 303.

About Liturgy

The Relationship between Music and Preaching, Part II: Continuing the discussion of the relationship between music and preaching, we remind ourselves of the types of liturgical music listed in the Constitution on the Sacred Liturgy (SC 30). There are acclamations, like "Alleluia," "Amen," "Blessed be God forever," and so on; responses such as "And with your Spirit" or "Thanks be to God"; psalmody not just in the responsorial psalm but also in the antiphons proper to the liturgy; antiphons at the entrance and communion rites, and also at the Liturgy of the Hours and other places; finally, songs, including hymns, canticles, the Gloria at Mass, and other pieces. Each sort of music enumerated here can fulfill, in some small or great way, a component of preaching, by content, structure, or other means.

For the purposes of this exploration, let's also spell out what is meant by "preaching" here. Most of the Christian faithful experience preaching in exactly one way, the homily at Eucharist. The word "homily" comes from the Greek word *homilia*, which means to have communion with or to communicate with another person. Please "put a pin" in that definition for a moment or two—it's important and we'll be returning to it later. The Constitution on the Sacred Liturgy also tells us its vision for the homily in a couple places: "It is from scripture that lessons are read and explained in the homily" (24) and "By means of the homily the mysteries of the faith and the guiding principles of the Christian life are expounded from the sacred text, during the course of the liturgical year; the homily, therefore, is to be highly esteemed as part of the liturgy itself" (52). Or, if you want to know what Google returns for "homily," it's this: "a religious discourse that is intended primarily for spiritual edification rather than doctrinal instruction; a sermon."

Preaching, therefore, is fundamentally similar to liturgical music. It strives to be communicative, and even dialogical in its own stilted way. It should help to unpack scriptural lessons, sacred theology, and indeed the whole Christian life and how these relate to one another. Lastly, both preaching and liturgical music ought to be primarily spiritual rather than doctrinal.

Yet preaching is simultaneously different from liturgical music. Music without words can express more of the ineffable divine mysteries as it operates on the level of symbolism, with melodies, harmonies, rhythms, etc., each expressing more broadly what words must do with more specificity. And a homily without words . . . ? St. Francis supposedly said, "Preach the Gospel at all times. When necessary, use words"—but that likely doesn't work very well within the liturgy itself, most of the time.

Most importantly, there should be an integrity in both music and preaching that might be best defined as the truth which only arises via communication and communion. In my experience, frequently both preaching and music seem to be concerned with truth that is more about worldview than about relationship and communication. (For a more in-depth look at truth in preaching, I highly recommend *Let's Talk about Truth* by Ann Garrido, from Ave Maria Press.)

Having defined our terms a bit, we will turn our attention to the relationship—the communication—between preaching and music, on future pages.

About Music

Taste and See Differently: It is wise to avoid, as mentioned briefly above, anything too "doctrinal" for this solemnity. Consider any of the myriad settings of Psalm 34, "Taste and See," perhaps picking one outside "the usual" and perhaps a stretch for your music ministers and assembly in terms of style or language. Your resources on hand no doubt offer several choices.

JUNE 19, 2022

THE MOST HOLY BODY AND BLOOD OF CHRIST (CORPUS CHRISTI)

GOSPEL ACCLAMATION
cf. Luke 1:76

R℣. Alleluia, alleluia.
You, child, will be called prophet of the Most
   High,
for you will go before the Lord to prepare his
   way.
R℣. Alleluia, alleluia.

Gospel   Luke 1:57-66, 80; L587

When the time arrived for Elizabeth
      to have her child
   she gave birth to a son.
Her neighbors and relatives heard
   that the Lord had shown his
      great mercy toward her,
   and they rejoiced with her.
When they came on the
      eighth day to circum-
      cise the child,
   they were going to call
      him Zechariah after
      his father,
   but his mother said in
      reply,
   "No. He will be called
      John."
But they answered her,
   "There is no one among
      your relatives who has this name."
So they made signs, asking his father
   what he wished him to be called.
He asked for a tablet and wrote, "John is
      his name,"
   and all were amazed.
Immediately his mouth was opened, his
      tongue freed,
   and he spoke blessing God.
Then fear came upon all their neighbors,
   and all these matters were discussed
      throughout the hill country of Judea.
All who heard these things took them to
      heart, saying,
   "What, then, will this child be?"
For surely the hand of the Lord was with
      him.

The child grew and became strong in
      spirit,
   and he was in the desert until the day
   of his manifestation to Israel.

See Appendix A, p. 304, for the other readings.

Reflecting on the Gospel

When Megan and Kyle brought their child to the church for the rite of Christian baptism, it was a ritual of joy and gratitude to God by parents and relatives alike. Christening is a ceremony of welcoming a newborn child to the household of God as parents, relatives, and friends gather as witnesses to the child's sacrament of Christian initiation. The child's full name is spoken aloud as the child is ritually claimed as a member of a family, community, and church. Zechariah's first public speech since his encounter with the angel of the Lord happened at John the Baptist's christening, at the public revelation of the child's name, the name that God has given to him.

The witnesses who have gathered at John the Baptist's christening acclaim: "the hand of the Lord was with him." By making this statement, Judeans, friends, and relatives of the parents of John the Baptist publicly acknowledge God's presence in the life of John the Baptist. "The hand of the Lord" represents the power of God that is at work in the life of John the Baptist. It is in fact the means through which God is present in the world through us in order to continue the divine plan to bring humankind into a permanent relationship with God. As John the Baptist begins his ministry in the desert of Jordan, he will call humankind into repentance. "What, then, will this child be?" Judeans and all who gathered at John the Baptist's christening query. The response to their inquiry is found in how God has chosen to be present in the world through John the Baptist—namely, by calling humankind to repentance. This is because everyone whom God foreknows is destined, therefore, to become the servant of God through whom God's presence manifests in the world.

John the Baptist's unusual lifestyle is another evidence that indeed "the hand of the Lord is with him," as he begins his ministry crying out in the wilderness and mending the pathways for the coming of our Lord (Mark 1:3). By choosing the lifestyle of self-deprivation, living in the Judean desert and feeding on wild nutrition, he shows his disposition to survive the harsh realities on his path because God's watchful hand is upon him. When he openly rebukes political leaders and the social elites to mend their ways and do right before God and humankind, he attests to the divine mandate and commissioning that drives his life and ministry. John the Baptist shows little or no concern that his public criticism of a political leader would cost him his life, which turned out to be the case (Mark 6:14-29).

Our celebration of the Nativity of John the Baptist reveals that God is with him, giving meaning to his life. His ministry calls us to embrace the values of the social life that create in us the consciousness of our common humanity. It is in fact the consciousness that moves us to aspire to do good toward one another, treating each other with justice, charity, and love. As a forerunner of Jesus Christ, John the Baptist carries out a ministry that cuts deep into the life of the social and political elites of his day, as they come to him seeking to know what they ought to do in order to be saved. Let our Christian life, like John the Baptist's life, lead others to experience the transforming presence of God so that they can welcome Christ into their lives.

Focusing the Gospel

Key words and phrases: "He asked for a tablet and wrote, 'John is his name,' and all were amazed."

To the point: The story of John's birth reads like a folktale. Elizabeth is assumed to be barren, but gives birth. She chooses a name that stuns her community, who do not know that she's been granted this gift by God. The name is particularly important, because, as in many other times in the Bible, a name indicates identity and carries much more weight than we might give it today. Her husband expresses solidarity with the choice of the unexpected name, or identity, and in doing so, he is healed. This miraculous cure convinces their community that the child, and his identity, are important, and come from God.

Model Penitential Act

Presider: As we celebrate John the Baptist, we honor someone who devoted his life to leading others to Christ. For the times we have not lived out our own call to follow Jesus, we ask for peace and forgiveness . . . *[pause]*

Lord Jesus, you are Son of God and son of Mary: Lord, have mercy.
Christ Jesus, you call us to yourself: Christ, have mercy.
Lord Jesus, you alone are our salvation: Lord, have mercy.

Model Universal Prayer (Prayer of the Faithful)

Presider: We raise our prayers today through the intercession of John the Baptist:

Response: Lord, hear our prayer.

That the church might follow the example of John the Baptist and actively bring others to Christ . . .

That all leaders be prophetic voices for the people under their care, especially those who are vulnerable and most in need . . .

That all who experience extended periods of loneliness, darkness, and depression might find care in loving friends and systems of support . . .

That all who experience persecution for their faith might remain confident and hopeful in their convictions . . .

Presider: Loving God, you called John the Baptist to prepare the way for your Son. May we, like John, decrease so that Christ may increase. We ask this through Christ our Lord. **Amen.**

About Liturgy

What to Call Someone or Something Is Important: Zechariah, his voice taken from him, only regains it when telling the world, in writing, his son's name. He is then freed to also proclaim the mighty works of God.

In our liturgical music and general discourse, we frequently use the word "bread" to mean the consecrated host, the Body of Christ, perceived by human senses in its "accidents" of bread. Yet allusions to the "bread of life" and similar phrases are all over our sacred Scriptures too. It's worth noting, however, that there are no scriptural warrants for using the word "wine" similarly; rather, "cup" or "chalice" is what Scriptures hand down to us.

Does using the word "bread" confuse the faithful if it's in reference to the consecrated host? Does that use contribute to a misunderstanding of "real presence" among our assemblies? Answers to these questions largely depend, it seems, on the catechesis given those in the pews, and each person's scriptural literacy. Instead of, perhaps, lamenting word choice, especially when considering the poetic texts of liturgical music, consider what else could be the issue and what the further ramifications of poor catechesis and lack of knowledge of scripture might be. Then, devise efforts to help these issues too!

COLLECT
Let us pray.

Pause for silent prayer

O God, who raised up Saint John the Baptist
to make ready a nation fit for Christ the
    Lord,
give your people, we pray,
the grace of spiritual joys
and direct the hearts of all the faithful
into the way of salvation and peace.
Through our Lord Jesus Christ, your Son,
who lives and reigns with you in the unity
    of the Holy Spirit,
God, for ever and ever. **Amen**.

FOR REFLECTION

• John the Baptist brought others to Christ by the way he lived. What are some ways you bring people to Christ through your everyday actions and interactions?

• John the Baptist knew and understood his role in salvation history. How is God acting in your life? In what ways might God be calling you today?

Homily Points

• John the Baptist's birth and circumcision show that John is part of the people of Israel, the line carried through his father. John and other people of Israel play a significant role in preparing for Christ and ultimately Christianity. This connection, which we see throughout Luke's gospel and Acts, cannot be ignored.

• Today's celebration affords us the opportunity to reflect on the many ways that both members of the Jewish faith and Christians respond to God's call in their lives. We pray for peace and continued dialogue with our Jewish brothers and sisters, so that we might all grow in relationship with the God who calls us to God's self.

GOSPEL ACCLAMATION
Matt 11:29ab

℟. Alleluia, alleluia.
Take my yoke upon you, says the Lord;
and learn from me, for I am meek and humble
    of heart.
℟. Alleluia, alleluia.

or

John 10:14

℟. Alleluia, alleluia.
I am the good shepherd says the
    Lord,
I know my sheep, and mine know me.
℟. Alleluia, alleluia.

Gospel

Luke 15:3-7; L172C

**Jesus addressed this
    parable to the
    Pharisees and
    scribes:
"What man among
    you having a hun-
    dred sheep and
    losing one of them
    would not leave the ninety-nine in the
        desert
    and go after the lost one until
        he finds it?
And when he does find it,
    he sets it on his shoulders with great
        joy
    and, upon his arrival home,
    he calls together his friends and
        neighbors and says to them,
    'Rejoice with me because I have
        found my lost sheep.'
I tell you, in just the same way
    there will be more joy in heaven over
        one sinner who repents
    than over ninety-nine righteous
        people
    who have no need of repentance."**

See Appendix A, p. 305, for the other readings.

Reflecting on the Gospel

One of the enduring identities of God in the Bible is the Shepherd of Israel. The image of God as the Shepherd of Israel comes about through the conception of the character of God's relationship with the people of Israel. In this relationship, the people of Israel confidently call God "my shepherd" (Ps 23:1). They trust in God's leadership as the shepherd of their lives, who leads them to pasture, comfort, and security. As the people of God, they have a history that is filled with stories of God's providential care and protection. Indeed, the first reading on this solemnity of the Most Sacred Heart of Jesus reveals the loving heart of God, the Shepherd of Israel. When God's children find themselves living among a much powerful overlord and nation like the Babylonians, God pledges to act on behalf of Israel as a shepherd will do for a sheep. God promises to seek out, rescue, gather, and bring back God's scattered children to dwell in one sheepfold, the land of Israel, under God's leadership as God shows affective disposition toward the well-being of God's children.

When Jesus was accused of ministering to the outcast and the rejected members of society, his response struck deep into the consciousness of our collective identity as God's children. He told his critics that finding the lost, the castoff, and the forgotten children of God is his ministerial priority and it is the main reason for his presence in the world. He identifies himself and his ministry with the image of a shepherd who will search diligently for a lost sheep, rejoice heartily after finding it, and bring it back to safety in the sheepfold.

Just as God identifies his relationship with the children of Israel with the image of a shepherd, likewise the image of the divine shepherd becomes part of Jesus's self-identity: "I am the good shepherd" (John 10:11). As a shepherd, God guides the people of Israel with tenderness, care, love, and compassion. The psalmist recounts God's goodness, mercy, and love as the divine shepherd. In the same vein, Jesus Christ shows compassion, love, and mercy on those whom society has forgotten and relegated to the margins of social life and prosperity. Jesus meets them at the edge of despair, despondency, and invisibility in their social life. With the heart of a shepherd he searches them out, finds them, and reinstates them right at the spot where the social elites notice their presence and recognize their membership in society. To further show that they belong to the household of God, Jesus Christ sits at table, having dinner with them. In this way, Jesus reminds them that like everyone else, they are members of God's household and so they will indeed share in the heavenly banquet.

The church invites us to celebrate the Most Sacred Heart of Jesus, the fountain of divine love, compassion, and mercy. Jesus is the shepherd of our lives; he is the savior who gathers God's children into onefold; he is our healer who nurses us back to life in the face of a debilitating illness, mental anguish, and emotional turmoil. As the shepherd of our lives, he gives his life on the cross so that we may have life eternal with God. Indeed, Jesus Christ displays an immensurable, affective, and heartfelt love for us. Let us do the same toward one another as brothers and sisters in the Lord.

Focusing the Gospel

Key words and phrases: "I tell you, in just the same way there will be more joy in heaven over one sinner who repents than over ninety-nine righteous people who have no need of repentance."

To the point: Call to mind areas in your spiritual life where you are consistently successful. Do you go to Mass every Sunday? Have you taught the children in your life to pray? Do you make helping vulnerable populations a priority? Now recall areas of your life where you struggle. What if, instead of focusing time and attention on the things you do well, you really put time and energy into growing where you know you're not the best? This is what Jesus is telling us in today's gospel: the work it takes to overcome one consistent sin is worthy of far more celebration than the areas of our life that are saintly without effort.

Model Penitential Act

Presider: Today's gospel on this celebration of the Sacred Heart of Jesus recalls the rejoicing in heaven over the repentance of God's children. With this, we confidently ask for God's pardon and peace . . . *[pause]*

Lord Jesus, you are the Good Shepherd: Lord, have mercy.

Christ Jesus, your love for us is infinite: Christ, have mercy.

Lord Jesus, you are merciful and show us the way to life in you: Lord, have mercy.

Model Universal Prayer (Prayer of the Faithful)

Presider: Trusting in the love and mercy of God, we bring our prayers and petitions through the intercession of the Sacred Heart of Jesus:

Response: Lord, hear our prayer.

That church leaders may follow Christ's example of love and mercy, standing always ready to welcome those seeking a spiritual home . . .

That national and world leaders might lead with humble mercy, working to protect the good of all people . . .

That all people who seek reconciliation might know the joy of peace in Christ . . .

That we might work for reform of the criminal justice system, remembering that we are called to walk the path of mercy in Christ . . .

Presider: Loving God, you know us intimately and shower us with your mercy. Hear the prayers we bring today and answer them according to your will. We ask this through Christ our Lord. **Amen.**

About Liturgy

The One That Needs Our Help: The readings today present strongly the image of the shepherd seeking out the lost and, in the gospel passage, elevating that lost sheep and rejoicing with it. Jesus leaves the ninety-nine sheep behind, not because they are worthless, not because they don't matter, but because it's the one lost sheep that needs attention, needs help, needs elevation. Once that has happened, all of the sheep are joyfully reunited in Christ.

The model to us in this parable is one in which the lost—the marginalized, the unseen—are, in their moment of greatest need, the ones on which we are called to focus our time and energies, even at great risk to ourselves.

Liturgically, are the lost, marginalized, and unseen given that same focus, even at risk to our own positions of power and authority? How can we share with our present assemblies, as if representing the ninety-nine sheep left behind by the shepherd, that they can be shepherds in their own ways too, seeking the one who needs to be elevated and joyfully celebrated?

COLLECT

Let us pray.

Grant, we pray, almighty God,
that we, who glory in the Heart of your beloved Son
and recall the wonders of his love for us,
may be made worthy to receive
an overflowing measure of grace
from that fount of heavenly gifts.
Through our Lord Jesus Christ, your Son,
who lives and reigns with you in the unity of the Holy Spirit,
God, for ever and ever. **Amen.**

or:

O God, who in the Heart of your Son,
wounded by our sins,
bestow on us in mercy
the boundless treasures of your love,
grant, we pray,
that, in paying him the homage of our devotion,
we may also offer worthy reparation.
Through our Lord Jesus Christ, your Son,
who lives and reigns with you in the unity of the Holy Spirit,
God, for ever and ever. **Amen.**

FOR REFLECTION

• Pope Francis proclaimed, "A little bit of mercy makes the world less cold and more just." How is God calling you to share a little bit of mercy today?

• While we are called to follow Christ's example of mercy, we sometimes find it difficult to love and forgive those who have hurt us. To whom might you ask for forgiveness? To whom might you extend forgiveness?

Homily Points

• Is there an image of God more familiar than the Good Shepherd? While we might be quick to resonate with this image, understanding our total dependence on God's love and mercy, we must also consider how we are called to extend God's love and mercy to others. We must be willing to be both sheep and shepherd—an arduous task to be sure, but essential if we are to truly understand and practice God's love and mercy as illuminated in the Sacred Heart of Jesus.

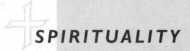

SPIRITUALITY

GOSPEL ACCLAMATION
1 Sam 3:9; John 6:68c

℟. Alleluia, alleluia.
Speak, Lord, your servant is listening;
you have the words of everlasting life.
℟. Alleluia, alleluia.

Gospel   Luke 9:51-62; L99C

When the days for Jesus'
    being taken up were
    fulfilled,
  he resolutely determined to
    journey to Jerusalem,
  and he sent messengers
    ahead of him.
On the way they entered a
    Samaritan village
  to prepare for his reception
    there,
  but they would not wel-
    come him
  because the destination of
    his journey was Jerusalem.
When the disciples James and John saw this
    they asked,
  "Lord, do you want us to call down fire
    from heaven
  to consume them?"
Jesus turned and rebuked them, and they
    journeyed to another village.

As they were proceeding on their journey
    someone said to him,
  "I will follow you wherever you go."
Jesus answered him,
  "Foxes have dens and birds of the sky
    have nests,
  but the Son of Man has nowhere to rest
    his head."

And to another he said, "Follow me."
But he replied, "Lord, let me go first and
    bury my father."
But he answered him, "Let the dead bury
    their dead.
But you, go and proclaim the kingdom of
    God."
And another said, "I will follow you, Lord,
    but first let me say farewell to my family
    at home."
To him Jesus said, "No one who sets a hand
    to the plow
  and looks to what was left behind is fit
    for the kingdom of God."

Reflecting on the Gospel

The road Jesus takes to Jerusalem is signposted with encounters, events, stopping places. This serves to universalize the way of discipleship; it has nothing to do with map reading or chronology, and everything to do with following Jesus in our own time and place. To help us along the way, Luke describes three encounters with would-be disciples. We hear the request, we listen to Jesus's response, but we learn nothing of the outcome of these meetings. It is as though, by this narrative silence, Jesus is saying to us: Listen to the answer your own life makes.

The first would-be disciple takes the initiative in approaching Jesus. He seems to be brashly confident, the enthusiast who needs to be tested for staying power, for readiness to be a powerless, homeless, and dispossessed disciple of a rejected Son of Man. Into Jesus's reply is woven the suggestion that in Roman-occupied Palestine everyone is at home except the true Israel. The "foxes" referred to are not just burrowing animals, but people like "that fox," Herod Antipas (Luke 13:32), who have dug themselves into politically secure positions. The "birds of the sky" were an apocalyptic symbol for the "roosting" Gentiles, the Romans who had disinherited Israel and now lord it over them. If you want to follow me, says Jesus, be prepared to be a powerless and dispossessed follower of a rejected Son of Man.

In the second encounter, it is Jesus who takes the initiative in calling the person to follow. We probably have a sneaking sympathy for this one who seems to make a very human and religious request of Jesus: "Let me go first and bury my father." But there is a cultural context to these words that persists even today in some Middle Eastern communities, and which throws a very different light on Jesus's demand. Sons were and sometimes still are expected to remain close to their family home at least until their father has passed away. In Jesus's invitation was the urgent and present call not to delay, not to put off the "today" demands of the reign of God. For all who answer the gospel call, there will be some contradiction of cultural expectations, some necessary reordering of priorities in our relationships. "Let the dead bury their dead" is Luke's literary device of exaggeration to emphasize the priority of Jesus's call. In no way does it deny the love for our parents that God explicitly commands.

The third would-be disciple wants to follow Jesus, but on condition that he is allowed to "first say farewell to my family at home." This seems a reasonable request, especially in the light of the first reading that describes how Elijah gave Elisha permission to go and say goodbye. But the following of Jesus has to be unswerving; not even this detour is allowed. The mini-parable of the plow explains further what is also Luke's literary device of exaggeration. The light Palestinian plow was guided with one hand, usually the left, while the plower's other hand carried a stick used to goad the oxen that pulled the plow. To make a furrow that was straight and of the right depth, to lift the plow over rocks that might shatter it, demanded great concentration and dexterity. To take one's eyes off the plow for a moment could spell disaster. So it is with his disciples, says Jesus. The eyes of our heart must be fixed on the reign of God with unwavering commitment so the field of this world may be well plowed and made ready for God's harvesting.

Focusing the Gospel

Key words and phrases: "But he answered him, 'Let the dead bury their dead. But you, go and proclaim the kingdom of God.'"

To the point: James and John realize the Samaritans are insulting their best friend, and they want to use his authority to make things right. They are refused housing in a town because of ethnic differences, and James and John essentially suggest throwing a fireball at the town. Predictably, Jesus "rebuked them."

As the journey continues, Jesus gives us three examples of demands that are made upon the lives of those who choose to follow him. The first is a warning that to follow Jesus is to lose the guarantee of a place to rest your head. The second is a reminder that our concern should not be with the dead, but with the living. The third is a call to look forward, and not at the past.

Connecting the Gospel

to the first and second readings: In the first reading, Elijah chooses Elisha to succeed him, and Elisha's first concern is saying good-bye to his family. In the second reading, Paul warns us that we are free in the Lord, but this freedom isn't to use on desires of the flesh. When we think of "desires of the flesh," we tend to think of lust or gluttony. What if it's a far less harmful desire—a desire to keep our familial relationships with those on earth just as they are, in the way that feels most comfortable? The psalm tells us, "You are my inheritance, O Lord." The psalmist replaces the linear gift of familial inheritance with a relationship with the Lord.

to experience: Our ultimate goal is not to transfer our families just as they are into the kingdom of heaven. We grow and leave our parents, and many of us become parents. Most likely we bury our parents, and our children will bury us. There is no moment in which our family freezes in place and becomes a perfect foretaste of heaven. The family is the domestic church, but it is one piece of a larger kingdom. This week we are reminded of the uncomfortable reality that our ultimate goal is God, and even though his love is mediated to us through our families, they are not the centerpiece of our faith—Jesus is.

Connecting the Responsorial Psalm

to the readings: This week's psalm describes a relationship with the Lord in which many familial roles are taken care of, especially that of parents. The Lord is someone in whom we can take refuge, someone who gives counsel, and someone who shows the path.

to psalmist preparation: Think of people in your life who have modeled these things to you. Who consoles you, and exhorts your heart? Who causes your heart to rejoice? Who makes you feel comfortable? Who has shown you good paths in life?

PROMPTS FOR FAITH-SHARING

Have you ever wanted to throw a fireball at someone for being rude? It's comforting to know that the apostles felt the same. How do you temper the desire for revenge with your faith?

If Jesus asked you to leave your family tomorrow in order to do his will, would you do it? Would you trust Jesus's words without understanding them? Why or why not?

Who in your life has become a chosen family member? How did you meet friends you consider family?

Which moment in your life can you point to and think, yes, that's when my family was truly a foretaste of heaven? What about this scene brings you comfort?

Model Penitential Act

Presider: Jesus invites each of us to follow him. For the times we have not followed Christ in our thoughts, words, and actions, we ask for God's healing and forgiveness . . . *[pause]*

Lord Jesus, you call, "Follow me": Lord, have mercy.

Christ Jesus, you teach us how to be faithful: Christ, have mercy.

Lord Jesus, you help us grow in patient, holy endurance: Lord, have mercy.

Homily Points

• Jesus must have been frustrated when his disciples completely missed the point of his mission and ministry. After being rejected, James and John ask Jesus if they should call down fire from heaven to consume those who did not receive them. Not surprisingly, Jesus rebukes them for this reaction. You can almost imagine Jesus looking at them and saying, "Really?"

• If we are honest with ourselves, there are times when each of us do the same thing. While we might not literally wish to call down fire upon others, there are times we respond to others in a way that is antithetical to Jesus's teaching. When someone makes us angry, our initial reaction might be to retaliate. If someone points out a flaw in our work, we might be quick to find flaws in everyone around us. If someone needs medical care or food or clothing, we might be happy to tell that person to work for those things just like everyone else.

• Following God's path is not always easy. In fact, Jesus's words about not saying goodbye to family or burying one's parent might seem incredibly harsh. Jesus is simply stating, however, that we will always be able to come up with excuses not to follow him. Building the kingdom of God must be our first priority. If we recognize this call, everything else will flow forth from it.

Model Universal Prayer (Prayer of the Faithful)

Presider: Jesus calls us to follow him. In faith, we raise our prayers and petitions:

Response: Lord, hear our prayer.

That the church might respond to Jesus's call with faithfulness and sincerity so to build up the kingdom of God . . .

That local and world leaders might work to dismantle systems of structural racism in our community and country . . .

That all who are grieving the loss of a loved one may find consolation in the outreach of others . . .

That we might commit ourselves to forgiveness instead of revenge and peace instead of conflict . . .

Presider: Loving God, hear our prayers today and answer them according to your will. Give us the strength and courage to respond to your call with conviction and sincerity. We ask this through Christ our Lord. **Amen.**

COLLECT

Let us pray.

Pause for silent prayer

O God, who through the grace of adoption
chose us to be children of light,
grant, we pray,
that we may not be wrapped in the
    darkness of error
but always be seen to stand in the bright
    light of truth.
Through our Lord Jesus Christ, your Son,
who lives and reigns with you in the unity
    of the Holy Spirit,
God, for ever and ever. **Amen.**

FIRST READING

1 Kgs 19:16b, 19-21

The LORD said to Elijah:
    "You shall anoint Elisha, son of
        Shaphat of Abel-meholah,
    as prophet to succeed you."

Elijah set out and came upon Elisha, son
    of Shaphat,
    as he was plowing with twelve yoke of
        oxen;
    he was following the twelfth.
Elijah went over to him and threw his
    cloak over him.
Elisha left the oxen, ran after Elijah,
    and said,
    "Please, let me kiss my father and
        mother goodbye,
    and I will follow you."
Elijah answered, "Go back!
Have I done anything to you?"
Elisha left him and, taking the yoke of
    oxen, slaughtered them;
    he used the plowing equipment for fuel
        to boil their flesh,
    and gave it to his people to eat.
Then Elisha left and followed Elijah as his
    attendant.

RESPONSORIAL PSALM

Ps 16:1-2, 5, 7-8, 9-10, 11

R℣. (cf. 5a) You are my inheritance, O Lord.

Keep me, O God, for in you I take refuge;
    I say to the LORD, "My Lord are you.
O LORD, my allotted portion and my cup,
    you it is who hold fast my lot."

R℣. You are my inheritance, O Lord.

I bless the LORD who counsels me;
    even in the night my heart exhorts me.
I set the LORD ever before me;
    with him at my right hand I shall not be
      disturbed.

R℣. You are my inheritance, O Lord.

Therefore my heart is glad and my soul
    rejoices,
    my body, too, abides in confidence
because you will not abandon my soul to
    the netherworld,
    nor will you suffer your faithful one to
      undergo corruption.

R℣. You are my inheritance, O Lord.

You will show me the path to life,
    fullness of joys in your presence,
    the delights at your right hand forever.

R℣. You are my inheritance, O Lord.

SECOND READING

Gal 5:1, 13-18

Brothers and sisters:
For freedom Christ set us free;
    so stand firm and do not submit again
      to the yoke of slavery.

For you were called for freedom, brothers
    and sisters.
But do not use this freedom
    as an opportunity for the flesh;
    rather, serve one another through love.
For the whole law is fulfilled in one
    statement,
    namely, *You shall love your neighbor as*
      yourself.
But if you go on biting and devouring one
    another,
    beware that you are not consumed by
      one another.

I say, then: live by the Spirit
    and you will certainly not gratify the
      desire of the flesh.
For the flesh has desires against the Spirit,
    and the Spirit against the flesh;
    these are opposed to each other,
    so that you may not do what you want.
But if you are guided by the Spirit, you
    are not under the law.

About Liturgy

The Relationship between Music and Preaching, Part III: Having defined music and preaching, and having briefly explored some of the foundational underpinnings of each, we can now turn our attention today to the relationship between music and preaching, and work to tease out some valuable insights.

First, focusing on the structures of each, we can study the composition of musical pieces and look for the potential similarities to the structures present in effective preaching. For instance, acclamations such as "Alleluia" and "Amen" are essentially "outbursts" of assent and praise. Such acclamations are common in many churches, particularly African American churches, from both preachers and assemblies. We ought to rightly wonder if there is more room for that in our own churches and whether there is a role for acclamations in preaching in other circumstances.

Turning next to responses, we might do well to seek out new, unique ways to engage the assembly in dialogue, a "lens" to view the whole of the text's content. Some pieces of music are dialogical in nature in just this way. For instance, Shannon Cerneka and I wrote "Fill Us, O God" (WLP/GIA) with a section that has a soloist sing "Take away our pride, fill us with your love," while the assembly maintains the mantra "Fill Us, O God." In further iterations, the word "pride" is replaced with other societal sins: envy, apathy, etc.

Regarding antiphons and other uses of psalms, we may recall that many psalms, in their completeness, take the singer on a journey, and the choice of refrain text and overall music can dramatically affect the reception and understanding of the text. Consider the many settings of Psalm 34 that you know, while also realizing that while "Taste and see the goodness of the Lord" is a refrain many times, so is "The Lord hears the cry of the poor"—often with similar verses of text but with very different styles of music.

While not explicitly mentioned in the Constitution on the Sacred Liturgy, litanies are a prevalent part of our liturgical music and prayer. They help us communicate to God while listening for God's voice, and they can help us, by creative and modern texts, engage in elaborating on any particular spiritual facet of our shared faith.

Liturgical music can also stand as a model for attending to both word choice and styles of delivery in preaching. Poetic language is always preferable: consider, for instance, the different sound and additional meaning that the word "lifeless" has in comparison to the word "dead," in this paraphrase of Psalm 31: "Empty, broken, lifeless: I give my spirit, Lord." Inserting the word "dead" for "lifeless" here would be an unfortunate mistake. Similarly, the tone of the text's delivery, be it through music or preaching, must match; this truly amplifies the text. Otherwise the words will have no chance of imparting the desired meaning or effect. Text painting, in music, does well to allow for silence in moments like Psalm 137, "Let my tongue be silenced," or to take on a more rapid urgency if the text demands that. Can our preaching borrow such techniques at the ambo too?

About Music

Matching Gospel, Tune, and Text: Ben Walther's "Make Your Home in Me" (OCP) is the perfect companion to this weekend's gospel, and, as described above, a perfect pairing of music and text, making this a powerful prayer to place on your assemblies' lips this weekend.

JUNE 26, 2022
THIRTEENTH SUNDAY
IN ORDINARY TIME

SAINTS PETER AND PAUL, APOSTLES

GOSPEL ACCLAMATION
Matt 16:18

R/. Alleluia, alleluia.
You are Peter and upon this rock I will build my
    Church,
and the gates of the netherworld shall not
    prevail against it.
R/. Alleluia, alleluia.

Gospel

Matt 16:13-19; L591

When Jesus went into
    the region of Cae-
    sarea Philippi
he asked his
    disciples,
"Who do people
    say that the
    Son of Man
    is?"
They replied, "Some
    say John the
    Baptist, others
    Elijah,
still others Jer-
    emiah or one of
    the prophets."
He said to them, "But who
    do you say that I am?"
Simon Peter said in reply,
    "You are the Christ, the Son of the
        living God."
Jesus said to him in reply, "Blessed are
    you, Simon son of Jonah.
For flesh and blood has not revealed
    this to you, but my heavenly
    Father.
And so I say to you, you are Peter,
    and upon this rock I will build my
        Church,
    and the gates of the netherworld
        shall not prevail against it.
I will give you the keys to the Kingdom
    of heaven.
Whatever you bind on earth shall be
    bound in heaven;
    and whatever you loose on earth
        shall be loosed in heaven."

See Appendix A, p. 306, for the other readings.

Reflecting on the Gospel

The story of St. Paul stands out as an example of what God is able to do in the life of anyone who is open to the movement of the Spirit of God in one's life. St. Paul's encounter with God on the road to Damascus and the subsequent revelation of Jesus Christ to him so that he will proclaim Christ to the Gentiles transform his life (Gal 1:12, 15). Also, it reveals his openness to the way that the Spirit of God is present in his life. His conviction of the validity of the encounter as coming from God is so strong that he wholeheartedly embraces the consequences of his apostolic commissioning. It is for this reason that he tells Timothy in today's second reading that through him the message of the good news of God's saving plan for the world through our Lord Jesus Christ is accomplished and the Gentiles have heard and embraced it (v. 17).

When St. Paul tells Timothy that "I have kept the faith" (v. 7), it reveals that the ministry of proclaiming the good news of Jesus Christ entrusted to him has been nothing less than successful. Indeed, St. Paul has fought the good fight of faith throughout the towns, regions, and provinces of the Roman Empire. In another letter, St. Paul stresses further the success of his ministry when he says to the Christian community in Rome that he is proud of what Christ has accomplished through his ministry, and "from Jerusalem all the way around to Illyricum I have finished preaching the gospel of Christ" (Rom 15:19). St. Paul carries the good news of Christ to all parts of the Roman Empire, both by sea and by road. His message is eloquent, convincing, and transformational, as his audience turn away from their former ways of life "to serve the living and true God" (1 Thess 1:9). The influence that St. Paul has on the communities he founded in the Roman Empire is also seen in the lives of the individuals he touched in a significant way. His companions are both men and women who are motivated as he is to do what God is doing in the world through faith in Christ. It is on this basis that he confidently says that his life has been poured out as a libation (v. 6) for the churches and individuals who received from him the message of the good news of Christ.

As one who has kept the faith, St. Paul is confident that "a crown of righteousness awaits [him], which the Lord, the just judge, will award" (v. 8) because from the moment of his encounter with God and Jesus Christ, he embraced his divine commissioning; he proclaimed the faith courageously, notwithstanding the physical, emotional, and mental challenges he faced; and indeed, many have come to believe in Jesus Christ as a result of his ministry. Likewise, many have come to believe in Christ on account of the ministry of St. Peter in spite of the adversity he faced proclaiming Christ (Acts 12:1-11). On this note, both Sts. Peter and Paul teach us the importance of our faith in Christ—namely, to bring others to experience faith in Christ so that the human family may know the salvation of God in Christ. In the same way, our experience of faith in Christ demands that we live as people of faith and bring others to have faith in Christ.

Focusing the Gospel

Key words and phrases: "You are the Christ, the Son of the living God."

To the point: In today's gospel, Peter is the first person to say out loud what Jesus's inner circle has probably been thinking. Notice that this is not the first answer the apostles give. The first thing they do is tell Jesus what everyone else has been thinking, and only after he specifically asks them does Peter speak up. It's possible that this was the first time the apostles told Jesus, to his face, that they suspected he might be the Messiah. Jesus points out that voicing this theory takes a lot of faith. Today we celebrate the unabashed honesty that Peter lived and led the church with. It is this truth, which is unafraid, that we celebrate and seek to emulate in our church today.

Model Penitential Act

Presider: Today we celebrate the great faith of Sts. Peter and Paul. But even with great faith, we sometimes fall short of who we are called to be. Mindful of this we ask for God's healing and forgiveness . . . *[pause]*

Lord Jesus, you are the Way, the Truth, and the Life: Lord, have mercy.
Christ Jesus, you are the Christ, the Son of the living God: Christ, have mercy.
Lord Jesus, you call us to follow you: Lord, have mercy.

Model Universal Prayer (Prayer of the Faithful)

Presider: Confident that God hears us, we offer our prayers today through the intercession of Sts. Peter and Paul:

Response: Lord, hear our prayer.

That the pope and all church leaders may work with humility to share Christ's message with the world . . .

That all social leaders might work with a conviction that defends the dignity of all persons . . .

That all who are persecuted for their faith might find resolve and consolation amid their difficult circumstances . . .

That our local community might build a church that is welcoming of all people, especially people who hold different political, religious, or ideological beliefs . . .

Presider: Loving God, you heard the prayers of your servants Sts. Peter and Paul as they answered your call. Hear our prayers today that we might live with the same conviction of Sts. Peter and Paul, always trusting in you so to grow in charity and love. We ask this through Christ our Lord. **Amen.**

About Liturgy

A Big Church: (These words appeared on this date, in just this way, last year. They are worth repeating in this space again.)

Have you ever had one of those moments in which you pause to consider a certain person or a liturgical practice the person espouses and wonder how it is you and he or she can coexist in the same church?

We don't know everything there is to know about Sts. Peter and Paul, but a lot of what we do know shows them frequently disagreeing. Indeed, at times their relationship is argumentative and strained to the point where any one of us might have just given up.

Yet it is divine wisdom that pairs these two, liturgically and otherwise, in the hearts and minds of the faithful. The church as we know it would not exist with only one half of this pair. So, too, we must keep in mind the church they helped build is broad and deep, vast and nearly immeasurable in every conceivable direction. If devotional practices to, for instance, Divine Mercy aren't your cup of tea, they do appeal and are helpful to someone you know. So, too, lay-led Liturgy of the Hours, or adoration, or Taizé prayer, or . . .

It's a big church, Peter and Paul can remind us, if we allow it to be.

COLLECT

Let us pray.

Pause for silent prayer

O God, who on the Solemnity of the Apostles Peter and Paul
give us the noble and holy joy of this day,
grant, we pray, that your Church
may in all things follow the teaching
of those through whom she received
the beginnings of right religion.
Through our Lord Jesus Christ, your Son,
who lives and reigns with you in the unity of the Holy Spirit,
God, for ever and ever. **Amen.**

FOR REFLECTION

• How do you respond when Jesus asks you, "[W]ho do you say that I am?"

• How might today's gospel serve as an invitation to reevaluate your priorities, those things that occupy your time, talent, and treasure?

• Who have been important figures in your own faith foundation and formation?

Homily Points

• There is a fundamental difference between knowing about God and actually knowing God through relationship. It is easy, however, for us to substitute our knowledge of God for that authentic relationship. When Jesus asks, "[W]ho do you say that I am?" he is not asking Peter for a theological discourse. Rather, Jesus asks Peter about his personal relationship with God that has been formed through years of prayer, conversation, and experiences. The same must be true for us.

• Today's gospel is often used to support the significance of apostolic tradition, and rightly so! We must remember, however, in the words of Pope Francis, that the church must also be a field hospital, ready to warmly welcome and care for all the people of God. We can follow the examples of St. Peter, St. Paul, Pope Francis, and the many holy men and women who have shown and continue to show by their lives how to follow Christ. What a great family to be counted among!

169

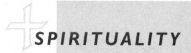

SPIRITUALITY

GOSPEL ACCLAMATION
Col 3:15a, 16a

℞. Alleluia, alleluia.
Let the peace of Christ control your hearts;
let the word of Christ dwell in you richly.
℞. Alleluia, alleluia.

Gospel Luke 10:1-12, 17-20; L102C

At that time the Lord appointed sev-
    enty-two others
    whom he sent ahead of him in pairs
    to every town and place he intended
        to visit.
He said to them,
    "The harvest is abundant but the la-
        borers are few;
    so ask the master of the harvest
    to send out laborers for his harvest.
Go on your way;
    behold, I am sending you like lambs
        among wolves.
Carry no money bag, no sack, no
    sandals;
    and greet no one along the way.
Into whatever house you enter, first say,
    'Peace to this household.'
If a peaceful person lives there,
    your peace will rest on him;
    but if not, it will return to you.
Stay in the same house and eat and
        drink what is offered to you,
    for the laborer deserves his payment.
Do not move about from one house to
    another.
Whatever town you enter and they wel-
    come you,
    eat what is set before you,
    cure the sick in it and say to them,
    'The kingdom of God is at hand for
        you.'
Whatever town you enter and they do
    not receive you,
    go out into the streets and say,
    'The dust of your town that clings to
        our feet,
    even that we shake off against you.'

Continued in Appendix A, p. 307,

or Luke 10:1-9, in Appendix A, p. 307.

Reflecting on the Gospel

"Mission statements" are the order of the day for communities of all kinds. Luke presents today's gospel as the early church's "mission statement" and a practical handbook for its implementation. Our society is different; travel, communication, economics, multiculturalism, and multi-faith contacts have changed greatly from a generation ago, let alone almost two millennia. So how is this gospel relevant today? How can we distill the essence of its truth so it can inform our current mission?

First, the world needs the mission of Christians because there is a plentiful harvest waiting to be reaped. Second, prayer to "the master of the harvest" is essential for the empowering of the harvesters. Third, because it is Jesus who sends us on mission, we can go in confident of his active protection. This is not to discount the fourth missionary principle: the reminder that there are "wolves" to be confronted on the way—personal, communal, and structural realities that will try to hunt down and consume those who proclaim the gospel. Every generation of Christians needs the gift of discernment so we can name and recognize these "wolves."

Fifth, in our mobile society we know that to travel well is to travel lightly. When the goal of our journey is the reign of God, then money, possessions (or perhaps possessiveness), or concern with status can be hindering baggage. "Carry no money bag, no sack, no sandals" is again a device of exaggeration that would have been understood by Luke's communities as emphasizing the urgency of the mission. The same is true for the sixth warning to "greet no one," not a recommendation for brash impoliteness, but a condemnation of social dalliance and time-consuming gossip.

Whether accepted or rejected, the precious gift of Christ's healing peace, not a false or conventional greeting, is to be offered to the household that the missionaries visit. This seventh instruction puts into the disciples' mouths Jesus's own resurrection greeting of Easter eve, "Peace be with you" (Luke 24:36), to be freely accepted or rejected.

Hospitality that is graciously accepted and allows the host to dictate the "menu" not only at meals but also in the broader cultural context of the table of life, is the eighth principle. Good missionaries do not impose their own cultural expectations on others but are nourished by whatever the host offers, both personal and social. This does not deny efforts to dismantle social barriers, and the mention of the curing of the sick reminds us that this is a work of loving service that speaks a universal language of care and respect for suffering humanity, no matter what a person's culture or social status. Accepted (v. 9) or rejected (v. 11), the message is the same: "The kingdom of God is at hand." And so the ninth missionary principle is the realistic expectation of failure, of being resisted and rejected as Jesus was.

The tenth and last principle of the missionary charter is that, no matter what, we persevere in our proclamation of the reign of God by our words, our relationships, and our rituals. The closing mention of Sodom is not in reference to any sexual immorality, but to the great sin of denying hospitality to God's messengers (Gen 13:13). This is what disciples of Jesus are. Those who deny them a welcome will be judged by what they reject—the reign of God.

Focusing the Gospel

Key words and phrases: "Whatever town you enter and they welcome you, eat what is set before you, cure the sick in it and say to them, 'The kingdom of God is at hand for you.'"

To the point: This week we learn more about what it means to be a disciple of Christ. Jesus sends out his followers to all of the towns he intends to visit en route to Jerusalem and tells them to bring good news about the harvest, referencing both the crop planted and himself, the Bread of Life.

Jesus delegates. He sends out a number of teams, not individuals, to bring peace on behalf of himself. No one goes alone. Partnership is valued, and when Jesus gives instructions, he trusts that his disciples will follow them.

Connecting the Gospel

to the first and second readings: In the second reading, Paul reminds us that signs of holiness are not, in fact, holiness. Circumcision is a sign of dedication to the Lord, but it is not dedication to the Lord. When Paul boasts, or is successful, it is not he who is successful, but the Lord, through Paul.

The first reading is an intimate discovery of a maternal relationship, with the Lord as the mother who nurses us. There is perhaps no more tender a relationship than that of a mother nursing her child, comforting and giving life.

to experience: The Trinity is our model of relationship, both with the Lord and one another. Even monks who commit to hermitage are in relationship with the Lord, emptying themselves in contemplation and prayer to be filled by God. We are given this striking image from Isaiah when he says, "Oh, that you may suck fully / of the milk of her comfort, / that you may nurse with delight / at her abundant breasts!" Can you imagine that kind of intimate relationship with the Lord?

Connecting the Responsorial Psalm

to the readings: Today's psalm has a story's layout, giving us an opportunity to see the relationship we are in with God. Verse one is an exclamation of praise. Verse two is an invitation to see the works of the Lord. Verse three is a list of these works. The fourth verse is a testament of joy for what the Lord has done.

to psalmist preparation: Begin your work with this verse: "Hear now, all you who fear God, while I declare what he has done for me." This is, essentially, how you approach the work of sharing the psalm every week. Though the psalms contain a great deal of poetry, much of your work is to make it personal, so that when you share these words with the congregation, you are doing so as a colleague of the first psalmist.

PROMPTS FOR FAITH-SHARING

Who are your partners in your daily work or career? Who are your partners in your faith?

Jesus tells his disciples, "Carry no money bag, no sack, no sandals; and greet no one along the way." How does this direction make you feel? Could you pick up and go out into the world without any luggage? This would make most people uncomfortable. Why do you think Jesus asks it?

In our reading from Isaiah, we see a vivid and tender image of the Lord. What imagery do you use to understand the Lord's care for you? How does the image of a nursing mother feel? Do you feel that the Lord does indeed care for you this way, or is this explicitly maternal image somewhat new?

What do you think it means to shake off the dust of a town that doesn't receive you?

Model Penitential Act

Presider: Jesus sends us out to follow his example and love in his name. For the times we have not loved as we should, we ask for God's forgiveness . . . *[pause]*

Lord Jesus, you are all goodness and truth: Lord, have mercy.

Christ Jesus, in you we find life lived for others: Christ, have mercy.

Lord Jesus, you invite us to labor in your fields: Lord, have mercy.

Homily Points

• There is urgency in today's gospel. Jesus not only proclaims that the kingdom of God is at hand, but he also gives some specific instructions for how to go forth to build the kingdom. God's kingdom is ever-present in the world, yet there are still signs of injustice and violence and hatred everywhere we look. At first it seems that these are contrasting ideologies, but we must remember that the kingdom of God is both "here" and "not yet."

• In sending out the seventy-two, Jesus insists that his disciples travel together in pairs. While our relationship with Jesus is personal, it cannot only be personal. We do not exist as isolated individuals, no matter how much we may want to. We hear throughout Hebrew and Christian Scripture that God calls us to community, for it is through and with others that we grow in relationship with God. The Acts of the Apostles tells us that the early disciples committed themselves to prayer and the breaking of bread.

• But the communal nature of Jesus's call is not limited to working and praying with those who share our same beliefs. Rather, we are called to preach and heal and pray with all people, especially people who might be typically ignored or forgotten. How do we share the kingdom of God with people who struggle with addiction, who live without a home, who love differently than we do, or who are not from our country of origin? With confidence in Christ and as a community of believers, we have the responsibility to build God's kingdom here on earth as we wait for the fulfillment of God's kingdom at the end of time.

Model Universal Prayer (Prayer of the Faithful)

Presider: You send us out to do your will and to build your kingdom. We bring you our prayers today so that we might continue to grow in our call and mission.

Response: Lord, hear our prayer.

That church leaders may recommit themselves to living for and among our community of believers . . .

That national leaders reject "us first" ideologies and remember our common solidarity with all people . . .

That all farmers and field workers may know just working conditions that value their labors for the good of all . . .

That our local community might expand our understanding of the kingdom of God and reach beyond our walls to people most in need of God's love and peace . . .

Presider: Loving God, you invite us to labor in your fields. Hear our prayers today so that we might be strengthened in mission and continue to rely on you and your saving work. We ask this through Christ our Lord. **Amen.**

COLLECT

Let us pray.

Pause for silent prayer

O God, who in the abasement of your Son
have raised up a fallen world,
fill your faithful with holy joy,
for on those you have rescued from slavery
    to sin
you bestow eternal gladness.
Through our Lord Jesus Christ, your Son,
who lives and reigns with you in the unity
    of the Holy Spirit,
God, for ever and ever. **Amen.**

FIRST READING

Isa 66:10-14c

Thus says the LORD:
Rejoice with Jerusalem and be glad
        because of her,
    all you who love her;
exult, exult with her,
    all you who were mourning over her!
Oh, that you may suck fully
    of the milk of her comfort,
that you may nurse with delight
    at her abundant breasts!
    For thus says the LORD:
Lo, I will spread prosperity over Jerusalem
        like a river,
    and the wealth of the nations like an
        overflowing torrent.
As nurslings, you shall be carried in her
        arms,
    and fondled in her lap;
as a mother comforts her child,
    so will I comfort you;
    in Jerusalem you shall find your
        comfort.

When you see this, your heart shall rejoice
    and your bodies flourish like the grass;
the LORD's power shall be known to his
    servants.

RESPONSORIAL PSALM
Ps 66:1-3, 4-5, 6-7, 16, 20

R̸. (1) Let all the earth cry out to God with joy.

Shout joyfully to God, all the earth,
  sing praise to the glory of his name;
  proclaim his glorious praise.
Say to God, "How tremendous are your
  deeds!"

R̸. Let all the earth cry out to God with joy.

"Let all on earth worship and sing praise
  to you,
  sing praise to your name!"
Come and see the works of God,
  his tremendous deeds among the
    children of Adam.

R̸. Let all the earth cry out to God with joy.

He has changed the sea into dry land;
  through the river they passed on foot;
  therefore let us rejoice in him.
He rules by his might forever.

R̸. Let all the earth cry out to God with joy.

Hear now, all you who fear God,
  while I declare what he has done for me.
Blessed be God who refused me not
  my prayer or his kindness!

R̸. Let all the earth cry out to God with joy.

SECOND READING
Gal 6:14-18

Brothers and sisters:
May I never boast except in the cross of
  our Lord Jesus Christ,
  through which the world has been
    crucified to me,
  and I to the world.
For neither does circumcision mean
  anything, nor does uncircumcision,
  but only a new creation.
Peace and mercy be to all who follow this
  rule
  and to the Israel of God.

From now on, let no one make troubles
  for me;
  for I bear the marks of Jesus on my
    body.

The grace of our Lord Jesus Christ be
  with your spirit,
  brothers and sisters. Amen.

About Liturgy

The Relationship between Music and Preaching, Part IV: Today we take some time to ponder, as the end of last Sunday's writing asked, whether preaching can borrow musical techniques. We also revisit the importance of exploring the relationship of liturgical music and preaching.

First, we should ask: Is the liturgy "over-texted" already? The danger of any of the various texts at liturgy is they, even though words themselves are signs, can actually be an obstacle that blocks the transcendent communication the liturgy is meant to use and be. The preaching and the musical lyrics are the places where that danger is perhaps highest.

Yet we know, too, that being concise and succinct is especially difficult in both arenas, and risks miscommunication, either by leaving out important details or, frankly, by not being very good at interpreting poetry. On the whole, though, we will still likely find it easier and be more successful by preaching on the poetry and symbolism of the Trinity, for instance, rather than explaining the doctrine of it; we will find it easier and be more successful by preaching the poetry and symbolism of the resurrection than explaining how it happened; we will find it easier and be more successful by preaching on the poetry and symbolism of Eucharist rather than describing how it is confected:

> The myst'ry of your presence, Lord,
> No mortal tongue can tell:
> Whom all the world cannot contain
> Comes in our hearts to dwell. ("Gift of Finest Wheat" by Omer Westendorf)

This is not to say that music and preaching should never dwell in specifics or in present reality—they can and must do so. Our faith, fundamentally, is one of mystery, paradox, the supernatural, things unseen but believed. Music and the poetry it tries to set and amplify both operate most successfully on the level of symbolism and are, therefore, perhaps best suited to express and make real within us this faith. Can our preaching do likewise, with relevance to a present context? I would hope so.

The Pew Research Center, in August 2016, released an analysis of data regarding Christians who seek new congregations. The percentage of adults who listed "quality of sermons" as an important factor in their search topped the list, at 83 percent. When we pair that with the earlier-mentioned admonition from Sing to the Lord, "Faith grows when it is well expressed in celebration. Good celebrations can foster and nourish faith. Poor celebrations may weaken it" (5), the importance of pursuing the best quality of preaching and music ministry cannot be overstated. Our church depends on it.

About Music

Music of Evangelization: The gospel passage today speaks of the seventy-two being sent out on a mission of evangelization. They are to take little with them, relying on those they meet for sustenance and lodging. Notably, Jesus sends them out in pairs, indicating that he expects a reliance on each other and the relationship the two share together. Our work of evangelization should not seem as if it's something we are called to alone, as if it's something unsupported by the whole of the Christian community and specifically by one other, with us on that mission, that journey.

A piece that speaks directly to these aspects of evangelization is Omer Westendorf's text "God's Blessing Sends Us Forth" (WLP/GIA), paired in the *One in Faith* hymnal with the ST. ELIZABETH hymn tune, more familiar perhaps as "Beautiful Savior."

SPIRITUALITY

GOSPEL ACCLAMATION
cf. John 6:63c, 68c

℟. Alleluia, alleluia.
Your words, Lord, are Spirit and life;
you have the words of everlasting life.
℟. Alleluia, alleluia.

Gospel

Luke 10:25-37; L105C

There was a scholar of the
 law who stood up to test
 Jesus and said,
 "Teacher, what must I do to
 inherit eternal life?"
Jesus said to him, "What is
 written in the law?
How do you read it?"
He said in reply,
 "You shall love the Lord,
 your God,
 with all your heart,
 with all your being,
 with all your strength,
 and with all your mind,
 and your neighbor as
 yourself."
He replied to him, "You have
 answered correctly;
 do this and you will live."

But because he wished to justify himself, he said to Jesus,
 "And who is my neighbor?"
Jesus replied,
 "A man fell victim to robbers
 as he went down from Jerusalem to
 Jericho.
They stripped and beat him and went
 off leaving him half-dead.
A priest happened to be going down
 that road,
 but when he saw him, he passed by
 on the opposite side.
Likewise a Levite came to the place,
 and when he saw him, he passed by
 on the opposite side.

Continued in Appendix A, p. 307.

Reflecting on the Gospel

The parable of the Good Samaritan is a "shocking" story, intended to make us think about alternatives in our relationships with God and one another. It is introduced with the lawyer's determined effort to justify himself with regard to the two great commandments: love of God and love of neighbor. Self-justification is centered on "I" and "my": "[W]hat must *I* do to inherit eternal life?" he asks, and Jesus responds with two questions of his own: "What is written in the law? How do you read it?" The lawyer is quick to answer; he has all the right and holy words, can quote his source documents perfectly, and adopts the faultless theological stance of Deuteronomy 6:4-5 and Leviticus 19:17-18. But Jesus urges him from right answering to right living: "[D]o this and you will live."

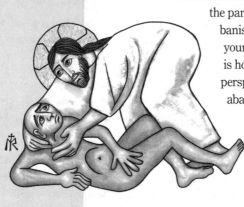

But the lawyer continues to seek self-justification rather than truth, responding: "And who is *my* neighbor?" Everything is in reference to himself. But discipleship does not start with myself, with asking whom I shall or shall not love or what are the boundaries of my responsibility. At the end of the parable, Jesus will ask the lawyer another question that banishes self from center stage: "Which of these three, in your opinion, was neighbor to the robbers' victim?" This is how our commitment to Jesus is to be defined: from the perspective of the half-dead, the fallen, the wounded, the abandoned ones, the person with whom every other character in the parable comes into either negative or positive contact.

After being ignored and avoided by the priest and the Levite, the abandoned man is approached, shockingly, by a Samaritan, a "corrupted" and despised Jew. The Samaritan is the one who *did* mercy. In the New Testament, "mercy" is a remarkable verb; one *does* mercy. In Luke's gospel, it is used only in reference to Jesus in this parable and that of the Prodigal Son. In Hebrew, "mercy" derives from the word for "womb," and in Greek it has the sense of the gut feeling that embraces the situation of another. The implication of these gospel references is that we can be compassionate only in Jesus, who makes flesh the creating, sustaining, and birthing love of God. This is what the Samaritan does.

To go on to Jericho or back to Jerusalem to find lodging for himself and the half-dead traveler was a further act of the Samaritan's brave compassion. Palestinian inns hardly offered five-star accommodation, especially if you arrived with a battered body slung over your donkey's back! Jesus's listeners might well imagine that the morning after the Samaritan's vigil with the patient there could be a thankless awakening when the traveler found himself ministered to by a Samaritan. After all, how would we feel about being helped by someone whose sexual, racial, political, or social status we find extremely distasteful? And are we, ourselves, ready for the sometime thankless responses after long nights of our ministries?

The innkeeper is told to take care of the man and given the resources to do so until the Samaritan returns, when the innkeeper will be repaid for anything he has spent on the care of the wounded one. In this sense, Jesus is telling us, as well as the lawyer, that we are all innkeepers, entrusted by Jesus with the care of the wounded, asked to respond to the prophetic call that sounds through the centuries. Jesus shouts most loudly at us—"I desire mercy, not sacrifice" (Matt 9:13)—until his return at the end of human history when we will be repaid for our compassion, or lack of it.

Focusing the Gospel

Key words and phrases: "Jesus said to him, 'What is written in the law? How do you read it?'"

To the point: Anyone who has taught in any capacity can relate to Jesus and the scholar of the law. Thinking that he can pin Jesus down, the scholar asks what he feels is a challenging question. Jesus spins it back, asking the scholar how the scholar himself interprets it. Classic Socratic method. Jesus commends him, but the scholar isn't finished! He asks Jesus a question that may have been intended as petty or insulting, but Jesus answers with one of the most unexpected and memorable parables in all of the gospels: the story of the Good Samaritan, a man who treated an enemy with love and care, doing more than his enemy's own community.

This is a parable that invites the reader to imagine all roles he or she has played. Have you been the man beaten, and then helped by a stranger you thought was an enemy? Have you been the Samaritan? Have you been the priest or the judge who saw something happen and kept walking? The brilliance of this story is that humanity is expressed in all of the characters, those who offer help and those who turn away. We will, at different points in our life, be each of these characters. The goal, of course, is to be the Samaritan.

Connecting the Gospel

to the first reading: Moses's words are just as biting and relevant today as they were thousands of years ago. "[T]his command that I enjoin on you today is not too mysterious and remote for you." He's telling the Israelites that this isn't some unattainable goal only for the privileged few. We can imagine Moses standing up and holding the scrolls, looking at his family and neighbors with dogged frustration. The answers aren't up in the sky or across the sea—they're here, in this book! The Lord gave them to us! Commandments and statutes, that's it, and they're right here! Similarly, Jesus isn't speaking in a coded language. He wants the Jews to be like the Samaritan in his story, to help one another and to reach out to their enemies. This isn't rocket science. It's love.

to experience: Sometimes it's hard to be a Christian. It's easier to follow the trends of the times and do whatever we need to do to fit in with society. But if you read the gospels and listen at Mass, you realize it's not that hard. There's no great secret to being a good person. The saints in heaven didn't stumble upon magical information. They loved the people around them, and God most of all. Do good, love others, and let yourself be renewed and animated by the Eucharist. One can imagine Jesus is just as attentive to the scholar questioning him as Moses was with the Israelites. "And who is my neighbor?" Everyone.

Connecting the Responsorial Psalm

to the readings: Death is our greatest human fear. All other fears stem from this, anthropologically. In this week's psalm, we hear that if we turn to the Lord in need, we're not just taken care of or comforted, but we will live. It immediately addresses the root of all of our fears, as does our faith as a whole. If you turn to the Lord, you will not die. You will survive. The gospel today is a parable about how a Samaritan saves a Jewish man from death, but in doing so demonstrates that if we become the Samaritan, we ourselves are saved from death as well.

to psalmist preparation: These words could easily come from the man beaten and left on the road in the parable from this week's gospel. "I am afflicted and in pain / Let your saving help, O God, protect me." Put yourself in that place this week, and let these be the words of the man saved by the Good Samaritan.

PROMPTS FOR FAITH-SHARING

Which character in today's gospel do you identify with the most? Is it the scholar questioning Jesus? Is it the man of faith who walks by the man in need? Why do you feel drawn to this particular character?

Who is a neighbor with whom you can spend more time being a Samaritan?

Have you ever sidestepped an issue because it made you uncomfortable? Do you see yourself in those who passed by the beaten man?

Who is your enemy?

Model Penitential Act

Presider: Today we hear the parable of the Good Samaritan. For the times we have failed to love as we are called, we ask God for healing and forgiveness . . . *[pause]*

Lord Jesus, you abound in life and love: Lord, have mercy.

Christ Jesus, you extend your arms and welcome those in need: Christ, have mercy.

Lord Jesus, your words are spirit and life: Lord, have mercy.

Homily Points

• How often do legalism and love seem to compete in our lives and our church? Jesus shares the parable of the Good Samaritan in response to a legal expert asking about the process for inheriting eternal life. In this story of the good Samaritan, Jesus shows that love must take precedence over legalism. Mercy must triumph over strict adherence. This must have been unsettling for some people to hear. If we are honest, it might also unsettle us a bit. Authentic love is not legalistic.

• This idea of love of God and love of neighbor is radical. We know we are to love God, but sometimes loving our neighbor isn't easy. It is important to note that the merciful person in this story is not a religious leader but a Samaritan, often considered to be the enemy of the Jewish people. If even our enemies can show mercy, how much more should we be able to be merciful in our lives?

• As we grow in relationship with Christ, we also come to realize that we are not always the Good Samaritan in this story. Sometimes we must be the recipient of mercy shown by others. And that is a good thing! Part of living in relationship with others is a constant sharing and receiving of love, mercy, and forgiveness. This is the way of Christ. This must be the way of the Christian.

Model Universal Prayer (Prayer of the Faithful)

Presider: We are called to recognize all people as our neighbor, especially people who are most in need. With confidence, we raise our prayers and petitions to the God of love and mercy.

Response: Lord, hear our prayer.

That the church might build ecumenical and interfaith relations so to be neighbor to all people . . .

That all civic leaders may work to abolish laws that do not promote a consistent ethic of life from conception until natural death . . .

That all first responders, paramedics, doctors, nurses, and all who offer comfort and healing may find support for their work within the community . . .

That all who feel excluded from our church community might experience the warm embrace of hospitality and welcome . . .

Presider: Loving God, hear the prayers we raise today for us and for all our neighbors. We know you will mercifully answer these prayers according to your will. We ask this through Christ our Lord. **Amen.**

COLLECT

Let us pray.

Pause for silent prayer

O God, who show the light of your truth to those who go astray,
so that they may return to the right path,
give all who for the faith they profess
are accounted Christians
the grace to reject whatever is contrary to
   the name of Christ
and to strive after all that does it honor.
Through our Lord Jesus Christ, your Son,
who lives and reigns with you in the unity
   of the Holy Spirit,
God, for ever and ever. **Amen.**

FIRST READING
Deut 30:10-14

Moses said to the people:
   "If only you would heed the voice of the
      LORD, your God,
   and keep his commandments and
      statutes
   that are written in this book of the law,
   when you return to the LORD, your God,
   with all your heart and all your soul.

"For this command that I enjoin on you
      today
   is not too mysterious and remote for
      you.
It is not up in the sky, that you should say,
   'Who will go up in the sky to get it for
      us
   and tell us of it, that we may carry it
      out?'
Nor is it across the sea, that you should
      say,
   'Who will cross the sea to get it for us
   and tell us of it, that we may carry it
      out?'
No, it is something very near to you,
   already in your mouths and in your
      hearts;
   you have only to carry it out."

RESPONSORIAL PSALM
Ps 69:14, 17, 30-31, 33-34, 36, 37

℟. (cf. 33) Turn to the Lord in your need,
   and you will live.

I pray to you, O LORD,
   for the time of your favor, O God!
In your great kindness answer me
   with your constant help.
Answer me, O LORD, for bounteous is your
      kindness:
   in your great mercy turn toward me.

℟. Turn to the Lord in your need, and you
   will live.

I am afflicted and in pain;
    let your saving help, O God, protect me.
I will praise the name of God in song,
    and I will glorify him with
        thanksgiving.

R⁊. Turn to the Lord in your need, and you
    will live.

"See, you lowly ones, and be glad;
    you who seek God, may your hearts
        revive!
For the LORD hears the poor,
    and his own who are in bonds he spurns
        not."

R⁊. Turn to the Lord in your need, and you
    will live.

For God will save Zion
    and rebuild the cities of Judah.
The descendants of his servants shall
        inherit it,
    and those who love his name shall
        inhabit it.

R⁊. Turn to the Lord in your need, and you
    will live.

or

RESPONSORIAL PSALM
Ps 19:8, 9, 10, 11

See Appendix A, p. •••.

SECOND READING
Col 1:15-20

Christ Jesus is the image of the invisible
        God,
    the firstborn of all creation.
For in him were created all things in
        heaven and on earth,
    the visible and the invisible,
    whether thrones or dominions or
        principalities or powers;
    all things were created through him and
        for him.
He is before all things,
    and in him all things hold together.
He is the head of the body, the church.
He is the beginning, the firstborn from the
        dead,
    that in all things he himself might be
        preeminent.
For in him all the fullness was pleased to
        dwell,
    and through him to reconcile all things
        for him,
    making peace by the blood of his cross
    through him, whether those on earth or
        those in heaven.

About Liturgy

Never Deny, Seldom Affirm, Always Distinguish: In today's gospel, Jesus teaches us to love our neighbors as we love ourselves. When he is pressed further on who our neighbors are, Jesus's parable reveals that we should strive to see all people, including those we might call enemies, as neighbor.

There are many people in a parish setting we might not always get along with very well, due to any number of factors: divergent political, philosophical, or liturgical tendencies to name but a very few. "May God bless and keep you . . . far away from me" might be a prayer muttered under our breath more than once, but unless a relationship has truly reached the "shake the dust from your feet" stage, it's not helpful. So, what might be helpful as we strive for better communication, better community in our faith experiences?

There is a Dominican (that is, Order of Preachers, OP) maxim, "Never deny, seldom affirm, always distinguish." It's attributed to St. Thomas Aquinas and gives a framework for a path forward, especially when embarking on difficult discussions—which, of course, never happens in the world of liturgy or liturgical music . . .

"Never deny" means that the listener should, by charity, assume the goodwill of the other and seek in what is being said some even partial truth, perhaps in one very specific detail or in an overarching sentiment—or possibly even in a "meta-message" behind the content. For example, if someone suggests needing more relevant and engaging preaching, to the point of absurd suggestions like having the pastor learn magic tricks or dress up like a mime, the meta-message here might be that, more broadly, the preaching needs to be more engaging, more relevant, even if the proposed methodology is on shaky ground.

By "seldom affirm," the listener avoids traps by fully and only aligning on one side of any given discussion. It even disallows the avoidance technique of "agreeing to disagree" and forces those in conversation to further explore opportunities for better answers, more agreement.

By "always distinguish," the maxim allows all parties to accomplish the first two ideas here while still allowing for room both to disagree and object and also to seek areas of agreement and truth. By mandating that the speaker choose words carefully, discussion freely continues with care and respect.

For instance, helpful phrases when pursuing this methodology include:

"If by X, you mean XYZ, then no; I see X meaning rather ABC."
"It would be helpful to distinguish here between X and Y."
"I believe X to be accurate, but not necessarily a cause of Y."

Reflexive listening is also helpful here: "What I just heard you say is . . ." as this technique ensures both speaker and listener are in agreement with what is being communicated.

If such discussions presume charity and a sincere desire to explore, communicate, and learn, then reason is also allowed into the exchange of ideas, and both truth and community are allowed to emerge from even the most divergent ideas and approaches.

About Music

Love for Others: Consider "Certainly, Lord," an African American spiritual arrangement found in *Lead Me, Guide Me* (GIA) among other places, for a text about loving others as commanded by God. Another option would be one of many pieces based on the familiar reading from 1 Corinthians, the treatise on love heard at many weddings. "Love Goes On" (OCP) by Bernadette Farrell is one, with an easy-to-learn melody reminiscent of American folk tunes.

JULY 10, 2022
FIFTEENTH SUNDAY
IN ORDINARY TIME

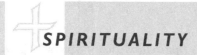

SPIRITUALITY

GOSPEL ACCLAMATION
cf. Luke 8:15

℞. Alleluia, alleluia.
Blessed are they who have kept the word with a
    generous heart
and yield a harvest through perseverance.
℞. Alleluia, alleluia.

Gospel

Luke 10:38-42; L108C

Jesus entered a village
    where a woman whose name was
        Martha welcomed him.
She had a sister named Mary
    who sat beside the Lord at his feet
        listening to him speak.
Martha, burdened with much serving,
    came to him and said,
    "Lord, do you not care
    that my sister has left me by myself
        to do the serving?
Tell her to help me."
The Lord said to her in reply,
    "Martha, Martha, you are anxious
        and worried about many things.
There is need of only one thing.
Mary has chosen the better part
    and it will not be taken from her."

Reflecting on the Gospel

When Jesus arrives at Mary and Martha's house, he and his companions are on a journey, and it is hardly possible that Jesus left them outside the door and presented himself as a privileged solo guest to the house at Bethany. Quite a crowd enters! Martha emerges as the dominant sister: the house is described as her home; she is the one who "welcomed" him; Mary is her sister. What distracts Martha is her service, her *diakonia*, a word that had a much broader meaning than only domestic duties in the early church (see Acts 6:4 and the apostles' *diakonia* of the Word). She complains that Mary sitting at Jesus's feet in silence is no help to her ministry. She, Martha, has been left to cope on her own. Rather like the lawyer in last week's parable, Martha is indulging in self-justification.

In response, Jesus admonishes the one who criticizes and he defends the criticized. Mary has chosen the better part on this occasion, he says, but it is only a *part* of the way the two sisters are to be of service of Jesus, not the whole picture; nor is either sister's service of Jesus constant or unwavering. Only both sisters, together, can accommodate Jesus in the way he should be welcomed.

We do not have to divide the world between competing poets, prophets, and pragmatists, nor do we need to choose once and for all between contemplation and action. Rather, what will unite us is to welcome all, to respect our differences, or to accept that we may be sometimes one and sometimes the other.

Some medieval legends describe Martha and Mary as traveling together to France, where Martha became a dragon-slayer. And yet Mary was there too, teaching and preaching as an active servant of the word she had once heard at Jesus's feet. Many women in our own times who have been at the forefront in slaying political "dragons" are also women of prayer like, for example, the "Women in Black." This movement began in 1988 with Israeli and Palestinian women united in keeping weekly public and prayerful vigils at the Western Wall in Jerusalem to protest against the Israeli occupation of the West Bank and Gaza. Since then the movement has spread worldwide to different situations and places of prayer as a peaceful protest about social injustices.

Many people, especially the young, are eager for both social action and service to the disadvantaged, while also searching for a spirituality that is contemplative but does not retreat into introspection. A wonderful example of this is the Sant'Egidio Community, a lay community founded in Rome in 1968 by university students, and now comprising over 50,000 members in more than seventy countries and four continents. Its solidarity with and ministry to the poor, efforts for peace and ecumenism, are founded on personal and communal prayer. Every night at the church of Santa Maria in Trastevere, hundreds gather with members of the community for Evening Prayer and the sharing of the Word. To divide and divorce the Martha and Mary in each of us is a real temptation. Both are needed to keep vigil and to be present to Christ when he is again in agony in our suffering brothers and sisters.

Focusing the Gospel

Key words and phrases: "Martha, Martha, you are anxious and worried about many things. There is need of only one thing."

To the point: Martha has a perfectly reasonable objection to what Mary is doing. Martha is making her guest's comfort the priority by serving him. She's probably making sure he's comfortable where he's sitting, as well as taking care of the food. But it turns out that the best way to ensure Jesus's comfort as a guest isn't material care, but attention. Mary is honoring Jesus by giving him her full attention, even physically sitting at his feet. Perhaps the message we can take from this week's gospel is not just a call to rest, but viewing hospitality as an act of attention and listening. Jesus tells Martha that the best way to serve him isn't feeding him, it's listening to him. What if we applied this work to our own guests, and put listening and being attentive above cleaning sheets and serving food? What if we began to view the homeless through this lens, and worked not only to house them, but to dignify them with our time and attention?

Connecting the Gospel

to the first reading: The story of Abraham and the three visitors is a basic narrative of our faith, but also has the hallmarks of a secular fairy tale. Abraham offers hospitality to three strangers, and in return, his greatest wish is granted. The power of this story reaches far beyond the Torah, and by pairing it with this week's gospel, we are reminded of the power and grace of welcoming the stranger.

to experience: Hospitality is an act in which everyone can participate, regardless of age or material wealth. When we encounter others, whether it's in school, the workplace, a restaurant, a store, or in a social setting, we have an opportunity to engage with openness and attention, or to engage in a purely transactional way. Sometimes we're tired or drained of energy, but think of Mary in the gospel: her gift was to listen, to sit and be present. It isn't motion and forced conversation; it is the ministry of presence.

Connecting the Responsorial Psalm

to the readings: The first reading and the gospel this week tell us stories of people who encountered God in their homes and responded with welcome. The psalm tells how we can enter into the house of the Lord, and partake in his hospitality. "Who harms not his fellow man, / nor takes up a reproach against his neighbor; / by whom the reprobate is despised, / while he honors those who fear the LORD." That is who will live in the house of the Lord.

to psalmist preparation: The psalm is one of the times during Mass when the congregation is invited to engage beyond just listening. You, in a way, bring the "Martha option" for participation, by inviting those around you to share their voices and physically participate. How can you use the psalm as a time of hospitality and welcome?

PROMPTS FOR FAITH-SHARING

How do you tend to show hospitality? What is the first thing you do when you know someone is coming to your home?

What does "the ministry of presence" mean to you? How can you participate in this ministry?

Have you ever been welcomed by a stranger? Where did this happen? How did it make you feel?

Think of someone in your life who is constantly annoying. How can you welcome that person? What small things can you change in the way you encounter him or her to let the person feel more welcomed in your presence?

Model Penitential Act

Presider: In today's gospel we hear of Martha and Mary and their love for Jesus. For the times we have not loved God and others as we should, we ask for forgiveness . . . *[pause]*

> Lord Jesus, you are the master teacher: Lord, have mercy.
>
> Christ Jesus, you call us to friendship with you: Christ, have mercy.
>
> Lord Jesus, you forgive us in your infinite love: Lord, have mercy.

Homily Points

• Women hold an important role throughout Luke's gospel narrative. Beginning with Mary and Elizabeth, we see that women play an active role in salvation history. We also see Luke uphold the example of faithful women—for example, the widow who shares her coin or the raising of Jairus's daughter or the curing of the hemorrhaging woman. Later, it is women who remain with Jesus on the cross and it is women who first witness to Jesus's resurrection.

• Today's account of Martha and Mary further illustrates the important role of women in discipleship. In fact, the kingdom of God is dependent on people like Martha and Mary who offer hospitality to visitors, listen intently, and ultimately boldly proclaim what they have seen and heard. What is important, however, is that Luke highlights these women as models of discipleship for all of us.

• Sometimes discipleship requires meeting physical needs, like we see in Martha preparing food. But Jesus reminds us that discipleship is also about truly being present with and for others. It is only when we are attentive to those we encounter that we can fully respond. It is only when we are attentive to Jesus that we can hear his voice and follow his invitation and command. May we look to Martha and Mary, and all the holy women throughout Scripture, as examples of discipleship and life in Christ. If we focus on Christ, everything else will fall into place.

Model Universal Prayer (Prayer of the Faithful)

Presider: In today's gospel, Jesus tells Martha not to be anxious about many things. With this, we bring our prayers to God, confident that they will be heard.

Response: Lord, hear our prayer.

That the institutional church will continue to listen to and uphold the voice and witness of women . . .

That leaders of cities and nations may work tirelessly to end all forms of sexism and discrimination . . .

That all who live with anxiety and depression may find comfort in Christ through their relationship with others . . .

That all gathered here might more attentively listen to the voice of Christ in our midst and set aside what distracts us from this listening . . .

Presider: Loving God, hear the prayers we bring to you this day. Answer them according to your will and give us the strength to follow you. We ask this through Christ our Lord. **Amen.**

COLLECT

Let us pray.

Pause for silent prayer

Show favor, O Lord, to your servants
and mercifully increase the gifts of your
  grace,
that, made fervent in hope, faith and
  charity,
they may be ever watchful in keeping your
  commands.
Through our Lord Jesus Christ, your Son,
who lives and reigns with you in the unity
  of the Holy Spirit,
God, for ever and ever. **Amen.**

FIRST READING

Gen 18:1-10a

The LORD appeared to Abraham by the
    terebinth of Mamre,
  as he sat in the entrance of his tent,
  while the day was growing hot.
Looking up, Abraham saw three men
    standing nearby.
When he saw them, he ran from the
    entrance of the tent to greet them;
  and bowing to the ground, he said:
  "Sir, if I may ask you this favor,
  please do not go on past your servant.
Let some water be brought, that you may
    bathe your feet,
  and then rest yourselves under the tree.
Now that you have come this close to your
    servant,
  let me bring you a little food, that you
    may refresh yourselves;
  and afterward you may go on your
    way."
The men replied, "Very well, do as you
    have said."

Abraham hastened into the tent and told
    Sarah,
  "Quick, three measures of fine flour!
    Knead it and make rolls."
He ran to the herd, picked out a tender,
    choice steer,
  and gave it to a servant, who quickly
    prepared it.
Then Abraham got some curds and milk,
  as well as the steer that had been
    prepared,
  and set these before the three men;
  and he waited on them under the tree
    while they ate.

They asked Abraham, "Where is your
    wife Sarah?"
He replied, "There in the tent."
One of them said, "I will surely return to
    you about this time next year,
  and Sarah will then have a son."

RESPONSORIAL PSALM

Ps 15:2-3, 3-4, 5

R̸. (1a) He who does justice will live in the presence of the Lord.

One who walks blamelessly and does justice;
who thinks the truth in his heart
and slanders not with his tongue.

R̸. He who does justice will live in the presence of the Lord.

Who harms not his fellow man,
nor takes up a reproach against his neighbor;
by whom the reprobate is despised,
while he honors those who fear the LORD.

R̸. He who does justice will live in the presence of the Lord.

Who lends not his money at usury
and accepts no bribe against the innocent.
One who does these things
shall never be disturbed.

R̸. He who does justice will live in the presence of the Lord.

SECOND READING

Col 1:24-28

Brothers and sisters:
Now I rejoice in my sufferings for your sake,
and in my flesh I am filling up
what is lacking in the afflictions of Christ
on behalf of his body, which is the church,
of which I am a minister
in accordance with God's stewardship given to me
to bring to completion for you the word of God,
the mystery hidden from ages and from generations past.
But now it has been manifested to his holy ones,
to whom God chose to make known the riches of the glory
of this mystery among the Gentiles;
it is Christ in you, the hope for glory.
It is he whom we proclaim,
admonishing everyone and teaching everyone with all wisdom,
that we may present everyone perfect in Christ.

About Liturgy

Temperance, Balance, Moderation: The Christian virtue of temperance "is the moral virtue that moderates the attraction of pleasures and provides balance in the use of created goods. It ensures the will's mastery over instincts and keeps desires within the limits of what is honorable. The temperate person directs the sensitive appetites toward what is good and maintains a healthy discretion" (*Catechism of the Catholic Church* 1809).

In consideration of Mary and Martha as presented in today's gospel, we must remind ourselves that our calling is not, broadly, to always be either "a Mary" or "a Martha," even though Jesus says Mary has chosen the better part. Rather, we should be mindful that hospitality takes many forms and relies on certain gifts that each of us has in differing ways, and at different times. A moderate and balanced approach is necessary and healthy.

Temperance, as described above, is the virtue that helps provide that sense of balance, not just in pursuit and use of "goods" but in all our daily living. In fact, the *Catechism* goes on to quote St. Augustine in that regard: "To live well is nothing other than to love God with all one's heart, with all one's soul and with all one's efforts; from this it comes about that love is kept whole and uncorrupted (through temperance). No misfortune can disturb it (and this is fortitude). It obeys only [God] (and this is justice), and is careful in discerning things, so as not to be surprised by deceit or trickery (and this is prudence)" (1809).

This particular cardinal virtue can impact how we approach all we say and do, and so influences how we might carry out any particular liturgical ministry. Especially if our role is one of making liturgical decisions, it is almost always wise to ensure not only that a decision is reached with all the information and potential consequences in front of us, but also that our disposition in the moment of deciding is one of balance and moderation.

One way of living temperance, balance, and moderation is (more secularly) embodied in the Virtue Continuum as created by Jim Lanctot in 2007. Temperance is one of eight virtues on the continuum, which lists extremes of "deficiency" and "excess" for each virtue. A deficiency of temperance leads to licentiousness; an excess of temperance leads to strictness. Neither is healthy or good, and shows us yet another example of the saying, "Everything in moderation, including moderation." I encourage you to explore the rest of the Virtue Continuum as you are able.

For the moment, ponder how temperance, balance, and moderation can better serve your liturgical ministry, especially if it is one of coordination or direction. Even if not, one of the goals of any liturgical ministry is to better create, form, and hold together the Christian community, which is almost always best served not by extremism or zealotry, but by love, mercy, and communion.

About Music

Hymns of Hospitality: When deciding on hymnody this weekend, remember that "welcome" is different from "hospitality." We have many obvious choices when it comes to music of welcome (recently mentioned on these pages) but fewer obvious candidates for music that truly speaks of hospitality. "Here at This Table" by Janét Sullivan Whitaker (OCP) is one; the *Psallite* refrain "Listen: I Stand at the Door and Knock" (Liturgical Press) would be another appropriate choice.

JULY 17, 2022
SIXTEENTH SUNDAY IN ORDINARY TIME

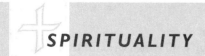

SPIRITUALITY

GOSPEL ACCLAMATION
Rom 8:15bc

℟. Alleluia, alleluia.
You have received a Spirit of adoption,
through which we cry, Abba, Father.
℟. Alleluia, alleluia.

Gospel

Luke 11:1-13; L111C

Jesus was praying in a certain place,
    and when he had finished,
    one of his disciples said to him,
    "Lord, teach us to pray just as John
        taught his disciples."
He said to them, "When you pray, say:
    Father, hallowed be your name,
        your kingdom come.
        Give us each day our daily bread
        and forgive us our sins
        for we ourselves forgive everyone
            in debt to us,
        and do not subject us to the final
            test."

And he said to them, "Suppose one of
    you has a friend
    to whom he goes at midnight and says,
    'Friend, lend me three loaves of bread,
    for a friend of mine has arrived at
        my house from a journey
    and I have nothing to offer him,'
    and he says in reply from within,
    'Do not bother me; the door has al-
        ready been locked
    and my children and I are already in
        bed.
I cannot get up to give you anything.'
I tell you,
    if he does not get up to give the
        visitor the loaves
    because of their friendship,
    he will get up to give him whatever
        he needs
    because of his persistence.

Continued in Appendix A, p. 308.

Reflecting on the Gospel

Why do we pray? It is not to impose our will on God, but to ask God to make us available to the divine will and to share our concerns with God, to place these under God's loving judgment. It is, therefore, not an effort to change God, but to change ourselves. Of all the evangelists, it is Luke who speaks most about prayer. His gospel begins (1:10) and ends (24:53) in the context of prayer. At significant moments in his life, Jesus prays, and his example leads the disciples to ask him, "Lord, teach us to pray just as John taught his disciples" (11:1). The Lukan version of Jesus's response is direct, shorter, simpler than Matthew's (Matt 6:9-13) and expresses the deepest reality of Jesus's relationship with his God, into which he wants his disciples to be drawn. The words are no magic formula; they help us to realize the personal reality of the One to whom we pray. Our familiarity with the Lord's Prayer may blunt our appreciation of its radical, even subversive, teaching about prayer. It is to be the prayer of a community that is conscious both of its intimate relationship with God and its presence in and respon- sibility for the world. In both testaments, God is "Father," a metaphor vastly different from that of the powerful Roman emperor, the "father of the homeland," or the au- thoritarian father of the family social unit. Especially in the gospels, God is the Abba of Jesus, in loving, faithful, and intimate relationship with the Beloved Son. The kingdom for which disciples pray is not a kingdom of political power, but one that belongs to the poor, the liberated, excluded women, forgiven sinners. That we may be changed, we pray for bread, forgiveness, and deliverance.

Given Luke's emphasis on hospitality, prayer for "our daily bread" is prob- ably a request for this basic necessity that should be shared with the poor. We also need to be nourished with one another's forgiveness, because God will never starve us of forgiveness, and God's behavior must be the norm for his sons and daughters. To live in this way will save us at the time of "the final test." The only other time that Luke uses the same word for "test" or temptation is again in the context of prayer in Gethsemane, when he urges the disciples, who slept while Jesus prayed, to "[g]et up and pray that you may not undergo the test" (22:46).

The Lord's Prayer is no magic formula. It is an instruction about the Father to whom Jesus and his disciples pray. Jesus affirms what should be the qual- ity of our prayer by telling two parables, both of which describe situations to which the response to "Just suppose" would be "Never!" What is described in the parable of the Friend at Midnight concerns three friends: the one who arrives unexpectedly, the host, and the one to whom the latter goes to ask for bread because he has run out of his own supply. To fail in hospitality by not being able to offer the barest sustenance to a friend and guest would be shame- ful, and if the third friend did not unbolt his door and help out, his shame would be the talk of his neighbors who no doubt would hear the midnight disturbance!

If we are in an enduring relationship as prayerful "friends" with God, we can be assured that God will be hospitable to us in our need.

Focusing the Gospel

Key words and phrases: "Give us each day our daily bread."

To the point: What is your daily bread? What is the thing that feeds you, that makes you feel whole, and that keeps you going? It can be many things—the love of a spouse, the dignity of a satisfying job, the Eucharist. Whatever it is, it is probably based on relationship. We say the Our Father many times in Catholic life, so much so that it becomes a passing set of words, more meditative than active. This week we have an opportunity to reflect on the true value of a petition to the Lord. Every time we pray, "Give us each day our daily bread," we are the man knocking on the door of his neighbor. We are heard, even if we don't always remember that we are asking.

Connecting the Gospel

to the first reading: In the first reading, Abraham is the petitioner, asking God a straightforward question, but inferring that Abraham himself is concerned for the good people of Sodom. He keeps lowering the number of good people in the city, asking if God will destroy it if that many good people remain.

to experience: How many times have you looked at the failing aspects of your faith and wondered if you were worthy of grace? Anxiety and doubt are a part of being human and will inevitably creep in over and over during the lifetime of a Christian. As the Lord calms Abraham's fears, we can be calmed by the knowledge that, like Sodom, we may be pardoned by the Lord as long as some small good remains in us.

Connecting the Responsorial Psalm

to the readings: This week's psalm is a celebration of prayers answered. In the gospel we are reminded of the power of asking for what we need. "And I tell you, ask and you will receive; seek and you will find; knock and the door will be opened to you." You have the privilege of sharing the words "When I called you answered me; / you built up strength within me."

to psalmist preparation: Recall a moment in your life when you asked for something over and over, and your needs were met. Did you feel that you were being too insistent? Or were you committed to that need and not willing to give up? Sometimes we need to be a "holy nuisance."

PROMPTS FOR FAITH-SHARING

If you had to retell the text of the Our Father in colloquial, modern terms, how would you say it?

What is an example in your life when you were persistent and achieved the desired result? What aspect of that experience do you credit with your success?

Have you ever acquiesced to a friend because of his or her constant petition?

If a neighbor showed up at your home in the middle of the night asking for help, what would you do?

Model Penitential Act

Presider: In the Lord's Prayer, we call on God to forgive us our sins just as we forgive those who have wronged us. For the times we have sinned or failed to extend forgiveness, we ask for God's healing and peace . . . *[pause]*

Lord Jesus, you teach us how to pray: Lord, have mercy.

Christ Jesus, you are one with the Father and Spirit: Christ, have mercy.

Lord Jesus, your words are spirit and life: Lord, have mercy.

Homily Points

• In today's gospel the disciples ask Jesus to teach them how to pray. This is an interesting request, as the disciples have been following Jesus for some time now. They have surely seen Christ pray before. If we look throughout the gospels, we see accounts of Jesus praying in any number of circumstances or situations. Jesus prays prayers of blessing and benediction. Jesus prays prayers of gratitude and thanksgiving. Jesus prays communally and privately. With this, the Lord's Prayer is situated within a much larger context of Jesus teaching his followers to pray in the everyday events of their lives.

• The Lord's Prayer is a prayer *par excellence* in the sense that it not only affirms our ultimate dependence on God but also insists that we as the people of God must be invested in our prayer. Jesus says, "[F]orgive us our sins for we ourselves forgive everyone in debt to us" and continues with the story of the friend who asks for bread. Pope Francis attested, "You pray for the hungry. Then you feed them. That's how prayer works." Prayer is a way of living in relationship with God and others.

• We must also remember that the answers to prayer do not always look like what we might expect. When Jesus asks who would give a scorpion instead of an egg, or a snake instead of a fish, our immediate response is "No one would ever do that." But this is a human way of thinking. Perhaps the scorpion or snake are actually answered prayers, as God answers prayer according to God's will, not ours. May we be open to all possibilities of God's answered prayer.

Model Universal Prayer (Prayer of the Faithful)

Presider: Jesus tells us, "Ask and you will receive; seek and you will find; knock and the door will be opened to you." Confident that God hears us, we confidently raise our prayers and petitions.

Response: Lord, hear our prayer.

That the church might celebrate liturgical prayer in a way that is both unified and culturally responsive . . .

That government leaders might listen to the needs of the people they serve and recommit themselves to working for the common good . . .

That all who are struggling to pray may find the peace that comes from simply being present to God . . .

That all gathered here might grow in our relationship with God and others through our prayer . . .

Presider: Loving God, we know you hear our prayers when we come to you. Answer them not according to our will, but your will, as we trust that you provide for us when we call on you. We ask this through Christ our Lord. **Amen.**

COLLECT

Let us pray.

Pause for silent prayer

O God, protector of those who hope in you,
without whom nothing has firm
foundation, nothing is holy,
bestow in abundance your mercy upon us
and grant that, with you as our ruler and
guide,
we may use the good things that pass
in such a way as to hold fast even now
to those that ever endure.
Through our Lord Jesus Christ, your Son,
who lives and reigns with you in the unity
of the Holy Spirit,
God, for ever and ever. **Amen.**

FIRST READING
Gen 18:20-32

In those days, the LORD said: "The outcry
against Sodom and Gomorrah is so
great,
and their sin so grave,
that I must go down and see whether or
not their actions
fully correspond to the cry against them
that comes to me.
I mean to find out."

While Abraham's visitors walked on
farther toward Sodom,
the LORD remained standing before
Abraham.
Then Abraham drew nearer and said:
"Will you sweep away the innocent with
the guilty?
Suppose there were fifty innocent people
in the city;
would you wipe out the place, rather
than spare it
for the sake of the fifty innocent people
within it?
Far be it from you to do such a thing,
to make the innocent die with the guilty
so that the innocent and the guilty
would be treated alike!
Should not the judge of all the world act
with justice?"
The LORD replied,
"If I find fifty innocent people in the
city of Sodom,
I will spare the whole place for their sake."
Abraham spoke up again:
"See how I am presuming to speak to
my Lord,
though I am but dust and ashes!
What if there are five less than fifty
innocent people?
Will you destroy the whole city because of
those five?"
He answered, "I will not destroy it, if I find
forty-five there."
But Abraham persisted, saying, "What if
only forty are found there?"

He replied, "I will forbear doing it for the
    sake of the forty."
Then Abraham said, "Let not my Lord
    grow impatient if I go on.
What if only thirty are found there?"
He replied, "I will forbear doing it if I can
    find but thirty there."
Still Abraham went on,
    "Since I have thus dared to speak to my
      Lord,
    what if there are no more than twenty?"
The LORD answered, "I will not destroy it,
    for the sake of the twenty."
But he still persisted:
    "Please, let not my Lord grow angry if I
      speak up this last time.
What if there are at least ten there?"
He replied, "For the sake of those ten, I will
    not destroy it."

RESPONSORIAL PSALM
Ps 138:1-2, 2-3, 6-7, 7-8

R̈/. (3a) Lord, on the day I called for help,
    you answered me.

I will give thanks to you, O LORD, with all
    my heart,
    for you have heard the words of my
      mouth;
    in the presence of the angels I will sing
      your praise;
I will worship at your holy temple
    and give thanks to your name.

R̈/. Lord, on the day I called for help, you
    answered me.

Because of your kindness and your truth;
    for you have made great above all things
    your name and your promise.
When I called you answered me;
    you built up strength within me.

R̈/. Lord, on the day I called for help, you
    answered me.

The LORD is exalted, yet the lowly he sees,
    and the proud he knows from afar.
Though I walk amid distress, you preserve
    me;
    against the anger of my enemies you
      raise your hand.

R̈/. Lord, on the day I called for help, you
    answered me.

Your right hand saves me.
    The LORD will complete what he has
      done for me;
    your kindness, O LORD, endures forever;
    forsake not the work of your hands.

R̈/. Lord, on the day I called for help, you
    answered me.

SECOND READING
Col 2:12-14

See Appendix A, p. 308.

CATECHESIS

About Liturgy

Cost Is Not the Same as Value: This particular passage from Genesis is one of my favorites in the Lectionary, especially if it is proclaimed well, with understanding and emotion. I've heard it a few times elicit laughter from the congregation, which is not inappropriate, as time after time Abraham pleads with God to spare the lives of those in Sodom and Gomorrah. The point Abraham is making here is that human lives are of incalculable value. It's not how many lives are spared, ultimately; it's that they all should be, if at all possible. Said another, more economic way, cost and value are not the same things.

Consider this scenario. Suppose you need your house painted. One bid comes in at $500, but is only guaranteed for six months. Another comes in at $2,500, and is guaranteed for a year. Finally, a third bid quotes a figure of $20,000, but is guaranteed for the life of the home. Which is the best cost? Which is the best value? This is not dissimilar to an earlier discussion on these pages of the Pareto Principle, in that both point us toward a sort of cost/benefit analysis in our everyday lives.

Take the above paint job scenario and now apply it toward liturgical life. One instance might be regarding digital and pipe organs. Digital organs are significantly cheaper in the short term and have fantastic abilities to mimic the sounds of a pipe organ these days. Their life expectancy, though, is still far, far shorter than a true pipe organ; in the long run, pipe organs are still the better investment. (Which says nothing about the authenticity and integrity of pipe organs compared to their digital siblings.) This same line of thinking can rightly be extended to pianos and other instruments, liturgical furnishings, even flooring and more utilitarian components of a church building or the worship experience that happens inside.

Another similar analysis is what I call the good-fast-cheap scenario. In almost every instance, you can meet exactly two of those three descriptors, and in almost every instance, you cannot have all three simultaneously. For example, if the parish desires a new Advent wreath later this year, if you start looking for one now, you will likely find one that is of good quality and less expensive than if you wait until mid-November. By then, the wreath would have to be produced quickly, so you'd have to choose between the wreath being "good and costly" or "not good and cheap."

This scenario extends beyond monetary economics into human resources, the "human cost," person-hours, so to speak. If the parish sets aside only two hours to set up its art and environment for Christmastide, you'll either need a lot of humans to do a nice job, or you'll have to settle for something less at a lesser "human cost."

Ultimately, value is still not the same as cost, and even using phrases like "human cost" make me a little uncomfortable! Humans, all creation, has infinite value in God's eyes. At least as a thought exercise, it is worth our time to ponder how we utilize and "spend" both our monetary and human resources in creating and executing liturgies for our communities of faith. What is the cost? What is the value?

About Music

Persistent Prayer: A piece that aligns well with the idea in today's Scripture of the power of persistent prayer is "As It Is in Heaven" (WN) by Ed Cash and Matt Maher. It borrows text from the Lord's Prayer and expands beautifully on each component of it, longing for the reign of God to be brought to earth.

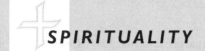

SPIRITUALITY

GOSPEL ACCLAMATION
Matt 5:3

R⁊. Alleluia, alleluia.
Blessed are the poor in spirit,
for theirs is the kingdom of heaven.
R⁊. Alleluia, alleluia.

Gospel   Luke 12:13-21; L114C

Someone in the crowd said to Jesus,
  "Teacher, tell my brother to share
      the inheritance with me."
He replied to him,
  "Friend, who appointed me as your
      judge and arbitrator?"
Then he said to the crowd,
  "Take care to guard against all greed,
  for though one may be rich,
  one's life does not consist of
      possessions."

Then he told them a parable.
"There was a rich man whose land pro-
      duced a bountiful harvest.
He asked himself, 'What shall I do,
  for I do not have space to store my
      harvest?'
And he said, 'This is what I shall do:
  I shall tear down my barns and build
      larger ones.
There I shall store all my grain and
      other goods
  and I shall say to myself, "Now as for
      you,
  you have so many good things stored
      up for many years,
  rest, eat, drink, be merry!"'
But God said to him,
  'You fool, this night your life will be
      demanded of you;
  and the things you have prepared, to
      whom will they belong?'
Thus will it be for all who store up
      treasure for themselves
  but are not rich in what matters to
      God."

Reflecting on the Gospel

Failures in big business enterprises, ups and downs on the stock exchange, court cases about disputed family inheritances: economic issues hit the headlines in our mass media and so often intrude tragically into the lives of hardworking, hard-saving people. When the annual lists of the world's richest individuals and nations are published, the discrepancy between the top and

bottom rungs of the economic ladder may raise our eyebrows if not, unfortunately, our consciences. It is often said that it would profit us if we read the Scriptures with a Bible in one hand and the daily newspaper in the other, discerning how the words and deeds announced by both are related.

The gospel this week begins with a question to Jesus from a man in the crowd who tries to draw him into an inheritance dispute with his brother. The Mosaic teaching of Numbers and Deuteronomy is clear (Num 27:1-11; Deut 21:15-17), and Jesus refuses the role of interpreter, only cautioning his questioner about greed. Nor does Jesus refer to the tough words like that of the Preacher (Qoheleth) in the first reading from the wisdom book of Ecclesiastes. Only once every three years do we hear this sobering voice proclaim, "[V]anity of vanities! All things are vanity!" "Vanity" in Hebrew can mean "vapor," a transitory, fleeting breath—and material wealth is like this. Jesus chooses to make his point as a storyteller, putting imaginative flesh on wisdom teaching with the parable of the Rich Fool.

The man is introduced as already rich, with a surplus harvest. He does not see that this blessing is from God, nor of the Jewish religious tradition and human prudence that demanded he make provision for himself and his whole community in case of any famine that might follow years of plenty. His "retirement plan" is a self-centered recital of "I will, I will, I will," well-punctuated by references to "my." The rich man considers that he owns everything: crops, barns, grains, and even his own soul. In a culture where a transaction at a street stall involved long and animated discussion between buyer and seller, the inappropriateness of such self-talk would not be lost on Jesus's audience. Likewise, it was expected that important decisions would be made in community, but this man has no one with whom he can or wants to talk—no family, cronies, advisers. His calculated option is to make and live in an isolated and alienating vacuum. This cannot be the option of Jesus's disciples.

Ironically, the parable uses the prophetic language of "tear[ing] down" and "build[ing] up" (Jer 1:10), but in a sadly cheapened context. The rich man is the opposite of the courageous prophet who does this in the name of and for the purposes of God. Tithes and offerings were set aside in landowners' barns for the priests and Levites to collect, but for this man, barns are just for hoarding. For the early Christians, the storage barns of the community were to be the mouths of the poor (Rom 15:25-28) and the collection for the poor of Jerusalem. A contemporary and tragic irony persists with the silos that are stocked with nuclear "abundance" or "deterrence" while many of those living almost in their destructive shadows are hungry and disadvantaged. Closer to home, perhaps our Christian families, parishes, or communities need to have annual "discipleship garage sales" to dispose of our surplus and give the profits to those in need.

Focusing the Gospel

Key words and phrases: "Thus will it be for all who store up treasure for themselves but are not rich in what matters to God."

To the point: This is a classic cautionary tale, with an irony that is sweeping. The rich man prioritized storing his goods, and when the time came to enjoy them, it was too late. This is reminiscent of Matthew's gospel and the Gospel of Luke that we will hear next week, in which Jesus tells us to store our goods in heaven. God isn't angry with the rich man, but instead calls him a fool. It is not God who misses out, but the rich man.

Connecting the Gospel

to the first reading: The first reading draws the connection between the toils of the rich man in today's gospel and vanity. "Here is one who has labored with wisdom and knowledge and skill, / and yet to another who has not labored over it, / he must leave property." However, it's not just the work of gaining property; it is the anxiety that accompanies just pursuits. "For what profit comes to man from all the toil and anxiety of heart / with which he has labored under the sun?"

to experience: It is good to ensure the care and safety of our families and communities. Jesus emphasizes the necessity of worldly care when he calls us, over and over, to ensure basic necessities for the poor. However, this gospel is clear in its message, and Jesus does not shy away from being critical of a man who spent his time ensuring the accumulation of and ability to sustain his personal wealth. We have a tendency in the modern era to immediately extrapolate what this means for the distribution of wealth among nations and implications for economies. This is noble work, but try reading this gospel as a message for you, and only you. Start with your own life. We have such a tendency to get ahead of ourselves, especially when we work for the church. This week, allow the gospel to be a love letter of instruction to you.

Connecting the Responsorial Psalm

to the readings: This week's psalm expresses the transience of human life, and how quickly we come and go. "You make an end of them in their sleep; / the next morning they are like the changing grass, / which at dawn springs up anew, / but by evening wilts and fades." Because of the briefness of life, we must focus our attention on the things that matter to the Lord, and not what the world values. "Teach us to number our days aright, / that we may gain wisdom of heart." The message in this week's psalm is that the sooner we listen to the Lord, the more time we have to focus on true wealth.

to psalmist preparation: Where do you find wealth in your life, outside of material things? Do you have a wealth of relationships? Do you have a wealth of satisfying work, or a wealth of time to enjoy the natural world? Name things in your life that you have in abundance. Allow these gifts to inform your presence this week.

PROMPTS FOR FAITH-SHARING

What does "wealth" mean to you? Who do you consider a "wealthy" person?

What is something that faded away before you realized its value? How would you approach that situation differently today?

If the Lord called you home tonight, would you be pleased with how you have or have not prioritized worldly wealth? Why or why not?

What does it mean to "labor in wisdom"?

CELEBRATION

Model Penitential Act

Presider: In today's gospel Jesus warns us to guard ourselves against greed. For the times we have been greedy in our thoughts, words, and actions, we ask for God's healing forgiveness and restorative peace . . . *[pause]*

Lord Jesus, you practice selfless love in your paschal mystery: Lord, have mercy.

Christ Jesus, you know the deepest longings of our hearts: Christ, have mercy.

Lord Jesus, you invite us to place our trust in you and the kingdom of God: Lord, have mercy.

Homily Points

• Jesus specifically states his point in today's gospel before using a parable to illustrate it. Jesus says, "Take care to guard against all greed, for though one may be rich, one's life does not consist of possessions." Easier said than done, right? Greed creeps into our boardroom meetings as we challenge colleagues and assert our dominance. Greed appears in families where children might not be willing to share material objects or even one's attention. We can be greedy in ways that are not monetary.

• If we are to combat greed, it is important to step back and evaluate what we treasure and value. The answer for the rich man in today's parable is obvious: He values a bountiful harvest and the ability and freedom to store up his riches for himself. But this control is fleeting, as his material goods will do nothing for him after his untimely death. Jesus invites us to look at this example and reflect on our own lives. What are we looking for? What will satisfy us? And ultimately, in what ways do we continue to grab and hoard and live with greed instead of practicing hospitality and generosity and self-gift?

• St. Augustine writes, "Our hearts are restless until they rest in you, O God." Nothing can satisfy us except for relationship with God. When we come to realize that God is our greatest desire, the one whom we seek above all else, we begin to notice that material things are not as important. Likewise, when we recognize that relationship with God is our deepest longing, we come to know that part of this relationship is caring for others by sharing the gifts God has given us. We do not exist as isolated individuals. Life in God fundamentally means life in community.

Model Universal Prayer (Prayer of the Faithful)

Presider: Jesus calls us to reevaluate our physical needs and deepest desires. Knowing that God hears us, we confidently ask for what we need and long for.

Response: Lord, hear our prayer.

That church leaders might reject power and glamor in favor of self-gift and humility . . .

That local and world leaders might share wealth and riches with others, recognizing that we are part of a single human family . . .

That all who struggle with debt or financial difficulties, and all who are unemployed or underemployed, might know their value and find the resources they need to live in health and dignity . . .

That members of our church finance council might share their work with transparency and refuse to bow to the powers of money present in our community . . .

Presider: Loving God, we know you sustain us and give us life. As we strive to grow in relationship with you, hear our prayers and answer them according to your will that we might discern what we truly value and uphold. We ask this through Christ our Lord. **Amen.**

COLLECT

Let us pray.

Pause for silent prayer

Draw near to your servants, O Lord,
and answer their prayers with unceasing kindness,
that, for those who glory in you as their Creator and guide,
you may restore what you have created
and keep safe what you have restored.
Through our Lord Jesus Christ, your Son,
who lives and reigns with you in the unity of the Holy Spirit,
God, for ever and ever. **Amen.**

FIRST READING

Eccl 1:2; 2:21-23

Vanity of vanities, says Qoheleth,
vanity of vanities! All things are vanity!

Here is one who has labored with wisdom and knowledge and skill,
and yet to another who has not labored over it,
he must leave property.
This also is vanity and a great misfortune.
For what profit comes to man from all the toil and anxiety of heart
with which he has labored under the sun?
All his days sorrow and grief are his occupation;
even at night his mind is not at rest.
This also is vanity.

RESPONSORIAL PSALM

Ps 90:3-4, 5-6, 12-13, 14 and 17

R. (8) If today you hear his voice, harden not your hearts.

You turn man back to dust,
saying, "Return, O children of men."
For a thousand years in your sight
are as yesterday, now that it is past,
or as a watch of the night.

R. If today you hear his voice, harden not your hearts.

You make an end of them in their sleep;
the next morning they are like the changing grass,
which at dawn springs up anew,
but by evening wilts and fades.

R. If today you hear his voice, harden not your hearts.

Teach us to number our days aright,
that we may gain wisdom of heart.
Return, O Lord! How long?
Have pity on your servants!

℞. If today you hear his voice, harden not
your hearts.

Fill us at daybreak with your kindness,
that we may shout for joy and gladness
all our days.
And may the gracious care of the Lord
our God be ours;
prosper the work of our hands for us!
Prosper the work of our hands!

℞. If today you hear his voice, harden not
your hearts.

SECOND READING

Col 3:1-5, 9-11

Brothers and sisters:
If you were raised with Christ, seek what
is above,
where Christ is seated at the right hand
of God.
Think of what is above, not of what is on
earth.
For you have died,
and your life is hidden with Christ in
God.
When Christ your life appears,
then you too will appear with him in
glory.

Put to death, then, the parts of you that
are earthly:
immorality, impurity, passion, evil
desire,
and the greed that is idolatry.
Stop lying to one another,
since you have taken off the old self
with its practices
and have put on the new self,
which is being renewed, for knowledge,
in the image of its creator.
Here there is not Greek and Jew,
circumcision and uncircumcision,
barbarian, Scythian, slave, free;
but Christ is all and in all.

About Liturgy

Spirituality of Stewardship: This may be a good weekend, both within and outside of the homily, to talk with your church's assemblies about stewardship: their gifts of time, talent, and treasure to the local community (and beyond). You can pair this stewardship message with preaching that focuses on how all life itself and all that fills it is a gift from God; we all need frequent reminders that nothing, not even our next breath, is our possession. This is foundational in a spirituality of tithing and sacrificial gifts of the firstfruits of our labors—and sometimes our first labors too.

Consider, too, exploring what it means to be a steward: a person who "takes care of" something, not in an "accomplish the task" sense, but in a true sense of being responsible for the other and for the whole community. Placing the needs of "the other" ahead of our own is what it means, fundamentally, to love like Christ loved us, and continues to.

It is most wise to reserve the time of the homily to highlight the spiritual aspects of giving, saving any practical words regarding parish budgets for before or after the liturgy.

About Liturgical Documents

Built of Living Stones—*An Overview:* Having been several weeks since we've explored the documents that guide our worship, we turn our attention next to *Built of Living Stones: Art, Architecture, and Worship*, which was promulgated by the USCCB in November 2000. Often overlooked, or at least set aside for later consideration, the architecture and worship environment of a church building informs nearly every aspect of a parish's living ecclesiology—from the layout of altar and pews, to the location of music ministry, to whether a church building has a dedicated narthex or gathering space. Even whether that space is called a narthex or a gathering space may be telling!

Practically, this document was "presented to assist the faithful involved in the building or renovation of churches, chapels, and oratories of the Latin Church in the United States. In addition, the document is intended for use by architects, liturgical consultants and artists, contractors, and other professionals engaged in the design and/or construction of these places of worship" (*Built of Living Stones* [BLS] 3).

Theologically, the affect that a church building has on the church that gathers within it is immense, and that affect is addressed in the document, beginning with these words:

> Churches, therefore, must be places "suited to sacred celebrations," "dignified," and beautiful. Their suitability for worship is determined by their ability through the architectural design of space and the application of artistic gifts to embody God's initiative and the community's faithful response. Church buildings and the religious artworks that beautify them are forms of worship themselves and both inspire and reflect the prayer of the community as well as the inner life of grace. Conversely, church buildings and religious artifacts that are trivial, contrived, or lack beauty can detract from the community's liturgy. Architecture and art become the joint work of the Holy Spirit and the local community, that of preparing human hearts to receive God's word and to enter more fully into communion. (BLS 18)

In the coming weeks, we shall delve more deeply into how a church's specific architecture, art, and environment impact worship and ecclesiology, and what our bishops' suggestions and guidelines for these liturgical elements teach us and recommend to us.

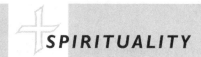

SPIRITUALITY

GOSPEL ACCLAMATION
Matt 24:42a, 44

℟. Alleluia, alleluia.
Stay awake and be ready!
For you do not know on what day your Lord
   will come.
℟. Alleluia, alleluia.

Gospel   Luke 12:32-48; L117C

Jesus said to his disciples:
   "Do not be afraid any longer, little
      flock,
   for your Father is pleased to give
      you the kingdom.
Sell your belongings and give alms.
Provide money bags for yourselves
      that do not wear out,
   an inexhaustible treasure in heaven
   that no thief can reach nor moth
      destroy.
For where your treasure is, there also
   will your heart be.

"Gird your loins and light your lamps
   and be like servants who await
      their master's return from a
      wedding,
   ready to open immediately when he
      comes and knocks.
Blessed are those servants
   whom the master finds vigilant on
      his arrival.
Amen, I say to you, he will gird
      himself,
   have them recline at table, and pro-
      ceed to wait on them.
And should he come in the second or
      third watch
   and find them prepared in this way,
   blessed are those servants.
Be sure of this:
   if the master of the house had
      known the hour
   when the thief was coming,
   he would not have let his house be
      broken into.

Continued in Appendix A, p. 308,

or Luke 12:35-40 in Appendix A, p. 308.

Reflecting on the Gospel

The sayings and parables of today's gospel are stitched together with the themes of vigilance, preparedness, and fidelity. Christians are to be "girded," ready for action. The biblical memory behind the parable's action is the Passover from Egypt when the Hebrews had to be girded, clothed, and belted up suitably so they would be ready to escape into freedom (see Exod 12:11). The early church lived in expectation of Christ's return during the great Easter night, yet unfolding history showed that the watch for the Parousia would be long.

In the first parable, addressed to disciples in general, the faithful servants are eagerly awaiting their master's return from a wedding banquet, a favorite biblical image of the end time. This Lectionary selection may seem more appropriate to Advent, but the positioning of it in the middle of Luke's gospel and halfway through the journey to Jerusalem reminds us to be alert at all times so we may recognize the Lord when he comes. He comes in those we meet, in the circumstances of our daily lives, and in the signs of our times. In a very real sense, every hour is an hour of the Lord's coming and knocking, and our response to this will either prepare for or hinder its final fulfillment.

For those who open the doors of their hearts to Jesus, the parable has a dramatic reversal of roles: the Master will be our "God-in-an-apron" who serves his watchful servants. The hospitality of God, incarnate in Jesus, serves us at every eucharistic table. At each Eucharist, too, we have some form of the "anamnesis," the "not-forgetting" prayer that recalls the death and resurrection of Jesus and the need to "look forward to his second coming" (Eucharistic Prayer III). It is a reminder, too, that one Eucharist will be our last, that our life and world history will both end. Then we will go to meet the ascended and risen One who stands in the heavens waiting for and waiting on those who have lived a lifestyle of ready welcome to him, especially as he comes to us in the poor and marginalized. The Lord's arrival will be as unexpected as a night thief, and the Eucharist is the sacrament of vigilant hope that nourishes and strengthens us for such eager service.

Whereas the first part of the gospel was lovingly addressed to the whole Christian community, Jesus's "little flock," the second parable is told in response to Peter's question and is more specifically directed at the leaders of that flock. Jesus has gifted them with a share of his authority over the household of God's people, but they still remain servants of the Master. A leader's authority, therefore, is an authority of service. If a steward becomes drunk with power and status, physically or psychologically abusing the members of the household (Luke typically mentions both sexes), he will earn the Master's great displeasure at his return. The church's leaders are not exempt from the demands of discipleship.

As Augustine told his people: "For you I am a bishop; with you I am a Christian"—and a Christian of whom even more will be expected because of the gifts that are entrusted to a leader. This gospel throws into tragic relief the shadows cast over the church by the sexual abuse, financial misappropriation, or lavish lifestyles of some of its leaders. The word "punish," which is translated in some lectionaries as "cut off" (*dichotomein*), literally means "to cut in two" and, in the context of the parable, is a fittingly ironic and symbolic statement about the fate of one who lives a double, "divided" life.

Focusing the Gospel

Key words and phrases: "Then Peter said, 'Lord, is this parable meant for us or for everyone?'"

To the point: The gospel passage opens with a tender consolation from Jesus. "Do not be afraid any longer, little flock, for your Father is pleased to give you the kingdom." Jesus refers to his disciples with the phrase "little flock," which not only places him as the shepherd, but refers to us with a diminutive term of endearment. Jesus wants us to be vigilant and place our treasure in heaven, not because it is the right thing to do, but because he loves us and wants to encourage our own happiness. Peter asks one of the great questions of the gospels: Is this parable meant for Jesus's disciples, with him at that moment, or for all of us? Jesus responds by telling Peter that the servant who knows the correct thing to do, and doesn't do it, will be punished, but the servant who is ignorant about the correct things will be punished less. The disciples, and all of us who seek to follow Christ, have no excuse.

Connecting the Gospel

to the second reading: In the second reading, Paul does a beautiful job of describing the Israelite's faith and journey from a physical homeland to the spiritual one. "They did not receive what had been promised but saw it and greeted it from afar and acknowledged themselves to be strangers and aliens on earth, for those who speak thus show that they are seeking a homeland."

to experience: The gospel and the readings today call us to keep our focus on things unseen. The book of Wisdom describes the Israelites waiting for the first Passover. In the gospel, Jesus tells us to place our treasure in heaven and stay vigilant here on earth. Paul tells the Hebrews, "Faith is the realization of what is hoped for and evidence of things not seen." All of these words are urging us to look forward and plan our lives according to salvation, not earthly satisfaction, so that we may "desire a better homeland, a heavenly one."

Connecting the Responsorial Psalm

to the readings: If the readings this week are all encouraging us to look forward, the psalm is here to remind us that, as we focus on God, God also focuses on us. Even as "Our soul waits for the LORD, who is our help and our shield," we know that "the eyes of the LORD are upon those who fear him, / upon those who hope for his kindness, / to deliver them from death."

to psalmist preparation: Do you feel chosen to be "God's own"? What in your life reminds you that you are chosen and called by God? This week's readings contain a number of challenges for us as believers, calling us to step up and be prepared. When you share the psalm this week, invite the congregation to feel comfort and care. Make space for your fellow believers to understand the love and tenderness our Lord has for us.

PROMPTS FOR FAITH-SHARING

Think about your long-term goals and how you are preparing for them. Are you more excited for retirement or salvation?

Jesus refers to his disciples as "little flock." Is there a term of endearment you use with children, or you remember your parents or grandparents used for you? How does using a diminutive form invite tenderness?

What is your treasure? Where do you keep it?

What do you do to "light your lamps" in preparation for the coming of the Lord?

Model Penitential Act

Presider: In today's gospel Jesus tells us, "Do not be afraid." For the times we have allowed fear to control our thoughts and actions, we ask for God's healing and peace . . . [pause]

Lord Jesus, your love is eternal: Lord, have mercy.

Christ Jesus, you call us to yourself: Christ, have mercy.

Lord Jesus, you hear us when we cry out to you: Lord, have mercy.

Homily Points

• When Jesus tells us, "Do not be afraid any longer, little flock," he knows just how paralyzing fear can be. When we act (or do not act) out of fear, we bow to feelings of insecurity and misperception. These feelings are not of God. Fear is not of God. We know this throughout Hebrew and Christian Scripture, as God (or God's representatives) command, "Do not be afraid." Taking these words to heart, however, can be challenging, as the fears we encounter every day are very real. Jesus is telling us, however, to trust in God during these times of fear.

• This theme continues throughout the gospel as Jesus addresses in whom or what we place our trust. Jesus says, "For where your treasure is, there also will your heart be." This statement is an invitation to reflect on what it is we truly value and treasure in our lives, for what we value is where we place our hearts. Do we place our hearts in relationships with God and others? Do we place our hearts in gratitude and peace? Do we place our hearts in *agapic*, self-giving love? Or do we place our hearts elsewhere?

• The gospel ends with a sense of urgency, as Jesus reminds us that there will be a time when the Son of Man will come. As we do not know the day or the hour, we must constantly live in relationship with God, practicing what we claim to value. This is not fear or cowardice or an act of apprehension. Rather, our constant relationship with God shows trust in what we truly treasure.

Model Universal Prayer (Prayer of the Faithful)

Presider: Jesus tells his disciples, "Do not be afraid." Confident that God provides for our every need, we raise our prayers and petitions with conviction.

Response: Lord, hear our prayer.

That the church will continue to value people over profit and relationships over power . . .

That leaders of cities and countries may reject fear-mongering tactics and instead sow seeds of hope . . .

That all who live in constant fear of violence and persecution might find the comfort and safety they long for . . .

That all gathered here might value relationship with God so to prepare our hearts and minds for the reign of the kingdom of God . . .

Presider: Loving God, hear the prayers we raise today. We do not offer them out of fear, but instead out of a genuine trust that you hear us and provide for us. We ask this through Christ our Lord. **Amen.**

COLLECT

Let us pray.

Pause for silent prayer

Almighty ever-living God,
whom, taught by the Holy Spirit,
we dare to call our Father,
bring, we pray, to perfection in our hearts
the spirit of adoption as your sons and
    daughters,
that we may merit to enter into the
    inheritance
which you have promised.
Through our Lord Jesus Christ, your Son,
who lives and reigns with you in the unity
    of the Holy Spirit,
God, for ever and ever. **Amen.**

FIRST READING

Wis 18:6-9

The night of the passover was known
    beforehand to our fathers,
    that, with sure knowledge of the oaths
      in which they put their faith,
    they might have courage.
Your people awaited the salvation of the
    just
    and the destruction of their foes.
For when you punished our adversaries,
    in this you glorified us whom you had
      summoned.
For in secret the holy children of the good
      were offering sacrifice
    and putting into effect with one accord
      the divine institution.

RESPONSORIAL PSALM

Ps 33:1, 12, 18-19, 20-22

R︎. (12b) Blessed the people the Lord has chosen to be his own.

Exult, you just, in the LORD;
    praise from the upright is fitting.
Blessed the nation whose God is the LORD,
    the people he has chosen for his own
        inheritance.

R︎. Blessed the people the Lord has chosen to be his own.

See, the eyes of the LORD are upon those
    who fear him,
    upon those who hope for his kindness,
to deliver them from death
    and preserve them in spite of famine.

R︎. Blessed the people the Lord has chosen to be his own.

Our soul waits for the LORD,
    who is our help and our shield.
May your kindness, O LORD, be upon us
    who have put our hope in you.

R︎. Blessed the people the Lord has chosen to be his own.

SECOND READING

Heb 11:1-2, 8-19

Brothers and sisters:
Faith is the realization of what is hoped for
    and evidence of things not seen.
Because of it the ancients were well attested.

By faith Abraham obeyed when he was
        called to go out to a place
    that he was to receive as an inheritance;
    he went out, not knowing where he was
        to go.
By faith he sojourned in the promised land
        as in a foreign country,
    dwelling in tents with Isaac and Jacob,
        heirs of the same promise;
    for he was looking forward to the city
        with foundations,
    whose architect and maker is God.
By faith he received power to generate,
    even though he was past the normal age
    —and Sarah herself was sterile—
    for he thought that the one who had
        made the promise was trustworthy.

Continued in Appendix A, p. 309,

or Heb 11:1-2, 8-12

in Appendix A, p. 309.

About Liturgy

Anamnesis—Looking Back, Looking Ahead: The Lectionary, for the epistle today, provides this reading summary: "[Abraham] was looking forward to the city . . . whose architect and maker is God." This, too, is what our liturgy does, more apparently when it is done well. The liturgy, principally the eucharistic prayer, dwells in anamnesis, a remembrance of the events of the paschal mystery—suffering, death, resurrection, and ascension—in a way that makes us present at those salvific moments. We are brought to the Last Supper, the cross, the tomb as we pray together, led by the priest *in persona Christi capitis,* in the person of Christ the head. There is, simultaneously, a forward-looking, at least from our perspective, anamnesis to the heavenly banquet in what is often called "the new Jerusalem."

From our perspective in time, *chronos,* we are both looking back and looking forward from the particular moment of time we are at Mass. Within God's time, *kairos,* these are all the same events, the same moments, and we are given a glimpse into that mystery.

This is just scratching the surface of anamnesis. Next week, we'll look more deeply at what it is, examine more fully at how it functions, and consider other places in liturgy one may look for it and pray with it.

About Liturgical Documents

Built of Living Stones—*A Church for an Assembly:* Even the title of this liturgical document speaks to the church being first and foremost the faithful people; paragraphs 30 and 31 emphasize this ecclesiology, in that the church building must be assembly-focused: "The general plan of the building should be such that 'in some way it conveys the image of the gathered assembly. It should also allow the participants to take the place most appropriate to them and assist all to carry out their function properly.' The church building fosters participation in the liturgy. Because liturgical actions by their nature are communal celebrations, they are celebrated with the presence and active participation of the Christian faithful whenever possible."

So, then, we have the foundation here of how a church building begins to impact the execution of worship and the vision of the assembly as church. Consider for a moment a grand cathedral, cruciform in shape, with rows and rows of pews on either side of a long center aisle that leads to an altar very near one wall of the building. Alongside that image, place a more recently constructed church, built in the round, perhaps with curving pews, and the altar in the center of the space. Which space communicates more strongly that the eucharistic celebration is sacrifice? Which one communicates more that it is a memorial banquet of thanksgiving? Eucharist is both; it is important and necessary that it is, of course. Which space has perhaps a 150-foot-high ceiling with mosaics or frescoes, drawing the worshippers' gaze "toward heaven"? Which has a more simple style, drawing more attention to the liturgical furnishings?

Neither of these sorts of spaces are right or wrong, mind you. Yet they are different and speak to different modes of participation, which in turn must create different sensibilities about who church is and what church does.

About Music

Be Ready, Be Responsible: Our gospel reading this weekend, sounds a bit like Advent has snuck up on us, with Jesus admonishing his followers to be ready, to be responsible. Tom Booth's "Find Us Ready" (OCP) speaks well to this passage, without seeming as if lifted from the Advent portion of a hymnal.

AUGUST 7, 2022
NINETEENTH SUNDAY IN ORDINARY TIME

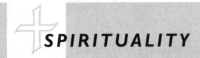

SPIRITUALITY

GOSPEL ACCLAMATION
John 10:27

℟. Alleluia, alleluia.
My sheep hear my voice, says the Lord;
I know them, and they follow me.
℟. Alleluia, alleluia.

Gospel

Luke 12:49-53; L120C

Jesus said to his disciples:
"I have come to set the earth on
   fire,
and how I wish it were already
   blazing!
There is a baptism with which I must
   be baptized,
and how great is my anguish until
   it is accomplished!
Do you think that I have come to establish peace on the earth?
No, I tell you, but rather division.
From now on a household of five will
   be divided,
three against two and two against
   three;
a father will be divided against his
   son
and a son against his father,
a mother against her daughter
and a daughter against her mother,
a mother-in-law against her
   daughter-in-law
and a daughter-in-law against her
   mother-in-law."

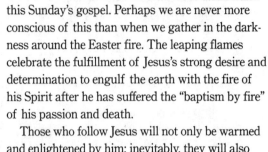

Reflecting on the Gospel

The Jewish heritage of Jesus is full of imagery of elusive, purifying fire. "I AM" speaks out of it; the pillar of God's fiery presence leads the Hebrews through the desert nights, sparks out on Sinai, burns in temple lampstands of pure gold, licks up the waters of Carmel, and anoints the lips of prophets. In the fullness of time, the holy fire takes flesh in Jesus, the Earth Firelighter of this Sunday's gospel. Perhaps we are never more conscious of this than when we gather in the darkness around the Easter fire. The leaping flames celebrate the fulfillment of Jesus's strong desire and determination to engulf the earth with the fire of his Spirit after he has suffered the "baptism by fire" of his passion and death.

Those who follow Jesus will not only be warmed and enlightened by him; inevitably, they will also feel the painful heat of their association. Sadly, some aspects of even the most intimate relationships with family and friendship may be scorched, or even totally destroyed. Earlier in Luke's gospel (3:16-17), that uncompromising precursor, John the Baptist, spoke of a baptism that would be greater than his purificatory rite: a baptism with the fire of the Holy Spirit that the Messiah would enkindle. Those whose lives were husks, empty of any repentance or commitment to the Coming One, would not be harvested into the kingdom, but would be burned in "unquenchable fire." Read in context, what John is speaking about so strongly are issues of social justice: sharing with the disadvantaged, nonviolence, and economic integrity. From the time he announced his mission in the Nazareth synagogue, this was also the burning social commitment of Jesus (Luke 4:16-21).

A fire that was familiar to the inhabitants of Jerusalem was the garbage being burned regularly in the Valley of Hinnon (Gehenna) just outside the city. But there is another and blessed fire that is to be lit from the person of Jesus himself, who burns with a wild love for the world. This is emphasized by the personal repetition: "I have come," "I wish," "I must be baptized," "I have come" (a second time), "I tell you." For Jesus to speak of himself in the first person in the Synoptic Gospels is extremely rare. It is an indication of the urgency that he wishes to communicate to his listeners. The adult Jesus who is speaking was the child whose birth was announced as heralding peace (Luke 2:14) but was also recognized by Simeon as a source of division (2:34). The two are not incompatible. Jesus's peace is not a warm, fuzzy glow, a comfortable satisfaction with the status quo. Rather, it is a burning decisiveness that results from the self-discovery and discernment Jesus experienced in the wilderness—that fierce place of temptation and commitment. Out of the wilderness he was driven on mission by the power of the Spirit, ready to live, suffer, and die for his God (3:1-14) and the salvation of the world.

This mission has nothing to do with the *pax Romana* (or the *pax Americana*). Those who follow Jesus share his experience by becoming part of it. It is significant that, in this gospel text, Jesus speaks so passionately not of extraordinary, dramatic suffering but of the intimate, painful divisions and misunderstanding that the choice of discipleship can cause in families. A close and faithful relationship to Jesus will influence all our other relationships in terms of values and priorities.

Focusing the Gospel

Key words and phrases: "I have come to set the earth on fire, and how I wish it were already blazing!"

To the point: Jesus's words in this gospel seem at odds with the rest of his message. Establishing division? That doesn't sound like a Christian worldview. However, Jesus is inviting us to recognize the reality of following him in our world: it will cause division. A follower of Christ, who willingly flips the assumptions and desires of the material world, will inevitably cause division. We are called to "set the world on fire," challenging the self-serving order of civilization and placing love at the center. Inviting people to serve God and others before themselves is an inflammatory suggestion.

Connecting the Gospel

to the first reading: In the first reading, the princes are mad at Jeremiah because they consider what he is preaching to be a threat to the well-being of their city. They find that, by speaking as a prophet, Jeremiah is "not interested in the welfare of our people, but in their ruin." Jeremiah is speaking right before the Israelites are going to be taken over by the Babylonians. They are about to be destroyed, and when Jeremiah calls them to better their faith, it's too much. They can't stand him.

to experience: Sometimes in life we are so focused on surviving from one day to the next that the call to focus on living the gospel feels like an imposition. How can God ask so much of us? But like the princes in Jeremiah, we cannot throw that call away and hope it disappears, just because we find it inconvenient.

Connecting the Responsorial Psalm

to the readings: This psalm can be read from the point of view of Jeremiah, who was thrown into a literal pit of destruction. The psalmist here implores the Lord with the verse "Lord, come to my aid," while detailing all the ways in which the Lord has done this. Aid from the Lord is not a singular event, but a constant petition, the results of which can be seen over and over.

to psalmist preparation: There are many great images in this psalm. The Lord "made firm my steps" and "put a new song into my mouth." Is there a time when you were dejected, and perhaps feeling like you were in the "pit of destruction," and the Lord pulled you out?

PROMPTS FOR FAITH-SHARING

Is there an issue that you get "fired up" about? Maybe it's a political issue, or a sports team, or a hobby. Why are you passionate about it? Is this issue tied to your faith? If not, is there a situation in which you might feel this same passion about your faith?

Has there ever been a point in your life when you were so hyper-focused on a task that making space for the Lord felt like an imposition? Why do you think you felt like this?

Have you ever been in a situation that felt like a "pit of destruction," in which you could not move forward or escape? How did you move through it? Was God present in this work? Is it ongoing?

How do you treat the Jeremiahs in your life? How do you encounter those who call you to more sincere faith? Do you ignore them, or actively reject them? Do you welcome them? Does Jeremiah's call inspire you, or make you uncomfortable?

Model Penitential Act

Presider: In today's reading from the letter to the Hebrews, we are charged to "rid our-selves of every burden and sin that clings to us." With this, we ask for God's healing and forgiveness . . . *[pause]*

Lord Jesus, you are the Light of the World: Lord, have mercy.

Christ Jesus, you are the Prince of Peace: Christ, have mercy.

Lord Jesus, you are the Son of God: Lord, have mercy.

Homily Points

• Jesus's words in today's gospel seem rather surprising coming from the Prince of Peace. At first glance, it may even sound like Jesus is promoting division and violence. If we look at today's passage within the overall gospel narrative, however, we find that Jesus's words remain consistent with what he has taught thus far and will continue to preach through his death and resurrection. Essentially, Jesus reminds us that we all have a choice to respond to God's invitation. Some will accept the invitation and others will reject it. Because of this, there will be division among people and families. We must also remember the context of Jesus's mission and ministry. Many people were upset that Jesus would teach and preach about the kingdom of God in a way that seemingly contradicted their established religious beliefs. There was a real tension present when Jesus spoke.

• The fire and water imagery point to a cleansing and refining that will be found at the end of time. For the past few weeks our gospel readings have discussed preparing for the eschaton, and today's reading highlights just how significant of an event this will be. We know how destructive fire and water can be, but we also know the life that can come from these primordial elements.

• Our reading from Hebrews reminds us that as consequential as this reality is, it is not something to necessarily fear with great trepidation. Rather, we can find consolation that we journey with "so great a cloud of witnesses" that support and walk with us on our journey to follow Christ. We live not as isolated individuals but as a profound community of believers. With this, we can follow Christ with confidence and look forward with joy to the coming of the reign of God.

Model Universal Prayer (Prayer of the Faithful)

Presider: Today's readings remind us of the reality of division in our world. With this, we pray for a unity that comes only from God and raise our prayers in confidence.

Response: Lord, hear our prayer.

That all members of the church might work together for the kingdom of God instead of breaking into factions that divide instead of unify . . .

That government leaders may seek nonviolent responses to the disunity that may arise among their own people and with people of other nations . . .

That all who feel the hurt of exclusion and rejection might find comfort in God's wel-come embrace . . .

That our local community might daily set aside differences so to walk and work with unity and peace . . .

Presider: Loving God, hear these prayers we raise. Be with us as we work to share the peace that comes from you alone, and guide us in our efforts to celebrate unity, not uni-formity. We ask this through Christ our Lord. **Amen.**

COLLECT

Let us pray.

Pause for silent prayer

O God, who have prepared for those who love you
good things which no eye can see,
fill our hearts, we pray, with the warmth of your love,
so that, loving you in all things and above all things,
we may attain your promises,
which surpass every human desire.
Through our Lord Jesus Christ, your Son,
who lives and reigns with you in the unity of the Holy Spirit,
God, for ever and ever. **Amen.**

FIRST READING
Jer 38:4-6, 8-10

In those days, the princes said to the king:
  "Jeremiah ought to be put to death;
    he is demoralizing the soldiers who are left in this city,
    and all the people, by speaking such things to them;
    he is not interested in the welfare of our people,
    but in their ruin."
King Zedekiah answered: "He is in your power";
    for the king could do nothing with them.
And so they took Jeremiah
    and threw him into the cistern of Prince Malchiah,
    which was in the quarters of the guard,
    letting him down with ropes.
There was no water in the cistern, only mud,
    and Jeremiah sank into the mud.

Ebed-melech, a court official,
    went there from the palace and said to him:
    "My lord king,
    these men have been at fault
    in all they have done to the prophet Jeremiah,
    casting him into the cistern.
He will die of famine on the spot,
    for there is no more food in the city."
Then the king ordered Ebed-melech the Cushite
    to take three men along with him,
    and draw the prophet Jeremiah out of the cistern before he should die.

RESPONSORIAL PSALM
Ps 40:2, 3, 4, 18

R∕. (14b) Lord, come to my aid!

I have waited, waited for the LORD,
  and he stooped toward me.

R∕. Lord, come to my aid!

The LORD heard my cry.
He drew me out of the pit of destruction,
  out of the mud of the swamp;
he set my feet upon a crag;
  he made firm my steps.

R∕. Lord, come to my aid!

And he put a new song into my mouth,
  a hymn to our God.
Many shall look on in awe
  and trust in the LORD.

R∕. Lord, come to my aid!

Though I am afflicted and poor,
  yet the LORD thinks of me.
You are my help and my deliverer;
  O my God, hold not back!

R∕. Lord, come to my aid!

SECOND READING
Heb 12:1-4

Brothers and sisters:
Since we are surrounded by so great a
    cloud of witnesses,
  let us rid ourselves of every burden and
      sin that clings to us
  and persevere in running the race that
      lies before us
  while keeping our eyes fixed on Jesus,
    the leader and perfecter of faith.
For the sake of the joy that lay before him
  he endured the cross, despising its
      shame,
  and has taken his seat at the right of
      the throne of God.
Consider how he endured such opposition
    from sinners,
  in order that you may not grow weary
      and lose heart.
In your struggle against sin
  you have not yet resisted to the point of
      shedding blood.

About Liturgy

More on Anamnesis: Last week we began looking at anamnesis and its critical role in our worship. Our liturgical anamnesis, while principally about the events of the paschal mystery, has its roots in Jewish prayer, specifically the celebration of Passover. Theologically speaking, the remembrance of the Passover events makes the efficacy of that first Passover present in modern times. So, when Jesus, at the Last Supper, says, "Do this in memory of me," we could say he is not only reinterpreting the Passover event and theology, not only inserting himself into that story of salvation, but in fact is saying, "Do this as my anamnesis" or "Do this as my presencing."

It is not just at Eucharist and in the eucharistic prayer where one prays by anamnesis, though that instance might be called liturgical anamnesis *par excellence*. There are many other texts, postures, gestures, and even silences that serve an anamnestic function, serve as memorial. The whole of liturgy is anamnestic too.

We should be careful to note that we ought not confuse anamnesis with a sort of allegorical interpretation of our liturgical rites—for instance, in the manner that some medieval theologians likened the various parts of the Mass, by the use of foreshadowing known sometimes as "type/antitype," directly to various parts of Christ's passion. No, anamnesis is much more profound, more imbued with mystery and presence.

Outside of Eucharist, we may find several instances of anamnesis in the rites of baptism. Some of those moments were mentioned in the writings here several months ago for the Baptism of the Lord. Further, we can look for or even create anamnetic moments through the careful selection of music to begin the rites, by the way we greet the person to be baptized at the church doors—which are themselves a reminder that Jesus is the gate of salvation—and in the moment the child is given his or her baptismal name, which is reminiscent of all those in Scripture who were given a new name to symbolize their new faith-filled purpose, indeed their very consecration.

Scripture is perhaps the most useful anamnetic tool, most fully realized with effective and relevant preaching. If it is part of the rite—or whenever it is prayed—the Litany of the Saints makes present to those assembled the church of history and the church already united with God in heaven.

The blessing of the water of baptism is a tour de force memorial of aquatic salvation history. Prior to the words of blessing, great moments of God's breaking into our lives are recalled: the creation narrative, Noah and the flood, the exodus through the sea, Jesus's baptism, the blood and water that flowed from his side at the crucifixion, and the disciples being sent to baptize are all memorialized.

There are many other moments in this rite and so many others, but space precludes them from being mentioned here. Last week I wrote briefly about a "forward-looking" anamnesis, to the eternal and heavenly banquet. We could always do more of this kind of "forward memorial," including, too, the Parousia—the second coming of Christ.

Lastly, anamnesis that has Scripture at its roots could provide a unique inroad for ecumenical dialogue, liturgical or otherwise, as it seems possible to more successfully seek agreements in theology and in liturgy specifically by pursuing conversations and agreements from the angle of such liturgical anamnesis.

About Music

Fiery Faith: Rory Cooney's "Canticle of the Turning" (GIA) is a fiery paraphrase of Mary's *Magnificat* that is appropriate for today and calls to mind tomorrow's solemnity.

AUGUST 14, 2022

TWENTIETH SUNDAY IN ORDINARY TIME

THE ASSUMPTION OF THE BLESSED VIRGIN MARY

R. Alleluia, alleluia.
Mary is taken up to heaven;
a chorus of angels exults.
R. Alleluia, alleluia.

Gospel

Luke 1:39-56; L622

Mary set out
and traveled to the hill country in haste
to a town of Judah,
where she entered the house of
Zechariah
and greeted Elizabeth.
When Elizabeth heard Mary's greeting,
the infant leaped in her womb,
and Elizabeth, filled with the Holy
Spirit,
cried out in a loud voice and said,
"Blessed are you among women,
and blessed is the fruit of your
womb.
And how does this happen to me,
that the mother of my Lord
should come to me?
For at the moment the sound of
your greeting reached my ears,
the infant in my womb leaped for
joy.
Blessed are you who believed
that what was spoken to you by the
Lord
would be fulfilled."

And Mary said:

"My soul proclaims the greatness of
the Lord;
my spirit rejoices in God my Savior
for he has looked with favor on his
lowly servant.
From this day all generations will call
me blessed:
the Almighty has done great things
for me,
and holy is his Name.
He has mercy on those who fear him
in every generation.
He has shown the strength of his arm,
and has scattered the proud in their
conceit.

Continued in Appendix A, p. 310.

See Appendix A, p. 310, for the other readings.

198

Reflecting on the Gospel

Whenever we celebrate the feast of the Blessed Virgin Mary, we honor her motherhood, her openness to the presence of God in her life and her willingness to cooperate with God for the salvation of the world. When her divine maternity was threatened by King Herod, who was determined to kill her child, God intervened to save the child from the king's murderous plans by sending the child and his mother to safety in Egypt. Similarly, the reading from the book of Revelation for the assumption of the Blessed Virgin Mary presents us with the apparitions of an expectant heavenly mother and the vicious ancient dragon (12:1, 3). The ancient dragon desires to devour the child of the heavenly mother as soon as he is born because he is to rule the nations. But God acts to protect the heavenly mother and her child, and God sends her away to safety in the wilderness out of sight of the ancient dragon.

When the Blessed Virgin Mary declares in the canticle that she has found favor with God, her experience of God's favor includes protection for her and her child from the murderous scheme of King Herod. She experiences God's protection as a young mother during her brief sojourn in a foreign land. As a young mother who is away from her relatives and friends, missing out on the help and support that her closely knit family ties in her native country among her people would have afforded her during the weening stage of her child, the Blessed Mother and her child nevertheless experience the protection of God throughout their stay in Egypt. God's favor is with her as the prophecy of Simeon pierces her heart with concern and worry for the direction of the life of her son. God continues to do great things in her life by keeping her calm and tranquil during difficult times when she is filled with sorrow for the safety of her child whom she has not seen for three days since the end of the festival in Jerusalem. Sorrow and distress overwhelm her as she holds the remains of her son, an image famously celebrated in the *Pietà*. In all these experiences, the strength of God's arm that gives her courage in adversity is with her.

We celebrate the Assumption of the Blessed Virgin Mary on the firm belief that her dormition to heaven is the climax of her experience of God's favor. God lifted up the Blessed Mother by granting her the divine favor of a heavenly home. From her immaculate conception to her glorious assumption into heaven, the Blessed Mother enjoyed the gratuitous gift of God's favor. She was a faithful servant of God and her faithfulness led to her experience of heavenly habitation. Likewise, our faithfulness to God no matter the circumstances of our life is the sure hope of our own experience of being judged as righteous before God.

Focusing the Gospel

Key words and phrases: "Mary remained with her about three months and then returned to her home."

To the point: Today's gospel contains the *Magnificat*, the Canticle of Mary. Mary shares these words after arriving at Elizabeth's home to help her through her pregnancy. The self-gift of Mary is immense. Not only has she said yes to bearing the Lord, but her first impulse is to join her cousin and help with

Elizabeth's pregnancy. As soon as she arrives, Mary bursts forth with beautiful words about the Lord, filled with gratitude. The orientation of Mary is always toward self-gift. Her life has been completely disrupted, and her engagement endangered, and yet Mary's response is complete trust and thanksgiving to the Lord for the great things he has done for her. She has a sense of the bigger picture that is never shaken.

Model Penitential Act

Presider: Today on the Assumption we celebrate Mary's life, a life lived in total service to God and others. For the times we have not lived as we are called, we ask for God's healing and peace . . . *[pause]*

Lord Jesus, you are Son of God and son of Mary: Lord, have mercy.
Christ Jesus, you long for relationship with your people: Christ, have mercy.
Lord Jesus, your words are spirit and life: Lord, have mercy.

Model Universal Prayer (Prayer of the Faithful)

Presider: Just as Mary expressed her complete trust in God we, too, raise our prayers and petitions, confident that God hears and answers them.

Response: Lord, hear our prayer.

That the church might practice selflessness and humility in all its teaching . . .

That leaders might choose healthy vulnerability, lowering themselves so that others might be raised up . . .

That all mothers and mothers-to-be might find both the economic and spiritual support they need to raise their children . . .

That all gathered here might open our hearts to God's voice and respond with courage and conviction . . .

Presider: Loving God, like Mary we trust that you work great things in each of us. Hear the prayers we bring today and answer them according to your will, that we might proclaim your greatness by our lives. We ask this through Christ our Lord. **Amen.**

About Liturgy

Truly Living Liturgy: Mary was the first disciple of Christ even as she was his mother and teacher. We should be mindful today of women's voices, teaching us how to live liturgically and turn that spirituality into a life of active and tangible faith outside the doors of the church. We turn today to these words from Dorothy Day: "Living the liturgical day as much as we are able, beginning with prime, using the missal, ending the day with compline and so going through the liturgical year we find that it is now not us, but Christ in us, who is working to combat injustice and oppression. We are on our way to becoming 'other Christs.' We cannot build up the idea of the apostolate of the laity without the foundation of the liturgy" (*The Catholic Worker*, January 1936).

Our acts of service, our evangelizing, our every word and deed must be connected to the prayer of the church and the intertwined worshipper and worshipped. All are united in prayer, in love, in life.

FOR REFLECTION

• Which line of Mary's *Magnificat* particularly resonates with you today? How do these words both challenge and inspire you?

• Mary traveled "in haste" to visit Elizabeth. To whom do you move "in haste" to spend time and grow in relationship with?

• Like Mary, God chooses each of us for God's self. When have you encountered this sacred belovedness?

Homily Points

• So often we think about creation as something that happened in the past, completed years ago when God first breathed life into the universe. Mary's proclamation today reminds us, however, that God's creative powers are ongoing and will continue until the end of time. As Mary states, in the fulfillment of God's kingdom the hungry will be fed, the powerless will know dignity, and those who have been relegated to the margins of society will be held in esteem as chosen and beloved.

• As "co-creators" we are called to work to bring about this reality. We must advocate for economic justice. We must actively denounce racism, sexism, homophobia, and xenophobia. We must protect children and refugees and those who are sick and suffering in any way. Do we dare pray the words of Mary's *Magnificat*? If we do, we have some work to do.

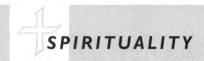

SPIRITUALITY

GOSPEL ACCLAMATION
John 14:6

R̸. Alleluia, alleluia.
I am the way, the truth and the life, says the Lord;
no one comes to the Father, except through me.
R̸. Alleluia, alleluia.

Gospel

Luke 13:22-30; L123C

Jesus passed through towns and villages,
    teaching as he went and making his
        way to Jerusalem.
Someone asked him,
    "Lord, will only a few people be
        saved?"
He answered them,
    "Strive to enter through the narrow
        gate,
    for many, I tell you, will attempt to
        enter
    but will not be strong enough.
After the master of the house has arisen
    and locked the door,
    then will you stand outside knocking
        and saying,
    'Lord, open the door for us.'
He will say to you in reply,
    'I do not know where you are from.'
And you will say,
    'We ate and drank in your company
        and you taught in our streets.'
Then he will say to you,
    'I do not know where you are from.
Depart from me, all you evildoers!'
And there will be wailing and grinding of
        teeth
    when you see Abraham, Isaac, and Jacob
    and all the prophets in the kingdom of
        God
    and you yourselves cast out.
And people will come from the east and
        the west
    and from the north and the south
    and will recline at table in the kingdom
        of God.
For behold, some are last who will be first,
    and some are first who will be last."

Reflecting on the Gospel

This Sunday's gospel opens with a reminder that Jesus is still journeying to Jerusalem, answering questions and telling stories along the way to explain what is expected of a disciple. "Lord, will only a few people be saved?" asks someone—no doubt with the unspoken hope "along with me!" The anonymity of the questioner drags us all into both the question and Jesus's reply. This reply is not a direct answer, but a parable about the effort needed to be saved. Central to the parable is the image of the narrow door. It is not a locked door, but one that requires disciples to give up self-indulgent ways and go into a spiritual training

program that will slim us down and enable us to pass through this door into the kingdom. The media is full of stories about the demanding regime athletes have to follow in their training. To squeeze into a sports team, especially as a representative of one's country, is a cause for celebration; to be citizens who squeeze into the kingdom of God (Phil 3:20) is an eternal joy beyond compare. It is in Jerusalem, where Jesus is heading to suffer, that the narrow door of salvation will be forced sufficiently wide for us by his crucified and risen body.

The Letter to the Hebrews maintains that for the spiritual olympiad, suffering is part of our training. Flagging disciples must never lose sight of Jesus and his endurance of the cross if they, too, are to endure in the face of hostility from without and lack of commitment from within themselves and their community. In an era when we are made privy to all the details of an injured sport hero's physical therapy routine ("punishing," as it is often described!), we need to reflect on our own routines for enduring the kingdom race as we strive to reach heaven.

The second image in the gospel, the second door, is a locked one. The door to the kingdom of God will not remain open forever. There comes a time when, for each one of us personally in death, and cosmically at the second coming of Christ, the door will be closed. Jesus, the risen Christ, is the Master of God's household who "arises" to shut the door. He will not open it to name-dropping or pleas of casual associates who by their protests only indicate how shallow their relationship with Jesus has been. In fact, says the gospel, Jesus will be busy at the back door with those who are too ashamed to come to the front: the strangers, the beggars, those healed in their bodies and psyches, the abused women, the repentant sinners, and all those who may not have known much about God. But they were known by God as the last who deserved to be first in the kingdom. This is a scene of gospel reversal, with graphic language to impress on Jesus's audience that those who expect to be the guests at the messianic banquet, who considered themselves holy, may be disappointed. They will have no place in the history of salvation and will not sit at table with Abraham, Isaac, Jacob, and all the prophets; others will take their place. We should remember that Jesus's words are admonitions rather than predictions. If we are honest with ourselves, especially our self-righteous selves, we will admit that we still find it rather scandalous and upsetting that "those people," with their contemporary name tags we choose to write and their categorizations we describe, might be invited into the feast—or at least have a more favored place at table than we do.

Focusing the Gospel

Key words and phrases: "Strive to enter through the narrow gate, for many, I tell you, will attempt to enter but will not be strong enough."

To the point: This part of the gospel is where Jesus lays out the reality of the kingdom of God: not everyone will make it. This feels counterintuitive—that the same Jesus who goes in search of a lost sheep, and embraces the Prodigal Son, will tell evildoers to depart. However, there is a satisfaction in the agency we are granted in this week's gospel. We have the choice within our own hearts, and exemplified by our actions, to love others as Christ loves us, or to not. "Strive to enter through the narrow gate, for many, I tell you, will attempt to enter but will not be strong enough." It is easy to desire to do good. It is far more challenging to put it into practice.

Connecting the Gospel

to the second reading: In the second reading, Paul explains the benefits of discipline. This pairs well with the message of the gospel, in that we are called to push ourselves and, frequently, to act in ways that are not easy. "At the time, all discipline seems a cause not for joy but for pain, yet later it brings the peaceful fruit of righteousness to those who are trained by it."

to experience: Following Jesus is work. It is counterintuitive, calls us to put others before ourselves, and is frequently in conflict with the messages told to us by the secular world. It requires discipline and being uncomfortable. "So strengthen your drooping hands and your weak knees. Make straight paths for your feet, that what is lame may not be disjointed but healed." If you want to follow Christ, you have to put yourself in the position to succeed. If you want to be better at a sport or an instrument, you practice. If we want to be better at loving God and others, we have to practice. Saints don't just happen. All of them, regardless of natural disposition, had to make the decision to put God first in their own life and circumstances.

Connecting the Responsorial Psalm

to the readings: Alongside readings exhorting the benefits of discipline, we get a psalm that tells us to go out and tell the Good News. It is through telling the Good News that we practice discipline. When we are living a life that glorifies the Lord, we are putting into practice the work that Paul tells us to do to strengthen our hands and knees.

to psalmist preparation: Today's psalm offers an opportunity to balance out the warnings that come in the other readings and gospel. In the midst of Paul's call to discipline and Jesus's story of those who are cast out, the psalm offers us hope and reminds us that "steadfast is his kindness toward us, / and the fidelity of the LORD endures forever." God does not desire to punish us, but draw us near.

Model Penitential Act

Presider: In today's gospel Jesus instructs us to strive to enter through the narrow gate. For the times we have rejected this invitation, we ask for healing and forgiveness . . . [pause]

Lord Jesus, you call all people to yourself: Lord, have mercy.

Christ Jesus, you show us the path to your kingdom: Christ, have mercy.

Lord Jesus, you are the narrow way: Lord, have mercy.

Homily Points

• In order to understand today's gospel, we must first know something about life in Jesus's day. When Jesus says, "Strive to enter through the narrow gate, for many, I tell you, will attempt to enter but will not be strong enough," we immediately think of Jesus putting some sort of restriction on our relationship with him and the ultimate entrance into heaven. While it may be a foreign concept to us, this image of the narrow gate would have been well-known by Jesus's followers. Traditional city gates at the time typically had one large, central entrance arch and two smaller portals off to each side. Caravans of goods and livestock and camels used the main entryway, but travelers without a cart or baggage could avoid this main line and enter through the narrow side gates.

• Grounded in the context of this image, we can recognize that Jesus is not the one who limits who will be saved. We know that Jesus's salvation is offered to all. We also know, however, that not everyone will accept this invitation. Our own baggage—our daily actions and lived reality, our possessions, our status—determine whether or not we can enter the narrow gate.

• If we are truly willing to leave all for Christ, we find comfort in today's gospel when Jesus says, "[P]eople will come from the east and the west and from the north and the south and will recline at table in the kingdom of God." All are welcome in the kingdom of God. We encounter this theme throughout Luke's narrative, as we constantly see Jesus reaching out to people whom society might typically reject. Jesus upholds and welcomes relationship with women and tax collectors and Pharisees and those who are deemed "unclean." Indeed, the last are first and the first are last.

Model Universal Prayer (Prayer of the Faithful)

Presider: As we strive to enter the narrow gate, we raise our needs and concerns to the God who loves us and beckons us to follow.

Response: Lord, hear our prayer.

That the church might foster authentic inclusivity and serve as a model of acceptance and welcome . . .

That all who hold leadership positions might use their authority to end the divisions that seek to separate us . . .

That all might work to end the systemic injustice that stems from the sin of racism . . .

That all gathered here might respond to God's call with renewed integrity and resolve to serve . . .

Presider: Loving God, you invite us to follow you and remind us of your incredible generosity. Renew our resolve to leave what holds us back so that we might grow as disciples and enter the kingdom you promise. We ask this through Christ our Lord. **Amen.**

COLLECT

Let us pray.

Pause for silent prayer

O God, who cause the minds of the faithful to unite in a single purpose,
grant your people to love what you command
and to desire what you promise,
that, amid the uncertainties of this world,
our hearts may be fixed on that place where true gladness is found.
Through our Lord Jesus Christ, your Son,
who lives and reigns with you in the unity of the Holy Spirit,
God, for ever and ever. **Amen.**

FIRST READING

Isa 66:18-21

Thus says the LORD:
I know their works and their thoughts,
and I come to gather nations of every language;
    they shall come and see my glory.
I will set a sign among them;
    from them I will send fugitives to the nations:
    to Tarshish, Put and Lud, Mosoch, Tubal and Javan,
    to the distant coastlands
    that have never heard of my fame, or seen my glory;
    and they shall proclaim my glory among the nations.
They shall bring all your brothers and sisters from all the nations
    as an offering to the LORD,
    on horses and in chariots, in carts, upon mules and dromedaries,
    to Jerusalem, my holy mountain, says the LORD,
    just as the Israelites bring their offering to the house of the LORD in clean vessels.
Some of these I will take as priests and Levites, says the LORD.

RESPONSORIAL PSALM
Ps 117:1, 2

R̂. (Mark 16:15) Go out to all the world
and tell the Good News.
or
R̂. Alleluia.

Praise the Lᴏʀᴅ, all you nations;
glorify him, all you peoples!

R̂. Go out to all the world and tell the
Good News.
or
R̂. Alleluia.

For steadfast is his kindness toward us,
and the fidelity of the Lᴏʀᴅ endures
forever.

R̂. Go out to all the world and tell the
Good News.
or
R̂. Alleluia.

SECOND READING
Heb 12:5-7, 11-13

Brothers and sisters,
You have forgotten the exhortation
addressed to you as children:
"My son, do not disdain the discipline
of the Lord
or lose heart when reproved by him;
for whom the Lord loves, he disciplines;
he scourges every son he
acknowledges."
Endure your trials as "discipline";
God treats you as sons.
For what "son" is there whom his father
does not discipline?
At the time,
all discipline seems a cause not for joy
but for pain,
yet later it brings the peaceful fruit of
righteousness
to those who are trained by it.

So strengthen your drooping hands and
your weak knees.
Make straight paths for your feet,
that what is lame may not be disjointed
but healed.

About Liturgy

What about "Liturgical East"?: "And people will come from the east and the west and from the north and the south and will recline at table in the kingdom of God" (Luke 13:29). Our Scripture points us this weekend toward images of worship, if slightly obliquely. Paired with the recent discussions here from *Built of Living Stones* on how church architecture imparts and impacts ecclesiology and identity to and onto the people in the pews, valuable consideration may be given to the growing practice of *ad orientem* worship. This is the liturgical practice most simply known as when the celebrant and the assembly face together in the same ordinal direction for at least the presidential prayers of the liturgy.

Our church is one of symbols being grounded in reality; that is, the stuff of our worship is real: water, bread, fire, ashes . . . The list goes on and on. Yet, *ad orientem* (literally, "to the east") worship does not seem to be, over 2,000 years of Christianity, embodied in a long tradition of all churches built so that everyone could, on Sunday morning, face actual east. There is some scholarship that shows that was a practice in the earliest churches, including house worship. In more recent times, though, even St. Peter's Basilica in Vatican City is west-facing, so to speak—though again there is some scholarship that shows in such situations the assembly would turn to face east at least some of the time.

There is indeed value in both *ad orientem* and *versus populi* worship, in a very Catholic "both/and" way to approach the topic. Those who try to say otherwise should probably reconsider their stance. It's certainly fine to have a preference, perhaps even if that means the exclusion of the other. But some seem to say there is no worth at all in the type of worship they do not prefer—and that must surely be incorrect, in this case.

It seems likely that some years down the road we might find more than a few churches who have, during the year, occasional *ad orientem* worship along with our more common *versus populi* arrangement. Perhaps it changes seasonally (Advent/Lent, etc.) like other liturgical elements change, sometimes by rule, sometimes tradition. During Lent, for instance, turning from and returning to the Lord could be made manifest in such a way; during Advent, we would wait for the Lord who comes: "People, look east, the time is near!"

And what could churches built in the round do? More about that next week!

About Music

Songs for the Banquet: "Table of Plenty" (OCP) by Dan Schutte would be a good fit with today's Scripture readings. Also consider the *Psallite* refrains "This Is My Body" or "Behold the Lamb of God!" to emphasize the banquet at which all are gathered (Liturgical Press).

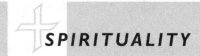

SPIRITUALITY

GOSPEL ACCLAMATION
Matt 11:29ab

R⁊. Alleluia, alleluia.
Take my yoke upon you, says the Lord;
and learn from me, for I am meek and humble
    of heart.
R⁊. Alleluia, alleluia.

Gospel   Luke 14:1, 7-14; L126C

On a sabbath Jesus went to dine
    at the home of one of the leading
        Pharisees,
    and the people there were observing
        him carefully.

He told a parable to those who had
        been invited,
    noticing how they were choosing the
        places of honor at the table.
"When you are invited by someone to
    a wedding banquet,
    do not recline at table in the place
        of honor.
A more distinguished guest than you
        may have been invited by him,
    and the host who invited both of you
        may approach you and say,
    'Give your place to this man,'
    and then you would proceed with
        embarrassment
    to take the lowest place.
Rather, when you are invited,
    go and take the lowest place
    so that when the host comes to you
        he may say,
    'My friend, move up to a higher
        position.'
Then you will enjoy the esteem of your
        companions at the table.
For everyone who exalts himself will
        be humbled,
    but the one who humbles himself will
        be exalted."

Continued in Appendix A, p. 310.

Reflecting on the Gospel

Anyone who has ever had to juggle seating arrangements—at anywhere from a family wedding to political conference dinners—knows the hazards! Where, with whom, do we sit people to avoid frosty silences, heated arguments, exhausting prattle, or offended sulking? In today's gospel, Jesus lays down the rules for "gospel seating," Christian table etiquette, and the compilation of guest lists. He himself is the guest at a Sabbath meal hosted by a leading Pharisee. The Lectionary omits the preceding verses that describe how Jesus heals the man with dropsy and is watched with silent disapproval by the lawyers and Pharisees who are at table with him. This, then, is the charged atmosphere in which Jesus does not hesitate to tell his parables. Luke structures his narrative in such a way that the hostility of Jesus's opponents provokes sympathy in his followers.

In Palestinian society of the first century, honor and shame were powerful social influences. A guest was expected to show appreciation for the hospitality offered, no matter how meager it might be. To criticize the host's action or the circumstances of the meal would be considered shameful for both the host and the guest, so Jesus takes the more subtle approach of storytelling. His first parable rebukes the social competitiveness of those who jockey for the best seats at table. The fact that Luke calls Jesus's words "a parable" indicates that more than social commentary is at stake. Jesus is about to serve a gospel ethic to those who sit at table with him.

Jesus deliberately invites into the parable the lawyers and Pharisees whose motive for dining with Jesus seems to be more to "catch him at something he might say" (Luke 11:54) than to enjoy his companionship. "When you are invited," Jesus begins. Today, as a eucharistic assembly, we too are invited to the table and into the parable. Jesus describes how a guest at a wedding banquet loses face when asked by the host to move to a lower place because someone more important has arrived. To presume self-importance is great foolishness. On the contrary, to be humble, and consequently free from the promotion push, is an honorable attitude and is recognized as such by the host's invitation to take a more important place at the table. But the parable is more than a piece of conventional social wisdom. A wedding banquet is frequently a biblical image of the heavenly banquet, and so we can hear this parable as a warning that it will be much more painful if, at the kingdom banquet, we find ourselves put down for those who had no such grandiose opinions of themselves. Those who are most distinguished in God's eyes because of their humble love may be the very ones whom we blindly consider to be of little worth. What we do "now" is preparing for our "not yet" reception in God's house. In our contemporary situation, it is not so much the grab for seats at a meal, but the "wannabe" culture that, in so many contexts, tempts us to elbow others out as we try to climb the ladder of self-importance and success.

Yet we should not confuse attitudes of false humility and passive resignation with taking the lower place. Those at the top and bottom of the social ladder will only meet when the poor are empowered by advocacy, education, and just health and economic policies to climb up to a more equitable future, and the rich relinquish some of their privileges in order to go down and share with those in need.

Focusing the Gospel
Key words and phrases: "[B]lessed indeed will you be because of their inability to repay you."

To the point: This gospel opens with a well-known parable about the last being first. The second half has a message not for the guests, but for the host. "When you hold a lunch or a dinner, do not invite your friends or your brothers or your relatives or your wealthy neighbors, in case they may invite you back and you have repayment." Jesus is describing an invitation that is transactional. It isn't a gift, because it comes with an expectation. Instead, Jesus proposes inviting those who cannot repay the host for such a meal. If the host were to "invite the poor, the crippled, the lame, the blind," it would be a meal gifted out of love, not expectation.

Connecting the Gospel
to the first reading: The first reading from Sirach lays down blunt and beautiful words on what it means to be humble. Someone who is humble is "loved more than a giver of gifts." This is an odd thing to say because one would assume that everyone wants to be around a gift giver. But think about it. Are you more interested in the company of someone who basks in his or her own greatness, even if it comes with perks, or would you rather spend time with someone who downplays his or her accomplishments and greets you with interest and authenticity?

to experience: There is likely something in your life in which you take great pride. How do you talk about this? Do you have a healthy ego about what you can do? Do you downplay it because you are anxious that others might belittle you? Do not mistake a lack of confidence for humility. You are allowed to be proud of good things you do. The line that Jesus asks us to walk in the gospel is that of knowing the difference between self-aggrandizement that separates ourselves from others and healthy self-knowledge that is wrapped in gratitude. If we are confident in our abilities and use them to point to the Lord, humility is easy, because our accomplishments speak for themselves.

Connecting the Responsorial Psalm
to the readings: This week's psalm beautifully details all the ways in which God rights the wrong of the world. "The father of orphans and the defender of widows / is God in his holy dwelling. / God gives a home to the forsaken; / he leads forth prisoners to prosperity." In these words, God places the last first.

to psalmist preparation: Think of someone in your life who gives his or her all but never seems to get the recognition or reward he or she deserves. Give yourself a moment to reflect on this person, who toils in humility. When you sing this psalm, sing it for this person.

PROMPTS FOR FAITH-SHARING

What is your "banquet"? What are the areas of your life in which you show your best self? Whom do you share these with?

Who might the poor, the crippled, the lame, and the blind be in the banquet of your life? Who do you meet in life who you know cannot repay you for what you give?

Can you recall a situation when you felt truly poor? Who "housed" you?

What do you think of when you read from the letter to the Hebrews, "the sprinkled blood that speaks more eloquently than that of Abel"? What do you think this means?

Model Penitential Act

Presider: In today's gospel Jesus commands us to humble ourselves, part of which is recognizing our own weaknesses and wounds. For the times we have not been who we are called to be, we ask for God's healing and peace . . . *[pause]*

Lord Jesus, you call us your friends and invite us to table: Lord, have mercy.

Christ Jesus, you show us how to be humble through your paschal mystery: Christ, have mercy.

Lord Jesus, you raise the lowly with your compassionate presence: Lord, have mercy.

Homily Points

• The entirety of the Christian message can be summarized by Jesus's words in today's gospel: "[E]veryone who exalts himself will be humbled, but the one who humbles himself will be exalted." This is the message of the cross *par excellence*. Christ gives us a model of how we must lower ourselves so as to not cling to power or riches but to find strength in humility and lowliness. While this message takes the form of a parable, it might better be described as a wisdom saying or a foundation for one's approach to life.

• If Christianity is a celebration of humility and lowliness, it is also a celebration of the vulnerable. There is something unsettling about vulnerability. Even the etymology would suggest that it is something to avoid, as it comes from the Latin noun *vulnus* or "wound." Why would we want to open ourselves to being hurt? This is where we must make an important distinction. We know all too well, especially in our church, that there are times when vulnerability, or the capacity to be physically or emotionally open, transparent, and even wounded, has been taken advantage of.

• Christ's invitation to humility and vulnerability is grounded in self-knowledge. This concept is so difficult to grasp because it seems to go against everything within us. Rather than climbing up the ladder of power and prestige, wealth and success, Christ invites us to descend, to lower ourselves, to understand and welcome our own weakness and wounds. Instead of exalting ourselves, Christ invites us to follow his example and humble ourselves.

Model Universal Prayer (Prayer of the Faithful)

Presider: Knowing that we can do nothing without you, we raise our prayers and petitions, confident that you hear us when we pray.

Response: Lord, hear our prayer.

That church leaders might follow Jesus's command to embrace lowliness and reject the glamour of power and status . . .

That employers might treat their employees with fairness and respect, always upholding their God-given dignity . . .

That all who experience poverty might find concrete support as they strive to meet their daily needs . . .

That all gathered here might work to raise others up instead of putting them down . . .

Presider: Loving God, hear these prayers we offer today. Listen to them and help us grow in humility, following the example of your Son. We ask this through Christ our Lord. **Amen.**

COLLECT

Let us pray.

Pause for silent prayer

God of might, giver of every good gift,
put into our hearts the love of your name,
so that, by deepening our sense of
    reverence,
you may nurture in us what is good
and, by your watchful care,
keep safe what you have nurtured.
Through our Lord Jesus Christ, your Son,
who lives and reigns with you in the unity
    of the Holy Spirit,
God, for ever and ever. **Amen.**

FIRST READING
Sir 3:17-18, 20, 28-29

My child, conduct your affairs with
    humility,
    and you will be loved more than a giver
        of gifts.
Humble yourself the more, the greater
    you are,
    and you will find favor with God.
What is too sublime for you, seek not,
    into things beyond your strength search
        not.
The mind of a sage appreciates proverbs,
    and an attentive ear is the joy of the
        wise.
Water quenches a flaming fire,
    and alms atone for sins.

RESPONSORIAL PSALM

Ps 68:4-5, 6-7, 10-11

℟. (cf. 11b) God, in your goodness, you
have made a home for the poor.

The just rejoice and exult before God;
they are glad and rejoice.
Sing to God, chant praise to his name;
whose name is the LORD.

℟. God, in your goodness, you have made
a home for the poor.

The father of orphans and the defender of
widows
is God in his holy dwelling.
God gives a home to the forsaken;
he leads forth prisoners to prosperity.

℟. God, in your goodness, you have made
a home for the poor.

A bountiful rain you showered down, O
God, upon your inheritance;
you restored the land when it
languished;
your flock settled in it;
in your goodness, O God, you provided
it for the needy.

℟. God, in your goodness, you have made
a home for the poor.

SECOND READING

Heb 12:18-19, 22-24a

Brothers and sisters:
You have not approached that which could
be touched
and a blazing fire and gloomy darkness
and storm and a trumpet blast
and a voice speaking words such that
those who heard
begged that no message be further
addressed to them.
No, you have approached Mount Zion
and the city of the living God, the
heavenly Jerusalem,
and countless angels in festal gathering,
and the assembly of the firstborn
enrolled in heaven,
and God the judge of all,
and the spirits of the just made perfect,
and Jesus, the mediator of a new
covenant,
and the sprinkled blood that speaks
more eloquently than that of Abel.

About Liturgy

More about **Ad Orientem:** Let's return to last week's discussion on *ad orientem* worship and the notion of something called "liturgical east." This would seem to be an issue in contemporary church architecture, where churches are frequently built in the round, or some approximation of it. Could we not just as easily be one body, facing one direction, as we gather around the eucharistic table—using "toward the altar" as if a cardinal direction, like east is used?

Perhaps east isn't a substance, but is a real thing with a real answer if someone asks, just as the rising sun is a real object we look to in the sky, even if we can't, and shouldn't, touch it. ("Billy, stop trying to touch the sun— it's hot and will hurt you!") Must we face together only east? Why not toward the altar? If we are facing "to the Lord as one," there are myriad places that might be, including the assembly the priest sees from his unique vantage point. After all, it's not as if God is only located fifteen feet over in that direction, or some other specific place and time.

Some may justly raise an objection: none of this matters unless the liturgy moves one to, and sustains one in, going out and serving the poor, priests included. Others might also note that, at their parish, they worship *ad projectionem*. These are valid points to discuss but are probably better discussed independently of the initial broader concerns of ecclesiology—at least before melding all those discussions into one.

A wise liturgist friend of mine (who wishes to remain anonymous) also noted to me, a few years ago, this observation:

> If it's not necessary to change something, then perhaps it's necessary to not change something. If an overzealous pastor starts saying the canon of the Mass in Latin, changes the orientation of the altar and the posture for receiving Communion, etc., many longtime parishioners will flee to the parish next door while handfuls of others from across town will start showing up, turning a neighborhood parish into a quasi-oratory for like-minded worshippers. Those leaving will likely outnumber those joining, attendance and the collection will drop, and the whole experiment will come to an early end, the damage already being done. It's ironic how those who decry contemporary liturgical experimentation will gladly say, "Let's start doing these purportedly ancient things that no other church in town does."

Ultimately, it's in sorting out "how the rubber meets the road" when dealing with some of the more theological portions of our liturgical guiding documents. Even the loftiest of ideas has to have some practical implementation at the end of the day, and those implementations (or lack of implementations) have real and lasting consequences, for good or for ill.

About Music

The Last Shall Be First: There are many references in today's readings, and those of the last few Sundays, regarding how Christians ought to seek the lowest places, pursue humility, and understand the needs of the most poor and meek to be paramount in society. "No Greater Love" (WN) by Audrey Assad, Chris Tomlin, and Matt Maher is a powerful contemporary anthem that amplifies these thoughts. Shirley Erena Murray's "A Place at the Table" has settings by both Lori True and Joy F. Patterson (WLP/GIA), with these powerful words (among others) in verse 4: "In anger, in hurt, a mindset of mercy, / For just and unjust, a new way to live."

✠ SPIRITUALITY

GOSPEL ACCLAMATION
Ps 119:135

℟. Alleluia, alleluia.
Let your face shine upon your servant;
and teach me your laws.
℟. Alleluia, alleluia.

Gospel   Luke 14:25-33; L129C

Great crowds were traveling with
    Jesus,
    and he turned and addressed them,
    "If anyone comes to me without hat-
        ing his father and mother,
    wife and children, brothers and
        sisters,
    and even his own life,
    he cannot be my disciple.
Whoever does not carry his
        own cross and come after me
    cannot be my disciple.
Which of you wishing to construct a
        tower
    does not first sit down and calculate
        the cost
    to see if there is enough for its
        completion?
Otherwise, after laying the foundation
    and finding himself unable to finish the
        work
    the onlookers should laugh at him and
        say,
    'This one began to build but did not
        have the resources to finish.'
Or what king marching into battle would
        not first sit down
    and decide whether with ten thousand
        troops
    he can successfully oppose another
        king
    advancing upon him with twenty thou-
        sand troops?
But if not, while he is still far away,
    he will send a delegation to ask for
        peace terms.
In the same way,
    anyone of you who does not renounce
        all his possessions
    cannot be my disciple."

Reflecting on the Gospel

We know how we can get into trouble by neglecting to read the small print on documents like guarantees or advertisements for apparently wonderful bargains! Jesus wants us to be quite sure that we understand the "small print" of the gospel demands on his disciples. There are three conditions that disciples must be clear about. The first is to prefer intimacy with Jesus to all other intimacies; the second is to accept the cross—not only that of the ordinary, painful suffering that is part of being human, but also of the persecution, ridicule, and conflict that may come with discipleship; and the third is to surrender possessions and possessiveness. To impress on his hearers the importance of these demands, Jesus tells two parables about two possible fools: one at work, the other at war.

The first foolish man is a landowner who decides to build a tower, probably a watch-tower, on his property. He is a captive of his wild, momentary enthusiasms. He wants a tower; let there be a tower! But he has no finances to raise anything on the foundations except the ridicule of the onlookers who scoff at his lack of foresight and planning. The other man is a king who engages in the serious business of war. He would be a fool not to weigh the possibilities of succeeding with a smaller army than his opponent and try to negotiate for peace rather than engage in war. As builder and king, these men are people of some substance, so to fail in what they set out to do will cause great shame. Jesus seems to suggest that the disciples with some material and social means at their disposal need to consider the cost of discipleship most carefully, because they will pay a greater price in terms of social status and possessions if they give up these to follow him. With memories of the mission of the seventy (or seventy-two) disciples in Luke 10:1-12, some may be expected to be itinerant missionaries, leaving the security of home and family but finding a new security and sense of belonging in the household of the church.

In *The Cost of Discipleship*, Dietrich Bonhoeffer compared "costly grace" and "cheap grace." The latter is grace without the cross, and so without Jesus Christ. As leader of the German Confessing Church, which confessed Jesus in opposition to the Nazis, Bonhoeffer "hated" (to use the word in today's gospel) his own life to the extent of being executed on April 9, 1945, only a few weeks before World War II ended in Europe. In comparing these two "graces," Bonhoeffer writes of "the person who hears the call to discipleship and wants to follow but feels obliged to insist on his own terms to the level of human understanding. The disciple places himself at the Master's disposal, but at the same time retains the right to dictate his own terms. But then discipleship is no longer discipleship, but a program of our own to be arranged to suit ourselves, and to be judged in accordance with the standards of rational ethic."

How ready are we to pay the cost of Christian discipleship in our own times by doing works of justice, by sacrificing reputation and advancement because we confess the needs of the disadvantaged? How can those who are disadvantaged be enabled to achieve self-advocacy and self-respect? Are there aspects of our lives in which we are wild enthusiasts for the gospel—but with no staying power? Today's gospel provides both encouragement and challenge.

Focusing the Gospel

Key words and phrases: "Whoever does not carry his own cross and come after me cannot be my disciple."

To the point: In this week's gospel, Jesus continues to lay out the reality of what it means to follow him. When a disciple makes the decision to give up the pursuits of this world to center life and love on Christ, that can be very scary, especially for family members who have expectations and assumptions based on their own experiences. Jesus uses metaphors of an architect making calculations and a king planning for a battle. In each of these situations, Jesus makes the point that massive projects take intentional foresight. If we are to align our lives with the work of Christ, we have to take stock of what it will affect in our life and, to that end, who might be hurt by our decision. Just because someone chooses to follow the gospel doesn't mean that everyone will understand it. Other Christians may not understand it. In that same vein, we have to be aware of how following Christ will alter our own desires and comfort. Jesus doesn't want us to bite off more than we can chew, or expect too much of ourselves without proper preparation.

Connecting the Gospel

to the first reading: The book of Wisdom gets to the heart of the matter outlined in the gospel: "For the deliberations of mortals are timid, and unsure are our plans." Wisdom is telling us the same thing that Jesus does: it will be difficult to follow God, not just because of the actions one makes when one is oriented toward Christ, but because of the planning and foresight. Following the Lord isn't something that just happens. It takes intention.

to experience: How many times in your life have you recommitted to being a "better person" and decided to "love more"? If you're like most Catholics, you've gone through the motions of commitment more than a few times. We do it multiple times a year in the liturgy when we renew our baptismal promises. But, as Catholics know, making a commitment to following the gospel and church teaching is not the same as following them, because it's hard to reorient our lives toward Christ. It takes planning and decisive action. It takes effort to follow the Lord. "For the corruptible body burdens the soul / and the earthen shelter weighs down the mind that has many concerns."

Connecting the Responsorial Psalm

to the readings: This week's psalm reminds us of the scope of the Lord: ageless. While we're here toiling and fretting and planning and forgetting, the Lord is seeing the big picture and the consistent march toward salvation. Is it possible for us to back up and take in a sliver of that view as well?

to psalmist preparation: This psalm is about the big picture and the overarching view that God has of our lives and history. Instead of suggesting that we are insignificant, this psalm invites us to wonder and share awe at the grand scope of our whole world. Bring that wonder and awe with you as you share these words.

PROMPTS FOR FAITH-SHARING

Have you ever had a disagreement with someone you love about how to be a Christian? How did you approach this difference? Did you reconcile the situation?

What is the hardest part about following Christ?

Do you ever "plan" your methods of being a better Christian? What does this mean to you? How might you plan your own spiritual improvement?

Read over the psalm. What emotions does it bring up in you?

CELEBRATION

Model Penitential Act

Presider: In today's gospel Jesus tells us that we must carry our crosses and follow after him. For the times we have rejected Christ's gift of self-love, we ask for forgiveness and healing . . . *[pause]*

Lord Jesus, you invite us to follow you: Lord, have mercy.

Christ Jesus, you call us to be faithful: Christ, have mercy.

Lord Jesus, in your cross we find life and light: Lord, have mercy.

Homily Points

• "Ave crux, spes unica. Hail the Cross, our only Hope." This mantra probably sounds ridiculous to those unfamiliar with the Christian story. Why would anyone ever willingly glorify an instrument of torture and death? We must remember that as Christians, we are called to "see with Easter eyes," for we know the story of Christ does not end with death. This post-resurrection mantra allows us to see the cross as more than what immediately meets the eye. Instead of death, we see life. Instead of rejection, we see glorification.

• Imagine how strange it must have felt, then, for Jesus's disciples to hear him say, "Whoever does not carry his own cross and come after me cannot be my disciple." Not only is this terrifying in itself, but this is the second time in Luke's gospel where Jesus speaks of taking up one's cross. The disciples will soon realize, if they haven't already, that the cross is not something to be avoided but embraced.

• The cross is an image of complete self-gift. Jesus gives himself totally for us through his death on the cross. We, too, are called to share the gift of ourselves, even when we might not literally be called to die for our faith. We practice self-gift when we give our time to others, listening attentively instead of checking our phone. We practice self-gift when we make decisions that benefit the good of others instead of ourselves. We practice self-gift when we recognize that we do not exist as isolated individuals and all of God's creation does not revolve around us. Indeed, let us follow Jesus's command to carry our cross after him that we might know the joy that comes in living for others.

Model Universal Prayer (Prayer of the Faithful)

Presider: Knowing that accepting the invitation to discipleship is not always easy, we bring our needs to the God who loves and sustains us.

Response: Lord, hear our prayer.

That all who follow Christ might practice self-gift in their interactions with others . . .

That all who are unemployed or underemployed might find work that offers just wages and safe working conditions . . .

That all who live in fear by perpetuating divisiveness might find friendship in those with whom they disagree . . .

That our local community might embrace the cross of Christ so to witness to the life and love that flow from vulnerability . . .

Presider: Loving God, your Son calls us to carry our crosses on our journey of discipleship. Be with us as we journey together and grow in faith, for we trust that you hear the prayers we raise. We ask this through Christ our Lord. **Amen.**

COLLECT

Let us pray.

Pause for silent prayer

O God, by whom we are redeemed and
    receive adoption,
look graciously upon your beloved sons
    and daughters,
that those who believe in Christ
may receive true freedom
and an everlasting inheritance.
Through our Lord Jesus Christ, your Son,
who lives and reigns with you in the unity
    of the Holy Spirit,
God, for ever and ever. **Amen.**

FIRST READING

Wis 9:13-18b

Who can know God's counsel,
    or who can conceive what the LORD
        intends?
For the deliberations of mortals are timid,
    and unsure are our plans.
For the corruptible body burdens the soul
    and the earthen shelter weighs down
        the mind that has many concerns.
And scarce do we guess the things on
    earth,
    and what is within our grasp we find
      with difficulty;
    but when things are in heaven, who can
      search them out?
Or who ever knew your counsel, except
    you had given wisdom
    and sent your holy spirit from on high?
And thus were the paths of those on earth
    made straight.

RESPONSORIAL PSALM

Ps 90:3-4, 5-6, 12-13, 14 and 17

℞. (1) In every age, O Lord, you have been
    our refuge.

You turn man back to dust,
    saying, "Return, O children of men."
For a thousand years in your sight
    are as yesterday, now that it is past,
    or as a watch of the night.

℞. In every age, O Lord, you have been
    our refuge.

You make an end of them in their sleep;
    the next morning they are like the
      changing grass,
which at dawn springs up anew,
    but by evening wilts and fades.

℞. In every age, O Lord, you have been
    our refuge.

Teach us to number our days aright,
    that we may gain wisdom of heart.
Return, O LORD! How long?
    Have pity on your servants!

R︎︎. In every age, O Lord, you have been
    our refuge.

Fill us at daybreak with your kindness,
    that we may shout for joy and gladness
        all our days.
And may the gracious care of the LORD
    our God be ours;
    prosper the work of our hands for us!
    Prosper the work of our hands!

R︎︎. In every age, O Lord, you have been
    our refuge.

SECOND READING
Phlm 9-10, 12-17

I, Paul, an old man,
    and now also a prisoner for Christ Jesus,
    urge you on behalf of my child
        Onesimus,
    whose father I have become in my
        imprisonment;
    I am sending him, that is, my own heart,
        back to you.
I should have liked to retain him for
        myself,
    so that he might serve me on your
        behalf
    in my imprisonment for the gospel,
    but I did not want to do anything
        without your consent,
    so that the good you do might not be
        forced but voluntary.
Perhaps this is why he was away from you
        for a while,
    that you might have him back forever,
    no longer as a slave
    but more than a slave, a brother,
    beloved especially to me, but even more
        so to you,
    as a man and in the Lord.
So if you regard me as a partner, welcome
        him as you would me.

About Liturgy

Planning Ahead: In college, I had a choir director who used to joke that it was his goal to "rehearse himself out of a job." That is, he desired to teach us a piece so completely that, come concert time, we wouldn't even need him, but perhaps to start the piece together. While the goal was understandable, it also seemed to miss the possibility that a piece of music might need differing interpretations based on the building it's performed in, the composition of the audience there to hear it, and other contextual information, like current events, the readiness of the performers, even the time of day.

In brief, it's wise to plan ahead, if only to have something to work off of when that plan goes awry or is, by external changes, rendered unusable. So often that can be the case with our liturgical preparations too. Having a liturgical "outline" or "script" is helpful, but must not be rigidly clung to when the tornado siren goes off, or when a guest presider appears because the pastor wakes up with the flu.

In today's gospel, Christ teaches us the value of planning ahead in the context of being his disciple and knowing what the cost will be ahead of time. Jesus asks for our whole selves, the same selves we must offer to him in prayer and worship. At times this is an easy offering, but most often it requires work and sacrifice. And, sometimes, that sacrifice involves giving up on our well-laid plans for what is more pastoral in a given liturgical moment and context.

About Liturgical Documents

Built of Living Stones—*Music Ministry:* When speaking of music ministry, *Built of Living Stones* always takes care to regard these ministers as part of the congregation—that is, they are part of the parish family, engaging in peer ministry, and so the architecture and layout of the physical church building should reflect that. At times in church history members of the choir held a privileged role, and at times today directors of music ministry still regard these ministers, wrongly, in that way. There are times, too, where music ministry can take on the trappings of "performance" or, perhaps said more kindly, ministering *to* instead of ministering *with.* So, what does this document add to the conversation?

"The ministers of music could also be located in the body of the church since they lead the entire assembly in song as well as by the example of their reverent attention and prayer" (BLS 51). By placing the ministers within the assembly, *Built of Living Stones* reinforces that they are part of that family of faith and are indeed leading from within. This is later reemphasized: "Because the roles of the choirs and cantors are exercised within the liturgical community, the space chosen for the musicians should clearly express that they are part of the assembly of worshipers" (89).

Given that there is a wide variety of church buildings and that many structures, especially historic ones, will not lend themselves easily to this philosophy of music ministry, a vivid "pastoral imagination" may be called for to achieve this vision for music ministry. This vision is not one of separation, of performance, or of even "visual leadership." Rather, it is one of peer ministry, leading from within, and enabling the voice of the faith community to lift up their sung prayer earnestly and fully.

About Music

Take Up Your Cross: "Take Up Your Cross" has both a traditional setting with text by Charles Everest (usually to the tune ERHALT UNS, HERR) and a new text and tune by Jaime Cortez (OCP), both appropriate for this weekend.

SEPTEMBER 4, 2022
TWENTY-THIRD SUNDAY
IN ORDINARY TIME

✠ SPIRITUALITY

R̝. Alleluia, alleluia.
God was reconciling the world to
   himself in Christ
and entrusting to us the message of
   reconciliation.
R̝. Alleluia, alleluia.

Gospel   Luke 15:1-32; L132C

Tax collectors and sinners were
   all drawing near to listen to
   Jesus,
   but the Pharisees and scribes
      began to complain,
      saying,
   "This man welcomes sinners
      and eats with them."
So to them he addressed this
   parable.
"What man among you having
   a hundred sheep and losing
   one of them
   would not leave the ninety-nine in the
      desert
   and go after the lost one until he
      finds it?
And when he does find it,
   he sets it on his shoulders with great
      joy
   and, upon his arrival home,
   he calls together his friends and
      neighbors and says to them,
   'Rejoice with me because I have
      found my lost sheep.'
I tell you, in just the same way
   there will be more joy in heaven over
      one sinner who repents
   than over ninety-nine righteous people
   who have no need of repentance.

"Or what woman having ten coins and
   losing one
   would not light a lamp and sweep the
      house,
   searching carefully until she finds it?

Continued in Appendix A, p. 311,

or Luke 15:1-10, p. 311.

Reflecting on the Gospel

The parable of the Prodigal Son can be regarded as the gospel in miniature, announcing as it does the compassionate love of God that forgives and welcomes home the sinner. In first-century Middle Eastern culture, a father might apportion his property to his children before his death, though they were not to use it until their father had died. "So the father divided the property between them," continues Jesus. The word "them" often escapes our notice, yet it should alert us to the fact that the elder son also took his share of the inheritance without protest and without any attempt, as the elder, to be the expected go-between in the reconciliation of his father and brother.

In giving his sons their inheritance, the father makes his first gesture of radical, "foolish" love, and allows the younger boy the freedom to leave home. When he left, this son had no intention of ending up in a pigsty, but that is where he eventually finds himself—starving and impoverished, both materially and spiritually. With all his inheritance squandered, enslaved by a Gentile boss, and looking after his pigs, he also makes himself ritually unclean and ostracized from his Jewish inheritance. So sitting down, he came "to his senses." He proceeds to work it all out . . . *himself*: the initiative he will take to return home, the suggestion he will make to his father about being taken on as a hired, wage-earning hand and so able to work off the debt of his inheritance and repay his father. But coming to his senses will not save the son; coming home to the father will.

A second time the father shows his foolish, costly love. There is no cool, reserved reception of his son, but a running welcome, a kiss, a compassionate embrace that squeezes all the preconceived plans out of his son. All the boy can say is: "Father, I have sinned against heaven and against you; I no longer deserve to be called your son." And from their dead relationships, his father raises him to new life, newly clothed and feasted.

In his book *The Road to Daybreak*, Henri Nouwen described his "homecoming" from academically successful but personally unsatisfying professorships at Harvard and Yale to his life working with men and women with disabilities in the L'Arche Daybreak community in Canada. With these wounded but loving and unpretentious people, Nouwen gradually learned to let go of his drive to do things and prove things. He was able to be his vulnerable, unadorned, and unmasked self, able to receive and give so much love. The parable of the Prodigal Son shows us an image of our Father who is also prodigal—a spendthrift with his love for each one of us, his unadorned and vulnerable children.

For the third time, the father is a foolish lover when, at the cost of being considered both rude and stupid, he ignores his guests in order to plead with his elder son to join in the communal rejoicing over his brother's return. But he refuses to be reconciled; he, too, has to learn what it means to be a son. He describes himself as one who has (as the NRSV translates it) "been working like a slave" for his father. He refuses to say "my brother," speaking only of "your son."

Abruptly, we are left with the elder son on the threshold of choice: to accept or reject the father's love, to be reconciled or unreconciled with a brother or sister. Jesus invites us, today's listeners, to write the conclusion to the parable with our lives.

Focusing the Gospel

Key words and phrases: "This man welcomes sinners and eats with them."

To the point: This week's gospel has three parables, all built around the theme of celebrating a sinner who turns back to God. In the first story, when a shepherd loses a sheep, he drops everything to retrieve it. When a woman misplaces a coin, she cleans the whole house in search of it. And when a wealthy father sees his wayward son walking home, he throws a blowout party. The joy and relief in the return of what has been lost is so overwhelming that the celebration is extended to include all. All of these stories are told in response to the Pharisees. The religious leaders are critical of a man who associates with those deemed harmful, those who exist outside the scope of appropriate society. Has this changed at all? Do you avoid "bad people" and situations with sinners, because you are afraid they will lead you to sin? Or do you view these encounters as an opportunity to be and give love?

Throughout his ministry, Jesus models accompaniment. He accompanies sinners, walking with them and eating with them, dignifying them with his presence.

Connecting the Gospel

to the first and second readings: In the first reading, Moses pleads on behalf of his sinful countrymen that God will forgive them and give them a chance to return to faithfulness. In the second reading, Paul praises the Lord who allowed him the opportunity to turn away from sin. "I was once a blasphemer and a persecutor and arrogant, but I have been mercifully treated because I acted out of ignorance in my unbelief."

to experience: The four readings today, from Moses, the psalmist, Luke, and Paul, give us a coherent snapshot of salvation history. The story of Moses and the golden calf demonstrates how the Israelites' understanding of God is a Lord who expresses wrath and is dependent upon a transactional form of faith. Moses begs God to spare the Israelites and give them an opportunity to repent. The psalmist puts faith in the Lord to "clean" his heart, putting the agency of transformation on God. But then we encounter Jesus, who demonstrates the way to move people away from sin is not with ultimatums and punishment but with accompaniment, and then we have Paul, who is grateful for receiving such patience. Paul tells us, "I was once a blasphemer and a persecutor and arrogant, but I have been mercifully treated because I acted out of ignorance in my unbelief. Indeed, the grace of our Lord has been abundant." We see the development of the human relationship with God, from the Torah to the early church.

Connecting the Responsorial Psalm

to the readings: Today's psalm has both action from God ("Thoroughly wash me from my guilt / and of my sin cleanse me") as well as personal agency ("I will rise and go to my father"). It's a bridge between the understanding of God in the time of Abraham, a God of covenants and rules to teach faithfulness, and the God of the New Testament, who is present in the person of Jesus Christ.

to psalmist preparation: Think about the graces God has placed in your life, as well as the movements you have made to position yourself to receive and recognize grace. Our faith is a conversation with God and with our community. This week, reflect on how you have both given and received in these relationships.

PROMPTS FOR FAITH-SHARING

When you think of forgiveness, do you focus on the act of repentance from the person who has done wrong, or the forgiveness of the person who was wronged? Which person's actions do you think are more important?

Do you spend time with sinners? Who do you consider a "sinner"?

When you want to turn away from sin, do you rely more on God or on yourself? Why?

Have you ever stopped a sinful habit because of a relationship with someone who chose to walk with you through it? What was this accompaniment like?

Model Penitential Act

Presider: In today's gospel we hear the parable of the Prodigal Son, perhaps better called the parable of the Merciful Father. Knowing that God is abundant in mercy, we call to mind our own sins and ask for God's forgiveness and healing . . . *[pause]*

Lord Jesus, you call our name when we are lost: Lord, have mercy.

Christ Jesus, you welcome us back after we turn away: Christ, have mercy.

Lord Jesus, you are loving and full of mercy: Lord, have mercy.

Homily Points

• In today's gospel we once again have people complaining that Jesus spends time eating with tax collectors and sinners. Luke groups these three parables together, each addressing something of value lost and found so to illustrate Jesus's message to the scribes and Pharisees. While the items range from a lost sheep to a lost son, the message is the same: God's mercy defies our conventional understandings.

• The first of the three parables is actually rather humorous if you think about it. Jesus asks the rhetorical question, "[Who] among you having a hundred sheep and losing one of them would not leave the ninety-nine in the desert and go after the lost one until he finds it?" If we are to answer that question, we might look at Jesus in astonishment and say, "No one would ever do that. That is ridiculous." But God's love is rather ridiculous, for it is merciful.

• One way to define mercy is "kindness beyond what is expected in a given situation." Perhaps there is no clearer example of mercy than the father who welcomes home his son. After the son demands his inheritance and then squanders it on "a life of dissipation," the situation certainly would not call for the father to show kindness. Even so, while his son was still a long way off, the father sees his homecoming and rejoices. The father's love is limitless and unmatched. The same is true of God's love for us, all sinners in our own ways. In these three stories the worth of the lost item increases from a sheep to a coin to a son. Likewise, the worth of each person only increases in God's eyes.

Model Universal Prayer (Prayer of the Faithful)

Presider: Knowing that God sees each of us while we are still a long way off, we can confidently raise our prayers, knowing they will be heard.

Response: Lord, hear our prayer.

That all who return to the church after any period of absence will be welcomed with abundant joy and radical hospitality . . .

That all people in leadership roles might celebrate the inherent worth and dignity of all people they serve regardless of status . . .

That all who feel lost or separated from family or friends might find comfort in the God who always reaches out . . .

That our church might be a safe space for all people, including immigrants, refugees, those fleeing abusive relationships, and members of the LGBTQ community . . .

Presider: Loving God, you are kind and abundant in mercy. Hear us as we call to you, for we know you rejoice in our presence. We ask this through Christ our Lord. **Amen.**

COLLECT

Let us pray.

Pause for silent prayer

Look upon us, O God,
Creator and ruler of all things,
and, that we may feel the working of your mercy,
grant that we may serve you with all our heart.
Through our Lord Jesus Christ, your Son,
who lives and reigns with you in the unity of the Holy Spirit,
God, for ever and ever. **Amen.**

FIRST READING
Exod 32:7-11, 13-14

The LORD said to Moses,
    "Go down at once to your people,
    whom you brought out of the land of Egypt,
    for they have become depraved.
They have soon turned aside from the way
        I pointed out to them,
    making for themselves a molten calf
        and worshiping it,
    sacrificing to it and crying out,
    'This is your God, O Israel,
    who brought you out of the land of Egypt!'
I see how stiff-necked this people is,"
        continued the LORD to Moses.
"Let me alone, then,
    that my wrath may blaze up against
        them to consume them.
Then I will make of you a great nation."

But Moses implored the LORD, his God, saying,
    "Why, O LORD, should your wrath blaze
        up against your own people,
    whom you brought out of the land of Egypt
    with such great power and with so
        strong a hand?
Remember your servants Abraham, Isaac, and Israel,
    and how you swore to them by your
        own self, saying,
    'I will make your descendants as
        numerous as the stars in the sky;
    and all this land that I promised,
    I will give your descendants as their
        perpetual heritage.'"
So the LORD relented in the punishment
    he had threatened to inflict on his people.

CATECHESIS

RESPONSORIAL PSALM
Ps 51:3-4, 12-13, 17, 19

℟. (Luke 15:18) I will rise and go to my
    father.

Have mercy on me, O God, in your
        goodness;
    in the greatness of your compassion
        wipe out my offense.
Thoroughly wash me from my guilt
    and of my sin cleanse me.

℟. I will rise and go to my father.

A clean heart create for me, O God,
    and a steadfast spirit renew within me.
Cast me not out from your presence,
    and your Holy Spirit take not from me.

℟. I will rise and go to my father.

O Lord, open my lips,
    and my mouth shall proclaim your
        praise.
My sacrifice, O God, is a contrite spirit;
    a heart contrite and humbled, O God,
        you will not spurn.

℟. I will rise and go to my father.

SECOND READING
1 Tim 1:12-17

Beloved:
I am grateful to him who has strengthened
    me, Christ Jesus our Lord,
    because he considered me trustworthy
    in appointing me to the ministry.
I was once a blasphemer and a persecutor
    and arrogant,
    but I have been mercifully treated
    because I acted out of ignorance in my
        unbelief.
Indeed, the grace of our Lord has been
        abundant,
    along with the faith and love that are in
        Christ Jesus.
This saying is trustworthy and deserves
    full acceptance:
    Christ Jesus came into the world to save
        sinners.
Of these I am the foremost.
But for that reason I was mercifully
        treated,
    so that in me, as the foremost,
    Christ Jesus might display all his
        patience as an example
    for those who would come to believe in
        him for everlasting life.
To the king of ages, incorruptible,
    invisible, the only God,
    honor and glory forever and ever. Amen.

About Liturgy / About Liturgical Documents

Built of Living Stones—*Transcendent Art:* Today's gospel is best proclaimed in long form, keeping this small collection of parables together and in relationship with one another. They each speak to seeking out the return and reconciliation of the lost as important in the ministry of Christ and for us as well.

It is tempting for a preacher, or for anyone in the context of Bible study, to attempt to "explain" parables, to determine exactly what each character, each object, each moment, represents. Parables, though, are not allegories, are not analogies, and do not have, typically, a "one-to-one" explanation, even if once or twice Jesus explains them that way in the gospels. Rather, they are to speak to us, in a similar way to many liturgical elements, on the level of symbol, leaving a lot of interpretation up to the listener, the viewer, the receiver.

In the parable of the Prodigal Son, it's tempting to declare this person or that one to be God, for instance. It's better for our understanding of this parable, and most parables, though, if we try to find ourselves in each component of the story. What understandings are gained if we insert ourselves as the father, the wayward son, the loyal son, even the pigs that are tended to, or as one of the anonymous guests at the party? Parables are, in a way, a room with many doors, each one a portal to somewhere unknown, none of them necessarily right or wrong.

So, too, liturgical art should not be so explicit as to remove any act of interpretation from the receiver. Liturgical art that engages in a beautification of texts is common, from stained glass windows to illuminated manuscripts. While such art is beautiful, the text is always there, commanding a certain starting point for viewers, perhaps even a destination, in their journey of perception and reflection.

I once sang a piece of music that set the famed letter that President Lincoln wrote to Mrs. Bixby, who was believed to have lost five sons in the Civil War. This particular setting, by Ulysses Kay, took all of the text of the letter and put it to music, including the handwritten "letterhead," which included the words "Executive Mansion." Normally, the second syllable of the word "Executive" is stressed. This setting, though, sets the words that way initially, but then later puts the stress on the word's first syllable (*EXecutive*), changing entirely the meaning. It turned the adjective from one meaning, that of "having the power to put plans, actions, or laws into effect," to more a statement on what the composer thought of the president from his time and his place: Ulysses Kay was an African American, and this piece dates from the late 1950s, just ahead of the profound Civil Rights movements of the 1960s. By forcing the listener to hear the word "executive" in both ways, so much more meaning is imparted and contemplation demanded.

Liturgical art demands the attention and interpretation of the receiver. "In the Christian community's place of prayer, art evokes and glorifies 'the transcendent mystery of God—the surpassing invisible beauty of truth and love visible in Christ'" (BLS 142). That transcendent mystery demands that artists not be too explicit: "A truly worthy and beautiful artwork can transform the artist and the community for which it is intended. The dialogue with God that an artwork mediates can persuade and invite; however, it does not force its meanings upon individuals or communities" (BLS 151).

In these ways, liturgical art and parables share a common "mode of being" and relationship with those of the faith community who receive, interpret, and ultimately "live" both into being.

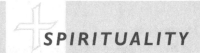

SPIRITUALITY

GOSPEL ACCLAMATION
cf. 2 Cor 8:9

R⁊. Alleluia, alleluia.
Though our Lord Jesus Christ was rich, he
    became poor,
so that by his poverty you might become
    rich.
R⁊. Alleluia, alleluia.

Gospel

Luke 16:1-13; L135C

Jesus said to his disciples,
    "A rich man had a steward
    who was reported to him for
        squandering his property.
He summoned him and said,
    'What is this I hear about you?
Prepare a full account of your
        stewardship,
    because you can no longer be
        my steward.'
The steward said to himself,
    'What shall I do,
    now that my master is taking
        the position of steward away
        from me?
I am not strong enough to dig and I am
        ashamed to beg.
I know what I shall do so that,
    when I am removed from the
        stewardship,
    they may welcome me into their
        homes.'
He called in his master's debtors one
        by one.
To the first he said,
    'How much do you owe my master?'
He replied, 'One hundred measures of
        olive oil.'
He said to him, 'Here is your promis-
        sory note.
Sit down and quickly write one for fifty.'
Then to another the steward said, 'And
        you, how much do you owe?'
He replied, 'One hundred kors of wheat.'

Continued in Appendix A, p. 312,

or Luke 16:10-13, p. 312.

Reflecting on the Gospel

In last Sunday's gospel we met a prodigal son; this week we meet a prodigal steward or business manager. Both squandered property. Whether the steward's wastefulness was because of negligence, incompetence, or malice, we are not told. Where he is efficient, however, is in the speedy formulation of a plan that will ensure his future now that he has been denounced. He thinks quickly and shrewdly. Without the physical strength to become a laborer or the humility to beg, he has to act before the news of his dismissal spreads throughout the village. So he decides to grant favors—debt reductions—and this, the debtors will presume, will be at his master's generous initiative, not his own. They would never imagine, rightly, that the manager would have such authority. The debtors gladly rewrite their promissory notes with the percentage cut offered by the manager, and there is much consequent praise of both the master and his employee. The latter has now feathered his own reputation nest and assured himself of receiving another debt, one of gratitude, which will result in making him welcome in the homes of those who have benefited from what the debtors consider the manager's speedy and efficient carrying out of his employer's generous decision. When he hears of his manager's actions, the master can do nothing more than make the best of the situation. To renege would mean a shameful loss of face and honor, unthinkable in that culture.

So the master wryly praises his manager, not for his business ethics, but for his flair and roguish intelligence in a time of crisis. The "children of this world," those like the manager who are driven by material values and are knowledgeable about the way to save their own unethical skins, show themselves resourceful in social dealings. The barb of the parable is that the "children of light," those enlightened by Jesus and his gospel proclamation, should be even more alert and enterprising, more ready to risk everything because they rely on the mercy and honor of their Master. "What will I do?" is a question for each of us as a disciple and trusty steward of the rich property of God's household, not only of the material resources that are to be shared with those in need, but especially of the mysteries of God (1 Cor 4:1). To some degree, we are all like the manager, a mix of the despicable and the commendable.

Probably none of us will ever feature in the list of the world's top billionaires but, says Jesus, the one who can be trusted with little things can also be trusted with the great and so win a rich inheritance in the kingdom. It is all too easy to be irresponsible with and indifferent to the familiar, everyday tasks, lacking the manager's honest self-knowledge and harboring the illusion that we will be reliable and committed when the big demands come. But in the near future, most of us will not have a stunning success on the stock market, launch a scheme for global economic recovery, or die a martyr's death. More likely, we will contribute to or disregard our parish planned giving; buy or resist purchasing what we don't really need; recycle our garbage or destroy a few more trees. The mundane is rich in opportunities for storing up treasure in heaven. If we are tainted with acquisitiveness, the best thing to do with our money is to give it away to those in need. Although we may not be introduced to them until we meet in the kingdom, our generous initiative will win us friends among the poor who are raised up, the hungry who are filled.

Focusing the Gospel

Key words and phrases: "The person who is trustworthy in very small matters is also trustworthy in great ones; and the person who is dishonest in very small matters is also dishonest in great ones."

To the point: Character counts. We hear this a lot growing up, but what it really means is what Jesus is talking about here. When we are asked to do things, we should not weigh them on a scale of what benefits us and what we can "get away with," but what is correct, as if all of our dealings were made public. In fact, they are public, in the eyes of the Lord.

Jesus tells us that we cannot serve both God and the world. What good is it if we make a show of devotion and prayer, while designing a life of ensured financial comfort? Where is the line between appropriate care for one's well-being and family, and exaggerated need based on secular expectations? Or the line between respect from one's neighbors and awe because of boasted accomplishment? These are age-old questions, and the struggle to serve our true Master, and no one else, is a struggle in which we all participate.

Connecting the Gospel

to the first reading: Amos is giving us a glimpse into the age-old act of cheating. He's speaking of his contemporaries, who are fixing the scales in order to get a little more pay for a little less of their dry goods, but this urge is universal. We'd all love to receive more for less work. And if we can get away with it, why not? Because the Lord knows when we are disingenuous.

to experience: Even more than the Lord knowing our transgressions done in secret, the act of cheating distances us from God. It doesn't just affect our relationship with God; it affects our relationship with ourselves. When we are focused on personal gain so much that we harm others in the process, or cheat them, we are harming ourselves and conditioning ourselves to separate from God and goodness.

Connecting the Responsorial Psalm

to the readings: The psalm calls us to identify with the poor, as in, place our identity there. Over and over in the Bible we are reminded of the special status the Lord of Abraham gives to the poor, and this is reiterated when Jesus places them above everyone else throughout his ministry. This is counterintuitive in any society, but it's a message that is so central to salvation that it will continue to appear, and you will continue to be its steward.

to psalmist preparation: Have you ever been "poor" in some way, and lifted up by the Lord? Have you ever found someone poor, whether in finances, relationships, or dignity, and lifted him or her up? This week, enter into the verse of this psalm from all points of view. "He raises up the lowly from the dust; / from the dunghill he lifts up the poor / to seat them with princes, / with the princes of his own people."

PROMPTS FOR FAITH-SHARING

What does it mean to "trample on the needy"?

Have you ever lied/cheated because you knew no one was watching? How did it play out? Do you regret it or try to forget it?

In what ways are you poor? In what ways can you lift up the poor?

Have you ever reconciled with another person, and felt it affected your faith? Does reconciling with others help you grow in relationship with the Lord?

Model Penitential Act

Presider: In today's gospel Jesus reminds us we cannot serve two masters. For the times we have placed other people or things before God, we ask for forgiveness . . . *[pause]*

Lord Jesus, your words are Spirit and life: Lord, have mercy.

Christ Jesus, you share yourself with us so that we might grow in holiness: Christ, have mercy.

Lord Jesus, you call us by name and invite us to relationship with you: Lord, have mercy.

Homily Points

- When Jesus says, "You cannot serve both God and mammon," we typically define *mammon* as wealth or riches, which certainly makes sense in the context of this story. But *mammon* also means anything that we might rely on, including power and privilege. When Jesus tells us we cannot serve God and mammon, he essentially insists that we cannot serve both God and anything that might prevent us from fully serving God.

- As we strive to serve God, we must intentionally discern what is of God and what is not of God. St. Ignatius of Loyola, a spiritual master on discernment, teaches that this discernment is something we do every day. Ignatius tells us that feelings and desires that bring us joy and happiness or experiences of faith, hope, and love are all of God. On the contrary, when we experience fear, inadequacy, doubt, or sadness, we recognize these feelings are not of God. As we grow in faith and relationship with God, we are better able to discern what is of God—namely, what brings us spiritual consolation—as well as those things that are not of God and bring spiritual desolation.

- Another important practice of discernment is learning how we might use our gifts to best serve God. While our lives and experiences take different forms and paths, all of us are called to respond to God's invitation in our lives. How do we respond? Do we use our time and talents to work for justice and the betterment of others? Do we share our gifts with people who might benefit from them? Do we serve God in our daily decisions? Or are we distracted, placing our trust in things that are fleeting? Today, we pray that we may listen attentively to Jesus's command to serve God.

Model Universal Prayer (Prayer of the Faithful)

Presider: As we strive to use our gifts to make God known, loved, and served, we offer our prayers and petitions, knowing that God hears and answers them.

Response: Lord, hear our prayer.

That church leaders may be faithful stewards not only in matters of wealth but in all their actions and interactions . . .

That world leaders may work to protect the gifts of God's creation through environmental stewardship and care for our common home . . .

That all who are discerning how to best use their gifts for the service of others might listen to God's call in their lives . . .

That all gathered here might treat each other with respect and work to dissolve the cliques and factions present within our church community . . .

Presider: Loving God, hear the prayers of your faithful people. Help us to grow as stewards of the resources with which you bless us so that we might share these gifts generously. We ask this through Christ our Lord. **Amen.**

COLLECT

Let us pray.

Pause for silent prayer

O God, who founded all the commands of
your sacred Law
upon love of you and of our neighbor,
grant that, by keeping your precepts,
we may merit to attain eternal life.
Through our Lord Jesus Christ, your Son,
who lives and reigns with you in the unity
of the Holy Spirit,
God, for ever and ever. **Amen.**

FIRST READING

Amos 8:4-7

Hear this, you who trample upon the
needy
and destroy the poor of the land!
"When will the new moon be over," you
ask,
"that we may sell our grain,
and the sabbath, that we may display
the wheat?
We will diminish the ephah,
add to the shekel,
and fix our scales for cheating!
We will buy the lowly for silver,
and the poor for a pair of sandals;
even the refuse of the wheat we will
sell!"
The LORD has sworn by the pride of Jacob:
Never will I forget a thing they have
done!

RESPONSORIAL PSALM

Ps 113:1-2, 4-6, 7-8

℟. (cf. 1a, 7b) Praise the Lord, who lifts up
the poor.
or
℟. Alleluia.

Praise, you servants of the LORD,
praise the name of the LORD.
Blessed be the name of the LORD
both now and forever.

℟. Praise the Lord, who lifts up the poor.
or
℟. Alleluia.

High above all nations is the LORD;
above the heavens is his glory.
Who is like the LORD, our God, who is
enthroned on high
and looks upon the heavens and the
earth below?

℟. Praise the Lord, who lifts up the poor.
or
℟. Alleluia.

He raises up the lowly from the dust;
    from the dunghill he lifts up the poor
to seat them with princes,
    with the princes of his own people.

R℣. Praise the Lord, who lifts up the poor.
    or
R℣. Alleluia.

SECOND READING
1 Tim 2:1-8

Beloved:
First of all, I ask that supplications,
        prayers,
    petitions, and thanksgivings be offered
        for everyone,
    for kings and for all in authority,
    that we may lead a quiet and tranquil
        life
    in all devotion and dignity.
This is good and pleasing to God our
        savior,
    who wills everyone to be saved
    and to come to knowledge of the truth.
        For there is one God.
        There is also one mediator between God
            and men,
        the man Christ Jesus,
        who gave himself as ransom for all.
This was the testimony at the proper time.
For this I was appointed preacher and
        apostle
    —I am speaking the truth, I am not
        lying—,
    teacher of the Gentiles in faith and
        truth.

It is my wish, then, that in every place the
        men should pray,
    lifting up holy hands, without anger
        or argument.

About Liturgy

Enlarging, Belonging: There is a familiar expression, "When the only tool you have is a hammer, everything looks like a nail." To elaborate, the sentiment here is that if you only know one way to solve a problem or fix something that is broken, eventually that limitation will lead to troubles. Not every situation in life can be solved using the same tool—that is, by the same approach, methodology, words, or actions.

Similarly, there is a corollary in reverse, so to speak. Imagine a test designed to determine which wild animal is the smartest. If that test is "how well can it climb a tree," the monkey is likely to do very well, while the whale or salmon is not.

When it comes to planning and implementing liturgies, these brief examples teach us a few important lessons. First, good liturgists need lots of tools in their tool belt. Liturgists are often found in "middle management"—which is to say they have someone, a priest/pastor, for instance, who supervises them—and sometimes they retain much of the liturgical power or authority, making them "coordinators" of sorts, rather than directors. Most liturgists also have several folks to wrangle and organize, including lectors, servers, musicians, and often a few people who manage those subgroups. It's a tricky position that requires many different approaches to people, contexts, situations, and outcomes. More education, more workshops, more reading, and more relationships can provide additional tools that a successful liturgist can rely on from moment to moment, navigating the sometimes-tricky paths of divine worship.

Second, an ability to assess the gifts and skills that those around us can bring to our liturgies can increase the size of our liturgical circles and not only make the liturgy more representative of our local communities, but give the individuals who make up those communities a sense of belonging and ownership in our worship. A critical skill in this regard is honing the facility to see not only what is specifically being offered, but also a larger sense of the person(s) offering it and what else might be drawn forth. Occasionally, someone will offer himself or herself as a lector, for instance, but not have the skills needed to effectively proclaim the word of God at liturgy. The ability to see the gift offered as gift is essential in our response, as is the skill to see if there is a possibility for growth into that ministry, or to see if there is something else that could be drawn forth to enhance and enlarge a community's worship.

The more tools we have in larger tool belts, and the more we can see those around us as individuals with specific gifts and talents, the better we will be in our liturgical roles and the better the community's worship will be because of it.

About Music

Music of Service: We may already be familiar with "Servant Song" (OCP) by Donna McGargill, or "The Servant Song" by Richard Gillard, found in several hymnals. Consider, too, "Till I Die, Till I Die" in *Lead Me, Guide Me* (GIA) or the *Psallite* refrain "Love the Lord Your God" (Liturgical Press).

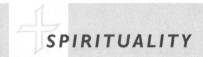

SPIRITUALITY

GOSPEL ACCLAMATION
cf. 2 Cor 8:9

℟. Alleluia, alleluia.
Though our Lord Jesus Christ was rich, he
    became poor,
so that by his poverty you might become rich.
℟. Alleluia, alleluia.

Gospel

Luke 16:19-31; L138C

Jesus said to the Pharisees:
    **"There was a rich man who dressed
        in purple garments and fine linen
    and dined sumptuously each day.
And lying at his door was a poor man
        named Lazarus, covered with
        sores,
who would gladly have eaten his fill
        of the scraps
that fell from the rich man's table.
Dogs even used to come and lick his
        sores.
When the poor man died,
    he was carried away by angels to the
        bosom of Abraham.
The rich man also died and was buried,
    and from the netherworld, where he
        was in torment,
    he raised his eyes and saw Abraham
        far off
    and Lazarus at his side.
And he cried out, 'Father Abraham,
    have pity on me.
Send Lazarus to dip the tip of his fin-
        ger in water and cool my tongue,
for I am suffering torment in these
        flames.'
Abraham replied,
    'My child, remember that you
        received
    what was good during your lifetime
    while Lazarus likewise received what
        was bad;
    but now he is comforted here,
        whereas you are tormented.**

Continued in Appendix A, p. 312.

Reflecting on the Gospel

In today's gospel, Jesus is speaking to the Pharisees who, we learn just before this passage begins, "loved money" (Luke 16:14) and who were ridiculing Jesus over what he had said about idolizing wealth over the worship of God. This Sunday, poverty and wealth, the "haves" and the "have-nots," are given human faces in the parable about a beggar at the gate of a rich man who sits comfort-

ably, securely, and blindly in his splendid dwelling. Likewise, the Lukan beatitude, "Blessed are you who are poor, for the kingdom of God is yours" (6:20), and the woe, "woe to you who are rich, for you have received your consolation" (6:24), become narrative in this parable. The beggar is the only character in any of Jesus's parables who is given a personal name. He is called "Lazarus," meaning "God has helped." The rich man is often referred to as "Dives," a name not used in the gospel text; it is simply the Latin for "rich man." In our society, it is usually the poor who are nameless while the mass media screams at us the names and faces of the rich, along with their often-inconsequential doings. This is an early hint of the gospel paradox that Jesus will proclaim in this parable.

Both Lazarus and the rich man die. Lazarus has some wonderful friends, the angels, who carry him from his dumping place to the loving and intimate company of Abraham, the model of Old Testament hospitality—hospitality he never received from the rich man. The rich man is dismissed abruptly; dead and buried, he ends up in Hades. All of a sudden, stirred by self-interest, he does notice Lazarus, and even knows his name. But even in Hades, the rich man cannot throw off his pride, his total self-centeredness, and his indifference to any suffering except his own. During his life, he prepared his own sorry future, but he refuses to admit responsibility for this. He wants Lazarus to be his slave, his water carrier, and his messenger boy.

We listen to this parable in the assembly as brothers and sisters in the house of living stones, gathered together by the one who has risen from the dead and comes to us in his Word and sacrament. Is our liturgical celebration securely and comfortably "gated" from the "poor" outside? Or does it challenge us to welcome and serve them? Do we ever try to put a human face on those who lie at the gates of our institutions and nations or allow ourselves to be challenged by those who are covered with contemporary sores: the unemployed, people with disabilities, asylum seekers, abused women and children? (The latter are the most numerous "Lazaruses" in our world today.) When "the poor" are just an abstract concept, they continue to be separated by a great chasm from their more fortunate sisters and brothers. The success of human interest stories in our newspapers and on TV bear witness to the impact of faces and names.

We must try to bridge the chasm in whatever way we can: through personal generosity, individual and group advocacy, information that stirs the heart to outreach, ethical business investments, or responsible voting; we are called to respond to the word of God in *this* life. Like the rich man and his five brothers, no signs, no miracles, not even the word of God can break into and convert our hearts if we are determined to lock out the disadvantaged from our lives, because in them our poor brother Jesus still sits begging at our gates.

Focusing the Gospel
Key words and phrases: "They have Moses and the prophets. Let them listen to them."

To the point: This week's gospel continues with variations on a theme of poverty above riches. The story of Lazarus is a simple dichotomy: the rich man has separated himself from love and reaps the result, and the poor man receives the mercy of God upon death. The twist here is that the rich man realizes his mistake and, in an act of selflessness that's too late, asks to warn his family, so they might not come to his fate. But God points out the obvious: "If they will not listen to Moses and the prophets, neither will they be persuaded if someone should rise from the dead."

This may feel unfair. The rich man has repented—why not allow him to warn his brothers? But Jesus reminds us that we have received warnings and road signs for life over and over through the prophets and through his own ministry. We, in this age, have also inherited the witness of the saints. What, then, is our excuse?

Connecting the Gospel
to the second reading: Paul's letter to Timothy contains an interesting line: "Compete well for the faith." Compete? Against what? Against whom? "I charge you before God . . . to keep the commandment without stain or reproach." The competition is between Timothy and himself. Paul is challenging Timothy to remain faithful against all odds. "Lay hold of eternal life, to which you were called when you made the noble confession in the presence of many witnesses."

to experience: The call of Timothy to keep his eyes on the prize is a necessary act of cheerleading, because, as the rich man in the gospel shows us, following the Law and the Prophets isn't always the obvious thing to do. It's easy for Catholics to attend Mass every week, pray before meals, and say we are laying hold to the promise of our baptism. But commonplace, outwards acts of faith are not the benchmark against which to measure our goals of faith. If we want to be competitive, in the realm of salvation, we are called to compete inwardly, with our hearts as well as our bodies.

Connecting the Responsorial Psalm
to the readings: In the psalm today, the Lord "sets captives free" and "raises up those who were bowed down." We see that happen for Lazarus, who is freed from his life of poverty and illness. This continues the theme from last week, placing value and success outside the realm of material comfort.

to psalmist preparation: This week, place yourself in the position of Lazarus, "covered with sores, who would gladly have eaten his fill of the scraps that fell from the rich man's table." Jesus crafts this story with moving language that is vivid and repulsive. He wants us to feel the despondence of Lazarus. Keep this parable in mind when you proclaim, "Blessed is he who keeps faith forever, / secures justice for the oppressed, / gives food to the hungry."

PROMPTS FOR FAITH-SHARING

Do you identify more with Lazarus or the rich man? Why?

Do you think it's fair that God won't let the rich man return to earth to warn his brothers? How do you feel about this?

What do you think is the biggest competition you hold with yourself when it comes to your faith? In what area do you feel you constantly stagnate? Where do you succeed?

Imagine you die today and stand before the gates of heaven and St. Paul asks you, "Did you listen to the gospel? Did you follow Jesus? It's all there, you know. You had all of the materials to be successful." Will you feel satisfied or nervous? Confident or upset?

Model Penitential Act

Presider: There are times in our lives that we fall short of living who we are called to be. Knowing this, we ask for God's forgiveness and healing . . . *[pause]*

Lord Jesus, you raise up the lowly: Lord, have mercy.

Christ Jesus, you teach us how to share: Christ, have mercy.

Lord Jesus, you call us to community and solidarity: Lord, have mercy.

Homily Points

• In an address to the United Nations on September 25, 2020, Pope Francis writes, "We are faced, then, with a choice between two possible paths. One path leads to the consolidation of multilateralism as the expression of a renewed sense of global co-responsibility, a solidarity grounded in justice and the attainment of peace and unity within the human family, which is God's plan for our world. The other path emphasizes self-sufficiency, nationalism, protectionism, individualism and isolation; it excludes the poor, the vulnerable and those dwelling on the peripheries of life. That path would certainly be detrimental to the whole community, causing self-inflicted wounds on everyone. It must not prevail."

• Today's parable of Lazarus and the Rich Man invites us to consider these words of Pope Francis. How do we reconcile the fact that while some people live in extravagance, others are struggling to eat? By including details about the rich man's "purple garments and fine linen," Luke reveals that this person is not just well-off. Rather, as purple dye was expensive and difficult to obtain, this man was the richest of the rich, living a luxurious lifestyle. Throughout the gospels, Jesus does not necessarily condemn people who are wealthy simply for having wealth. Rather, as we have seen in the readings for the past several Sundays, Jesus denounces people who have an excess of resources that they are unwilling to share with others.

• In true Lukan fashion, care for people who are poor or marginalized in some way is the essence of Jesus's mission and ministry. The rich man had the opportunity to be in relationship with Lazarus but chose not to share his time or treasure with him. We also have the opportunity to grow in relationship with people who are hurting and lonely, and sick and hungry. How do we choose to respond?

Model Universal Prayer (Prayer of the Faithful)

Presider: Knowing our need for relationship with God and others, we raise our prayers and petitions, trusting they will be heard and answered.

Response: Lord, hear our prayer.

That the church might always stand on the side of people who are hurting and vulnerable . . .

That civic leaders may work for a fair and just distribution of resources so that all people may flourish . . .

That all who experience hunger might be filled with good things to nourish and sustain them . . .

That our local community might be attentive to the needs of those in our midst, especially those who are hurting . . .

Presider: Loving God, hear the prayers we raise to you. In your great love and mercy hear and answer them that we might continue to build your kingdom and care for all of your creation. We ask this through Christ our Lord. **Amen.**

COLLECT

Let us pray.

Pause for silent prayer

O God, who manifest your almighty power
above all by pardoning and showing
mercy,
bestow, we pray, your grace abundantly
upon us
and make those hastening to attain your
promises
heirs to the treasures of heaven.
Through our Lord Jesus Christ, your Son,
who lives and reigns with you in the unity
of the Holy Spirit,
God, for ever and ever. **Amen.**

FIRST READING

Amos 6:1a, 4-7

Thus says the LORD, the God of hosts:
Woe to the complacent in Zion!
Lying upon beds of ivory,
stretched comfortably on their couches,
they eat lambs taken from the flock,
and calves from the stall!
Improvising to the music of the harp,
like David, they devise their own
accompaniment.
They drink wine from bowls
and anoint themselves with the best oils;
yet they are not made ill by the collapse
of Joseph!
Therefore, now they shall be the first to go
into exile,
and their wanton revelry shall be done
away with.

RESPONSORIAL PSALM

Ps 146:7, 8-9, 9-10

R̸. (1b) Praise the Lord, my soul!
or
R̸. Alleluia.

Blessed is he who keeps faith forever,
secures justice for the oppressed,
gives food to the hungry.
The LORD sets captives free.

R̸. Praise the Lord, my soul!
or
R̸. Alleluia.

The LORD gives sight to the blind.
The LORD raises up those who were
bowed down.
The LORD loves the just.
The LORD protects strangers.

R̸. Praise the Lord, my soul!
or
R̸. Alleluia.

The fatherless and the widow he sustains,
    but the way of the wicked he thwarts.
The Lᴏʀᴅ shall reign forever;
    your God, O Zion, through all
        generations. Alleluia.

R℣. Praise the Lord, my soul!
  or
R℣. Alleluia.

SECOND READING
1 Tim 6:11-16

But you, man of God, pursue righteousness,
    devotion, faith, love, patience, and
        gentleness.
Compete well for the faith.
Lay hold of eternal life, to which you were
    called
    when you made the noble confession in
        the presence of many witnesses.
I charge you before God, who gives life to
    all things,
    and before Christ Jesus,
    who gave testimony under Pontius
        Pilate for the noble confession,
to keep the commandment without stain
    or reproach
until the appearance of our Lord Jesus
    Christ
that the blessed and only ruler
will make manifest at the proper time,
the King of kings and Lord of lords,
who alone has immortality, who dwells
    in unapproachable light,
and whom no human being has seen or
    can see.
To him be honor and eternal power. Amen.

CATECHESIS

About Liturgy

Just Labors, Just Rewards: In recent years, organizations like the American Guild of Organists (AGO) and National Association of Pastoral Musicians (NPM), as well as several dioceses, have had to remove public documents pertaining to just and equitable pay scales for music and liturgy professionals, due to legal challenges. That these no longer exist in many places is of course no reason for parishes, schools, and dioceses not to pay such laborers a just and earned compensation, taking into account their skills, experience, education, and hours worked.

Scripture frequently tells us, "The laborer deserves his keep" (Matt 10:10) and similar sentiments. That may vary based on the cost of living and the factors mentioned above; a professional, in any case, deserves just hours and just compensation—all part of working together to build God's reign on earth.

About Liturgical Documents

Built of Living Stones—*Stewardship of Resources:* While there is much more that could be explored in this document, space precludes us from doing so. The last element we'll investigate is what *Built of Living Stones* tells us about the financial implications of building, renovating, or beautifying a church: "[T]he cost of an item is not the only consideration in planning for construction and renovation. Every faith community, even the financially poorest, is called to use all the powers of human ingenuity at its disposal to provide beautiful, uplifting, and enriching places of worship that also serve basic human needs" (191).

We've all been in a conversation where another person decries the cost of something a parish has done, be it a new building, a renovation, or some artistic element. "Could not that money have been used to support the poor and hungry?" we might have heard. Sometimes, an outsider might not know the true cost of a project or an object, or may not realize that, for instance, the new beautiful cantor stand was made by a parishioner over many months of loving labor.

Still, *Built of Living Stones* sees both sides of this sort of discussion: "Building a beautiful church is itself an act of worship because beauty is a reflection of God and 'a call to transcendence.' All church buildings and their contents should mirror divine beauty, which is not to be confused with lavish display. Whatever the style of architecture adopted, extravagant expenditures on the construction of a church should be avoided in light of the obligation to share the resources of the earth in an equitable manner" (192).

Built of Living Stones goes on to remind us, recalling the Constitution on the Sacred Liturgy's call to the liturgy embodying "noble simplicity" (SC 34), that there can be beauty and elegance in simplicity, humility, and creativity.

The ways in which a church's architecture and its art and environment form the community and impact its worship is myriad and cannot be overstated, even while being perhaps the least-considered element of divine worship. I urge everyone to explore this document as foundational to our ecclesiology and our missionary and evangelical zeal.

About Music

Equity and Integrity: "More Like Jesus" (WN) is a contemporary and earnest prayer of conversion and offering our dreams and desires to that which Jesus wills, loving service and evangelization, reminiscent of today's epistle.

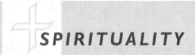

SPIRITUALITY

GOSPEL ACCLAMATION
1 Pet 1:25

℟. Alleluia, alleluia.
The word of the Lord remains forever.
This is the word that has been proclaimed
    to you.
℟. Alleluia, alleluia.

Gospel

Luke 17:5-10; L141C

**The apostles said to the Lord,
    "Increase our faith."
The Lord replied,
    "If you have faith the size of a
        mustard seed,
    you would say to this mulberry
        tree,
    'Be uprooted and planted in the
        sea,' and it would obey you.**

**"Who among you would say to
        your servant
    who has just come in from
        plowing or tending sheep in
        the field,
    'Come here immediately and take
        your place at table'?
Would he not rather say to him,
    'Prepare something for me to eat.
Put on your apron and wait on me
        while I eat and drink.
You may eat and drink when I am
        finished'?
Is he grateful to that servant because
        he did what was commanded?
So should it be with you.
When you have done all you have been
        commanded,
    say, 'We are unprofitable servants;
    we have done what we were obliged
        to do.'"**

Reflecting on the Gospel

This gospel comes immediately after Jesus speaks some hard words to his disciples: warnings about being a stumbling block for others on the journey of discipleship. What is needed is correction, repentance, and forgiveness that is generous and uncalculating, even in aggravating circumstances. It all seems a bit too much for the disciples, so they ask, "Increase our faith." "Quality, not quantity" is a cliché that we often use, seriously or frivolously, with reference to many different situations. In this one, the apostles (not the larger group of disciples) are asking Jesus for "more" faith, but Jesus responds with a qualitative image of faith: faith that is like a tiny mustard seed that the sower God plants in our hearts. Buried deep, it germinates in darkness, but if we fail to tend the seed it will never break through its protective membrane and push into our lives. When disciples do live by faith, even "mustard seed faith," they can continue to do extraordinary things like persisting in the forgiveness about which Jesus has just spoken in the verse preceding the Lectionary text.

To impress us with this truth, Jesus uses another image: an uprooted mulberry tree. These trees can grow up to seventy feet high, and their root system is extraordinarily invasive. Those of us who have coped with root damage to plumbing systems would appreciate the first-century Palestinian law that prohibited the planting of mulberry trees near cisterns. Using exaggeration to make his point, Jesus says that the word of a disciple empowered with mustard seed faith would be able to lift up a mulberry tree and transplant it into the sea! Such is the metaphorical strength that God bestows on the person of faith, even in impossible, ridiculous situations.

Our faith is to be the faith of "slaves," not in the abusive sense, but in the way that Paul refers to himself as "a slave of Christ Jesus, called to be an apostle and set apart for the gospel of God" (Rom 1:1). Since Jesus's audience comprises those who are to be the apostolic leaders of communities, the parable of the Master and Servant (or slave) is directed first to them and then, by further extension, to all Christians. The servant's duties are described as shepherding, plowing, and serving his master at table. The ministry of Christian leaders is to care for their flocks, plow the field of their communities to make them ready for the sowing of God's word, and feed their people at the Lord's table. There is to be no self-adulation or congratulations, no expectation of special rewards or entitlements, no elevation of themselves to domineer over "their flock," as this always belongs to the Master. Such servants are to consider themselves unworthy of any special reward, because what they do is to be expected of them in response to the grace of God that has been so generously given to them. A significant title of the pope is "servant of the servants of God."

A lack of humility can result in leaders who become self-righteous and adopt an attitude of spiritual superiority that hinders their shepherding and serving of the Christian community and that makes it difficult for the "little ones," especially, to approach and trust them. No disciple is exempt from personal sinfulness and immersion in the sin of the world. To judge ourselves as more worthwhile, more deserving than others puts us under the judgment of God. In the center of this parable is the master's table; at the center of our lives, at this Sunday Eucharist, is the table before which, priest and people together, we profess, "Lord, I am not worthy." For our integrity as disciples, our lives must witness what our lips proclaim.

Focusing the Gospel

Key words and phrases: "The apostles said to the Lord, 'Increase our faith.'"

To the point: Here the disciples are building on the lessons we've heard the past few weeks. Knowing that following Jesus takes planning, intention, and lots of hard work, they ask for an increase in their faith. This isn't just the ability to do good, but the desire to do good. It is a request "to want" to follow Christ.

This is a very good place to start. Thomas Merton famously said, "I believe that the desire to please you does in fact please you." Our hearts must be in it. And if they aren't, it's okay to ask for help not only with our work, but in the intentions of our work.

Connecting the Gospel

to the first reading: In Habakkuk we hear the prophet lay out the physical, immediate needs of his people. "Destruction and violence are before me; there is strife, and clamorous discord." By the end of the passage, however, the call is not for physical protection, but for an increase in faith. "The rash one has no integrity; but the just one, because of his faith, shall live." We see this interplay between faith and physical safety, and how the prophet is connecting an increase in faith to increased protection.

to experience: The gospel this week gives us more insight into how fully God, in the person of Jesus, understands humanity. It's not enough to tell us to do good; Jesus leads his disciples in such a way that they realize they can pray for the desire to change their actions and to grow their faith, instead of just changing their actions and being done with it. This level of personal agency gets at the heart of true Christian formation. It's deeper than following Christ in word and deed. It also requires working toward orienting one's heart toward Christ.

Connecting the Responsorial Psalm

to the readings: What does a "hard heart" mean? We tend to use it colloquially to mean someone who is callus and unfeeling toward those who need help. It can also be a heart that is immovable, someone we don't perceive as having compassion. So if we are tasked with making sure our hearts are not hardened, this means we must allow ourselves to be moved not only by the word of God, but by the cries for help from our brothers and sisters on earth.

to psalmist preparation: Twice in this psalm you say to the congregation, "Come." You are not giving them a command, but an invitation. The psalm says "let us," not "let you." You are a part of the community to which you preach. In that vein, invite the congregation to harden not their hearts by making sure that you, yourself, are also open to hearing God's voice.

PROMPTS FOR FAITH-SHARING

Have you ever prayed for an increase in faith? Is it part of your regular prayer practice? Why or why not?

Reflect on Thomas Merton's words, "I believe that the desire to please you does in fact please you." Do you desire to please God?

Is an increase in faith the result of your decision, or the grace of God? Which do you think you rely on more? Which do you think is more important to you at this moment in your life?

What is a "hard heart"? What do you do to ensure that your heart remains soft?

CELEBRATION

Model Penitential Act

Presider: In today's gospel the disciples ask Jesus to increase their faith. For the times we have not been faithful to God's call in our lives, we ask for forgiveness and healing . . . [pause]

Lord Jesus, you are Alpha and Omega: Lord, have mercy.
Christ Jesus, you are peace and justice: Christ, have mercy.
Lord Jesus, you are hope for all who trust in you: Lord, have mercy.

Homily Points

• In the literary masterpiece *The Fellowship of the Ring*, J.R.R. Tolkien writes, "Faithless is he that says farewell when the road darkens." While it is easy to discuss the notion of faith in the abstract, having faith becomes much more challenging when one is in the midst of a difficult situation. This is perhaps why Jesus does not end his discussion of faith with the story of the mustard seed and mulberry tree. The story of the servant reminds us that, no matter how much good we may do, we are all unprofitable or seemingly useless servants if we do not rely on God. Faith is no longer an abstract concept but a lived reality.

• The dialogue between God and the prophet Habakkuk in the first reading reinforces this idea that faith is necessary, but not necessarily easy. The prophet exclaims, "I cry for help but you do not listen!" We continue to cry out today. We cry out in response to racial injustice and senseless killings. We cry out for all who are sick and suffering in body, mind, or spirit. We cry out against the destruction of our common home. We cry out to God.

• We might think about these realities and be tempted to believe that God does not care about us or that God does not or cannot intervene. Instead, we are called to recognize that God's creative works continue now and through the end of time. God continues to create and re-create our world and our lives, inching us ever closer to the day when God's glory will be fully realized at the eschaton. Faith keeps us looking forward to this day and gives us the strength and courage to be co-creators with God, for God's kingdom is both "here" and "not yet."

Model Universal Prayer (Prayer of the Faithful)

Presider: Just as the disciples prayed, "[Lord,] [i]ncrease our faith," we also ask God to hear the prayers we offer today.

Response: Lord, hear our prayer.

That our church may always be grounded in a spirit of humility and stewardship . . .

That our leaders may work for lasting peace that upholds each person's fundamental human dignity . . .

That catechists, teachers, and all who help others grow in faith may remain grounded in their relationship with God . . .

That our faith might increase so to boldly proclaim our knowledge of Christ and concern for others . . .

Presider: Loving God, hear the prayers we raise today. We trust that you will hear them and know that you will answer them according to your will, not ours. We ask this through Christ our Lord. **Amen.**

COLLECT
Let us pray.

Pause for silent prayer

Almighty ever-living God,
who in the abundance of your kindness
surpass the merits and the desires of
    those who entreat you,
pour out your mercy upon us
to pardon what conscience dreads
and to give what prayer does not dare to
    ask.
Through our Lord Jesus Christ, your Son,
who lives and reigns with you in the unity
    of the Holy Spirit,
God, for ever and ever. **Amen.**

FIRST READING
Hab 1:2-3; 2:2-4

How long, O LORD? I cry for help
    but you do not listen!
I cry out to you, "Violence!"
    but you do not intervene.
Why do you let me see ruin;
    why must I look at misery?
Destruction and violence are before me;
    there is strife, and clamorous discord.
Then the LORD answered me and said:
    Write down the vision clearly upon the
        tablets,
    so that one can read it readily.
For the vision still has its time,
    presses on to fulfillment, and will not
        disappoint;
if it delays, wait for it,
    it will surely come, it will not be late.
The rash one has no integrity;
    but the just one, because of his faith,
        shall live.

RESPONSORIAL PSALM

Ps 95:1-2, 6-7, 8-9

R. (8) If today you hear his voice, harden
    not your hearts.

Come, let us sing joyfully to the LORD;
    let us acclaim the Rock of our salvation.
Let us come into his presence with
    thanksgiving;
    let us joyfully sing psalms to him.

R. If today you hear his voice, harden not
    your hearts.

Come, let us bow down in worship;
    let us kneel before the LORD who made us.
For he is our God,
    and we are the people he shepherds, the
        flock he guides.

R. If today you hear his voice, harden not
    your hearts.

Oh, that today you would hear his voice:
    "Harden not your hearts as at Meribah,
    as in the day of Massah in the desert,
where your fathers tempted me;
    they tested me though they had seen
        my works."

R. If today you hear his voice, harden not
    your hearts.

SECOND READING

2 Tim 1:6-8, 13-14

Beloved:
I remind you to stir into flame
    the gift of God that you have through the
        imposition of my hands.
For God did not give us a spirit of
        cowardice
    but rather of power and love and
        self-control.
So do not be ashamed of your testimony
    to our Lord,
    nor of me, a prisoner for his sake;
    but bear your share of hardship for the
        gospel
with the strength that comes from God.

Take as your norm the sound words that
    you heard from me,
    in the faith and love that are in Christ
        Jesus.
Guard this rich trust with the help of the
    Holy Spirit
    that dwells within us.

About Liturgy

Signs on the Journey: On retreats with young people, I frequently lead an exercise that uses road signs to help give language and expression to one's relationship with God. In practice, a couple dozen road signs are projected on a screen, and the participants are invited to pick a sign—or some other sign that didn't make it into our graphic—that describes how they walk with God right now. Then they are invited to pick another sign that describes how they would like that relationship to change.

Often, people pick the "Pedestrian Crossing" sign, the yellow, five-sided one with a pair of people walking, as how they walk with God right now, with a variety of explanations. When I give an example of how I want my personal relationship with God to change, I often pick the "No Passing Zone" sign, because frequently my life is so busy and full of demands and obligations that, even when those things are at the service of my faith, I can sometimes forget that God needs to be a part of all these activities, and not left behind.

Using this approach not only gives the young people vivid imagery and a language they might not otherwise have access to when speaking about their faith lives, but it also plants the seed that faith itself is a journey, to God and with God, of questions, of discipleship, of holiness.

Back when the newest translation of the Missal came out, I used this exercise with a parish youth group gathering to talk about their experience of the Mass: which sign described their experience with Mass at their parish; which sign described how they hoped that experience would change. We spent some time talking about what some of the textual changes in the Missal would be and both how the Mass was about to change, for better or worse, and how they might consider changing their approach to the liturgy, including how they chose to pray at it, both individually and corporately.

Today's psalm invites the singer to keep a soft and open heart to God's voice. We all must be continually open to new information and new insights, both in our own faith journeys and when it comes to how we help communities pray together liturgically. If we are able to maintain such a stance, our expressions of faith can expand and grow in ways beneficial to the whole local community.

Sometimes new insights come to us like a punch in the gut, or like a barrier placed on a comfortable path. These are times that may require contemplation and more study. Sometimes these new insights are more like a bright light or blazing fire and seem to compel us to immediate action and change. And truly, sometimes that change is necessary, in short order. The reading today from Habakkuk seems to speak to all such discernments, at least from the vantage point of seeing violence and destruction before us. Note the last line of the passage though: "The rash one has no integrity; / but the just one, because of his faith, shall live" (Hab 2:4). In all we do, in how we respond to new insights and make them tangible, let us do so with integrity and faith!

About Music

Faith into Action: To pair with today's readings on turning faith into action, consider "Age to Age" by Janet Vogt (OCP) or the *Psallite* refrain "Don't Be Afraid" (Liturgical Press): "Your faith will save you: only believe."

OCTOBER 2, 2022
TWENTY-SEVENTH SUNDAY
IN ORDINARY TIME

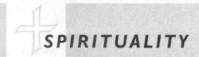

SPIRITUALITY

GOSPEL ACCLAMATION

1 Thess 5:18

R7. Alleluia, alleluia.
In all circumstances, give thanks,
for this is the will of God for you in Christ
    Jesus.
R7. Alleluia, alleluia.

Gospel

Luke 17:11-19; L144C

As Jesus continued his journey to
    Jerusalem,
    he traveled through Samaria and
        Galilee.
As he was entering a village, ten lep-
    ers met him.
They stood at a distance from him
    and raised their voices, saying,
    "Jesus, Master! Have pity on us!"
And when he saw them, he said,
    "Go show yourselves to the
        priests."
As they were going they were
    cleansed.
And one of them, realizing he had been
    healed,
    returned, glorifying God in a loud
        voice;
    and he fell at the feet of Jesus and
        thanked him.
He was a Samaritan.
Jesus said in reply,
    "Ten were cleansed, were they not?
Where are the other nine?
Has none but this foreigner returned to
    give thanks to God?"
Then he said to him, "Stand up and go;
    your faith has saved you."

Reflecting on the Gospel

With Jesus we are traveling along the border between Galilee and Samaria, still on the way to Jerusalem. No one would really take such a circuitous route, but Luke is not interested in geography except as it serves his theology. He wishes to remind us that Jesus is at the territorial boundary of Samaria, whose people were despised by the Jews for their "hybrid" faith. The Samaritans reciprocated with their own expressions of hostility to the Jews, whom they consid-ered religious and social outcasts. In the miracle that follows, Jesus is a marginal person with the marginalized: with the ten men who must keep their distance because of an infectious skin disease, referred to in the Scriptures as "leprosy," but not to be equated with today's leprosy (Hansen's disease). So abhorrent was this condition that description, taboos, and rituals connected with it were detailed in the Book of Leviticus (chapters 13 and 14). The Greek text and some contemporary translations describe them not just as "lepers," but also as *men*. It may seem a subtle point, but it is a humanizing note that respects personal dignity, just as today we prefer to use the phrase "people with disabilities," not "the disabled." What is more significant is the personhood, not the disability.

Keeping their distance, the men do not shout the prescribed warning words, "Unclean! Unclean!" (see Lev 13:45-46) or ask for alms, but as one they call out for Jesus's mercy. They name him as "Master," a title not found in Luke's gospel on the lips of anyone except the disciples. Jesus offers no healing touch, no eyes raised to heaven, no prayer over them; there is no tugging at his robe with diseased fin-gers. All he offers is his word that crosses the gap between them. *Before* they are healed, Jesus challenges the ten lepers to the obedience of faith in his word. He tells them to go and observe the ritual that was usually ob-served *after* the healing of a leper, when a clean bill of health obtained from a Jewish priest would enable a person to reenter society. They obey. "As they were going they were cleansed."

The significance of "seeing" is repeated throughout this gospel. Jesus sees those who need mercy; the lepers see that they are healed; and one of them sees the power and presence of God in his healing by Jesus. Disciples need to learn how to "see" and be moved with the compassion of Jesus and the gratitude of the Samaritan. Thomas Merton, in *The Sign of Jonas*, describes being over-whelmed on a street corner in Louisville in one of his infrequent excursions out-side the monastery of Gethsemane in 1948: "I found that everything stirred me with a deep and mute sense of compassion. Perhaps some of the people we saw going about the streets were hard and tough—but I did not observe it because I seemed to have lost an eye for merely exterior detail and to have discovered, instead, a deep sense of respect and love."

Do we see today's "lepers" in the isolated, the alienated, the "untouchables" in our society and respond with compassion? And what of the "leper" in each one of us: that weakest, least acceptable, and most unattractive aspect of myself that seems to put me at a distance from God, from my sisters and brothers, and from my own self-acceptance? For all this we, too, need to cry out with faith, "Jesus, Master! Have pity on us!"

Focusing the Gospel

Key words and phrases: "And one of them, realizing he had been healed, returned, glorifying God in a loud voice; and he fell at the feet of Jesus and thanked him."

To the point: In the first century, disease was considered an outward sign of inward sin, or the result of familial sin. Lepers were avoided not because others fear being sick, but because they are "unclean" spiritually. Jesus's healing involves lepers a few times in the gospel, and each time it is utterly shocking to those around him.

The way Jesus heals the lepers in this week's gospel is by telling them to go to the priests. Jesus doesn't lay hands upon them or draw them close to him, but instead gives them a direction, and by following Jesus's directions, the lepers are healed. The only person who returns to thank Jesus for healing him is a foreigner.

Connecting the Gospel

to the first reading: The first reading gives us a parallel story to the gospel. Namaan is cleansed of his leprosy in a foreshadowing of baptism by the prophet Elisha. Once healed, Namaan is filled with gratitude and tries to thank him with a gift. Elisha refuses, and Namaan turns his gratitude into faith in Elisha's God.

to experience: Elisha does not want a material gift from Namaan, and when Namaan realizes this, Namaan turns his gratitude into joining Elisha in faith. Instead of a transaction of a material gift, Namaan expresses gratitude by allying himself with the values of the man who saved him.

Both Namaan and the ten lepers of the gospel are healed because they follow the directions of one who seeks to help them. Neither Namaan nor the lepers are healed instantly. Namaan must go to the river Jordan and dunk himself seven times. The lepers must go to the priests. In both of these situations, though the healer could have made it instantaneous, those who are to be healed need to express a desire for healing and act upon it.

Connecting the Responsorial Psalm

to the readings: What do all of the readings—Namaan healed of leprosy by following Elisha, in the first reading; the call to bear suffering in order to join Christ, in the second reading, and the gospel of Jesus healing ten lepers—tell us to remember? That God is a healer and will always carry saving power. "Sing to the Lord a new song, / for he has done wondrous deeds" could be spoken by Namaan, the lepers, and Paul writing to Timothy. We sing a new song, because we ourselves are made new.

to psalmist preparation: Has there been a situation in your life in which you have been renewed, or made new? Perhaps this was a graduation, a medical treatment, a sacrament, or a meaningful exchange within a relationship. What part of you was "saved" in this situation?

PROMPTS FOR FAITH-SHARING

Have you ever forgotten to be thankful for something someone else did for you? What would happen if you reached out now?

Why do you think Jesus told the lepers to go to the priest, instead of healing them on the spot?

Have you ever, like Elisha, refused a gift of gratitude that someone was trying to give you? Why?

What is a situation in which the Lord revealed to you the saving power of his love?

Model Penitential Act

Presider: In today's gospel ten lepers call out to Jesus, "Have pity on us!" Knowing there are places in our own lives in need of healing, we ask for God's forgiveness and peace . . . *[pause]*

Lord Jesus, you hear us when we call to you: Lord, have mercy.

Christ Jesus, you heal us when we are hurting: Christ, have mercy.

Lord Jesus, you are the Son of the living God: Lord, have mercy.

Homily Points

• Today's gospel celebrates gratitude. If we look at the details of the story, however, we notice that there is more to this seemingly simple narrative. We already know Luke's emphasis on upholding and including people who are often oppressed and marginalized, so it should not be too surprising that this story of the cleansing of the ten lepers only appears in Luke's gospel. By the nature of their illness, people with leprosy lived in exile from the rest of society, even standing "at a distance" from Jesus when they called to him. Already there is an image of Jesus living in relationship with people who are often ignored.

• But there is another level of inclusion and exclusion in this story. Jesus comments that only a foreigner—a Samaritan—has returned to give thanks after being healed. We know that in Jesus's time, Jews and Samaritans generally did not have the best relationship with each other, making it almost unheard of that a Samaritan would be the one who is lauded for his gratitude. It is all the more surprising, then, when Jesus tells the healed person, "[Y]our faith has saved you." Jesus does not just say, "You are healed," but instead promises salvation. Jesus lauds the faith of the one who might typically be regarded as faithless. For Luke, faith is intimately connected with salvation, and salvation is promised to even the "outsiders" of the day.

• As Paul proclaims in today's second reading, "[T]he word of God is not chained" to human understanding. God's love transcends the human barriers we create. Let us celebrate this reality. In the words of the psalmist, may we "Sing to the LORD a new song, for he has done marvelous deeds."

Model Universal Prayer (Prayer of the Faithful)

Presider: Just as the lepers knew they could call out to Jesus, we know that when we call out to God our prayers are heard and answered.

Response: Lord, hear our prayer.

That the church might continue to celebrate and uphold the voices of women and all people who are too often ignored or forgotten . . .

That cities and nations may focus on what unifies rather than what divides so to create a safe and welcoming home for all people . . .

That all who are excluded due to sickness or varying abilities might find welcome in others and a home in Christ Jesus . . .

That all gathered here might practice gratitude in our daily lives, thanking God for God's wonderous works . . .

Presider: Loving God, hear the prayers we raise today as we strive to more closely follow you and so grow in relationship with others. Through hospitality and gratitude may we continue to build your kingdom on earth. We ask this through Christ our Lord. **Amen.**

COLLECT

Let us pray.

Pause for silent prayer

May your grace, O Lord, we pray,
at all times go before us and follow after
and make us always determined
to carry out good works.
Through our Lord Jesus Christ, your Son,
who lives and reigns with you in the unity
    of the Holy Spirit,
God, for ever and ever. **Amen.**

FIRST READING

2 Kgs 5:14-17

Naaman went down and plunged into the
    Jordan seven times
    at the word of Elisha, the man of God.
His flesh became again like the flesh of a
    little child,
    and he was clean of his leprosy.

Naaman returned with his whole retinue
    to the man of God.
On his arrival he stood before Elisha and
    said,
    "Now I know that there is no God in all
    the earth,
    except in Israel.
Please accept a gift from your servant."

Elisha replied, "As the Lord lives whom
    I serve, I will not take it";
    and despite Naaman's urging, he still
    refused.
Naaman said: "If you will not accept,
    please let me, your servant, have two
    mule-loads of earth,
    for I will no longer offer holocaust or
    sacrifice
    to any other god except to the LORD."

RESPONSORIAL PSALM
Ps 98:1, 2-3, 3-4

R℣. (cf. 2b) The Lord has revealed to the
  nations his saving power.

Sing to the LORD a new song,
  for he has done wondrous deeds;
his right hand has won victory for him,
  his holy arm.

R℣. The Lord has revealed to the nations
  his saving power.

The LORD has made his salvation known:
  in the sight of the nations he has
    revealed his justice.
He has remembered his kindness and his
  faithfulness
  toward the house of Israel.

R℣. The Lord has revealed to the nations
  his saving power.

All the ends of the earth have seen
  the salvation by our God.
Sing joyfully to the LORD, all you lands:
  break into song; sing praise.

R℣. The Lord has revealed to the nations
  his saving power.

SECOND READING
2 Tim 2:8-13

Beloved:
Remember Jesus Christ, raised from the
  dead, a descendant of David:
  such is my gospel, for which I am
    suffering,
  even to the point of chains, like a
    criminal.
But the word of God is not chained.
Therefore, I bear with everything for the
  sake of those who are chosen,
  so that they too may obtain the
    salvation that is in Christ Jesus,
  together with eternal glory.
This saying is trustworthy:
  If we have died with him
    we shall also live with him;
  if we persevere
    we shall also reign with him.
  But if we deny him
    he will deny us.
  If we are unfaithful
    he remains faithful,
    for he cannot deny himself.

About Liturgy

True Colors: We are all familiar with the expression "true colors," when people let their "real selves" finally show through their usual outward expressions of self and reveal more of their heart and soul to the community. Sometimes people have "true colors" that show them to be much more caring and warmer than their usual hard and cold exterior demonstrates; sometimes those true colors show people to be much more hard, judgmental, and angry than their exterior reveals. (None of this, of course, has anything to do with a person's skin color!)

The liturgy has true colors too, which reveal something of the inner character of the celebration or season. White is used as a color of resurrection and new life; violet for penitence; red for the blood of martyrs or the fire of the Spirit; green in ordinary time symbolizes life and hope.

Yet the symbolism of colors can sometimes be problematic, especially in a global church with cultures and peoples with customs and practices very different from the Roman/European one that shaped our liturgical practices. In China, Korea, and some other Asian countries, white represents death, mourning, and bad luck, and is traditionally worn at funerals—not as a symbol of resurrection, but in the same way that mourners in America wear black at funerals. And in some cases, where white is used to indicate purity (along the lines of the customary white wedding dress), such symbolism can instantly become problematic.

There are two lesser-used liturgical colors too, rose and black. Black especially had been nearly forgotten for many years, but is, in some instances, returning, at least to vestments. As already noted, black symbolizes death and mourning. It may be used at funeral Masses, the feast of All Souls (in a few weeks' time), or the anniversary of a loved one's death. Following Vatican II, white is the preferred color since it reminds us of the resurrection and our baptism.

A brief note, too, about silver and gold: one little-known tidbit awaits in the GIRM, to perhaps surprise us and expand our horizons: "The colors gold or silver may be worn on more solemn occasions in the Dioceses of the United States of America" (346). In practice, gold and silver have become a sort of "super-white," perhaps worn for Christmas, Easter, or a local patronal feast. Now, how it came to be that enough places in the United States were using gold and silver vestments that it became a part of the nation's liturgical law (but not universal law) is a matter for more academic writing and more space on the page than this volume affords.

Today's readings each show us someone revealing their "true colors," or, in the epistle, one pathway of doing so. When we use and talk about liturgical colors and symbolism, let us be mindful of the intended representations, the potential difficult other meanings, and all the options available to more fully celebrate liturgy Sunday by Sunday, feast by feast, season by season.

About Music

Faithful Gratitude: "Imela" is a Nigerian traditional melody, translated by John Bell (GIA), short and simple enough to be quickly learned and prayed by any assembly. The traditional favorite "Now Thank We All Our God," found in many hymnals, would also be at home this weekend, with its sturdy and repetitive stepwise melodies.

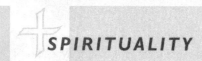

SPIRITUALITY

GOSPEL ACCLAMATION

Heb 4:12

R℣. Alleluia, alleluia.
The word of God is living and effective,
discerning reflections and thoughts of the
    heart.
R℣. Alleluia, alleluia.

Gospel

Luke 18:1-8; L147C

Jesus told his disciples a parable
    about the necessity for them to
        pray always without becom-
        ing weary.
He said, "There was a judge in a
    certain town
who neither feared God nor re-
    spected any human being.
And a widow in that town used to
    come to him and say,
    'Render a just decision for me
        against my adversary.'
For a long time the judge was
    unwilling, but eventually he
    thought,
    'While it is true that I neither fear God
        nor respect any human being,
    because this widow keeps bothering me
    I shall deliver a just decision for her
    lest she finally come and strike me.'"
The Lord said, "Pay attention to what the
    dishonest judge says.
Will not God then secure the rights of his
    chosen ones
who call out to him day and night?
Will he be slow to answer them?
I tell you, he will see to it that justice is
    done for them speedily.
But when the Son of Man comes, will he
    find faith on earth?"

Reflecting on the Gospel

As Jesus travels with his disciples to Jerusalem, today's gospel describes how he tells stories that smash some stereotypes. We meet an insistent widow and an unjust judge whom she gets the better of. The parable is prefaced with Jesus's comment about the need to pray always and not lose heart, but it is a parable that not only illustrates the importance of persistent prayer but also concerns the persistent pursuit of justice. The world of the parable is a difficult world, especially for a woman who is widowed and apparently without any sons or male relatives, since she represents herself before the judge. It is a world of injustice, suspected bribery, contemptuous judiciary, struggling and marginalized women. Yet if we look beyond the cultural context, we can recognize similarities in the way human beings relate to one another today. Huge backlogs of court cases for the poor who cannot afford expert legal help; judges who jockey for positions behind the scenes while cultivating the government that appoints them; charges of bribery among keepers of law and order that are either upheld or dismissed: such are the headlines in our own daily papers.

The judge of the parable is everything he is *not* supposed to be according to Sirach 35:14-19, which is a portrait of a just judge who is especially attentive to the supplications of widows and orphans. The widow of this parable, however, does not dissolve into tears at her unjust treatment. She is no silent figure hovering in the shadows of her disregarded gender and marital status. She comes in from the margins of society loudly demanding justice of the judge who fears neither God nor anyone else. He is apparently shameless in a culture where honor and shame largely defined one's social response and reputation. There is also a lurking suspicion that the widow's opponent may have bribed favor from the judge. In the end, the judge gives in to the woman, admitting that what she asks are her just rights and she "keeps bothering me." The widow reveals the power of weakness, as Jesus himself will soon do in his passion, death, and resurrection.

The judge is described as dishonest and contemptuous in order to put him in sharp contrast with God and to establish the argumentative technique of "from the lesser to the greater." If even a judge like this one gave in to the widow because of self-interest and suspect motives, how much more, suggests Jesus, will our compassionate God do justice for those who persist in their prayer and their faith. The destitute and the despised, those with no voting power, those on the losing side are offered in the person of Jesus the presence and grace of God. Jesus's disciples, therefore, are to persist in prayer and be accountable for justice, advocating for people on the margins and enabling the defenseless to find their own voices, because what is not just is not of God.

To prayer that is persistent and constant must also be added the qualities of trust and patience that support the belief that God answers persevering prayer when and how God wills. That the timeline may be lengthy is suggested by the "sandwiching" of the parable between the preceding narrative about the "last days" (see Luke 17:20-37) and the last verse of today's reading (18:8). Our faith should be "night and day" faith like Anna's, the first widow whom we meet in Luke's gospel (2:37), faith that endures until the coming of the Son of Man at the end of both our own personal life and the Second Coming at the end of human history.

Focusing the Gospel

Key words and phrases: "Will not God then secure the rights of his chosen ones who call out to him day and night?"

To the point: In this gospel, Jesus uses the example of someone who won't give up, who continues to ask, over and over, for what she justly deserves until a disinterested party, the judge, relents and gives in. If this judge, who can't be bothered to do his job, relents in the face of persistence, how much more will our Lord, who desires to help us, be moved? Bearing this in mind, we should not give up when it seems that our prayers aren't being answered.

Connecting the Gospel

to the second reading: Paul tells Timothy the uses of the Scriptures and how necessary they are for salvation. When he's writing, Paul doesn't know that his letters will themselves be added to the canon of Scripture. In this way, Paul is able to speak not only from the authority of an author inspired by the Holy Spirit, but as one of us, hoping to understand more fully how to follow Jesus Christ. In his letters, Paul offers us an opportunity to go through the steps of someone discerning how to live a life inspired by Christ. He tells us directly, "All Scripture is inspired by God and is useful for teaching, for refutation, for correction, and for training in righteousness, so that one who belongs to God may be competent, equipped for every good work."

to experience: Paul reminds Timothy to remain constant in his goals, as Jesus tells us in the gospel. He tells Timothy to "be persistent whether it is convenient or inconvenient; convince, reprimand, encourage through all patience and teaching." Jesus uses the example to refer to prayer without weariness, and Paul expands that to following all of the Scriptures and the person of Jesus Christ.

Connecting the Responsorial Psalm

to the readings: This week's psalm employs a narrative structure. The first stanza is the psalmist telling us, "I lift up my eyes toward the mountains; whence shall help come to me?" The second stanza is directed toward an audience, as the psalmist says, "May he not suffer your foot to slip; / may he slumber not who guards you." The last two stanzas explain who the Lord is to us. "The LORD is your guardian; the LORD is your shade; / he is beside you at your right hand."

to psalmist preparation: The psalm today is one speaking from the point of view of the community. "Our help is from the Lord, who made heaven and earth." It's our help, for all of us. This isn't a personal prayer of the psalmist; it is a prayer on behalf of your entire congregation.

PROMPTS FOR FAITH-SHARING

Have you ever achieved something because of pure, dogged persistence? What was so important that you refused to give up on it?

Have you ever given into someone because of his or her persistence? Did you find this annoying? Did you relent because you were annoyed, or because you realized how important this was for the other person?

What is something you pray about constantly that has yet to be fulfilled or answered? Why do you keep praying?

What do you use Scripture for? What is its main purpose in your life? How do you use it as a tool?

CELEBRATION

Model Penitential Act

Presider: In today's gospel Jesus reminds his disciples of the importance of praying without becoming weary. For the times we have grown weary in prayer or discipleship, we ask for God's healing and peace . . . *[pause]*

 Lord Jesus, you call us to faithfulness: Lord, have mercy.

 Christ Jesus, you invite us to pray always without ceasing: Christ, have mercy.

 Lord Jesus, you will return in glory to judge the living and the dead: Lord, have mercy.

Homily Points

• To do anything without ceasing is difficult. Perhaps this is why there is often an urge to dismiss Jesus's command in today's gospel as utterly impractical and unrealistic. If we are to understand Jesus's words, however, we must begin to understand prayer as a lived reality, something we do every day. Only when we live our lives as a prayer—when we know that everything we do connects us to the God who loves us—can we begin to pray without ceasing. Prayer, then, is less about what we do or say and more about relationship with God.

• Part of growing in relationship with God is growing in transparency with God. We do not tell God our needs and petitions to let God know what is on our hearts. God knows us better than we know ourselves and God knows our needs better than we can possibly express. Instead, we share our needs with God so that we might grow in greater transparency with God. Part of growing in relationship with anyone is practicing authenticity, where one can simply be one's self around another person. When we are able to live authentically and grow as the person we are called to be, we are indeed living lives of prayer.

• Pope Francis also reminds us that to pray without ceasing is to be keenly aware of the needs of our brothers and sisters. Every time we work for justice and peace and unity we articulate our prayer through our lives. When we put someone else's needs before our own or help meet the spiritual or physical needs of someone, we grow in relationship with Christ. There is a popular phrase attributed to Pope Francis: "You pray for the hungry and then you feed them. This is how prayer works." When we live in right relationship with God and others, we can heed Jesus's command and truly pray without ceasing.

Model Universal Prayer (Prayer of the Faithful)

Presider: As Jesus instructs us to pray without ceasing, we confidently bring our prayers to God, both the prayers we speak and those we hold in the silence of our hearts.

Response: Lord, hear our prayer.

That church leaders might witness to lives of prayer through their relationship with God and others . . .

That leaders of cities and nations might listen attentively to the needs of the people they serve so to create spaces for authentic human flourishing . . .

That all who struggle to pray might find peace and consolation in the reality that someone is always holding them in prayer through our personal devotions and communal celebrations . . .

That all gathered here might encourage others to join us in our liturgical prayer, offering a place of hospitality and welcome . . .

Presider: Loving God, listen to the prayers we bring before you today. As we strive to pray without ceasing, give us the endurance and strength to move past periods of dryness in prayer, knowing that we are always in relationship with you. We ask this through Christ our Lord. **Amen.**

May he not suffer your foot to slip;
    may he slumber not who guards you:
indeed he neither slumbers nor sleeps,
    the guardian of Israel.

R̟. Our help is from the Lord, who made
    heaven and earth.

The LORD is your guardian; the LORD is
    your shade;
he is beside you at your right hand.
The sun shall not harm you by day,
    nor the moon by night.

R̟. Our help is from the Lord, who made
    heaven and earth.

The LORD will guard you from all evil;
    he will guard your life.
The LORD will guard your coming and
    your going,
both now and forever.

R̟. Our help is from the Lord, who made
    heaven and earth.

SECOND READING
2 Tim 3:14–4:2

Beloved:
Remain faithful to what you have learned
    and believed,
    because you know from whom you
        learned it,
    and that from infancy you have known
        the sacred Scriptures,
    which are capable of giving you
        wisdom for salvation
    through faith in Christ Jesus.
All Scripture is inspired by God
    and is useful for teaching, for refutation,
        for correction,
    and for training in righteousness,
    so that one who belongs to God may be
        competent,
    equipped for every good work.

I charge you in the presence of God and of
    Christ Jesus,
    who will judge the living and the dead,
    and by his appearing and his kingly
        power:
    proclaim the word;
    be persistent whether it is convenient or
        inconvenient;
    convince, reprimand, encourage through
        all patience and teaching.

About Liturgy

The Holiness of Saying "No": Weariness can set upon any of us, especially as with each passing day it seems we are both called to do more and more, and find it more and more difficult to say "no" to requests of our time and talents. Yet one of the holiest words there is (in addition to the word "and") is "no." God indeed often answers prayers with a "no," or at least a "not right now" or an "I have something even better in mind."

The ability to say "no" is a necessary skill for any pastoral minister. This response should not be seen as withholding God's love and grace from those in need, but rather as preserving your time and energy to devote to obligations already taken on. Stretching yourself too thin can result in fulfilling commitments in a partial, incomplete, or tardy manner, or bringing on stress, anxiety, and burnout to yourself, which is both unhealthy and unhelpful in the long run. Every minister must practice self-care: loving your neighbor as you love yourself means, it seems absurd to point out, loving yourself! Know your limits, take time to rest and rejuvenate, and return a strong servant of the Lord.

Self-control is lauded as a needed Christian virtue, from the book of Proverbs to Paul's second letter to Timothy and beyond. In the present context, the most helpful Bible verse may be this: "Let your 'Yes' mean 'Yes,' and your 'No' mean 'No.' Anything more is from the evil one" (Matt 5:37).

About Liturgical Documents

About Dies Domini—*Keeping Holy the Sabbath:* The last liturgical document we will spend significant time considering in this volume is *Dies Domini* (DD), an apostolic letter promulgated by Pope John Paul II on July 30, 1998. It stands as a modern-day reminder of all the various things Sunday symbolizes and represents to the Christian believer, but five broad ideas come to the fore: creation, resurrection, Eucharist, Sabbath, and time.

Without any real additions to liturgical law per se, this document does indicate a philosophy and approach to keeping the Lord's Day holy, as indicated in the ancient commandment (Exod 20:8). The core of the document, because it is the core of our faith, is the paschal mystery, the "full revelation of the mystery of the world's origin, the climax of the history of salvation and the anticipation of the eschatological fulfilment of the world. What God accomplished in Creation and wrought for his People in the Exodus has found its fullest expression in Christ's Death and Resurrection, though its definitive fulfilment will not come until the Parousia, when Christ returns in glory. In him, the 'spiritual' meaning of the Sabbath is fully realized, as Saint Gregory the Great declares: 'For us, the true Sabbath is the person of our Redeemer, our Lord Jesus Christ'" (DD 18).

Placing the paschal mystery as part of God's continuing creation points the believer to Sunday as the "Eighth Day," the day of new creation by Christ's victory over death. Sunday, then, becomes both a celebration of the day of rest at the end of God's initial creation and a celebration of being made new by God's son: "We move from the 'Sabbath' to the 'first day after the Sabbath,' from the seventh day to the first day: the *dies Domini* becomes the *dies Christi!*" (DD 18).

About Music

Music of Perseverance: "No Turning Back" by Jason Ingram, Matt Maher, and Chris Tomlin (WN) is a strong piece on strength and dedication in discipleship, as is "Take from My Heart" (WLP/GIA) by Karen Schneider Kirner and John T. Kyler.

OCTOBER 16, 2022
TWENTY-NINTH SUNDAY IN ORDINARY TIME

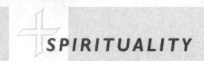

SPIRITUALITY

GOSPEL ACCLAMATION

2 Cor 5:19

R⁄. Alleluia, alleluia.
God was reconciling the world to himself
    in Christ,
and entrusting to us the message of
    salvation.
R⁄. Alleluia, alleluia.

Gospel

Luke 18:9-14; L150C

Jesus addressed this parable
    to those who were convinced of
        their own righteousness
    and despised everyone else.
"Two people went up to the temple
        area to pray;
    one was a Pharisee and the other
        was a tax collector.
The Pharisee took up his posi-
        tion and spoke this prayer to
        himself,
    'O God, I thank you that I am not
        like the rest of humanity—
    greedy, dishonest, adulterous—or
        even like this tax collector.
I fast twice a week, and I pay tithes on
    my whole income.'
But the tax collector stood off at a
    distance
    and would not even raise his eyes to
        heaven
    but beat his breast and prayed,
    'O God, be merciful to me a sinner.'
I tell you, the latter went home justified,
    not the former;
    for whoever exalts himself will be
        humbled,
    and the one who humbles himself will
        be exalted."

Reflecting on the Gospel

In the homily he preached at the funeral Mass of his friend Cardinal Basil Hume, OSB, Bishop John Crowley described the cardinal's reaction when he learned of his terminal cancer two months earlier. Hume told him that at first he was tempted to feel: "If only . . . If only I could start all over again, I would be a much better monk, a much better abbot, a much better bishop. But then I

thought, [these are Hume's own words] then I thought how much better if I can come before God when I die not to say thank you that I was such a good monk, a good abbot, a good bishop, but rather, 'God, be merciful to me a sinner.' For if I come empty-handed then I will be ready to receive God's gift. 'God, be merciful to me, a sinner.'" For that reason, Basil Hume himself chose for his funeral Mass gospel the parable of the Pharisee and the Tax Collector that we hear this Sunday.

Last Sunday's gospel spoke about persistent prayer; this week it is about both presumptuous prayer and humble prayer. The parable praises those who, like Basil Hume, realize the wisdom of coming before God not only with awareness of their sins, but also with abiding trust in God's mercy. Luke notes that Jesus told this parable to those who trusted in their own goodness and regarded others with contempt, but there is no indication in the text that Jesus's audience consisted only of Pharisees.

The setting for the parable is public temple worship, not private devotions. From beginning to end, Jesus draws a sharp contrast between the two men who go there to pray. The Pharisee, a pious lay leader, stood and prayed about himself. His prayer is a litany of self-congratulation, self-advertisement, and self-aggrandizement, a litany of "I . . , I . . , I . . , I . . , I . . ." Exalted in his own eyes, the Pharisee looks down on others, adding the tax collector to his list of undesirable companions or worshippers. In the custom of the time, the Pharisee's prayer would be audible, a litany of moral virtue for which he himself, not God, is responsible. It is announced not only to God (in case God doesn't know) but also to the other worshippers around him. His tithing and fasting are beyond what was required, but his boasting gives the lie to his claim to virtue. If we are regular churchgoers, reasonably generous financial supporters of our parish, it might be rather shocking, but sobering, to stand with the Pharisee, rather than the tax collector, and look into our own hearts. How dependent on God do we acknowledge ourselves to be? How self-satisfied are we about our religious observance? Are we dismissive of or mean-spirited about those who are on the margins of church and society, or outside both? And how do such attitudes and judgments affect our relationship with God and our prayer life?

The love of God can so easily turn into idolatrous self-love. If we regard God's gift as our possession, the gift is canceled out. Prayer is distorted into boasting by comparisons with and judgment of our sisters and brothers. The Pharisee becomes another kind of "tax collector" of exorbitant self-adulation.

Focusing the Gospel

Key words and phrases: "Jesus addressed this parable to those who were convinced of their own righteousness and despised everyone else."

To the point: The opening scene in which this parable is told is almost as charged with meaning as the parable itself. Jesus is addressing it to "those who were convinced of their own righteousness and despised everyone else." Not only are those who think so highly of themselves righteous, but the necessary result of their self-satisfaction is that those around them are despised. The Pharisee in the parable isn't just pleased with himself; his pleasure in his own deeds twists his perception of those in his community so much that he views them as lesser than himself.

Connecting the Gospel

to the first reading: This week's readings build upon the call to persistent prayer of last week. Sirach tells us, "The Lord is a God of justice, who knows no favorites," which would be a disappointing thing for the Pharisee to hear. Sirach gives us specific characteristics of those whom God hears: the orphan, the widow, the one who serves God willingly, and the lowly.

to experience: The four groups that Sirach names are three people who are marginalized by circumstance and one who makes a choice to serve God. It's possible to see that all whom God hears fall into one of these four categories. "Though not unduly partial toward the weak, yet he hears the cry of the oppressed."

Connecting the Responsorial Psalm

to the readings: What does it mean to be poor? Does it mean financial, material, social, or spiritual lacking? Is a poor person someone who struggles to keep up relationships, or who has lost a family member to sickness or an accident? Is it a person with addiction? Is it the Christian who can't bear to go to church anymore because of a negative experience with someone in the church? The truth is we may all be poor in some way, and from that position, when we cry to God, we are heard.

to psalmist preparation: Think of people in your life, and perhaps yourself, who are poor in a variety of ways. Go through a list of each of these people and pray for them, holding them in your heart for a moment. When you share this week's psalm, speak to the poverty that comes in all forms.

PROMPTS FOR FAITH-SHARING

Are you the Pharisee or the tax collector? Which traits do you feel you share with one or the other today?

Do you consider yourself to be righteous? Why or why not? How do you feel about this?

When you "serve the poor," whom do you think of first? How does God call you to continue to "serve the poor"?

Do you consider yourself to be poor? In what way?

Model Penitential Act

Presider: In today's gospel Jesus invites us to humble ourselves so that we might be exalted. For the times we have not practiced humility, we ask for God's forgiveness . . . *[pause]*

> Lord Jesus, you lift up the oppressed and exalt the humble: Lord, have mercy.
> Christ Jesus, you call us to live lives of reconciliation and mercy: Christ, have mercy.
> Lord Jesus, you embody compassion and kindness to all: Lord, have mercy.

Homily Points

• As we have seen the last several weeks, salvation in Christ is not found in the typical norms or structures of this world. Instead, salvation in Christ is the ultimate reversal of traditional models of power. The hungry are fed. The lowly are raised. The dead live. However, Jesus does not fault the Pharisee in today's gospel for his good works. Fasting, tithing, and honesty are all important. With this, we must remember that the gospel does not condemn pious practices. Instead, it invites us to consider our own interior dispositions to prayer.

• While we certainly bring our entire selves to prayer, we do not pray to boost our own self-esteem or tell God about how great we are. Instead, like the tax collector, we come humbly before God, aware of our own shortfalls and inadequacies. We name these realities and place our trust in the God of mercy.

• In our own pride we can sometimes fall into the trap of comparing ourselves to others: *Certainly, I know more than she does. At least I didn't screw up as badly as he did.* It is easy for us to become frustrated when our worldly understandings of success and failure are not necessarily the same as God's. We would do well, then, to consider the words of the author of Sirach: "The Lord is a God of justice, who knows no favorites. Though not unduly partial toward the weak, yet he hears the cry of the oppressed."

Model Universal Prayer (Prayer of the Faithful)

Presider: Inspired by the example of the tax collector in today's gospel, we come humbly before God, raising our prayers and petitions.

Response: Lord, hear our prayer.

That church may always be a home for people seeking forgiveness and right relationship with God and others . . .

That leaders may govern with authority grounded in humility, putting the needs of others before their own . . .

That all who feel overwhelmed by their sinfulness may find comfort and healing in the compassion of Christ . . .

That all gathered here might put aside our judgments of others and see each person as an image of the invisible God . . .

Presider: Loving God, we recognize that we rely on you for all things and trust in your manifold works. Listen to us as we cry out to you. We ask this through Christ our Lord. **Amen.**

COLLECT
Let us pray.

Pause for silent prayer

Almighty ever-living God,
increase our faith, hope and charity,
and make us love what you command,
so that we may merit what you promise.
Through our Lord Jesus Christ, your Son,
who lives and reigns with you in the unity
    of the Holy Spirit,
God, for ever and ever. **Amen.**

FIRST READING
Sir 35:12-14, 16-18

The Lord is a God of justice,
    who knows no favorites.
Though not unduly partial toward the
    weak,
    yet he hears the cry of the oppressed.
The Lord is not deaf to the wail of the
    orphan,
    nor to the widow when she pours out
      her complaint.
The one who serves God willingly is
    heard;
    his petition reaches the heavens.
The prayer of the lowly pierces the clouds;
    it does not rest till it reaches its goal,
nor will it withdraw till the Most High
    responds,
    judges justly and affirms the right,
and the Lord will not delay.

RESPONSORIAL PSALM
Ps 34:2-3, 17-18, 19, 23

℞. (7a) The Lord hears the cry of the poor.

I will bless the Lord at all times;
    his praise shall be ever in my mouth.
Let my soul glory in the Lord;
    the lowly will hear me and be glad.

℞. The Lord hears the cry of the poor.

The Lord confronts the evildoers,
    to destroy remembrance of them from
      the earth.
When the just cry out, the Lord hears
    them,
    and from all their distress he rescues
      them.

℞. The Lord hears the cry of the poor.

The LORD is close to the brokenhearted;
  and those who are crushed in spirit he
  saves.
The LORD redeems the lives of his
  servants;
  no one incurs guilt who takes refuge in
  him.

R̸. The Lord hears the cry of the poor.

SECOND READING
2 Tim 4:6-8, 16-18

Beloved:
I am already being poured out like a
  libation,
  and the time of my departure is at
  hand.
I have competed well; I have finished the
  race;
  I have kept the faith.
From now on the crown of righteousness
  awaits me,
  which the Lord, the just judge,
  will award to me on that day, and not
    only to me,
  but to all who have longed for his
    appearance.

At my first defense no one appeared on
  my behalf,
  but everyone deserted me.
May it not be held against them!
But the Lord stood by me and gave me
  strength,
  so that through me the proclamation
    might be completed
  and all the Gentiles might hear it.
And I was rescued from the lion's mouth.
The Lord will rescue me from every evil
  threat
  and will bring me safe to his heavenly
    kingdom.
To him be glory forever and ever. Amen.

About Liturgy

Being a Fool for Christ: There is a familiar Christian paradox of finding strength in weakness. This is perhaps most manifest today when people "lead from behind," exercising servant leadership by washing feet in multiple ways and leading by example and relationship rather than by power and authority.

We sometimes hear, too, about becoming a "Clown of God," as in the Italian folktale retold famously by Tomie dePaola, or a "Fool for Christ." This can be both the hardest lesson for a disciple to learn and the most difficult to live from day to day, particularly when modern society pulls us in precisely the opposite direction and holds up as good and valuable the drive to achieve status and acquire power, fame, and wealth.

Those of us in leadership roles: let us bring this mode of discipleship to our ministries; let us bring not hierarchy and caste to our structures, but communion, humility, and service, to the point of being seen as a clown and fool perhaps by the world around us. Let us bring about the worship of Christ in the manner in which he lived: loving, sacrificial service to all, especially to the least among us.

About Liturgical Documents

About Dies Domini—*Resurrection and Eucharist:* As *Dies Domini* continues its exploration of the Day of the Lord, it next turns its attention to Sunday as a "Weekly Easter," the day of resurrection and new creation. Last time this space mentioned Sunday as the "Eighth Day" and that facet is expanded now as not just a single day but an image of eternity: "Saint Basil explains that Sunday symbolizes that truly singular day which will follow the present time, the day without end which will know neither evening nor morning, the imperishable age which will never grow old; Sunday is the ceaseless foretelling of life without end which renews the hope of Christians and encourages them on their way" (DD 26).

This day also remembers anamnetically Sunday as the day of the gift of light (via the rising sun), the gift of the Spirit, and the gift of faith itself. In such a way, Sunday stands "as an indispensable element of our Christian identity" (DD 30).

The Eucharist—that is, the gathering of the assembly on Sundays for liturgy, for making the Lord present—is the fundamental way for Christians to keep Sunday holy. The Day of the Lord is also the Day of the Church (DD 35), the gathered people of God. It is a day of unity, of pilgrimage, and hope. At the table of the Word and the table of the Body of Christ, all partake in sacrifice and banquet, and are given mission into the world. "[T]he faithful must realize that, because of the common priesthood received in Baptism, 'they participate in the offering of the Eucharist.' Although there is a distinction of roles, they still 'offer to God the divine victim and themselves with him. Offering the sacrifice and receiving holy communion, they take part actively in the liturgy,' finding in it light and strength to live their baptismal priesthood and the witness of a holy life" (DD 51).

Dies Domini also notes that there are places and situations where the faithful cannot celebrate Eucharist for a variety of reasons. And, while shunning "minimalism and mediocrity at the level of faith" (DD 52), it opens the door to other expressions of faith that help keep the Sabbath holy: Liturgy of the Hours, pilgrimages, and praying the Mass via radio and television (and by extension, the internet, computers, tablets, and smartphones in today's times).

OCTOBER 23, 2022
THIRTIETH SUNDAY
IN ORDINARY TIME

✠ SPIRITUALITY

GOSPEL ACCLAMATION
John 3:16

℟. Alleluia, alleluia.
God so loved the world that he gave his only Son,
so that everyone who believes in him might have
    eternal life.
℟. Alleluia, alleluia.

Gospel   Luke 19:1-10;
L153C

At that time, Jesus came to
    Jericho and intended to
    pass through the town.
Now a man there named
    Zacchaeus,
    who was a chief tax col-
        lector and also a
        wealthy man,
    was seeking to see who
        Jesus was;
    but he could not see
        him because of the
        crowd,
    for he was short in
        stature.
So he ran ahead and climbed
    a sycamore tree in
    order to see Jesus,
    who was about to pass
        that way.
When he reached the place, Jesus looked up
    and said,
    "Zacchaeus, come down quickly,
    for today I must stay at your house."
And he came down quickly and received
    him with joy.
When they all saw this, they began to grum-
    ble, saying,
    "He has gone to stay at the house of a
        sinner."
But Zacchaeus stood there and said to the
    Lord,
    "Behold, half of my possessions, Lord, I
        shall give to the poor,
    and if I have extorted anything from
        anyone
    I shall repay it four times over."
And Jesus said to him,
    "Today salvation has come to this house
    because this man too is a descendant of
        Abraham.
For the Son of Man has come to seek
    and to save what was lost."

Reflecting on the Gospel

Jesus passes through the city of Jericho and into Zacchaeus's life, plucking him from the tree like good fruit ripe for discipleship. He looks up and sees Zacchaeus, and the urgency of his call adds to the vitality of this encounter. Even with the crowd following him, Jesus stops for just one person, up a tree, and calls him by name. He tells Zacchaeus to hurry and come down, because Jesus *must* stay at his house, and do so *today*. This imperative is associated with the urgency of Jesus's mission: for example, with the prediction of his passion (Luke 9:22) and the preparation of the Passover lamb (22:7). "[T]o seek and to save what was lost" is also the demanding and continuing mission of the Son of Man.

Zacchaeus responds to Jesus's call with eager joy and ready hospitality that shine out against the dark background of the crowd's judgmental murmuring. Throughout Luke's gospel and down the ages, the prophecy of Simeon will be fulfilled: Jesus is destined for the falling and rising of many and will be a sign to be opposed (Luke 2:34). The murmurers oppose both Jesus and Zacchaeus; they are not able to see either of them for what they really are. They stereotype Zacchaeus as a sinner and, by association with him, Jesus is also judged as contaminated. When Zacchaeus stops on the way home to publicly profess his financial dealings in front of the crowd, he speaks in the present continuous tense, suggesting that his determination to give to the poor and make restitution to anyone he has defrauded was not going to be a one-shot burst of enthusiasm, but an ongoing conversion and commitment over and above the demands of the Mosaic Law. The fault does not lie in being rich, but in how one had become that way and what is done with one's wealth, as Luke reminds us in the Acts of the Apostles where Barnabas, Lydia, and Dorcas are all acclaimed disciples and people of economic means who generously share their wealth.

Jesus does not respond to Zacchaeus with any probing questions about his dealings; he gives no lengthy sermon or moralizing instruction; Jesus just accepts his seeking and his longing to see him. Are there implications here for the way in which we ritualize and celebrate the sacrament of forgiveness in today's church?

Jesus invites himself to Zacchaeus's house; he is host rather than guest, offering the tax collector the hospitality of salvation and calling him a "descendant of Abraham," worthy of the inheritance of the Abrahamic promises—such is the dignity of the forgiven Zacchaeus. Jesus longs to be welcomed into our homes, our parishes, our communities and to be received there with joy—the expansive Lukan response to the good news. Then, to our surprise, we too will find ourselves hosted into new life and love.

The murmuring crowd is nameless, and we can ask ourselves if we are in its midst: rejecting others because of prejudice and cynical superiority that "knows" what certain people are like and that they cannot change. Yet Jesus keeps company with "the lost," and the vividness of the account gives Zacchaeus a very human face. Although a meal at Zacchaeus's house is not part of the narrative, it is only a threshold away. Because Jesus so often encounters despised people and offers them hospitality, questions are surely raised for the church: "Who should we welcome into the reign of God?" and "With whom should we eat?" The answer to the first is universal; the answer to the second is an ongoing quest that dares to question.

Focusing the Gospel

Key words and phrases: "Behold, half of my possessions, Lord, I shall give to the poor, and if I have extorted anything from anyone I shall repay it four times over."

To the point: Zacchaeus is "seeking to see who Jesus was." He's curious. He's probably heard about Jesus, and being a man who is successful in his own endeavors, he likely wants to get a better look at the man who's causing such a fuss in Jericho. There's a determination here that's unique to Zacchaeus. Instead of crying out for Jesus, or muscling his way through the crowd, he climbs up a tree to see what's going on. It's remarkably innovative, and yet delightfully mundane. (And probably a little undignified.) But Jesus sees this burning curiosity and chooses to honor Zacchaeus by entering his home.

This bothers everyone who knows Zacchaeus, because Zacchaeus is a religious sellout, working as tax collector for the Roman occupiers. He's benefited from the system and is probably resented by a lot of his community. Jesus chooses this person. Why on earth would Jesus choose the person who has hurt members of the community? Because Jesus knows the path to conversion is engagement. He honors Zacchaeus, enters his home, and Zacchaeus has a total conversion experience. Jesus chooses to engage, and enters the space of the sinner, in order to invite him to seek better things.

Connecting the Gospel

to the first reading: The passage from Wisdom offers us perspective we rarely get: the awesomeness of the Lord is overwhelming, and yet, though we are tiny grains in the grander scope of history, God loves us, because he made us. "For you love all things that are / and loathe nothing that you have made; / for what you hated, you would not have fashioned." Even Zacchaeus, sinful and selfish by choice, is loved by the Lord.

to experience: "Therefore you rebuke offenders little by little, / warn them and remind them of the sins they are committing." Think about places in your life where you tend to fall into sin. Maybe it's a habit; maybe it's a sinful reaction born from an understandable desire for self-preservation. Maybe it's a place in your life where you're overwhelmed and can't be bothered to put effort into self-correction. How does God rebuke you, little by little? What small signs do you see that remind you to turn back toward the Lord? "But you have mercy on all, because you can do all things; / and you overlook people's sins that they may repent."

Connecting the Responsorial Psalm

to the readings: In today's psalm we have what can be considered the "thesis statement" of all of the psalms: "The LORD is gracious and merciful, / slow to anger and of great kindness. / The LORD is good to all / and compassionate toward all his works." This is, perhaps, the place we all start when we begin an encounter with the Lord, or when he begins to encounter us. What is our response to this? To praise his name forever, as our king and our God.

to psalmist preparation: The psalm begins in the first-person, naming the actions of the psalmist, and then moves to a description of the Lord, inviting all "his works" to give thanks. Move through this narrative yourself. Bring to mind how you, in your daily life, praise the Lord. Now think of all the ways the Lord has blessed you and lifted you up. Our relationship with God is a conversation in words and deeds.

PROMPTS FOR FAITH-SHARING

Have you ever desired to see something so much that you've gone to ridiculous lengths to get there? Perhaps a concert or show? How does this help you relate to Zacchaeus climbing a tree to see Jesus?

Think of a known sinner in the world who blatantly disregards the gospel. What would you do if Jesus told you he was going to that person's home to share a meal? Would you be jealous? Angry? Confused?

Have you ever sought out the company of someone who has wronged you, seeking reconciliation? Would you ever consider, instead of seeking an apology, asking to go over to the person's home for a meal?

"Before the LORD the whole universe is as a grain from a balance / or a drop of morning dew come down upon the earth." How does this make you feel? Is it comforting or discouraging?

CELEBRATION

Model Penitential Act

Presider: In today's gospel Zacchaeus turns to Jesus and acknowledges his sins. Let us do the same, asking for God's pardon and peace . . . *[pause]*

Lord Jesus, you invite us to follow you: Lord, have mercy.
Christ Jesus, you call sinners to yourself: Christ, have mercy.
Lord Jesus, you are the Son of God: Lord, have mercy.

Homily Points

• In today's gospel we often look at Zacchaeus as the sinner who turned to Jesus that he might be saved. If we focus only on his sinfulness, however, we miss an important part of the story. When Zacchaeus climbed the tree, he put himself in a position where he was readily available to Jesus. He sought out the Lord and did what was necessary to make himself present to God. How do we change our hearts and our lives so that we might be more present to God calling us?

• At the end of the gospel when Jesus proclaims, "[T]he Son of Man has come to seek and to save what was lost," we might also immediately think of sinfulness. To be lost, however, simply means to be in the wrong place. Zacchaeus was physically in the wrong place, so he did what was necessary to move toward Jesus, but his promise to care for the poor and repay what he owed shows his conversion of heart. Zacchaeus, once lost, now finds himself in the right place—in relationship with Jesus.

• This relationship with God is not something new. In the reading from the book of Wisdom we hear that God loves all things God has made, making God's relationship with God's people intimate. It is important to remember that just as God chooses God's people in Hebrew Scripture and Jesus chooses Zacchaeus, God also chooses each of us. The "LORD and lover of souls" calls us by name. How do we, like Zacchaeus, avail ourselves to this relationship?

Model Universal Prayer (Prayer of the Faithful)

Presider: Let us bring our prayers to the God of love who constantly seeks us and desires relationship with us.

Response: Lord, hear our prayer.

That the church might make itself available to all people, always seeking to help restore relationship with Christ . . .

That financial leaders might have the zeal to treat all people with fairness, justice, and compassion . . .

That all who are yearning for relationship with God might know that they are already beloved and chosen in God . . .

That our community might always strive to turn away from grumbling and gossip . . .

Presider: Loving God, you call us to yourselves. Hear the prayers we bring, for we know we are in relationship with you. We ask this through Christ our Lord. **Amen.**

COLLECT
Let us pray.

Pause for silent prayer

Almighty and merciful God,
by whose gift your faithful offer you
right and praiseworthy service,
grant, we pray,
that we may hasten without stumbling
to receive the things you have promised.
Through our Lord Jesus Christ, your Son,
who lives and reigns with you in the unity
    of the Holy Spirit,
God, for ever and ever. **Amen.**

FIRST READING
Wis 11:22–12:2

Before the LORD the whole universe is as a
        grain from a balance
    or a drop of morning dew come down
        upon the earth.
But you have mercy on all, because you
        can do all things;
    and you overlook people's sins that they
        may repent.
For you love all things that are
    and loathe nothing that you have made;
    for what you hated, you would not have
        fashioned.
And how could a thing remain, unless you
        willed it;
    or be preserved, had it not been called
        forth by you?
But you spare all things, because they are
        yours,
    O LORD and lover of souls,
    for your imperishable spirit is in all
        things!
Therefore you rebuke offenders little by
        little,
    warn them and remind them of the sins
        they are committing,
    that they may abandon their wickedness
        and believe in you, O LORD!

RESPONSORIAL PSALM
Ps 145:1-2, 8-9, 10-11, 13, 14

℟. (cf. 1) I will praise your name forever,
        my king and my God.

I will extol you, O my God and King,
    and I will bless your name forever and
        ever.
Every day will I bless you,
    and I will praise your name forever and
        ever.

℟. I will praise your name forever, my
        king and my God.

The LORD is gracious and merciful,
  slow to anger and of great kindness.
The LORD is good to all
  and compassionate toward all his
    works.

R̸. I will praise your name forever, my
    king and my God.

Let all your works give you thanks, O
    LORD,
  and let your faithful ones bless you.
Let them discourse of the glory of your
    kingdom
  and speak of your might.

R̸. I will praise your name forever, my
    king and my God.

The LORD is faithful in all his words
  and holy in all his works.
The LORD lifts up all who are falling
  and raises up all who are bowed down.

R̸. I will praise your name forever, my
    king and my God.

SECOND READING
2 Thess 1:11—2:2

Brothers and sisters:
We always pray for you,
  that our God may make you worthy of
    his calling
  and powerfully bring to fulfillment
    every good purpose
  and every effort of faith,
  that the name of our Lord Jesus may be
    glorified in you,
  and you in him,
  in accord with the grace of our God and
    Lord Jesus Christ.

We ask you, brothers and sisters,
  with regard to the coming of our Lord
    Jesus Christ
  and our assembling with him,
  not to be shaken out of your minds
    suddenly, or to be alarmed
  either by a "spirit," or by an oral
    statement,
  or by a letter allegedly from us
  to the effect that the day of the Lord is
    at hand.

About Liturgy

The "How" of Sharing Truths: A sentiment often attributed to Maya Angelou is, apparently, rooted in the Church of Jesus Christ of Latter-day Saints (LDS). Richard L. Evans was a prominent figure in the LDS and in 1971 published a collection titled *Richard Evans' Quote Book.* In this book, the following statement was ascribed to Carl W. Buehner, a high-level official in the Church of Jesus Christ of Latter-day Saints: "They may forget what you said—but they will never forget how you made them feel."

The sentiment, of course, doesn't mean that harsh truths ought never be spoken, nor that we must always place the feelings of others above what needs to be shared. There are instances where abrupt and immediate truth must reign above all. Usually, though, we have opportunity to measure how we will share truth, so it may be received well and be effective in those to whom we speak. In these instances, the "how" it is we share truth must be resonant, consistent with the truth being shared. Catholic morality would tell us something similar, that the ends do not justify the means (see *Catechism* 1753, 1759, and surrounding).

There are times when our preaching and music selection is immediately impacted by current events on a global, national, or local level. Particularly in the homily, you may feel compelled, rightly so, to make strong statements on a given situation—to allow the "how" of the truth to match its substance. At the same time, you must be aware of who is in the pews that particular Sunday: sinners, victims, allies, bystanders, and more. Frequently, any one individual is one or two of those, or all at the same time. Each person will need to hear the same truth, the capital-T Truth, which is God and divine wholeness and holiness. Each will hear the same words—your words of preaching, or the words of selected hymnody—incomplete and perhaps even elusive, in quite different ways. Further, each might have difficulty hearing the words as if from the vantage point of other people, with their very different background and context.

Our faith's social teaching instructs us to show a preferential option for the poor and vulnerable. Who are these, in our midst, in this moment, in this time? How can we best, by the words we choose, show them Christ's love and solidarity, Christ's admonishment and outstretched arms, Christ's love and unity?

About Music

Saints and Sinners: When phrases like "What would Jesus do (WWJD)?" or "Love like Christ loved" are inserted into conversation, the intended meaning is usually along the lines of "Stop judging, that you may not be judged" (Matt 7:1) or that one should love in a self-giving, sacrificial way. Both of these attributes are embodied in today's gospel, in which Jesus does not shun a sinner who is despised by the community, but rather invites himself over for dinner at the sinner's home. While the people grumble, Zacchaeus emerges from that encounter a converted soul, won for God by Christ.

While we must always stand with and support those harmed by sinful people, we must also hope for, if not work for, the repentance and conversion of the sinners. If such are exiled from community, they may struggle to learn, grow, express sorrow and regret, and ultimately may never fully—or even partially—rejoin the Christian community. Sinners and those they have wronged, depending on context, will likely find difficulty remaining in relationship; it may even not be advisable in many circumstances. Saints and sinners, broadly speaking, must remain in conversation, and even in communion with one another.

Pieces that speak to this well include "Table of Plenty" by Dan Schutte (OCP) and "Will the Circle Be Unbroken?" by Tony Alonso (GIA).

OCTOBER 30, 2022
THIRTY-FIRST SUNDAY
IN ORDINARY TIME

GOSPEL ACCLAMATION
Matt 11:28

℟. Alleluia, alleluia.
Come to me, all you who labor and are burdened,
and I will give you rest, says the Lord.
℟. Alleluia, alleluia.

Gospel

Matt 5:1-12a; L667

When Jesus saw the crowds, he
went up the mountain,
and after he had sat down, his
disciples came to him.
He began to teach them, saying:

"Blessed are the poor in spirit,
for theirs is the Kingdom of
heaven.
Blessed are they who
mourn,
for they will be
comforted.
Blessed are the
meek,
for they will in-
herit the land.
Blessed are they
who hunger
and thirst for
righteousness,
for they will be satisfied.
Blessed are the merciful,
for they will be shown mercy.
Blessed are the clean of heart,
for they will see God.
Blessed are the peacemakers,
for they will be called children of
God.
Blessed are they who are persecuted
for the sake of righteousness,
for theirs is the Kingdom of
heaven.
Blessed are you when they insult you
and persecute you
and utter every kind of evil against
you falsely because of me.
Rejoice and be glad,
for your reward will be great in
heaven."

See Appendix A., p. 313, for the other readings.

Reflecting on the Gospel

The reading from the book of Revelation calls the saints "servants of our God" (7:3) who have come from all the peoples of the earth. Like every believer, they were also baptized in Christ and they kept their robes white as a sign of their commitment to their baptismal promises. They were servants of God because they shared in God's plan for the salvation of the world and their presence to everyone was a testament of their identity as "children of God" (1 John 3:1) who were obedient only to the will and plan of God. They were the ones who, by touching our lives in remarkable ways, are judged to be people of prayer who lived their lives according to the fruits of the Holy Spirit and at the same time shared the seed of these fruits with everyone (Gal 5:22-23). They heard Jesus's Sermon on the Mount and embraced it as a rule of life (Matt 5:1-12). Conforming one's life according to the Sermon on the Mount that we hear in the gospel reading is not just for the purpose of attaining the promise of eternal life; more so, it is about making the moral choice to live every day in such a manner that our lifestyle leaves a positive impression on others and draws them closer to God.

Jesus's Sermon on the Mount is a way of life for the saints who have chosen to be "poor in spirit." As children of God, they are untroubled by the worries of life and, to this effect, allow their tranquil presence to be felt by those they encounter. The saints aspire to deal justly in their actions, doing what is right and upright before God and humankind. They eschew good conscience, uprightness, and integrity in their relationship and interaction with others. Their presence in our lives and in society help us see beyond our differences, conflicts, and divisions and work toward unity, harmony, and peace. As apostles of peace, the saints will diffuse any volatile situation and they will never speak in a language that will demean and degrade any other child of God. When slandered and vilified for their manner of life, they will neither respond with confrontation nor speak back to their detractors. They are the first to deescalate volatile situations with their presence and words, showing mercy and working toward reconciliation. In the words of Pope Francis in *Fratelli Tutti*, the saints only speak "words of comfort, strength, consolation and encouragement and not words that demean, sadden, anger or show scorn." As the children of God who have committed themselves to the teachings of Jesus and the Christian life, they are entreated to rejoice because they'll inherit eternal life.

Our liturgical celebration today honors the saints for their forbearing life of holiness and faith in Christ by inviting us to imitate their Christian life. They have experienced God's promise of eternal reward as they join the company of angels in perpetual worship of God (Rev 7:9-12). Their life of holiness before God and humanity has earned them our devotion. On their part, they were simply living the values of their familial relationship with God on account of their baptism in Christ. Like us, they were members of a family, community, and nation who lived a life of holiness and Christian charity according to the teachings of Jesus Christ. This is the same kind of life that each one of us is called to live.

Focusing the Gospel

Key words and phrases: "Rejoice and be glad, for your reward will be great in heaven."

To the point: This is the summation of Jesus's ministry. All of the parables and acts of healing, all of the stories and moments of compassion, all leading up to the sacrifice at Calvary, are contained in the Beatitudes.

"Beatitude" comes from the Latin word for happiness. The Beatitudes are, then, a recipe for happiness. And what do we achieve if we live a life of beatific happiness? Sainthood, in which we join the communion of saints to look upon the beatific vision, the face of God. That is true happiness. The gospel today is Jesus giving us the road map, the directions, for how to lead a life that is not only fulfilling and joyful while we are on earth, but conditions us for heaven, to join those whom we celebrate today.

Model Rite for the Blessing and Sprinkling of Water
Presider: Today's celebration of All Saints reminds us that you call each of us to holiness. May this water remind us of our own baptismal vocation . . . *[pause]*
[continue with The Roman Missal, *Appendix II]*

Model Universal Prayer (Prayer of the Faithful)
Presider: Through the intercession of the saints and all holy men and women who have gone before us, we offer our prayers and petitions.

Response: Lord, hear our prayer.

That the church might find strength in the witness of the men and women who have lived for Christ throughout the ages . . .

That leaders might embody the Beatitudes, bringing about the reversal of strength and power that comes from God . . .

That all who feel isolated from friends, family, and community might find comfort through the outreach of others and the peace of Christ . . .

That all gathered here might respond to our universal call to holiness, following the examples of the saints who have gone before us . . .

Presider: Loving God, you call us to grow in relationship with others and with you. Help us as we strive to embody holiness in our lives and hear the prayers we bring to you today. We ask this through Christ our Lord. **Amen.**

About Liturgy
Hymn Tunes and Hymn Texts: "For All the Saints" is a hymn one will likely hear in many churches today. The usual tune for these words was composed by Ralph Vaughn Williams, who gave it the name "SINE NOMINE"—literally, "Without Name." Many of your favorite hymns likely have tune names, which are usually presented in all caps. (So you understand, I and they are not screaming their names at you!) "God of Day and God of Darkness" uses the tune BEACH SPRING; "Love Divine, All Loves Excelling" uses HYFRYDOL; "All Creatures of Our God and King" uses "LASST UNS ERFREUEN." You probably know other words to each of these tunes: "As a Fire Is Meant for Burning" or "Alleluia, Sing to Jesus" or "Jesus Is Risen." Further, you could sing some of these words to different tunes: try "Love Divine, All Loves Excelling" to the "Ode to Joy" tune sometime! Hymn texts and tunes are usually cataloged with numbers, like 8787, which serve to inform you how many syllables there are in each line. All this intentional utility of hymn tunes and hymn texts, this interchangeability, is meant to help assemblies learn and sing prayers quickly and strongly. Take advantage of that!

COLLECT
Let us pray.

Pause for silent prayer

Almighty ever-living God,
by whose gift we venerate in one celebration
the merits of all the Saints,
bestow on us, we pray,
through the prayers of so many intercessors,
an abundance of the reconciliation with you
for which we earnestly long.
Through our Lord Jesus Christ, your Son,
who lives and reigns with you in the unity of
    the Holy Spirit,
God, for ever and ever. **Amen.**

FOR REFLECTION

• As we celebrate All Saints, which saints do you most resonate with? Is there something inspiring about their stories? How might you be called to share in the witness of the saints?

• Is there a particular image or visual representation of a saint or saints that has particularly inspired you?

Homily Points

• It is easy to hear the Beatitudes and picture an idyllic world that we hope to someday experience. While we know that what Jesus describes will be true in the kingdom of heaven, his words also speak to a lived reality in the moment. There are people who are poor, who mourn, who are meek, who hunger, who are merciful and make peace in our world today. With this, Jesus's words are both an affirmation and a challenge.

• As we celebrate All Saints we have a similar affirmation and challenge. Today's celebration honors and affirms those who have built up the kingdom of God here on earth. But it does not end there. Inspired by these examples, we are each challenged and called to continue this witness, this way of living our own lives. Do we dare accept the challenge?

GOSPEL ACCLAMATION
See John 6:40

This is the will of my Father, says the Lord,
that everyone who sees the Son and believes in
      him
may have eternal life.

Gospel   John 6:37-40; L668

Jesus said to the crowds:
"Everything that the Father gives me
      will come to me,
   and I will not reject anyone who
         comes to me,
   because I came down from heaven
         not to do my own will
   but the will of the one who sent me.
And this is the will of the one who sent
      me,
   that I should not lose anything of
         what he gave me,
   but that I should raise it on the last
      day.
For this is the will of my Father,
   that everyone who sees the Son and
         believes in him
   may have eternal life,
   and I shall raise him on the last day."

See Appendix A., p. 314, for the other readings.

Additional reading choices are in the Lectionary
for Mass *(L668) or those given in the Masses for
the Dead (L1011–1016).*

246

Reflecting on the Gospel

To celebrate the feast of All Souls, my parish erects an altar of the dead at the corner of the sanctuary and parishioners place pictures of deceased relatives on the altar. One of the pictures is of a woman whose funeral I celebrated. I remembered that her family was overwhelmed with sorrow and a deep sense of loss because she was the family matriarch—she held the family together and she exuded love with her home cooking and presence at family get-togethers and celebrations. Upon seeing her picture, I was filled with happy remembrance that those we remember at the liturgy of All Souls had touched our lives remarkably with their leadership and love.

Our remembrance of our deceased relatives on the feast of All Souls comes from a place of conviction and Christian belief that they have joined the company of the holy ones in the presence of God. More so, we believe that their difference-making presence in our lives and that of others through their virtuous Christian life was based on their faith in Christ through their baptism. Christian baptism is an initiation into the life of Christ (Rom 6:3). Being baptized into Christ means also to identify with Christ's life, death, and resurrection because baptism in Christ makes the believer one with Christ: "For all of you who were baptized into Christ have clothed yourselves with Christ" (Gal 3:27). The benefits of this relationship between Christ and the believer reaches its fullness in the believer's experience of resurrection from the dead and the newness of life (Rom 6:4).

We believe that Jesus fulfills God's will by uniting believers to himself through baptism and offering every believer an opportunity to enjoy the benefits of the new life that God promises to humanity. To this effect, Jesus Christ declares in the gospel reading that no one who comes to him through baptismal initiation will experience rejection, but rather unity and concord. When believers conform their lives according to the demands of their baptismal commitment in Christ by love of God and neighbor, then they will have eternal life as Christ promises. Those who are initiated through baptism in the "name of Christ Jesus" live like Christ, whose identity they have embraced. Christ is alive in the world through them, as they represent in words and deeds the presence of Christ by touching our lives in the manner that Christ himself would have done. By modeling their lives according to Christ's, they enjoyed the benefit of experiencing death just as Christ did, and they have risen to eternal life by experiencing the resurrection from the dead just as Christ experienced (Rom 6:5).

When one of my parishioners placed the picture of his mother on our parish altar for the dead, he exclaimed that his mother was God's gift to the family and to all who encountered her. This was his conviction because his mother lived her life according to her baptismal commitment with the full knowledge that Christ was present through her to her family and to all those who seek reassurance (Gal 2:20). On this feast of All Souls, he knows that she is in the presence of God, praying for the family that continues to feel a close bond with her. Let us turn our memorial for the faithful departed into an occasion for us to renew our baptismal commitment to God through Christ and be present to one another.

Focusing the Gospel

Key words and phrases: "For this is the will of my Father, that everyone who sees the Son and believes in him may have eternal life, and I shall raise him on the last day."

To the point: Here we have two directions: to see the Son and to believe in him. That's it! Our lives—waking up, caring for our families, going to work, giving charity in word and deed—are the medium through which this is achieved. Do we love others? Put the Lord first in our daily lives and goals? Do we set our hearts on Christ and seek the intercession of his mother? Do we "see" the Son in everyone we meet? Do we believe in Christ and follow him? Everyone is invited to do this. Today, we celebrate all of those who have gone before us, knowing that we are all called to fulfill the task at hand.

Model Penitential Act

Presider: As we commemorate those who have died, we recognize and name the times in our lives where we have failed to respond to God's invitation to love and ask for healing and forgiveness . . . *[pause]*

 Lord Jesus, you are merciful and forgiving: Lord, have mercy.
 Christ Jesus, you break the bonds of sin and death: Christ, have mercy.
 Lord Jesus, you invite us to the heavenly banquet: Lord, have mercy.

Model Universal Prayer (Prayer of the Faithful)

Presider: Together we raise our prayer with the faithful departed, our brothers and sisters who have fallen asleep in the peace of Christ in hope of the resurrection.

Response: Lord, hear our prayer.

That the church might be a place of safety for people who are grieving . . .

That local, national, and world leaders might enact legislation and just practices that protect the sanctity of life from conception until natural death . . .

That all who experience any form of loss might find comfort and peace in this community of believers . . .

That all who have died may rest in the peace of Christ and know the glory of the resurrection . . .

Presider: Loving God, hear the prayers we raise today and answer them according to your will, for we know that life always triumphs over death. **Amen.**

About Liturgy

Resurrection Choirs: Does your church have a resurrection choir? By this, I mean a group of singers dedicated to providing music ministry at your community's funerals and memorial Masses. Frequently this would be a group of older parishioners who have availability during those midweek daytime hours when such liturgies are usually held. Consider forming a list of community members who would like an opportunity to minister to their families and friends in this way during an hour of need. Such a choir need not be especially accomplished; strong singing of congregational melodies is sufficient for most funerals. In these circumstances, music ministry by a choir, as opposed to an individual cantor, can communicate to the grieving just how much support and solidarity their faith community has to offer. Keeping repertoire consistent and limited for a resurrection choir will be key to its success in ministry. Consider preparing binders of music or acquiring from publishers small hymnals prepared specifically for funerals and memorial Masses. This choir could then, too, sing at an annual Mass of Remembrance (mentioned last year in this space) on this date, extending their ministerial reach and relationship with the community at prayer.

COLLECT (from the first Mass)
Let us pray.

Pause for silent prayer

Listen kindly to our prayers, O Lord,
and, as our faith in your Son,
raised from the dead, is deepened,
so may our hope of resurrection for your
  departed servants
also find new strength.
Through our Lord Jesus Christ, your Son,
who lives and reigns with you in the unity of
  the Holy Spirit,
God, for ever and ever. **Amen.**

FOR REFLECTION

• How might you be a source of comfort to those who are experiencing loss and grieving?

• What are your own experiences of loss? What role did/does your faith play in these experiences?

Homily Points

• One of the amazing things about liturgy is that it transcends time and space. When we celebrate, we do so united not only with people around the world, but also with the generations of holy men and women who have gone before us. We are a family in Christ.

• This gives us hope, for as we hear in today's gospel, "For this is the will of my Father, that everyone who sees the Son and believes in him may have eternal life, and I shall raise him on the last day." Not only do we look forward in hope to the eternal life of our friends and family who have died, but we also look forward to sharing that same reality ourselves.

✠ SPIRITUALITY

GOSPEL ACCLAMATION
Rev 1:5a, 6b

℟. Alleluia, alleluia.
Jesus Christ is the firstborn of the dead;
to him be glory and power, forever and ever.
℟. Alleluia, alleluia.

Gospel   Luke 20:27-38; L156C

Some Sadducees, those who deny that
there is a resurrection,
came forward and put this question to
Jesus, saying,
"Teacher, Moses wrote for us,
If someone's brother dies leaving a wife
but no child,
his brother must take the wife
and raise up descendants for his
brother.
Now there were seven brothers;
the first married a woman but
died childless.
Then the second and the third married
her,
and likewise all the seven died
childless.
Finally the woman also died.
Now at the resurrection whose wife will
that woman be?
For all seven had been married to her."
Jesus said to them,
"The children of this age marry and
remarry;
but those who are deemed worthy to attain to the coming age
and to the resurrection of the dead
neither marry nor are given in marriage.
They can no longer die,
for they are like angels;
and they are the children of God
because they are the ones who will rise.
That the dead will rise
even Moses made known in the passage
about the bush,
when he called out 'Lord,'
the God of Abraham, the God of Isaac,
and the God of Jacob;
and he is not God of the dead, but of the
living,
for to him all are alive."

or Luke 20:27, 34-38 in Appendix A, p. 315.

Reflecting on the Gospel

Not *Seven Brides for Seven Brothers* in the old Hollywood musical style, but one bride for all of them, death after death, is the setting for this Sunday's gospel. Jesus is confronted by the Sadducees—articulate, conservative, and aristocratic, successful cultivators of lucrative contracts with the Roman governors and others in positions of power. This earned them privileges and the consequent desire to keep things as they were. They could smell danger to their status in the air around Jesus and in the company he kept, and so the Sadducees were determined to show that he is either crazy, irrelevant, disobedient to the Mosaic teaching and traditions, or a threat to established authority, especially their own. To have the common people excited about possibilities of change and a new quality of life is the last thing the Sadducees want. To disturb the status quo would threaten their powerful influence in the comfortable world they have created for themselves, and this world is all that matters to the Sadducees who, unlike the Pharisees, held that there could be nothing as radically new as resurrection from the dead. A concept of an afterlife had only been clearly articulated in Judaism about two centuries before Christ, in the Second Book of Maccabees (which is today's first reading) and in Daniel 12:2, but the Sadducees' rejection underlines their conservative stance.

In the midst of all the concerns with social oppression that were current in Palestine, it is surprising that the Sadducees should raise an issue based on Deuteronomy 25:2-6. They use this text as the basis of either cynicism or absurd exaggeration with which to provoke Jesus. Deuteronomy taught that if brothers live together and one of them dies leaving no son to carry on his name into the next generation, his brother must marry the widow. The first son of this marriage will bear the name of the dead husband. This was known as the "Levirate law" (from Hebrew *levir*, meaning "a husband's brother"). Its original purpose, though seeming strange to us, was to strengthen family bonds and provide for the widow. The Sadducees push the brotherly mortality rate through the six other brothers! To ridicule the idea of resurrection from the dead, the Sadducees put the question: "[A]t the resurrection whose wife will that woman be?"—with the implication that this question could only be considered by those who are stupid enough to believe in such a resurrection. Any answer that Jesus gives, therefore, will reveal the supposed absurdity of this belief.

Jesus refuses to play number games or indulge in trivial biblical pursuit. The power of resurrection is utterly new and overwhelmingly transformative. To be children of the resurrection is to be ready to commit ourselves into the hands of God, accepting that our relationship with God surpasses any other human relationship, no matter how intimate and loving. Jesus shows the Sadducees that they are playing with fire when they try to use the word of God against him. He replies in a traditional Jewish method, answering their reference to one biblical text with another, and giving it a meaning that extends beyond that of the original author. Unlike the Sadducees' biblical reference, the text that Jesus quotes is radical and central to Jewish faith: the event of the burning bush (Exod 3). Here, says Jesus, God names himself as the "I AM," the God of Abraham, Isaac, and Jacob, a God in a continuing and personal relationship with the Hebrew ancestors that transcends death. This is "not God of the dead, but of the living, / for to him all are alive." This is the fierce faith that is the central focus and challenge of the gospel.

Focusing the Gospel

Key words and phrases: "They can no longer die, for they are like angels; and they are the children of God because they are the ones who will rise."

To the point: Part of the basic beliefs of the Sadducees is that there is no such thing as resurrection. They are a Jewish sect active at the time of Jesus, but they differ from the Pharisees because they are solely focused on the physical reality of life right now. Aspects of the spiritual realm—angels, demons, the afterlife—are not entertained by Sadducees. When they approach Jesus to challenge him with a hypothetical question, they know it's silly, and they want to point out how ridiculous Jesus is. Jesus, of course, sees right through their motives and responds by leaning into the very things the Sadducees don't accept: an afterlife that is not governed by the rules of this world.

Connecting the Gospel

to the first reading: The first reading demonstrates that belief in the resurrection has existed since the time of Moses. "You accursed fiend, you are depriving us of this present life, / but the King of the world will raise us up to live again forever. / It is for his laws that we are dying." This idea of salvation after mortal life is not new in the time of Jesus, but has been included in the belief of the Israelites since the formation of the Torah.

to experience: If no one had ever introduced the idea of resurrection to you, would you believe we live after death? Resurrection is one of the most shocking and necessary beliefs of a Christian. The whole system hinges on this idea that we are worth more than this life, that there is an eternal joy, for which we condition ourselves here. We train ourselves for resurrection by loving others, putting others first, and seeking goodness in all things. Does the notion of life after death ever shock you or surprise you? Do you ever struggle to believe it?

Connecting the Responsorial Psalm

to the readings: This week's psalm is forward-looking and anticipates the resurrection spoken of in the first reading and the gospel. "Lord, when your glory appears, / my joy will be full." What do you think the Lord's glory is? Is it the resurrection of Jesus Christ? Is it the Second Coming? Is it a moment of personal revelation in the heart of the psalmist?

to psalmist preparation: The psalm implores the Lord, "Keep me as the apple of your eye, / hide me in the shadow of your wings." What does this imagery feel like to you? One is an image of preference, the other of protection. Which image makes you feel closer to God? Why?

PROMPTS FOR FAITH-SHARING

Has there ever been a time in your life when you've questioned the validity of resurrection, perhaps the death of a loved one? Does the idea of resurrection fill you with hope, anxiety, or both?

How would you have responded to the question posed by the Sadducees?

What does it mean to be the apple of God's eye?

Paul tells the Thessalonians, "We are confident of you in the Lord that what we instruct you, you are doing and will continue to do." What would you say if Paul wrote these words to you, today? Would you agree? Would you feel you are worthy of his confidence?

Model Penitential Act

Presider: Today the psalmist proclaims, "My steps have been steadfast in your paths, my feet have not faltered." For the times we have not been steadfast and turned away from God, we ask for forgiveness, healing, and peace . . . *[pause]*

Lord Jesus, you were raised from the dead: Lord, have mercy.

Christ Jesus, you invite us to follow you so to grow in life: Christ, have mercy.

Lord Jesus, you are the one whom we seek: Lord, have mercy.

Homily Points

• As Jesus inches ever closer to his passion and death, his opponents continue to argue with him. While today's dialogue between the Sadducees and Jesus is centered on the reality of the resurrection, their questioning of Jesus seems more like a method of self-preservation. The Jesus who dined with sinners and welcomed the outcast was gaining popularity among the people. The Sadducees in today's gospel, like the Pharisees previously, want to assert, ensure, and preserve their own power.

• As we move closer to our celebration of Christ the King and the end of this liturgical year, the readings continue to invite us to reflect on the sources of power in our lives. Where does power come from? While God is the obvious answer, and true authority comes from God, it might be more helpful to consider the things we prioritize over God in our own lives. To whom or what do we bow? Do we prostrate ourselves to false power? Do we genuflect to greed and status? Do we try to assert our own power or authority by putting other people down or trying to intentionally confuse them, as the Sadducees do in today's gospel?

• May our prayer today be the prayer of Paul in the second letter to the Thessalonians: "May the Lord direct [our] hearts to the love of God and to the endurance of Christ." For when we direct our hearts to God, we come to intimately know and believe God is not a God of the dead, but rather the God of the living.

Model Universal Prayer (Prayer of the Faithful)

Presider: We cry out to the God of the living who hears and answers our prayers.

Response: Lord, hear our prayer.

That the church may continue the work of the first disciples and always witness to the resurrection of Christ . . .

That public servants might work to unite people rather than create chasms of separation and segregation . . .

That all who have lost a loved one might find comfort in the God of the living, trusting in the resurrection and life everlasting . . .

That our local community might better serve all who grieve, walking with them as they mourn and learn to live a life that is changed, not ended . . .

Presider: Loving God, you are the God of life and of the living. Hear the prayers of your people—those we raise today and those we hold in the silence of our hearts—that we might always testify to your life and love. We ask this through Christ our Lord. **Amen.**

COLLECT

Let us pray.

Pause for silent prayer

Almighty and merciful God,
graciously keep from us all adversity,
so that, unhindered in mind and body alike,
we may pursue in freedom of heart
the things that are yours.
Through our Lord Jesus Christ, your Son,
who lives and reigns with you in the unity of the Holy Spirit,
God, for ever and ever. **Amen.**

FIRST READING 2 Macc 7:1-2, 9-14

It happened that seven brothers with their mother were arrested
    and tortured with whips and scourges by the king,
    to force them to eat pork in violation of God's law.
One of the brothers, speaking for the others, said:
    "What do you expect to achieve by questioning us?
We are ready to die rather than transgress the laws of our ancestors."

At the point of death he said:
    "You accursed fiend, you are depriving us of this present life,
    but the King of the world will raise us up to live again forever.
It is for his laws that we are dying."

After him the third suffered their cruel sport.
He put out his tongue at once when told to do so,
    and bravely held out his hands, as he spoke these noble words:
    "It was from Heaven that I received these;
    for the sake of his laws I disdain them;
    from him I hope to receive them again."
Even the king and his attendants marveled at the young man's courage,
    because he regarded his sufferings as nothing.

After he had died,
    they tortured and maltreated the fourth brother in the same way.
When he was near death, he said,
    "It is my choice to die at the hands of men with the hope God gives of being raised up by him;
    but for you, there will be no resurrection to life."

RESPONSORIAL PSALM

Ps 17:1, 5-6, 8, 15

℟. (15b) Lord, when your glory appears,
   my joy will be full.

Hear, O LORD, a just suit;
   attend to my outcry;
   hearken to my prayer from lips without
      deceit.

℟. Lord, when your glory appears, my joy
   will be full.

My steps have been steadfast in your
      paths,
   my feet have not faltered.
I call upon you, for you will answer me,
      O God;
   incline your ear to me; hear my word.

℟. Lord, when your glory appears, my joy
   will be full.

Keep me as the apple of your eye,
   hide me in the shadow of your wings.
But I in justice shall behold your face;
   on waking I shall be content in your
      presence.

℟. Lord, when your glory appears, my joy
   will be full.

SECOND READING

2 Thess 2:16–3:5

Brothers and sisters:
May our Lord Jesus Christ himself and
      God our Father,
   who has loved us and given us
      everlasting encouragement
   and good hope through his grace,
   encourage your hearts and strengthen
      them in every good deed and word.

Finally, brothers and sisters, pray for us,
   so that the word of the Lord may speed
      forward and be glorified,
   as it did among you,
   and that we may be delivered from
      perverse and wicked people,
   for not all have faith.
But the Lord is faithful;
   he will strengthen you and guard you
      from the evil one.
We are confident of you in the Lord that
      what we instruct you,
   you are doing and will continue to do.
May the Lord direct your hearts to the love
      of God
   and to the endurance of Christ.

About Liturgy

Successful Psalms: When choosing musical settings of responsorial psalms, it is helpful to understand a couple differences between metrical and chanted psalms that may not be obvious, yet are worth our attention. These musical moments are in a way a lynchpin of the Liturgy of the Word, and as such they may demand a certain attention not given to other portions of sung liturgy.

Chanted psalms of various sorts, be they Gregorian, monastic (Meinrad psalm tones and similar), or those of Gelineau or Guimont or other composers, have certain strengths that are hard to attain in metrical settings. Setting aside the brief refrains that might be either metrical or chanted, chanted verses allow the texts of the psalms to be delivered and heard in a more speech-like fashion, which can increase their clarity and understandability over some metrical settings that may break clauses up unnaturally or put odd word stresses where they would not be otherwise.

Chanted psalms are also usually quite a bit shorter than their metrical counterparts. There are some metrical settings of psalms, those with four or five verses, that on their own are longer than the other readings combined. In this way, they can become a bit overbearing and take on an undue stature that might obscure the significance of the other readings.

Let me be quick to add, of course, that there are quite lovely and usable metrical settings of psalms for use in our Sunday celebrations of Eucharist! Perhaps consider chanted psalms for most of the year, and fuller metrical ones for celebrations that would benefit from their unique character.

About Liturgical Documents

About Dies Domini—*Sabbath and Time:* In addition to noting the traditional connotations of the weekly Sabbath, rest and joy, *Dies Domini* notably links these to the social teaching of solidarity. Solidarity, in short, means recognizing others as our brothers and sisters and actively working for their good. So, even though Sunday is a day of rest, "Ever since Apostolic times, the Sunday gathering has in fact been for Christians a moment of fraternal sharing with the very poor. 'On the first day of the week, each of you is to put aside and save whatever extra you earn' (1 Cor 16:2), says Saint Paul referring to the collection organized for the poor Churches of Judaea" (DD 70).

Further, this solidarity is not just an economic act of mercy, but a true creation of a *"culture of sharing"* (DD 70), in which "the whole of Sunday becomes a great school of charity, justice and peace" (DD 73).

Inasmuch as the Divine Trinity exists outside of time, when the triune God breaks into human time and space, Sunday takes on a certain importance in its revelation of the meaning of time and in fact the whole liturgical calendar. "Sunday emerges therefore as the natural model for understanding and celebrating these feast-days of the Liturgical Year, which are of such value for the Christian life that the Church has chosen to emphasize their importance by making it obligatory for the faithful to attend Mass and to observe a time of rest, even though these feast-days may fall on variable days of the week" (DD 79).

The letter gracefully concludes: "In coming to know the Church, which every Sunday joyfully celebrates the mystery from which she draws her life, may the men and women of the Third Millennium come to know the Risen Christ. And constantly renewed by the weekly commemoration of Easter, may Christ's disciples be ever more credible in proclaiming the Gospel of salvation and ever more effective in building the civilization of love. My blessing to you all!" (DD 87).

NOVEMBER 6, 2022
THIRTY-SECOND SUNDAY
IN ORDINARY TIME

✝ SPIRITUALITY

GOSPEL ACCLAMATION
Luke 21:28

R̸. Alleluia, alleluia.
Stand erect and raise your heads
because your redemption is at hand.
R̸. Alleluia, alleluia.

Gospel

Luke 21:5-19; L159C

While some people were speaking about
  how the temple was adorned
    with costly stones and votive
    offerings,
  Jesus said, "All that you see
    here—
  the days will come when there
    will not be left
  a stone upon another stone that
    will not be thrown down."

Then they asked him,
  "Teacher, when will this happen?
And what sign will there be when all
    these things are about to happen?"
He answered,
"See that you not be deceived,
  for many will come in my name,
    saying,
  'I am he,' and 'The time has come.'
Do not follow them!
When you hear of wars and
    insurrections,
  do not be terrified; for such things
    must happen first,
  but it will not immediately be the
    end."
Then he said to them,
  "Nation will rise against nation, and
    kingdom against kingdom.
There will be powerful earthquakes,
    famines, and plagues
  from place to place;
  and awesome sights and mighty signs
    will come from the sky.

Continued in Appendix A, p. 315.

Reflecting on the Gospel

With our contemporary technology, we are almost instantly aware of global crises—social, ecological, political, and even in outer space, that would have been beyond the imagination of the Lukan communities. Related to this can be an awareness that nothing in this world lasts forever: not the second temple refurbished by Herod, not the twin towers of the World Trade Center, not a booming economy, not human lives. On the other hand, our awareness and mindfulness can be anesthetized by the bombardment of technology and the mass media. At times we seem to be citizens of a rather random, chaotic, and disordered world, desperately in need of encouragement and hope. It is such a hope that is central to this Sunday's gospel and the discussion precipitated by Jesus's words about the destruction of the temple. It would appear that from the perspective of Luke's gospel, this event lies in the future, but when Luke actually wrote his gospel this cataclysmic event had happened about fifteen years earlier in 70 CE. Many of those to whom Luke is writing the good news may have witnessed the event, and so the purpose of this narrative becomes not prediction but hope—hope for those who profess the gospel in the face of its opponents. But no matter what the disasters, Jesus promises that spiritual resources to remain faithful will always be available.

Jesus warns his followers of every age against opportunists who will claim leadership in his name but, in fact, are only concerned with exploiting people when they are most frightened and vulnerable. Jesus tells those around him to watch out for—but not be deceived by or panicked because of—prophets of doom. There will be persecutions and suffering, betrayals even by family and friends, but these are opportunities to bear witness to one's faith with the eloquent wisdom that is the gift of the Spirit of Jesus, and so there is no need to worry about what to say. The Lord will never allow his faithful witness to perish.

Jesus is not forecasting the end *of* the world; he is urging his followers to be confident in and obedient to God in the face of the tough demands of their present and future discipleship that is *for* the world. In the Acts of the Apostles, Luke describes how the early church suffered the various trials Jesus speaks about in this gospel: imprisonment, persecution at the hands of Jews and Gentiles, hatred of those who held political power. But this was countered by the bold wisdom of Stephen, the empowerment of the apostles to work miracles on hearts and bodies, their steadfastness in prison or under flogging, and, ultimately, martyrdom. This is what Jesus himself suffered, and with Jesus we can let go of our precious, protected selves, confident that, no matter what the disaster, if we die into his love, we will also rise with him.

In Chaim Potok's novel *The Chosen*, the gentle and progressive Orthodox scholar David Malter speaks to his son Reuven about the pain that is in human life and its short span when measured against eternity. It is, he says, like the blink of an eye. A blink of an eye is nothing but, he continues, the person who blinks—no matter if that person's life is long or short—is of infinite value. It is not the quantity but the quality of a person's life that is important. And quality consists in filling the life we are given with meaning. This is always hard work—a continuous, active endeavor before and with God, not just passive expectation that meaning will be given automatically.

Focusing the Gospel

Key words and phrases: "You will be hated by all because of my name, but not a hair on your head will be destroyed."

To the point: The gospel this week begins with entering a temple and some of Jesus's disciples pointing out how lovely it is inside. Jesus uses this moment to caution everyone that what is coming isn't an easy life, "adorned with costly stones and votive offerings." Jesus tells them that destruction is coming and those who follow him will be persecuted. Understandably worried, they ask when it will happen and how they will know it's going to happen. Jesus responds in an eschatological way, referencing the end of the world—probably not what his disciples were expecting on a routine trip to the local temple. No matter where he is in his ministry, Jesus maintains a clear-eyed view of the future and wants his disciples to know the weight of what he's asking of them.

Connecting the Gospel

to the first reading: In the first reading, Malachi tells of horrible destruction, but it's for the enemies of the Lord, not those who "fear [his] name." This appears to run in contrast to what Jesus is telling his disciples in the gospel—that they themselves will experience persecution. However, both Malachi and Jesus are seeing the big picture and the long game. The Israelites in Malachi's time are experiencing horrible physical destruction, but Malachi puts their sights on the Lord and the "sun of justice." Jesus tells his disciples that they may lose their lives, but, "By your perseverance you will secure your lives."

to experience: How many times do we endure something hard, because we know a benefit lies at the end of the struggle? A challenging year of school, a hard workout, a difficult conversation with a spouse? Our species has evolved to avoid pain, as any animal, and yet as creatures made in the image and likeness of God, we have the ability to choose to endure hard things because we can perceive the benefit of going through them.

Connecting the Responsorial Psalm

to the readings: This week's psalm is forward-looking, anticipating the Lord coming to rule with justice. Though the Lord is with us always—guiding the Israelites, accompanying us on earth in the person of Jesus Christ, and active in the person of the Holy Spirit—we are still moving steadily toward the New Jerusalem. This psalm reminds us that, regardless of the evil and destruction in the world today, "he will rule the world with justice and the peoples with equity."

to psalmist preparation: When we, in our words and deeds, create a world of justice and equity, we anticipate the coming of the Lord and help bring about the kingdom of God. What are a few small, mundane ways that you have brought about justice in your life? Do you break up fights between siblings? Provide a calm, helping hand to friends?

PROMPTS FOR FAITH-SHARING

If you were traveling with Jesus, how do you think you would have reacted to his words in the gospel?

_____

_____

_____

_____

What is something you worked for in the midst of enduring pain? Is there a current goal you're working toward that requires discipline?

_____

_____

_____

_____

What does the psalm's imagery "let the rivers clap their hands, the mountains shout with them for joy" make you think? Can you imagine a river clapping its hands or mountains shouting for joy?

_____

_____

_____

_____

Have you ever, as Paul describes, been someone who "conduct[s] themselves . . . in a disorderly way, by not keeping busy but minding the business of others"? How do you push through this attitude, when it inevitably comes, throughout your life?

_____

_____

_____

_____

CELEBRATION

Model Penitential Act

Presider: As we come to the end of the liturgical year, we take a moment to reflect on the ways we have failed to be the people God calls us to be and ask for God's forgiveness . . . *[pause]*

Lord Jesus, you work signs and wonders: Lord, have mercy.

Christ Jesus, you bring light to those in darkness: Christ, have mercy.

Lord Jesus, you are seated at the right hand of the Father: Lord, have mercy.

Homily Points

• Jesus's words in today's gospel could easily describe our lives today. Nations continue to rise against nations. Families continue to rise against families. Even our own church community often seems to be at odds. Fires, earthquakes, famines, floods, and plagues are such an everyday occurrence that we might even ignore them, imagining that they are not actually part of the current reality. Even so, we can take comfort in Jesus's words: "By your perseverance you will secure your lives."

• Perseverance takes a number of forms. Sometimes it looks like choosing to love your spouse and children every day, even when it seems impossible. Sometimes it looks like fighting injustice by condemning the racist or sexist comments we hear our friends make. Sometimes perseverance is simply taking time for prayer. In all of these cases and more, our relationship with God grounds us and gives us life.

• The images in today's gospel are certainly apocalyptic, but they are also eschatological. This reading comes from what is often referred to as the "Lukan eschatological discourse," where we see not only what the end of time might look like, but more importantly, what it reveals about God and our relationship with God. Jesus's command is so significant because it offers an essential disposition to each of us: "[D]o not be terrified." Do not be afraid.

Model Universal Prayer (Prayer of the Faithful)

Presider: Taking comfort in Jesus's command to not be afraid, we confidently offer our prayers and petitions to God, knowing that God hears us.

Response: Lord, hear our prayer.

That our church might be a sign of hope and unity for the world in the midst of so much unrest . . .

That leaders might respond to the signs of the times, always upholding the dignity of each person . . .

That all might work to reduce waste, conserve and protect natural resources, and combat climate change in stewardship of our common home . . .

That all gathered here might cultivate peace in their homes, schools, workplaces, and community . . .

Presider: Loving God, hear these prayers we offer to you and answer them according to your will so that we might grow in unity as we work to spread your reign on earth. We ask this through Christ our Lord. **Amen.**

COLLECT

Let us pray.

Pause for silent prayer

Grant us, we pray, O Lord our God,
the constant gladness of being devoted
    to you,
for it is full and lasting happiness
to serve with constancy
the author of all that is good.
Through our Lord Jesus Christ, your Son,
who lives and reigns with you in the unity
    of the Holy Spirit,
God, for ever and ever. **Amen.**

FIRST READING

Mal 3:19-20a

Lo, the day is coming, blazing like an oven,
    when all the proud and all evildoers will
        be stubble,
and the day that is coming will set them
    on fire,
    leaving them neither root nor branch,
    says the LORD of hosts.
But for you who fear my name, there will
    arise
    the sun of justice with its healing rays.

254

RESPONSORIAL PSALM

Ps 98:5-6, 7-8, 9

R℣. (cf. 9) The Lord comes to rule the earth
   with justice.

Sing praise to the LORD with the harp,
   with the harp and melodious song.
With trumpets and the sound of the horn
   sing joyfully before the King, the LORD.

R℣. The Lord comes to rule the earth with
   justice.

Let the sea and what fills it resound,
   the world and those who dwell in it;
let the rivers clap their hands,
   the mountains shout with them for joy.

R℣. The Lord comes to rule the earth with
   justice.

Before the LORD, for he comes,
   for he comes to rule the earth;
he will rule the world with justice
   and the peoples with equity.

R℣. The Lord comes to rule the earth with
   justice.

SECOND READING

2 Thess 3:7-12

Brothers and sisters:
You know how one must imitate us.
For we did not act in a disorderly way
      among you,
   nor did we eat food received free from
      anyone.
On the contrary, in toil and drudgery,
      night and day
   we worked, so as not to burden any of
      you.
Not that we do not have the right.
Rather, we wanted to present ourselves as
      a model for you,
   so that you might imitate us.
In fact, when we were with you,
   we instructed you that if anyone was
      unwilling to work,
   neither should that one eat.
We hear that some are conducting
      themselves among you in a disorderly
      way,
   by not keeping busy but minding the
      business of others.
Such people we instruct and urge in the
      Lord Jesus Christ to work quietly
   and to eat their own food.

About Liturgy

Don't Overlook the Universal Norms: Many Sundays in this book took time to explore in depth a few liturgical documents that inform our celebrations. Some of these perhaps were already familiar to you in some way, hopefully! Each deserves a much fuller treatment than the space allowed here, and it is a good idea to return to them from time to time for a fuller reading or rereading, to remind ourselves of certain details—or indeed grand and broad values—that may have faded from our memory.

One document that is often overlooked or sometimes even forgotten is the Universal Norms on the Liturgical Year (UN) and the General Roman Calendar. This *motu proprio* was issued by Pope Paul VI in 1969 to clarify some elements of the Constitution on the Sacred Liturgy and provide, unsurprisingly, some lucidity on the liturgical year and sanctoral cycle, given the new rite that emanated from Vatican II and those who worked to implement its changes.

Unlike many liturgical documents, this letter is not very long and is written with a brevity and intelligibility that such texts are not always known for. It's also easily found online, as well as near the front of the Roman Missal.

First, there is an introduction that places the new norms in the context of previous pontiffs and liturgical expressions. It further notes that in earlier calendars, "more feasts of the Saints were introduced than was appropriate" (Universal Norms, Introduction, II) and that a simpler, clearer approach would be needed.

If you've even wondered what the difference is between a solemnity, a feast, and a memorial and how any of these do or do not interact with Sunday as "the primordial feast day" (Universal Norms 4), this is the document for you! It also not only offers practicalities concerning the cycle of the liturgical year—more on that next Sunday— but also delves into the character of each season and certain details regarding their celebration.

Chapter II of this letter delves into much detail concerning the ordering of Proper of Time for use not only universally, but in certain countries or dioceses, or within religious orders, etc. The document concludes with a table of precedence for the most common universal celebrations, which can become quite handy if you deal with daily Masses regularly, for instance at religious schools.

Be sure to keep a copy of this document—and all the others discussed this year— handy, whether in a published volume of such texts or perhaps as a collection of bookmarks in a web browser. While it's helpful to know them well, it's often more helpful to know which document might quickly provide an answer to a question you or someone else might have, and to be able to locate each document quickly as well!

About Music

Coming to the End: As our Scriptures this time of year call us to contemplate the end times and the second coming of Christ, our music ought to reflect these circumstances too. There is a certain "doom and gloom" that must be tempered by hope and promise as well. Today's gospel might bring to mind Rory Cooney's "Canticle of the Turning" (GIA). Look, too, at "The King Shall Come When Morning Dawns" in either its traditional setting or with more contemporary music from Joe Mattingly or Christian Cosas (WLP/GIA).

NOVEMBER 13, 2022
THIRTY-THIRD SUNDAY
IN ORDINARY TIME

✝ SPIRITUALITY

GOSPEL ACCLAMATION
Mark 11:9, 10

℟. Alleluia, alleluia.
Blessed is he who comes in the name of the
  Lord!
Blessed is the kingdom of our father David
  that is to come!
℟. Alleluia, alleluia.

Gospel

Luke 23:35-43; L162C

The rulers sneered at Jesus and
  said,
  "He saved others, let him save
    himself
  if he is the chosen one, the Christ
    of God."
Even the soldiers jeered at him.
As they approached to offer him
  wine they called out,
  "If you are King of the Jews, save
    yourself."
Above him there was an inscription
  that read,
  "This is the King of the Jews."

Now one of the criminals hanging there
  reviled Jesus, saying,
  "Are you not the Christ?
Save yourself and us."
The other, however, rebuking him, said
  in reply,
  "Have you no fear of God,
  for you are subject to the same
    condemnation?
And indeed, we have been condemned
  justly,
  for the sentence we received corre-
    sponds to our crimes,
  but this man has done nothing
    criminal."
Then he said,
  "Jesus, remember me when you come
    into your kingdom."
He replied to him,
  "Amen, I say to you,
  today you will be with me in
    Paradise."

Reflecting on the Gospel

Stumbling along, sometimes backtracking, we have tried to follow Jesus through another year of grace. With the many people we have met along the Lukan way, we have accepted or refused the hospitality of God that invites us each Sunday to be fed at the tables of both Word and sacrament so that

we might go out to nourish with compassion our sisters and brothers, especially the most hungry and thirsty whose lives are in ruins. And so we come to the Sunday that closes Year C and are confronted with the stark realism of the gospel choice for this Solemnity of Our Lord Jesus Christ, King of the Universe.

The end of the Jerusalem journey is not Mount Zion, "the fortress . . . , which is the City of David" (2 Sam 5:7) and the site of Solomon's temple and the second temple. We finish outside the city walls, on an unremarkable outcrop shaped like a skull, a place of execution of criminals. There Jesus is brutally enthroned and reigns as king from the cross that can never be separated from his resurrection. As was customary with crucifixion, a notation of the crime for which the person was condemned is placed on the cross, so above Jesus could be read: "This is the King of the Jews." For some this will prompt abusive derision; for others it will be a proclamation of faith. And Simeon's prophecy of division, of people's falling or rising because of Jesus, will be played out around the temple of his body (Luke 2:34). We listen and watch, knowing where we should be as his disciples, but also knowing at times the temptation to join the jeering, the mocking, the raging or to be among the absent ones.

To the end, Jesus endures the wilderness temptations, not on the pinnacle of the temple but from the height of the cross: "Are you not the Christ? Save yourself and us." The leaders glory in their shabby triumphalism; the soldiers hang around Jesus in a kind of bored representation of officialdom and offer sour wine to this One who drinks our sinfulness to the dregs; one of the criminals who was crucified with Jesus derides him as no good to himself or anyone else.

Around Jesus, too, are people who will rise because of him: those who stand by not just watching but "contemplating" their crucified king and the other criminal who recognizes in Jesus an authority so different from that which has condemned them both. Luke gives to this man the voice of a traditional Jewish hope for the end time that was envisaged as a return to the primeval innocence and peace of the garden ("Paradise" in the Greek translation of the Hebrew Scriptures). Throughout his life, Jesus associated with and befriended outcasts; again and again he sought out and forgave the lost and the sinners, and he will do this even as he is dying. One of the crucified criminals rebukes the other for his cynical messianic taunting of Jesus and dares to ask Jesus for a late invitation into the kingdom. This criminal addresses him not with the title of the inscription hanging above him, but simply and familiarly as "Jesus." And then a faint, future hope becomes a "today" event of salvation for the one whom we have come to call "the good thief," the man for whom the compassion of Jesus throws open the door of the kingdom and allows him to steal Paradise.

Focusing the Gospel

Key words and phrases: "And indeed, we have been condemned justly, for the sentence we received corresponds to our crimes, but this man has done nothing criminal."

To the point: This scene from Luke's gospel has multiple stories and journeys taking place. The soldiers next to the three crosses are making fun of Jesus. By dehumanizing the people they are executing, the Roman soldiers are able to justify their actions. Sneering and jeering at Jesus are ways for the soldiers to signify that Jesus is "other" and worthy of being killed.

One of the criminals executed with Jesus joins in the opportunity to separate himself from Jesus, who is currently reviled by the crowd. But the second criminal goes against all expectations. He not only defends Jesus, but places Jesus above himself by asking Jesus to remember him when Jesus enters his kingdom, showing all those gathered that he believes Jesus's claims to be true and submits himself to Jesus in suppliance. Jesus, of course, responds with mercy.

Connecting the Gospel

to the second reading: In this week's second reading, Paul works very hard to describe just who Jesus is, and it's not a simple explanation. "He is before all things, / and in him all things hold together. / He is the head of the body, the church. / He is the beginning, the firstborn from the dead, / that in all things he himself might be preeminent." Paul is doing what every inspired writer of the Bible attempts to do: describe God using human language. This week we celebrate Jesus as King of the Universe, which is a scope of power that is hard to adequately describe.

to experience: The gospel gives a "micro" demonstration of Jesus's position as King of the Universe, when a criminal condemned to die next to Jesus experiences a turn of heart and asks Jesus, while hanging on a cross next to him, to remember him in Jesus's kingdom. The second reading gives us a "macro" version of this kingship, as Paul describes the varied and awesome ways in which Jesus is the "firstborn of all creation." These two readings are paired to give us varied entries into this idea of Jesus as ruler of all that is and all that will be. One is personal, and one is poetic.

Connecting the Responsorial Psalm

to the readings: As the liturgical year comes to a close this week, the psalm gives us the perfect way to tie it all up: "Let us go rejoicing to the house of the Lord." This is the final scene in a year spent journeying through the Gospel of Luke. What is the house of the Lord? It is the church, the Church, and the kingdom to which we hope to one day gain entry, joining the man crucified next to Jesus, St. Paul, and all those who have gone before us in faith.

to psalmist preparation: Think back over the last year. How has proclaiming the psalm changed you? Has it been a task to complete, or an opportunity to savor? Has it brought stress or joy? Or perhaps all of the above? Take a moment to reflect on your work as a minister, and allow space to be thankful and proud.

PROMPTS FOR FAITH-SHARING

Do you feel you have more tendency to model the criminal questioning the power of Jesus, or the one asking to be remembered? Why?

Do you go "rejoicing" to church, or is it more of a task? How can you better orient your heart so that your work is more of a joy and less of an obligation?

Which image from Paul's letter to the Colossians stands out to you? Why?

Bring to mind the biggest struggle in your life right now. How does it look when placed in the context of Jesus as King of the Universe, knowing Jesus holds power over all things?

Model Penitential Act

Presider: In today's gospel the repentant thief calls out to Jesus on the cross and asks for mercy. We, too, ask for God's forgiveness for the times we have failed to love as we should . . . *[pause]*

> Lord Jesus, you are King of Kings: Lord, have mercy.
> Christ Jesus, you are Lord of Lords: Christ, have mercy.
> Lord Jesus, you are ruler of heaven and earth: Lord, have mercy.

Homily Points

• As we enter into today's celebration of Our Lord Jesus Christ, King of the Universe, it is helpful to go back to the beginning of Jesus's public ministry. Luke writes of Jesus's temptation in the desert: "When the devil had finished every temptation, he departed from him for a time." The devil does not leave Jesus forever, but waits for opportune times to resume temptation. As we read these words in concert with today's gospel, the soldiers' shouts seem even more significant: "If you are King of the Jews, save yourself."

• Jesus is the epitome of kingship precisely because he rejects these false notions of power and authority. Jesus does not act in self-interest. As always, Jesus lives and loves for others, and calls us to do the same. The Lord, robed in majesty, offers salvation to the repentant thief and to all of us. The psalmist today embodies our elation: "I rejoiced because they said to me, 'We will go up to the house of the Lord.'"

• As we look forward to the new liturgical year that begins in Advent, may we remember this image of Christ the King and turn to it often, for it helps us understand the realities of Christianity: Power comes from humility, selfishness falls to sacrifice, and death springs from life.

Model Universal Prayer (Prayer of the Faithful)

Presider: Just as the thief called out to Jesus on the cross, we offer our needs and intentions to the God who intimately knows us and hears our prayers.

Response: Lord, hear our prayer.

That the church may celebrate Christ the King by raising up the lowly, supporting the oppressed, and caring for the most vulnerable among us . . .

That all leaders might govern by lowering themselves so to raise up others . . .

That all who suffer from violence and persecution might find safe refuge, and that the senseless killings in our country and world will end . . .

That all who face temptation might find courage and resolve to make choices that bring life . . .

Presider: Loving God, hear the prayers we offer today. Help us follow the example of your Son, that we might truly be Christ for others in all we think, say, and do. We ask this through Christ our Lord. **Amen.**

COLLECT

Let us pray.

Pause for silent prayer

Almighty ever-living God,
whose will is to restore all things
in your beloved Son, the King of the
    universe,
grant, we pray,
that the whole creation, set free from
    slavery,
may render your majesty service
and ceaselessly proclaim your praise.
Through our Lord Jesus Christ, your Son,
who lives and reigns with you in the unity
    of the Holy Spirit,
God, for ever and ever. **Amen.**

FIRST READING

2 Sam 5:1-3

In those days, all the tribes of Israel came
    to David in Hebron and said:
    "Here we are, your bone and your flesh.
In days past, when Saul was our king,
    it was you who led the Israelites out and
        brought them back.
And the Lord said to you,
    'You shall shepherd my people Israel
    and shall be commander of Israel.'"
When all the elders of Israel came to
    David in Hebron,
    King David made an agreement with
        them there before the Lord,
    and they anointed him king of Israel.

RESPONSORIAL PSALM

Ps 122:1-2, 3-4, 4-5

℟. (cf. 1) Let us go rejoicing to the house
    of the Lord.

I rejoiced because they said to me,
    "We will go up to the house of the
        Lord."
And now we have set foot
    within your gates, O Jerusalem.

℟. Let us go rejoicing to the house of the
    Lord.

Jerusalem, built as a city
    with compact unity.
To it the tribes go up,
    the tribes of the Lord.

℟. Let us go rejoicing to the house of the
    Lord.

According to the decree for Israel,
    to give thanks to the name of the Lord.
In it are set up judgment seats,
    seats for the house of David.

℟. Let us go rejoicing to the house of the
    Lord.

SECOND READING
Col 1:12-20

Brothers and sisters:
Let us give thanks to the Father,
  who has made you fit to share
  in the inheritance of the holy ones in
    light.
He delivered us from the power of
  darkness
and transferred us to the kingdom of
  his beloved Son,
in whom we have redemption, the
  forgiveness of sins.

He is the image of the invisible God,
  the firstborn of all creation.
For in him were created all things in
  heaven and on earth,
  the visible and the invisible,
  whether thrones or dominions or
    principalities or powers;
all things were created through
  him and for him.
He is before all things,
  and in him all things hold together.
He is the head of the body, the
  church.
He is the beginning, the firstborn
  from the dead,
  that in all things he himself might
    be preeminent.
For in him all the fullness was
  pleased to dwell,
  and through him to reconcile all
    things for him,
  making peace by the blood of his
    cross
  through him, whether those on
    earth or those in heaven.

About Liturgy

Cyclical Nature of Liturgy: Our liturgical year, as it has come to us in the 2,000 years since Jesus's time physically with us, is cyclical, as we are likely already aware. This should not be surprising. Our very lives, owing to the rotations and revolutions of the Earth, hurtling through space, return us to each season—spring, summer, fall, and winter—in due course. Just as the sun "rises and falls" as the Earth, tilted on its axis, gives portions of our planet more or less sun certain times of year, so too our human activities change; and by close observation of the sun, moon, and stars, humankind has for many centuries marked the cyclical passing of time.

Our liturgy is also cyclical. The church has given us a Lectionary that, by three cycles on Sunday and two on weekdays, opens the treasures of Scripture to us in a fuller way since the reforms of Vatican II. The end of each Lectionary cycle, with its emphasis on end times and the Second Coming, leads us almost imperceptibly into the season of Advent and our preparations for Christmas as a celebration of both incarnation and Parousia. It's noteworthy—and I hope an intentional wink to us by the framers of the Lectionary—that the last responsorial psalm of Cycle C, today's Psalm 122, "Let us go rejoicing to the house of the Lord," is the same as the psalm for the first Sunday of Advent in Cycle A! (Next Sunday has two additional verses, however.)

It can be tempting, for both homilists and those who program music for the liturgy, especially in our digital age, to refer back to words and music from three years ago when preparing current liturgies. The cyclical nature of the liturgy puts the same Scripture and prayers before us, time after time. I propose, though, that the more valuable image for the passing of time, for our purposes here, is a spiral. Imagine a childhood Slinky toy, stretched out a bit to allow some space between the coils. If you look through the coils from one end, as if a telescope, tracing one loop a full 360 degrees does in fact bring you back to the same point where you began. Looking at the coils from the side, though, reveals that tracing the loop has actually brought you to a different geographical spot.

While the liturgical cycle brings us, in one manner of consideration, back to where we were, we are also three years along in our lives, and almost certainly very different individuals, very different people than three years ago. As you are reading this, three years ago would have been just a few short months before a pandemic disrupted nearly every aspect of life as we knew it. What is it about life that is different now than it was then? Which words and texts from three years ago might be valuable today; which ones ought to change; which ones, without changing, will be heard and valued differently?

About Music

An Unexpected King: Christ's ministry on earth upended what people expected from a messianic king. Does our liturgical music today reflect that? Consider "Unwavering" by Matt Maher (WN), which allows congregations to sing the Beatitudes and their unexpected words of blessing and holiness. The *Psallite* refrain "Blest Are the Poor in Spirit" would serve a similar function in a different style (Liturgical Press).

Readings *(continued)*

The Immaculate Conception of the Blessed Virgin Mary, December 8, 2021

Gospel (cont.)
Luke 1:26-38; L689

He will be great and will be called Son of the Most High,
 and the Lord God will give him the throne of David his father,
 and he will rule over the house of Jacob forever,
 and of his Kingdom there will be no end."
But Mary said to the angel,
 "How can this be,
 since I have no relations with a man?"
And the angel said to her in reply,
 "The Holy Spirit will come upon you,
 and the power of the Most High will overshadow you.
Therefore the child to be born
 will be called holy, the Son of God.

And behold, Elizabeth, your relative,
 has also conceived a son in her old age,
 and this is the sixth month for her who was called barren;
 for nothing will be impossible for God."
Mary said, "Behold, I am the handmaid of the Lord.
May it be done to me according to your word."
Then the angel departed from her.

FIRST READING
Gen 3:9-15, 20

After the man, Adam, had eaten of the tree,
 the Lᴏʀᴅ God called to the man and asked
 him, "Where are you?"
He answered, "I heard you in the garden;
 but I was afraid, because I was naked,
 so I hid myself."
Then he asked, "Who told you that you were
 naked?
You have eaten, then,
 from the tree of which I had forbidden you
 to eat!"
The man replied, "The woman whom you put
 here with me—
 she gave me fruit from the tree, and so I
 ate it."
The Lᴏʀᴅ God then asked the woman,
 "Why did you do such a thing?"
The woman answered, "The serpent tricked
 me into it, so I ate it."

Then the Lᴏʀᴅ God said to the serpent:
 "Because you have done this, you shall be
 banned
 from all the animals
 and from all the wild creatures;
 on your belly shall you crawl,
 and dirt shall you eat
 all the days of your life.
I will put enmity between you and the
 woman,
 and between your offspring and hers;
 he will strike at your head,
 while you strike at his heel."

The man called his wife Eve,
 because she became the mother of all the
 living.

RESPONSORIAL PSALM
Ps 98:1, 2-3ab, 3cd-4

℟. (1a) Sing to the Lord a new song, for he has
 done marvelous deeds.

Sing to the Lᴏʀᴅ a new song,
 for he has done wondrous deeds;
His right hand has won victory for him,
 his holy arm.

℟. Sing to the Lord a new song, for he has
 done marvelous deeds.

The Lᴏʀᴅ has made his salvation known:
 in the sight of the nations he has revealed
 his justice.
He has remembered his kindness and his
 faithfulness
 toward the house of Israel.

℟. Sing to the Lord a new song, for he has
 done marvelous deeds.

All the ends of the earth have seen
 the salvation by our God.
Sing joyfully to the Lᴏʀᴅ, all you lands;
 break into song; sing praise.

℟. Sing to the Lord a new song, for he has
 done marvelous deeds.

SECOND READING
Eph 1:3-6, 11-12

Brothers and sisters:
Blessed be the God and Father of our Lord
 Jesus Christ,
 who has blessed us in Christ
 with every spiritual blessing in the heavens,
 as he chose us in him, before the foundation
 of the world,
 to be holy and without blemish before him.
In love he destined us for adoption to himself
 through Jesus Christ,
 in accord with the favor of his will,
 for the praise of the glory of his grace
 that he granted us in the beloved.

In him we were also chosen,
 destined in accord with the purpose of the
 One
 who accomplishes all things according to
 the intention of his will,
 so that we might exist for the praise of his
 glory,
 we who first hoped in Christ.

Gospel (cont.)
Luke 1:26-38; L690A

He will be great and will be called Son of the Most High,
  and the Lord God will give him the throne of David his father,
  and he will rule over the house of Jacob forever,
  and of his Kingdom there will be no end."
But Mary said to the angel,
  "How can this be,
  since I have no relations with a man?"
And the angel said to her in reply,
  "The Holy Spirit will come upon you,
  and the power of the Most High will overshadow you.
Therefore the child to be born
  will be called holy, the Son of God.
And behold, Elizabeth, your relative,
  has also conceived a son in her old age,
  and this is the sixth month for her who was called barren;
  for nothing will be impossible for God."
Mary said, "Behold, I am the handmaid of the Lord.
May it be done to me according to your word."
Then the angel departed from her.

or Luke 1:39-47

Mary set out
  and traveled to the hill country in haste
  to a town of Judah,
  where she entered the house of Zechariah
  and greeted Elizabeth.
When Elizabeth heard Mary's greeting,
  the infant leaped in her womb,
  and Elizabeth, filled with the Holy Spirit,
  cried out in a loud voice and said,
  "Most blessed are you among women,
  and blessed is the fruit of your womb.
And how does this happen to me,
  that the mother of my Lord should come to me?
For at the moment the sound of your greeting reached my ears,
  the infant in my womb leaped for joy.
Blessed are you who believed
  that what was spoken to you by the Lord
  would be fulfilled."

And Mary said:

  "My soul proclaims the greatness of the Lord;
  my spirit rejoices in God my savior."

FIRST READING
Rev 11:19a; 12:1-6a, 10ab

God's temple in heaven was opened,
  and the ark of his covenant could be seen
    in the temple.

A great sign appeared in the sky, a woman
    clothed with the sun,
  with the moon under her feet,
  and on her head a crown of twelve stars.
She was with child and wailed aloud in pain
    as she labored to give birth.
Then another sign appeared in the sky;
  it was a huge red dragon, with seven heads
      and ten horns,
  and on its heads were seven diadems.
Its tail swept away a third of the stars in the
    sky
  and hurled them down to the earth.
Then the dragon stood before the woman
      about to give birth,
  to devour her child when she gave birth.
She gave birth to a son, a male child,
  destined to rule all the nations with an iron
    rod.
Her child was caught up to God and his
    throne.
The woman herself fled into the desert
  where she had a place prepared by God.

Then I heard a loud voice in heaven say:
  "Now have salvation and power come,
    and the Kingdom of our God
    and the authority of his Anointed."

or Zech 2:14-17

Sing and rejoice, O daughter Zion!
See, I am coming to dwell among you, says
      the LORD.
Many nations shall join themselves to the
      LORD on that day,
  and they shall be his people,
  and he will dwell among you,
  and you shall know that the LORD of hosts
      has sent me to you.
The LORD will possess Judah as his portion in
      the holy land,
  and he will again choose Jerusalem.
Silence, all mankind, in the presence of the
      LORD!
  For he stirs forth from his holy dwelling.

RESPONSORIAL PSALM
Judith 13:18bcde, 19

R̸. (15:9d) You are the highest honor of our
    race.

Blessed are you, daughter, by the Most High
    God,
  above all the women on earth;
  and blessed be the LORD God,
  the creator of heaven and earth.

R̸. You are the highest honor of our race.

Your deed of hope will never be forgotten
  by those who tell of the might of God.

R̸. You are the highest honor of our race.

Gospel (cont.)
Matt 1:1-25; L13ABC

Asaph became the father of Jehoshaphat,
    Jehoshaphat the father of Joram,
    Joram the father of Uzziah.
Uzziah became the father of Jotham,
    Jotham the father of Ahaz,
    Ahaz the father of Hezekiah.
Hezekiah became the father of Manasseh,
    Manasseh the father of Amos,
    Amos the father of Josiah.
Josiah became the father of Jechoniah and his brothers
    at the time of the Babylonian exile.

After the Babylonian exile,
    Jechoniah became the father of Shealtiel,
    Shealtiel the father of Zerubbabel,
    Zerubbabel the father of Abiud.
Abiud became the father of Eliakim,
    Eliakim the father of Azor,
    Azor the father of Zadok.
Zadok became the father of Achim,
    Achim the father of Eliud,
    Eliud the father of Eleazar.
Eleazar became the father of Matthan,
    Matthan the father of Jacob,
    Jacob the father of Joseph, the husband of Mary.
Of her was born Jesus who is called the Christ.

Thus the total number of generations
    from Abraham to David
    is fourteen generations;
    from David to the Babylonian exile,
    fourteen generations;
    from the Babylonian exile to the Christ,
    fourteen generations.

Now this is how the birth of Jesus Christ came about.
When his mother Mary was betrothed to Joseph,
    but before they lived together,
    she was found with child through the Holy Spirit.
Joseph her husband, since he was a righteous man,
    yet unwilling to expose her to shame,
    decided to divorce her quietly.
Such was his intention when, behold,
    the angel of the Lord appeared to him in a dream and said,
    "Joseph, son of David,
    do not be afraid to take Mary your wife into your home.
For it is through the Holy Spirit
    that this child has been conceived in her.
She will bear a son and you are to name him Jesus,
    because he will save his people from their sins."
All this took place to fulfill
    what the Lord had said through the prophet:
      Behold, the virgin shall conceive and bear a son,
        and they shall name him Emmanuel,
    which means "God is with us."
When Joseph awoke,
    he did as the angel of the Lord had commanded him
    and took his wife into his home.
He had no relations with her until she bore a son,
    and he named him Jesus.

or Matt 1:18-25

This is how the birth of Jesus Christ came about.
When his mother Mary was betrothed to Joseph,
    but before they lived together,
    she was found with child through the Holy Spirit.
Joseph her husband, since he was a righteous man,
    yet unwilling to expose her to shame,
    decided to divorce her quietly.
Such was his intention when, behold,
    the angel of the Lord appeared to him in a dream and said,
    "Joseph, son of David,
    do not be afraid to take Mary your wife into your home.
For it is through the Holy Spirit
    that this child has been conceived in her.
She will bear a son and you are to name him Jesus,
    because he will save his people from their sins."
All this took place to fulfill
    what the Lord had said through the prophet:
      Behold, the virgin shall conceive and bear a son,
        and they shall name him Emmanuel,
    which means "God is with us."
When Joseph awoke,
    he did as the angel of the Lord had commanded him
    and took his wife into his home.
He had no relations with her until she bore a son,
    and he named him Jesus.

FIRST READING

Isa 62:1-5

For Zion's sake I will not be silent,
  for Jerusalem's sake I will not be quiet,
until her vindication shines forth like the
    dawn
  and her victory like a burning torch.

Nations shall behold your vindication,
  and all the kings your glory;
you shall be called by a new name
  pronounced by the mouth of the LORD.
You shall be a glorious crown in the hand of
    the LORD,
  a royal diadem held by your God.
No more shall people call you "Forsaken,"
  or your land "Desolate,"
but you shall be called "My Delight,"
  and your land "Espoused."
For the LORD delights in you
  and makes your land his spouse.
As a young man marries a virgin,
  your Builder shall marry you;
and as a bridegroom rejoices in his bride
  so shall your God rejoice in you.

RESPONSORIAL PSALM

Ps 89:4-5, 16-17, 27, 29

R̦. (2a) For ever I will sing the goodness of
  the Lord.

I have made a covenant with my chosen one,
  I have sworn to David my servant:
forever will I confirm your posterity
  and establish your throne for all
    generations.

R̦. For ever I will sing the goodness of the
  Lord.

Blessed the people who know the joyful shout;
  in the light of your countenance, O LORD,
    they walk.
At your name they rejoice all the day,
  and through your justice they are exalted.

R̦. For ever I will sing the goodness of the
  Lord.

He shall say of me, "You are my father,
  my God, the rock, my savior."
Forever I will maintain my kindness toward
    him,
  and my covenant with him stands firm.

R̦. For ever I will sing the goodness of the
  Lord.

SECOND READING

Acts 13:16-17, 22-25

When Paul reached Antioch in Pisidia and
    entered the synagogue,
  he stood up, motioned with his hand, and
    said,
    "Fellow Israelites and you others who are
      God-fearing, listen.
The God of this people Israel chose our
    ancestors
  and exalted the people during their sojourn
    in the land of Egypt.
With uplifted arm he led them out of it.
Then he removed Saul and raised up David
    as king;
  of him he testified,
  'I have found David, son of Jesse, a man
      after my own heart;
  he will carry out my every wish.'
From this man's descendants God, according
    to his promise,
  has brought to Israel a savior, Jesus.
John heralded his coming by proclaiming a
      baptism of repentance
  to all the people of Israel;
  and as John was completing his course, he
      would say,
  'What do you suppose that I am? I am not
      he.
Behold, one is coming after me;
  I am not worthy to unfasten the sandals of
    his feet.'"

Gospel (cont.)

Luke 2:1-14; L14ABC

She wrapped him in swaddling clothes and laid him in a manger,
  because there was no room for them in the inn.

Now there were shepherds in that region living in the fields
  and keeping the night watch over their flock.
The angel of the Lord appeared to them
  and the glory of the Lord shone around them,
  and they were struck with great fear.
The angel said to them,
  "Do not be afraid;
  for behold, I proclaim to you good news of great joy
  that will be for all the people.
For today in the city of David
  a savior has been born for you who is Christ and Lord.
And this will be a sign for you:
  you will find an infant wrapped in swaddling clothes
  and lying in a manger."

And suddenly there was a multitude of the heavenly host with the
    angel,
  praising God and saying:
    "Glory to God in the highest
      and on earth peace to those on whom his favor rests."

The Nativity of the Lord, December 25, 2021 (Mass at Midnight)

FIRST READING
Isa 9:1-6

The people who walked in darkness
   have seen a great light;
upon those who dwelt in the land of gloom
   a light has shone.
You have brought them abundant joy
   and great rejoicing,
as they rejoice before you as at the harvest,
   as people make merry when dividing spoils.
For the yoke that burdened them,
   the pole on their shoulder,
and the rod of their taskmaster
   you have smashed, as on the day of Midian.
For every boot that tramped in battle,
   every cloak rolled in blood,
   will be burned as fuel for flames.
For a child is born to us, a son is given us;
   upon his shoulder dominion rests.
They name him Wonder-Counselor, God-Hero,
   Father-Forever, Prince of Peace.
His dominion is vast
   and forever peaceful,
from David's throne, and over his kingdom,
   which he confirms and sustains
by judgment and justice,
   both now and forever.
The zeal of the LORD of hosts will do this!

RESPONSORIAL PSALM
Ps 96:1-2, 2-3, 11-12, 13

R̖. (Luke 2:11) Today is born our Savior,
   Christ the Lord.

Sing to the LORD a new song;
   sing to the LORD, all you lands.
Sing to the LORD; bless his name.

R̖. Today is born our Savior, Christ the Lord.

Announce his salvation, day after day.
   Tell his glory among the nations;
   among all peoples, his wondrous deeds.

R̖. Today is born our Savior, Christ the Lord.

Let the heavens be glad and the earth rejoice;
   let the sea and what fills it resound;
   let the plains be joyful and all that is in
     them!
Then shall all the trees of the forest exult.

R̖. Today is born our Savior, Christ the Lord.

They shall exult before the LORD, for he
   comes;
   for he comes to rule the earth.
He shall rule the world with justice
   and the peoples with his constancy.

R̖. Today is born our Savior, Christ the Lord.

SECOND READING
Titus 2:11-14

Beloved:
The grace of God has appeared, saving all
   and training us to reject godless ways and
     worldly desires
   and to live temperately, justly, and devoutly
     in this age,
   as we await the blessed hope,
   the appearance of the glory of our great
     God
   and savior Jesus Christ,
   who gave himself for us to deliver us from
     all lawlessness
   and to cleanse for himself a people as his
     own,
   eager to do what is good.

The Nativity of the Lord, December 25, 2021 (Mass at Dawn)

FIRST READING
Isa 62:11-12

See, the LORD proclaims
   to the ends of the earth:
say to daughter Zion,
   your savior comes!
Here is his reward with him,
   his recompense before him.
They shall be called the holy people,
   the redeemed of the LORD,
and you shall be called "Frequented,"
   a city that is not forsaken.

RESPONSORIAL PSALM
Ps 97:1, 6, 11-12

R̖. A light will shine on us this day: the Lord
   is born for us.

The LORD is king; let the earth rejoice;
   let the many isles be glad.
The heavens proclaim his justice,
   and all peoples see his glory.

R̖. A light will shine on us this day: the Lord
   is born for us.

Light dawns for the just;
   and gladness, for the upright of heart.
Be glad in the LORD, you just,
   and give thanks to his holy name.

R̖. A light will shine on us this day: the Lord
   is born for us.

SECOND READING
Titus 3:4-7

Beloved:
When the kindness and generous love
   of God our savior appeared,
not because of any righteous deeds we had
     done
   but because of his mercy,
he saved us through the bath of rebirth
   and renewal by the Holy Spirit,
whom he richly poured out on us
   through Jesus Christ our savior,
so that we might be justified by his grace
   and become heirs in hope of eternal life.

Gospel (cont.)
John 1:1-18; L16ABC

And the Word became flesh
and made his dwelling among us,
and we saw his glory,
the glory as of the Father's only Son,
full of grace and truth.
John testified to him and cried out, saying,
"This was he of whom I said,
'The one who is coming after me ranks ahead of me
because he existed before me.'"
From his fullness we have all received,
grace in place of grace,
because while the law was given through Moses,
grace and truth came through Jesus Christ.
No one has ever seen God.
The only Son, God, who is at the Father's side,
has revealed him.

or John 1:1-5, 9-14

In the beginning was the Word,
and the Word was with God,
and the Word was God.
He was in the beginning with God.

All things came to be through him,
and without him nothing came to be.
What came to be through him was life,
and this life was the light of the human race;
the light shines in the darkness,
and the darkness has not overcome it.
The true light, which enlightens everyone,
was coming into the world.
He was in the world,
and the world came to be through him,
but the world did not know him.
He came to what was his own,
but his own people did not accept him.

But to those who did accept him
he gave power to become children of God,
to those who believe in his name,
who were born not by natural generation
nor by human choice nor by a man's decision
but of God.
And the Word became flesh
and made his dwelling among us,
and we saw his glory,
the glory as of the Father's only Son,
full of grace and truth.

FIRST READING
Isa 52:7-10

How beautiful upon the mountains
are the feet of him who brings glad tidings,
announcing peace, bearing good news,
announcing salvation, and saying to Zion,
"Your God is King!"

Hark! Your sentinels raise a cry,
together they shout for joy,
for they see directly, before their eyes,
the Lord restoring Zion.
Break out together in song,
O ruins of Jerusalem!
For the Lord comforts his people,
he redeems Jerusalem.
The Lord has bared his holy arm
in the sight of all the nations;
all the ends of the earth will behold
the salvation of our God.

RESPONSORIAL PSALM
Ps 98:1, 2-3, 3-4, 5-6

R̸. (3c) All the ends of the earth have seen the
saving power of God.

Sing to the Lord a new song,
for he has done wondrous deeds;
his right hand has won victory for him,
his holy arm.

R̸. All the ends of the earth have seen the
saving power of God.

The Lord has made his salvation known:
in the sight of the nations he has revealed
his justice.
He has remembered his kindness and his
faithfulness
toward the house of Israel.

R̸. All the ends of the earth have seen the
saving power of God.

All the ends of the earth have seen
the salvation by our God.
Sing joyfully to the Lord, all you lands;
break into song; sing praise.

R̸. All the ends of the earth have seen the
saving power of God.

Sing praise to the Lord with the harp,
with the harp and melodious song.
With trumpets and the sound of the horn
sing joyfully before the King, the Lord.

R̸. All the ends of the earth have seen the
saving power of God.

SECOND READING
Heb 1:1-6

Brothers and sisters:
In times past, God spoke in partial and
various ways
to our ancestors through the prophets;
in these last days, he has spoken to us
through the Son,
whom he made heir of all things
and through whom he created the universe,
who is the refulgence of his glory,
the very imprint of his being,
and who sustains all things by his mighty
word.
When he had accomplished purification
from sins,
he took his seat at the right hand of the
Majesty on high,
as far superior to the angels
as the name he has inherited is more
excellent than theirs.

For to which of the angels did God ever say:
*You are my son; this day I have begotten
you?*
Or again:
*I will be a father to him, and he shall be a
son to me?*
And again, when he leads the firstborn into
the world, he says:
Let all the angels of God worship him.

Gospel (cont.)
Luke 2:41-52; L17C

When his parents saw him,
    they were astonished,
    and his mother said to him,
    "Son, why have you done this to us?
Your father and I have been looking for you with great anxiety."
And he said to them,
    "Why were you looking for me?
Did you not know that I must be in my Father's house?"
But they did not understand what he said to them.
He went down with them and came to Nazareth,
    and was obedient to them;
    and his mother kept all these things in her heart.
And Jesus advanced in wisdom and age and favor
    before God and man.

FIRST READING
Sir 3:2-6, 12-14

God sets a father in honor over his children;
    a mother's authority he confirms over her
        sons.
Whoever honors his father atones for sins,
    and preserves himself from them.
When he prays, he is heard;
    he stores up riches who reveres his mother.
Whoever honors his father is gladdened by
        children,
    and, when he prays, is heard.
Whoever reveres his father will live a long life;
    he who obeys his father brings comfort to
        his mother.

My son, take care of your father when he is
        old;
    grieve him not as long as he lives.
Even if his mind fail, be considerate of him;
    revile him not all the days of his life;
kindness to a father will not be forgotten,
    firmly planted against the debt of your sins
    —a house raised in justice to you.

RESPONSORIAL PSALM
Ps 128:1-2, 3, 4-5

℞. (cf. 1) Blessed are those who fear the Lord
    and walk in his ways.

Blessed is everyone who fears the LORD,
    who walks in his ways!
For you shall eat the fruit of your handiwork;
    blessed shall you be, and favored.

℞. Blessed are those who fear the Lord and
    walk in his ways.

Your wife shall be like a fruitful vine
    in the recesses of your home;
your children like olive plants
    around your table.

℞. Blessed are those who fear the Lord and
    walk in his ways.

Behold, thus is the man blessed
    who fears the LORD.
The LORD bless you from Zion:
    may you see the prosperity of Jerusalem
    all the days of your life.

℞. Blessed are those who fear the Lord and
    walk in his ways.

SECOND READING
Col 3:12-21

Brothers and sisters:
Put on, as God's chosen ones, holy and
        beloved,
    heartfelt compassion, kindness, humility,
        gentleness, and patience,
    bearing with one another and forgiving one
        another,
    if one has a grievance against another;
    as the Lord has forgiven you, so must you
        also do.
And over all these put on love,
    that is, the bond of perfection.
And let the peace of Christ control your
        hearts,
    the peace into which you were also called in
        one body.
And be thankful.
Let the word of Christ dwell in you richly,
    as in all wisdom you teach and admonish
        one another,
    singing psalms, hymns, and spiritual songs
    with gratitude in your hearts to God.
And whatever you do, in word or in deed,
    do everything in the name of the Lord
        Jesus,
    giving thanks to God the Father through
        him.

Wives, be subordinate to your husbands,
    as is proper in the Lord.
Husbands, love your wives,
    and avoid any bitterness toward them.
Children, obey your parents in everything,
    for this is pleasing to the Lord.
Fathers, do not provoke your children,
    so they may not become discouraged.

or Col 3:12-17

Brothers and sisters:
Put on, as God's chosen ones, holy and beloved,
    heartfelt compassion, kindness, humility,
        gentleness, and patience,
    bearing with one another and forgiving one
        another,
    if one has a grievance against another;
    as the Lord has forgiven you, so must you
        also do.
And over all these put on love,
    that is, the bond of perfection.
And let the peace of Christ control your
        hearts,
    the peace into which you were also called in
        one body.
And be thankful.
Let the word of Christ dwell in you richly,
    as in all wisdom you teach and admonish
        one another,
    singing psalms, hymns, and spiritual songs
    with gratitude in your hearts to God.
And whatever you do, in word or in deed,
    do everything in the name of the Lord
        Jesus,
    giving thanks to God the Father through
        him.

Solemnity of Mary, the Holy Mother of God, *January 1, 2022*

FIRST READING
Num 6:22-27

The Lord said to Moses:
    "Speak to Aaron and his sons and tell them:
    This is how you shall bless the Israelites.
Say to them:
    The Lord bless you and keep you!
    The Lord let his face shine upon
        you, and be gracious to you!
    The Lord look upon you kindly and
        give you peace!
So shall they invoke my name upon the
        Israelites,
    and I will bless them."

RESPONSORIAL PSALM
Ps 67:2-3, 5, 6, 8

R̸. (2a) May God bless us in his mercy.

May God have pity on us and bless us;
    may he let his face shine upon us.
So may your way be known upon earth;
    among all nations, your salvation.

R̸. May God bless us in his mercy.

May the nations be glad and exult
    because you rule the peoples in equity;
    the nations on the earth you guide.

R̸. May God bless us in his mercy.

May the peoples praise you, O God;
    may all the peoples praise you!
May God bless us,
    and may all the ends of the earth fear him!

R̸. May God bless us in his mercy.

SECOND READING
Gal 4:4-7

Brothers and sisters:
When the fullness of time had come, God sent
        his Son,
    born of a woman, born under the law,
    to ransom those under the law,
    so that we might receive adoption as sons.
As proof that you are sons,
    God sent the Spirit of his Son into our
        hearts,
    crying out, "Abba, Father!"
So you are no longer a slave but a son,
    and if a son then also an heir, through God.

The Epiphany of the Lord, *January 2, 2022*

Gospel (cont.)
Matt 2:1-12; L20ABC

Then Herod called the magi secretly
    and ascertained from them the time of the star's appearance.
He sent them to Bethlehem and said,
    "Go and search diligently for the child.
When you have found him, bring me word,
    that I too may go and do him homage."
After their audience with the king they set out.
And behold, the star that they had seen at its rising preceded them,
    until it came and stopped over the place where the child was.
They were overjoyed at seeing the star,
    and on entering the house
    they saw the child with Mary his mother.
They prostrated themselves and did him homage.
Then they opened their treasures
    and offered him gifts of gold, frankincense, and myrrh.
And having been warned in a dream not to return to Herod,
    they departed for their country by another way.

The Baptism of the Lord, *January 9, 2022*

SECOND READING
Titus 2:11-14; 3:4-7

Beloved:
The grace of God has appeared, saving all
 and training us to reject godless ways and
   worldly desires
 and to live temperately, justly, and devoutly
   in this age,
 as we await the blessed hope,
 the appearance of the glory of our great
   God
 and savior Jesus Christ,
 who gave himself for us to deliver us from
   all lawlessness
 and to cleanse for himself a people as his
   own,
 eager to do what is good.
  When the kindness and generous love
   of God our savior appeared,
  not because of any righteous deeds we
    had done
   but because of his mercy,
  he saved us through the bath of rebirth
   and renewal by the Holy Spirit,
  whom he richly poured out on us
   through Jesus Christ our savior,
  so that we might be justified by his grace
   and become heirs in hope of eternal
     life.

FIRST READING
Isa 42:1-4, 6-7

Thus says the LORD:
Here is my servant whom I uphold,
 my chosen one with whom I am pleased,
upon whom I have put my spirit;
 he shall bring forth justice to the nations,
not crying out, not shouting,
 not making his voice heard in the street.
A bruised reed he shall not break,
 and a smoldering wick he shall not quench,
until he establishes justice on the earth;
 the coastlands will wait for his teaching.

I, the LORD, have called you for the victory of
   justice,
 I have grasped you by the hand;
I formed you, and set you
 as a covenant of the people,
 a light for the nations,
to open the eyes of the blind,
 to bring out prisoners from confinement,
 and from the dungeon, those who live in
   darkness.

RESPONSORIAL PSALM
Ps 29:1-2, 3-4, 9-10

R℣. (11b) The Lord will bless his people with
   peace.

Give to the LORD, you sons of God,
 give to the LORD glory and praise,
give to the LORD the glory due his name;
 adore the LORD in holy attire.

R℣. The Lord will bless his people with peace.

The voice of the LORD is over the waters,
 the LORD, over vast waters.
The voice of the LORD is mighty;
 the voice of the LORD is majestic.

R℣. The Lord will bless his people with peace.

The God of glory thunders,
 and in his temple all say, "Glory!"
The LORD is enthroned above the flood;
 the LORD is enthroned as king forever.

R℣. The Lord will bless his people with peace.

SECOND READING
Acts 10:34-38

Peter proceeded to speak to those gathered
 in the house of Cornelius, saying:
 "In truth, I see that God shows no
   partiality.
Rather, in every nation whoever fears him and
   acts uprightly
 is acceptable to him.
You know the word that he sent to the
   Israelites
 as he proclaimed peace through Jesus
   Christ, who is Lord of all,
 what has happened all over Judea,
 beginning in Galilee after the baptism
 that John preached,
 how God anointed Jesus of Nazareth
 with the Holy Spirit and power.
He went about doing good
 and healing all those oppressed by the
   devil,
 for God was with him."

Gospel (cont.)

Luke 1:1-4; 4:14-21; L69C

He has sent me to proclaim liberty to captives
and recovery of sight to the blind,
to let the oppressed go free,
and to proclaim a year acceptable to the Lord.

Rolling up the scroll, he handed it back to the attendant and sat down,
and the eyes of all in the synagogue looked intently at him.
He said to them,
"Today this Scripture passage is fulfilled in your hearing."

SECOND READING

1 Cor 12:12-30

Brothers and sisters:
As a body is one though it has many parts,
and all the parts of the body, though many, are one body,
so also Christ.
For in one Spirit we were all baptized into one body,
whether Jews or Greeks, slaves or free persons,
and we were all given to drink of one Spirit.

Now the body is not a single part, but many.
If a foot should say,
"Because I am not a hand I do not belong to the body,"
it does not for this reason belong any less to the body.
Or if an ear should say,
"Because I am not an eye I do not belong to the body,"
it does not for this reason belong any less to the body.
If the whole body were an eye, where would the hearing be?
If the whole body were hearing, where would the sense of smell be?
But as it is, God placed the parts,
each one of them, in the body as he intended.
If they were all one part, where would the body be?
But as it is, there are many parts, yet one body.
The eye cannot say to the hand, "I do not need you,"
nor again the head to the feet, "I do not need you."
Indeed, the parts of the body that seem to be weaker
are all the more necessary,
and those parts of the body that we consider less honorable

we surround with greater honor,
and our less presentable parts are treated with greater propriety,
whereas our more presentable parts do not need this.
But God has so constructed the body
as to give greater honor to a part that is without it,
so that there may be no division in the body,
but that the parts may have the same concern for one another.
If one part suffers, all the parts suffer with it;
if one part is honored, all the parts share its joy.

Now you are Christ's body, and individually parts of it.
Some people God has designated in the church
to be, first, apostles; second, prophets; third, teachers;
then, mighty deeds;
then gifts of healing, assistance, administration,
and varieties of tongues.
Are all apostles? Are all prophets? Are all teachers?
Do all work mighty deeds? Do all have gifts of healing?
Do all speak in tongues? Do all interpret?

SECOND READING

1 Cor 12:31–13:13

Brothers and sisters:
Strive eagerly for the greatest spiritual gifts.
But I shall show you a still more excellent way.

If I speak in human and angelic tongues,
but do not have love,
I am a resounding gong or a clashing cymbal.
And if I have the gift of prophecy,
and comprehend all mysteries and all knowledge;
if I have all faith so as to move mountains,
but do not have love, I am nothing.
If I give away everything I own,
and if I hand my body over so that I may boast,
but do not have love, I gain nothing.

Love is patient, love is kind.
It is not jealous, it is not pompous,
it is not inflated, it is not rude,
it does not seek its own interests,
it is not quick-tempered, it does not brood over injury,
it does not rejoice over wrongdoing
but rejoices with the truth.
It bears all things, believes all things,
hopes all things, endures all things.

Love never fails.
If there are prophecies, they will be brought to nothing;
if tongues, they will cease;
if knowledge, it will be brought to nothing.
For we know partially and we prophesy partially,

but when the perfect comes, the partial will pass away.
When I was a child, I used to talk as a child,
think as a child, reason as a child;
when I became a man, I put aside childish things.
At present we see indistinctly, as in a mirror,
but then face to face.
At present I know partially;
then I shall know fully, as I am fully known.
So faith, hope, love remain, these three;
but the greatest of these is love.

Gospel (cont.)
Luke 5:1-11; L75C

When Simon Peter saw this, he fell at the knees of Jesus and said,
    "Depart from me, Lord, for I am a sinful man."
For astonishment at the catch of fish they had made seized him
    and all those with him,
    and likewise James and John, the sons of Zebedee,
    who were partners of Simon.
Jesus said to Simon, "Do not be afraid;
    from now on you will be catching men."
When they brought their boats to the shore,
    they left everything and followed him.

SECOND READING
1 Cor 15:1-11

I am reminding you, brothers and sisters,
    of the gospel I preached to you,
    which you indeed received and in which
        you also stand.
Through it you are also being saved,
    if you hold fast to the word I preached to
        you,
    unless you believed in vain.
For I handed on to you as of first importance
        what I also received:
    that Christ died for our sins
        in accordance with the Scriptures;
    that he was buried;
    that he was raised on the third day
        in accordance with the Scriptures;
    that he appeared to Cephas, then to the
        Twelve.

After that, he appeared to more
        than five hundred brothers at once,
    most of whom are still living,
    though some have fallen asleep.
After that he appeared to James,
    then to all the apostles.
Last of all, as to one born abnormally,
    he appeared to me.
For I am the least of the apostles,
    not fit to be called an apostle,
    because I persecuted the church of God.
But by the grace of God I am what I am,
    and his grace to me has not been
        ineffective.
Indeed, I have toiled harder than all of them;
    not I, however, but the grace of God that is
        with me.
Therefore, whether it be I or they,
    so we preach and so you believed.

Gospel (cont.)
Luke 6:27-38; L81C

But rather, love your enemies and do good to them,
    and lend expecting nothing back;
    then your reward will be great
    and you will be children of the Most High,
    for he himself is kind to the ungrateful and the wicked.
Be merciful, just as your Father is merciful.

"Stop judging and you will not be judged.
Stop condemning and you will not be condemned.
Forgive and you will be forgiven.
Give, and gifts will be given to you;
    a good measure, packed together, shaken down, and overflowing,
    will be poured into your lap.
For the measure with which you measure
    will in return be measured out to you."

Gospel (cont.)
Matt 6:1-6, 16-18; L219

"When you fast,
  do not look gloomy like the hypocrites.
They neglect their appearance,
  so that they may appear to others to be fasting.
Amen, I say to you, they have received their reward.
But when you fast,
  anoint your head and wash your face,
  so that you may not appear to be fasting,
  except to your Father who is hidden.
And your Father who sees what is hidden will repay you."

FIRST READING
Joel 2:12-18

Even now, says the LORD,
  return to me with your whole heart,
  with fasting, and weeping, and mourning;
Rend your hearts, not your garments,
  and return to the LORD, your God.
For gracious and merciful is he,
  slow to anger, rich in kindness,
  and relenting in punishment.
Perhaps he will again relent
  and leave behind him a blessing,
Offerings and libations
  for the LORD, your God.

Blow the trumpet in Zion!
  proclaim a fast,
  call an assembly;
Gather the people,
  notify the congregation;
Assemble the elders,
  gather the children
  and the infants at the breast;
Let the bridegroom quit his room
  and the bride her chamber.
Between the porch and the altar
  let the priests, the ministers of the LORD,
    weep,
And say, "Spare, O LORD, your people,
  and make not your heritage a reproach,
  with the nations ruling over them!
Why should they say among the peoples,
  'Where is their God?'"

Then the LORD was stirred to concern for his
    land
  and took pity on his people.

RESPONSORIAL PSALM
Ps 51:3-4, 5-6ab, 12-13, 14 and 17

R̸. (see 3a) Be merciful, O Lord, for we have
    sinned.

Have mercy on me, O God, in your goodness;
  in the greatness of your compassion wipe
    out my offense.
Thoroughly wash me from my guilt
  and of my sin cleanse me.

R̸. Be merciful, O Lord, for we have sinned.

For I acknowledge my offense,
  and my sin is before me always:
"Against you only have I sinned,
  and done what is evil in your sight."

R̸. Be merciful, O Lord, for we have sinned.

A clean heart create for me, O God,
  and a steadfast spirit renew within me.
Cast me not out from your presence,
  and your Holy Spirit take not from me.

R̸. Be merciful, O Lord, for we have sinned.

Give me back the joy of your salvation,
  and a willing spirit sustain in me.
O Lord, open my lips,
  and my mouth shall proclaim your praise.

R̸. Be merciful, O Lord, for we have sinned.

SECOND READING
2 Cor 5:20—6:2

Brothers and sisters:
We are ambassadors for Christ,
  as if God were appealing through us.
We implore you on behalf of Christ,
  be reconciled to God.
For our sake he made him to be sin who did
    not know sin,
  so that we might become the righteousness
    of God in him.

Working together, then,
  we appeal to you not to receive the grace of
    God in vain.
For he says:

  *In an acceptable time I heard you,
    and on the day of salvation I helped you.*

Behold, now is a very acceptable time;
  behold, now is the day of salvation.

SECOND READING
Rom 10:8-13 *(cont.)*

For the Scripture says,
No one who believes in him will be put to shame.
For there is no distinction between Jew and Greek;
the same Lord is Lord of all,
enriching all who call upon him.
For "everyone who calls on the name of the Lord will be saved."

SECOND READING
Phil 3:20–4:1

Brothers and sisters:
Our citizenship is in heaven,
and from it we also await a savior, the Lord Jesus Christ.
He will change our lowly body
to conform with his glorified body
by the power that enables him also
to bring all things into subjection to himself.

Therefore, my brothers and sisters,
whom I love and long for, my joy and crown,
in this way stand firm in the Lord, beloved.

Gospel
Luke 2:41-51a; L543

Each year Jesus' parents went to Jerusalem for the feast of Passover,
  and when he was twelve years old,
  they went up according to festival custom.
After they had completed its days, as they were returning,
  the boy Jesus remained behind in Jerusalem,
  but his parents did not know it.
Thinking that he was in the caravan,
  they journeyed for a day
  and looked for him among their relatives and acquaintances,
  but not finding him,
  they returned to Jerusalem to look for him.
After three days they found him in the temple,
  sitting in the midst of the teachers,
  listening to them and asking them questions,
  and all who heard him were astounded
  at his understanding and his answers.
When his parents saw him,
  they were astonished,
  and his mother said to him,
  "Son, why have you done this to us?
Your father and I have been looking for you with great anxiety."

And he said to them,
  "Why were you looking for me?
Did you not know that I must be in my Father's house?"
But they did not understand what he said to them.
He went down with them and came to Nazareth,
  and was obedient to them.

FIRST READING
2 Sam 7:4-5a, 12-14a, 16

The Lord spoke to Nathan and said:
"Go, tell my servant David,
  'When your time comes and you rest with
    your ancestors,
  I will raise up your heir after you, sprung
    from your loins,
  and I will make his kingdom firm.
It is he who shall build a house for my name.
And I will make his royal throne firm forever.
I will be a father to him,
  and he shall be a son to me.
Your house and your kingdom shall endure
    forever before me;
  your throne shall stand firm forever.'"

RESPONSORIAL PSALM
Ps 89:2-3, 4-5, 27 and 29

R︦. (37) The son of David will live for ever.

The promises of the Lord I will sing forever,
  through all generations my mouth will
    proclaim your faithfulness,
For you have said, "My kindness is
    established forever";
  in heaven you have confirmed your
    faithfulness.

R︦. The son of David will live for ever.

"I have made a covenant with my chosen one;
  I have sworn to David my servant:
Forever will I confirm your posterity
  and establish your throne for all
    generations."

R︦. The son of David will live for ever.

"He shall say of me, 'You are my father,
  my God, the Rock, my savior.'
Forever I will maintain my kindness toward
    him,
  and my covenant with him stands firm."

R︦. The son of David will live for ever.

SECOND READING
Rom 4:13, 16-18, 22

Brothers and sisters:
It was not through the law
  that the promise was made to Abraham
    and his descendants
  that he would inherit the world,
  but through the righteousness that comes
    from faith.
For this reason, it depends on faith,
  so that it may be a gift,
  and the promise may be guaranteed to all
    his descendants,
  not to those who only adhere to the law
  but to those who follow the faith of
    Abraham,
  who is the father of all of us, as it is
    written,
I have made you father of many nations.
He is our father in the sight of God,
  in whom he believed, who gives life to the
    dead
  and calls into being what does not exist.
He believed, hoping against hope,
  that he would become *the father of many
    nations,*
  according to what was said, *Thus shall your
    descendants be.*
That is why *it was credited to him as
    righteousness.*

SECOND READING
1 Cor 10:1-6, 10-12

I do not want you to be unaware, brothers and
    sisters,
    that our ancestors were all under the cloud
    and all passed through the sea,
    and all of them were baptized into Moses
        in the cloud and in the sea.
All ate the same spiritual food,
    and all drank the same spiritual drink,
    for they drank from a spiritual rock that
        followed them,
    and the rock was the Christ.
Yet God was not pleased with most of them,
    for they were struck down in the desert.

These things happened as examples for us,
    so that we might not desire evil things, as
        they did.

Do not grumble as some of them did,
    and suffered death by the destroyer.
These things happened to them as an
        example,
    and they have been written down as a
        warning to us,
    upon whom the end of the ages has come.
Therefore, whoever thinks he is standing
        secure
    should take care not to fall.

Gospel

John 4:5-42; L28A

Jesus came to a town of Samaria called Sychar,
　　near the plot of land that Jacob had given to his son Joseph.
Jacob's well was there.
Jesus, tired from his journey, sat down there at the well.
It was about noon.

A woman of Samaria came to draw water.
Jesus said to her,
　　"Give me a drink."
His disciples had gone into the town to buy food.
The Samaritan woman said to him,
　　"How can you, a Jew, ask me, a Samaritan woman, for a drink?"
—For Jews use nothing in common with Samaritans.—
Jesus answered and said to her,
　　"If you knew the gift of God
　　and who is saying to you, 'Give me a drink,'
　　you would have asked him
　　and he would have given you living water."
The woman said to him,
　　"Sir, you do not even have a bucket and the cistern is deep;
　　where then can you get this living water?
Are you greater than our father Jacob,
　　who gave us this cistern and drank from it himself
　　with his children and his flocks?"
Jesus answered and said to her,
　　"Everyone who drinks this water will be thirsty again;
　　but whoever drinks the water I shall give will never thirst;
　　the water I shall give will become in him
　　a spring of water welling up to eternal life."
The woman said to him,
　　"Sir, give me this water, so that I may not be thirsty
　　or have to keep coming here to draw water."

Jesus said to her,
　　"Go call your husband and come back."
The woman answered and said to him,
　　"I do not have a husband."
Jesus answered her,
　　"You are right in saying, 'I do not have a husband.'
For you have had five husbands,
　　and the one you have now is not your husband.
What you have said is true."
The woman said to him,
　　"Sir, I can see that you are a prophet.
Our ancestors worshiped on this mountain;
　　but you people say that the place to worship is in Jerusalem."
Jesus said to her,
　　"Believe me, woman, the hour is coming
　　when you will worship the Father
　　neither on this mountain nor in Jerusalem.
You people worship what you do not understand;
　　we worship what we understand,
　　because salvation is from the Jews.
But the hour is coming, and is now here,
　　when true worshipers will worship the Father in Spirit and truth;
　　and indeed the Father seeks such people to worship him.
God is Spirit, and those who worship him
　　must worship in Spirit and truth."
The woman said to him,

"I know that the Messiah is coming, the one called the Christ;
　　when he comes, he will tell us everything."
Jesus said to her,
　　"I am he, the one speaking with you."

At that moment his disciples returned,
　　and were amazed that he was talking with a woman,
　　but still no one said, "What are you looking for?"
　　or "Why are you talking with her?"
The woman left her water jar
　　and went into the town and said to the people,
　　"Come see a man who told me everything I have done.
Could he possibly be the Christ?"
They went out of the town and came to him.
Meanwhile, the disciples urged him, "Rabbi, eat."
But he said to them,
　　"I have food to eat of which you do not know."
So the disciples said to one another,
　　"Could someone have brought him something to eat?"
Jesus said to them,
　　"My food is to do the will of the one who sent me
　　and to finish his work.
Do you not say, 'In four months the harvest will be here'?
I tell you, look up and see the fields ripe for the harvest.
The reaper is already receiving payment
　　and gathering crops for eternal life,
　　so that the sower and reaper can rejoice together.
For here the saying is verified that 'One sows and another reaps.'
I sent you to reap what you have not worked for;
　　others have done the work,
　　and you are sharing the fruits of their work."

Many of the Samaritans of that town began to believe in him
　　because of the word of the woman who testified,
　　"He told me everything I have done."
When the Samaritans came to him,
　　they invited him to stay with them;
　　and he stayed there two days.
Many more began to believe in him because of his word,
　　and they said to the woman,
　　"We no longer believe because of your word;
　　for we have heard for ourselves,
　　and we know that this is truly the savior of the world."

or
John 4:5-15, 19b-26, 39a, 40-42; L28A

Jesus came to a town of Samaria called Sychar,
　　near the plot of land that Jacob had given to his son Joseph.
Jacob's well was there.
Jesus, tired from his journey, sat down there at the well.
It was about noon.

A woman of Samaria came to draw water.
Jesus said to her,
　　"Give me a drink."
His disciples had gone into the town to buy food.
The Samaritan woman said to him,
　　"How can you, a Jew, ask me, a Samaritan woman, for a drink?"
—For Jews use nothing in common with Samaritans.—
Jesus answered and said to her,

"If you knew the gift of God
and who is saying to you, 'Give me a drink,'
you would have asked him
and he would have given you living water."
The woman said to him,
"Sir, you do not even have a bucket and the cistern is deep;
where then can you get this living water?
Are you greater than our father Jacob,
who gave us this cistern and drank from it himself
with his children and his flocks?"
Jesus answered and said to her,
"Everyone who drinks this water will be thirsty again;
but whoever drinks the water I shall give will never thirst;
the water I shall give will become in him
a spring of water welling up to eternal life."
The woman said to him,
"Sir, give me this water, so that I may not be thirsty
or have to keep coming here to draw water.

"I can see that you are a prophet.
Our ancestors worshiped on this mountain;
but you people say that the place to worship is in Jerusalem."
Jesus said to her,
"Believe me, woman, the hour is coming
when you will worship the Father

neither on this mountain nor in Jerusalem.
You people worship what you do not understand;
we worship what we understand,
because salvation is from the Jews.
But the hour is coming, and is now here,
when true worshipers will worship the Father in Spirit and truth;
and indeed the Father seeks such people to worship him.
God is Spirit, and those who worship him
must worship in Spirit and truth."
The woman said to him,
"I know that the Messiah is coming, the one called the Christ;
when he comes, he will tell us everything."
Jesus said to her,
"I am he, the one speaking with you."

Many of the Samaritans of that town began to believe in him.
When the Samaritans came to him,
they invited him to stay with them;
and he stayed there two days.
Many more began to believe in him because of his word,
and they said to the woman,
"We no longer believe because of your word;
for we have heard for ourselves,
and we know that this is truly the savior of the world."

FIRST READING
Exod 17:3-7

In those days, in their thirst for water,
the people grumbled against Moses,
saying, "Why did you ever make us leave
Egypt?
Was it just to have us die here of thirst
with our children and our livestock?"
So Moses cried out to the LORD,
"What shall I do with this people?
A little more and they will stone me!"
The LORD answered Moses,
"Go over there in front of the people,
along with some of the elders of Israel,
holding in your hand, as you go,
the staff with which you struck the river.
I will be standing there in front of you on the
rock in Horeb.
Strike the rock, and the water will flow from it
for the people to drink."
This Moses did, in the presence of the elders
of Israel.
The place was called Massah and Meribah,
because the Israelites quarreled there
and tested the LORD, saying,
"Is the LORD in our midst or not?"

RESPONSORIAL PSALM
Ps 95:1-2, 6-7, 8-9

R⁊. (8) If today you hear his voice, harden not
your hearts.

Come, let us sing joyfully to the LORD;
let us acclaim the Rock of our salvation.
Let us come into his presence with
thanksgiving;
let us joyfully sing psalms to him.

R⁊. If today you hear his voice, harden not
your hearts.

Come, let us bow down in worship;
let us kneel before the LORD who made us.
For he is our God,
and we are the people he shepherds, the
flock he guides.

R⁊. If today you hear his voice, harden not
your hearts.

Oh, that today you would hear his voice:
"Harden not your hearts as at Meribah,
as in the day of Massah in the desert,
Where your fathers tempted me;
they tested me though they had seen my
works."

R⁊. If today you hear his voice, harden not
your hearts.

SECOND READING
Rom 5:1-2, 5-8

Brothers and sisters:
Since we have been justified by faith,
we have peace with God through our Lord
Jesus Christ,
through whom we have gained access by
faith
to this grace in which we stand,
and we boast in hope of the glory of God.

And hope does not disappoint,
because the love of God has been poured
out into our hearts
through the Holy Spirit who has been given
to us.
For Christ, while we were still helpless,
died at the appointed time for the ungodly.
Indeed, only with difficulty does one die for a
just person,
though perhaps for a good person one
might even find courage to die.
But God proves his love for us
in that while we were still sinners Christ
died for us.

Gospel (cont.)
Luke 1:26-38; L545

But Mary said to the angel,
  "How can this be,
  since I have no relations with a man?"
And the angel said to her in reply,
  "The Holy Spirit will come upon you,
  and the power of the Most High will
    overshadow you.
Therefore the child to be born
  will be called holy, the Son of God.
And behold, Elizabeth, your relative,
  has also conceived a son in her old age,
  and this is the sixth month for her who was
    called barren;
  for nothing will be impossible for God."
Mary said, "Behold, I am the handmaid of the
  Lord.
May it be done to me according to your word."
Then the angel departed from her.

FIRST READING
Isa 7:10-14; 8:10

The Lord spoke to Ahaz, saying:
Ask for a sign from the Lord, your God;
  let it be deep as the nether world, or high as
    the sky!
But Ahaz answered,
  "I will not ask! I will not tempt the Lord!"
Then Isaiah said:
  Listen, O house of David!
Is it not enough for you to weary people,
  must you also weary my God?
Therefore the Lord himself will give you this
    sign:
  the virgin shall be with child, and bear a son,
  and shall name him Emmanuel,
  which means "God is with us!"

RESPONSORIAL PSALM
Ps 40:7-8a, 8b-9, 10, 11

R̥. (8a and 9a) Here I am, Lord; I come to do
  your will.

Sacrifice or offering you wished not,
  but ears open to obedience you gave me.
Holocausts and sin-offerings you sought not;
  then said I, "Behold, I come."

R̥. Here I am, Lord; I come to do your will.

"In the written scroll it is prescribed for me,
To do your will, O God, is my delight,
  and your law is within my heart!"

R̥. Here I am, Lord; I come to do your will.

I announced your justice in the vast assembly;
  I did not restrain my lips, as you, O Lord,
    know.

R̥. Here I am, Lord; I come to do your will.

Your justice I kept not hid within my heart;
  your faithfulness and your salvation I have
    spoken of;
I have made no secret of your kindness and
    your truth
  in the vast assembly.

R̥. Here I am, Lord; I come to do your will.

SECOND READING
Heb 10:4-10

Brothers and sisters:
It is impossible that the blood of bulls and
    goats
  takes away sins.
For this reason, when Christ came into the
    world, he said:

  "Sacrifice and offering you did not desire,
    but a body you prepared for me;
  in holocausts and sin offerings you took no
    delight.
  Then I said, 'As is written of me in the scroll,
  behold, I come to do your will, O God.'"

First Christ says, "Sacrifices and offerings,
  holocausts and sin offerings,
  you neither desired nor delighted in."
These are offered according to the law.
Then he says, "Behold, I come to do your will."
He takes away the first to establish the second.
By this "will," we have been consecrated
  through the offering of the Body of Jesus
    Christ once for all.

Gospel (cont.)
Luke 15:1-3, 11-32; L33C

I no longer deserve to be called your son;
   treat me as you would treat one of your hired workers."'
 So he got up and went back to his father.
While he was still a long way off,
   his father caught sight of him, and was filled with compassion.
He ran to his son, embraced him and kissed him.
His son said to him,
   'Father, I have sinned against heaven and against you;
   I no longer deserve to be called your son.'
But his father ordered his servants,
   'Quickly bring the finest robe and put it on him;
   put a ring on his finger and sandals on his feet.
Take the fattened calf and slaughter it.
Then let us celebrate with a feast,
   because this son of mine was dead, and has come to life again;
   he was lost, and has been found.'
Then the celebration began.
Now the older son had been out in the field
   and, on his way back, as he neared the house,
   he heard the sound of music and dancing.
He called one of the servants and asked what this might mean.

The servant said to him,
   'Your brother has returned
   and your father has slaughtered the fattened calf
   because he has him back safe and sound.'
He became angry,
   and when he refused to enter the house,
   his father came out and pleaded with him.
He said to his father in reply,
   'Look, all these years I served you
   and not once did I disobey your orders;
   yet you never gave me even a young goat to feast on with
      my friends.
But when your son returns
   who swallowed up your property with prostitutes,
   for him you slaughter the fattened calf.'
He said to him,
   'My son, you are here with me always;
   everything I have is yours.
But now we must celebrate and rejoice,
   because your brother was dead and has come to life again;
   he was lost and has been found.'"

Gospel
John 9:1-41; L31A

As Jesus passed by he saw a man blind from birth.
His disciples asked him,
    "Rabbi, who sinned, this man or his parents,
    that he was born blind?"
Jesus answered,
    "Neither he nor his parents sinned;
    it is so that the works of God might be made visible through him.
We have to do the works of the one who sent me while it is day.
Night is coming when no one can work.
While I am in the world, I am the light of the world."
When he had said this, he spat on the ground
    and made clay with the saliva,
    and smeared the clay on his eyes, and said to him,
    "Go wash in the Pool of Siloam"—which means Sent—.
So he went and washed, and came back able to see.

His neighbors and those who had seen him earlier as a beggar said,
    "Isn't this the one who used to sit and beg?"
Some said, "It is,"
    but others said, "No, he just looks like him."
He said, "I am."
So they said to him, "How were your eyes opened?"
He replied,
    "The man called Jesus made clay and anointed my eyes
    and told me, 'Go to Siloam and wash.'
So I went there and washed and was able to see."
And they said to him, "Where is he?"
He said, "I don't know."

They brought the one who was once blind to the Pharisees.
Now Jesus had made clay and opened his eyes on a sabbath.
So then the Pharisees also asked him how he was able to see.
He said to them,
    "He put clay on my eyes, and I washed, and now I can see."
So some of the Pharisees said,
    "This man is not from God,
    because he does not keep the sabbath."
But others said,
    "How can a sinful man do such signs?"
And there was a division among them.
So they said to the blind man again,
    "What do you have to say about him,
    since he opened your eyes?"
He said, "He is a prophet."

Now the Jews did not believe
    that he had been blind and gained his sight
    until they summoned the parents of the one who had gained his
        sight.
They asked them,
    "Is this your son, who you say was born blind?
How does he now see?"
His parents answered and said,
    "We know that this is our son and that he was born blind.
We do not know how he sees now,
    nor do we know who opened his eyes.
Ask him, he is of age;
    he can speak for himself."
His parents said this because they were afraid of the Jews,

for the Jews had already agreed
    that if anyone acknowledged him as the Christ,
    he would be expelled from the synagogue.
For this reason his parents said,
    "He is of age; question him."

So a second time they called the man who had been blind
    and said to him, "Give God the praise!
We know that this man is a sinner."
He replied,
    "If he is a sinner, I do not know.
One thing I do know is that I was blind and now I see."
So they said to him,
    "What did he do to you?
    How did he open your eyes?"
He answered them,
    "I told you already and you did not listen.
Why do you want to hear it again?
Do you want to become his disciples, too?"
They ridiculed him and said,
    "You are that man's disciple;
    we are disciples of Moses!
We know that God spoke to Moses,
    but we do not know where this one is from."
The man answered and said to them,
    "This is what is so amazing,
    that you do not know where he is from, yet he opened my eyes.
We know that God does not listen to sinners,
    but if one is devout and does his will, he listens to him.
It is unheard of that anyone ever opened the eyes of a person born
        blind.
If this man were not from God,
    he would not be able to do anything."
They answered and said to him,
    "You were born totally in sin,
    and are you trying to teach us?"
Then they threw him out.

When Jesus heard that they had thrown him out,
    he found him and said, "Do you believe in the Son of Man?"
He answered and said,
    "Who is he, sir, that I may believe in him?"
Jesus said to him,
    "You have seen him,
    and the one speaking with you is he."
He said,
    "I do believe, Lord," and he worshiped him.
Then Jesus said,
    "I came into this world for judgment,
    so that those who do not see might see,
    and those who do see might become blind."

Some of the Pharisees who were with him heard this
    and said to him, "Surely we are not also blind, are we?"
Jesus said to them,
    "If you were blind, you would have no sin;
    but now you are saying, 'We see,' so your sin remains."

Fourth Sunday of Lent, *March 27, 2022*

Gospel

John 9:1, 6-9, 13-17, 34-38; L31A

As Jesus passed by he saw a man blind from birth.
He spat on the ground and made clay with the saliva,
   and smeared the clay on his eyes, and said to him,
   "Go wash in the Pool of Siloam"—which means Sent—.
So he went and washed, and came back able to see.

His neighbors and those who had seen him earlier as a beggar said,
   "Isn't this the one who used to sit and beg?"
Some said, "It is,"
   but others said, "No, he just looks like him."
He said, "I am."

They brought the one who was once blind to the Pharisees.
Now Jesus had made clay and opened his eyes on a sabbath.
So then the Pharisees also asked him how he was able to see.
He said to them,
   "He put clay on my eyes, and I washed, and now I can see."
So some of the Pharisees said,
   "This man is not from God,
   because he does not keep the sabbath."
But others said,
   "How can a sinful man do such signs?"
And there was a division among them.

So they said to the blind man again,
   "What do you have to say about him,
   since he opened your eyes?"
He said, "He is a prophet."

They answered and said to him,
   "You were born totally in sin,
   and are you trying to teach us?"
Then they threw him out.

When Jesus heard that they had thrown him out,
   he found him and said, "Do you believe in the Son of Man?"
He answered and said,
   "Who is he, sir, that I may believe in him?"
Jesus said to him,
   "You have seen him,
   and the one speaking with you is he."
He said,
   "I do believe, Lord," and he worshiped him.

FIRST READING   1 Sam 16:1b, 6-7, 10-13a

The LORD said to Samuel:
   "Fill your horn with oil, and be on your way.
I am sending you to Jesse of Bethlehem,
   for I have chosen my king from among his
      sons."

As Jesse and his sons came to the sacrifice,
   Samuel looked at Eliab and thought,
   "Surely the LORD's anointed is here before
      him."
But the LORD said to Samuel:
   "Do not judge from his appearance or from
      his lofty stature,
   because I have rejected him.
Not as man sees does God see,
   because man sees the appearance
   but the LORD looks into the heart."
In the same way Jesse presented seven sons
      before Samuel,
   but Samuel said to Jesse,
   "The LORD has not chosen any one of these."
Then Samuel asked Jesse,
   "Are these all the sons you have?"
Jesse replied,
   "There is still the youngest, who is tending
      the sheep."
Samuel said to Jesse,
   "Send for him;
   we will not begin the sacrificial banquet
      until he arrives here."
Jesse sent and had the young man brought to
      them.
He was ruddy, a youth handsome to behold
   and making a splendid appearance.

The LORD said,
   "There—anoint him, for this is the one!"
Then Samuel, with the horn of oil in hand,
   anointed David in the presence of his
      brothers;
   and from that day on, the spirit of the LORD
      rushed upon David.

RESPONSORIAL PSALM   Ps 23:1-3a, 3b-4, 5, 6

℟. (1) The Lord is my shepherd; there is noth-
      ing I shall want.

The LORD is my shepherd; I shall not want.
   In verdant pastures he gives me repose;
beside restful waters he leads me;
   he refreshes my soul.

℟. The Lord is my shepherd; there is nothing
      I shall want.

He guides me in right paths
   for his name's sake.
Even though I walk in the dark valley
   I fear no evil; for you are at my side
with your rod and your staff
   that give me courage.

℟. The Lord is my shepherd; there is nothing
      I shall want.

You spread the table before me
   in the sight of my foes;
you anoint my head with oil;
   my cup overflows.

℟. The Lord is my shepherd; there is nothing
      I shall want.

Only goodness and kindness follow me
   all the days of my life;
and I shall dwell in the house of the LORD
   for years to come.

℟. The Lord is my shepherd; there is nothing
      I shall want.

SECOND READING
Eph 5:8-14

Brothers and sisters:
You were once darkness,
   but now you are light in the Lord.
Live as children of light,
   for light produces every kind of goodness
   and righteousness and truth.
Try to learn what is pleasing to the Lord.
Take no part in the fruitless works of
      darkness;
   rather expose them, for it is shameful even
         to mention
   the things done by them in secret;
   but everything exposed by the light
         becomes visible,
   for everything that becomes visible is light.
Therefore, it says:
   "Awake, O sleeper,
   and arise from the dead,
   and Christ will give you light."

Gospel
John 11:1-45; L34A

Now a man was ill, Lazarus from Bethany,
  the village of Mary and her sister Martha.
Mary was the one who had anointed the Lord with perfumed oil
  and dried his feet with her hair;
  it was her brother Lazarus who was ill.
So the sisters sent word to Jesus saying,
  "Master, the one you love is ill."
When Jesus heard this he said,
  "This illness is not to end in death,
  but is for the glory of God,
  that the Son of God may be glorified through it."
Now Jesus loved Martha and her sister and Lazarus.
So when he heard that he was ill,
  he remained for two days in the place where he was.
Then after this he said to his disciples,
  "Let us go back to Judea."
The disciples said to him,
  "Rabbi, the Jews were just trying to stone you,
  and you want to go back there?"
Jesus answered,
  "Are there not twelve hours in a day?
If one walks during the day, he does not stumble,
  because he sees the light of this world.
But if one walks at night, he stumbles,
  because the light is not in him."
He said this, and then told them,
  "Our friend Lazarus is asleep,
  but I am going to awaken him."
So the disciples said to him,
  "Master, if he is asleep, he will be saved."
But Jesus was talking about his death,
  while they thought that he meant ordinary sleep.
So then Jesus said to them clearly,
  "Lazarus has died.
And I am glad for you that I was not there,
  that you may believe.
Let us go to him."
So Thomas, called Didymus, said to his fellow disciples,
  "Let us also go to die with him."

When Jesus arrived, he found that Lazarus
  had already been in the tomb for four days.
Now Bethany was near Jerusalem, only about two miles away.
And many of the Jews had come to Martha and Mary
  to comfort them about their brother.
When Martha heard that Jesus was coming,
  she went to meet him;
  but Mary sat at home.
Martha said to Jesus,
  "Lord, if you had been here,
  my brother would not have died.
But even now I know that whatever you ask of God,
  God will give you."
Jesus said to her,
  "Your brother will rise."
Martha said to him,
  "I know he will rise,
  in the resurrection on the last day."
Jesus told her,

"I am the resurrection and the life;
  whoever believes in me, even if he dies, will live,
  and everyone who lives and believes in me will never die.
Do you believe this?"
She said to him, "Yes, Lord.
I have come to believe that you are the Christ, the Son of God,
  the one who is coming into the world."

When she had said this,
  she went and called her sister Mary secretly, saying,
  "The teacher is here and is asking for you."
As soon as she heard this,
  she rose quickly and went to him.
For Jesus had not yet come into the village,
  but was still where Martha had met him.
So when the Jews who were with her in the house comforting her
  saw Mary get up quickly and go out,
  they followed her,
  presuming that she was going to the tomb to weep there.
When Mary came to where Jesus was and saw him,
  she fell at his feet and said to him,
  "Lord, if you had been here,
  my brother would not have died."
When Jesus saw her weeping and the Jews who had come with her
    weeping,
  he became perturbed and deeply troubled, and said,
  "Where have you laid him?"
They said to him, "Sir, come and see."
And Jesus wept.
So the Jews said, "See how he loved him."
But some of them said,
  "Could not the one who opened the eyes of the blind man
  have done something so that this man would not have died?"

So Jesus, perturbed again, came to the tomb.
It was a cave, and a stone lay across it.
Jesus said, "Take away the stone."
Martha, the dead man's sister, said to him,
  "Lord, by now there will be a stench;
  he has been dead for four days."
Jesus said to her,
  "Did I not tell you that if you believe
  you will see the glory of God?"
So they took away the stone.
And Jesus raised his eyes and said,
  "Father, I thank you for hearing me.
I know that you always hear me;
  but because of the crowd here I have said this,
  that they may believe that you sent me."
And when he had said this,
  he cried out in a loud voice,
  "Lazarus, come out!"
The dead man came out,
  tied hand and foot with burial bands,
  and his face was wrapped in a cloth.
So Jesus said to them,
  "Untie him and let him go."

Now many of the Jews who had come to Mary
  and seen what he had done began to believe in him.

Gospel

John 11:3-7, 17, 20-27, 33b-45; L34A

The sisters of Lazarus sent word to Jesus saying,
  "Master, the one you love is ill."
When Jesus heard this he said,
  "This illness is not to end in death,
  but is for the glory of God,
  that the Son of God may be glorified through it."
Now Jesus loved Martha and her sister and Lazarus.
So when he heard that he was ill,
  he remained for two days in the place where he was.
Then after this he said to his disciples,
  "Let us go back to Judea."

When Jesus arrived, he found that Lazarus
  had already been in the tomb for four days.
When Martha heard that Jesus was coming,
  she went to meet him;
  but Mary sat at home.
Martha said to Jesus,
  "Lord, if you had been here,
  my brother would not have died.
But even now I know that whatever you ask of God,
  God will give you."
Jesus said to her,
  "Your brother will rise."
Martha said,
  "I know he will rise,
  in the resurrection on the last day."
Jesus told her,
  "I am the resurrection and the life;
  whoever believes in me, even if he dies, will live,
  and everyone who lives and believes in me will never die.
Do you believe this?"
She said to him, "Yes, Lord.
I have come to believe that you are the Christ, the Son of God,
  the one who is coming into the world."

He became perturbed and deeply troubled, and said,
  "Where have you laid him?"
They said to him, "Sir, come and see."
And Jesus wept.
So the Jews said, "See how he loved him."
But some of them said,
  "Could not the one who opened the eyes of the blind man
  have done something so that this man would not have died?"

So Jesus, perturbed again, came to the tomb.
It was a cave, and a stone lay across it.
Jesus said, "Take away the stone."
Martha, the dead man's sister, said to him,
  "Lord, by now there will be a stench;
  he has been dead for four days."
Jesus said to her,
  "Did I not tell you that if you believe
  you will see the glory of God?"
So they took away the stone.
And Jesus raised his eyes and said,
  "Father, I thank you for hearing me.
I know that you always hear me;
  but because of the crowd here I have said this,
  that they may believe that you sent me."
And when he had said this,
  he cried out in a loud voice,
  "Lazarus, come out!"
The dead man came out,
  tied hand and foot with burial bands,
  and his face was wrapped in a cloth.
So Jesus said to them,
  "Untie him and let him go."

Now many of the Jews who had come to Mary
  and seen what he had done began to believe in him.

FIRST READING

Ezek 37:12-14

Thus says the Lord GOD:
  O my people, I will open your graves
  and have you rise from them,
  and bring you back to the land of Israel.
Then you shall know that I am the LORD,
  when I open your graves and have you rise
      from them,
  O my people!
I will put my spirit in you that you may live,
  and I will settle you upon your land;
  thus you shall know that I am the LORD.
I have promised, and I will do it, says the LORD.

RESPONSORIAL PSALM

Ps 130:1-2, 3-4, 5-6, 7-8

℟. (7) With the Lord there is mercy and
    fullness of redemption.

Out of the depths I cry to you, O LORD;
  LORD, hear my voice!

Let your ears be attentive
  to my voice in supplication.

℟. With the Lord there is mercy and fullness
    of redemption.

If you, O LORD, mark iniquities,
  LORD, who can stand?
But with you is forgiveness,
  that you may be revered.

℟. With the Lord there is mercy and fullness
    of redemption.

I trust in the LORD;
  my soul trusts in his word.
More than sentinels wait for the dawn,
  let Israel wait for the LORD.

℟. With the Lord there is mercy and fullness
    of redemption.

For with the LORD is kindness
  and with him is plenteous redemption;
and he will redeem Israel
  from all their iniquities.

℟. With the Lord there is mercy and fullness
    of redemption.

SECOND READING

Rom 8:8-11

Brothers and sisters:
Those who are in the flesh cannot please God.
But you are not in the flesh;
  on the contrary, you are in the spirit,
  if only the Spirit of God dwells in you.
Whoever does not have the Spirit of Christ
  does not belong to him.
But if Christ is in you,
  although the body is dead because of sin,
  the spirit is alive because of righteousness.
If the Spirit of the One who raised Jesus from
      the dead dwells in you,
  the One who raised Christ from the dead
  will give life to your mortal bodies also,
  through his Spirit dwelling in you.

Gospel at the Procession with Palms (cont.)

Luke 19:28-40; L37C

They proclaimed:
  "Blessed is the king who comes
    in the name of the Lord.
  Peace in heaven
    and glory in the highest."
Some of the Pharisees in the crowd said to him,
  "Teacher, rebuke your disciples."
He said in reply,
  "I tell you, if they keep silent,
  the stones will cry out!"

Gospel at Mass

Luke 22:14–23:56; L38ABC

When the hour came,
  Jesus took his place at table with the apostles.
He said to them,
  "I have eagerly desired to eat this Passover with you before I suffer,
  for, I tell you, I shall not eat it again
  until there is fulfillment in the kingdom of God."
Then he took a cup, gave thanks, and said,
  "Take this and share it among yourselves;
  for I tell you that from this time on
  I shall not drink of the fruit of the vine
  until the kingdom of God comes."
Then he took the bread, said the blessing,
  broke it, and gave it to them, saying,
  "This is my body, which will be given for you;
  do this in memory of me."
And likewise the cup after they had eaten, saying,
  "This cup is the new covenant in my blood,
  which will be shed for you.

"And yet behold, the hand of the one who is to betray me
  is with me on the table;
  for the Son of Man indeed goes as it has been determined;
  but woe to that man by whom he is betrayed."
And they began to debate among themselves
  who among them would do such a deed.

Then an argument broke out among them
  about which of them should be regarded as the greatest.
He said to them,
  "The kings of the Gentiles lord it over them
  and those in authority over them are addressed as 'Benefactors';
  but among you it shall not be so.
Rather, let the greatest among you be as the youngest,
  and the leader as the servant.
For who is greater:
  the one seated at table or the one who serves?
Is it not the one seated at table?
I am among you as the one who serves.
It is you who have stood by me in my trials;
  and I confer a kingdom on you,
  just as my Father has conferred one on me,
  that you may eat and drink at my table in my kingdom;
  and you will sit on thrones
  judging the twelve tribes of Israel.

"Simon, Simon, behold Satan has demanded
  to sift all of you like wheat,
  but I have prayed that your own faith may not fail;
  and once you have turned back,
  you must strengthen your brothers."
He said to him,
  "Lord, I am prepared to go to prison and to die with you."
But he replied,
  "I tell you, Peter, before the cock crows this day,
  you will deny three times that you know me."

He said to them,
  "When I sent you forth without a money bag or a sack or sandals,
  were you in need of anything?"
"No, nothing," they replied.
He said to them,
  "But now one who has a money bag should take it,
  and likewise a sack,
  and one who does not have a sword
  should sell his cloak and buy one.
For I tell you that this Scripture must be fulfilled in me,
  namely, *He was counted among the wicked;*
  and indeed what is written about me is coming to fulfillment."
Then they said,
  "Lord, look, there are two swords here."
But he replied, "It is enough!"

Then going out, he went, as was his custom, to the Mount of Olives,
  and the disciples followed him.
When he arrived at the place he said to them,
  "Pray that you may not undergo the test."
After withdrawing about a stone's throw from them and kneeling,
  he prayed, saying, "Father, if you are willing,
  take this cup away from me;
  still, not my will but yours be done."
And to strengthen him an angel from heaven appeared to him.
He was in such agony and he prayed so fervently
  that his sweat became like drops of blood
  falling on the ground.
When he rose from prayer and returned to his disciples,
  he found them sleeping from grief.
He said to them, "Why are you sleeping?
Get up and pray that you may not undergo the test."

While he was still speaking, a crowd approached
  and in front was one of the Twelve, a man named Judas.
He went up to Jesus to kiss him.
Jesus said to him,
  "Judas, are you betraying the Son of Man with a kiss?"
His disciples realized what was about to happen, and they asked,
  "Lord, shall we strike with a sword?"
And one of them struck the high priest's servant
  and cut off his right ear.
But Jesus said in reply,
  "Stop, no more of this!"
Then he touched the servant's ear and healed him.
And Jesus said to the chief priests and temple guards
  and elders who had come for him,
  "Have you come out as against a robber, with swords and clubs?
Day after day I was with you in the temple area,
  and you did not seize me;
  but this is your hour, the time for the power of darkness."

After arresting him they led him away
  and took him into the house of the high priest;
  Peter was following at a distance.

They lit a fire in the middle of the courtyard and sat around it,
    and Peter sat down with them.
When a maid saw him seated in the light,
    she looked intently at him and said,
    "This man too was with him."
But he denied it saying,
    "Woman, I do not know him."
A short while later someone else saw him and said,
    "You too are one of them";
    but Peter answered, "My friend, I am not."
About an hour later, still another insisted,
    "Assuredly, this man too was with him,
    for he also is a Galilean."
But Peter said,
    "My friend, I do not know what you are talking about."
Just as he was saying this, the cock crowed,
    and the Lord turned and looked at Peter;
    and Peter remembered the word of the Lord,
    how he had said to him,
    "Before the cock crows today, you will deny me three times."
He went out and began to weep bitterly.
The men who held Jesus in custody were ridiculing and beating him.
They blindfolded him and questioned him, saying,
    "Prophesy! Who is it that struck you?"
And they reviled him in saying many other things against him.

When day came the council of elders of the people met,
    both chief priests and scribes,
    and they brought him before their Sanhedrin.
They said, "If you are the Christ, tell us,"
    but he replied to them, "If I tell you, you will not believe,
    and if I question, you will not respond.
But from this time on the Son of Man will be seated
    at the right hand of the power of God."
They all asked, "Are you then the Son of God?"
He replied to them, "You say that I am."
Then they said, "What further need have we for testimony?
We have heard it from his own mouth."

Then the whole assembly of them arose and brought him before Pilate.
They brought charges against him, saying,
    "We found this man misleading our people;
    he opposes the payment of taxes to Caesar
    and maintains that he is the Christ, a king."
Pilate asked him, "Are you the king of the Jews?"
He said to him in reply, "You say so."
Pilate then addressed the chief priests and the crowds,
    "I find this man not guilty."
But they were adamant and said,
    "He is inciting the people with his teaching
        throughout all Judea,
    from Galilee where he began even to here."

On hearing this Pilate asked if the man was a Galilean;
    and upon learning that he was under Herod's jurisdiction,
    he sent him to Herod who was in Jerusalem at that time.
Herod was very glad to see Jesus;
    he had been wanting to see him for a long time,
    for he had heard about him
    and had been hoping to see him perform some sign.
He questioned him at length,
    but he gave him no answer.
The chief priests and scribes, meanwhile,
    stood by accusing him harshly.
Herod and his soldiers treated him contemptuously and mocked him,
    and after clothing him in resplendent garb,
    he sent him back to Pilate.
Herod and Pilate became friends that very day,
    even though they had been enemies formerly.
Pilate then summoned the chief priests, the rulers, and the people
    and said to them, "You brought this man to me
    and accused him of inciting the people to revolt.
I have conducted my investigation in your presence
    and have not found this man guilty
    of the charges you have brought against him,
    nor did Herod, for he sent him back to us.
So no capital crime has been committed by him.
Therefore I shall have him flogged and then release him."

But all together they shouted out,
    "Away with this man!
    Release Barabbas to us."
—Now Barabbas had been imprisoned for a rebellion
    that had taken place in the city and for murder.—
Again Pilate addressed them, still wishing to release Jesus,
    but they continued their shouting,
    "Crucify him! Crucify him!"
Pilate addressed them a third time,
    "What evil has this man done?
    I found him guilty of no capital crime.
Therefore I shall have him flogged and then release him."
With loud shouts, however,
    they persisted in calling for his crucifixion,
    and their voices prevailed.
The verdict of Pilate was that their demand should be granted.
So he released the man who had been imprisoned
    for rebellion and murder, for whom they asked,
    and he handed Jesus over to them to deal with as they wished.

As they led him away
    they took hold of a certain Simon, a Cyrenian,
    who was coming in from the country;
    and after laying the cross on him,
    they made him carry it behind Jesus.
A large crowd of people followed Jesus,
    including many women who mourned and lamented him.
Jesus turned to them and said,
    "Daughters of Jerusalem, do not weep for me;
    weep instead for yourselves and for your children
    for indeed, the days are coming when people will say,
    'Blessed are the barren,
    the wombs that never bore
    and the breasts that never nursed.'
At that time people will say to the mountains,
    'Fall upon us!'
    and to the hills, 'Cover us!'
    for if these things are done when the wood is green
    what will happen when it is dry?"
Now two others, both criminals,
    were led away with him to be executed.

When they came to the place called the Skull,
    they crucified him and the criminals there,
    one on his right, the other on his left.
Then Jesus said,
    "Father, forgive them, they know not what they do."

They divided his garments by casting lots.
The people stood by and watched;
   the rulers, meanwhile, sneered at him and said,
    "He saved others, let him save himself
    if he is the chosen one, the Christ of God."
Even the soldiers jeered at him.
As they approached to offer him wine they called out,
    "If you are King of the Jews, save yourself."
Above him there was an inscription that read,
    "This is the King of the Jews."

Now one of the criminals hanging there reviled Jesus, saying,
    "Are you not the Christ?
    Save yourself and us."
The other, however, rebuking him, said in reply,
    "Have you no fear of God,
    for you are subject to the same condemnation?
And indeed, we have been condemned justly,
    for the sentence we received corresponds to our crimes,
    but this man has done nothing criminal."
Then he said,
    "Jesus, remember me when you come into your kingdom."
He replied to him,
    "Amen, I say to you,
    today you will be with me in Paradise."

It was now about noon and darkness came over the whole land
    until three in the afternoon
    because of an eclipse of the sun.
Then the veil of the temple was torn down the middle.
Jesus cried out in a loud voice,
    "Father, into your hands I commend my spirit";
    and when he had said this he breathed his last.

Here all kneel and pause for a short time.

The centurion who witnessed what had happened glorified God and said,
    "This man was innocent beyond doubt."
When all the people who had gathered for this spectacle
    saw what had happened,
    they returned home beating their breasts;
    but all his acquaintances stood at a distance,
    including the women who had followed him from Galilee
    and saw these events.

Now there was a virtuous and righteous man named Joseph who,
    though he was a member of the council,
    had not consented to their plan of action.
He came from the Jewish town of Arimathea
    and was awaiting the kingdom of God.
He went to Pilate and asked for the body of Jesus.
After he had taken the body down,
    he wrapped it in a linen cloth
    and laid him in a rock-hewn tomb
    in which no one had yet been buried.
It was the day of preparation,
    and the sabbath was about to begin.
The women who had come from Galilee with him followed behind,
    and when they had seen the tomb
    and the way in which his body was laid in it,
    they returned and prepared spices and perfumed oils.
Then they rested on the sabbath according to the commandment.

or Luke 23:1-49

The elders of the people, chief priests and scribes,
    arose and brought Jesus before Pilate.
They brought charges against him, saying,
    "We found this man misleading our people;
    he opposes the payment of taxes to Caesar
    and maintains that he is the Christ, a king."
Pilate asked him, "Are you the king of the Jews?"
He said to him in reply, "You say so."
Pilate then addressed the chief priests and the crowds,
    "I find this man not guilty."
But they were adamant and said,
    "He is inciting the people with his teaching
        throughout all Judea,
    from Galilee where he began even to here."

On hearing this Pilate asked if the man was a Galilean;
    and upon learning that he was under Herod's jurisdiction,
    he sent him to Herod who was in Jerusalem at that time.
Herod was very glad to see Jesus;
    he had been wanting to see him for a long time,
    for he had heard about him
    and had been hoping to see him perform some sign.
He questioned him at length,
    but he gave him no answer.
The chief priests and scribes, meanwhile,
    stood by accusing him harshly.
Herod and his soldiers treated him contemptuously and mocked him,
    and after clothing him in resplendent garb,
    he sent him back to Pilate.
Herod and Pilate became friends that very day,
    even though they had been enemies formerly.
Pilate then summoned the chief priests, the rulers, and the people
    and said to them, "You brought this man to me
    and accused him of inciting the people to revolt.
I have conducted my investigation in your presence
    and have not found this man guilty
    of the charges you have brought against him,
    nor did Herod, for he sent him back to us.
So no capital crime has been committed by him.
Therefore I shall have him flogged and then release him."

But all together they shouted out,
    "Away with this man!
    Release Barabbas to us."
—Now Barabbas had been imprisoned for a rebellion
    that had taken place in the city and for murder.—
Again Pilate addressed them, still wishing to release Jesus,
    but they continued their shouting,
    "Crucify him! Crucify him!"
Pilate addressed them a third time,
    "What evil has this man done?
    I found him guilty of no capital crime.
Therefore I shall have him flogged and then release him."
With loud shouts, however,
    they persisted in calling for his crucifixion,
    and their voices prevailed.
The verdict of Pilate was that their demand should be granted.
So he released the man who had been imprisoned
    for rebellion and murder, for whom they asked,
    and he handed Jesus over to them to deal with as they wished.

Gospel (cont.)
Luke 23:1-49

As they led him away
    they took hold of a certain Simon, a Cyrenian,
    who was coming in from the country;
    and after laying the cross on him,
    they made him carry it behind Jesus.
A large crowd of people followed Jesus,
    including many women who mourned and lamented him.
Jesus turned to them and said,
    "Daughters of Jerusalem, do not weep for me;
    weep instead for yourselves and for your children
    for indeed, the days are coming when people will say,
    'Blessed are the barren,
    the wombs that never bore
    and the breasts that never nursed.'
At that time people will say to the mountains,
    'Fall upon us!'
    and to the hills, 'Cover us!'
    for if these things are done when the wood is green
    what will happen when it is dry?"
Now two others, both criminals,
    were led away with him to be executed.

When they came to the place called the Skull,
    they crucified him and the criminals there,
    one on his right, the other on his left.
Then Jesus said,
    "Father, forgive them, they know not what they do."
They divided his garments by casting lots.
The people stood by and watched;
    the rulers, meanwhile, sneered at him and said,
    "He saved others, let him save himself
    if he is the chosen one, the Christ of God."
Even the soldiers jeered at him.

As they approached to offer him wine they called out,
    "If you are King of the Jews, save yourself."
Above him there was an inscription that read,
    "This is the King of the Jews."

Now one of the criminals hanging there reviled Jesus, saying,
    "Are you not the Christ?
    Save yourself and us."
The other, however, rebuking him, said in reply,
    "Have you no fear of God,
    for you are subject to the same condemnation?
And indeed, we have been condemned justly,
    for the sentence we received corresponds to our crimes,
    but this man has done nothing criminal."
Then he said,
    "Jesus, remember me when you come into your kingdom."
He replied to him,
    "Amen, I say to you,
    today you will be with me in Paradise."

It was now about noon and darkness came over the whole land
    until three in the afternoon
    because of an eclipse of the sun.
Then the veil of the temple was torn down the middle.
Jesus cried out in a loud voice,
    "Father, into your hands I commend my spirit";
    and when he had said this he breathed his last.

Here all kneel and pause for a short time.

The centurion who witnessed what had happened glorified God and said,
    "This man was innocent beyond doubt."
When all the people who had gathered for this spectacle
    saw what had happened,
    they returned home beating their breasts;
    but all his acquaintances stood at a distance,
    including the women who had followed him from Galilee
    and saw these events.

Gospel (cont.)
John 13:1-15; L39ABC

For he knew who would betray him;
  for this reason, he said, "Not all of you are clean."

So when he had washed their feet
  and put his garments back on and reclined at table again,
  he said to them, "Do you realize what I have done for you?
You call me 'teacher' and 'master,' and rightly so, for indeed I am.
If I, therefore, the master and teacher, have washed your feet,
  you ought to wash one another's feet.
I have given you a model to follow,
  so that as I have done for you, you should also do."

FIRST READING
Exod 12:1-8, 11-14

The LORD said to Moses and Aaron in the land
    of Egypt,
  "This month shall stand at the head of
    your calendar;
  you shall reckon it the first month of the
    year.
Tell the whole community of Israel:
  On the tenth of this month every one of
    your families
  must procure for itself a lamb, one apiece
    for each household.
If a family is too small for a whole lamb,
  it shall join the nearest household in
    procuring one
  and shall share in the lamb
  in proportion to the number of persons
    who partake of it.
The lamb must be a year-old male and
    without blemish.
You may take it from either the sheep or the
    goats.
You shall keep it until the fourteenth day of
    this month,
  and then, with the whole assembly of Israel
    present,
  it shall be slaughtered during the evening
    twilight.
They shall take some of its blood
  and apply it to the two doorposts and the
    lintel
  of every house in which they partake of
    the lamb.
That same night they shall eat its roasted
    flesh
  with unleavened bread and bitter herbs.

"This is how you are to eat it:
  with your loins girt, sandals on your feet
    and your staff in hand,
  you shall eat like those who are in flight.

It is the Passover of the LORD.
For on this same night I will go through
    Egypt,
  striking down every firstborn of the land,
    both man and beast,
  and executing judgment on all the gods of
    Egypt—I, the LORD!
But the blood will mark the houses where you
    are.
Seeing the blood, I will pass over you;
  thus, when I strike the land of Egypt,
  no destructive blow will come upon you.

"This day shall be a memorial feast for you,
  which all your generations shall celebrate
  with pilgrimage to the LORD, as a perpetual
    institution."

RESPONSORIAL PSALM
Ps 116:12-13, 15-16bc, 17-18

R̸. (cf. 1 Cor 10:16) Our blessing-cup is a
    communion with the Blood of Christ.

How shall I make a return to the LORD
  for all the good he has done for me?
The cup of salvation I will take up,
  and I will call upon the name of the LORD.

R̸. Our blessing-cup is a communion with the
    Blood of Christ.

Precious in the eyes of the LORD
  is the death of his faithful ones.
I am your servant, the son of your handmaid;
  you have loosed my bonds.

R̸. Our blessing-cup is a communion with the
    Blood of Christ.

To you will I offer sacrifice of thanksgiving,
  and I will call upon the name of the LORD.
My vows to the LORD I will pay
  in the presence of all his people.

R̸. Our blessing-cup is a communion with the
    Blood of Christ.

SECOND READING
1 Cor 11:23-26

Brothers and sisters:
I received from the Lord what I also handed
    on to you,
  that the Lord Jesus, on the night he was
    handed over,
  took bread, and, after he had given thanks,
  broke it and said, "This is my body that is
    for you.
Do this in remembrance of me."
In the same way also the cup, after supper,
    saying,
  "This cup is the new covenant in my blood.
Do this, as often as you drink it, in
    remembrance of me."
For as often as you eat this bread and drink
    the cup,
  you proclaim the death of the Lord until he
    comes.

Gospel (cont.)

John 18:1–19:42; L40ABC

So the band of soldiers, the tribune, and the Jewish guards seized Jesus,
    bound him, and brought him to Annas first.
He was the father-in-law of Caiaphas,
    who was high priest that year.
It was Caiaphas who had counseled the Jews
    that it was better that one man should die rather than the people.

Simon Peter and another disciple followed Jesus.
Now the other disciple was known to the high priest,
    and he entered the courtyard of the high priest with Jesus.
But Peter stood at the gate outside.
So the other disciple, the acquaintance of the high priest,
    went out and spoke to the gatekeeper and brought Peter in.
Then the maid who was the gatekeeper said to Peter,
    "You are not one of this man's disciples, are you?"
He said, "I am not."
Now the slaves and the guards were standing around a charcoal fire
    that they had made, because it was cold,
    and were warming themselves.
Peter was also standing there keeping warm.

The high priest questioned Jesus
    about his disciples and about his doctrine.
Jesus answered him,
    "I have spoken publicly to the world.
I have always taught in a synagogue
    or in the temple area where all the Jews gather,
    and in secret I have said nothing. Why ask me?
Ask those who heard me what I said to them.
They know what I said."
When he had said this,
    one of the temple guards standing there struck Jesus and said,
    "Is this the way you answer the high priest?"
Jesus answered him,
    "If I have spoken wrongly, testify to the wrong;
    but if I have spoken rightly, why do you strike me?"
Then Annas sent him bound to Caiaphas the high priest.

Now Simon Peter was standing there keeping warm.
And they said to him,
    "You are not one of his disciples, are you?"
He denied it and said,
    "I am not."
One of the slaves of the high priest,
    a relative of the one whose ear Peter had cut off, said,
    "Didn't I see you in the garden with him?"
Again Peter denied it.
And immediately the cock crowed.

Then they brought Jesus from Caiaphas to the praetorium.
It was morning.
And they themselves did not enter the praetorium,
    in order not to be defiled so that they could eat the Passover.
So Pilate came out to them and said,
    "What charge do you bring against this man?"
They answered and said to him,
    "If he were not a criminal,
    we would not have handed him over to you."
At this, Pilate said to them,
    "Take him yourselves, and judge him according to your law."

The Jews answered him,
    "We do not have the right to execute anyone,"
    in order that the word of Jesus might be fulfilled
    that he said indicating the kind of death he would die.
So Pilate went back into the praetorium
    and summoned Jesus and said to him,
    "Are you the King of the Jews?"
Jesus answered,
    "Do you say this on your own
    or have others told you about me?"
Pilate answered,
    "I am not a Jew, am I?
Your own nation and the chief priests handed you over to me.
What have you done?"
Jesus answered,
    "My kingdom does not belong to this world.
If my kingdom did belong to this world,
    my attendants would be fighting
    to keep me from being handed over to the Jews.
But as it is, my kingdom is not here."
So Pilate said to him,
    "Then you are a king?"
Jesus answered,
    "You say I am a king.
For this I was born and for this I came into the world,
    to testify to the truth.
Everyone who belongs to the truth listens to my voice."
Pilate said to him, "What is truth?"

When he had said this,
    he again went out to the Jews and said to them,
    "I find no guilt in him.
But you have a custom that I release one prisoner to you at Passover.
Do you want me to release to you the King of the Jews?"
They cried out again,
    "Not this one but Barabbas!"
Now Barabbas was a revolutionary.

Then Pilate took Jesus and had him scourged.
And the soldiers wove a crown out of thorns and placed it on his head,
    and clothed him in a purple cloak,
    and they came to him and said,
    "Hail, King of the Jews!"
And they struck him repeatedly.
Once more Pilate went out and said to them,
    "Look, I am bringing him out to you,
    so that you may know that I find no guilt in him."
So Jesus came out,
    wearing the crown of thorns and the purple cloak.
And he said to them, "Behold, the man!"
When the chief priests and the guards saw him they cried out,
    "Crucify him, crucify him!"
Pilate said to them,
    "Take him yourselves and crucify him.
I find no guilt in him."
The Jews answered,
    "We have a law, and according to that law he ought to die,
    because he made himself the Son of God."
Now when Pilate heard this statement,

he became even more afraid,
and went back into the praetorium and said to Jesus,
"Where are you from?"
Jesus did not answer him.
So Pilate said to him,
"Do you not speak to me?
Do you not know that I have power to release you
and I have power to crucify you?"
Jesus answered him,
"You would have no power over me
if it had not been given to you from above.
For this reason the one who handed me over to you
has the greater sin."
Consequently, Pilate tried to release him; but the Jews cried out,
"If you release him, you are not a Friend of Caesar.
Everyone who makes himself a king opposes Caesar."

When Pilate heard these words he brought Jesus out
and seated him on the judge's bench
in the place called Stone Pavement, in Hebrew, Gabbatha.
It was preparation day for Passover, and it was about noon.
And he said to the Jews,
"Behold, your king!"
They cried out,
"Take him away, take him away! Crucify him!"
Pilate said to them,
"Shall I crucify your king?"
The chief priests answered,
"We have no king but Caesar."
Then he handed him over to them to be crucified.

So they took Jesus, and, carrying the cross himself,
he went out to what is called the Place of the Skull,
in Hebrew, Golgotha.
There they crucified him, and with him two others,
one on either side, with Jesus in the middle.
Pilate also had an inscription written and put on the cross.
It read,
"Jesus the Nazorean, the King of the Jews."
Now many of the Jews read this inscription,
because the place where Jesus was crucified was near the city;
and it was written in Hebrew, Latin, and Greek.
So the chief priests of the Jews said to Pilate,
"Do not write 'The King of the Jews,'
but that he said, 'I am the King of the Jews.'"
Pilate answered,
"What I have written, I have written."

When the soldiers had crucified Jesus,
they took his clothes and divided them into four shares,
a share for each soldier.
They also took his tunic, but the tunic was seamless,
woven in one piece from the top down.
So they said to one another,
"Let's not tear it, but cast lots for it to see whose it will be,"
in order that the passage of Scripture might be fulfilled that says:
They divided my garments among them,
and for my vesture they cast lots.
This is what the soldiers did.

Standing by the cross of Jesus were his mother
and his mother's sister, Mary the wife of Clopas,
and Mary of Magdala.
When Jesus saw his mother and the disciple there whom he loved
he said to his mother, "Woman, behold, your son."
Then he said to the disciple,
"Behold, your mother."
And from that hour the disciple took her into his home.

After this, aware that everything was now finished,
in order that the Scripture might be fulfilled,
Jesus said, "I thirst."
There was a vessel filled with common wine.
So they put a sponge soaked in wine on a sprig of hyssop
and put it up to his mouth.
When Jesus had taken the wine, he said,
"It is finished."
And bowing his head, he handed over the spirit.

Here all kneel and pause for a short time.

Now since it was preparation day,
in order that the bodies might not remain
on the cross on the sabbath,
for the sabbath day of that week was a solemn one,
the Jews asked Pilate that their legs be broken
and that they be taken down.
So the soldiers came and broke the legs of the first
and then of the other one who was crucified with Jesus.
But when they came to Jesus and saw that he was already dead,
they did not break his legs,
but one soldier thrust his lance into his side,
and immediately blood and water flowed out.
An eyewitness has testified, and his testimony is true;
he knows that he is speaking the truth,
so that you also may come to believe.
For this happened so that the Scripture passage might be fulfilled:
Not a bone of it will be broken.
And again another passage says:
They will look upon him whom they have pierced.

After this, Joseph of Arimathea,
secretly a disciple of Jesus for fear of the Jews,
asked Pilate if he could remove the body of Jesus.
And Pilate permitted it.
So he came and took his body.
Nicodemus, the one who had first come to him at night,
also came bringing a mixture of myrrh and aloes
weighing about one hundred pounds.
They took the body of Jesus
and bound it with burial cloths along with the spices,
according to the Jewish burial custom.
Now in the place where he had been crucified there was a garden,
and in the garden a new tomb, in which no one had yet been buried.
So they laid Jesus there because of the Jewish preparation day;
for the tomb was close by.

FIRST READING
Isa 52:13–53:12

See, my servant shall prosper,
   he shall be raised high and greatly exalted.
Even as many were amazed at him—
   so marred was his look beyond human
      semblance
   and his appearance beyond that of the sons
      of man—
so shall he startle many nations,
   because of him kings shall stand
      speechless;
for those who have not been told shall see,
   those who have not heard shall ponder it.

Who would believe what we have heard?
   To whom has the arm of the LORD been
      revealed?
He grew up like a sapling before him,
   like a shoot from the parched earth;
there was in him no stately bearing to make
      us look at him,
   nor appearance that would attract us to him.
He was spurned and avoided by people,
   a man of suffering, accustomed to infirmity,
one of those from whom people hide their
      faces,
   spurned, and we held him in no esteem.

Yet it was our infirmities that he bore,
   our sufferings that he endured,
while we thought of him as stricken,
   as one smitten by God and afflicted.
But he was pierced for our offenses,
   crushed for our sins;
upon him was the chastisement that makes
      us whole,
   by his stripes we were healed.
We had all gone astray like sheep,
   each following his own way;
but the LORD laid upon him
   the guilt of us all.

Though he was harshly treated, he submitted
   and opened not his mouth;
like a lamb led to the slaughter
   or a sheep before the shearers,
   he was silent and opened not his mouth.
Oppressed and condemned, he was taken away,
   and who would have thought any more of
      his destiny?
When he was cut off from the land of the
      living,
   and smitten for the sin of his people,
a grave was assigned him among the wicked
   and a burial place with evildoers,
though he had done no wrong
   nor spoken any falsehood.
But the LORD was pleased
   to crush him in infirmity.

If he gives his life as an offering for sin,
   he shall see his descendants in a long life,
   and the will of the LORD shall be
      accomplished through him.

Because of his affliction
   he shall see the light
      in fullness of days;
through his suffering, my servant shall justify
      many,
   and their guilt he shall bear.
Therefore I will give him his portion among
      the great,
   and he shall divide the spoils with the
      mighty,
because he surrendered himself to death
   and was counted among the wicked;
and he shall take away the sins of many,
   and win pardon for their offenses.

RESPONSORIAL PSALM
Ps 31:2, 6, 12-13, 15-16, 17, 25

R̸. (Luke 23:46) Father, into your hands I
      commend my spirit.

In you, O LORD, I take refuge;
   let me never be put to shame.
In your justice rescue me.
Into your hands I commend my spirit;
   you will redeem me, O LORD, O faithful God.

R̸. Father, into your hands I commend my
      spirit.

For all my foes I am an object of reproach,
   a laughingstock to my neighbors, and a
      dread to my friends;
   they who see me abroad flee from me.
I am forgotten like the unremembered dead;
   I am like a dish that is broken.

R̸. Father, into your hands I commend my
      spirit.

But my trust is in you, O LORD;
   I say, "You are my God.
In your hands is my destiny; rescue me
   from the clutches of my enemies and my
      persecutors."

R̸. Father, into your hands I commend my
      spirit.

Let your face shine upon your servant;
   save me in your kindness.
Take courage and be stouthearted,
   all you who hope in the LORD.

R̸. Father, into your hands I commend my
      spirit.

SECOND READING
Heb 4:14-16; 5:7-9

Brothers and sisters:
Since we have a great high priest who has
      passed through the heavens,
   Jesus, the Son of God,
   let us hold fast to our confession.
For we do not have a high priest
   who is unable to sympathize with our
      weaknesses,
   but one who has similarly been tested in
      every way,
   yet without sin.
So let us confidently approach the throne of
      grace
   to receive mercy and to find grace for
      timely help.

In the days when Christ was in the flesh,
   he offered prayers and supplications with
      loud cries and tears
   to the one who was able to save him from
      death,
   and he was heard because of his reverence.
Son though he was, he learned obedience from
      what he suffered;
   and when he was made perfect,
   he became the source of eternal salvation
      for all who obey him.

FIRST READING
Gen 1:1–2:2

In the beginning, when God created the
heavens and the earth,
the earth was a formless wasteland, and
darkness covered the abyss,
while a mighty wind swept over the waters.

Then God said,
"Let there be light," and there was light.
God saw how good the light was.
God then separated the light from the
darkness.
God called the light "day," and the darkness
he called "night."
Thus evening came, and morning followed—
the first day.

Then God said,
"Let there be a dome in the middle of the
waters,
to separate one body of water from the
other."
And so it happened:
God made the dome,
and it separated the water above the dome
from the water below it.
God called the dome "the sky."
Evening came, and morning followed—the
second day.

Then God said,
"Let the water under the sky be gathered
into a single basin,
so that the dry land may appear."
And so it happened:
the water under the sky was gathered into
its basin,
and the dry land appeared.
God called the dry land "the earth,"
and the basin of the water he called "the
sea."
God saw how good it was.
Then God said,
"Let the earth bring forth vegetation:
every kind of plant that bears seed
and every kind of fruit tree on earth
that bears fruit with its seed in it."
And so it happened:
the earth brought forth every kind of plant
that bears seed
and every kind of fruit tree on earth
that bears fruit with its seed in it.
God saw how good it was.
Evening came, and morning followed—the
third day.

Then God said:
"Let there be lights in the dome of the sky,
to separate day from night.
Let them mark the fixed times, the days and
the years,

and serve as luminaries in the dome of the
sky,
to shed light upon the earth."
And so it happened:
God made the two great lights,
the greater one to govern the day,
and the lesser one to govern the night;
and he made the stars.
God set them in the dome of the sky,
to shed light upon the earth,
to govern the day and the night,
and to separate the light from the darkness.
God saw how good it was.
Evening came, and morning followed—the
fourth day.

Then God said,
"Let the water teem with an abundance of
living creatures,
and on the earth let birds fly beneath the
dome of the sky."
And so it happened:
God created the great sea monsters
and all kinds of swimming creatures with
which the water teems,
and all kinds of winged birds.
God saw how good it was, and God blessed
them, saying,
"Be fertile, multiply, and fill the water of
the seas;
and let the birds multiply on the earth."
Evening came, and morning followed—the
fifth day.

Then God said,
"Let the earth bring forth all kinds of living
creatures:
cattle, creeping things, and wild animals of
all kinds."
And so it happened:
God made all kinds of wild animals, all
kinds of cattle,
and all kinds of creeping things of the
earth.
God saw how good it was.
Then God said:
"Let us make man in our image, after our
likeness.
Let them have dominion over the fish of the
sea,
the birds of the air, and the cattle,
and over all the wild animals
and all the creatures that crawl on the
ground."
God created man in his image;
in the image of God he created him;
male and female he created them.
God blessed them, saying:
"Be fertile and multiply;
fill the earth and subdue it.
Have dominion over the fish of the sea, the
birds of the air,

and all the living things that move on the
earth."
God also said:
"See, I give you every seed-bearing plant all
over the earth
and every tree that has seed-bearing fruit
on it to be your food;
and to all the animals of the land, all the
birds of the air,
and all the living creatures that crawl on
the ground,
I give all the green plants for food."
And so it happened.
God looked at everything he had made, and he
found it very good.
Evening came, and morning followed—the
sixth day.

Thus the heavens and the earth and all their
array were completed.
Since on the seventh day God was finished
with the work he had been doing,
he rested on the seventh day from all the
work he had undertaken.

or

Gen 1:1, 26-31a

In the beginning, when God created the
heavens and the earth,
God said: "Let us make man in our image,
after our likeness.
Let them have dominion over the fish of the
sea,
the birds of the air, and the cattle,
and over all the wild animals
and all the creatures that crawl on the
ground."
God created man in his image;
in the image of God he created him;
male and female he created them.
God blessed them, saying:
"Be fertile and multiply;
fill the earth and subdue it.
Have dominion over the fish of the sea, the
birds of the air,
and all the living things that move on the
earth."
God also said:
"See, I give you every seed-bearing plant all
over the earth
and every tree that has seed-bearing fruit
on it to be your food;
and to all the animals of the land, all the
birds of the air,
and all the living creatures that crawl on
the ground,
I give all the green plants for food."
And so it happened.
God looked at everything he had made, and
found it very good.

RESPONSORIAL PSALM

Ps 104:1-2, 5-6, 10, 12, 13-14, 24, 35

R̰. (30) Lord, send out your Spirit, and renew
the face of the earth.

Bless the LORD, O my soul!
O LORD, my God, you are great indeed!
You are clothed with majesty and glory,
robed in light as with a cloak.

R̰. Lord, send out your Spirit, and renew the
face of the earth.

You fixed the earth upon its foundation,
not to be moved forever;
with the ocean, as with a garment, you
covered it;
above the mountains the waters stood.

R̰. Lord, send out your Spirit, and renew the
face of the earth.

You send forth springs into the watercourses
that wind among the mountains.
Beside them the birds of heaven dwell;
from among the branches they send forth
their song.

R̰. Lord, send out your Spirit, and renew the
face of the earth.

You water the mountains from your palace;
the earth is replete with the fruit of your
works.
You raise grass for the cattle,
and vegetation for man's use,
producing bread from the earth.

R̰. Lord, send out your Spirit, and renew the
face of the earth.

How manifold are your works, O LORD!
In wisdom you have wrought them all—
the earth is full of your creatures.
Bless the LORD, O my soul!

R̰. Lord, send out your Spirit, and renew the
face of the earth.

or

Ps 33:4-5, 6-7, 12-13, 20 and 22

R̰. (5b) The earth is full of the goodness of
the Lord.

Upright is the word of the LORD,
and all his works are trustworthy.
He loves justice and right;
of the kindness of the LORD the earth is full.

R̰. The earth is full of the goodness of the Lord.

By the word of the LORD the heavens were
made;
by the breath of his mouth all their host.
He gathers the waters of the sea as in a flask;
in cellars he confines the deep.

R̰. The earth is full of the goodness of the Lord.

Blessed the nation whose God is the LORD,
the people he has chosen for his own
inheritance.
From heaven the LORD looks down;
he sees all mankind.

R̰. The earth is full of the goodness of the Lord.

Our soul waits for the LORD,
who is our help and our shield.
May your kindness, O LORD, be upon us
who have put our hope in you.

R̰. The earth is full of the goodness of the Lord.

SECOND READING

Gen 22:1-18

God put Abraham to the test.
He called to him, "Abraham!"
"Here I am," he replied.
Then God said:
"Take your son Isaac, your only one, whom
you love,
and go to the land of Moriah.
There you shall offer him up as a holocaust
on a height that I will point out to you."
Early the next morning Abraham saddled his
donkey,
took with him his son Isaac and two of his
servants as well,
and with the wood that he had cut for the
holocaust,
set out for the place of which God had told
him.

On the third day Abraham got sight of the
place from afar.
Then he said to his servants:
"Both of you stay here with the donkey,
while the boy and I go on over yonder.
We will worship and then come back to you."
Thereupon Abraham took the wood for the
holocaust
and laid it on his son Isaac's shoulders,
while he himself carried the fire and the
knife.
As the two walked on together, Isaac spoke to
his father Abraham:
"Father!" Isaac said.
"Yes, son," he replied.
Isaac continued, "Here are the fire and the
wood,
but where is the sheep for the holocaust?"
"Son," Abraham answered,
"God himself will provide the sheep for the
holocaust."
Then the two continued going forward.

When they came to the place of which God
had told him,
Abraham built an altar there and arranged
the wood on it.

Next he tied up his son Isaac,
and put him on top of the wood on the
altar.
Then he reached out and took the knife to
slaughter his son.
But the LORD's messenger called to him from
heaven,
"Abraham, Abraham!"
"Here I am," he answered.
"Do not lay your hand on the boy," said the
messenger.
"Do not do the least thing to him.
I know now how devoted you are to God,
since you did not withhold from me your
own beloved son."
As Abraham looked about,
he spied a ram caught by its horns in the
thicket.
So he went and took the ram
and offered it up as a holocaust in place of
his son.
Abraham named the site Yahweh-yireh;
hence people now say, "On the mountain
the LORD will see."

Again the LORD's messenger called to
Abraham from heaven and said:
"I swear by myself, declares the LORD,
that because you acted as you did
in not withholding from me your beloved
son,
I will bless you abundantly
and make your descendants as countless
as the stars of the sky and the sands of the
seashore;
your descendants shall take possession
of the gates of their enemies,
and in your descendants all the nations of
the earth
shall find blessing—
all this because you obeyed my command."

or

Gen 22:1-2, 9a, 10-13, 15-18

God put Abraham to the test.
He called to him, "Abraham!"
"Here I am," he replied.
Then God said:
"Take your son Isaac, your only one, whom
you love,
and go to the land of Moriah.
There you shall offer him up as a holocaust
on a height that I will point out to you."

When they came to the place of which God
had told him,
Abraham built an altar there and arranged
the wood on it.
Then he reached out and took the knife to
slaughter his son.

But the LORD's messenger called to him from
heaven,
"Abraham, Abraham!"
"Here I am," he answered.
"Do not lay your hand on the boy," said the
messenger.
"Do not do the least thing to him.
I know now how devoted you are to God,
since you did not withhold from me your
own beloved son."
As Abraham looked about,
he spied a ram caught by its horns in the
thicket.
So he went and took the ram
and offered it up as a holocaust in place of
his son.

Again the LORD's messenger called to
Abraham from heaven and said:
"I swear by myself, declares the LORD,
that because you acted as you did
in not withholding from me your beloved
son,
I will bless you abundantly
and make your descendants as countless
as the stars of the sky and the sands of the
seashore;
your descendants shall take possession
of the gates of their enemies,
and in your descendants all the nations of
the earth
shall find blessing—
all this because you obeyed my command."

RESPONSORIAL PSALM
Ps 16:5, 8, 9-10, 11

R℣. (1) You are my inheritance, O Lord.

O LORD, my allotted portion and my cup,
you it is who hold fast my lot.
I set the LORD ever before me;
with him at my right hand I shall not be
disturbed.

R℣. You are my inheritance, O Lord.

Therefore my heart is glad and my soul
rejoices,
my body, too, abides in confidence;
because you will not abandon my soul to the
netherworld,
nor will you suffer your faithful one to
undergo corruption.

R℣. You are my inheritance, O Lord.

You will show me the path to life,
fullness of joys in your presence,
the delights at your right hand forever.

R℣. You are my inheritance, O Lord.

THIRD READING
Exod 14:15–15:1

The LORD said to Moses, "Why are you crying
out to me?
Tell the Israelites to go forward.
And you, lift up your staff and, with hand
outstretched over the sea,
split the sea in two,
that the Israelites may pass through it on
dry land.
But I will make the Egyptians so obstinate
that they will go in after them.
Then I will receive glory through Pharaoh and
all his army,
his chariots and charioteers.
The Egyptians shall know that I am the LORD,
when I receive glory through Pharaoh
and his chariots and charioteers."

The angel of God, who had been leading
Israel's camp,
now moved and went around behind them.
The column of cloud also, leaving the front,
took up its place behind them,
so that it came between the camp of the
Egyptians
and that of Israel.
But the cloud now became dark, and thus the
night passed
without the rival camps coming any closer
together all night long.
Then Moses stretched out his hand over the
sea,
and the LORD swept the sea
with a strong east wind throughout the
night
and so turned it into dry land.
When the water was thus divided,
the Israelites marched into the midst of the
sea on dry land,
with the water like a wall to their right and
to their left.

The Egyptians followed in pursuit;
all Pharaoh's horses and chariots and
charioteers went after them
right into the midst of the sea.
In the night watch just before dawn
the LORD cast through the column of the
fiery cloud
upon the Egyptian force a glance that
threw it into a panic;
and he so clogged their chariot wheels
that they could hardly drive.
With that the Egyptians sounded the retreat
before Israel,
because the LORD was fighting for them
against the Egyptians.

Then the LORD told Moses, "Stretch out your
hand over the sea,
that the water may flow back upon the
Egyptians,
upon their chariots and their charioteers."
So Moses stretched out his hand over the sea,
and at dawn the sea flowed back to its
normal depth.
The Egyptians were fleeing head on toward
the sea,
when the LORD hurled them into its midst.
As the water flowed back,
it covered the chariots and the charioteers
of Pharaoh's whole army
which had followed the Israelites into the sea.
Not a single one of them escaped.
But the Israelites had marched on dry land
through the midst of the sea,
with the water like a wall to their right and
to their left.
Thus the LORD saved Israel on that day
from the power of the Egyptians.
When Israel saw the Egyptians lying dead on
the seashore
and beheld the great power that the LORD
had shown against the Egyptians,
they feared the LORD and believed in him
and in his servant Moses.

Then Moses and the Israelites sang this song
to the LORD:
I will sing to the LORD, for he is gloriously
triumphant;
horse and chariot he has cast into the sea.

RESPONSORIAL PSALM
Exod 15:1-2, 3-4, 5-6, 17-18

R℣. (1b) Let us sing to the Lord; he has covered
himself in glory.

I will sing to the LORD, for he is gloriously
triumphant;
horse and chariot he has cast into the sea.
My strength and my courage is the LORD,
and he has been my savior.
He is my God, I praise him;
the God of my father, I extol him.

R℣. Let us sing to the Lord; he has covered
himself in glory.

The LORD is a warrior,
LORD is his name!
Pharaoh's chariots and army he hurled into
the sea;
the elite of his officers were submerged in
the Red Sea.

R℣. Let us sing to the Lord; he has covered
himself in glory.

The flood waters covered them,
   they sank into the depths like a stone.
Your right hand, O Lᴏʀᴅ, magnificent in
      power,
   your right hand, O Lᴏʀᴅ, has shattered the
      enemy.

R℣. Let us sing to the Lord; he has covered
   himself in glory.

You brought in the people you redeemed
   and planted them on the mountain of your
      inheritance—
the place where you made your seat, O Lᴏʀᴅ,
   the sanctuary, Lᴏʀᴅ, which your hands
      established.
The Lᴏʀᴅ shall reign forever and ever.

R℣. Let us sing to the Lord; he has covered
   himself in glory.

FOURTH READING
Isa 54:5-14

The One who has become your husband is
      your Maker;
   his name is the Lᴏʀᴅ of hosts;
your redeemer is the Holy One of Israel,
   called God of all the earth.
The Lᴏʀᴅ calls you back,
   like a wife forsaken and grieved in spirit,
   a wife married in youth and then cast off,
      says your God.
For a brief moment I abandoned you,
   but with great tenderness I will take you
      back.
In an outburst of wrath, for a moment
   I hid my face from you;
but with enduring love I take pity on you,
   says the Lᴏʀᴅ, your redeemer.
This is for me like the days of Noah,
   when I swore that the waters of Noah
   should never again deluge the earth;
so I have sworn not to be angry with you,
   or to rebuke you.
Though the mountains leave their place
   and the hills be shaken,
my love shall never leave you
   nor my covenant of peace be shaken,
   says the Lᴏʀᴅ, who has mercy on you.
O afflicted one, storm-battered and
      unconsoled,
   I lay your pavements in carnelians,
   and your foundations in sapphires;
I will make your battlements of rubies,
   your gates of carbuncles,
   and all your walls of precious stones.
All your children shall be taught by the Lᴏʀᴅ,
   and great shall be the peace of your children.

In justice shall you be established,
   far from the fear of oppression,
   where destruction cannot come near you.

RESPONSORIAL PSALM
Ps 30:2, 4, 5-6, 11-12, 13

R℣. (2a) I will praise you, Lord, for you have
   rescued me.

I will extol you, O Lᴏʀᴅ, for you drew me clear
   and did not let my enemies rejoice over me.
O Lᴏʀᴅ, you brought me up from the
      netherworld;
   you preserved me from among those going
      down into the pit.

R℣. I will praise you, Lord, for you have
   rescued me.

Sing praise to the Lᴏʀᴅ, you his faithful ones,
   and give thanks to his holy name.
For his anger lasts but a moment;
   a lifetime, his good will.
At nightfall, weeping enters in,
   but with the dawn, rejoicing.

R℣. I will praise you, Lord, for you have
   rescued me.

Hear, O Lᴏʀᴅ, and have pity on me;
   O Lᴏʀᴅ, be my helper.
You changed my mourning into dancing;
   O Lᴏʀᴅ, my God, forever will I give you
      thanks.

R℣. I will praise you, Lord, for you have
   rescued me.

FIFTH READING
Isa 55:1-11

Thus says the Lᴏʀᴅ:
All you who are thirsty,
   come to the water!
You who have no money,
   come, receive grain and eat;
come, without paying and without cost,
   drink wine and milk!
Why spend your money for what is not bread,
   your wages for what fails to satisfy?
Heed me, and you shall eat well,
   you shall delight in rich fare.
Come to me heedfully,
   listen, that you may have life.
I will renew with you the everlasting covenant,
   the benefits assured to David.
As I made him a witness to the peoples,
   a leader and commander of nations,
so shall you summon a nation you knew not,
   and nations that knew you not shall run
      to you,

because of the Lᴏʀᴅ, your God,
   the Holy One of Israel, who has glorified
      you.
Seek the Lᴏʀᴅ while he may be found,
   call him while he is near.
Let the scoundrel forsake his way,
   and the wicked man his thoughts;
let him turn to the Lᴏʀᴅ for mercy;
   to our God, who is generous in forgiving.
For my thoughts are not your thoughts,
   nor are your ways my ways, says the Lᴏʀᴅ.
As high as the heavens are above the earth,
   so high are my ways above your ways
   and my thoughts above your thoughts.

For just as from the heavens
   the rain and snow come down
and do not return there
   till they have watered the earth,
   making it fertile and fruitful,
giving seed to the one who sows
   and bread to the one who eats,
so shall my word be
   that goes forth from my mouth;
my word shall not return to me void,
   but shall do my will,
   achieving the end for which I sent it.

RESPONSORIAL PSALM
Isa 12:2-3, 4, 5-6

R℣. (3) You will draw water joyfully from the
   springs of salvation.

God indeed is my savior;
   I am confident and unafraid.
My strength and my courage is the Lᴏʀᴅ,
   and he has been my savior.
With joy you will draw water
   at the fountain of salvation.

R℣. You will draw water joyfully from the
   springs of salvation.

Give thanks to the Lᴏʀᴅ, acclaim his name;
   among the nations make known his deeds,
   proclaim how exalted is his name.

R℣. You will draw water joyfully from the
   springs of salvation.

Sing praise to the Lᴏʀᴅ for his glorious
      achievement;
   let this be known throughout all the earth.
Shout with exultation, O city of Zion,
   for great in your midst
   is the Holy One of Israel!

R℣. You will draw water joyfully from the
   springs of salvation.

SIXTH READING
Bar 3:9-15, 32–4:4

Hear, O Israel, the commandments of life:
  listen, and know prudence!
How is it, Israel,
  that you are in the land of your foes,
  grown old in a foreign land,
defiled with the dead,
  accounted with those destined for the
    netherworld?
You have forsaken the fountain of wisdom!
  Had you walked in the way of God,
  you would have dwelt in enduring peace.
Learn where prudence is,
  where strength, where understanding;
that you may know also
  where are length of days, and life,
  where light of the eyes, and peace.
Who has found the place of wisdom,
  who has entered into her treasuries?

The One who knows all things knows her;
  he has probed her by his knowledge—
The One who established the earth for all time,
  and filled it with four-footed beasts;
  he who dismisses the light, and it departs,
  calls it, and it obeys him trembling;
before whom the stars at their posts
  shine and rejoice;
when he calls them, they answer, "Here we are!"
  shining with joy for their Maker.
Such is our God;
  no other is to be compared to him:
he has traced out the whole way of
    understanding,
  and has given her to Jacob, his servant,
  to Israel, his beloved son.

Since then she has appeared on earth,
  and moved among people.
She is the book of the precepts of God,
  the law that endures forever;
all who cling to her will live,
  but those will die who forsake her.
Turn, O Jacob, and receive her:
  walk by her light toward splendor.
Give not your glory to another,
  your privileges to an alien race.
Blessed are we, O Israel;
  for what pleases God is known to us!

RESPONSORIAL PSALM
Ps 19:8, 9, 10, 11

℞. (John 6:68c) Lord, you have the words of
  everlasting life.

The law of the LORD is perfect,
  refreshing the soul;
the decree of the LORD is trustworthy,
  giving wisdom to the simple.

℞. Lord, you have the words of everlasting life.

The precepts of the LORD are right,
  rejoicing the heart;
the command of the LORD is clear,
  enlightening the eye.

℞. Lord, you have the words of everlasting life.

The fear of the LORD is pure,
  enduring forever;
the ordinances of the LORD are true,
  all of them just.

℞. Lord, you have the words of everlasting life.

They are more precious than gold,
  than a heap of purest gold;
sweeter also than syrup
  or honey from the comb.

℞. Lord, you have the words of everlasting life.

SEVENTH READING
Ezek 36:16-17a, 18-28

The word of the LORD came to me, saying:
  Son of man, when the house of Israel lived
    in their land,
  they defiled it by their conduct and deeds.
Therefore I poured out my fury upon them
  because of the blood that they poured out
    on the ground,
  and because they defiled it with idols.
I scattered them among the nations,
  dispersing them over foreign lands;
  according to their conduct and deeds I
    judged them.
But when they came among the nations
    wherever they came,
  they served to profane my holy name,
  because it was said of them: "These are the
    people of the LORD,
  yet they had to leave their land."
So I have relented because of my holy name
  which the house of Israel profaned
  among the nations where they came.
Therefore say to the house of Israel: Thus
    says the Lord GOD:
  Not for your sakes do I act, house of Israel,
  but for the sake of my holy name,
  which you profaned among the nations to
    which you came.
I will prove the holiness of my great name,
  profaned among the nations,
  in whose midst you have profaned it.
Thus the nations shall know that I am the
    LORD, says the Lord GOD,
  when in their sight I prove my holiness
    through you.
For I will take you away from among the nations,
  gather you from all the foreign lands,
  and bring you back to your own land.
I will sprinkle clean water upon you
  to cleanse you from all your impurities,
  and from all your idols I will cleanse you.

I will give you a new heart and place a new
    spirit within you,
  taking from your bodies your stony hearts
  and giving you natural hearts.
I will put my spirit within you and make you
    live by my statutes,
  careful to observe my decrees.
You shall live in the land I gave your fathers;
  you shall be my people, and I will be your
    God.

RESPONSORIAL PSALM
Ps 42:3, 5; 43:3, 4

℞. (42:2) Like a deer that longs for running
  streams, my soul longs for you, my God.

Athirst is my soul for God, the living God.
  When shall I go and behold the face of God?

℞. Like a deer that longs for running streams,
  my soul longs for you, my God.

I went with the throng
  and led them in procession to the house of God,
amid loud cries of joy and thanksgiving,
  with the multitude keeping festival.

℞. Like a deer that longs for running streams,
  my soul longs for you, my God.

Send forth your light and your fidelity;
  they shall lead me on
and bring me to your holy mountain,
  to your dwelling-place.

℞. Like a deer that longs for running streams,
  my soul longs for you, my God.

Then will I go in to the altar of God,
  the God of my gladness and joy;
then will I give you thanks upon the harp,
  O God, my God!

℞. Like a deer that longs for running streams,
  my soul longs for you, my God.

or

Isa 12:2-3, 4bcd, 5-6

℞. (3) You will draw water joyfully from the
  springs of salvation.

God indeed is my savior;
  I am confident and unafraid.
My strength and my courage is the LORD,
  and he has been my savior.
With joy you will draw water
  at the fountain of salvation.

℞. You will draw water joyfully from the
  springs of salvation.

Give thanks to the LORD, acclaim his name;
  among the nations make known his deeds,
  proclaim how exalted is his name.

℞. You will draw water joyfully from the
  springs of salvation.

Sing praise to the LORD for his glorious
achievement;
let this be known throughout all the earth.
Shout with exultation, O city of Zion,
for great in your midst
is the Holy One of Israel!

R̸. You will draw water joyfully from the
springs of salvation.

or

Ps 51:12-13, 14-15, 18-19

R̸. (12a) Create a clean heart in me, O God.

A clean heart create for me, O God,
and a steadfast spirit renew within me.
Cast me not out from your presence,
and your Holy Spirit take not from me.

R̸. Create a clean heart in me, O God.

Give me back the joy of your salvation,
and a willing spirit sustain in me.
I will teach transgressors your ways,
and sinners shall return to you.

R̸. Create a clean heart in me, O God.

For you are not pleased with sacrifices;
should I offer a holocaust, you would not
accept it.
My sacrifice, O God, is a contrite spirit;
a heart contrite and humbled, O God, you
will not spurn.

R̸. Create a clean heart in me, O God.

EPISTLE
Rom 6:3-11

Brothers and sisters:
Are you unaware that we who were baptized
into Christ Jesus
were baptized into his death?
We were indeed buried with him through
baptism into death,
so that, just as Christ was raised from the
dead
by the glory of the Father,
we too might live in newness of life.

For if we have grown into union with him
through a death like his,
we shall also be united with him in the
resurrection.
We know that our old self was crucified with
him,
so that our sinful body might be done away
with,
that we might no longer be in slavery to sin.
For a dead person has been absolved from sin.
If, then, we have died with Christ,
we believe that we shall also live with him.
We know that Christ, raised from the dead,
dies no more;
death no longer has power over him.
As to his death, he died to sin once and for all;
as to his life, he lives for God.
Consequently, you too must think of
yourselves as being dead to sin
and living for God in Christ Jesus.

RESPONSORIAL PSALM
Ps 118:1-2, 16-17, 22-23

R̸. Alleluia, alleluia, alleluia.

Give thanks to the LORD, for he is good,
for his mercy endures forever.
Let the house of Israel say,
"His mercy endures forever."

R̸. Alleluia, alleluia, alleluia.

The right hand of the LORD has struck with
power;
the right hand of the LORD is exalted.
I shall not die, but live,
and declare the works of the LORD.

R̸. Alleluia, alleluia, alleluia.

The stone which the builders rejected
has become the cornerstone.
By the LORD has this been done;
it is wonderful in our eyes.

R̸. Alleluia, alleluia, alleluia.

Gospel
Luke 24:1-12; L41C

At daybreak on the first day of the week
  the women who had come from Galilee with Jesus
  took the spices they had prepared
  and went to the tomb.
They found the stone rolled away from the tomb;
  but when they entered,
  they did not find the body of the Lord Jesus.
While they were puzzling over this, behold,
  two men in dazzling garments appeared to them.
They were terrified and bowed their faces to the ground.
They said to them,
  "Why do you seek the living one among the dead?
He is not here, but he has been raised.
Remember what he said to you while he was still in Galilee,
that the Son of Man must be handed over to sinners
  and be crucified, and rise on the third day."
And they remembered his words.
Then they returned from the tomb
  and announced all these things to the eleven
  and to all the others.
The women were Mary Magdalene, Joanna, and Mary the mother of James;
  the others who accompanied them also told this to the apostles,
  but their story seemed like nonsense
  and they did not believe them.
But Peter got up and ran to the tomb,
  bent down, and saw the burial cloths alone;
  then he went home amazed at what had happened.

at an afternoon or evening Mass

Gospel
Luke 24:13-35; L46

That very day, the first day of the week,
  two of Jesus' disciples were going
  to a village seven miles from Jerusalem called Emmaus,
  and they were conversing about all the things that had occurred.
And it happened that while they were conversing and debating,
  Jesus himself drew near and walked with them,
  but their eyes were prevented from recognizing him.
He asked them,
  "What are you discussing as you walk along?"
They stopped, looking downcast.
One of them, named Cleopas, said to him in reply,
  "Are you the only visitor to Jerusalem
  who does not know of the things
  that have taken place there in these days?"
And he replied to them, "What sort of things?"
They said to him,
  "The things that happened to Jesus the Nazarene,
  who was a prophet mighty in deed and word
  before God and all the people,
  how our chief priests and rulers both handed him over
  to a sentence of death and crucified him.
But we were hoping that he would be the one to redeem Israel;
  and besides all this,
  it is now the third day since this took place.
Some women from our group, however, have astounded us:
  they were at the tomb early in the morning
  and did not find his body;
  they came back and reported
  that they had indeed seen a vision of angels
  who announced that he was alive.
Then some of those with us went to the tomb
  and found things just as the women had described,
  but him they did not see."
And he said to them, "Oh, how foolish you are!
How slow of heart to believe all that the prophets spoke!
Was it not necessary that the Christ should suffer these things
  and enter into his glory?"
Then beginning with Moses and all the prophets,
  he interpreted to them what referred to him
  in all the Scriptures.
As they approached the village to which they were going,
  he gave the impression that he was going on farther.
But they urged him, "Stay with us,
  for it is nearly evening and the day is almost over."
So he went in to stay with them.
And it happened that, while he was with them at table,
  he took bread, said the blessing,
  broke it, and gave it to them.
With that their eyes were opened and they recognized him,
  but he vanished from their sight.
Then they said to each other,
  "Were not our hearts burning within us
  while he spoke to us on the way and opened the Scriptures to us?"
So they set out at once and returned to Jerusalem
  where they found gathered together
  the eleven and those with them who were saying,
  "The Lord has truly been raised and has appeared to Simon!"
Then the two recounted
  what had taken place on the way
  and how he was made known to them in the breaking of the bread.

FIRST READING
Acts 10:34a, 37-43

Peter proceeded to speak and said:
    "You know what has happened all over Judea,
    beginning in Galilee after the baptism
    that John preached,
    how God anointed Jesus of Nazareth
    with the Holy Spirit and power.
He went about doing good
    and healing all those oppressed by the devil,
    for God was with him.
We are witnesses of all that he did
    both in the country of the Jews and in
        Jerusalem.
They put him to death by hanging him on a tree.
This man God raised on the third day and
        granted that he be visible,
    not to all the people, but to us,
    the witnesses chosen by God in advance,
    who ate and drank with him after he rose
        from the dead.
He commissioned us to preach to the people
    and testify that he is the one appointed by God
    as judge of the living and the dead.
To him all the prophets bear witness,
    that everyone who believes in him
    will receive forgiveness of sins through his
        name."

RESPONSORIAL PSALM
Ps 118:1-2, 16-17, 22-23

℟. (24) This is the day the Lord has made; let
    us rejoice and be glad.
    or:
℟. Alleluia.

Give thanks to the Lord, for he is good,
    for his mercy endures forever.
Let the house of Israel say,
    "His mercy endures forever."

℟. This is the day the Lord has made; let us
    rejoice and be glad.
    or:
℟. Alleluia.

"The right hand of the Lord has struck with
        power;
    the right hand of the Lord is exalted.
I shall not die, but live,
    and declare the works of the Lord."

℟. This is the day the Lord has made; let us
    rejoice and be glad.
    or:
℟. Alleluia.

The stone which the builders rejected
    has become the cornerstone.
By the Lord has this been done;
    it is wonderful in our eyes.

℟. This is the day the Lord has made; let us
    rejoice and be glad.
    or:
℟. Alleluia.

SECOND READING
Col 3:1-4

Brothers and sisters:
If then you were raised with Christ, seek what
        is above,
    where Christ is seated at the right hand of
        God.
Think of what is above, not of what is on
        earth.
For you have died, and your life is hidden with
    Christ in God.
When Christ your life appears,
    then you too will appear with him in glory.

or
1 Cor 5:6b-8

Brothers and sisters:
Do you not know that a little yeast leavens all
        the dough?
Clear out the old yeast,
    so that you may become a fresh batch of
        dough,
    inasmuch as you are unleavened.
For our paschal lamb, Christ, has been
        sacrificed.
Therefore, let us celebrate the feast,
    not with the old yeast, the yeast of malice
        and wickedness,
    but with the unleavened bread of sincerity
        and truth.

SEQUENCE

Victimae paschali laudes
Christians, to the Paschal Victim
    Offer your thankful praises!
A Lamb the sheep redeems;
    Christ, who only is sinless,
    Reconciles sinners to the Father.
Death and life have contended in that combat
        stupendous:
    The Prince of life, who died, reigns
        immortal.
Speak, Mary, declaring
    What you saw, wayfaring.
"The tomb of Christ, who is living,
    The glory of Jesus' resurrection;
Bright angels attesting,
    The shroud and napkin resting.
Yes, Christ my hope is arisen;
    To Galilee he goes before you."
Christ indeed from death is risen, our new life
        obtaining.
    Have mercy, victor King, ever reigning!
    Amen. Alleluia.

Second Sunday of Easter (or of Divine Mercy), *April 24, 2022*

Gospel (cont.)
John 20:19-31; L45C

Then he said to Thomas, "Put your finger here and see my hands,
    and bring your hand and put it into my side,
    and do not be unbelieving, but believe."
Thomas answered and said to him, "My Lord and my God!"
Jesus said to him, "Have you come to believe because you have seen me?
Blessed are those who have not seen and have believed."

Now Jesus did many other signs in the presence of his disciples
    that are not written in this book.
But these are written that you may come to believe
    that Jesus is the Christ, the Son of God,
    and that through this belief you may have life in his name.

Gospel (cont.)
John 21:1-19; L48C

When they climbed out on shore,
  they saw a charcoal fire with fish on it and bread.
Jesus said to them, "Bring some of the fish you just caught."
So Simon Peter went over and dragged the net ashore
  full of one hundred fifty-three large fish.
Even though there were so many, the net was not torn.
Jesus said to them, "Come, have breakfast."
And none of the disciples dared to ask him, "Who are you?"
  because they realized it was the Lord.
Jesus came over and took the bread and gave it to them,
  and in like manner the fish.
This was now the third time Jesus was revealed to his disciples
  after being raised from the dead.

When they had finished breakfast, Jesus said to Simon Peter,
  "Simon, son of John, do you love me more than these?"
Simon Peter answered him, "Yes, Lord, you know that I love you."
Jesus said to him, "Feed my lambs."
He then said to Simon Peter a second time,
  "Simon, son of John, do you love me?"
Simon Peter answered him, "Yes, Lord, you know that I love you."
Jesus said to him, "Tend my sheep."
Jesus said to him the third time,
  "Simon, son of John, do you love me?"
Peter was distressed that Jesus had said to him a third time,
  "Do you love me?" and he said to him,
  "Lord, you know everything; you know that I love you."
Jesus said to him, "Feed my sheep.
Amen, amen, I say to you, when you were younger,
  you used to dress yourself and go where you wanted;
  but when you grow old, you will stretch out your hands,
  and someone else will dress you
  and lead you where you do not want to go."
He said this signifying by what kind of death he would glorify God.
And when he had said this, he said to him, "Follow me."

or John 21:1-14; L48C

At that time, Jesus revealed himself again to his disciples at the Sea of
    Tiberias.
He revealed himself in this way.
Together were Simon Peter, Thomas called Didymus,
    Nathanael from Cana in Galilee,
    Zebedee's sons, and two others of his disciples.
Simon Peter said to them, "I am going fishing."
They said to him, "We also will come with you."
So they went out and got into the boat,
    but that night they caught nothing.
When it was already dawn, Jesus was standing on the shore;
    but the disciples did not realize that it was Jesus.
Jesus said to them, "Children, have you caught anything to eat?"
They answered him, "No."
So he said to them, "Cast the net over the right side of the boat
    and you will find something."
So they cast it, and were not able to pull it in
    because of the number of fish.
So the disciple whom Jesus loved said to Peter, "It is the Lord."
When Simon Peter heard that it was the Lord,
    he tucked in his garment, for he was lightly clad,
    and jumped into the sea.
The other disciples came in the boat,
    for they were not far from shore, only about a hundred yards,
    dragging the net with the fish.
When they climbed out on shore,
    they saw a charcoal fire with fish on it and bread.
Jesus said to them, "Bring some of the fish you just caught."
So Simon Peter went over and dragged the net ashore
    full of one hundred fifty-three large fish.
Even though there were so many, the net was not torn.
Jesus said to them, "Come, have breakfast."
And none of the disciples dared to ask him, "Who are you?"
    because they realized it was the Lord.
Jesus came over and took the bread and gave it to them,
    and in like manner the fish.
This was now the third time Jesus was revealed to his disciples
    after being raised from the dead.

Fourth Sunday of Easter, *May 8, 2022*

SECOND READING
Rev 7:9, 14b-17

I, John, had a vision of a great multitude,
  which no one could count,
  from every nation, race, people, and tongue.
They stood before the throne and before the
    Lamb,
  wearing white robes and holding palm
    branches in their hands.

Then one of the elders said to me,
  "These are the ones who have survived the
    time of great distress;

they have washed their robes
and made them white in the blood of the
  Lamb.

  "For this reason they stand before God's
    throne
  and worship him day and night in his
    temple.
The one who sits on the throne will
  shelter them.
They will not hunger or thirst anymore,
  nor will the sun or any heat strike
    them.

For the Lamb who is in the center of the
    throne
  will shepherd them
  and lead them to springs of life-giving
    water,
  and God will wipe away every tear
    from their eyes."

Sixth Sunday of Easter, *May 22 2022*

SECOND READING

Rev 21:10-14, 22-23

The angel took me in spirit to a great, high
mountain
and showed me the holy city Jerusalem
coming down out of heaven from God.
It gleamed with the splendor of God.
Its radiance was like that of a precious stone,
like jasper, clear as crystal.
It had a massive, high wall,
with twelve gates where twelve angels were
stationed
and on which names were inscribed,
the names of the twelve tribes of the
Israelites.

There were three gates facing east,
three north, three south, and three west.
The wall of the city had twelve courses of
stones as its foundation,
on which were inscribed the twelve names
of the twelve apostles of the Lamb.

I saw no temple in the city
for its temple is the Lord God almighty and
the Lamb.
The city had no need of sun or moon to shine
on it,
for the glory of God gave it light,
and its lamp was the Lamb.

The Ascension of the Lord, *May 26 (Thursday) or May 29, 2022*

SECOND READING

Eph 1:17-23

Brothers and sisters:
May the God of our Lord Jesus Christ, the
Father of glory,
give you a Spirit of wisdom and revelation
resulting in knowledge of him.
May the eyes of your hearts be enlightened,
that you may know what is the hope that
belongs to his call,
what are the riches of glory
in his inheritance among the holy ones,
and what is the surpassing greatness of
his power
for us who believe,
in accord with the exercise of his great
might,
which he worked in Christ,
raising him from the dead
and seating him at his right hand in the
heavens,
far above every principality, authority,
power, and dominion,
and every name that is named
not only in this age but also in the one to
come.

And he put all things beneath his feet
and gave him as head over all things to the
church,
which is his body,
the fullness of the one who fills all things
in every way.

or

Heb 9:24-28; 10:19-23

Christ did not enter into a sanctuary made by
hands,
a copy of the true one, but heaven itself,
that he might now appear before God on
our behalf.
Not that he might offer himself repeatedly,
as the high priest enters each year into the
sanctuary
with blood that is not his own;
if that were so, he would have had to suffer
repeatedly
from the foundation of the world.
But now once for all he has appeared at the
end of the ages
to take away sin by his sacrifice.
Just as it is appointed that men and women
die once,

and after this the judgment, so also Christ,
offered once to take away the sins of many,
will appear a second time, not to take away
sin
but to bring salvation to those who eagerly
await him.

Therefore, brothers and sisters, since through
the blood of Jesus
we have confidence of entrance into the
sanctuary
by the new and living way he opened for us
through the veil,
that is, his flesh,
and since we have "a great priest over the
house of God,"
let us approach with a sincere heart and in
absolute trust,
with our hearts sprinkled clean from an
evil conscience
and our bodies washed in pure water.
Let us hold unwaveringly to our confession
that gives us hope,
for he who made the promise is
trustworthy.

SECOND READING
Rom 8:8-17

Brothers and sisters:
Those who are in the flesh cannot please
God.
But you are not in the flesh;
on the contrary, you are in the spirit,
if only the Spirit of God dwells in you.
Whoever does not have the Spirit of Christ
does not belong to him.
But if Christ is in you,
although the body is dead because of sin,
the spirit is alive because of righteousness.
If the Spirit of the one who raised Jesus from
the dead dwells in you,
the one who raised Christ from the dead
will give life to your mortal bodies also,
through his Spirit that dwells in you.
Consequently, brothers and sisters,
we are not debtors to the flesh,
to live according to the flesh.
For if you live according to the flesh, you
will die,
but if by the Spirit you put to death the
deeds of the body,
you will live.

For those who are led by the Spirit of God are
sons of God.
For you did not receive a spirit of slavery to
fall back into fear,
but you received a Spirit of adoption,
through whom we cry, "Abba, Father!"
The Spirit himself bears witness with our
spirit
that we are children of God,
and if children, then heirs,
heirs of God and joint heirs with Christ,
if only we suffer with him
so that we may also be glorified with him.

or

1 Cor 12:3b-7, 12-13

Brothers and sisters:
No one can say, "Jesus is Lord," except by the
Holy Spirit.

There are different kinds of spiritual gifts but
the same Spirit;
there are different forms of service but the
same Lord;
there are different workings but the same God
who produces all of them in everyone.
To each individual the manifestation of the
Spirit
is given for some benefit.

As a body is one though it has many parts,
and all the parts of the body, though many,
are one body,
so also Christ.
For in one Spirit we were all baptized into one
body,
whether Jews or Greeks, slaves or free
persons,
and we were all given to drink of one Spirit.

SEQUENCE
Veni, Sancte Spiritus

Come, Holy Spirit, come!
And from your celestial home
Shed a ray of light divine!
Come, Father of the poor!
Come, source of all our store!
Come, within our bosoms shine.
You, of comforters the best;
You, the soul's most welcome guest;
Sweet refreshment here below;
In our labor, rest most sweet;
Grateful coolness in the heat;
Solace in the midst of woe.
O most blessed Light divine,
Shine within these hearts of yours,
And our inmost being fill!
Where you are not, we have naught,
Nothing good in deed or thought,
Nothing free from taint of ill.
Heal our wounds, our strength renew;
On our dryness pour your dew;
Wash the stains of guilt away:
Bend the stubborn heart and will;
Melt the frozen, warm the chill;
Guide the steps that go astray.
On the faithful, who adore
And confess you, evermore
In your sevenfold gift descend;
Give them virtue's sure reward;
Give them your salvation, Lord;
Give them joys that never end. Amen.
Alleluia.

OPTIONAL SEQUENCE

Lauda Sion

Laud, O Zion, your salvation,
Laud with hymns of exultation,
  Christ, your king and shepherd true:

Bring him all the praise you know,
He is more than you bestow.
  Never can you reach his due.

Special theme for glad thanksgiving
Is the quick'ning and the living
  Bread today before you set:

From his hands of old partaken,
As we know, by faith unshaken,
  Where the Twelve at supper met.

Full and clear ring out your chanting,
Joy nor sweetest grace be wanting,
  From your heart let praises burst:

For today the feast is holden,
When the institution olden
  Of that supper was rehearsed.

Here the new law's new oblation,
By the new king's revelation,
  Ends the form of ancient rite:

Now the new the old effaces,
Truth away the shadow chases,
  Light dispels the gloom of night.

What he did at supper seated,
Christ ordained to be repeated,
  His memorial ne'er to cease:

And his rule for guidance taking,
Bread and wine we hallow, making
  Thus our sacrifice of peace.

This the truth each Christian learns,
Bread into his flesh he turns,
  To his precious blood the wine:

Sight has fail'd, nor thought conceives,
But a dauntless faith believes,
  Resting on a pow'r divine.

Here beneath these signs are hidden
Priceless things to sense forbidden;
  Signs, not things are all we see:

Blood is poured and flesh is broken,
Yet in either wondrous token
  Christ entire we know to be.

Whoso of this food partakes,
Does not rend the Lord nor breaks;
  Christ is whole to all that taste:

Thousands are, as one, receivers,
One, as thousands of believers,
  Eats of him who cannot waste.

Bad and good the feast are sharing,
Of what divers dooms preparing,
  Endless death, or endless life.

Life to these, to those damnation,
See how like participation
  Is with unlike issues rife.

When the sacrament is broken,
Doubt not, but believe 'tis spoken,

That each sever'd outward token
  doth the very whole contain.

Nought the precious gift divides,
Breaking but the sign betides
  Jesus still the same abides,
    still unbroken does remain.

The shorter form of the sequence begins here.

Lo! the angel's food is given
To the pilgrim who has striven;
  See the children's bread from heaven,
    which on dogs may not be spent.

Truth the ancient types fulfilling,
Isaac bound, a victim willing,
  Paschal lamb, its lifeblood spilling,
    manna to the fathers sent.

Very bread, good shepherd, tend us,
Jesu, of your love befriend us,
  You refresh us, you defend us,
    Your eternal goodness send us
In the land of life to see.

You who all things can and know,
Who on earth such food bestow,
  Grant us with your saints, though lowest,
    Where the heav'nly feast you show,
Fellow heirs and guests to be. Amen. Alleluia.

FIRST READING
Isa 49:1-6

Hear me, O coastlands,
    listen, O distant peoples.
The LORD called me from birth,
    from my mother's womb he gave me my
        name.
He made of me a sharp-edged sword
    and concealed me in the shadow of his arm.
He made me a polished arrow,
    in his quiver he hid me.
You are my servant, he said to me,
    Israel, through whom I show my glory.

Though I thought I had toiled in vain,
    and for nothing, uselessly, spent my
        strength,
yet my reward is with the LORD,
    my recompense is with my God.
For now the LORD has spoken
    who formed me as his servant from the
        womb,
that Jacob may be brought back to him
    and Israel gathered to him;
and I am made glorious in the sight of the
        LORD,
    and my God is now my strength!
It is too little, he says, for you to be my
        servant,
    to raise up the tribes of Jacob,
    and restore the survivors of Israel;
I will make you a light to the nations,
    that my salvation may reach to the ends of
        the earth.

RESPONSORIAL PSALM
Ps 139:1b-3, 13-14ab, 14c-15

R̸. (14a) I praise you, for I am wonderfully
    made.

O LORD, you have probed me, you know me;
    you know when I sit and when I stand;
    you understand my thoughts from afar.
My journeys and my rest you scrutinize,
    with all my ways you are familiar.

R̸. I praise you, for I am wonderfully made.

Truly you have formed my inmost being;
    you knit me in my mother's womb.
I give you thanks that I am fearfully,
        wonderfully made;
    wonderful are your works.

R̸. I praise you, for I am wonderfully made.

My soul also you knew full well;
    nor was my frame unknown to you
When I was made in secret,
    when I was fashioned in the depths of the
        earth.

R̸. I praise you, for I am wonderfully made.

SECOND READING
Acts 13:22-26

In those days, Paul said:
"God raised up David as their king;
    of him God testified,
    I have found David, son of Jesse, a man
        after my own heart;
    he will carry out my every wish.
From this man's descendants God, according
        to his promise,
    has brought to Israel a savior, Jesus.
John heralded his coming by proclaiming a
        baptism of repentance
    to all the people of Israel;
    and as John was completing his course, he
        would say,
    'What do you suppose that I am? I am not
        he.
Behold, one is coming after me;
    I am not worthy to unfasten the sandals of
        his feet.'

"My brothers, sons of the family of Abraham,
    and those others among you who are God-
        fearing,
    to us this word of salvation has been sent."

The Solemnity of the Most Sacred Heart of Jesus, *June 24, 2022*

FIRST READING
Ezek 34:11-16

Thus says the Lord GOD:
  I myself will look after and tend my sheep.
As a shepherd tends his flock
  when he finds himself among his scattered
    sheep,
  so will I tend my sheep.
I will rescue them from every place where
    they were scattered
  when it was cloudy and dark.
I will lead them out from among the peoples
  and gather them from the foreign lands;
  I will bring them back to their own country
  and pasture them upon the mountains of
    Israel
  in the land's ravines and all its inhabited
    places.
In good pastures will I pasture them,
  and on the mountain heights of Israel
  shall be their grazing ground.
There they shall lie down on good grazing
    ground,
  and in rich pastures shall they be pastured
  on the mountains of Israel.
I myself will pasture my sheep;
  I myself will give them rest, says the Lord
    GOD.
The lost I will seek out,
  the strayed I will bring back,
  the injured I will bind up,
  the sick I will heal,
  but the sleek and the strong I will destroy,
  shepherding them rightly.

RESPONSORIAL PSALM
Ps 23:1-3a, 3b-4, 5, 6

℟. (1) The Lord is my shepherd; there is nothing I shall want.

The LORD is my shepherd; I shall not want.
  In verdant pastures he gives me repose;
beside restful waters he leads me;
  he refreshes my soul.

℟. The Lord is my shepherd; there is nothing
  I shall want.

He guides me in right paths
  for his name's sake.
Even though I walk in the dark valley
  I fear no evil; for you are at my side
with your rod and your staff
  that give me courage.

℟. The Lord is my shepherd; there is nothing
  I shall want.

You spread the table before me
  in the sight of my foes;
you anoint my head with oil;
  my cup overflows.

℟. The Lord is my shepherd; there is nothing
  I shall want.

Only goodness and kindness follow me
  all the days of my life;
and I shall dwell in the house of the LORD
  for years to come.

℟. The Lord is my shepherd; there is nothing
  I shall want.

SECOND READING
Rom 5:5b-11

Brothers and sisters:
The love of God has been poured out into our
    hearts
  through the Holy Spirit that has been given
    to us.
For Christ, while we were still helpless,
  died at the appointed time for the ungodly.
Indeed, only with difficulty does one die for a
    just person,
  though perhaps for a good person
  one might even find courage to die.
But God proves his love for us
  in that while we were still sinners Christ
    died for us.
How much more then, since we are now
    justified by his blood,
  will we be saved through him from the
    wrath.
Indeed, if, while we were enemies,
  we were reconciled to God through the
    death of his Son,
  how much more, once reconciled,
  will we be saved by his life.
Not only that,
  but we also boast of God through our Lord
    Jesus Christ,
  through whom we have now received
    reconciliation.

FIRST READING
Acts 12:1-11

In those days, King Herod laid hands upon
    some members of the Church to harm
    them.
He had James, the brother of John, killed by
    the sword,
    and when he saw that this was pleasing to
        the Jews
    he proceeded to arrest Peter also.
—It was the feast of Unleavened Bread.—
He had him taken into custody and put in
    prison
    under the guard of four squads of four
        soldiers each.
He intended to bring him before the people
    after Passover.
Peter thus was being kept in prison,
    but prayer by the Church was fervently
        being made
    to God on his behalf.

On the very night before Herod was to bring
    him to trial,
    Peter, secured by double chains,
    was sleeping between two soldiers,
    while outside the door guards kept watch
        on the prison.
Suddenly the angel of the Lord stood by him,
    and a light shone in the cell.
He tapped Peter on the side and awakened
    him, saying,
    "Get up quickly."
The chains fell from his wrists.
The angel said to him, "Put on your belt and
    your sandals."
He did so.
Then he said to him, "Put on your cloak and
    follow me."
So he followed him out,
    not realizing that what was happening
        through the angel was real;
    he thought he was seeing a vision.
They passed the first guard, then the second,
    and came to the iron gate leading out to the
        city,
    which opened for them by itself.
They emerged and made their way down an
    alley,
    and suddenly the angel left him.
Then Peter recovered his senses and said,
    "Now I know for certain
    that the Lord sent his angel
    and rescued me from the hand of Herod
    and from all that the Jewish people had
        been expecting."

RESPONSORIAL PSALM
Ps 34:2-3, 4-5, 6-7, 8-9

℟. (8) The angel of the Lord will rescue those
    who fear him.

I will bless the LORD at all times;
    his praise shall be ever in my mouth.
Let my soul glory in the LORD;
    the lowly will hear me and be glad.

℟. The angel of the Lord will rescue those
    who fear him.

Glorify the LORD with me,
    let us together extol his name.
I sought the LORD, and he answered me
    and delivered me from all my fears.

℟. The angel of the Lord will rescue those
    who fear him.

Look to him that you may be radiant with joy,
    and your faces may not blush with shame.
When the poor one called out, the LORD heard,
    and from all his distress he saved him.

℟. The angel of the Lord will rescue those
    who fear him.

The angel of the LORD encamps
    around those who fear him, and delivers
        them.
Taste and see how good the LORD is;
    blessed the man who takes refuge in him.

℟. The angel of the Lord will rescue those
    who fear him.

SECOND READING
2 Tim 4:6-8, 17-18

I, Paul, am already being poured out like a
    libation,
    and the time of my departure is at hand.
I have competed well; I have finished the race;
    I have kept the faith.
From now on the crown of righteousness
    awaits me,
    which the Lord, the just judge,
    will award to me on that day, and not only
        to me,
    but to all who have longed for his
        appearance.

The Lord stood by me and gave me strength,
    so that through me the proclamation might
        be completed
    and all the Gentiles might hear it.
And I was rescued from the lion's mouth.
The Lord will rescue me from every evil threat
    and will bring me safe to his heavenly
        Kingdom.
To him be glory forever and ever. Amen.

Fourteenth Sunday in Ordinary Time, July 3, 2022

Gospel (cont.)
Luke 10:1-12, 17-20; L102C

Yet know this: the kingdom of God is at hand.
I tell you,
  it will be more tolerable for Sodom on that day than for that town."

The seventy-two returned rejoicing, and said,
  "Lord, even the demons are subject to us because of your name."
Jesus said, "I have observed Satan fall like lightning from the sky.
Behold, I have given you the power to 'tread upon serpents' and
    scorpions
  and upon the full force of the enemy and nothing will harm you.
Nevertheless, do not rejoice because the spirits are subject to you,
  but rejoice because your names are written in heaven."

or Luke 10:1-9; L102C

At that time the Lord appointed seventy-two others
  whom he sent ahead of him in pairs
  to every town and place he intended to visit.
He said to them,
  "The harvest is abundant but the laborers are few;
  so ask the master of the harvest
  to send out laborers for his harvest.
Go on your way;
  behold, I am sending you like lambs among wolves.
Carry no money bag, no sack, no sandals;
  and greet no one along the way.
Into whatever house you enter, first say,
  'Peace to this household.'
If a peaceful person lives there,
  your peace will rest on him;
  but if not, it will return to you.
Stay in the same house and eat and drink what is offered to you,
  for the laborer deserves his payment.
Do not move about from one house to another.
Whatever town you enter and they welcome you,
  eat what is set before you,
  cure the sick in it and say to them,
  'The kingdom of God is at hand for you.'"

Fifteenth Sunday in Ordinary Time, July 10, 2022

Gospel (cont.)
Luke 10:25-37; L105C

But a Samaritan traveler who came upon him
  was moved with compassion at the sight.
He approached the victim,
  poured oil and wine over his wounds and bandaged them.
Then he lifted him up on his own animal,
  took him to an inn, and cared for him.
The next day he took out two silver coins
  and gave them to the innkeeper with the instruction,
  'Take care of him.
If you spend more than what I have given you,
  I shall repay you on my way back.'
Which of these three, in your opinion,
  was neighbor to the robbers' victim?"
He answered, "The one who treated him with mercy."
Jesus said to him, "Go and do likewise."

RESPONSORIAL PSALM
Ps 19:8, 9, 10, 11

R̸. (9a) Your words, Lord, are Spirit and life.

The law of the LORD is perfect,
  refreshing the soul;
the decree of the LORD is trustworthy,
  giving wisdom to the simple.

R̸. Your words, Lord, are Spirit and life.

The precepts of the LORD are right,
  rejoicing the heart;
the command of the LORD is clear,
  enlightening the eye.

R̸. Your words, Lord, are Spirit and life.

The fear of the LORD is pure,
  enduring forever;
the ordinances of the LORD are true,
  all of them just.

R̸. Your words, Lord, are Spirit and life.

They are more precious than gold,
  than a heap of purest gold;
sweeter also than syrup
  or honey from the comb.

R̸. Your words, Lord, are Spirit and life.

Seventeenth Sunday in Ordinary Time, *July 24, 2022*

Gospel (cont.)
Luke 11:1-13; L111C

"And I tell you, ask and you will receive;
  seek and you will find;
  knock and the door will be opened to you.
For everyone who asks, receives;
  and the one who seeks, finds;
  and to the one who knocks, the door will be opened.
What father among you would hand his son a snake
  when he asks for a fish?
Or hand him a scorpion when he asks for an egg?
If you then, who are wicked,
  know how to give good gifts to your children,
  how much more will the Father in heaven
  give the Holy Spirit to those who ask him?"

SECOND READING
Col 2:12-14

Brothers and sisters:
You were buried with him in baptism,
  in which you were also raised with him
  through faith in the power of God,
  who raised him from the dead.
And even when you were dead
  in transgressions and the uncircumcision of your flesh,
  he brought you to life along with him,
  having forgiven us all our transgressions;
  obliterating the bond against us, with its legal claims,
  which was opposed to us,
  he also removed it from our midst, nailing it to the cross.

Nineteenth Sunday in Ordinary Time, *August 7, 2022*

Gospel (cont.)
Luke 12:32-48; L117C

You also must be prepared, for at an hour you do not expect,
  the Son of Man will come."

Then Peter said,
  "Lord, is this parable meant for us or for everyone?"
And the Lord replied,
  "Who, then, is the faithful and prudent steward
  whom the master will put in charge of his servants
  to distribute the food allowance at the proper time?
Blessed is that servant whom his master on arrival finds doing so.
Truly, I say to you, the master will put the servant
  in charge of all his property.
But if that servant says to himself,
  'My master is delayed in coming,'
  and begins to beat the menservants and the maidservants,
  to eat and drink and get drunk,
  then that servant's master will come
  on an unexpected day and at an unknown hour
  and will punish the servant severely
  and assign him a place with the unfaithful.
That servant who knew his master's will
  but did not make preparations nor act in accord with his will
  shall be beaten severely;
  and the servant who was ignorant of his master's will
  but acted in a way deserving of a severe beating
  shall be beaten only lightly.
Much will be required of the person entrusted with much,
  and still more will be demanded of the person entrusted with more."

or Luke 12:35-40

Jesus said to his disciples:
"Gird your loins and light your lamps
and be like servants who await their master's return from a wedding,
ready to open immediately when he comes and knocks.
Blessed are those servants
  whom the master finds vigilant on his arrival.
Amen, I say to you, he will gird himself,
  have them recline at table, and proceed to wait on them.
And should he come in the second or third watch
  and find them prepared in this way,
  blessed are those servants.
Be sure of this:
  if the master of the house had known the hour
  when the thief was coming,
  he would not have let his house be broken into.
You also must be prepared, for at an hour you do not expect,
  the Son of Man will come."

SECOND READING

Heb 11:1-2, 8-19 *(cont.)*

So it was that there came forth from one man,
    himself as good as dead,
    descendants as numerous as the stars in
        the sky
    and as countless as the sands on the
        seashore.

All these died in faith.
They did not receive what had been promised
    but saw it and greeted it from afar
    and acknowledged themselves to be
        strangers and aliens on earth,
    for those who speak thus show that they
        are seeking a homeland.
If they had been thinking of the land from
        which they had come,
    they would have had opportunity to return.
But now they desire a better homeland, a
        heavenly one.
Therefore, God is not ashamed to be called
        their God,
    for he has prepared a city for them.

By faith Abraham, when put to the test,
        offered up Isaac,
    and he who had received the promises was
        ready to offer his only son,
    of whom it was said,
    "Through Isaac descendants shall bear
        your name."
He reasoned that God was able to raise even
        from the dead,
    and he received Isaac back as a symbol.

or Heb 11:1-2, 8-12

Brothers and sisters:
Faith is the realization of what is hoped for
    and evidence of things not seen.
Because of it the ancients were well attested.

By faith Abraham obeyed when he was called
        to go out to a place
    that he was to receive as an inheritance;
    he went out, not knowing where he was to
        go.
By faith he sojourned in the promised land as
        in a foreign country,
    dwelling in tents with Isaac and Jacob,
        heirs of the same promise;
    for he was looking forward to the city with
        foundations,
    whose architect and maker is God.
By faith he received power to generate,
    even though he was past the normal age
    —and Sarah herself was sterile—
    for he thought that the one who had made
        the promise was trustworthy.
So it was that there came forth from one man,
    himself as good as dead,
    descendants as numerous as the stars in
        the sky
    and as countless as the sands on the
        seashore.

Gospel (cont.)
Luke 1:39-56; L622

He has cast down the mighty from their
    thrones,
    and has lifted up the lowly.
He has filled the hungry with good things,
    and the rich he has sent away empty.
He has come to the help of his servant
    Israel
    for he has remembered his promise of
      mercy,
    the promise he made to our fathers,
    to Abraham and his children forever."

Mary remained with her about three months
    and then returned to her home.

FIRST READING
Rev 11:19a; 12:1-6a, 10ab

God's temple in heaven was opened,
    and the ark of his covenant could be seen
      in the temple.

A great sign appeared in the sky, a woman
    clothed with the sun,
    with the moon under her feet,
    and on her head a crown of twelve stars.
She was with child and wailed aloud in pain
    as she labored to give birth.
Then another sign appeared in the sky;
    it was a huge red dragon, with seven heads
      and ten horns,
    and on its heads were seven diadems.

Its tail swept away a third of the stars in the
    sky
    and hurled them down to the earth.
Then the dragon stood before the woman
    about to give birth,
    to devour her child when she gave birth.
She gave birth to a son, a male child,
    destined to rule all the nations with an iron
      rod.
Her child was caught up to God and his
    throne.
The woman herself fled into the desert
    where she had a place prepared by God.

Then I heard a loud voice in heaven say:
    "Now have salvation and power come,
      and the Kingdom of our God
      and the authority of his Anointed One."

RESPONSORIAL PSALM
Ps 45:10, 11, 12, 16

R℣. (10bc) The queen stands at your right
    hand, arrayed in gold.

The queen takes her place at your right hand
    in gold of Ophir.

R℣. The queen stands at your right hand,
    arrayed in gold.

Hear, O daughter, and see; turn your ear,
    forget your people and your father's house.

R℣. The queen stands at your right hand,
    arrayed in gold.

So shall the king desire your beauty;
    for he is your lord.

R℣. The queen stands at your right hand,
    arrayed in gold.

They are borne in with gladness and joy;
    they enter the palace of the king.

R℣. The queen stands at your right hand,
    arrayed in gold.

SECOND READING
1 Cor 15:20-27

Brothers and sisters:
Christ has been raised from the dead,
    the firstfruits of those who have fallen asleep.
For since death came through man,
    the resurrection of the dead came also
      through man.
For just as in Adam all die,
    so too in Christ shall all be brought to life,
    but each one in proper order:
    Christ the firstfruits;
    then, at his coming, those who belong to
      Christ;
    then comes the end,
    when he hands over the Kingdom to his
      God and Father,
    when he has destroyed every sovereignty
    and every authority and power.
For he must reign until he has put all his
    enemies under his feet.
The last enemy to be destroyed is death,
    for "he subjected everything under his feet."

Gospel (cont.)
Luke 14:1, 7-14; L126C

Then he said to the host who invited him,
    "When you hold a lunch or a dinner,
    do not invite your friends or your brothers
    or your relatives or your wealthy neighbors,
    in case they may invite you back and you have repayment.
Rather, when you hold a banquet,
    invite the poor, the crippled, the lame, the blind;
    blessed indeed will you be because of their inability to repay you.
For you will be repaid at the resurrection of the righteous."

Gospel (cont.)
Luke 15:1-32; L132C

And when she does find it,
    she calls together her friends and neighbors
    and says to them,
    'Rejoice with me because I have found the coin that I lost.'
In just the same way, I tell you,
    there will be rejoicing among the angels of God
    over one sinner who repents."

Then he said,
    "A man had two sons, and the younger son said to his father,
    'Father give me the share of your estate that should come to me.'
So the father divided the property between them.
After a few days, the younger son collected all his belongings
    and set off to a distant country
    where he squandered his inheritance on a life of dissipation.
When he had freely spent everything,
    a severe famine struck that country,
    and he found himself in dire need.
So he hired himself out to one of the local citizens
    who sent him to his farm to tend the swine.
And he longed to eat his fill of the pods on which the swine fed,
    but nobody gave him any.
Coming to his senses he thought,
    'How many of my father's hired workers
    have more than enough food to eat,
    but here am I, dying from hunger.
I shall get up and go to my father and I shall say to him,
    "Father, I have sinned against heaven and against you.
I no longer deserve to be called your son;
    treat me as you would treat one of your hired workers."'
So he got up and went back to his father.
While he was still a long way off,
    his father caught sight of him,
    and was filled with compassion.
He ran to his son, embraced him and kissed him.
His son said to him,
    'Father, I have sinned against heaven and against you;
    I no longer deserve to be called your son.'
But his father ordered his servants,
    'Quickly bring the finest robe and put it on him;
    put a ring on his finger and sandals on his feet.
Take the fattened calf and slaughter it.
Then let us celebrate with a feast,
    because this son of mine was dead, and has come to life again;
    he was lost, and has been found.'
Then the celebration began.
Now the older son had been out in the field
    and, on his way back, as he neared the house,
    he heard the sound of music and dancing.
He called one of the servants and asked what this might mean.

The servant said to him,
    'Your brother has returned
    and your father has slaughtered the fattened calf
    because he has him back safe and sound.'
He became angry,
    and when he refused to enter the house,
    his father came out and pleaded with him.
He said to his father in reply,
    'Look, all these years I served you
    and not once did I disobey your orders;
    yet you never gave me even a young goat to feast on with my
        friends. But when your son returns,
    who swallowed up your property with prostitutes,
    for him you slaughter the fattened calf.'
He said to him,
    'My son, you are here with me always;
    everything I have is yours.
But now we must celebrate and rejoice,
    because your brother was dead and has come to life again;
    he was lost and has been found.'"

or Luke 15:1-10

Tax collectors and sinners were all drawing near to listen to Jesus,
    but the Pharisees and scribes began to complain, saying,
    "This man welcomes sinners and eats with them."
So to them he addressed this parable.
"What man among you having a hundred sheep and losing one of them
    would not leave the ninety-nine in the desert
    and go after the lost one until he finds it?
And when he does find it,
    he sets it on his shoulders with great joy
    and, upon his arrival home,
    he calls together his friends and neighbors and says to them,
    'Rejoice with me because I have found my lost sheep.'
I tell you, in just the same way
    there will be more joy in heaven over one sinner who repents
    than over ninety-nine righteous people
    who have no need of repentance.

"Or what woman having ten coins and losing one
    would not light a lamp and sweep the house,
    searching carefully until she finds it?
And when she does find it,
    she calls together her friends and neighbors
    and says to them,
    'Rejoice with me because I have found the coin that I lost.'
In just the same way, I tell you,
    there will be rejoicing among the angels of God
    over one sinner who repents."

Gospel (cont.)
Luke 16:1-13; L135C

The steward said to him, 'Here is your promissory note;
   write one for eighty.'
And the master commended that dishonest steward for acting
   prudently.

"For the children of this world
   are more prudent in dealing with their own generation
   than are the children of light.
I tell you, make friends for yourselves with dishonest wealth,
   so that when it fails, you will be welcomed into eternal dwellings.
The person who is trustworthy in very small matters
   is also trustworthy in great ones;
   and the person who is dishonest in very small matters
   is also dishonest in great ones.
If, therefore, you are not trustworthy with dishonest wealth,
   who will trust you with true wealth?
If you are not trustworthy with what belongs to another,
   who will give you what is yours?
No servant can serve two masters.
He will either hate one and love the other,
   or be devoted to one and despise the other.
You cannot serve both God and mammon."

or Luke 16:10-13

Jesus said to his disciples,
   "The person who is trustworthy in very small matters
   is also trustworthy in great ones;
   and the person who is dishonest in very small matters
   is also dishonest in great ones.
If, therefore, you are not trustworthy with dishonest wealth,
   who will trust you with true wealth?
If you are not trustworthy with what belongs to another,
   who will give you what is yours?
No servant can serve two masters.
He will either hate one and love the other,
   or be devoted to one and despise the other.
You cannot serve both God and mammon."

Gospel (cont.)
Luke 16:19-31; L138C

Moreover, between us and you a great chasm is established
   to prevent anyone from crossing who might wish to go
   from our side to yours or from your side to ours.'
He said, 'Then I beg you, father,
   send him to my father's house, for I have five brothers,
   so that he may warn them,
   lest they too come to this place of torment.'
But Abraham replied, 'They have Moses and the prophets.
Let them listen to them.'
He said, 'Oh no, father Abraham,
   but if someone from the dead goes to them, they will repent.'
Then Abraham said, 'If they will not listen to Moses and the prophets,
   neither will they be persuaded if someone should rise from the dead.'"

FIRST READING
Rev 7:2-4, 9-14

I, John, saw another angel come up from the
East,
  holding the seal of the living God.
He cried out in a loud voice to the four angels
  who were given power to damage the land
    and the sea,
    "Do not damage the land or the sea or the
      trees
    until we put the seal on the foreheads of
      the servants of our God."
I heard the number of those who had been
    marked with the seal,
  one hundred and forty-four thousand
    marked
  from every tribe of the children of Israel.

After this I had a vision of a great multitude,
  which no one could count,
  from every nation, race, people, and tongue.
They stood before the throne and before the
    Lamb,
  wearing white robes and holding palm
      branches in their hands.
They cried out in a loud voice:

  "Salvation comes from our God,
    who is seated on the throne,
  and from the Lamb."

All the angels stood around the throne
  and around the elders and the four living
    creatures.
They prostrated themselves before the throne,
  worshiped God, and exclaimed:

  "Amen. Blessing and glory, wisdom and
      thanksgiving,
    honor, power, and might
    be to our God forever and ever. Amen."

Then one of the elders spoke up and said to
    me,
  "Who are these wearing white robes, and
      where did they come from?"
I said to him, "My lord, you are the one who
    knows."
He said to me,
  "These are the ones who have survived the
      time of great distress;
  they have washed their robes
  and made them white in the Blood of the
      Lamb."

RESPONSORIAL PSALM
Ps 24:1bc-2, 3-4ab, 5-6

℟. (cf. 6) Lord, this is the people that longs to
    see your face.

The Lord's are the earth and its fullness;
  the world and those who dwell in it.
For he founded it upon the seas
  and established it upon the rivers.

℟. Lord, this is the people that longs to see
    your face.

Who can ascend the mountain of the Lord?
  or who may stand in his holy place?
One whose hands are sinless, whose heart is
    clean,
  who desires not what is vain.

℟. Lord, this is the people that longs to see
    your face.

He shall receive a blessing from the Lord,
  a reward from God his savior.
Such is the race that seeks him,
  that seeks the face of the God of Jacob.

℟. Lord, this is the people that longs to see
    your face.

SECOND READING
1 John 3:1-3

Beloved:
See what love the Father has bestowed on us
    that we may be called the children of God.
Yet so we are.
The reason the world does not know us
  is that it did not know him.
Beloved, we are God's children now;
  what we shall be has not yet been revealed.
We do know that when it is revealed we shall
    be like him,
  for we shall see him as he is.
Everyone who has this hope based on him
    makes himself pure,
  as he is pure.

FIRST READING
Dan 12:1-3; L1011.7

In those days, I, Daniel, mourned
  and heard this word of the Lord:
At that time there shall arise
  Michael, the great prince,
  guardian of your people;
It shall be a time unsurpassed in distress
  since nations began until that time.
At that time your people shall escape,
  everyone who is found written in the book.

Many of those who sleep in the dust of the
    earth shall awake;
Some shall live forever,
  others shall be an everlasting horror and
    disgrace.
But the wise shall shine brightly
  like the splendor of the firmament,
And those who lead the many to justice
  shall be like the stars forever.

RESPONSORIAL PSALM
Ps 27:1, 4, 7, and 8b, and 9a, 13-14; L1013.3

℟. (1a) The Lord is my light and my
    salvation.
  or:
℟. (13) I believe that I shall see the good
    things of the Lord in the land of the
    living.

The LORD is my light and my salvation;
  whom should I fear?
The LORD is my life's refuge;
  of whom should I be afraid?

℟. The Lord is my light and my salvation.
  or:
℟. I believe that I shall see the good things of
    the Lord in the land of the living.

One thing I ask of the LORD;
  this I seek:
To dwell in the house of the LORD
  all the days of my life,
That I may gaze on the loveliness of the LORD
  and contemplate his temple.

℟. The Lord is my light and my salvation.
  or:
℟. I believe that I shall see the good things of
    the Lord in the land of the living.

Hear, O LORD, the sound of my call;
  have pity on me and answer me.
Your presence, O LORD, I seek.
  Hide not your face from me.

℟. The Lord is my light and my salvation.
  or:
℟. I believe that I shall see the good things of
    the Lord in the land of the living.

I believe that I shall see the bounty of the
    LORD
  in the land of the living.
Wait for the LORD with courage;
  be stouthearted, and wait for the LORD.

℟. The Lord is my light and my salvation.
  or:
℟. I believe that I shall see the good things of
    the Lord in the land of the living.

SECOND READING
Rom 6:3-9; L1014.3

Brothers and sisters:
Are you unaware that we who were baptized
    into Christ Jesus
  were baptized into his death?
We were indeed buried with him through
    baptism into death,
  so that, just as Christ was raised from the
    dead
  by the glory of the Father,
  we too might live in newness of life.

For if we have grown into union with him
    through a death like his,
  we shall also be united with him in the
    resurrection.
We know that our old self was crucified with
    him,
  so that our sinful body might be done away
    with,
  that we might no longer be in slavery to sin.
For a dead person has been absolved from sin.
If, then, we have died with Christ,
  we believe that we shall also live with him.
We know that Christ, raised from the dead,
    dies no more;
  death no longer has power over him.

Thirty-Second Sunday in Ordinary Time,
November 6, 2022

Gospel
Luke 20:27, 34-38; L156C

Some Sadducees, those who deny that there is a resurrection,
  came forward.

Jesus said to them,
  "The children of this age marry and remarry;
  but those who are deemed worthy to attain to the coming age
  and to the resurrection of the dead
  neither marry nor are given in marriage.
They can no longer die,
  for they are like angels;
  and they are the children of God
  because they are the ones who will rise.
That the dead will rise
  even Moses made known in the passage about the bush,
  when he called out 'Lord,'
  the God of Abraham, the God of Isaac, and the God of Jacob;
  and he is not God of the dead, but of the living,
  for to him all are alive."

Thirty-Third Sunday in Ordinary Time,
November 13, 2022

Gospel (cont.)
Luke 21:5-19; L159C

"Before all this happens, however,
  they will seize and persecute you,
  they will hand you over to the synagogues and to prisons,
  and they will have you led before kings and governors
  because of my name.
It will lead to your giving testimony.
Remember, you are not to prepare your defense beforehand,
  for I myself shall give you a wisdom in speaking
  that all your adversaries will be powerless to resist or refute.
You will even be handed over by parents, brothers, relatives, and
    friends,
  and they will put some of you to death.
You will be hated by all because of my name,
  but not a hair on your head will be destroyed.
By your perseverance you will secure your lives."

Lectionary Pronunciation Guide

Lectionary Word	Pronunciation
Aaron	EHR-uhn
Abana	AB-uh-nuh
Abednego	uh-BEHD-nee-go
Abel-Keramin	AY-b'l-KEHR-uh-mihn
Abel-meholah	AY-b'l-mee-HO-lah
Abiathar	uh-BAI-uh-ther
Abiel	AY-bee-ehl
Abiezrite	ay-bai-EHZ-rait
Abijah	uh-BAI-dzhuh
Abilene	ab-uh-LEE-neh
Abishai	uh-BIHSH-ay-ai
Abiud	uh-BAI-uhd
Abner	AHB-ner
Abraham	AY-bruh-ham
Abram	AY-br'm
Achaia	uh-KAY-yuh
Achim	AY-kihm
Aeneas	uh-NEE-uhs
Aenon	AY-nuhn
Agrippa	uh-GRIH-puh
Ahaz	AY-haz
Ahijah	uh-HAI-dzhuh
Ai	AY-ee
Alexandria	al-ehg-ZAN-dree-uh
Alexandrian	al-ehg-ZAN-dree-uhn
Alpha	AHL-fuh
Alphaeus	AL-fee-uhs
Amalek	AM-uh-lehk
Amaziah	am-uh-ZAI-uh
Amminadab	ah-MIHN-uh-dab
Ammonites	AM-uh-naitz
Amorites	AM-uh-raits
Amos	AY-muhs
Amoz	AY-muhz
Ampliatus	am-plee-AY-tuhs
Ananias	an-uh-NAI-uhs
Andronicus	an-draw-NAI-kuhs
Annas	AN-uhs
Antioch	AN-tih-ahk
Antiochus	an-TAI-uh-kuhs
Aphiah	uh-FAI-uh
Apollos	uh-PAH-luhs
Appius	AP-ee-uhs
Aquila	uh-KWIHL-uh
Arabah	EHR-uh-buh
Aram	AY-ram
Arameans	ehr-uh-MEE-uhnz
Areopagus	ehr-ee-AH-puh-guhs
Arimathea	ehr-uh-muh-THEE-uh
Aroer	uh-RO-er

Lectionary Word	Pronunciation
Asaph	AY-saf
Asher	ASH-er
Ashpenaz	ASH-pee-naz
Assyria	a-SIHR-ee-uh
Astarte	as-TAHR-tee
Attalia	at-TAH-lee-uh
Augustus	uh-GUHS-tuhs
Azariah	az-uh-RAI-uh
Azor	AY-sawr
Azotus	uh-ZO-tus
Baal-shalishah	BAY-uhl-shuh-LAI-shuh
Baal-Zephon	BAY-uhl-ZEE-fuhn
Babel	BAY-bl
Babylon	BAB-ih-luhn
Babylonian	bab-ih-LO-nih-uhn
Balaam	BAY-lm
Barabbas	beh-REH-buhs
Barak	BEHR-ak
Barnabas	BAHR-nuh-buhs
Barsabbas	BAHR-suh-buhs
Bartholomew	bar-THAHL-uh-myoo
Bartimaeus	bar-tih-MEE-uhs
Baruch	BEHR-ook
Bashan	BAY-shan
Becorath	bee-KO-rath
Beelzebul	bee-EHL-zee-buhl
Beer-sheba	BEE-er-SHEE-buh
Belshazzar	behl-SHAZ-er
Benjamin	BEHN-dzhuh-mihn
Beor	BEE-awr
Bethany	BEHTH-uh-nee
Bethel	BETH-el
Bethesda	beh-THEHZ-duh
Bethlehem	BEHTH-leh-hehm
Bethphage	BEHTH-fuh-dzhee
Bethsaida	behth-SAY-ih-duh
Beth-zur	behth-ZER
Bildad	BIHL-dad
Bithynia	bih-THIHN-ih-uh
Boanerges	bo-uh-NER-dzheez
Boaz	BO-az
Caesar	SEE-zer
Caesarea	zeh-suh-REE-uh
Caiaphas	KAY-uh-fuhs
Cain	kayn
Cana	KAY-nuh
Canaan	KAY-nuhn
Canaanite	KAY-nuh-nait
Canaanites	KAY-nuh-naits

Lectionary Word	Pronunciation
Candace	kan-DAY-see
Capernaum	kuh-PERR-nay-uhm
Cappadocia	kap-ih-DO-shee-u
Carmel	KAHR-muhl
carnelians	kahr-NEEL-yuhnz
Cenchreae	SEHN-kree-ay
Cephas	SEE-fuhs
Chaldeans	kal-DEE-uhnz
Chemosh	KEE-mahsh
Cherubim	TSHEHR-oo-bihm
Chislev	KIHS-lehv
Chloe	KLO-ee
Chorazin	kor-AY-sihn
Cilicia	sih-LIHSH-ee-uh
Cleopas	KLEE-o-pas
Clopas	KLO-pas
Corinth	KAWR-ihnth
Corinthians	kawr-IHN-thee-uhnz
Cornelius	kawr-NEE-lee-uhs
Crete	kreet
Crispus	KRIHS-puhs
Cushite	CUHSH-ait
Cypriot	SIH-pree-at
Cyrene	sai-REE-nee
Cyreneans	sai-REE-nih-uhnz
Cyrenian	sai-REE-nih-uhn
Cyrenians	sai-REE-nih-uhnz
Cyrus	SAI-ruhs
Damaris	DAM-uh-rihs
Damascus	duh-MAS-kuhs
Danites	DAN-aits
Decapolis	duh-KAP-o-lis
Derbe	DER-bee
Deuteronomy	dyoo-ter-AH-num-mee
Didymus	DID-I-mus
Dionysius	dai-o-NIHSH-ih-uhs
Dioscuri	dai-O-sky-ri
Dorcas	DAWR-kuhs
Dothan	DO-thuhn
dromedaries	DRAH-muh-dher-eez
Ebed-melech	EE-behd-MEE-lehk
Eden	EE-dn
Edom	EE-duhm
Elamites	EE-luh-maitz
Eldad	EHL-dad
Eleazar	ehl-ee-AY-zer
Eli	EE-lai
Eli Eli Lema Sabachthani	AY-lee AY-lee luh-MAH sah-BAHK-tah-nee

Lectionary Word	Pronunciation	Lectionary Word	Pronunciation	Lectionary Word	Pronunciation
Eliab	ee-LAI-ab	Gilead	GIHL-ee-uhd	Joppa	DZHAH-puh
Eliakim	ee-LAI-uh-kihm	Gilgal	GIHL-gal	Joram	DZHO-ram
Eliezer	ehl-ih-EE-zer	Golgotha	GAHL-guh-thuh	Jordan	DZHAWR-dn
Elihu	ee-LAI-hyoo	Gomorrah	guh-MAWR-uh	Joseph	DZHO-zf
Elijah	ee-LAI-dzhuh	Goshen	GO-shuhn	Joses	DZHO-seez
Elim	EE-lihm	Habakkuk	huh-BAK-uhk	Joshua	DZHAH-shou-ah
Elimelech	ee-LIHM-eh-lehk	Hadadrimmon	hay-dad-RIHM-uhn	Josiah	dzho-SAI-uh
Elisha	ee-LAI-shuh	Hades	HAY-deez	Jotham	DZHO-thuhm
Eliud	ee-LAI-uhd	Hagar	HAH-gar	Judah	DZHOU-duh
Elizabeth	ee-LIHZ-uh-bth	Hananiah	han-uh-NAI-uh	Judas	DZHOU-duhs
Elkanah	el-KAY-nuh	Hannah	HAN-uh	Judea	dzhou-DEE-uh
Eloi Eloi Lama Sabechthani	AY-lo-ee AY-lo-ee LAH-mah sah-BAHK-tah-nee	Haran	HAY-ruhn	Judean	dzhou-DEE-uhn
		Hebron	HEE-bruhn	Junia	dzhou-nih-uh
		Hermes	HER-meez	Justus	DZHUHS-tuhs
Elymais	ehl-ih-MAY-ihs	Herod	HEHR-uhd	Kephas	KEF-uhs
Emmanuel	eh-MAN-yoo-ehl	Herodians	hehr-O-dee-uhnz	Kidron	KIHD-ruhn
Emmaus	eh-MAY-uhs	Herodias	hehr-O-dee-uhs	Kiriatharba	kihr-ee-ath-AHR-buh
Epaenetus	ee-PEE-nee-tuhs	Hezekiah	heh-zeh-KAI-uh	Kish	kihsh
Epaphras	EH-puh-fras	Hezron	HEHZ-ruhn	Laodicea	lay-o-dih-SEE-uh
ephah	EE-fuh	Hilkiah	hihl-KAI-uh	Lateran	LAT-er-uhn
Ephah	EE-fuh	Hittite	HIH-tait	Lazarus	LAZ-er-uhs
Ephesians	eh-FEE-zhuhnz	Hivites	HAI-vaitz	Leah	LEE-uh
Ephesus	EH-fuh-suhs	Hophni	HAHF-nai	Lebanon	LEH-buh-nuhn
Ephphatha	EHF-uh-thuh	Hor	HAWR	Levi	LEE-vai
Ephraim	EE-fray-ihm	Horeb	HAWR-ehb	Levite	LEE-vait
Ephrathah	EHF-ruh-thuh	Hosea	ho-ZEE-uh	Levites	LEE-vaits
Ephron	EE-frawn	Hur	her	Leviticus	leh-VIH-tih-kous
Epiphanes	eh-PIHF-uh-neez	hyssop	HIH-suhp	Lucius	LOO-shih-uhs
Erastus	ee-RAS-tuhs	Iconium	ai-KO-nih-uhm	Lud	luhd
Esau	EE-saw	Isaac	AI-zuhk	Luke	look
Esther	EHS-ter	Isaiah	ai-ZAY-uh	Luz	luhz
Ethanim	EHTH-uh-nihm	Iscariot	ihs-KEHR-ee-uht	Lycaonian	lihk-ay-O-nih-uhn
Ethiopian	ee-thee-O-pee-uhn	Ishmael	ISH-may-ehl	Lydda	LIH-duh
Euphrates	yoo-FRAY-teez	Ishmaelites	ISH-mayehl-aits	Lydia	LIH-dih-uh
Exodus	EHK-so-duhs	Israel	IHZ-ray-ehl	Lysanias	lai-SAY-nih-uhs
Ezekiel	eh-ZEE-kee-uhl	Ituraea	ih-TSHOOR-ree-uh	Lystra	LIHS-truh
Ezra	EHZ-ruh	Jaar	DZHAY-ahr	Maccabees	MAK-uh-beez
frankincense	FRANGK-ihn-sehns	Jabbok	DZHAB-uhk	Macedonia	mas-eh-DO-nih-uh
Gabbatha	GAB-uh-thuh	Jacob	DZHAY-kuhb	Macedonian	mas-eh-DO-nih-uhn
Gabriel	GAY-bree-ul	Jairus	DZH-hr-uhs	Machir	MAY-kihr
Gadarenes	GAD-uh-reenz	Javan	DZHAY-van	Machpelah	mak-PEE-luh
Galatian	guh-LAY-shih-uhn	Jebusites	DZHEHB-oo-zaits	Magdala	MAG-duh-luh
Galatians	guh-LAY-shih-uhnz	Jechoniah	dzhehk-o-NAI-uh	Magdalene	MAG-duh-lehn
Galilee	GAL-ih-lee	Jehoiakim	dzhee-HOI-uh-kihm	magi	MAY-dzhai
Gallio	GAL-ih-o	Jehoshaphat	dzhee-HAHSH-uh-fat	Malachi	MAL-uh-kai
Gamaliel	guh-MAY-lih-ehl	Jephthah	DZHEHF-thuh	Malchiah	mal-KAI-uh
Gaza	GAH-zuh	Jeremiah	dzhehr-eh-MAI-uh	Malchus	MAL-kuhz
Gehazi	gee-HAY-zai	Jericho	DZHEHR-ih-ko	Mamre	MAM-ree
Gehenna	geh-HEHN-uh	Jeroham	dzhehr-RO-ham	Manaen	MAN-uh-ehn
Genesis	DZHEHN-uh-sihs	Jerusalem	dzheh-ROU-suh-lehm	Manasseh	man-AS-eh
Gennesaret	gehn-NEHS-uh-reht	Jesse	DZHEH-see	Manoah	muh-NO-uh
Gentiles	DZHEHN-tailz	Jethro	DZHEHTH-ro	Mark	mahrk
Gerasenes	DZHEHR-uh-seenz	Joakim	DZHO-uh-kihm	Mary	MEHR-ee
Gethsemane	gehth-SEHM-uh-ne	Job	DZHOB	Massah	MAH-suh
Gideon	GIHD-ee-uhn	Jonah	DZHO-nuh	Mattathias	mat-uh-THAI-uhs

Lectionary Word	Pronunciation	Lectionary Word	Pronunciation	Lectionary Word	Pronunciation
Matthan	MAT-than	Parmenas	PAHR-mee-nas	Sabbath	SAB-uhth
Matthew	MATH-yoo	Parthians	PAHR-thee-uhnz	Sadducees	SAD-dzhoo-seez
Matthias	muh-THAI-uhs	Patmos	PAT-mos	Salem	SAY-lehm
Medad	MEE-dad	Peninnah	pee-NIHN-uh	Salim	SAY-lim
Mede	meed	Pentecost	PEHN-tee-kawst	Salmon	SAL-muhn
Medes	meedz	Penuel	pee-NYOO-ehl	Salome	suh-LO-mee
Megiddo	mee-GIH-do	Perez	PEE-rehz	Salu	SAYL-yoo
Melchizedek	mehl-KIHZ-eh-dehk	Perga	PER-guh	Samaria	suh-MEHR-ih-uh
Mene	MEE-nee	Perizzites	PEHR-ih-zaits	Samaritan	suh-MEHR-ih-tuhn
Meribah	MEHR-ih-bah	Persia	PER-zhuh	Samothrace	SAM-o-thrays
Meshach	MEE-shak	Peter	PEE-ter	Samson	SAM-s'n
Mespotamia	mehs-o-po-TAY-mih-uh	Phanuel	FAN-yoo-ehl	Samuel	SAM-yoo-uhl
		Pharaoh	FEHR-o	Sanhedrin	san-HEE-drihn
Micah	MAI-kuh	Pharisees	FEHR-ih-seez	Sarah	SEHR-uh
Midian	MIH-dih-uhn	Pharpar	FAHR-pahr	Sarai	SAY-rai
Milcom	MIHL-kahm	Philemon	fih-LEE-muhn	saraph	SAY-raf
Miletus	mai-LEE-tuhs	Philippi	fil-LIH-pai	Sardis	SAHR-dihs
Minnith	MIHN-ihth	Philippians	fih-LIHP-ih-uhnz	Saul	sawl
Mishael	MIHSH-ay-ehl	Philistines	fih-LIHS-tihnz	Scythian	SIH-thee-uhn
Mizpah	MIHZ-puh	Phinehas	FEHN-ee-uhs	Seba	SEE-buh
Moreh	MO-reh	Phoenicia	fee-NIHSH-ih-uh	Seth	sehth
Moriah	maw-RAI-uh	Phrygia	FRIH-dzhih-uh	Shaalim	SHAY-uh-lihm
Mosoch	MAH-sahk	Phrygian	FRIH-dzhih-uhn	Shadrach	SHAY-drak
myrrh	mer	phylacteries	fih-LAK-ter-eez	Shalishah	shuh-LEE-shuh
Mysia	MIH-shih-uh	Pi-Hahiroth	pai-huh-HAI-rahth	Shaphat	Shay-fat
Naaman	NAY-uh-muhn	Pilate	PAI-luht	Sharon	SHEHR-uhn
Nahshon	NAY-shuhn	Pisidia	pih-SIH-dih-uh	Shealtiel	shee-AL-tih-ehl
Naomi	NAY-o-mai	Pithom	PAI-thahm	Sheba	SHEE-buh
Naphtali	NAF-tuh-lai	Pontius	PAHN-shus	Shebna	SHEB-nuh
Nathan	NAY-thuhn	Pontus	PAHN-tus	Shechem	SHEE-kehm
Nathanael	nuh-THAN-ay-ehl	Praetorium	pray-TAWR-ih-uhm	shekel	SHEHK-uhl
Nazarene	NAZ-awr-een	Priscilla	PRIHS-kill-uh	Shiloh	SHAI-lo
Nazareth	NAZ-uh-rehth	Prochorus	PRAH-kaw-ruhs	Shinar	SHAI-nahr
nazirite	NAZ-uh-rait	Psalm	Sahm	Shittim	sheh-TEEM
Nazorean	naz-aw-REE-uhn	Put	puht	Shuhite	SHOO-ait
Neapolis	nee-AP-o-lihs	Puteoli	pyoo-TEE-o-lai	Shunammite	SHOO-nam-ait
Nebuchadnezzar	neh-byoo-kuhd-NEHZ-er	Qoheleth	ko-HEHL-ehth	Shunem	SHOO-nehm
		qorban	KAWR-bahn	Sidon	SAI-duhn
Negeb	NEH-gehb	Quartus	KWAR-tuhs	Silas	SAI-luhs
Nehemiah	nee-hee-MAI-uh	Quirinius	kwai-RIHN-ih-uhs	Siloam	sih-LO-uhm
Ner	ner	Raamses	ray-AM-seez	Silvanus	sihl-VAY-nuhs
Nicanor	nai-KAY-nawr	Rabbi	RAB-ai	Simeon	SIHM-ee-uhn
Nicodemus	nih-ko-DEE-muhs	Rabbouni	ra-BO-nai	Simon	SAI-muhn
Niger	NAI-dzher	Rahab	RAY-hab	Sin (desert)	sihn
Nineveh	NIHN-eh-veh	Ram	ram	Sinai	SAI-nai
Noah	NO-uh	Ramah	RAY-muh	Sirach	SAI-rak
Nun	nuhn	Ramathaim	ray-muh-THAY-ihm	Sodom	SAH-duhm
Obed	O-behd	Raqa	RA-kuh	Solomon	SAH-lo-muhn
Olivet	AH-lih-veht	Rebekah	ree-BEHK-uh	Sosthenes	SAHS-thee-neez
Omega	o-MEE-guh	Rehoboam	ree-ho-BO-am	Stachys	STAY-kihs
Onesimus	o-NEH-sih-muhs	Rephidim	REHF-ih-dihm	Succoth	SUHK-ahth
Ophir	O-fer	Reuben	ROO-b'n	Sychar	SI-kar
Orpah	AWR-puh	Revelation	reh-veh-LAY-shuhn	Syene	sai-EE-nee
Pamphylia	pam-FIHL-ih-uh	Rhegium	REE-dzhee-uhm	Symeon	SIHM-ee-uhn
Paphos	PAY-fuhs	Rufus	ROO-fuhs	synagogues	SIHN-uh-gahgz

Lectionary Word	Pronunciation	Lectionary Word	Pronunciation	Lectionary Word	Pronunciation
Syrophoenician	SIHR-o fee-NIHSH-ih-uhn	Timon	TAI-muhn	Zebedee	ZEH-beh-dee
Tabitha	TAB-ih-thuh	Titus	TAI-tuhs	Zebulun	ZEH-byoo-luhn
Talitha koum	TAL-ih-thuh-KOOM	Tohu	TO-hyoo	Zechariah	zeh-kuh-RAI-uh
Tamar	TAY-mer	Trachonitis	trak-o-NAI-tis	Zedekiah	zeh-duh-KAI-uh
Tarshish	TAHR-shihsh	Troas	TRO-ahs	Zephaniah	zeh-fuh-NAI-uh
Tarsus	TAHR-suhs	Tubal	TYOO-b'l	Zerah	ZEE-ruh
Tekel	TEH-keel	Tyre	TAI-er	Zeror	ZEE-rawr
Terebinth	TEHR-ee-bihnth	Ur	er	Zerubbabel	zeh-RUH-buh-behl
Thaddeus	THAD-dee-uhs	Urbanus	er-BAY-nuhs	Zeus	zyoos
Theophilus	thee-AH-fih-luhs	Uriah	you-RAI-uh	Zimri	ZIHM-rai
Thessalonians	theh-suh-LO-nih-uhnz	Uzziah	yoo-ZAI-uh	Zion	ZAI-uhn
Theudas	THU-duhs	Wadi	WAH-dee	Ziph	zihf
Thyatira	thai-uh-TAI-ruh	Yahweh-yireh	YAH-weh-yer-AY	Zoar	ZO-er
Tiberias	tai-BIHR-ih-uhs	Zacchaeus	zak-KEE-uhs	Zorah	ZAWR-uh
Timaeus	tai-MEE-uhs	Zadok	ZAY-dahk	Zuphite	ZUHF-ait
		Zarephath	ZEHR-ee-fath		